Lecture Notes in Computer Science   9758

Commenced Publication in 1973
Founding and Former Series Editors:
Gerhard Goos, Juris Hartmanis, and Jan van Leeuwen

Editorial Board

More information about this series at http://www.springer.com/series/7409

Klaus Miesenberger · Christian Bühler
Petr Penaz (Eds.)

Computers Helping People with Special Needs

15th International Conference, ICCHP 2016
Linz, Austria, July 13–15, 2016
Proceedings, Part I

 Springer

Editors
Klaus Miesenberger
Institute Integriert Studieren
Universität Linz
Linz
Austria

Petr Penaz
Masaryk University
Brno
Czech Republic

Christian Bühler
Rehabilitationswissenschaften
Technische Universität Dortmund
Dortmund
Germany

ISSN 0302-9743   ISSN 1611-3349   (electronic)
Lecture Notes in Computer Science
ISBN 978-3-319-41263-4   ISBN 978-3-319-41264-1   (eBook)
DOI 10.1007/978-3-319-41264-1

Library of Congress Control Number: 2016943068

LNCS Sublibrary: SL3 – Information Systems and Applications, incl. Internet/Web, and HCI

Printed on acid-free paper

This Springer imprint is published by Springer Nature
The registered company is Springer International Publishing AG Switzerland

Preface

Twenty-seven years ago, a group of computer science experts from the Austrian Computer Society, led by Prof. Roland Wagner and Prof. A Min Tjoa, started ICCHP conference. Since the first conference in Vienna (Austria) back in 1989, ICCHP has evolved as a unique and one of the few long-term  references of R&D in the field and is evidence of how information and communication technology (ICT), assistive technology (AT), and eAccessibility have been implemented and have significantly contributed to the improvement of the life of people with disabilities. ICCHP had the honor of accompanying and supporting the revolutionary developments of Assistive Technology and eAccessibility over the last decades. It can be proud to serve as a platform for exchange and communication in this context. The UN Convention on the Rights of People with Disabilities (UNCRPD) is the globally accepted reference and expression of the societal transformation toward effective inclusion and participation of all people with disabilities in society. The UNCRPD refers to AT, eAccessibility, eInclusion, and design for all as a precondition and means of support. Exactly these issues are also the core science topics of ICCHP.

ICCHP's scientifically based mission for inclusion and participation in the information society strives for better AT for support, enhancement and restoration of resources of people with disabilities, and compensating limitations of standardized HCI. This mission continues to gain more importance owing to the ongoing ICT revolution (Internet/Web of Things/ubiquitous computing/cloud-based services). The ICT revolution brings along an increased potential for inclusion and participation, but also risks for exclusion and thus the responsibility for implementing eAccessibility. It provokes a growing number of challenging research questions. Old boundaries of concepts dissolve, new approaches and fresh thinking are needed: not only in technical terms but also in legal, social, economic, pedagogic, and other terms. ICCHP is open to all these aspects and invites one to, and provides a platform for, a holistic discussion for improving the lives of people with disabilities in every corner of our world.

ICCHP is proud of its history and to this day it provides one of the few comprehensive and complete collections of scientific work in the field of AT and eAccessibility. All proceedings covering more than 2,300 reviewed articles have been published by Springer in their *Lecture Notes in Computer Science Series*. Since 2006, they have been available online with more than 100,000 (some almost 200,000) downloads of articles. This makes ICCHP a well-recognized reference and a unique source for learning and understanding the theoretical, methodological, and pragmatic specializations of this growing and expanding R&D field.

The proceedings of the 15th edition constitute a collection of high-quality, well-reviewed submissions by scientists, users, practitioners, educators, and policy makers from around the world. Each of the 239 eligible submissions was carefully reviewed by at least by three members of the international Programme Committee composed of

129 experts from all over the world and listed herein. The panel of 18 conference chairs analyzed the review results and prepared the final decisions. Based on this intense and careful analysis, ICCHP 2016 accepted 115 submissions as full papers and 48 as short papers (acceptance rate 59 %). These data provide evidence of the highly competitive process guaranteeing for the scientific quality of the proceedings and the conference.

ICCHP 2016 in Linz hosts high-quality, well-reviewed submissions from scientists, users, practitioners, educators, and policy makers and discussions among more than 500 participants from around the world. In particular ICCHP welcomes young researchers, the next generation of experts in our field, and invites them to contribute to the Young Researchers Consortium as well as to the Coding for a Cause (C4C) competition. "Universal Learning Design" has become a central topic which is taken care of by the Teiresias Center at the Masaryk University Brno. The Roland Wagner ICCHP Award, the C4C Competition, the Young Researchers Consortium, the Summer University on Math, Science, and Statistics for Blind People, and a series of parallel workshops and meetings make ICCHP a unique meeting place to drive AT and eAccessibility forward.

We welcome the attendees valuable contribution to ICCHP 2016 and encourage them and their colleagues to become regular participants in its most important mission. It is here that research, innovation, and practical endeavors in important topics of AT and eAccessibility come together to be shared, explored, and discussed.

ICCHP 2016 is proud to be under the patronage of the United Nations Educational, Scientific, and Cultural Organization (UNESCO).

May 2016

Klaus Miesenberger
Christian Bühler
Petr Penaz

ICCHP Committees

General Chair

Bühler, C.   TU Dortmund University, FTB, Germany

Steering Board

Burger, D.   INSERM, France
Klaus, J.   Karlsruhe Institute of Technology, Germany
Murphy, H.J.   California State University Northridge, USA
Suzuki, M.   Kyushu University, Japan
Tjoa, A.M.   Technical University of Vienna, Austria
Wagner, R.   University of Linz, Austria

Publishing Chairs

Miesenberger, K.   University of Linz, Austria
Penaz, P.   University of Brno, Czech Republic

Programme Chairs

Archambault, D.   Université Paris 8, France
Fels, D.   Ryerson University, Canada
Kobayashi, M.   Tsukuba University of Technology, Japan
Kouroupetroglou, G.   University of Athens, Greece
Manduchi, R.   University of California at Santa Cruz, USA
Ramesh, S.K.   CSUN, USA
Weber, G.   Technische Universität Dresden, Germany

Young Researcher Consortium Chairs

Archambault, D.   Université Paris 8, France
Fels, D.   Ryerson University, Canada
Fitzpatrick, D.   Dublin City University, Ireland
Kobayashi, M.   Tsukuba University of Technology, Japan
Lam, S.   Project:Possibility, USA
Mihailidis, A.   University of Toronto, Canada
Morandell, M.   AIT Austrian Institute of Technology GmbH, Austria
Pontelli, E.   New Mexico State University, USA
Prazak-Aram, B.   AIT Austrian Institute of Technolog GmbH, Austria
Weber, G.   Technische Universität Dresden, Germany
Zimmermann, G.   Stuttgart Media University, Germany

Workshop Chairs

Petz, A.	University of Linz, Austria
Pühretmair, F.	KI-I, Austria

International Programme Committee

Abbott, C.	King's College London, UK
Abou-Zahra, S.	W3C Web Accessibility Initiative (WAI), Austria
Abu Doush, I.	Yarmouk University, Jordan
Andrich, R.	Polo Tecnologico Fondazione Don Carlo Gnocchi Onlus, Italy
Arató, A.	KFKI-RMKI, Hungary
Azevedo, L.	Instituto Superior Tecnico, Portugal
Banes	Qatar Assistive Technology Center, Qatar
Batusic, M.	Fabasoft, Austria
Bernareggi, C.	Università degli Studi di Milano, Italy
Bernier, A.	BrailleNet, France
Bosse, I.	Technische Universität Dortmund, Germany
Bu, J.	Zhejiang University, China
Chen, W.	Oslo and Akershus University College of Applied Sciences, Norway
Chorbev, I.	Ss. Cyrill and Methodius University in Skopje, Macedonia
Christensen, L.B.	Sensus, Denmark
Chutimaskul, W.	King Mongkut's University of Technology Thonburi, Thailand
Coughlan. J.	Smith-Kettlewell Eye Research Institute, USA
Craddock, G.	Centre for Excellence in Universal Design, Ireland
Crombie, D.	Utrecht School of the Arts, The Netherlands
Cudd, P.	University of Sheffield, UK
Darvishy, A.	Züricher Hochschule für Angewandte Wissenschaften, Switzerland
Darzentas, J.	University of the Aegean, Greece
Debevc, M.	University of Maribor, Slovenia
Debeljak, M.	University of Ljubljana, Slovenia
DeRuyter, F.	Duke University Medical Centre, USA
Diaz del Campo, R.	Antarq Tecnosoluciones, Mexico
Draffan, E.A.	University of Southampton, UK
Dupire, J.	CNAM, France
Emiliani, P.L.	Institute of Applied Physics Nello Carrara, Italy
Engelen, J.	Katholieke Universiteit Leuven, Belgium
Galinski, Ch.	InfoTerm, Austria
Gardner, J.	Oregon State University, USA
Hakkinen, M.T.	Educational Testing Service (ETS), USA
Harper, S.	University of Manchester, UK

Vlachogiannis, E.	Fraunhofer Institute for Applied Information Technology, Germany
Votis, K.	CERTH/ITI, Greece
Wada, C.	Kyushu Institute of Technology, Japan
Wagner, G.	Upper Austria University of Applied Sciences, Austria
Watanabe, T.	University of Niigata, Japan
Weber, H.	ITA, University of Kaiserslautern, Germany
Whitfield, M.	Ryerson University, Canada
Wöß, W.	University of Linz, Austria
Yamaguchi, K.	Nihon University, Japan
Yeliz Yesilada	Middle East Technical University, Cyprus

Organizing Committee

Bieber, R. (Chair)	CEO, Austrian Computer Society, Austria
Feichtenschlager, P.	Integriert Studieren, JKU Linz, Austria
Haider, S.	Integriert Studieren, JKU Linz, Austria
Heumader, P.	Integriert Studieren, JKU Linz, Austria
Jitngernmadan, P.	Integriert Studieren, JKU Linz, Austria
Klemen, M.D.	President, Austrian Computer Society, Austria
Koutny, R.	Integriert Studieren, JKU Linz, Austria
Kremser, W.	WG ICT with/for People with Disabilities, Austrian Computer Society, Austria
Miesenberger, K.	Integriert Studieren, JKU Linz, Austria
Murillo Morales, T.	Integriert Studieren, JKU Linz, Austria
Penaz, P.	Masaryk University Brno (ULD), Czech Republic
Petz, A.	Integriert Studieren, JKU Linz, Austria
Plhák, J.	Integriert Studieren, JKU Linz, Austria
Schult, Ch.	Integriert Studieren, JKU Linz, Austria
Wagner, R.	Integriert Studieren, JKU Linz, Austria

ICCHP Roland Wagner Award Nomination Committee

Andras Arato	KFKI Budapest, Hungary
Christian Bühler	TU Dortmund, FTB Vollmarstein, Germany
Deborah Fels	Ryerson University, Canada
Klaus Miesenberger	University of Linz, Austria
Wolfgang Zagler	Vienna University of Technology, Austria

We thank the Austrian Computer Society for announcing and sponsoring the *Roland Wagner Award on Computers Helping People with Special Needs*.

The Austrian Computer Society decided in September 2001 to endow this award in honor of Prof. Roland Wagner, the founder of ICCHP.

The Roland Wagner Award is a biannual award in the range of €3,000. It is handed over at the occasion of ICCHP conferences.

Award Winners:

- *Award 7:* Prof. Dr. Art Karshmer (⚕ 2015), University of San Francisco, USA and Prof. Dr. Masakazu Suzuki. Kyushu University, Japan, ICCHP 2014 in Paris.
- *Award 6:* The TRACE Centre of the University Wisconsin-Madison, USA, ICCHP 2012 in Linz
- *Award 5:* Harry Murphy Founder, Former Director and Member Advisory Board of the Centre on Disabilities USA and Joachim Klaus, Founder, Former Director of the Study Centre for Blind and Partially Sighted Students at the Karlsruhe Institute of Technology (KIT), Germany, ICCHP 2010 in Vienna
- *Award 4:* George Kersher, Daisy Consortium, ICCHP 2008 in Linz
- Special Award 2006: Roland Traunmüller, University of Linz
- *Award 3:* Larry Scadden, National Science Foundation, ICCHP 2006 in Linz
- *Award 2:* Paul Blenkhorn, University of Manchester, ICCHP 2004 in Paris
- Special Award 2003: A Min Tjoa, Vienna University of Technology on the occasion of his 50th birthday
- *Award 1:* WAI-W3C, ICCHP 2002 in Linz
- Award 0: Prof. Dr. Roland Wagner on the occasion of his 50th birthday, 2001

Once again we thank all those helping to put ICCHP in place and thereby supporting the AT field and a better quality of life for people with disabilities. Special thanks go to all our supporters and sponsors, displayed at: http://www.icchp.org/sponsors.

Contents – Part I

Technology for Inclusion and Participation

Ambient Assisted Living (AAL) for Aging and Disability

The Impact of PDF/UA on Accessible PDF

Standards, Tools and Procedures in Accessible eBook Production

Accessible eLearning - eLearning for Accessibility/AT

Inclusive Settings, Pedagogies and Approaches in ICT-Based Learning for Disabled and Non-disabled People

Digital Games Accessibility

Contents – Part II

Tactile Maps and Map Data for Orientation and Mobility

Mobility Support for Blind and Partially Sighted People

The Use of Mobile Devices by Individuals with Special Needs as an Assistive Tool

Mobility Support for People with Motor and Cognitive Disabilities

Towards e-Inclusion for People with Intellectual Disabilities

AT and Inclusion of People with Autism or Dyslexia

AT and Inclusion of Deaf and Hard of Hearing People

Art Karshmer Lectures in Access to Mathematics, Science and Engineering

Art Karshmer Lectures in Access to Mathematics, Science and Engineering

Introduction to the Special Thematic Session

Dominique Archambault[1]([⊠]), Katsuhito Yamaguchi[2],
Georgios Kouroupetroglou[3], and Klaus Miesenberger[4]

[1] Université Paris 8-Vincennes-Saint-Denis, Saint-Denis, France
`dominique.archambault@univ-paris8.fr`
[2] Nihon University, Tokyo, Japan
[3] National and Kapodistrian University of Athens, Athens, Greece
[4] Johannes Kepler Universität Linz, Linz, Austria

Abstract. This session is the continuation of the STS started by Pr Arthur I. Karshmer at ICCHP since 2002. It intends to bring together experts from around the world to present and discuss the state of the art, the actual research and development activities and the future perspectives in access to mathematics, science and statistics. Its aim is to find ways how the potential of ICT and AT could lead to advancements in education and career of disabled students, in particular, those with a print disability, in fields where advanced skills in mathematics are necessary.

Keyword: Accessibility to mathematics

In memoriam of Pr Arthur I. Karshmer, the founder and long serving chair of this STS.

1 A Few Words About Art

Professor Arthur I. Karshmer, our dear colleague, mentor and Computer Science guru, started a thematic session about access to Mathematics and Science at ICCHP in 2002 in Linz. He intended to have a session presenting *"new approaches to offer blind students a better access to math, to provide tools for doing math as well as to support teachers in teaching math."*

Since 2002, a session about access to Mathematics has always been present at ICCHP conference, chaired by Art. The Table 1 underlines that the STS founded and chaired by Art is one of the few and longer lasting series of references in this domain.

Art started to work in the area of Assistive Technologies in the mid 1980s [6] and was one of the first researchers to wonder how students with visual impairment could access to mathematical notation, and therefore to STEM subjects (Science, Technology, Engineering and Mathematics) [4]. Then he carried on a lot of researches to find ways to help them to understand formulas and to do calculations, and more widely to

Table 1. The "Access to Maths" STS at ICCHP since 2002

Conference		Title of the session	Papers
2002	Linz	*Access to Mathematics for Blind Students*	8
2004	Paris	*Blind People: Access to Mathematics*	12
2006	Linz	*Blind People: Access to Mathematics*	11
2008	Linz	*Access to Mathematics and Science*	15
2010	Vienna	*Blind and Partially Sighted People: Access to Mathematics*	6
2012	Linz	*Access to Mathematics and Science*	13
2014	Paris	*Access to Mathematics, Science and Music*	15
			80

learn Mathematics. He made several breakthrough in this domain and especially when he invented the idea of navigation within a formula using meaningful chunks, which came after studying how people understand Mathematics [5]. Very pragmatic, he understood very early the necessity to work in multi-disciplinary team, with colleagues from other disciplines, like psychology [3].

He was convinced that researchers need to meet, to share, to discuss: that's how new ideas come. He had an incredible number of visits in labs all around the world as invited professor or researcher. There, he would stay a few weeks, taking part of the laboratory life, advising Master and PhD students, giving a few talks and working on his mathematical software. Thereby he came to Paris, Nice, Linz, Finland, Spain, and lots of other places.

He created the STS in 2002 and at the same period he invited us to form a group, that we called iGUMA, for *International Group for Universal Maths Access*, including our teams from Florida, New Mexico, Texas, Dublin, Linz and Paris, soon joined by the infty group in Japan. This group was at the origin of the idea of working on a Universal Maths Conversion Library [2].

Two years ago Art chaired his last ICCHP session in Paris, where he was awarded, together with Pr Masakazu Suzuki, by the seventh ICCHP Roland Wagner Award.

Art was an outstanding researcher, an extraordinary pedagogue, who knew how to build on students knowledge to make them progress, and excellent speaker, who caught immediately his audience. But Art was also a wonderful friend. We were meeting all around, in Linz, Paris, San Francisco or anywhere else, like in his house in Tampa. Whatever time since last meeting, he always add new questions for you, new things he wanted to understand, but also he wanted to understand what you think of this or that, with your different culture and background.

Art passed away in November 2015. We miss him as a friend and researcher. ICCHP and the panel of experts in access to math and science he composed decided to dedicate this session to the memory of Art. We see it as our responsibility to keep its heritage up to date and bring it into the future.

2   The 2016 Session

The 2016 session is dedicated to Art. This year we will have 9 papers, 6 from 6 different European countries, one from the USA and 2 from Japan. 6 of these papers are focused on mathematics itself while 2 are about programming, and one about access to chemistry.

Several years ago, we introduced the following classification of works in the topic of access to Mathematics and Science [1], which appeared successively during the last 2 decades:

1. **accessing**: access to mathematical content, including conversion tools, OCR, *etc.*
2. **understanding**: how to understand mathematical content, including formula browsers, *etc.*
3. **doing**: solving mathematical problems, doing mathematics.

In this session, we have 3 papers about the first category, *"accessing"* including 2 about OCR of mathematical documents:

- *Recognition of E-Born PDF Including Mathematical Formulas*, Masakazu Suzuki and Katsuhito Yamaguchi, Japan;
- *Artificial neural networks and fuzzy logic for recognizing alphabet characters and mathematical symbols*, by Giuseppe Airó Farulla, Tiziana Armano, Anna Capietto, Nadir Murru, and Rosaria Rossini, Italy;

And one about converting mathemactical content into different mathematical braille codes

- *Braille Math extension to RoboBraille - A universal software solution for converting mathematical documents into Braille*, by Vlad Paul Cosma, Tanja Stevns and Lars Ballieu Christensen, Denmark;

Then 5 papers can be classified into the second category: *"undestanding"*, where 2 are about mathematical text-to-speech

- *An Evaluation Methodology of Math-to-Speech in non-English DAISY Digital Talking Books*, by Paraskevi Riga, Georgios Kouroupetroglou, and Polyxeni-Parthena Ioannidou, Greece;
- *Navigation of Mathematical Expressions Using Speech*, by Neil Soiffer, United States;

One about didactics of mathematics:

- *Analysis of Implicit Didactics in Math Schoolbooks for Interactive Non-visual User Interface Development*, by Prajaks Jitngernmadan, Andrea Petz, Bernhard Stöger, and Klaus Miesenberger, Austria;

And two papers about how to design accessible documents, in chemistry, and in computer modelisation.

- *Polyfilling Accessible Chemistry Diagrams*, by Volker Sorge, United Kingdom;

– *Guidelines for Accessible Textual UML Modeling Notations*, by Vanessa Petrausch and Stephan Seifermann, Germany;

Finally the last paper is about *"doing"*, with a method to teach programming using tangible objects.

– *Tangible Programming Gimmck using RFID Systems Considering the Use of Visually Impairments*, by Tatsuo Motoyoshi, Naoki Tetsumura, Hiroyuki Masuta, Kenihci Koyanagi, Toru Oshima and Hiroshi Kawakami, Japan.

References

1. Archambault, D.: Non visual access to mathematical contents: state of the art and prospective. In: Proceedings of WEIMS Conference 2009 (The Workshop on E-Inclusion in Mathematics and Science), pp. 43–52 (2009)
2. Archambault, D., Fitzpatrick, D., Gupta, G., Karshmer, A.I., Miesenberger, K., Pontelli, E.: Towards a universal maths conversion library. In: Miesenberger, K., Klaus, J., Zagler, W.L., Burger, D. (eds.) ICCHP 2004. LNCS, vol. 3118, pp. 664–669. Springer, Heidelberg (2004)
3. Karshmer, A., Gillan, D.: How well can we read equations to blind mathematics students: some answers from psychology. In: Proceedings of 10th International Conference on Human-Computer Interaction, Universal Access in HCI - Inclusive Design in the Information Society, vol. 4, pp. 1290–1294. Lawrence Erlbaum Associates, Mahwah, New Jersey, USA (2003)
4. Karshmer, A., Gupta, G., Geiger, S., Weaver, C.: Reading and writing mathematics: the MAVIS project. Behav. Inf. Technol. **18**(1), 2–10 (1998)
5. Karshmer, A.I., Bledsoe, C.: Introduction to the special thematic session. In: Miesenberger, K., Klaus, J., Zagler, W. (eds.) ICCHP 2002. LNCS, vol. 2398, pp. 471–476. Springer, Heidelberg (2002)
6. Karshmer, A.I., Oliver, R.L.: Special computer interfaces for the visually handicapped: F.O.B. the manufacturer. In: Bass, L.J., Unger, C., Gornostaev, J. (eds.) EWHCI 1993. LNCS, vol. 753, pp. 272–280. Springer, Heidelberg (1993)

Artificial Neural Networks and Fuzzy Logic for Recognizing Alphabet Characters and Mathematical Symbols

Giuseppe Airò Farulla[1], Tiziana Armano[2], Anna Capietto[2], Nadir Murru[2(✉)], and Rosaria Rossini[3]

[1] Department of Control and Computer Engineering, Politecnico di Torino,
Corso Duca Degli Abruzzi 24, Torino 10129, Italy
`giuseppe.airof@gmail.com`
[2] Department of Mathematics, University of Turin,
Via Carlo Alberto 10, Torino 10121, Italy
`{tiziana.armano,anna.capietto,nadir.murru}@unito.it`
[3] Center for Applied Research on ICT, Istituto Superiore Mario Boella,
Via Pier Carlo Boggio 61, Torino 10138, Italy
`rosaria.francesca.rossini@gmail.com`

Abstract. Optical Character Recognition software (OCR) are important tools for obtaining accessible texts. We propose the use of artificial neural networks (ANN) in order to develop pattern recognition algorithms capable of recognizing both normal texts and formulae. We present an original improvement of the backpropagation algorithm. Moreover, we describe a novel image segmentation algorithm that exploits fuzzy logic for separating touching characters.

Keywords: Artificial neural networks · Fuzzy logic · Kalman filter · Optical character recognition

1 Introduction

Currently, InftyReader is the unique OCR that performs automatic recognition of both normal texts and formulae [20]. The pattern recognition algorithm used by the authors of InftyReader is based on support vector machine learning [20]. In this paper, we propose to base the pattern recognition algorithm on artificial neural networks (ANNs). ANNs can be successfully exploited for developing pattern recognition algorithms [3]. Recently, several studies have been pointed out on ANNs for the automatic recognition of characters in different alphabets, such as Latin [18], Arabic [16] and many others. However, it appears that ANNs have not been exploited for recognizing both alphabet characters and mathematical

R. Rossini—This work has been developed in the framework of an agreement between IRIFOR/UICI (Institute for Research, Education and Rehabilitation/Italian Union for the Blind and Partially Sighted) and Turin University.

K. Miesenberger et al. (Eds.): ICCHP 2016, Part I, LNCS 9758, pp. 7–14, 2016.
DOI: 10.1007/978-3-319-41264-1_1

symbols in printed documents yet, since the large amount of different patterns to recognize does not allow fast convergence of the training algorithms. In this paper, we address this problem by means of an original use of the Kalman filter (mainly based on the work of Murru and Rossini [14]), with the aim of improving the rate of convergence in the training of ANNs even in presence of a large amount of patterns that must be recognized. In particular we study the backpropagation (BP) algorithm. It is well–known that convergence of BP is heavily affected by initial weights [1]. Different initialization techniques have been proposed such as adaptive step size methods [17], partial least squares method [9], interval based method [19]. Other different approaches can be found, e.g., in [2,5]. However, random weight initialization is still the most used method also due to its simplicity. Thus, the study of new initialization methods is an important research field in order to improve application of neural nets and deepen their knowledge.

Within an OCR, pattern segmentation is a required step before pattern analysis and recognition. The most common character segmentation algorithms are based on vertical projection, pitch estimation or character size, contour analysis, or segmentation–recognition coupled techniques [13]. Several methods for separating touching characters have been developed, see, e.g., [7,10,12,15]. In presence of formulae, separation of touching characters is harder since cutting positions can occur vertically, horizontally and diagonally. Several methods perform differently according to the features of the characters and their selection and use is an art rather than a technique. In other words, features selection mainly depends on the experience of the authors. Thus, in this context, fuzzy logic can be very useful, since it is widely used in applications where tuning of features is based on experience and it can be preferred to a deterministic approach. In this paper, we propose a method that combines, by means of a fuzzy logic based approach, some state–of–the–art features usually exploited one at a time.

In Sect. 2, we explain a novel method for the initialization of weights that improves performances of the backpropagation algorithm in order to train neural nets in the field of pattern recognition. In Sect. 3, we present a fuzzy based approach for performig segmentation of touching characters. Finally, Sects. 4 and 5 are devoted to numerical results and conclusions, respectively.

2 An Improvement of the Backpropagation Algorithm

Let us consider a neural network with L layers. Let $N(i)$ be the number of neurons in the layer i, for $i = 1, ..., L$, and $w_{ij}^{(k)}$ be the weight of connection between the i-th neuron in the layer k and the j-th neuron in the layer $k - 1$. An ANN is trained over a set of inputs so that it provides a fixed output for a given training input. Let us denote X the set of training inputs. An element $\mathbf{x} \in X$ is a vector (e.g., a string of bits representing a pattern). Let $a_i^{(k,\mathbf{x})}$ be the output of the i-th neuron in layer k when an input $\mathbf{x}$ is processed by the ANN. This output is computed as follows:

$$\begin{cases} a_i^{(1,\mathbf{x})} = f(x_i) \\ a_i^{(k,\mathbf{x})} = f\left(\sum_{j=1}^{N(k-1)} w_{ij}^{(k)} a_j^{(k-1,\mathbf{x})}\right), \quad k = 2, ..., L, \end{cases} \tag{1}$$

where f is the activation function (usually, the sigmoidal or hyperbolic tangent function). Finally, let $\mathbf{y}^{(\mathbf{x})}$ be the desired output of the neural network corresponding to the input $\mathbf{x}$. In other words, we would like that $\mathbf{a}^{(L,\mathbf{x})} = \mathbf{y}^{(\mathbf{x})}$, when neural net processes input $\mathbf{x}$. Clearly, this depends on weights $w_{ij}^{(k)}$ and it is not possible to know their correct values a priori. Thus, it is usual to randomly initialize values of weights and use a training algorithm in order to adjust their values. One of the most common and used training algorithm is the BP. In [14], Murru and Rossini proposed an original approach for the initialization of weights mainly based on a customization of the Kalman filter through a Bayesian approach, in order to improve performances of BP algorithm. The Kalman filter is a well–established technique to estimate the state $\mathbf{w}_t$ of a dynamic process at each time t. Specifically, the Kalman gain matrix balances prior estimations and measurements so that an estimation is provided as follows: $\tilde{\mathbf{w}}_t = \mathbf{w}_t^- + K_t(\mathbf{m}_t - \mathbf{w}_t^-)$, where $\mathbf{m}_t$ is a measurement of the process, $\mathbf{w}_t^-$ a prior estimation of the process, K_t the Kalman gain matrix. As in [14], we customize the Kalman filter modeling measurements and prior estimations by means of multivariate normal random variables $\mathbf{W}_t$ and $\mathbf{M}_t$ such that their density functions satisfy $g(\mathbf{W}_t) = \mathcal{N}(\mathbf{w}_t^-, Q_t)$, $g(\mathbf{M}_t|\mathbf{W}_t) = \mathcal{N}(\mathbf{m}_t^-, R_t)$, where Q_t and R_t are covariance matrices conveniently initialized. In this way, the posterior density is given by $g(\mathbf{W}_t|\mathbf{M}_t) \propto \mathcal{N}(\mathbf{w}_t^-, Q_t)\mathcal{N}(\mathbf{m}_t, R_t) = \mathcal{N}(\tilde{\mathbf{w}}_t, P_t)$, where $\tilde{\mathbf{w}}_t = (Q_t^{-1}+R_t^{-1})^{-1}(Q_t^{-1}\mathbf{w}_t^- +R_t^{-1}\mathbf{m}_t)$, $P_t = (Q_t^{-1}+R_t^{-1})^{-1}$. We can apply this technique to weights initialization considering processes $\mathbf{w}_t(k)$, for $k = 2, ..., L$, as non–time–varying quantities whose components are the unknown values of weights $w^{(k)}$, for $k = 2, ..., L$, of the neural net such that $\mathbf{a}^{(L,\mathbf{x})} = \mathbf{y}^{(\mathbf{x})}$. The goal is to provide an estimation of initial weights to reduce the number of steps that allows convergence of BP neural net. Thus, for each set $w^{(k)}$ we consider initial weights as unknown processes and we optimize randomly generated weights (which we consider as measurements of the processes) with the above approach. In these terms, we derive an optimal initialization of weights by means of the following equations:

$$\begin{cases} \mathbf{m}_t = Rnd(-h, h) \\ (R_t)_{ii} = \dfrac{1}{N(k)N(k-1)}\sum_{\mathbf{x}\in X} \|\mathbf{d}^{(k,\mathbf{x})}\|^2, \quad (R_t)_{lm} = 0.7 \\ \tilde{\mathbf{w}}_t = (Q_t^{-1} + R_t^{-1})^{-1}(Q_t^{-1}\mathbf{w}_t^- + R_t^{-1}\mathbf{m}_t) \\ Q_{t+1} = (Q_t^{-1} + R_t^{-1})^{-1}, \quad \mathbf{w}_{t+1}^- = \tilde{\mathbf{w}}_t \end{cases} \tag{2}$$

where $Rnd(-h, h)$ denotes the function that samples a random real number in the interval $(-h, h)$ and $\mathbf{d}^{(k,\mathbf{x})}$ is the usual error of the k–th layer when an input $\mathbf{x}$ is given.

3   Image Segmentation with Fuzzy Logic

In a binarized image, a pattern can be represented by a matrix whose entries are
0 (white pixels) and 1 (black pixels). Generally, methods for segmenting touching characters define a function based on some features that characterize cut
positions. Then, such a function is evaluated for each column (row, or diagonal)
of the matrix and the cut position is chosen depending on its values. Classical functions of this kind are the peak–to–valley function g and the function h
defined as

$$g(i) = \frac{V(l_i) - 2V(i) + V(r_i)}{V(i) + 1}, \quad h(i) = \frac{V(i-1) - 2V(i) + V(i+1)}{V(i)}, \quad (3)$$

where $V(i)$ denotes the vertical projection function for the i-th column (row or
diagonal), l_i and r_i are the peak positions on the left side and right side of i,
respectively. Let us denote by $\bar{g}$ and $\bar{h}$ the functions g and h normalized to $[0,1]$,
respectively. In the following, we will consider $\tilde{g} = 1 - \bar{g}$ and $\tilde{h} = 1 - \bar{h}$. Here,
we propose a fuzzy routine typically identifying a column, a row, or a diagonal
of the matrix that could be a cut point that conveniently separates the touching
characters.

Our fuzzy routine combines four state–of–the–art features: distance from the
center of the pattern; crossing count, i.e., the number of transitions from white
to black pixels, and viceversa; the function $\bar{g}$; the function $\bar{h}$. These features are
widely used in literature for determining cut positions in touching characters
[12]. However, they are usually managed separately and in a deterministic way.
In our approach, these features are combined by means of convenient fuzzy rules
in order to exploit the information given by each of these features.

Given a pattern in a binarized image, let A, m, n, and c be the matrix of
pixels of the binarized matrix, the number of rows of A, the number of columns
of A, and the central column of A, respectively. For the sake of simplicity, in the
following we only focus on columns of A and when we refer to a column i of A,
we refer to the i–th column of A, i.e., we are considering the vector of length
m whose elements are the entries of the i–th column. For each column i of A,
we define its normalized distance from the center of the pattern as $d(i) = \frac{|c-i|}{c}$.
Moreover, we indicate the crossing count function by f, i.e., the number of
transitions between white and black pixels.

To design a suitable fuzzy strategy, some steps are required, in order to
introduce the notion of a fuzzy degree qualifying a column i to be a cut position:
for short $\rho = \rho(i) \in [0,1]$. In our model, the low values of ρ locate good cut
positions. The strategy can be detailed by means of the fuzzification of the
functions d, f, $\tilde{g}$, $\tilde{h}$. Figure 1a, b and c show the fuzzy sets and the related
membership functions. Note that we have considered the same fuzzy sets and
membership functions for $\tilde{g}$, $\tilde{h}$, and ρ.

For each column i of A, the inference system combines the values $d(i)$, $f(i)$,
$\tilde{g}(i)$, $\tilde{h}(i)$ and produces the fuzzy output $\rho(i)$ by means of the following fuzzy
rules:

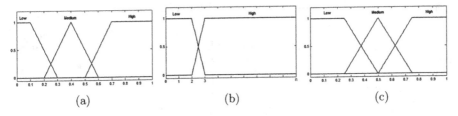

Fig. 1. Membership functions of the fuzzy sets related to, respectively, (a) d, (b) f, (c) $\tilde{g}$, $\tilde{h}$, and ρ.

1. if $d(i)$ is Low and $\tilde{g}(i), \tilde{h}(i)$ are not High and $f(i)$ is Low, then $\rho(i)$ is Low;
2. if $\tilde{g}(i), \tilde{h}(i)$ are Low and $d(i)$ is Medium and $f(i)$ is Low, then $\rho(i)$ is Low;
3. if $\tilde{g}(i)$ is Low and $d(i)$ is not High and $\tilde{h}(i)$ is not Low and $f(i)$ is Low, then $\rho(i)$ is Low;
4. if $d(i)$ is Low and $\tilde{g}(i), \tilde{h}(i)$ are not High and $f(i)$ is High, then $\rho(i)$ is Medium;
5. if $\tilde{g}(i), \tilde{h}(i)$ are Low and $d(i)$ is Medium and $f(i)$ is High, then $\rho(i)$ is Medium;
6. if $\tilde{g}(i)$ is Low and $d(i)$ is not High and $\tilde{h}(i)$ is not Low and $f(i)$ is High, then $\rho(i)$ is Medium;
7. if $\tilde{h}(i)$ is Low and $d(i)$ is not High and $g(i)$ is not Low and $f(i)$ is Low, then $\rho(i)$ is Medium;
8. if $d(i), \tilde{g}(i), \tilde{h}(i)$ are Medium and $f(i)$ is Low, then $\rho(i)$ is Medium;
9. otherwise $\rho(i)$ is High.

These fuzzy rules have been tuned using heuristic criteria taking into account that high values of g, h and low values of d, f usually identify cut positions. The inference engine is the basic Mamdani model with if–then rules, minimax set–operations, sum for composition of activated rules and defuzzification based on the centroid method. The Mamdani model is congenial to capture and to code expert-based knowledge.

4 Numerical Results

In this section, we describe the process to train neural networks in order to recognize both characters and mathematical symbols, comparing the rate of convergence of the BP algorithm with the Bayesian initialization (BI) presented in Sect. 2 against classical random initialization (RI).

Firstly, we use a training set composed by 26 Latin printed characters for 7 different fonts (Arial, Cambria, Courier, Georgia, Tahoma, Times New Roman, Verdana), 24 Greek letters, and 35 miscellaneous mathematical symbols, with 12 pt. In Fig. 2a, b and c performances of BP algorithm with BI and RI are compared for different values of h and η, where $(-h, h)$ is the interval where weights are sampled and η is the learning rate of the BP algorithm. The improvement in convergence rate due to BI is noticeable at a glance in these figures. In particular, we can see that BI approach is more resistant than RI with respect to high values of h. In fact, for large values of h, weights can range over a large

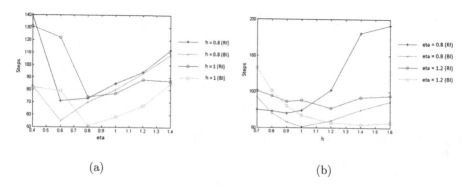

(a)   (b)

Fig. 2. Comparison between BI and RI for convergence of BP neural net with $L = 3$, $N(1) = 315$, $N(2) = 100$, $N(3) = 85$, and hyperbolic tangent activation function

interval. Consequently, RI produces weights scattered on a large interval causing a slower convergence of BP algorithm. On the other hand, BI seems to set initial weights on regions that allow a faster convergence of BP algorithm, despite the size of h. This could be very useful in complex problems where small values of h do not allow convergence of BP algorithm and large intervals are necessary, as the case of the realization of an OCR for both text and formulae, where the number of different patterns for training the neural net is very high and large values of h are necessary. Indeed, we can observe in our simulations that the best performances are generally obtained by BI with large values of h.

In Table 1, we have trained neural networks on the MNIST training set [11], composed by 60000 handwritten digits. Note that in the case of the MNIST database, if training is accomplished over all the training dataset, then BP algorithm for multilayer neural networks yields a very high accuracy in the recognition on the MNIST validation set composed by 10000 handwritten digits (more than 99 %, see, e.g., [4]).

The computational complexity to implement the classical Kalman filter is polynomial (see, e.g., [6] p. 226). Our customization is faster since it involves

Table 1. Comaprison between BI and RI for convergence of BP neural net trained on the MNIST database

	$L = 5, \eta = 1.5$		$L = 3, \eta = 3$	
	Random in.	Bayes in.	Random in.	Bayes in.
h	Steps	Steps	Steps	Steps
0.7	832	809	874	868
0.8	823	812	652	631
0.9	748	696	722	706
1	749	671	688	564
1.1	961	929	803	658
1.2	1211	1118	967	872

fewer number of operations (matrix multiplications) than usual Kalman filter and we use circulant matrices, whose inverse can be evaluated in a very fast way. Indeed, these matrices can be diagonalized by using the Discrete Fourier Transform ([8], p. 32); the Discrete Fourier Transform and the inverse of a diagonal matrix are immediate to evaluate. Thus, our initialization algorithm is faster than classical Kalman filter, moreover it is iterated for a low number of steps (usually twice). Surely, this approach has a time complexity greater than random initialization. However, looking at BP Algorithm, we can observe that Eq. 2 involve similar operations (i.e., matrix multiplications or multiplications between matrices and vectors) in a minor quantity; moreover it needs a smaller number of cycles. Furthermore, we have seen that BI generally leads to a noticeable decrease of steps necessary for the convergence of the BP algorithm with respect to random initialization. Thus, using BI we can reach a faster convergence, in terms of time, of the BP algorithm than using random initialization.

Finally, we report the results on the segmentation of 296 touching characters by means of the fuzzy method explained in the previous section. The dataset is composed by 66 touching characters font Verdana and 10 pt, 58 with font Times New Roman and 20 pt, 92 font Lucida and 25 pt, 40 Georgia and 20 pt, 54 Cambria and 20 pt. Our method correctly segments the 93.6 % of these touching characters, improving performances obtained by using functions g and h one at a time that perform a correct segmentation in 76.5 % and 71.1 % of cases, respectively.

5   Conclusion

We propose the development of an OCR able to recognize both alphabet characters and mathematical symbols. The pattern recognition algorithm is based on ANNs trained by means of an improvement of the backpropagation algorithm. The image segmentation algorithm is based on a fuzzy routine that combines some features usually exploited one at a time. Note that we are not proposing an OCR already completed and tuned. The proposed experimental results and simulations show that the approaches presented in this paper introduce improvements and benefits if compared with existing standard achievements.

Future works will deal with an extensive validation of the proposed system with visually impaired and blind subjects. Moreover, we will develop a novel architecture for character recognition, based on an array of ANNs which are applied in parallel to a given input pattern. This choice will enable us to reach better accuracy with respect to more traditional approaches based on a single ANN, with at the same time no appreciable degradation on performances.

References

1. Adam, S., Karras, D.A., Vrahatis, M.N.: Revisiting the problem of weight initialization for multi-layer perceptrons trained with back propagation. In: Köppen, M., Kasabov, N., Coghill, G. (eds.) ICONIP 2008, Part II. LNCS, vol. 5507, pp. 308–315. Springer, Heidelberg (2009)

2. Adam, S.P., Karras, D.A., Magoulas, G.D., Vrahatis, M.N.: Solving the linear interval tolerance problem for weight initialization of neural networks. Neural Netw. **54**, 17–37 (2014)
3. Bishop, C.M.: Neural Networks for Pattern Recognition. Clarendon Express, Oxford (1995)
4. Cireşan, D.C., Meier, U., Gambardella, L.M., Schmidhuber, J.: Deep big multilayer perceptrons for digit recognition. In: Montavon, G., Orr, G.B., Müller, K.-R. (eds.) Neural Networks: Tricks of the Trade. LNCS, vol. 7700, 2nd edn, pp. 581–598. Springer, Heidelberg (2012)
5. Erdogmus, D., Romero, O.F., Principe, J.C.: Linear-least-squares initialization of multilayer perceptrons through backpropagation of the desired response. IEEE Trans. Neural Netw. **16**(2), 325–336 (2005)
6. Hajiyev, C., Caliskan, F.: Fault Diagnosis and Reconfiguration in Flight Control Systems. Springer, Heidelberg (2003)
7. Garain, U., Chaudhuri, B.B.: Segmentation of touching symbols for OCR of printed mathematical expressions: an approach based on multifactorial analysis. In: 8th International Conference in Documents Analysis and Recognition, pp. 177–181 (2005)
8. Gray, R.M.: Toeplitz and circulant matrices: a review. Found. Trends Commun. Inf. Theor. **2**(3), 155–239 (2006)
9. Hsiao, T.C., Lin, C.W., Chiang, H.K.: Partial least squares algorithm for weight initialization of backpropagation network. Neurocomputing **5**, 237–247 (2003)
10. Kumar, A., Yadav, M., Patnaik, T., Kumar, B.: A survey on touching charcter segmentation. Int. J. Eng. Adv. Technol. **2**(3), 569–574 (2013)
11. Lecun, Y., Cortes, C., Burges, C.J.C.: The MNIST database of handwriteen digits. http://yann.lecun.com/exdb/mnist
12. Liang, S., Shridhar, M., Ahmadi, M.: Segmentation of touching characters in printed document recognition. Pattern Recogn. **27**(6), 825–840 (1994)
13. Lu, Y.: Machine printed character segmentation - an overview. Pattern Recogn. **28**(1), 67–80 (1995)
14. Murru, N., Rossini, R.: A Bayesian approach for initialization of weights in back-propagation neural net with application to character recognition. Neurocomputing (2016, to appear)
15. Saba, T., Sulong, G., Rahim, S., Rehman, A.: On the segmentation of multiple touched cursive characters: a heuristic approach. In: Das, V.V., Vijaykumar, R. (eds.) ICT 2010. CCIS, vol. 101, pp. 540–542. Springer, Heidelberg (2010)
16. Sahlol, A.T., Suen, C.Y., Elbasyouni, M.R., Sallam, A.A.: A proposed OCR algo-rithm for the recognition of handwritten Arabic characters. J. Pattern Recogn. Intell. Syst. **2**(1), 8–22 (2014)
17. Schrusolph, N.N.: Fast curvature matrix-vector products for second order gradient descent. Neural Comput. **14**(7), 1723–1738 (2002)
18. Shrivastava, V.: Artificial neural networks based optical character recognition. Sig. Image Process.: Int. J. **3**(5), 73–80 (2012)
19. Sodhi, S.S., Chandra, P.: Interval based weight initialization method for sigmoidal feedforward artificial neural networks. AASRI Procedia **6**, 19–25 (2014)
20. Suzuki, M., Kanahori, T., Ohtake, N., Yamaguchi, K.: An integrated OCR software for mathematical documents and its output with accessibility. In: Miesenberger, K., Klaus, J., Zagler, W.L., Burger, D. (eds.) ICCHP 2004. LNCS, vol. 3118, pp. 648–655. Springer, Heidelberg (2004)

Braille Math Extension to RoboBraille

A Universal Software Solution for Converting Math into Braille

Vlad Paul Cosma, Tanja Stevns, and Lars Ballieu Christensen[✉]

Sensus ApS, Hillerød, Denmark
{paul,tanja,lars}@sensus.dk

Abstract. While sighted mathematicians have long accepted the need for a uniform way of writing math, the situation amongst the blind is different: Rather than standardising, the tradition has been to develop language-, country- or even institution-specific codes for expressing math in Braille in addition to the national Braille codes for literary Braille. Using the RoboBraille service as a foundation, the paper describes an automated and flexible system that can shred, transcribe and reassemble documents containing math into Braille. Using existing components, the Braille Math extension to RoboBraille enables Braille readers to mix and match amongst supported national Braille codes and Braille math regimes, including Braille math systems like Nemeth and Marburg, and mainstream formats such as LaTeX and MathML. Finally, the paper discusses how the system may be enhanced to handle charts, graphs and tables.

Keywords: Braille math · Inclusive education for all · Automated transcription · RoboBraille · UMCL

1 Introduction

Math is important in mainstream education as it is an integral part of many subjects (math, biology, sociology, economics, and linguistics). As blind students are included in mainstream education, adequate transcription systems are required that can convert educational material containing mathematical notation into Braille in a timely, cost-efficient and easy way. Sighted mathematicians have long accepted the need for a unified way of expressing math. Using a common set of universally agreed mathematical symbols [1], this enables mathematicians from different cultures and countries to learn, exchange and discuss mathematical problems.

2 The Braille Math Challenge

In order to present math in Braille, the two-dimensional notation used by the sighted needs to be transcribed into a sequence of Braille characters. Although it has proven difficult to teach math to blind students and costly to transcribe textbook material in Braille, the approach in many countries has been to develop language-, country- or

© Springer International Publishing Switzerland 2016
K. Miesenberger et al. (Eds.): ICCHP 2016, Part I, LNCS 9758, pp. 15–18, 2016.
DOI: 10.1007/978-3-319-41264-1_2

even institution-specific Braille codes for math. Examples include Antoine (France), Marburg (Germany and others), as well as the British Math Braille code used in the UK and many commonwealth countries, the Nemeth code used in the US and many places in the Middle East and Asia, and many others. Some educational institutions experiment with using mainstream formats such as LaTeX and MathML directly.

For the text parts of the educational material, the situation is similar: The literary Braille codes differ from country to country and from language to language, with significant difference in how Braille signs are used to represent contractions, national characters, punctuation signs and more. Even though math Braille notation could likely benefit from standardisation (similar to the standardisation of music Braille), standardisation and international acceptance of a uniform way of expressing math in Braille is unlikely to happen in the foreseeable future.

3   Bringing Fragmented Solutions Together

To accommodate the blind, systems are required that allow to select between different national Braille codes and Braille math notation systems with minimum hassle.

Several solutions exist for transcribing math into Braille, including MathInBraille [2], LaBraDoor [3], BraMaNet [4], Math2Braille [5], Winsight [6] and many more.

The Braille Math extension to RoboBraille [7] consolidates several Braille transcription and math conversion libraries (Sensus SB4 [8], LibLouis [9], UMCL [10], fMath [11]) into a single solution, enabling users to mix and match amongst supported Braille codes and Braille math regimes.

4   The Braille Math Extension to RoboBraille (BMER)

The objective of the BMER was to create a system capable of automatically transcribing a digital representation of a mathematical schoolbook created for the sighted into a Braille book. As such, the BMER provides a unified interface to a range of efficient conversion tools specific for each document element (text, math, tables, graphics), under a single, accessible and user friendly interface that is universally available to students and others. Likely end-users are blind students and teachers that need books containing math equations converted into Braille.

The BMER comprises a set of programs and libraries designed to work together under a single web application. The BMER is based on a robust, vertically layered architecture, that is easily extendable to support the addition of new components. The BMER consists of three layers: 1. The Presentation Layer (top layer), the web application, handles the interaction between the user and the software. 2. The Domain Logic layer (middle layer) is responsible for transporting and manipulating data. And 3. The Data Source layer (bottom layer) contains the individual conversion libraries. They achieve the simple conversion tasks of transcribing text to literary Braille code, MathML to math Braille code or shapes to tactile graphics.

Once submitted for conversion, the document goes through three stages: (1) preparation; (2) processing; and (3) formatting. Stage 1 shreds the document into its basic elements (text, math, illustrations), while at the same time maintaining its structure. Stage 2 sends each element, along with relevant input parameters, to the appropriate data source layer library and retrieves the converted result. For consistency reasons, all results are represented within the unicode Braille range. Finally, stage 3 brings the elements back together to a single document and applies the final formatting, such as pagination, page numbering, conversion into the Portable Embosser Format (PEF) [12] or local character set transposition. Each mathematical equation is written on a new line, in order to distinguish text from math. For "Simplified LaTeX" conversions, the dollar symbol marks when an equation begins and ends, e.g., $ c - 1 = b $.

The domain logic layer constitutes the core implementation and functionality of the BMER. The layer is split into mechanisms for transportation and manipulation of data. Furthermore, it is responsible for linking the data source layer with the presentation layer. In order to achieve this, each of the four underlying libraries are encapsulated into their own unit of work that exposes their functionality through a clearly defined point of entry. Towards the presentation layer, communication is implemented with remote procedure calls to ensure extensibility and reliability.

Initially four libraries were selected to achieve the text and math conversions. Sensus SB4 and LibLouis are used for literary Braille conversions of text, while fMath and UMCL handle conversions from MathML to a variety of math Braille codes. fMath is used to convert MathML to LaTeX. UMCL is used to convert MathML into Braille math in Nemeth, Marburg, British, French, Italian and Czech Braille math codes.

5   Evaluation and Future Work

Following development and extensive testing, a few conclusions can be made: Mapping MathML constructs into their LaTeX representations appear accurate. The conversion of MathML into Nemeth, Marburg, British, French, Italian and Czech is limited due to the confines of the underlying UMCL as discussed in [13]; this limits the usefulness to cover only the curriculum until and including upper secondary level as concepts such as matrices, integrals, trigonometric functions or limits are not support-ed. Following final testing, the BMER is expected to be made publicly available as part of the RoboBraille service during the second half of 2016.

The resulting Braille text document reflects the structure of the source document. Reliability is assured by marking failed conversions in the resulting document, so that they may be resolved at a later time by manual intervention. The overall performance of the solution is linear to the size of the input file, which is a limitation of the underlying libraries. Utilizing messaging queues in a cloud-based architecture, multiple conversions can be handled in parallel.

During the development of the Braille Math extension to RoboBraille, several ide-as for improvements were identified: Support for scanned documents: The current implementation relies on documents in Microsoft Word with math equations composed using an equation editor. Charts and graphs: The current implementation does not support illustrations. As math material typically consists of text, mathematical notation as well as graphs and charts, a future solution would benefit from being able to export illustrations into documents that can be rendered as tactile graphics, 3D renditions or similar. Tables: The current implementation is capable of extracting table information from the document. A future solution could benefit from being able to map table data into a linearized Braille form.

References

1. ISO 80000-2:2009 Quantities and units - Part 2: Mathematical signs and symbols to be used in the natural sciences and technology. ISO (2009)
2. Miesenberger, K., Batusic, M., Heumader, P., Stöger, B.: MathInBraille online converter. In: Miesenberger, K., Karshmer, A., Penaz, P., Zagler, W. (eds.) ICCHP 2012, Part I. LNCS, vol. 7382, pp. 196–203. Springer, Heidelberg (2012)
3. Batusic, M., Miesenberger, K., Stöger, B.: Labradoor, a contribution to making mathematics accessible for the blind. In: Edwards, A., Arato, A., Zagler, W. (eds.) ICCHP 1998. Springer, Berlin (1998)
4. BraMaNet: http://handy.univ-lyon1.fr/MH/bramanet/bramanet.php
5. Crombie, D., Lenoir, R., McKenzie, N.R., Barker, A.: math2braille: opening access to mathematics. In: Miesenberger, K., Klaus, J., Zagler, W.L., Burger, D. (eds.) ICCHP 2004. LNCS, vol. 3118, pp. 670–677. Springer, Heidelberg (2004)
6. Gopal, D., Wang, Q., Gupta, G., Chitnis, S., Guo, H., Karshmer, Arthur I.: Winsight: towards completely automatic backtranslation of Nemeth code. In: Stephanidis, C. (ed.) HCI 2007. LNCS, vol. 4556, pp. 309–318. Springer, Heidelberg (2007)
7. Christensen, L.B.: RoboBraille – automated braille translation by means of an e-mail robot. In: Miesenberger, K., Klaus, J., Zagler, W.L., Karshmer, A.I. (eds.) ICCHP 2006. LNCS, vol. 4061, pp. 1102–1109. Springer, Heidelberg (2006)
8. Christensen, L.B.: Multilingual two-way braille translation. In: Klaus, J., et al. (eds.) Interdisciplinary Aspects on Computers Helping People with Special Needs, Österreichische Computer Gesellschaft/R. Oldenbourg Wien München (1996)
9. LibLouis: http://www.liblouis.org
10. Archambault, D., et al.: UMCL: https://sourceforge.net/projects/umcl
11. fMath: http://www.fmath.info
12. Portable Embosser Format (PEF): http://pef-format.org
13. Jamar, M.: Conversion of Mathematical Documents into Braille. Masaryk University, Faculty of Informatics (2012)

Analysis of Implicit Didactics in Math Schoolbooks for Interactive Non-visual User Interface Development

Prajaks Jitngernmadan[✉], Andrea Petz, Bernhard Stöger,
and Klaus Miesenberger

Johannes Kepler University, Linz, Austria
{prajaks.jitngernmadan, andrea.petz, bernhard.stoeger,
klaus.miesenberger}@jku.at

Abstract. Most math schoolbooks consist of practical and theoretical parts where the theoretical parts guide the students and explain the strategies on how to solve a given problem. These theoretical parts contain visual didactic information where the problem solving processes are explained using pictorial and spatial representations. So far, there is no workaround for non-visual user interfaces such as refreshable braille displays to represent this implicit visual information. This affects learning ability of visually impaired and blind students. In this paper, we present the results from analyzing these implicit notations and the possible strategies to help visually impaired and blind students benefiting from visual didactic information in math schoolbooks.

Keywords: Implicit didactics · Mathematics · Schoolbooks · Visual notation · Non-visual user interface

1 Introduction

In the didactics of teaching mathematics at primary school level, different teachers and/or educators try to use different strategies for catching students' attention. This reflects in math schoolbooks from different publishers. Generally, a classical math schoolbook consists of two parts of contents: a theoretical and a practical one. In order to understand how the didactics in math schoolbooks works, we considered to do a research on the theoretical part of three different math schoolbooks from three different Austrian publishers [1–3]. The educators who designed the lessons had applied the concepts that are based on visual representation where the problems and necessary steps to solve them are visualized and represented. This approach works perfectly fine for sighted students, especially the visualization in terms of the so-called spatial representation where the visualization provides objects' arrangement and their relations [4]. The visual (pictorial) representations are e.g. different colors for different place values, artifacts or objects representing digits and numbers, thin or thick lines representing borders, letters of different place values (in German H for hundreds, Z for tens, and E for ones) indicating real value of that digit, etc. The spatial representations are e.g. arrangement of digits by using tables or matrices, relations by using arrows,

© Springer International Publishing Switzerland 2016
K. Miesenberger et al. (Eds.): ICCHP 2016, Part I, LNCS 9758, pp. 19–26, 2016.
DOI: 10.1007/978-3-319-41264-1_3

alignment of digits in different rows, context-relevant instructions, etc. From analysis of these math schoolbooks, we categorized these kinds of notation into three domains of didactic teaching methods, namely (1) implicit visual notations, (2) context-relevant instructions, and (3) spatial arrangements.

Visually impaired or blind students who are assisted with assistive technologies (AT) such as refreshable braille displays or screen reader software would need a translation of those didactic approaches. The approaches would have to be converted into formats that can be accessed and represented by the AT. At the conversion, as used for mathematical contents in the moment, some of these visual and didactically valuable notations are simply ignored. Possible reasons for this are the developmental status of AT and traditional teaching approaches for blind students [5]. The lack of this implicit information of didactics, of course, affects the learning ability of the blind students.

Another problem that affects the conversion of visual didactic information into a non-visual format is the representation of formulae, which are rep-resented in 2-dimensional structures. In addition, educators may use spatial arrangements to give step-by-step instructions for more complex mathematical problem solving. Blind students usually use refreshable braille displays that can represent information only one line at a time (1-dimensional). In consequence of their features, this kind of AT cannot display information in 2-dimensional representation.

In our work, we concentrated on analyzing the didactics in math schoolbooks, especially concerning the theoretical part that contains valuable implicit information. This includes the visual notations, spatial arrangements, and 2-dimensional representation of mathematical formulae. Furthermore, it is important to describe valuable implicit information explicitly, in order to develop strategies for adapting/converting them to be used with non-visual user interfaces.

2   State of the Art

According to Stoeger and Miesenberger [6], the visually impaired or blind people can deal with mathematics in three different ways. These are (1) reading mathematics where it can be happened mostly in the continuous plaintext con-tents, (2) navigating within mathematical contents or formulae, and (3) doing mathematics or manipulating the mathematical contents, especially for those who are in the higher education or scientific institutions. Several researches tried to approach the solutions for these three problems. The approaches do solve some parts of the problem but not in total. None of the solutions can fulfill the problems completely [5].

2.1   Reading a Mathematical Formula

For reading mathematical formulae in a document, one has to be sure that the mathematical formulae will be transformed from 2-dimensional to linear presentation correctly. To distinguish the text braille codes from the mathematical one, the braille codes for mathematical expressions are defined. The code notation is not standardized worldwide. Different regions have different mathematical braille codes. Two problems can be identified here, the first one is the history of the braille code in different countries, and the second one is the technical development in that country. While the Nemeth Braille Code is popular in the USA and neighboring countries, the Marburg Braille Code is widely used in Germany and is a base for different mathematical braille codes in Europe. In addition, the mathematical braille codes are always long because of the special notations. The technologies affect the use of mathematical braille codes, too. The 6 dots and 8 dots braille codes let the representation of the codes differently. Furthermore, the standard of digital mathematical formula presentation, the MathML, is quite difficult to process for screen reader software. Another popular mathematical notation is LaTeX. The problem here is the learning curve of the notation and the screen reader software may not read out correctly, too. To convert between different mathematical braille codes, we can use some tools that work in a proper way: such as Universal Maths Conversion Library (UMCL) [7], MathInBraille online service [8], etc. Some of these tools can prepare math braille codes into regular plaintext for the screen reader software, and/or speak the text aloud by themselves, such as ASTER by Raman [9] or MathPlayer by Design Science [10].

2.2   Navigating a Mathematical Formula

To navigate through mathematical formulae is a step more complicated than reading them. The navigation throughout a mathematical formula needs a well-structured mathematical notation. For the sighted people, the eyes will register a mathematical formula in a whole, and then begin to navigate the detail items one by one. The 2-dimensional mathematical formula representation builds up a structure of the formula content indirectly. For the blind people, they will not receive the information of the formula as a whole in the first stage. They will start at the beginning of the mathematical formula and then go through the detail items one by one. This can lead to a major time consuming, misunderstanding, or even not understanding of this mathematical formula for the blind people. The tool called Math Genie [11] is one of speech-based solutions that uses the MathML format and let the blind users go through the structural tree. Other technologies, e.g. MAWEN prototype (MICOLE project) or gestured-based mathematical formulae browsing on touch screen [6] are in the researching activity and not yet well developed enough to be used in school.

2.3   Doing a Mathematical Formula

To manipulate mathematical formulae one has to deal with the complexity of the mathematical formulae [5]. For the sighted people, the eyes will move between the mathematic terms within the formula rapidly and gather necessary information during this action. The use of tools such as paper and pencil enables the cooperation between physical and psychological functions and builds up the cognitive psychology process [12, 13]. This enable the sighted people to under-stand and can compare the terms in the logical way, including (a) storing information, because the sighted people can take notes with paper and pencil, (b) orientation, for finding the clues, paths, or patterns easily, and (c) formula structure, for rearranging the mathematical formula into simple form. On the other side, the blind people depend on the assistive tools that are available. They may not understand the whole formula because of losing an overview and therefore cannot manipulate it correctly. Despite these obstacles, several tools are developed to help blind people to overcome these limitations. Tools that deal with mathematical calculation and function using assistants are, e.g. MAWEN Prototype that can deal with arithmetic and a tool that deals with algebra from PhD thesis of Flores and Archambault [14]. The existing mathematical editors, e.g. MATLAB/MuPAD from MathWorks, etc., can deal with the mathematical calculation, but some of them may not work properly with screen reader software or not suitable for the learning process in the basic state of mathematics learning.

3   Analysis and Model Development

3.1   Structure of Math Schoolbooks

Math schoolbooks from three different popular Austrian publishers (Veritas, Jugend und Volk, and Helbling) were analyzed. These books are used in primary schools and have the same structure (a theoretical and a practical part). The theoretical part contains didactic explanations and examples on how to solve the problems systematically. The practical part contains exercises, where the (sighted) students can practice what they have learned. In the theoretical part, the educators designed an exemplary problem solving process using several strategies to address different perceptual channels of (sighted) students. The most used strategy is the visual one, including pictorial and spatial representation. Figure 1 depicts an example of a typical theoretical part of a math schoolbook showing a long addition.

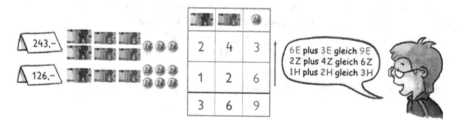

Fig. 1. Typical theoretical part of a mathematical schoolbook [1]

3.2   Analysis of the "Typical" Theoretical Part of a Math Schoolbook

The theoretical part of a math schoolbook contains different visual information anchoring in the explanation process. These paradigms are absorbed with or without awareness of the (sighted) students. For example, different colors for digits categorizing them automatically, relevant objects linking to the same meaning out of students' experience such as a 100€-banknote links to the place value "hundreds", or an arrangement of the digits builds up a meaningful structure of the process, etc.

In addition, a sighted student is able to create his/her own mental map that relates all of the represented information into a meaningful connection, which is important for anchoring and knowledge building.

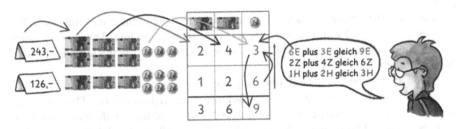

Fig. 2. Relationship between visual information in theoretical part [1]

In Fig. 2, the educators tried to guide the (sighted) students through the long addition solving process by using visual pictorial and spatial representation. They first separate the numbers into three different place values, namely Hundreds, Tens, and Ones (which are H, Z, and E in German respectively). The whole process is built up with 4 perceptible columns. Starting with a three-digit number from the left-hand side, followed by a representation of the number with banknotes and coins, then the arrangement (in form of a table or matrix) is built, and the context-relevant instruction is on the right-hand side. A sighted student may notice this as a whole, and then begin to build up relations between them systematically. For a visually distinct presentation of the single digits, they use table blocks and three different colors, namely red for hundreds, blue for tens, and green for ones. For consistency, these colors remain constant all over the book. Furthermore, the reference to daily life is secured by using banknotes and coins with values of 100€, 10€, and 1€ respectively. The concept of using money also helps with explaining principle of carryover, e.g. when it comes to 14, this value can be split into a 10€ banknote and four 1€ coins and separate them into their respective category.

The later-added color arrows show fictitious relations between adjacent objects and digits. From left to right, one can observe a successive flow of the digit representation. The context-relevant instructions guide the student through the solving process. The blue arrows show the relation between the first instruction and the first sub-calculation step in the table.

3.3 Implicit Didactic Information Extraction

From the analysis above, we categorized the implicit didactic information into three domains, which are (1) implicit visual notations, (2) context-relevant instructions, and (3) spatial arrangements. The implicit visual notations describe behaviors or properties of the used didactic teaching techniques. They highlight an important information for catching learners' attention, e.g. graphics, color-coded fonts, bold line technique, etc. This helps to distinguish upcoming (or relevant) information and non-relevant one.

This can be further differentiated into subdomains, including text attributes (e.g. color-codes, font weight, font size, decorations), graphics (e.g. characters, real-world objects, area representation, number line), symbols (e.g. bold lines, plus sign, pointing arrows), and grouping (e.g. group of ten ones to one ten, grouping by using colors, parentheses).

The context-relevant instructions are noted aside the current calculating step. The learners can read and follow the procedures described in the text. This can be differentiated into subdomains, including overview descriptions, calculation step instructions, and definitions.

The spatial arrangements describe the placement of one or more elements, defining their order (e.g. numbers) into (mostly) 2-dimensional representation. These arrangements are, e.g. table grids, columns of hundreds, tens, and ones with ones at the most right position, addition upwards, etc. This can be differentiated into subdomains, including position (the arrangement, which places the numbers into proper position. The writing of place value abbreviation, such as H, Z, or E, after the number, e.g. 5H + 2Z + 8E.), direction (the arrangement, which guides the learners to the next point, guided arrows, etc.), and boundary (the visible border, which distinguish numbers according to their place values).

The most important feature containing in the implicit didactic information is the relation between different objects. This allows both sighted and blind students build up their own mental map and therefore meaningful knowledge model. This concept of relation is taken into consideration in our model and prototype development.

4   Calculation Process Analysis

4.1   Long Addition Calculation Process Analysis

In order to operate a calculation process, one has to acquire the big picture of the whole assignment. One at least has to know the place value concept. Table 1 shows the steps and tasks used for solving an addition.

Table 1. Steps and tasks used for solving an addition

Step	Task
1	Define columns for hundreds, tens, and ones (H, Z, E)
2	Transcribe the first addend into the respective place value column from left to right
3	Transcribe the second addend into the respective place value column from left to right. Every single digit has to be placed directly below the first addend according to their place values
4	Add up the vertical ones from bottom to top. After finishing with the ones, sum up tens, and then hundreds respectively
5	In case of carryover of the place value ones, the digit that has value over 10 will be kept as an intermediate result, and "1" will be transferred to the place value tens, e.g. 5 + 9 = 14, 4 will be kept at ones and 1 will be transferred to tens
6	If place value tens is assigned with a carryover, this will be added up with the digits from place value tens. This occurs to place value hundreds, too

4.2   Long Addition Activity Diagram

To design our long addition calculation process, we created an activity diagram depicting relations between blind users and software objects. This can be used as a base for further development of our prototype. We implemented an "assistant concept" to guide the blind user throughout the calculating process. This compensates several implicit notations used in math schoolbooks, including, among others, color codes, 2-dimensional representation, spatial arrangement. Figure 3 depicts a part of activity diagram for long addition solving process as described above.

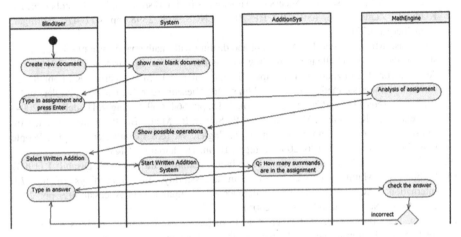

Fig. 3. Part of activity diagram for long addition calculation steps

5   Conclusion and Future Work

The theoretical part of math schoolbooks contains valuable implicit didactic information created from educators. This information can be pictorial and spatial representations, which work efficiently for sighted students. When it comes to conversion of this didactic information for blind students, who use AT such as refreshable braille displays or screen reader software, the implicit information gets lost. We analyzed this theoretical part of math schoolbooks and conceptual designed strategies supporting visually impaired and blind students solving mathematical problems. The presented approaches used in the long addition can be applied for analyzing other basic mathematical operations such as subtraction, multiplication, and division, too. Furthermore, this approach is potential to be applied for other educational contexts that have similar concepts as mathematics. In the near future, we plan to develop suitable prototypes and test our concept.

References

1. Grosser, N., Koth, M.: Alles klar! 3 Mathematik für wissbegierige Schulkinder. VERITAS Schulbuch Verlags- und Handelsges.mbH & Co. OG, Linz (2012)
2. Grurl, C., Liemer-Mair, M., Schoeller, H.: Die Mathe-Forscher/innen 3. Verlag Jugend und Volk GmbH, Wien (2012)
3. Wohlhart, D., Scharnreitner, M., Kleißner, E.: EINS PLUS 3 - ERARBEITUNGSTEIL. Helbling Verlagsgesellschaft mbH, Rum/Innsbruck (2011)
4. Hegarty, M., Kozhevnikov, M.: Types of visual–spatial representations and mathematical problem solving. J. Educ. Psychol. **91**, 684–689 (1999)
5. Karshmer, A.I., Bledsoe, C.: Access to mathematics by blind students. In: Miesenberger, K., Klaus, J., Zagler, W.L. (eds.) ICCHP 2002. LNCS, vol. 2398, pp. 471–476. Springer, Heidelberg (2002)
6. Stöger, B., Miesenberger, K.: Accessing and dealing with mathematics as a blind individual: state of the art and challenges. Enabling Access Persons Vis. Impairment **199** (2015)
7. Archambault, D., Fitzpatrick, D., Gupta, G., Karshmer, A.I., Miesenberger, K., Pontelli, E.: Towards a universal maths conversion library. In: Miesenberger, K., Klaus, J., Zagler, W.L., Burger, D. (eds.) ICCHP 2004. LNCS, vol. 3118, pp. 664–669. Springer, Heidelberg (2004)
8. Miesenberger, K., Batusic, M., Heumader, P., Stöger, B.: MathInBraille online converter. In: Miesenberger, K., Karshmer, A., Penaz, P., Zagler, W. (eds.) Computers Helping People with Special Needs, pp. 196–203. Springer, Berlin Heidelberg (2012)
9. Raman, T.V.: AsTeR: audio system for technical readings. Inf. Technol. Disabil. **1** (1994)
10. Soiffer, N.: MathPlayer: web-based math accessibility. In: Proceedings of the 7th International ACM SIGACCESS Conference on Computers and Accessibility, pp. 204–205. ACM, New York, NY, USA (2005)
11. Gillan, D.J., Barraza, P., Karshmer, A.I., Pazuchanics, S.: Cognitive analysis of equation reading: application to the development of the math genie. In: Miesenberger, K., Klaus, J., Zagler, W.L., Burger, D. (eds.) ICCHP 2004. LNCS, vol. 3118, pp. 630–637. Springer, Heidelberg (2004)
12. Longcamp, M., Boucard, C., Gilhodes, J.-C., Velay, J.-L.: Remembering the orientation of newly learned characters depends on the associated writing knowledge: a comparison between handwriting and typing. Hum. Mov. Sci. **25**, 646–656 (2006)
13. Michael, J.A.: Mental models and meaningful learning. J. Vet. Med. Educ. **31**, 1–5 (2004)
14. Flores, S.F., Archambault, D.: Multimodal interface for working with algebra: interaction between the sighted and the non sighted. In: Miesenberger, K., Fels, D., Archambault, D., Peňáz, P., Zagler, W. (eds.) ICCHP 2014, Part I. LNCS, vol. 8547, pp. 606–613. Springer, Heidelberg (2014)

An Evaluation Methodology of Math-to-Speech in Non-English DAISY Digital Talking Books

Paraskevi Riga[1,2], Georgios Kouroupetroglou[1,2(✉)],
and Polyxeni-Parthena Ioannidou[1]

[1] Department of Informatics and Telecommunications,
National and Kapodistrian University of Athens, Athens, Greece
{p.riga,koupe}@di.uoa.gr
[2] Accessibility Unit for Students with Disabilities, National and Kapodistrian
University of Athens, Athens, Greece

Abstract. The DAISY 3 MathML Modular Extension allows all of the features of a Digital Talking Book to work for math, just as they do for literary text. But this extension does not specify details about advanced MathML players on the localization (i.e. support of a specific native language), support of multilingual mathematical or textual content, cultural differences or user preferences. In this work we present the methodology, we have developed to evaluate in a systematic way the correctness of the Math-to-Speech rendering by investigating specific steps during the production and rendering phases for non-English DAISY Digital Talking Math Books. We define four types of errors in the math expressions: deletions (D), insertions (I), substitutions (S) and translations (T). More-over, we propose an appropriate corpus of mathematical expressions that facilitates the evaluation of the proposed methodology. Then, we have applied the above in the case of the Greek language, a not widespread inflectional natural language. The results of the evaluation for the Greek language and the Math-Player working with the ReadHear player are for each category of math expressions in the whole corpus: trigonometry = 2D, fractions = 3D, matrices = 18T & 4D, integrals = 10T, 12S & 4D, limits = 2T, 12S & 4D, powers-indicators = 8T, 4S & 1D and sets = 9T, 1S, 5D & 3I.

Keywords: DAISY · Digital talking books · Math-to-Speech · MathML · Accessible math

1 Introduction

DAISY (Digital Accessible Information SYstem) is a technical standard for digital audiobooks, periodicals and computerized text. DAISY is designed to be a complete audio substitute for print material and is specifically designed for use by people with "print disabilities", including blindness, impaired vision, and dyslexia. DAISY can be used as an electronic format for textbooks and other learning material.

To ensure that mathematics is accessible within DAISY books, the DAISY Consortium [1] developed a mechanism to include MathML support. MathML is a standard language for marking up mathematical formulas so that their content and structure can: (a) be displayed visually on the web, (b) be audio rendered by screen readers and

© Springer International Publishing Switzerland 2016
K. Miesenberger et al. (Eds.): ICCHP 2016, Part I, LNCS 9758, pp. 27–34, 2016.
DOI: 10.1007/978-3-319-41264-1_4

Text-to-Speech or (c) be converted to braille. This DAISY extension, entitled Digital Talking Book Modular Extension for Mathematics [2] (informally known as the DAISY 3 MathML [3] Modular Extension) allows all of the features of a Digital Talking Book (e.g., support for large print, customizable speech, braille, navigation, and synchronized highlighting) to work for math, just as they do for literary text. DAISY 3 has become officially the DAISY/NISO Z39.86 Specifications for the Digital Talking Book (DTB) [4]. DAISY 3 DTBs with MathML are commonly referred to as "full DAISY".

An Advanced DAISY player is a DTB reading system that incorporates a native understanding of MathML structures and semantics. It is able to render and navigate within the MathML content intelligently. Research into the best way to speak mathematics, navigate mathematical structure, and synchronously highlight mathematics is still ongoing. Localization (i.e. support of a specific native language), support of multilingual mathematical or textual content, cultural differences and user preferences are among the open challenging factors that influence the behavior of Advanced MathML players [5]. DAISY 3 MathML Extension does not specify details in these areas.

In this work we present the methodology, we have developed to evaluate in a systematic way the effectiveness of the Math-to-Speech transformation, by investigating specific steps output of the production and rendering pipeline of non-English DAISY Digital Talking Books. Moreover, we propose an appropriate corpus of mathematical expressions that facilitates this approach and can be further used for the evaluation of relative Math-to-Speech systems. Then, we test the above in the case of the Greek language, a not widespread inflectional natural language.

2 Related Work

Audio rendering of mathematics is not as straightforward as with text. It requires the cooperation of a number of software applications. In the last decade, several such applications were introduced towards to achieve accessible Math-to-Speech. Audio-Math [6] uses MathML to speak mathematics, MathTalk [7] is a system for speaking mathematical equations using speech recognition technology, MathSpeak, invented by Dr. Nemeth, incorporates a set of rules for speaking mathematical expressions non-ambiguously, later improved [8, 9] and became a component of MathPlayer [10].

The steps needed to get a working DAISY DTB with mathematics can be found by applying reverse engineering. The only advanced MathML DAISY player currently available to render mathematics is ReadHear (formerly gh Player) [11]. This player calls MathPlayer to display and render acoustically the MathML content. On the open-source side, there is yet no editor to produce full DAISY. DAISY Pipeline odt2braille is an open source extension for OpenOffice.org Writer that can convert ODT files into DAISY 3 books, however, it cannot produce DAISY with support for math [12]. On the commercial side, two solutions are available to create DTB with math content. Microsoft Word has the option to produce DAISY using the free Save-As-DAISY Word Plugin [13], but to convert the equations in the document to MathML, the use of MathDaisy [14] is required. ChattyInfty 3 [15] produces DAISY 2 textbooks supporting math, where all mathematical expressions are treated as images together with audio files, generated by the speech engine, as well as text-based information. For the present, Japanese and English versions are available, while support for French and some other language versions is under development. The support of one's native language in the Talking Book is a given necessity [5, 16, 17]. The AcceSciTech project [18] plans to create ZedAI, a framework that will finally produce EPUB 3, which covers full DAISY.

Thus, the only way, to date, to deliver full DAISY DTBs with support for math is presented in Fig. 1.

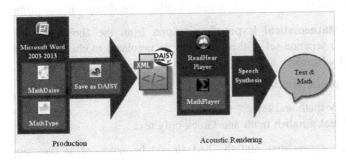

Fig. 1. Math-to-Speech workflow for the production and rendering of DAISY 3 Math Books.

3 The Proposed Methodology

3.1 Corpus Development

Mathematical Expressions. In an initial pilot study [19], the set of mathematical expressions for the demonstration of the AsTeR audio rendering system [20] was used. MathPlayer v.2 can render this set correctly in the Greek language. To further check the audio rendering of MathPlayer, or any relative system, a broader set of expressions has to be created. This corpus must have the following characteristics:

- Include all the symbols and formulae found in a national curriculum,
- Have an appropriate size to be usable during the evaluation,
- Be classified over math content,
- Have different and escalating complexity levels.

To create this corpus for Greek all the formal textbooks for mathematics from elementary school to high school were inspected for mathematical symbols and expressions. The expressions were classified in the following eight categories: (a) derivatives, (b) fractions, (c) integrals, (d) limits, (e) powers-indicators, (f) sets, (g) matrices, and (h) trigonometry. Relative classifications can also be found in the evaluation of Math-to-Speech systems [6, 21, 29]. Doing a cross-check, we found that MathPlayer actually supports all the expression categories found in Greek textbooks.

Next, we have to keep a representative set for every category, so we dismissed the excess of expressions that have similar structure and differ only in numerical values or operators. To add some more structural complexity in the expressions we also chose some expressions used in Spiegel's book [22], published math papers [23–27], and online school math material [28, 29].

In total 130 expressions were selected that were grouped in two main classes, depending on their complexity:

- Simple expressions, found in text books,
- Complex expressions, found mostly in scientific papers.

Moreover, a subset of the expressions was rewritten using a mix of Greek and English in the same expression to check how they are output. If the speech synthesis used supports both languages, then they should be rendered without problems.

Text with Mathematical Expressions. Apart from the above sets of core math expressions, a separate set of theorems was accumulated to check how text and math are rendered when they are entwined. In total 8 pages were accumulated.

In these pages one can find:

- Greek-only math and text,
- Mixed Greek-English math and Greek-only text.

The math expressions and the text should be rendered as they appear in the text-book, regarding order and content. Many times when writing math in Greek, some English symbols are used in the place of their Greek counterparts, such as 'x' instead of 'χ' (chi) and 'y' instead of 'ψ' (psi). In the case the Text-to-Speech system used sup-ports both languages, then the software under examination should also render these without problems.

3.2   Content Editing

To get mathematics successfully to DAISY 3 with MathDaisy they have to be written in a.doc(x) file with MathML. A popular WYSIWYG math editor and the one recommended by MathPlayer is MathType [30], a professional upgrade to the equation editor of MS Office. Other editors are standalone, i.e. one can only write MathML code using them and later embed it in a formatted document file. If the LaTeX source code is available, then a transformation to MathML can take place using either a free tool (e.g. TeX4HT [31]) to produce XHTML + MathML) or a commercial tool (e.g. GrindEQ [32]). The only tool available to recognize printed documents or PDF with math is ChattyInfty [15]. After correcting the OCR errors using InftyEditor [15] and LaTeX code, you can export the document to XHTML + MathML.

The math expressions of the corpus were written using MathType 6.9. The use of the alternative software tools mentioned above could produce non-identical MathML code and probably different audio rendering from the DAISY player. The evaluation method described in Sect. 3.3 can be used to compare the audio outcome correctness and effectiveness when different methods are used to write MathML.

3.3 Evaluation of Audio Rendering

As we have described above, the audio rendering of mathematics in DAISY books is a result of the sequential use of a set of software systems. Starting with a printed math book, it has to be transcribed to a.doc file with MathML. Then, it is transformed to full DAISY using a tool that supports math. In the end, the DAISY Math book is rendered using speech synthesis by a compatible DAISY Reader. Since, MathML is not altered during the conversion from.doc to DAISY, it is the MathML authoring tool and the MathML rendering tool which can impose errors in the final audio output.

Because of the appropriate size of the corpus, one is able to check one-by-one the correctness of the produced MathML of the expressions and theorems. Once, we certify that MathML is error free, we can move to the evaluation of the MathML rendering tool, which in our case is MathPlayer. The lexical cues which indicate the structural information of every possible expression have to be correctly adapted in the Greek language along with the different math symbols. Since, there is no way to check the infinite number of possible expressions one-by-one, the corpus described above can be used. The same set can be reused to check future editions of the DAISY player and MathPlayer or new rendering tools, not only for the Greek, but also for other non-English languages.

The content of the corpus is used in two rounds of trials:

- In the first round (Round 1), a sighted researcher (without any hearing loss), with proficient knowledge of the underlying math, has to listen to every expression while reading its 2D representation. During this run all the types of mathematical errors, i.e. deletions (D), insertions (I) and substitutions (S), are noted on the printed 2D representation. There is also a new type of errors called translation (T) where a part of the expression was not translated to the non-english language.
- In the second round (Round 2), the same researcher has to listen the rendering of each expression using a lower speech rate, without seeing it, and, at the same time, write down the 2D representation. Afterwards, (s)he would compare the 2D representation of the initial (reference) expression with the perceived expression and mark the math errors on the reference expression.

The researcher would take notes in both rounds, of errors on the expressions in Round 1 and of the perceived expression in Round 2, at the same time with the acoustical rendering, so that the acoustic memory of the researcher does not influence the results. Should the researcher be a person with low or no vision, (s)he would keep notes on a computer or a braille machine written in math code, such as Nemeth or Marburg. Afterwards, (s)he would rewrite them in MathML and measure errors using the metrics described in [33]. After the researcher has confirmed the correctness of every audio expression, and therefore of the math editing and rendering systems, a full study can take place to check the effectiveness of the system, with the participation of different target groups, such as people with low vision or people with dyslexia, using the method described in [19].

4 Results

Using the corpus for the acoustic rendering of math, the errors doubled when we moved from the initial localized edition 2.1, used as a plugin in Internet Explorer, to the edition 3.0 of MathPlayer, used in the DAISY player, (Table 1). The number of errors was not influenced by the number of subexpressions in an expression. Moreover, the errors in each category were repetitive, reaching a maximum of 6 unique errors per category. Even less errors were found on the second round since the listener, who could understand the English rendering, corrected the T errors.

The D and T errors are most likely produced by the localization of the rendering application to the native language, while I and S errors are most likely produced by the rendering program itself. Thus, the respective components have to be corrected to obtain an error-free rendering of Greek full DAISY books.

Table 1. Deletion (D), insertion (I), substitution (S) and translation (T) evaluation errors

Category	Errors of MathPlayer 2.1	Errors of MathPlayer 3.0
Derivatives	6T, 1S	10T, 3S, 1D
Fractions	0	3D
Integrals	8T	10T, 12S, 4D
Limits	1T, 1D	2T, 12S, 1D
Powers-indicators	7T, 1S	8T, 4S, 1D
Sets	3T, 7S	9T, 3I, 1S, 5D
Matrices	11T	18T, 4D
Trigonometry	0	2D

5 Conclusions

Nowadays, we know that a proven workflow for the delivery DAISY Digital Talking Math Books has been already introduced. This workflow includes the production and the rendering phases. In this work we have proposed a methodology, along with an appropriate math corpus, to examine the correctness of these phases for Math-to-Speech. The output of the MathML editor as well as the localization of the rendering application (MathPlayer) can be thoroughly tested by extracting deletion (D), insertion (I), substitution (S) and translation (T) errors. Having these errors as a compass, the involved software tools can be revised to produce correct Math-to-Speech.

The proposed evaluation methodology can be also used to test other MathML editing/creating software tools, in order to get a broader spectrum of applications that can effectively be used in the production phase of DAISY Math DTBs.

Our future plans include the effectiveness and usability study of the DAISY Math Books on various student groups, in connection with their disability, usage modality, user preferences, context of use, and language.

Acknowledgements. This research has been co-financed by the European Union (European Social Fund – ESF) and Greek national funds through the Operational Program "Education and Lifelong Learning" of the National Strategic Reference Framework (NSRF) under the Research Funding Project: "THALIS-University of Macedonia- KAIKOS: Audio and Tactile Access to Knowledge for Individuals with Visual Impairments", MIS 380442.

References

1. DAISY Consortium. www.daisy.org
2. Leas, D., Persoon, E., Soiffer, N., Zacherle, M.: Daisy 3: a standard for accessible multimedia books. IEEE Multimedia **4**, 28–37 (2008)
3. Ausbrooks, R., Buswell, S., Carlisle, D., Dalmas, S., Devitt, S., Diaz, A., Miner, R.: Mathematical Markup Language (MathML) version 2.0. W3C Recommendation. World Wide Web Consortium (2003)
4. ANSI/NISO 2008. Z39.83-2008 NISO Circulation Interchange Protocol. ISSN: 1041-5653, ISBN: 978-1-880124-97-0. NISO Press, Bethesda. http://www.niso.org/apps/group_public/download.php/5815/z39-83-2-2008_2_01.pdf. Accessed 24 Mar 2016
5. Yamaguchi, K., Suzuki, M.: On necessity of a new method to read out math contents properly in DAISY. In: Miesenberger, K., Klaus, J., Zagler, W., Karshmer, A. (eds.) ICCHP 2010, Part II. LNCS, vol. 6180, pp. 415–422. Springer, Heidelberg (2010)
6. Ferreira, H., Freitas, D.: AudioMath: using MathML for speaking mathematics. In: XATA 2005 (2005)
7. Stevens, R., Edwards, A., Harling, P.: Access to mathematics for visually disabled students through multimodal interaction. Hum.-Comput. Interact. **12**, 47–92 (1997)
8. Isaacson, M.D., Srinivasan, S., Lloyd, L.: Development of an algorithm for improving quality and information processing capacity of MathSpeak synthetic speech renderings. J. Disabil. Rehabil. Assistive Technol. **5**, 83–93 (2010)
9. Isaacson, M.D., Lloyd, L.L., Schleppenbach, D.: Reducing multiple interpretations of mathematical expressions with MathSpeak. In: 1st International Conference on Technology-Based Learning with Disability, pp. 1–10. Wright State University, Dayton, Ohio (2007)
10. Soiffer, N.: MathPlayer v2. 1: web-based math accessibility. In: Proceedings of the 9th International ACM SIGACCESS Conference on Computers and Accessibility, pp. 257–258. ACM Press, New York (2007)
11. ReadHear Player. https://www.gh-accessibility.com/
12. Strobbe, C., Engelen, J., Spiewak, V.: Generating DAISY books from OpenOffice.org. In: Miesenberger, K., Klaus, J., Zagler, W., Karshmer, A. (eds.) ICCHP 2010, Part 1. LNCS, vol. 6179, pp. 5–11. Springer, Heidelberg (2010)
13. Archambault, D., Spiewak, V.: OpenOffice.org Save-as-Daisy extension. In: Emiliani, P.L., et al. (eds.) Assistive Technology Research Series AAATE 2009, vol. 25, pp. 212–216. IOS Press, Amsterdam (2009)
14. Design Science. http://www.dessci.com/en/products/mathdaisy/
15. InftyProject. http://www.inftyproject.org/en/index.html
16. Yamaguchi, K., Suzuki, M.: Accessible authoring tool for DAISY ranging from mathematics to others. In: Miesenberger, K., Karshmer, A., Penaz, P., Zagler, W. (eds.) ICCHP 2012, Part I. LNCS, vol. 7382, pp. 130–137. Springer, Heidelberg (2012)
17. Davydov, M.V., Lozytskyy, O., Nikolskyy, Y.: Method of Automatic Formulas Reading in Ukrainian. Lviv Polytechnic National University MES of Ukraine, Ukraine (2013)

18. Bernier, A., Burger, D.: AcceSciTech: a global approach to make scientific and technical literature accessible. In: Stephanidis, C., Antona, M. (eds.) UAHCI 2013, Part III. LNCS, vol. 8011, pp. 283–290. Springer, Heidelberg (2013)

19. Kacorri, H., Riga, P., Kouroupetroglou, G.: EAR-math: evaluation of audio rendered mathematics. In: Stephanidis, C., Antona, M. (eds.) UAHCI 2014, Part II. LNCS, vol. 8514, pp. 111–120. Springer, Heidelberg (2014)

20. Raman, T.V.: ASTER-towards modality-independent electronic documents. Multimedia Tools Appl. **6**, 141–151 (1998)

21. Fitzpatrick, D.: Towards Accessible Technical Documents: Production of Speech and Braille Output from Formatted Documents. Doctoral dissertation, Dublin City University (1999)

22. Spiegel, M., Lipschutz, S., Liu, J.: Mathematical Handbook of Formulas and Tables, 3rd edn. McGraw-Hill, New York (1968)

23. Bradji, A., Fuhrmann, J.: Some error estimates in finite volume method for parabolic equations. In: Eymard, R., H´erard, J.-M. (eds.) Finite Volumes for Complex Applications V, Proceedings of the 5th International Symposium on Finite Volume for Complex Applications, pp. 233–240. Wiley, Chichester (2008)

24. Zhang, X., Zhou, Y.: Periodic solutions of non-autonomous second order Hamiltonian systems. J. Math. Anal. Appl. **345**, 929–933 (2008)

25. Hung, N.M., Long, H.V., Son, N.T.K.: On the asymptotics of solutions to the second initial boundary value problem for Schrödinger systems in domains with conical points. J. Appl. Math. **58**, 63–91 (2013)

26. Yao, Q.: Positive solutions for eigenvalue problems of fourth-order elastic beam equations. J. Appl. Math. Lett. **17**, 237–243 (2004)

27. Kubáček, L.: Seemingly unrelated regression models. Appl. Math. **58**, 111–123 (2013)

28. Argirakis, D., Vourganas, P., Mentis, K., Tsikopoulou, S., Chrisovergis, M.: Mathematics 3rd Class of Gymnasium, pp. 38–39. http://ebooks.edu.gr/courses/DSGYM-C104/document/4bddaea1n61y/52402801231s/52402823jhtj.pdf

29. Andreadakis, S., Katsargiris, V., Papastavridis, S., Polizos, G., Sverkos, A.: Mathematics 2nd Class of Lyceum, pp. 97–98. http://ebooks.edu.gr/courses/DSGL-B133/document/4e09fabdb67e/4e09fac5l2ig/4e5908d84hoj.pdf

30. Design Science. http://www.dessci.com/en/products/mathtype/

31. Polewczac, J.: LaTeX, MathML, and TEX4HT: Tools for creating accessible documents. Mathematics, CSUN, Northridge (2005)

32. GrindEq. http://www.grindeq.com/

33. Kacorri, H., Riga, P., Kouroupetroglou, G.: Performance metrics and their extraction methods for audio rendered mathematics. In: Miesenberger, K., Fels, D., Archambault, D., Peňáz, P., Zagler, W. (eds.) ICCHP 2014, Part I. LNCS, vol. 8547, pp. 614–621. Springer, Heidelberg (2014)

Recognition of E-Born PDF Including Mathematical Formulas

Masakazu Suzuki[1] and Katsuhito Yamaguchi[2(✉)]

[1] Institute of Mathematics for Industry, Kyushu University,
744, Motooka, Nishi-ku, Fukuoka 819-0395, Japan
suzuki@isit.or.jp
[2] Junior College Funabashi Campus, Nihon University,
7-24-1 Narashinodai, Funabashi, Chiba 274-8501, Japan
eugene@gaea.jcn.nihon-u.ac.jp

Abstract. A new method to recognize STEM contents in "e-born PDF," which is produced originally from an electronic file such as a Microsoft-Word document, LaTeX system, etc., is developed. Character information (the character code, the font type and the coordinates on a page) extracted directly from a document is combined with analysis technologies in Math OCR. It improves recognition rate for STEM contents in e-born PDF remarkably, compared with ordinary image-based OCR approaches. This new method is actually implemented in our math OCR system (InftyReader).

Keywords: STEM · OCR · E-born PDF · Accessibility

1 Introduction

We believe that one of the most serious problems in digitized STEM (science, technology, engineering and mathematics) contents, which are provided in PDF in most cases, is their poor accessibility. Not only on the web, but PDF is commonly used for the exchange of STEM contents among researchers or in various educational fields. To guarantee accessibility, it is now increasing that publishers provide print-disabled customers with a book in PDF as an alternative media for the printed one. In many cases, print-disabled people use OCR (optical character recognition) software to read those PDF; however, that is not always successful.

There have been many researches on computerized recognition for the scanned image of a document or PDF including mathematical formulas in aims of information retrieval, improving accessibility and so on [1]. Our research group also started the development of an OCR system for mathematical documents since the late 1990s and has already put software "InftyReader" to practical use [2–4]. It should be pointed out, however, that all of them are so-called "image-based" approaches, so far; that is, PDF is converted into image files once before getting into the analysis, and then, OCR process is applied. As far as they adopt totally image-based processing, a certain percentage of recognition errors should be unavoidable.

© Springer International Publishing Switzerland 2016
K. Miesenberger et al. (Eds.): ICCHP 2016, Part I, LNCS 9758, pp. 35–42, 2016.
DOI: 10.1007/978-3-319-41264-1_5

To make the situation much clearer, here, we classify PDF into two types. In this paper, we call as "e-born PDF" PDF that is produced originally from an electronic file such as a document in Microsoft Word, LaTeX, Adobe InDesign, etc. We refer to the other type as "image PDF," which is usually made by scanning and contains only images. When viewing them in a regular size, there may be no significant difference between them. However, while the quality of character images in the latter should commonly become worse in zooming up, it should be kept to be fine in the former no matter how large characters are magnified. From the viewpoint of computerized processing to convert it into accessible form, the most significant advantage of e-born PDF is that the information on each character/symbol such as its character code, font type, coordinates on a page is embedded in it.

Here, we show a new method to improve remarkably recognition rate for STEM contents in e-born PDF. After reviewing earlier studies on e-born PDF recognition, we introduce our new approach by combining the conventional image-based algorithm in our math OCR software, InftyReader, with character/symbol information extracted from e-born PDF by a PDF parser. Results of evaluation tests and (remaining) unsolved problems in the current version (future tasks) are also discussed.

2   E-Born PDF Recognition

In terms of e-born PDF recognition, during 2008–2013, Josef Baker supervised by Volker Sorge and Alan Sexton at the University of Birmingham intensively studied the methods to convert PDF into LaTeX or MathML, by using only the character information (the character code, the font type, the coordinates) embedded in the e-born PDF [5]. Based on the result, they also provide a pilot online service named "MaxTract" for evaluation purpose [6–8]. There were also recent works on the methods to extract math formulas from e-born PDF by Yu et al. [9] and Lin et al. [10]. However, those are still on the research level and have not been put to practical use, yet. Although only MathTract seems to have aimed at release for general users, unfortunately the service and the development are currently suspended.

In those works, they tried to extract math formulas and to analyze their structures (to recognize math expressions), based only on character information embedded in e-born PDF. However, it is not easy to detect all the character codes used in STEM PDF since various types of fonts are used in math formulas. Furthermore, the font rect-area (rectangular area) extracted from the PDF often differs significantly from the graphical rect-area of the original character image. Thus, math recognition based only on character information embedded in PDF has serious limit.

On the other hand, although InftyReader is totally image-based OCR software, it can recognize properly math documents in PDF if the image is fine enough, and if the document has simple layout. Currently, many print-disabled people in the world use InftyReader to read STEM contents in PDF including e-born ones. However, although its math-recognition capability is highly evaluated, there still remain several tasks that we should work on.

1. Characters/Symbols on color/pattern background are often misrecognized or missed.
2. Characters in text areas sometimes misrecognized as math characters/symbols due to recognition errors.
3. Documents with complicated-layout structures are out of scope at the current stage.

The purpose of this paper is to show the efficiency of the combination of conventional InftyReader algorithm and the character information (the character code, the font type, the coordinates) detected from e-born PDF (see Fig. 1 below). It is very effective to reduce the errors referred in the above items (1) and (2). As for the task in (3), it will be left for future works.

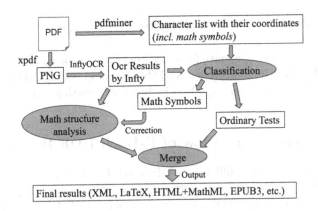

Fig. 1. Recognition flow of e-born PDF by InftyReader.

3   Extraction of Character Information from E-Born PDF

As is commonly known, the order of texts stored in a PDF file is usually different from its visual appearance. Consequently, the text extracted from the PDF becomes often in the wrong order and is difficult to understand as it stands. Furthermore, as far as a math part is concerned, we usually get nothing or a meaningless character/symbol sequence.

Thus, to obtain correctly information on an entire document including both text and math parts, at first, we have to analyze the inside of PDF. There are various powerful PDF parsers to do such works, but many of them are too expensive and it is difficult to incorporate them in InftyReader for redistribution purpose. By testing them, we know that two PDF parsers, TET of "PDFLib" [11] and "pdfminer" [12], are useful and powerful enough for InftyReader to get character/symbol information in PDF including math-expression areas. Taking account of several advantages, we have adopted pdfminer to incorporate in InftyReader.

Unfortunately, however, as same as the other PDF parsers, extracted character information by pdfminer cannot be used directly for STEM document recognition as it stands.

1. The font rect-area extracted from e-born PDF often differs significantly from the graphical rect-area of the original character image. Sometimes, the area size is even double or triple of the character/symbol image size. To illustrate this situation, some sample images are shown in Fig. 2.
2. Concerning special symbols in a math formula, pdfminer sometimes fails at getting character code correctly.

Fig. 2. Font rect-areas of symbols in math expressions.

To find the structure of a math formula properly by applying the conventional methods used in InftyReader, we do need the character codes and the graphical-image size of all the characters/symbols included in a math formula as accurately as possible.

4   Method and Work Flow of E-Born PDF Recognition

As is well known, the first difficult task in math OCR is to segment text lines including math formulas properly into ordinary texts and math parts. As was discussed in the paper [3], InftyReader uses commercial OCR engines to recognize ordinary texts and compares the result with the results by Infty math-OCR engine for the math-text segmentation.

On the other hand, in the new algorithm of InftyReader to recognize e-born PDF, character/symbol information extracted by pdfminer is used, instead of the commercial OCR engines (See Fig. 1). As the result, the new version of InftyReader does not require any additional commercial OCR engine to recognize e-born PDF even for multi-lingual documents including extended-Latin or Cyrillic characters.

In the recognition of e-born PDF by InftyReader, at first, the character information extracted by pdfminer is examined and classified into the following four groups of characters/symbols, based on the type of character code, the continuity of the font type and size, as well as the comparison with a result by Infty-OCR engine ("Classification" in Fig. 1).

1. Text1: Text characters having the corresponding character-image rect-area in the recognition result by Infty OCR, where the mismatching of code information between the two recognition result is allowed (just the compatibility of the character-image's coordinates is concerned).

2. Text2: Text characters with no corresponding character-image area in the recognition result by Infty OCR.
3. Math1: Characters/symbols in math area, character code of which were successfully obtained.
4. Math2: Characters/symbols in math area for which pdfminer detected "unknown" or an irregular code as the result. The irregularity is checked by comparing that with the Infty-OCR result.

Text2 characters are integrated with the Text1 characters after presumption of each character area, by taking account of information on the entire-word rect-area including them, together with the type of their character codes. The unified results are included in a final output as literal characters.

As was pointed out above, in the inside of math formulas, the font rect-area extracted from e-born PDF by pdfminer often differs significantly from the graphical area of the original character images (see Fig. 2), and cannot be used for math-structure analysis as it stands. Therefore, the conventional math OCR (InftyReader algorithm) is applied in the e-born PDF recognition by the new InftyReader, too. The Math1 character/symbol information extracted by pdfminer is used for correcting the character recognition results by Infty-OCR engine ("Correction" in the Fig. 1). The information of characters and symbols classified into Math2 is not used.

Subsequent steps of processing: analyzing math structures, integrating the math-OCR results with the text-OCR results, final checking the entire result are all same as the previous version of InftyReader (See the paper [3]).

5   Evaluation

The recognition method for e-born PDF discussed here has been already implemented in the recent version of InftyReader (Ver. 3.1.1.0 or later). Users can test freely how it works (up to 5 pages in a day). We therefore selected PDF files listed below, which are available online, for convenience of the readers in their own evaluation test. We took 8 e-born PDF files, which were found with Google search with math terms and keywords together with "PDF", such as "Integration by parts, PDF" and cut out five pages from each PDF except for the 2nd sample. As for the second one (here, we call it PDF2), it is a slide for presentation, and the number of characters included in each page is less than the other samples. Hence, we got the first 10 pages from it.

1. Elementary Algebra Textbook
   http://mathrev.redwoods.edu/ElemAlgText/ElementaryAlgebra.pdf, pp. 535–539,
2. Indefinite Integration
   https://www.plymouth.ac.uk/uploads/production/document/path/3/3734/PlymouthUniversity_MathsandStats_outreach_indefinite_integration.pdf, pp. 1–10 (Slides),

3. Integration by parts
   http://math.berkeley.edu/~ehallman/math1B/IntByParts.pdf,
   pp. 1–5,
4. Integrali Indefinite (Italian)
   http://calvino.polito.it/~terzafac/Corsi/analisi1/pdf/integrali-svolti.pdf,
   pp. 1–5,
5. Quadratic equations
   http://www.mathcentre.ac.uk/resources/uploaded/mc-ty-quadeqns-2009-1.pdf, pp. 1–5,
6. Solving quadratic equations
   http://mathsupport.mas.ncl.ac.uk/images/1/1e/Solving_quadratic_equatns.pdf, pp. 1–5,
7. The sum of an infinite series
   http://www.mathcentre.ac.uk/resources/uploaded/mc-ty-convergence-2009-1.pdf, pp. 1–5,
8. Weighted Inequalities (Math article by a Japanese blind mathematician)
   http://www.ms.u-tokyo.ac.jp/journal/pdf/jms060202.pdf, pp. 1–5.

PDF4 and PDF8 include many math expressions. In particular, PDF8 is a paper published on a professional-math journal and includes highly technical formulas.

Using those samples, we examined evaluations in two different manners. In the first one, they were converted into gray-scale (black and white) images of 600 DPI once with "xpdf" [13], and those images were recognized with the previous InftyReader without pdfminer but with the FineReader plug-in. We call this process IRFR. On the other hand, in the second, they were recognized with the new method described above using PDFminer, but without any commercial OCR engines. We refer to the second process as IRPM.

Table 1. Evaluation result.

	Char Num	Form Num	Form Len	AR Err (IRFR)	CR Err (IRFR)	FR Err (IRFR)	AR Err (IRPM)	CR Err (IRPM)	FR Err (IRPM)
PDF1	5669	125	3.98	1	1	1	0	1	1
PDF2	3835	75	8.44	0	0	2	0	0	0
PDF3	2830	87	12.80	1	5	2	0	2	2
PDF4	6149	162	18.98	0	6	2	0	3	2
PDF5	5540	115	7.16	1	4	1	0	2	1
PDF6	5538	45	16.69	2	5	1	0	5	1
PDF7	4987	104	8.23	3	2	1	0	1	1
PDF8	5083	101	12.40	0	5	0	0	1	0

Notations Used in the Table 1.

- Char Num = the total number of characters and symbols.

- Form Num = the number of the formulas, where "formula" is a connected math expression separated by spaces, line breaks or ordinary texts. We counted only the formulas which have either characters/symbols of special math fonts (Greek characters, operators, etc.), functions or math structures such as fractions, radicals, super/subscripts and so on.
- Form Len = the average number of the characters and symbols included in a formula.
- AR Error = the number of undetected text blocks
- CR Error = the number of errors in character/symbol recognition.
- FR Error = the number of the formulas including at-least-one error in math-structure analysis.

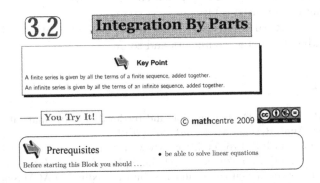

Fig. 3. List of the 6 types of undetected text blocks by IRFR.

The main difference between the two recognition methods is that, while in IRFR, background color, patterns or illustrations gave rise to failures at extracting text areas shown in the Fig. 3 above, they are all correctly extracted in IRPM. On the other hand, in the performance of character/symbol recognition and math-structure analysis, there are no significant differences between IRFR and IRPM, as it is shown in the Table 1. Since the quality of generated images from those PDF files were all very good, and recognition results by FineReader were accurate enough. Hence, IRFR also could recognize text characters almost successfully. There were few errors by IRFR such as "In x" instead of "$\ln x$" (logarithm), "da;" instead of "dx", etc., which did not occur in IRPM. Five character-recognition errors in the first page of PDF6, which occurred commonly in IRFR and IRPM, are of a "check mark" that is not included in the character-code list of InftyReader.

Thus, we can conclude that for both of text and math parts, our new method combining the InftyReader with the PDF parser (pdfminer) gives better recognition results than the previous method based on InftyReader with FineReader although the font rect-areas extracted by pdfminer often differ significantly from the graphical area of the original character images. Furthermore, although the previous method depending on only image-based OCR often fails at getting character information in a block with shading or other background illustrations, it is recognized correctly in the new method.

6   Future Tasks

To make e-born PDF fully accessible, there still remain unsolved problems that we have to work on. The most important one is to establish an efficient computerized method to analyze complicated layout, which may include:

- Improving the segmentation of figures, tables, and text blocks (including math).
- Analyzing the reading order of segmented text blocks.
- Recognizing complicated tables.
- Analyzing the logical structure of a document such as a title, authors, headings, an index, footnotes, comments and so on.

References

1. Zanibbi, R., Blostein, D.: Recognition and retrieval of mathematical expressions. Int. J. Doc. Anal. Recogn. **15**(4), 331–357 (2012)
2. Publication List at InftyProject. http://www.inftyproject.org/en/articles_ocr.html
3. Suzuki, M., Tamari, F., Fukuda, R., Uchida, S., Kanahori, T.: Infty - an integrated OCR system for mathematical documents. In: Proceedings of ACM Symposium on Document Engineering 2003, Grenoble, pp. 95–104 (2003)
4. InftyReader. http://www.sciaccess.net/en/InftyReader/
5. Baker   J.   at   Google   Scholar.   http://scholar.google.co.uk/citations? user=0g0TMuQAAAAJ&hl=en
6. Baker, J.B., Sexton, A.P., Sorge, V.: MaxTract: converting PDF to LaTeX, MathML and text. In: Jeuring, J., Campbell, J.A., Carette, J., Reis, G.D., Sojka, P., Wenzel, M., Sorge, V. (eds.) CICM 2012. LNCS, vol. 7362, pp. 422–426. Springer, Heidelberg (2012)
7. MathTract.   http://www.cs.bham.ac.uk/research/groupings/sdag/ maxtract.php
8. MathTract. http://researchblogs.cs.bham.ac.uk/math-access/
9. Yu, B., Tian, X., Luo, W.: Extracting mathematical components directly from PDF documents for mathematical expression recognition and retrieval. In: Tan, Y., Shi, Y., Coello, C.A.C. (eds.) ICSI 2014, Part II. LNCS, vol. 8795, pp. 170–179. Springer, Heidelberg (2014)
10. Lin, X., Gao, L., Tang, Z., Baker, J., Sorge, V.: Mathematical formula identification and performance evaluation in PDF documents. Int. J. Doc. Anal. Recogn. **17**, 239–255 (2014)
11. PDFLib. https://www.pdflib.com/
12. PDFMiner. http://www.unixuser.org/euske/python/pdfminer/
13. Xpdf. http://www.foolabs.com/xpdf/download.html

Polyfilling Accessible Chemistry Diagrams

Volker Sorge[1,2(✉)]

[1] School of Computer Science, University of Birmingham, Birmingham, UK
[2] Progressive Accessibility Solutions Ltd., Birmingham, UK
volker.sorge@gmail.com
http://www.cs.bham.ac.uk/~vxs
http://progressiveaccess.com

Abstract. We present a polyfill solution for replacing inaccessible images of molecules with fully web-accessible chemistry diagrams. Thereby marked up bitmap images on a client web site are extracted, server side recognised and semantically enriched to generate scalable vector graphics (SVG) with embedded chemical information. These graphics are then re-inserted into the original web page providing readers with accessibility features such as speech output and interactive exploration together with synchronised highlighting and magnification. Our solution works for most combinations of browsers and screen reading software on all major desktop platforms, and while it is currently only implemented for chemical diagrams, it is extensible to other STEM subject areas.

Keywords: Web accessibility · STEM accessibility · Chemistry diagrams

1 Introduction

Diagrams are an important means of conveying information in STEM subjects and they are ubiquitous in teaching material. Since they need to be understood in fine detail, their precise description is often very difficult and they thus present a major hurdle for inclusive education. Even in electronic teaching material, diagrams present an obstacle as they are generally given in raster-based image formats (e.g. gif, png, and jpeg), leaving them inaccessible for visually impaired learners: Screen readers can only pick up alternative texts that is usually not enough to convey a full description; and magnification tools struggle to deal with diagrams since magnification does not proportionally increase resolution leading to a loss of image quality.

To overcome this problem on the web, we present a new approach for making chemical diagrams accessible by automatically replacing inaccessible bitmap formats with fully web accessible scalable vector graphics (SVG) in web pages. The idea is implemented as a polyfill solution, that is, a JavaScript library that can be injected into any client web site, where marked up images are recognised and transformed server side into accessible SVG and re-inserted into the web page. In addition to recognising bitmap images, it can also exploit standard chemical markup notation to produce SVG diagrams.

© Springer International Publishing Switzerland 2016
K. Miesenberger et al. (Eds.): ICCHP 2016, Part I, LNCS 9758, pp. 43–50, 2016.
DOI: 10.1007/978-3-319-41264-1_6

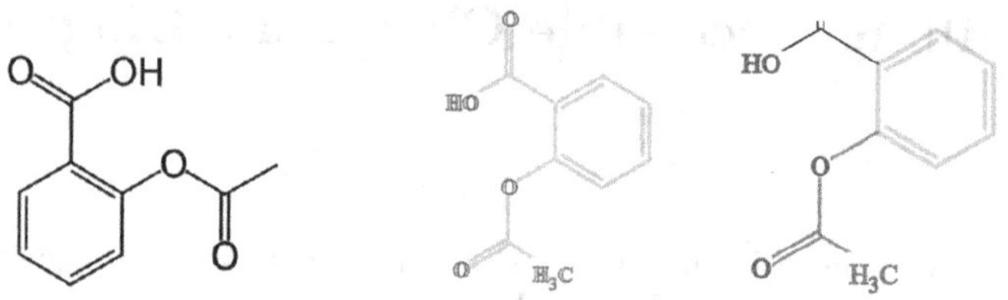

Fig. 1. Aspirin molecule as bitmap image left and as accessible, interactive SVG.

The library draws on our work in fully automatically generating web accessible chemical diagrams, without the need for specialist tools for authoring or reading the accessible diagrams [8]. Instead it employs image analysis to recognise diagrams, semantic enrichment to derive detailed information on their content, and regeneration into an annotated graphics format that makes them amenable to assistive technology. Web browsing software allows readers to interactively engage with diagrams by exploring them step-wise and on different layers, enabling aural rendering of diagrams and their individual components together with highlighting and magnification to assist readers with low vision or learning difficulties. And although originally developed as an assistive technology tool, the approach could also be exploited as a general teaching tool as well as extended to other STEM subject areas.

2   Producing Accessible Chemical Diagrams

Our approach is based on a procedure to recognise chemical diagrams from bitmap images and transform them into semantically enriched, fully web accessible SVG graphics. The procedure is fully automatic and combines three independent computational steps into a single software pipeline:

(1) Image analysis recognises molecule diagrams.
(2) Semantic enrichment computes detailed information on chemical molecules.
(3) Reproduction of diagrams in navigatable Scalable Vector Graphics (SVG).

We summarise how each of these steps proceeds in this section. For more details on the process see also [8]. As a running example we use the recognition and semantic enrichment of the chemical molecule for Aspirin, which is originally given as the bitmap image presented in Fig. 1 on the very left.

2.1   Image Analysis

The Image analysis that recognises molecule diagrams is based on our previous work [5], which has shown itself superior in a number of international recognition competitions [4,6]. It proceeds in two stages: *Image Segmentation* decomposes diagrams into a set of geometric primitives. *Diagram Recognition* uses chemical knowledge to assemble a basic representation of the diagram.

```
60;4;336;279;188.992693;206.825861
chargroup;0;258;223;287;257
chargroup;0;195;114;224;148
chargroup;0;6;5;35;39
chargroup;OH;132;5;192;39
line;normal;82;62;85;56;4;4611686018427387904.0
line;normal;83;130;82;63;4;4611686018427387904.0
              ...
line;normal;86;56;127;32;4;-0.575723
line;normal;85;55;39;28;4;0.580944
```

Fig. 2. Abbreviated list of geometric primitives for Aspirin.

```
<molecule id="m1" xmlns="http://www.xml-cml.org/schema">
  <atomArray>
    <atom id="a1" elementType="C" x2="1.4301" y2="-0.6083" hydrogenCount="3"/>
    <atom id="a2" elementType="C" x2="-0.4599" y2="-1.6683" hydrogenCount="1"/>
    ....
  </atomArray>
  <bondArray>
    <bond id="b1" atomRefs2="a3 a1" order="S"/>
    <bond id="b2" atomRefs2="a5 a4" order="S"/>
    ....
  </bondArray>
</molecule>
```

Fig. 3. Abbreviated CML for Aspirin molecule.

In the *Image Segmentation* step an image is vectorised in order to segment it into the main constituents making up the diagram, resulting in a set of distinct primitives like lines, circles, solid triangles, arcs, or character groups together with their geometric location in the original image. This process is robust not only with respect to the type of bitmap images (e.g., jpeg, png, tiff), but also with respect to differences in authoring styles or potential problems stemming from the image origin. For example, noise introduced by image capturing techniques such as scanning is removed in a pre-processing step. The result of the segmentation is then a textual representation of the geometric primitives. For our Aspirin example we get a set of 22 geometric primitives: 18 lines and 4 character groups. These are given partially in Fig. 2.

In the subsequent *Diagram Recognition* step the actual recognition of the molecule is performed by a rule engine, in which largely disjoint rules are repeatedly applied to the initial set of geometric primitives, rewriting it into a graph representation of the molecule diagram. Rules are defined in terms of preconditions and consequences. A rule is applicable if there exist geometric objects that satisfy its preconditions. Executing its consequence removes existing geometric objects while adding elements to the graph as well as possibly adding new geometric objects. In general, preconditions of different rules are mutually exclusive, and thus the order of rule application is irrelevant.

The graph structure resulting from the rewriting step serves as a basis from which efficient electronic representation formats can be generated. While these formats are largely equivalent, we concentrate on generating standard chemical file formats such as MOL and CML (Chemical Markup Language [2]), as well as InChI (International Chemical Identifier). For Aspirin the InChI is given as

InChI=1S/C9H8O4/c1-6(10)13-8-5-3-2-4-7(8)9(11)12/h2-5H,1H3,(H,11,12)

while the corresponding CML is given in parts in Fig. 3.

It is worth noting that the image segmentation is fully generic, that is, it is independent of the actual type of diagrams analysed. Only the diagram recognition actually uses information on the domain (i.e., chemistry). Consequently, the approach is portable other STEM diagrams using similar geometric primitives simply by replacing the set of rules used for recognition and graph rewriting.

2.2   Semantic Enrichment

While the result of the image analysis is sufficient to reproduce the diagram and to distinguish molecules, the extracted information is still only sufficient for a flat representation, in the sense of describing single components of a diagram and their relationship to their direct neighbours. However, they lack sufficiently rich semantic that would be necessary to provide meaningful explanations of the diagram. Therefore the most challenging part is to enrich this representation with sufficient semantic meaning to allow the automatic generation of diagram descriptions that emulate human reading behaviour in its different facets, such as taking a casual glance at a drawing, getting an initial abstract overview of its components, before diving deeper into single components.

In our semantic enrichment we analyse the graph representing the molecule structure in order to identify chemically interesting compounds such as ring systems, aliphatic chains and functional groups exploiting cheminformatics algorithms implemented in the Chemistry Development Kit (CDK) [9]. This imposes a hierarchical structure on the molecule that we can later exploit for navigation. In addition identified substructures are being automatically named using online web services (e.g., [3,10]) that generate common chemical names given a specification of a compound.

For the Aspirin molecule we identify three major components: a Benzene ring, two functional groups, Carboxylic Acid and Ester. These are depicted in Fig. 4 on the left. Once identified these components are combined and represented in the abstraction graph given in Fig. 4 on the right and names for them as well as for the overall molecule, i.e. Aspirin, are computed via ChemSpider [3]. The computed information is then represented as an XML structure to extend the basic CML representation to an enriched CML format that contains the administrative information for the abstraction graph as well as sufficient information on later generating speech strings for the diagram.

2.3   Annotated SVG Generation

Already the non-enriched, generated CML representation of a molecule can serve as the basis to compute the corresponding diagram as SVG. Although there exist

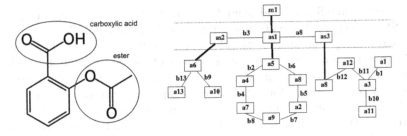

Fig. 4. Functional groups and abstraction graph for Aspirin molecule.

a number of solutions for this, these are exclusively geared towards rendering a diagram, discarding all chemical information in the process. That is, they will set all the geometric components, lines and characters, in a flat structure, losing information about bonds or atoms. As making a connection between the geometric component of the SVG and the bonds and atoms in the input CML file is important for the purpose of highlighting and magnification, we have implemented our own SVG renderer. It exploits SVG facilities to group elements together as well as to add attributes reflecting their chemical purpose and connecting them to their origins in CML.

3   Web Integration and Front End

The SVG resulting from the recognition process can directly be included into the rendered page. However, we also want to exploit the abstraction graph structure to overlay the SVG with a navigation model to enable users to explore diagrams interactively. Unfortunately, this is not doable by embedding the navigation structure into the SVG alone, as SVG is a tree structure, while the abstraction graph is a hierarchical graph with shared elements. Consequently, we need this structure independently in the web page, and connect it to the SVG via JavaScript functionality.

More technically, we employ AJAX to import the SVG together with the semantically enriched chemical information as an SVG+XML media type into the web page. Some injected JavaScript code then enables interactive exploration of diagrams. The main idea is that a user can enter a diagram and interactively browse through its components on different levels and in different granularity. The components are presented to the reader by making descriptions available for aural rendering by a screen reader through pushing text strings into a ARIA live region. Parts of the molecule structure can be focused, both by highlighting and optionally via magnification. These functions are implemented via CSS changes and moving the SVG viewport, respectively. All interactions and voicing operations are thus implemented browser, screen reader, and platform independent, exploiting HTML5, CSS and WAI-ARIA standards.

Considering again our example molecule Aspirin, its CML structure allows us to generate an SVG diagram that can be imported into any modern web browser.

It can then be highlighted and magnified using CSS modifications and changes of the SVG viewport. The SVG diagram already highlighted on the top molecule level, that corresponds to the entire Aspirin molecule is shown in the middle of Fig. 1. Browsing the molecule diagrams allows us to move vertically between the different levels of the graph presented in Fig. 4 as well as horizontally between nodes on a single level of the graph. For example, one can move from the top level Aspirin molecule, down to the major component level and around this level. The right most image in Fig. 1 depicts a move on the major component level, from the Benzene ring to the functional group Carboxylic Acid. This step is voiced as "Benzene ring with Carboxylic Acid at substitution 1".

4   Polyfilling Diagrams on the Web

Polyfills are a technology that aims to mask the discrepancy in provision of functionality and APIs from different web browsers and platforms by providing uniform APIs, allowing developers to implement a homogeneous user experience in a platform independent way [7]. While often intended to be of a temporary nature, to fill the gap between new web standards and their lack of browser implementation, and in particular ensuring backwards compatibility for old browsers, many have become permanent solutions over time. A prominent example is MathJax [1], that was originally designed as a stop gap for displaying mathematics on the web until the MathML standard would be implemented in all browsers. However, since only very few browsers implement MathML (and even then only incomplete), MathJax has become the de facto rendering solution for Mathematics. Moreover, it can deal not only with MathML but with the more prevalent formats of LaTeX and ASCIIMath, replacing those expressions in web pages by DOM components that produce the correct visual rendering.

We have chosen a similar approach to tackling the problem of inaccessible diagrams on the Web. The basic idea is to provide a polyfill solution in form of a JavaScript library called *DIAGcess* that can replace inaccessible chemical diagrams or notation by fully accessible SVG diagrams upon page load. *DIAGcess* can be included via a `script` tag into a website and bitmap images of chemical molecules can be marked for transformation. The actual transformation is performed server side and its result, the accessible SVG diagram, replaces the original bitmap image in the page, using the described AJAX functionality. We thereby support three different types of transformations, depending on the markup of an image element that includes Aspirin in a web page:

We thereby support three different types of transformations, depending on the markup of an image element. Figure 5 displays the HTML element for including Aspirin as a bitmap in a web page. The element contains three dedicated data attributes `data-chemistry-access`, `-cas`, and `-inchi`. If the former attribute is set to true, the image will be transformed and replaced. How exactly the transformation works depends on which of the two latter attributes are given:

– If only `data-chemistry-access` is given, *DIAGcess* will run the entire recognition process starting in step (2) of the procedure presented in Sect. 2.

```
<img src="aspirin.png" alt="Aspirin Molecule" width="200" height="175"
    data-chemistry-access="true" data-chemistry-cas="50-78-2"
    data-chemistry-inchi=
    "InChI=1S/C9H8O4/c1-6(10)13-8-5-3-2-4-7(8)9(11)12/h2-5H,1H3,(H,11,12)"
/>
```

Fig. 5. HTML element for including Aspirin image in page.

```
<div class="ChemAccess-element" tabindex="0" role="application"
    aria-label="Navigatable molecule" has-cml="true" has-svg="true">
  <div class="cml" aria-hidden="true">
    <molecule id="m1" xmlns="http://www.xml-cml.org/schema">
    ...
    </molecule>
  </div>
  <div class="svg" aria-hidden="true">
    <svg xmlns="http://www.w3.org/2000/svg" width="200" height="175" ...>
    ....
    </svg>
  </div>
</div>
```

Fig. 6. HTML element for including accessible SVG diagram of Aspirin in page.

- If `data-chemistry-inchi` is provided with a legal InChI code *DIAGcess* will directly generate the accessible SVG diagram, effectively starting at step (2) of the process, omitting image analysis.
- If only `data-chemistry-cas` is given, the attribute contains the unique registry number of the molecule provided by the American Chemical Society. *DIAGcess* will then call ChemSpider [3] to determine the corresponding InChI code and proceed as in the previous case.

Starting in either of the latter two steps has the obvious advantage that they will always yield fully correct diagrams as no recognition errors can be introduced. In all cases, the original image element in the web site will be replaced by a container element presented in Fig. 6 that wraps together both the semantically enriched CML structure (i.e., an augmented version of the one presented in Fig. 3) and the annotated SVG, tagged the appropriate ARIA elements.

5   Conclusions

The presented work flow transforms inaccessible molecule images into accessible interactive SVG diagrams without the need for manual intervention. It neither relies on authors to produce accessible content nor requires users to install and learn additional software tools. We have integrated this process into the JavaScript library *DIAGcess* that acts as a polyfill solution, allowing automatic transformation of images in web pages and easy inclusion into web content.

As the image analysis phase can introduce errors, we believe that the ability to generate accessible SVG from unique chemical identifiers is of great advantage in the context of *DIAGcess*, where we assume that web page authors have knowledge on the molecules included in a page and can thus provide the correct identifiers. The advantage of using a polyfill solution rather than immediately integrating the accessible SVG is, that it allows to exploit updates and improvements made in the library. Moreover, certain browsers do not support the inclusion of XML document structures, necessary for navigation, directly from source. In addition, the code for navigation does not need to be provided locally.

We have carried out user testing for the diagram navigation via a demonstrator page with a collection of accessible molecules. The feedback we have received was primarily positive, particularly commending the simplicity of the navigation model, but results are not yet statistically significant. However, we hope that making *DIAGcess* available will lead to more feedback, as it allows users to easily work with material they are interested in.

DIAGcess has been implemented as a platform independent tool, and can run in all major modern browsers that support SVG. Similarly the browser front-end that supports navigation, highlighting and aural rendering, works with the majority of modern screen readers that support ARIA live regions, on all major desktop platforms. The library has to be installed and included locally for now, however, we aim to eventually distribute it via content distribution network.

Although the server back-end has currently been realised for chemical diagrams, only, the approach is not restricted to chemistry but extensible to diagrams in other STEM subjects. In fact, both the image analysis and the semantic enrichment procedure are separated into a generic and a domain specific part, where the latter can be parameterised by providing rule sets for syntactic recognition and semantic interpretation, respectively. Consequently future work will consist of extending our ideas to diagrams in other STEM subjects, like mathematics, physics and biology.

References

1. MathJax Consortium: MathJax Version 2.5 (2014). http://www.mathjax.org
2. Murray-Rust, P., Rzepa, H.: Chemical markup, XML and the world-wide web. The CMLDOM. J. Chem. Inf. Comput. Sci. **41**(5), 1113–1123 (2001)
3. Royal Society of Chemistry: Chemspider. http://chemspider.com
4. Sadawi, N., Sexton, A.P., Sorge, V.: Performance of MolRec at TREC 2011: overview and analysis of results. In: Proceedings of TREC-2011. NIST (2011)
5. Sadawi, N., Sexton, A.P., Sorge, V.: Chemical structure recognition: a rule-based approach. In: Document Recognition and Retrieval XIX, vol. 8297. SPIE (2012)
6. Sadawi, N., Sexton, A.P., Sorge, V.: Molrec at CLEF 2012: overview and analysis of results. In: CLEF Evaluation Labs (2012). http://clef2012.org
7. Remy Sharp. What is a Polyfill? October 2010. https://remysharp.com/2010/10/08/what-is-a-polyfill
8. Sorge, V., Lee, M., Wilkinson, S.: End-to-end solution for accessible chemical diagrams. In: Proceedings of 12th Web for All Conference, p. 6. ACM (2015)
9. Steinbeck, C., Han, Y., Kuhn, S., Horlacher, O., Luttmann, E., Willighagen, E.: The chemistry development kit. J. Chem. Inf. Comput. Sci. **43**(2), 493–500 (2003)
10. CADD Group Chemoinformatics Tools and User Services: Chemical Identifier Resolver. http://cactus.nci.nih.gov/chemical/structure

Tangible Programming Gimmick Using RFID Systems Considering the Use of Visually Impairments

Tatsuo Motoyoshi[✉], Naoki Tetsumura, Hiroyuki Masuta,
Ken'ihci Koyanagi, Toru Oshima, and Hiroshi Kawakami

Department of Intelligent Systems Design Engineering,
Toyama Prefectural University, Toyama 939-0398, Japan
motoyosh@pu-toyama.ac.jp

Abstract. We developed P-CUBE as a tangible programming education tool for visually impairments or inexperienced persons in PC operation. Users are able to control a mobile robot simply by positioning blocks on a mat. The fundamental programming concepts taught by P-CUBE consist of three elements: sequences, branches and loops. These systems uses radio frequency identification (RFID) systems to identify the position of blocks or cards on the mat. Blocks utilize RFID tags alone. P-CUBE is designed to operate via tactile information for visually impaired.

We report on the system configurations of P-CUBE and programming workshop held for visually impairments. Then, we discuss merits of tangible programming tools using RFID systems.

1 Introduction

The number of people studying programming from elementary school has been increasing of late years We think there is a need for programming education tool, which is easy to operation for beginners who are inexperienced in PC operation including visually impaired. A number of studies on programming education tools for beginner or younger individuals have been conducted [1–3]. However, these tools are not designed for use by visually impaired individuals.

We are developing P-CUBE which is a tangible [4] programming education tool for beginners and visually impaired [5]. P-CUBE is intended to teach fundamental programming concept [6] in beginner-level by simple operation. The users can create program only placing blocks on the mat based on algorithm structure.

P-CUBE has some features such as the following. First, programming blocks have tactile information to distinguish programming blocks. Therefore, P-CUBE is easy for visually impairments to create program. Second, since users needs no complicated operation like connector connection, the system has high robustness for rough operation.

© Springer International Publishing Switzerland 2016
K. Miesenberger et al. (Eds.): ICCHP 2016, Part I, LNCS 9758, pp. 51–58, 2016.
DOI: 10.1007/978-3-319-41264-1_7

2   P-CUBE

2.1   System Configuration

P-CUBE consists of a program mat, programming blocks, and a PC [5]. Users are able to create four types programs (sequential OPEN, sequential LOOP, conditional branch - one sensor, and two sensors) for mobile robot using only by positioning programming blocks on the program mat. Programming blocks has tactile information like motion directions to present type of blocks to users. When using P-CUBE, users are able to make a program by easy operation without handling any precision mechanical equipments. Figure 1 shows the concept of P-CUBE. The programming procedure of P-CUBE is as follows.

1. Select a programming block
2. Place programming blocks on the program mat
3. Repeat 1 and 2
4. Read and transfer the position information of programming blocks to a mobile robot via a PC
5. Execute a program

Figure 2 shows flow chart of a sequential program and a line trace program, and positions of programing blocks on the program mat. Positional relation of programming blocks corresponds to a structure of program elements in a flow-chart. A user can learn the fundamental structure of a program like sequential processing, loop, or conditional branch.

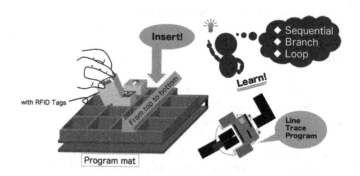

Fig. 1. Concept of P-CUBE

2.2   Program Mat

The program mat has 30 holes for attaching programming blocks, and each hole is equipped with an RFID reader. A user operates the slide bar for reading the information of RFID tags attached on the programming block. The block type information obtained from the programming block RFID tag is transmitted to the PC. After which, the information is conveyed to the mobile robot, using a SD card reader which has a wireless communication function. Figure 3 shows the system configuration of the Program mat. Figure 4 shows the transmitting process to the mobile robot.

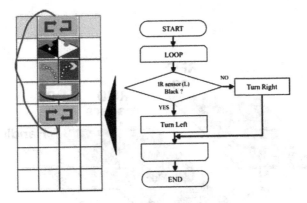

Fig. 2. Example of a program

2.3 Programming Block

Figure 5 shows all types of programming blocks. There are four types of programming blocks motion, timer, IF, and LOOP blocks. Programming blocks correspond program elements, the mobile robot movement, loop instruction and conditional branch instruction. Users complete program by arrangement programming block on the program mat adequately.

Motion Block. Motion blocks have four RFID tags on each face and instruct the mobile robot to move forward, back, or rotate depending on the face displayed to the sensors. Since each side of a motion block corresponds to a mobile robot motion, users can control movements of the mobile robot by changing the displayed side of the motion block. The blocks are made from Japanese cedar and weigh approximately 30 g.

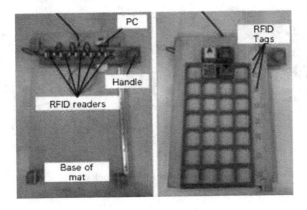

Fig. 3. Program mat

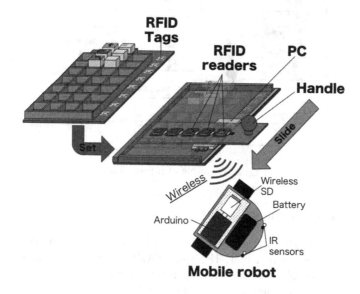

Fig. 4. Transmitting process

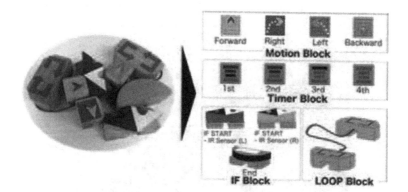

Fig. 5. Programming blocks

Timer Block. Timer blocks set the movement duration of the robot on a scale of one to four. Users have to set timer blocks next to motion blocks. The timer blocks are also made from cork and weigh approximately 16 g.

If Block. IF blocks correspond to the conditional branch functions depending on the information from two infrared (IR) sensors mounted in the mobile robot. Tactile information is incorporated into begin blocks by equipping them with silicone rubber dots, ethylene-vinyl acetate (EVA) sheets and drawing paper. The blocks are made from Japanese cedar and weigh approximately 60 g.

LOOP Block. LOOP blocks correspond to while loop functions. Mobile robot repeats the movements of blocks positioned between a pair of LOOP blocks. LOOP blocks are made from Japanese zelkova wood and weigh approximately 205 grams.

Figure 6 shows the shape and contents of information indicated on each programming block.

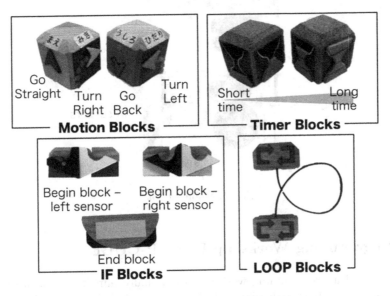

Fig. 6. Tactile information on the Programming blocks

2.4   Mobile Robot

The mobile robot, which is composed of an Arduino microcontroller board, a wireless SD shield, and batteries, receives RFID information via a microSD card. The frame of the robot is made from Japanese cedar board, to which two IR

sensors are attached. We designed the interface of the mobile robot to be operated easily for visually impairments. Since, there are no operating switches or
buttons except for executing button, a user can execute the program by pushing
the button attached on the backboard of the robot. Visually impairments do not
need to search the operating equipment. Furthermore, mobile robot informs its
own movements in real time to the visually impairments by some type of jingles.
Figure 7 shows the system configuration of the mobile robot.

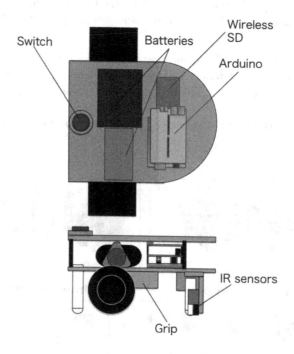

Fig. 7. Mobile robot

3   Programming Workshop Using P-CUBE

We conducted a programming workshop for visually impaired. The workshop
participants were four high school students. Two of them were sight persons
and one was very poor vision and another was absolutely blind who have no
experience in programing. All participants are engaged only in creating program
(placing programming blocks). Figure 8 shows a photograph of the participant
placing the programming block of P-CUBE. If participants made errors in the
program, a mobile did not move and played the error sound when they executed
their program.

Fig. 8. View of the workshop

All participants completed the tasks. Two sighted participants completed all tasks without any incidents. Two visually impaired take longer time for selecting and positioning programming blocks. Especially, distinguishing IF block are seemed to be difficult for visually impaired. The comments of visually impaired are as follows.

- I am interested in reading and executing program operations.
- Motion blocks and timer blocks are easy to distinguish.
- Weight, smell, and touch feeling of the block are available for selecting.
- I want to create a program for controlling another type robot i.e. for example which starts a conversation with me.

4   Discussion and Conclusions

We introduced the P-CUBE system, which is a tangible programming education tool for beginners and visually impaired. P-CUBE has three advantages. First, the P-CUBE system uses blocks with tactile information in the form of surface gaps in order to enable the system to be used by visually impaired individuals. We expect that the system will also be useful for younger individuals. Second, the interface that the user touches is robust. Since the blocks contain only RFID tags, they are difficult to break. This is convenient because of the target users of P-CUBE are younger individuals and visually impaired individuals. Furthermore, the P-CUBE system is relatively inexpensive.

In the future work, we will need to conduct a usability study of P-CUBE and improve design of the system. In addition, we intend to evaluate the learning effects of P-CUBE in programming learning for visually impairments. We hope P-CUBE becomes like an educational toy which anyone including visually impairments can use in anytime at any place freely.

References

1. Wang, D., Zhang, Y., Chen, S.: E-Block: a tangible programming tool with graphical blocks. In: Proceedings of Mathematical Problems in Engineering and MPE 2013, vol. 2013, Article ID 598547 (2013)
2. Horn, M.S., Solovey, E.T., Crouser, R.J., Jacob, R.J.K.: Comparing the use of tangible and graphical programming languages for informal science education. In: Proceedings of SIGCHI Conference on Human Factors in Computing Systems and CHI 2009, pp. 975–984 (2009)
3. Smith, A.C.: Symbols for children's tangible programming cubes: an explorative study. In: Proceedings of Annual Conference of the Southern African Computer Lecturers' Association and SACLA 2009, pp. 105–109 (2009)
4. Ishi, H., Ulmer, B.: Tangible bits: toward samless interface beeween people, bits and atoms. In: Proceedings of Conference on Human Factors in Computing System, CHI 1997, pp. 234–241 (1997)
5. Kakehashi, S., Motoyoshi, T., Koyanagi, K., Oshima, T., Kawakami, H.: Improvement of P-CUBE: algorithm education tool for visually impaired. In: Proceedings of IEEE Symposium Series on Computational Intelligence (SSCI), Orlando, USA, pp. 117–122 (2014)
6. Dijkstra, E.W.: Structured programming. In: Randell, B., Buxto, J.N. (eds.) Software Engineering Techniques, pp. 84–88. NATO Scientific Affairs Division, Brussels (1970)

A Study of Speech Versus Braille and Large Print of Mathematical Expressions

Neil Soiffer[✉]

Portland, OR, USA
soiffer@alum.mit.edu

Abstract. Several systems have been developed that allow mathematical expressions to be spoken and navigated. This paper describes studies involving the latest revision of the most widely used system: MathPlayer 4. This version includes features to allow navigation of mathematical expressions. Students with blindness or low vision used NVDA + MathPlayer to read Microsoft Word documents with math problems in them. The results were compared with the same students reading similar documents using their favorite modality (braille or large print). The results showed that speech augmented with navigation resulted in similar comprehension rates compared to when students used their preferred modality. This is an important finding because electronic documents are often available in situations where braille or large print documents are not.

Keywords: Speech generation · MathML · Print disabilities · Braille · Large print · Accessibility

1 Background

There exist several software aids for speaking mathematical expressions in web pages and elsewhere (e.g., MathPlayer, JAWS, Safari + VoiceOver, ChromeVox). A spoken expression is comprehensible when the expression being spoken is short. For most people, working memory is limited to around 7 words [1], and may be shorter when dealing with mathematics due to the density of its notation. This makes comprehension of larger expressions difficult via speech alone. One obvious solution is to allow users to navigate expressions so they can rehear parts and better understand the structure of the expression.

Several systems have implemented some form of navigation including the earliest systems for speaking math: Aster [2] and MathTalk [3]. Aster used a strict tree-based model of navigation. MathTalk and subsequent systems rejected that as too complicated and used a tree only for two-dimensional notations such as fractions and roots. Subsequent research efforts including MathGenie [4] and AudioMath [5] also supported navigation. Currently available math-to-speech systems include MathPlayer [6], ChattyInfty [7], ChromeVox [8], Safari + VoiceOver, and JAWS: all support navigation. ChromeVox, Safari + VoiceOver, and JAWS navigate math similar to MathPlayer's simple mode (see below); ChattyInfty's navigation is similar to MathPlayer's character mode.

© Springer International Publishing Switzerland 2016
K. Miesenberger et al. (Eds.): ICCHP 2016, Part I, LNCS 9758, pp. 59–66, 2016.
DOI: 10.1007/978-3-319-41264-1_8

In collaboration with the Educational Testing Service (ETS) as part of an IES grant, Design Science added the ability to move around/navigate expressions to MathPlayer. Both NVDA and Window-Eyes make use of MathPlayer to generate math speech, with several other assistive technology companies looking into using MathPlayer. The MathPlayer navigation work includes many capabilities not found in prior work; it is discussed in the next section.

Only MathTalk and MathGenie have published user studies and for both of them, studies were done with sighted users. The IES study is the first to use blind and low vision students to compare comprehension and usability of speech versus braille and large print for mathematical expressions. The findings are discussed in the remainder of this paper.

2   Implementation

Navigation was added to MathPlayer for a navigation study and modified some for the MathPlayer 4 release based on feedback from the study. Navigation in MathPlayer is performed via keyboard commands. Features include:

- Moving/Zooming: This is the basic mode of navigating. Three modes of moving around an expression are supported (see below). Arrow keys are used to move left/right and to zoom in/out of expressions.
- Descriptions/Overviews: Users can choose between hearing the expression read to them or hearing a description (overview) of the expression (e.g., "fraction plus something plus 1"). Overviews can be set as a default when moving around or can be heard via key commands.
- Place markers: 10 place markers are supported. At any point, users can set, move to, or hear what is at the place marker. This is particularly useful for cancelling fractions, marking coefficients for systems of equations, etc.
- Where am I: the ability to recall context without moving (e.g., "x + 1 inside of the fraction with numerator x + 1 and denominator x squared minus one"). The ability to get more and more context along with the ability to get the entire context is provided.

A unique aspect of MathPlayer's navigation is the ability to navigate in different modes: character, simple, and enhanced. To illustrate the differences, this sample expression is used:

$$2\sqrt{x^2 - 4} + 3a\sqrt{x + 1} \tag{1}$$

- Character/Word: navigate the leaves of the tree. E.g., moving to the right by typing the right arrow key in the above expression, results in the user hearing "2", "inside square root, in base, x", "in exponent, 2", "out of exponent, minus", etc. Character and Word mode differ only for multi-digit numbers such as 128 and multi-character identifiers/operators such as "sin".

- Simple: navigates by word except for 2D notations such as fractions and exponents. For these, the entire 2D notation is spoken. Users zoom into and out of the notation to hear parts of it. This is the common model that is implemented in many systems such as Safari, ChromeVox, and JAWS. In simple mode, moving to the right in the above expression, the user hears "2", "times the square root of x squared minus 4", "plus", "3", "a", "times the square root of x plus 1".
- Enhanced: infers what the expression tree is for the math and moving left/right uses that structure. E.g., in the example above, one would hear "2 times the square root of x squared minus 4", "plus", "3 a times the square root of x plus 1".

Another unique aspect of MathPlayer's navigation is "auto zoom in"/"auto zoom out". A description can be found in [6]. Several power users (those who read at very high TTS speeds) requested that auto zoom out be turned off. These users said that they commonly "bang" multiple times on the arrow key and want to use the end of a structure to act as a wall that stops them. No student in the IES study requested this. The ability to turn to turn off auto zoom out was added to the final release of Math-Player. "Shift arrow" will auto zoom out even if it is turned off. This provides a way to avoid having to "back out" (zoom out) of a nested 2D notation.

3 Study Results

The IES grant consisted of MathPlayer development along with four feedback studies and a final pilot study covering all aspects of the grant. The four feedback studies looked at a new speech style (ClearSpeak [9]), various forms of prosody and lexical cues to resolve speech ambiguities, navigation, and authoring documents (aimed at teachers). After making changes based on the studies, these features were evaluated in final pilot study [10]. This paper discusses the navigation study and the pilot study.

IRB approval of the studies was obtained and all participants signed consent forms. As thanks for participating in the study, the students received gift cards in amounts ranging between $25 and $125 depending upon the length of the study.

3.1 Navigation Study

The initial navigation study involved 20 students with blindness or low vision in classes ranging from algebra 1 to pre-calculus. Each participant read through an interactive tutorial to learn and practice MathPlayer's navigation features. Based upon their experiences from the tutorial for each of the navigation features, the study asked:"how easy/hard was it learn..." and "how likely are you to use...". The students found it easy to learn most features. On a scale ranging from 0-3, with three being "very easy," the mean was between 2.44 and 2.79. Three features were viewed as less likely to be used:

- Describe/Overview (1.78)
- Placemarkers (2.21)
- Where am I (2.28)

Describe/Overview mode was the least developed feature in MathPlayer, so it came as no surprise to us that it was the least liked feature. There are two problems with Describe/Overview that we were aware of:

- More effort needed to be spent determining the amount of detail to provide. E.g., the expression

$$x^2 + \frac{1}{x^2 + 1} + 1 \tag{2}$$

is read as "something plus fraction plus 1". It would probably be better to read it as "x squared plus one over something plus 1". That is only slightly longer, but it provides much more detail.[1]

- We debated using the words "term", "factor", "exponent", etc., instead of "something" in expressions. Ultimately, we used the generic word "something" because the semantics of the expression aren't fully known and we felt that using a wrong word might be misleading. One student suggested using "term", etc., when asked what they would like to see changed; most students had no suggestions for improvement.

There were two things about place markers that confused some students. As implemented (for simplicity of implementation), place markers are local to each expression: they can only reference the current expression and disappear when the expression being navigated is exited. A couple of students didn't seem to realize this and asked for a method to clear the place markers. One student asked for more than 10 place markers (place markers are currently bound to keys 0–9 for simplicity).

There were two comments about "where am I": one person wanted it to go from the bigger to the smaller (whole context then current location) and one person wanted an indication of how deeply nested they were. The rest either had no comment or thought it was fine the way it was.

In the final pilot (see next section), students were again asked about specific navigation features and how they helped their understanding and solving math problems in the pilot. Table 1 (below) shows the responses from the pilot study (one student didn't answer this question). As can be seen, the results are similar to those found in the navigation study. Several questions tried to get information about on how the students liked the three navigation modes. Students' answers varied widely as to their preferred mode, although many of students said they made use of all three modes and found each useful for different situations.

---

[1] This is *not* ambiguous because "over" is only used when the denominator is simple.

Table 1. Ratings of navigation features (adapted from [10])

Using feature made spoken math...	Much easier	Somewhat easier	Slightly easier	No easier
Arrow keys	14	4	2	0
Zoom in/out	14	5	0	1
Switch navigation modes	13	4	2	1
Place markers	7	4	6	3
Where-am-I	3	5	2	9
Describe	2	5	1	12

3.2   Final Pilot

The final pilot involved 21 students, 17 of whom had also participated in the navigation study. They were given two similar documents: a Word document with math problems (accessible via TTS + NVDA + MathPlayer + MathType[2]) and a braille, regular print for CCTV, or large print document based upon their preferences or previous usage. Students were divided randomly into two groups. Each group received paired documents in different orders (speech first or last), with each document containing 16 questions (32 total). This allowed a comparison between our speech-based solution and the student's preferred non-electronic format.

Prior to the experiment, students familiarized themselves with MathPlayer by going through a tutorial. On the day of their study participation, they practiced with two problems to make sure they remained comfortable with the system. Each part of the pilot began with a sample problem and answer followed by problems the student should solve. Here are a few examples:

1. How many zeroes are there to the right of the decimal point in the number 3.0000001?
2. The following questions are based on the polynomial

$$12x^6 + 18x^2 + 35x^7 + 5x^{15} + 45 + 16x^{12}$$

   (a) How many terms does the polynomial have?
   (b) What is the coefficient of x^2?
3. Simplify the expression $4 + 3x - 2 + 8y - 2x - 3y + 5 - 4y + 10x$
4. What is the value of the expression $3((6+5) - (8-4)) - 2$?
5. Simplify the algebraic fraction $\frac{(x+1)(2x-3)}{(2x+1)(x+1)(2x+3)}$.
   (a) What is the numerator of the simplified fraction?
   (b) What is the denominator of the simplified fraction?

---

[2] Nemeth refreshable braille is also supported by NVDA + MathPlayer, but the study did not allow students to use this feature.

64   N. Soiffer

Net scores were computed for the paired (spoken and other format) problems as follows:

- 0: student answered *both* the spoken question and its non-spoken clone correctly/incorrectly
- 1: student correctly answered the spoken question but not its non-spoken clone
- −1: student *incorrectly* answered spoken question but correctly answered its non-spoken clone

The average net score per question was 0.125 (Std. Dev. 2.73). This indicates that the students' performance using speech was similar to their performance using their usual format (insignificant bias towards speech). In other words, despite less familiarity with the speech solution, students performed comparably to the familiar but more costly printed solution.

Table 2 (below) shows that most students performed similarly on the two formats independent of the question with two exceptions: question 3.2 (example 3 above, much worse with speech) and question 4.3 (example 4 above, much better with speech).

Table 2. Performance on each question and format (adapted from [10])

Math question pair	All students (N = 21)			Print users (N = 13)			Braille users (N = 8)		
	Net	# correct spoken	# correct non-spoken	Net	# correct spoken	# correct print	Net	# correct spoken	# correct braille
1.1	−1	20	21	−1	12	13	0	8	8
1.2	−2	18	20	−2	10	12	0	8	8
2.1	0	19	19	−1	11	12	1	8	7
2.2	2	21	19	2	13	11	0	8	8
2.3	−2	19	21	−1	12	13	−1	7	8
2.4	2	21	19	2	13	11	0	8	8
2.5	0	20	20	0	12	12	0	8	8
3.1	−1	19	20	1	13	12	−2	6	8
3.2	−6	9	15	−2	6	8	−4	3	7
4.1	2	17	15	−1	10	11	3	7	4
4.2	0	7	7	0	4	4	0	3	3
4.3	6	13	7	3	9	6	3	4	1
5.1	2	13	11	1	9	8	1	4	3
5.2	−1	13	14	1	9	8	−2	4	6
6.1	3	20	17	1	12	11	2	8	6
6.2	−2	7	9	−1	5	6	−1	2	3

Table 3 shows the data per user along with their favorite modality for accessing math. The maximum net difference for a user was just 2, showing that speech is a viable option among all users in the study independent of their preferred format. Despite the students' similar performance across formats, on a feedback question,

Table 3. Net (spoken vs. non-spoken) and per-format scores by student (N = 21), aggregated across question pairs and sorted by net score, showing selected demographic information from the background questionnaire. *B = "blind", LV = "Low Vision" (Adapted from [10])

Net	Max score = 16			Current/most recent math class	Vision status*	Usual medium	Best medium
	Spoken	Print	Braille				
2	15	13	n/a	Algebra 1	LV	Large print	Large print
2	15	n/a	13	Algebra 1	B	Braille	Reader
2	16	14	n/a	Algebra 2	LV	CCTV	CCTV
2	13	11	n/a	Algebra 2	LV	CCTV	CCTV
2	14	n/a	12	Algebra 1	B	Reader	Braille
1	13	12	n/a	Geometry	LV	CCTV	Large print
1	13	12	n/a	Algebra 1	LV	CCTV	CCTV
0	14	14	n/a	Geometry	LV	Reader	CCTV
0	14	14	n/a	College Alg	LV	CCTV	CCTV
0	11	n/a	11	Geometry	B	Braille	Braille
0	10	n/a	10	Math models	B	Braille	Braille
0	13	n/a	13	Math models	LV	Braille	Braille
0	14	14	n/a	Algebra 2	LV	Screen Mag	Reader
−1	11	12	n/a	Geometry	LV	Large print	Large print
−1	9	10	n/a	Algebra 1	LV	Screen Mag	Screen Mag
−1	10	n/a	11	Algebra 1	B	Braille	Braille
−1	11	12	n/a	Geometry	LV	CCTV	CCTV
−1	5	6	n/a	Math models	LV	CCTV	Reader
−1	12	n/a	13	Statistics	B	Refreshable braille	Braille
−2	11	n/a	13	Algebra 1	B	Braille	Braille
−2	12	14	n/a	Algebra 1	LV	CCTV	CCTV

student's expressed a small preference for their usual format. We looked at the results for those who answered that they would always or would usually prefer their usual method. The data showed that their math scores were slightly higher for speech. Also, the time they spent on the problems in each method didn't correlate with their preference.

Students were asked at the end of each document how easy or difficult it was to understand the math in the document. Almost all of the students said understanding the speech was "somewhat easy", compared to "very easy" for their preferred format.

Acknowledgements. The study portion of the grant was carried out by Lois Frankel and Beth Brownstein at ETS. I am very thankful for their expertise in designing the study questions and hard work in getting IRB approval, lining up the students, and evaluating the results. Some tutorial material and student recruitment was carried out by Stephen Noble.

I had many late night discussions with Sina Bahram about how navigation should work. Many ideas were discussed and rejected until we came to the current design. The design was very much a joint effort.

The research reported here was supported by the Institute of Education Sciences, U.S. Department of Education, through Grant R324A110355 to the Educational Testing Service and Design Science. The opinions expressed are those of the author and do not represent views of the Institute or the U.S. Department of Education.

References

1. Miller, G.A.: The magical number seven, plus or minus two: some limits on our capacity for processing information. Psychol. Rev. **63**(2), 81 (1956)
2. Raman, T.V.: Audio system for technical readings. PhD thesis, Ithaca, NY, USA. UMI Order No. GAX95-11869 (1994)
3. Edwards, A.D., Harling, P.A., Stevens, R.D.: Access to mathematics for visually disabled students through multimodal interaction. Hum.-Comput. Interact. **12**, 47–92 (1997). doi:10.1207/s15327051hci1201&2_3
4. Gillan, D.J., Barraza, P., Karshmer, A.I., Pazuchanics, S.: Cognitive analysis of equation reading: application to the development of the math genie. In: Miesenberger, K., Klaus, J., Zagler, W.L., Burger, D. (eds.) ICCHP 2004. LNCS, vol. 3118, pp. 630–637. Springer, Heidelberg (2004)
5. Ferreira, H., Freitas, D.: AudioMath-using MathML for speaking mathematics. Presented at XML: Aplicacoes e Tecnologias Associadas, Braga, Portugal (2005)
6. Soiffer, N.: Browser-independent accessible math. In: Proceedings of the 12th Web for All Conference (W4A 2015), Article 28, 3 p. ACM, New York, NY, USA (2015). doi:10.1145/2745555.2746678
7. Sorge, V., Chen, C., Raman, T.V., Tseng, D.: Towards making mathematics a first class citizen in general screen readers. In: Proceedings of 11th Web for All Conference (W4A 2014), Article 40, 10 p. (2014). doi:10.1145/2596695.2596700
8. Science Accessibility Net. ChattyInfty, the Version 3 Series Manual (2014). http://www.sciaccess.net/en/ChattyInfty/ChattyInfty3_Eng_Manual.pdf
9. Frankel, L., Brownstein, B,, Soiffer, N.: Navigable, customizable TTS for algebra. J. Technol. Persons Disabil. **1** [22] (2013) http://scholarworks.csun.edu/handle/10211.3/121942
10. Frankel, L., Brownstein, B., Soiffer, N.: Expanding Audio Access to Mathematics Expressions by Students with Visual Impairments via MathML. To be published in ETS Research Report Series

Guidelines for Accessible Textual UML Modeling Notations

Vanessa Petrausch[1]([⊠]), Stephan Seifermann[2], and Karin Müller[1]

[1] Karlsruhe Institute of Technology, Karlsruhe, Germany
{vanessa.petrausch,karin.e.mueller}@kit.edu
[2] FZI Research Center for Information Technology, Karlsruhe, Germany
seifermann@fzi.de

Abstract. Textual representations of UML are basic requisites to make UML modeling accessible for visually impaired people. The accessibility, however, varies depending on the concrete realization. Constructing and rating accessible notations is challenging because the notation has to consider requirements of various assistive techniques including screen readers with audio and/or braille output. Neither accessibility metrics for existing textual notations nor comprehensive guidelines for constructing such notations exist. To bridge this gap, we design an interview for rating the accessibility of notations for UML class diagrams and conduct it with six participants for four textual notations. We use the results and related work to derive general design guidelines for accessible textual UML notations. The guidelines allow constructing accessible notations without deep understanding of assistive technologies and can serve as a benchmark for existing notations.

Keywords: UML · Textual notation · Survey · Accessibility · Formal modeling · Language design · Guidelines

1 Introduction

Modeling is frequently used in the software engineering process to describe various aspects of a system in an abstract way. The Unified Modeling Language (UML) is the most commonly used modeling language. It provides a complete graphical notation but only patchy textual notations for parts of diagram types. The lack of a standardized accessible notation impedes equal participation of visually impaired software developers and engineers even if the demand for IT experts is high.

Textual notations are considered accessible in general but their concrete realization influences accessibility. For instance, a verbose notation hinders the usage of braille displays since reading the notation is onerous and reduces the working efficiency. Furthermore, most existing notations do not focus on accessibility and thus do not consider the needs of assistive technologies.

© Springer International Publishing Switzerland 2016
K. Miesenberger et al. (Eds.): ICCHP 2016, Part I, LNCS 9758, pp. 67–74, 2016.
DOI: 10.1007/978-3-319-41264-1_9

Accessibility ratings for existing textual notations do not exist. Creating such a rating is, however, challenging because of missing rating criteria or notation design guidelines for deriving such criteria.

The contribution of this paper is a comprehensive set of design guidelines for constructing accessible textual UML notations. Notation designers do not need to have extensive accessibility experience to use them. The guidelines also serve as a benchmark for existing notations. We derived the guidelines from related work and an accessibility survey for existing textual UML notations. We drafted an interview sheet for UML class diagram notations that can be reused for further accessibility assessments. Two blind computer scientists, two researchers in the field of assistive technology and two researchers in the field of computer science participated in interviews using those interview sheets.

As a result, we derived five guideline categories covering usability, accessibility and technical aspects. The guidelines contain 18 concrete recommendations for textual UML notations which are not only applicable for class diagrams but for other UML diagram types as well.

The remainder of the paper is structured as follows: Sect. 2 shows related work. We describe our research methodology for the accessibility survey in Sect. 3 and present the results in Sect. 4. Section 5 describes the design guidelines derived from related work and the survey results. We conclude and outline future work in Sect. 6.

2   Related Work

Textual notations are beneficial from an accessibility and a general usability point of view. Loitsch and Weber [4] state that textual notations exploit existing assistive techniques such as screen readers although they focus on tactile displays to make UML diagrams accessible. Various approaches for transforming UML models into haptic representations such as 3D printing [1] exist but lack editing support. Grönniger et al. [2] present advantages of textual notations for general usability including fast editing, layouting and conciseness.

Many surveys on textual notations for UML modeling exist. Luque et al. [5] surveyed 27 and Müller [7] three approaches that exploit textual notations for making UML diagrams accessible. Seifermann and Groenda [11] surveyed 31 notations with focus on UML coverage, editing experience and applicability in engineering teams. No survey focused on rating the accessibility of notations.

Additionally, research on guidelines for textual notations exists. Patil et al. [9] define design guidelines for making textual information accessible. When designing UML notations, the suggestions of naturally expressing concepts and supporting the user's environment are applicable. The other guidelines given by Patil focus on tool support rather than the notation. The W3C formulated general accessibility principles for websites [12] that partially apply to textual UML notations. Karsai et al. [3] derive general design guidelines for improving the usability of languages and cover language purpose, realization, content as well as the concrete and abstract syntax. We cannot apply the guidelines for language content and abstract syntax because the UML [8] already defines them. Mazanec and Macek [6] also define general usability guidelines for textual notations.

3 Methodology for Deriving Accessible Notation Concepts

The overall objective is the definition of design guidelines that allow creating accessible textual UML notations. We mine the available general guidelines for textual notations from the related work section and complement them with rules we derive from expert interviews on accessible realization concepts of textual notations. The following paragraphs describe the selection of representative textual notations and their elements, the interview sheet and the interview conduction.

The interview shall cover commonly used realization concepts of textual notations. For our initial interview sheet, we restrict the interview to elements usually found in class diagrams to not overcharge our participants. We base the selection of representative notations on our previous survey on textual UML notations [11]. We categorize the notations in two dimensions: *Modeling Focus* and *Modeling Objectives*. Notations in the same category express aspects in a similar way. Figure 1 gives an overview on the categories and the selected notations.

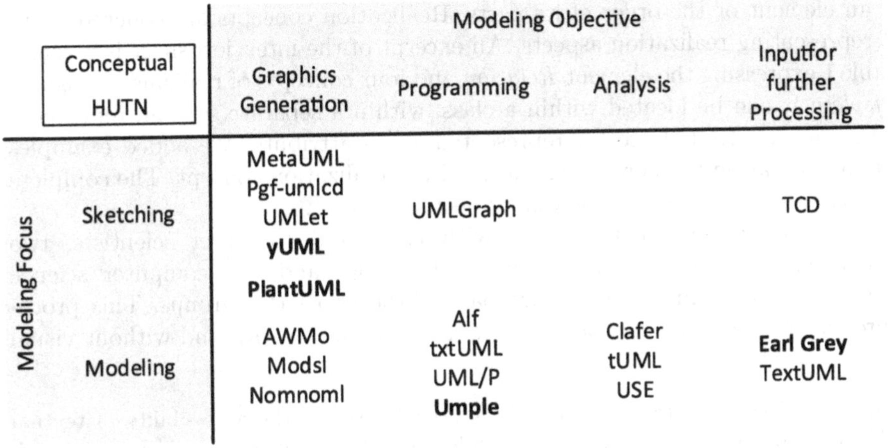

		Modeling Objective			
Conceptual HUTN		Graphics Generation	Programming	Analysis	Inputfor further Processing
Modeling Focus	Sketching	MetaUML Pgf-umlcd UMLet **yUML**	UMLGraph		TCD
	Modeling	**PlantUML** AWMo Modsl Nomnoml	Alf txtUML UML/P **Umple**	Clafer tUML USE	**Earl Grey** TextUML

Fig. 1. Categorization of the analyzed textual notations

The *Modeling Focus* covers the modeled element's type. *Sketching* focuses on graphic-oriented elements. Notations fall into this category if users have to describe graphical shapes rather than concepts. *Modeling* produces layout agnostic elements. The *Modeling Objective* covers the motivation for modeling. The classification into the categories *Graphics Generation*, *Programming* and *Analysis* relies on the intended usage stated by the notation vendors. We also define the objective of a notation to be *Programming* if the language is based on a programming language. If tools generate formal UML models without defining later usage, the objective is *Providing Input for Further Processing*.

We selected at most one textual notation from each combination of *Modeling Focus* and *Modeling Objectives* because notations in such a group express UML concepts in a similar way. We do not consider *Analysis* notations because these are usually tailored for a specific need and therefore often not applicable for general purpose modeling. We considered yUML from sketching because it has a concise, pure graphical notation and thus is an interesting candidate for comparison. We omit other sketching notations because TCD is basically text-based visual art (also called ASCII art) and therefore are not accessible by definition. The syntax of UMLGraph is too close to corresponding notations in the *Modeling* category to gain more insights. For the *Programming* objective, we select Umple over the other candidates because it is well established, covers many language constructs, has a comprehensible documentation, is not fully based on a programming language and is concise. For the *Input for further Processing* objective, we select Earl Grey over TextUML because the former focuses on usability, which often implies accessibility.

In order to compare the notations, we draft an interview sheet that distinguishes between available elements, realization aspects and realization concepts. Available elements are the UML elements that can be modeled. A realization aspect groups realization concepts for a certain purpose such as the location of an element or the order of its parts. Realization concepts are concrete ways of representing realization aspects. An excerpt of the interview sheet is given in Table 1 expressing the element *Relation* and four concepts of realizing the aspect *Display*: It can be located within a class, within a separate section, repeatedly within all involved classes or represented as an attribute. We added examples for each notation to allow easier rating of the realization concept. The complete interview sheet is available on our project's website[1].

We conduct expert interviews with two blind computer scientists, two researchers in the field of assistive technologies and two computer science researchers. The three authors are part of the two latter groups. This procedure ensures that our notation fits the needs of people with and without visual

Table 1. Excerpt of the interview sheet used for rating the accessibility of textual UML class diagram notations. The example shows how a relation could be displayed. The users rated three times for PlantUML and three times for the realization as a separate section.

Realization	Example	Notation example
Within a class	class ClassA { − > ClassB }	Umple: class A{ *− > * B; }
Separate section	relation { from Element A; to Element B; }	PlantUML: class A − > class B
Within all involved classes	class ClassA { − > ClassB } class ClassB { − > ClassA }	
Like attribute	class ClassA { ClassB reference; }	

---

[1] http://www.cooperate-project.de/icchp2016.

impairment and supports formal modeling as well. Participants are asked to rate the concept or concrete notation example they prefer to realize the given aspect.

4   Results of Our Accessibility Survey

The experts rated 29 aspects for 21 class diagram elements. Because of size limitations, we cannot publish all results here. Nevertheless, we elaborate on our general findings. The complete raw results are available on the project's website[2]. The participants rated the different notations due to accessibility, easy comprehensibility and technical feasibility in case of the two computer science researchers. Participants chose the best notation for each element and its different aspects of the class diagram from their point of view. In total, PlantUML is chosen for 21 out of 29 aspects, Umple for eight aspects, Earl Grey for three aspects and yUML never. Choosing means that at least one participant rated the notation best. PlantUML is chosen in more than 50 % of all aspects and thus seems to be preferred. In 13 ratings, all participants chose the same realization concept of an aspect, even if they chose different notations. For example, all participants decided using a *separate section* (see Table 1) for relations, although three chose PlantUML, one Earl Grey and two chose the concept rather than a concrete notation. Table 2 visualizes the relation location representation in the surveyed notations by a simple directional relation from class "Teacher" with an attribute "subject:String" to class "Pupil". PlantUML, yUML and Earl Grey use a separate association section, whereas Umple represents associations like attributes. The ratings indicate that the participants preferred graphical imitations for relations instead of verbose textual descriptions like used in Earl Grey. Pure graphical representations such as yUML are uncomfortable.

In cases of disjoint opinions, further research and discussions will be done to gain more insights. The results, however, show that participants prefer a mix of graphical imitations and textual descriptions, separated blocks for defining elements like classes and prefer compact notations rather than verbose ones although this reduces intuitive understanding of an element. The complete results are summarized within our derived guidelines in the next section.

Table 2. Excerpt from simple class diagram modeled in four different textual notations

PlantUML	Umple	Earl Grey	yUML
```class Teacher{ subject: String } Teacher -> Pupil```	```class Teacher{ String subject; 1 -> 1 Pupil; }```	```class Teacher subject: String end association Teacher[1] Pupil[1] end```	```[Teacher|subject: String] [Teacher]->[Pupil]```

---

[2] http://www.cooperate-project.de/icchp2016.

5 Design Guidelines for Accessible Textual UML Notations

We derive our design guidelines from the results of the expert interviews and the analysis of existing guidelines for accessibility and language design in general. Our guidelines cover accessibility and usability conditions but also technical feasibility to provide an easy integration within development frameworks. The literally fundamentals of the guidelines are taken from Groenninger et al. [2], Mazanec and Mace [6], Patil et al. [9] and Paige et al. [10]. We extend or filter these guidelines based on the results of our expert interview. We reviewed existing guidelines and our final guidelines from three different viewpoints to develop a notation most suitable for diversity teams. We primarily focus on the view of software developers with visual impairments, secondly the view of people working in a diversity team and last from technical feasibility.

The resulting guidelines shown in Fig. 2 include five top-level categories with several concrete realizations:(1) Usability of Textual Notation, (2) Accessibility Support for Visually Impaired, (3) Notation Realization, (4) Concrete Syntax and (5) Functional Interaction between Notation and Tools.

Usability of Textual Notations. Usability plays an important role to allow all participants working efficiently. Thus, the notation should be simple, easy to learn and intuitively comprehensible. Notations fulfilling these criteria guarantee team members working with two different representations (visual vs. textual) a smooth communication and efficient working. Furthermore, if the concepts are consistently designed, learning is facilitated.

Accessibility Support for Visually Impaired. The notation is mainly designed to improve access to UML for visually impaired people and thus we focus on accessibility features. The reading techniques of persons with visual impairment differ significantly from those of sighted persons. They cannot skim texts to pick certain information. Thus, it is important to provide mechanisms which compensate skimming to allow a fast overview and easy search in a textual notation. The identified compensation mechanisms proved to be beneficial in many consulting sessions with visually impaired persons.

Notation Realization. This category focuses on general notation conditions. Mimicking some graphical shapes with ASCII code is compact and intuitively understandable by sighted users, e.g. PlantUML uses (*) for the starting point in activity diagrams. Although compactness is preferred by blind persons, they have to learn these arbitrary letter sequences by heart as visual mnemonics are not available. In contrast to the finding in our study, we follow the objections of our blind participants regarding visual mnemonics. We choose textual realizations such as abbreviations based on natural language as they are compact and more easily to learn and to remember. It is also helpful to reuse meaningful text elements used in other notations.

Concrete Syntax. The concrete syntax defines the concrete representation of the modeled elements by graphics, texts, or other ways. Browsing code can be very cumbersome. Thus, it helps using (a) brackets to show element belongings and ease searching for certain elements (b) the same styles for each abstraction level (c) programming syntax for programming paradigms. Furthermore, ambiguity of expressions should not be allowed.

Functional Interaction Between Notation and Tools. Textual notations for software development are designed to be used in digital form especially when visually impaired persons are involved. A tool should support both sighted and visually impaired persons in editing. Code completion can be used by both groups whereas syntax highlighting can be used by sighted users only. Tools should provide similar support for both groups. Moreover, it is necessary that notations are usable across different platforms and support version control mechanisms.

1. **Usability of Language**
   (a) Keep the language simple and consistent
   (b) Create an intuitive language
   (c) Easy to learn
   (d) Ensure consistency of concepts
2. **Accessibility Support for Visually Impaired**
   (a) Constrain certain general structure
   (b) Use title for main structures
   (c) Enable transcribing mechanisms (Braille, Voice, Text)
3. **Language Realization**
   (a) Minimize graphical realizations
   (b) Use textual realizations based on natural language
   (c) Use descriptive notations, based on common known keywords
   (d) Adopt existing notations if appropriate
4. **Concrete Syntax**
   (a) Use special characters to provide organizational structures
   (b) Allow the same style for every abstraction level
   (c) Use programming syntax for programming paradigms
   (d) Use unambiguous expressions
5. **Functional Interaction between Notation and Tools**
   (a) Provide platform independence
   (b) Support writing by certain mechanisms for sighted and visual impaired persons
   (c) Provide version control mechanisms

Fig. 2. Overview of all guidelines

6 Conclusion and Future Work

Textual notations make UML modeling accessible. However, comprehensive guidelines for designing and rating such notations do not exist. We bridge this gap by drafting an interview sheet for assessing the accessibility of textual notations for UML class diagrams. We conduct an expert interview with six participants and rate four representative textual notations covering 29 realization aspects. Our participants often chose the same realization concepts independently of a potential visual impairment or working domain.

Textual notation designers can use our interview sheet to survey the accessibility of their notation. Additionally, they can construct new sheets for other diagram types by applying our method described in Sect. 3.

Based on the results of our survey and existing guidelines for designing textual notations, we derive our design guidelines for the notation developed in the Cooperate project. The guidelines are organized in five main categories and cover aspects for accessibility, usability and implementation feasibility. The guidelines give 18 concrete instructions in total for designing a textual UML notation.

Our next step is to evaluate the effect of editing support such as code completion on accessibility and whether editing support can compensate insufficiencies of textual notations. We will also evaluate how notations constructed according to our guidelines fit the requirements of screen readers and Braille displays and how they enhance working processes for UML diagrams.

Acknowledgements. This work has been funded by the German Federal Ministry of Labour and Social Affairs under grant 01KM141108.

References

1. Doherty, B., Cheng, B.H.C.: UML modeling for visually-impaired persons. In: HuFaMo 2015, pp. 4–10 (2015)
2. Grönninger, H., Krahn, H., Rumpe, B., Schindler, M., Völkel, S.: Textbased modeling. In: ATEM 2007 (2007)
3. Karsai, G., Krahn, H., Pinkernell, C., Rumpe, B., Schindler, M., Völkel, S.: Design guidelines for domain specific languages. In: DSM 2009 (2014)
4. Loitsch, C., Weber, G.: Viable haptic UML for blind people. In: Miesenberger, K., Karshmer, A., Penaz, P., Zagler, W. (eds.) ICCHP 2012, Part II. LNCS, vol. 7383, pp. 509–516. Springer, Heidelberg (2012)
5. Luque, L., de Oliveira Brandão, L., Tori, R., Brandão, A.A.F.: On the inclusion of blind people in UML e-learning activities. In: RBIE 2015, vol. 23, no. 02, p. 18 (2015)
6. Mazanec, M., Macek, O.: On general-purpose textual modeling languages. In: DATESO 2012, pp. 1–12 (2012)
7. Müller, K.: How to make unified modeling language diagrams accessible for blind students. In: ICCHP 2012, pp. 186–190 (2012)
8. OMG: Unified Modeling Language (UML)- Version 2.5, March 2015. http://www.omg.org/spec/UML/2.5/PDF
9. Patil, B., Maetzel, K., Neuhold, E.J.: Universal usability issues of textual information structures, commands, and languages of native visually challenged users: an inclusive design framework. In: Miesenberger, K., Klaus, J., Zagler, W.L. (eds.) ICCHP 2002. LNCS, vol. 2398, p. 403. Springer, Heidelberg (2002)
10. Paige, R.F., Ostro, J.S., Brooke, P.J.: Principles for modeling language design. Inf. Softw. Technol. **42**(10), 665–675 (2000)
11. Seifermann, S., Groenda, H.: Survey on textual notations for the unified modeling language. In: MODELSWARD 2016, pp. 20–31. SciTePress (2016)
12. W3C: Accessibility Principles - How People with Disabilities Use the Web, August 2012. https://www.w3.org/WAI/intro/people-use-web/principles. Accessed 28 Jan 2016

Technology for Inclusion
and Participation

Technology for Inclusion and Participation

Introduction to the Special Thematic Session

Christian Bühler[1(✉)] and Bastian Pelka[2]

[1] Rehabilitation Technology, School of Rehabilitation Science, TU Dortmund University, Research Cluster Technology for Inclusion and Participation (TIP), Dortmund, Germany
christian.buehler@tu-dortmund.de
[2] Social Research Centre - Central Scientific Institute, TU Dortmund University, Research Cluster Technology for Inclusion and Participation (TIP), Dortmund, Germany
pelka@sfs-dortmund.de

Abstract. This paper introduces to "Technology for Inclusion and Participation" and an STS of the "15th International Conference on Computers Helping People with Special Needs" (ICCHP), 13th–15th July 2016. It threads contributions of the STS topics along two strands: addressing technological developments and the embeddedness of technology in social settings, underpinning the need to address discriminating environments by social means. The paper reveals the insight, that both perspectives can't be seen without the other and blends both strands into the discourse on social innovation – the co-creation of innovative solutions for better tackling social needs.

Keywords: Assistive technology · Accessibility · Universal design · Social innovation

1 ICT: Paramount Potentials for Inclusion and Participation

The UN CONVENTION ON THE RIGHTS OF PERSONS WITH DISABILITIES has put a new perspective and reinforced emphasis on the full and equal enjoyment of all human rights and freedoms by all persons with disabilities. The use of available technologies is seen as a central precondition and tool towards the implementation of inclusion and participation. This requests the use of traditional rehabilitation technology, but also new media and new technology. The ICCHP with its 18 topics[1] suggests a thematic framework for needed research by combining technological challenges with a target group approach and contributes to the concept of the International Classification of Functioning, Disability and Health (ICF) of the World Health Organization (WHO), which highlights the role of technology for inclusion and participation.

In this context ICT for inclusion and participation seems to be an overarching perspective on inclusion, regardless of target groups. Questions on the embedding of technology in social settings have to be addressed: How can technology and

---

[1] See: http://www.icchp.org/topics-16.

non-technological assistance be linked, in which places and by which persons with which competences [1]? The function and power of social innovations [2] need more thorough research [3]. Multidisciplinary cooperation is needed that includes end users, target group representatives and intermediaries. Strands of action involve also policy advice, workshops and trainings and evaluation.

It is the basic understanding of the members of the TIP Cluster [4] and reflected in the session "Technology for Inclusion and Participation" that digital technology has paramount potentials for inclusion and empowerment as well in digital, as in physical spaces. This insight is framed by the finding that technology needs to be embedded in social support settings, aiming at improving the inclusiveness of environments [5]. A wide interdisciplinary perspective has to be taken which comprises technology, user experiences, user expertise [6] and user and society related research.

2   Technological and Social Innovations Need to Be Blended

The session TIP is blending two strands of research and development:

Firstly, latest findings and developments in technological innovations have to be identified and their role for inclusion and participation scrutinized. Technology is addressed in three ways: assistive technology, accessibility and universal design (design for all [7]). The focus in this thematic session is mainly on new media and digital technology while "traditional" technology is rarely addressed. In countries and situations where little has been made available policy and research need to cover up and improve. Highly developed countries and societies are requested to make use of the potential of technologies. Universal design is one of the concepts supporting inclusion. A valuable contribution is presented in [8] from the Norwegian practice. Cloud computing in inclusive education [9] is a closely related approach with high potential. The use of mobile apps at the workplace [10] or technology based speech interventions [11] constitute two examples if ICT based assistive technology. Many more can be found in the ICCHP proceedings.

Secondly, in order to create benefit for people beyond the mere technology, social aspects need attention. A most recent discourse on the way to change social settings has spun around the notion of civil society based initiatives, coined as "social innovations". This new paradigm is characterized by the innovation process opening up to society, a stronger role of civil society and stakeholders in co-creation processes and its orientation towards major societal challenges [4, 5]. Social innovations themselves are understood as intentional new configurations of social practices, exceeding traditional innovation concepts relying on technology as well as a normative understanding of innovations. Service delivery plays a major role in this context and new ways need to be found to reach out [12]. A global perspective like the GATE initiative of the WHO[2] of bridging the gap between available assistive technology and actual provision is needed. The STS presentation "Closing the gap between assistive technology need and provision: Towards a Global Research Agenda" tries to achieve progress here. Often

---

[2] http://www.who.int/disabilities/technology/gate/en/ .

not in focus, but very relevant are standardization and standards [13]. Only through the interoperability of technologies and services and user orientation the full potential of technology can be exploited. For the implementation of the elements of the UNCRPD strategies to create and maintain accessible environments based on social communities are required, where an example from Germany is described in [14]. Research and innovation themselves need new user oriented approaches heading for inclusive research, e.g. co-creation [15] or the use of working prototypes in participatory design [16], or education towards inclusive mindedness [17].

Seeing these contributions from a bird's eye perspective, two insights are noticeable: Firstly, ICT seems to be a technology connected to high expectations from an inclusion point of view. On the other side, the progressing digitalization of developed countries' social systems urges people to use ICT in order to participate in social environments – with high expectations towards competences and equipment. Secondly, ICT is not seen as a pure technological artifact, but as socio-digital innovations, embedded in social environments. Needs of people with disabilities, impairments or disadvantages can only be addressed by a blended approach of technological and social innovation.

Acknowledgements. This paper builds in parts on the results of the research projects "Social Innovation – Driving Force of Social Change" (SI-DRIVE) and SIMPACT – "Boosting the Impact of Social Innovation in Europe through Economic Underpinnings". Both have received funding from the EU's 7th Framework Programme under GA No. 612870 and 613411.

References

1. Kaletka, C., Pelka, B.: (Digital) social innovation through public internet access points. In: Antona, M., Stephanidis, C. (eds.) UAHCI 2015. LNCS, vol. 9175, pp. 201–212. Springer, Heidelberg (2015)
2. Howaldt, J., Schwarz, M.: Social innovation: concepts, research fields and international trends. In: Henning, K., Hees, F. (eds.) Studies for Innovation in a Modern Working Environment - International Monitoring, vol. 5 (2010). http://www.sfs-dort-mund.de/odb/Repository/Publication/Doc%5C1289%5CIMO_Trendstudie_Howaldt_Schwarz_englische_Version.pdf
3. Howaldt, J., Butzin, A., Domanski, D., Kaletka, C. (eds.): Theoretical approaches to social innovation - a critical literature review. In: A Deliverable of the Project: 'Social Innovation: Driving Force of Social Change' (SI-DRIVE). sfs, Dortmund (2014)
4. Research Cluster TIP (2016). http://tip.tu-dortmund.de Accessed 2 Mar 2016
5. Bühler, C., Pelka, B.: Empowerment by digital media of people with disabilities. In: Miesenberger, K., Fels, D., Archambault, D., Peňáz, P., Zagler, W. (eds.) ICCHP 2014, Part I. LNCS, vol. 8547, pp. 17–24. Springer, Heidelberg (2014)
6. Bühler, C.: Guidelines for participation of users with disabilities in R&D projects. In: Assistive Technology – Added Value to the Quality of Life - AAATE 2001, pp. 104–109 (2001). ISBN: 978-1-58603-195-4
7. Bühler, C.: Managing the process of design for all. In: Stephanidis, C. (ed.) The Universal Access Handbook, pp. 56-1–56-12. CRC-Press, Boca Raton (2001). ISBN 978-0-8058-6280-5

8. Eileen, M., Begnum, N.: Methodology for universal design of ICTs – practices among norwegian domain experts. In: Miesenberger, K., Bühler, C., Penaz, P. (eds.) ICCHP 2016, Part I. LNCS, vol. 9758, pp. 121–128. Springer, Heidelberg (2016)

9. Bosse, I.: Cloud computing in European schools – the impact on inclusive education. In: Miesenberger, K., Bühler, C., Penaz, P. (eds.) ICCHP 2016, Part I. LNCS, vol. 9758, pp. 1–4. Springer, Heidelberg (2016)

10. Feldmann, A., Padberg, M., Brausch, C., Bühler, C.: Supported employment - electronic job-coach (EJO). In: Miesenberger, K., Bühler, C., Penaz, P. (eds.) ICCHP 2016, Part I. LNCS, vol. 9758, pp. 1–8. Springer, Heidelberg (2016)

11. Mühlhaus, J.: Developing technology-based speech interventions for acquired speech motor impairment: a psychological approach. In: Miesenberger, K., Bühler, C., Penaz, P. (eds.) ICCHP 2016, Part I. LNCS, vol. 9758, pp. 93–100. Springer, Heidelberg (2016)

12. Andrich, R.: Re-thinking assistive technology service delivery models in the light of the UN Convention. In: Miesenberger, K., Bühler, C., Penaz, P. (eds.) ICCHP 2016, Part I. LNCS, vol. 9758, pp. 1–8. Springer, Heidelberg (2016)

13. Galinski, C., Giraldo, B.S.: Standards related to eAccessibility and eInclusion – dimensions of interoperability based on standards with respect to eAcessibility and eInclusion. In: Miesenberger, K., Bühler, C., Penaz, P. (eds.) ICCHP 2016, Part I. LNCS, vol. 9758, pp. 1–4. Springer, Heidelberg (2016)

14. Hubert, M., et al.: IMPLEMENTING UNCRPD – strategies of accessibility promotion and assistive technology transfer in North Rhine-Westphalia. In: Miesenberger, K., Bühler, C., Penaz, P. (eds.) ICCHP 2016, Part I. LNCS, vol. 9758, pp. 1–4. Springer, Heidelberg (2016)

15. Parsons, S.: Co-creating an online TimeBank for inclusive research. In: Miesenberger, K., Bühler, C., Penaz, P. (eds.) ICCHP 2016, Part I. LNCS, vol. 9758, pp. 1–8. Springer, Heidelberg (2016)

16. Hamidi, F.: Theme and variations: using working prototypes for participatory design with people with disabilities. In: Miesenberger, K., Bühler, C., Penaz, P. (eds.) ICCHP 2016, Part I. LNCS, vol. 9758, pp. 134–141. Springer, Heidelberg (2016)

17. Miura, S., Hayashi, N., Ogoshi, S., Nishi, H., Yoshioka, T., Yamaguchi, Y., Ogoshi, Y.: Fostering the development of inclusively minded engineers. In: Miesenberger, K., Bühler, C., Penaz, P. (eds.) ICCHP 2016, Part I. LNCS, vol. 9758, pp. 113–116. Springer, Heidelberg (2016)

Co-creating an Online TimeBank
for Inclusive Research

Sarah Parsons[1]([✉]), Andrew Power[1], Melanie Nind[1], Ken Meacham[2],
Clare Hooper[2], Anne Collis[3], Mal Cansdale[3], and Alan Armstrong[3]

[1] University of Southampton, Southampton, UK
{S.J.Parsons,a.power,m.a.nind}@soton.ac.uk
[2] IT Innovation, The University of Southampton, Southampton, UK
{kem,cjh}@it-innovation.soton.ac.uk
[3] Barod, Community Interest Company, Bangor, UK
{Anne,Mal,Alan}@barod.org

Abstract. Participatory and inclusive approaches to research have
become more common as researchers recognize the benefits of enabling
the meaningful involvement of representative community users in the
development of accessible technologies. One of the major challenges in
this context is how the involvement of community members can be
appropriately supported in project-related activities: payment for time
and contributions is a particularly difficult and longstanding issue. This
paper discusses the inclusive development of an online Timebank involving community members with intellectual disabilities. The TimeBank
is conceived as a tool that enables people to contribute their different
expertise on the basis of time, rather than monetary reward. The development process of the TimeBank is described as well as the challenges
faced by the research team. There is much potential in the Timebank
idea, although considerable further research is needed to establish an
accessible, usable, credible and trustworthy resource.

Keywords: Participatory research · User involvement · Intellectual disabilities · Equity · Inclusion

1 Introduction

Participatory design of technology encompasses a range of approaches to inclusive research that has developed within the field of human-computer interaction
over the past 30 years [7]. Within this context and timeframe, there has also been
increasing recognition of the value and importance of taking participatory and
inclusive approaches to research in the intellectual disability field. While 'learning disability' is a preferred term in the UK, we use the more internationally
recognised term 'intellectual disability', referring to a person's need for support
in understanding complex information and/or communicating. This paper introduces an inclusively designed online TimeBank as a tool for (a) supporting the
engagement and interaction of inclusive researchers, and (b) ensuring that time

© Springer International Publishing Switzerland 2016
K. Miesenberger et al. (Eds.): ICCHP 2016, Part I, LNCS 9758, pp. 81–88, 2016.
DOI: 10.1007/978-3-319-41264-1_10

contributed to research is equitably recognized, valued and rewarded for inclusive researchers based at universities as well as for those based outside them e.g. in third sector and other community-based organisations.

Inclusive research is an umbrella term for methodological approaches that seek to provide greater sharing of power and decision-making in research [15]. Inclusive and participatory approaches share core principles through their focus:

"...on a process of sequential reflection and action, carried out with and by local people rather than on them. Local knowledge and perspectives are not only acknowledged but form the basis for research and planning" [8, p. 1667].

The 'local people' and 'local knowledge' in this context refer to the expertise of community members who are not, or traditionally have not been, initiators of, or partners in, research i.e. those from outside academia who have tended to be marginalised from research or been the subjects of it [20]. Such inclusive research in the intellectual disability field has made important contributions to knowledge regarding the priorities and issues that matter in the lives of people with intellectual disabilities e.g. [2,13], as well as empowering people through the development of skills, awareness, confidence, friendships and advocacy (e.g. [3]).

In a similar way, the participatory design of technologies has been identified as a key driver for ethically aware and appropriate development that seeks to ensure that technologies are usable and accessible to all [1]. Moreover, [4] suggest that the co-design and co-development of technologies with traditionally marginalised groups can promote digital empowerment and social inclusion, echoing the importance and strength of inclusivity that can be achieved by working 'with' others rather than researching 'on' others (cf. [8,20]). Crucially, [1] argue that disabled people should be involved from the 'first steps' (p. 486) of technology development in order to aim for more universal, accessible design.

However, there are challenges to participatory design research and inclusive research more broadly. Firstly, within inclusive research generally, there are important discussions about the extent to which all members of a research project can or should be included at all stages of the work, for example, including data analysis and interpretation (e.g. [14]). In participatory technology design, there are similar discussions that relate to the roles of community partners or intended 'end users' e.g. from tester and user, through to informant, and design partner [9], which have very different implications for the extent to which power and decision-making are shared. Indeed, [18] suggest that more equitable inclusive approaches to technology development may be especially challenging and thorny, not least because it may be unclear who the experts are regarding what a technology should be able to do. In other words, while inclusive research that focuses on the everyday lives of people with intellectual disabilities recognises and prioritises the expertise that individuals have on their own experiences, the same may not be true for technology development where a possible technological solution is novel and none of the individuals involved may be experts on all aspects of making the novel solution a reality [17].

Another major issue for inclusive and participatory research is how the involvement of community members can be appropriately supported in project-related activities. Payment for time and contributions is a particularly difficult and longstanding issue, both on a practical and ethical basis. Practically, payments for (often) unsalaried community users, or community users working in other jobs (such as schools), can be highly problematic because payments for research contributions may affect benefits and other income [12]. Ethically, if there is an aspiration to include community members from the very earliest stages of projects, including project planning and initial ideas, then there is a fundamental inequity between academic researchers who are usually salaried and paid for their time irrespective of whether project funding is in place vs. community members whose involvement is likely to be more dependent on securing project-specific funding [16].

Our proposed solution to this problem is to inclusively co-design an online TimeBank that enables university researchers and community members to be rewarded equitably for the time they contribute to inclusive research [11]. This paper outlines the process of initiation and development of the TimeBank idea, and discusses the extent to which co-design was achievable at all stages of the project. In other words, we document an inclusive research approach to solving an inclusive research problem, highlighting the challenges and opportunities for the design process and its outcome in the form of an online prototype.

1.1   TimeBanking as a Solution to the Problem of Equity and Payment in Inclusive Research

TimeBanks are 'community-based mutual volunteering schemes whereby participants give and receive services in exchange for time credits' [19, p. 63], that is, time becomes currency [5]. The TimeBanking concept was originated in the US by Edgar Cahn who proposed that TimeBanks can enable democratic and reciprocal working partnerships, and the building of social capital, because people contribute their different expertise on the basis of time, rather than on the basis of any actual or perceived hierarchical monetary reward [6]. In this sense, a TimeBank is potentially a very inclusive device, enabling reciprocal and equitable exchanges for all participants [16].

TimeBanks have been developed to meet a diverse range of community-based needs in the UK and internationally [5,10]. While there seems to be increasing awareness and use of TimeBanks for supporting non-monetised exchanges [5] there has not yet, to the best of our knowledge, been a TimeBank targeted at inclusive researchers or developed through inclusive, participatory design processes. Beyond the core principles of instantiating equity and reciprocity of time, such a TimeBank could have numerous benefits, including:

- formalising and auditing currently invisible exchanges of time;
- enabling new and wider networks to be formed, moving beyond existing and local contacts;

- improving the quality of research proposals and potential for wider impact through being able to involve the right people at the right time, particularly before and after grant-funded work;
- creating an inclusive space to encourage and enable more people with intellectual disabilities to express an interest in research.

2   Methodology and Results: Co-designing the TimeBank

Barod, a Community Interest Company run by people with and without intellectual disability, had the initial idea that TimeBanks could help inclusive research, and discussed the idea with university-based researchers. Internal funding was obtained for a small-scale project from the University of Southampton's Web Science Institute. Our 'core design' team (those who initially applied for the funding) therefore comprised three community-based inclusive researchers from Barod and four university-based researchers from different disciplines and areas of expertise including disability studies and web design. The project also involved a web developer who came on-board after initial scoping to help design and build the prototype. We called the project PRICE [Participation and Responsible Innovation in Co-Design for Exchange] and henceforth refer to the 'PRICE TimeBank'. Our methodology for developing the PRICE TimeBank comprised four main steps, each involving a number of activities, which are summarised next.

2.1   Scoping and Agreeing the Initial Idea

Each member of the team was tasked with searching for information to inform the development of the inclusive TimeBank, either from the academic research literature or from the web more broadly. Topics for searching included: examples of TimeBanking and accessible websites; history of the development of TimeBanks; web accessibility research; and digital tools for supporting and documenting communication and networking within the project. Our findings from these search exercises were shared with each other in a face-to-face meeting using accessible slides to show key ideas. We made plans at this meeting for the next stages of the project which were designed to inform the development of the online PRICE TimeBank prototype.

2.2   Validating and Extending the Initial Idea

We organised two main activities to further inform, validate and develop the PRICE TimeBank idea: (1) a face-to-face focus group and (2) a Twitter discussion. The focus group comprised 15 inclusive researchers in addition to members of the research team, specifically eight academic researchers and seven researchers with intellectual disabilities or autism. The Twitter discussion was a two-hour session in which contributors were able to tweet ideas and comments using a dedicated hashtag 'pricestudy'. There were 108 relevant contributions from 38 different Twitter accounts. Both activities contributed valuable ideas about how accessibility, online safety, trust, and reciprocity of the time exchanges could be managed, and reminded us of the need for caution in these areas. More information about the findings of these activities can be found in [11, 16].

2.3 Development of the Idea into a Prototype

Following the feedback from these activities, each core member of the design team submitted a 'walkthrough' describing the main features of the prototype that they felt were needed and how they would expect to be able to access, input and retrieve information from the PRICE TimeBank. These 'walkthroughs' were collated into an overall wish list which we negotiated with our web developer. The core design team provided feedback on specific features through a series of short iterative cycles based on visual mockups of the TimeBank over approximately two months, after which an early prototype of the online PRICE TimeBank was made available for preliminary evaluation.

2.4 Evaluation and Feedback

We approached seven people, already known to us, and asked them to try out the prototype individually; the seven people were: two inclusive researchers who had taken part in the focus group; two experts in web accessibility; one academic doing collaborative work in health; and two people with intellectual disabilities (one familiar with TimeBanks but not using the Web and one familiar with the Web but not TimeBanks). Each person was sent the link and asked to set up a user account, login, and explore the TimeBank. They were asked to feedback about current usability and accessibility, make suggestions for improvements, and comment on whether they felt the idea was understandable and useful.

Overall, feedback showed that these users liked the idea and felt there was a need for the TimeBank. There were many helpful suggestions for how the accessibility and usability of the TimeBank could be improved, for example by focusing on the overall layout in terms of text/visuals as well as the navigation between tabs and screens. There were also some suggestions for how the concept of the TimeBank might be conveyed more clearly, for example, it was felt that the TimeBank logo/image we used was not especially illuminating, and that we needed to be much clearer about what people with intellectual disabilities get back out of the Timebank. The use of specific examples and short videos was suggested as being potentially very helpful for providing this information.

3 Outcomes and Contribution

We have produced an early prototype of an online TimeBank for inclusive research and established, amongst members of the inclusive research community as well as the intellectual disability field more widely, that there is strong support for the idea. Current web accessibility guidelines do not provide information about how to make a website equally accessible to people with intellectual disabilities and academics, and we are in a good position to draft, test and refine guidelines as we further develop the PRICE TimeBank.

Nevertheless, there remained challenges about the extent to which all aspects of the design and development were fully inclusive. Our 'core design team' contributed equally to the initial scoping of the idea (Stage 1 above) and decision-making about the main aspects of the TimeBank (Stage 3). Thus, the core design team were design partners in the sense that [9, p. 4] describes. i.e. '...as equal stakeholders in the design of new technologies throughout the entire experience ...[who] contribute to the process in ways that are appropriate for [them] and the process'. Although Druin's work focused on children, her framework for thinking about the different roles of stakeholders in technology design processes can be applied much more widely, including people with intellectual disabilities. Indeed, she [9, p. 19] emphasizes that different stakeholders can offer 'special experiences and viewpoints ...that other partners may not be capable of contributing'. This position is very much aligned with the fundamental ethos of inclusive research more broadly, as noted in the Introduction.

However, in terms of evaluation and further iterations outside our core design team, we were selective and targeted about whose views we sought at different stages. For example, in validating the idea (Stage 2) we invited members of our known networks to join discussions, either face-to-face or via Twitter. These participants were not design partners but were informants to the project which, according to [9], is when stakeholders are invited to contribute ideas before the technology is developed, often using low-tech methods to visualise concepts or ideas. We then involved other stakeholders as testers of the prototype TimeBank during the evaluation of the prototype (Stage 4). Testers usually evaluate prototypes before they are finalised and released for wider use and, therefore, can have quite immediate impacts on iterations as prototypes become more robust during further development [9]. However, only two out of the seven people involved at this stage had also contributed as informants via the focus group and so most knew very little about the project objectives.

There were some concerns within our core design team about the exclusion of many of our informants from the testing phase. This decision was made because it was felt the prototype was not yet accessible enough to be tested appropriately by all of the people who attended the focus group hence their invited involvement would have been excluding for them and, therefore, unethical. Nevertheless, although this decision was made for good pragmatic and ethical reasons, it was experienced as uncomfortable by the design team because questions arose about the extent to which we were able to be appropriately inclusive in all of our activities. This illustrates the specific challenge for technology development within inclusive and participatory research frameworks, as suggested by [17,18].

4   Conclusions and Next Steps

We have established an inclusive research partnership that works well, is trusting and open, and has produced a prototype online TimeBank for inclusive research. Despite all of our experiences in inclusive research, we were still challenged by some of the practical and ethical implications of co-design within technology development. We need to research, develop and test an improved version for the online TimeBank because, although we showed the concept works from our early version, we are painfully aware of its inadequacies. We also need to explore the concept of online trust, how to build trust and how to keep the TimeBank trustworthy in order to ensure that people's time and goodwill are not exploited. We intend to apply for further research funding to continue this work. It will be essential to maintain the strong involvement of people with intellectual disabilities in all of our plans and activities in order to ensure that issues of trust, relevance and credibility are appropriately investigated and addressed within future iterations of the TimeBank.

Acknowledgements. This project was funded by the WebScience Stimulus Fund at the University of Southampton, UK.

References

1. Abascal, J., Nicolle, C.: Moving towards inclusive design guidelines for socially and ethically aware HCI. Interact. Comput. **17**(5), 484–505 (2005)
2. Abbott, S., McConkey, R.: The barriers to social inclusion as perceived by people with intellectual disabilities. J. Intellect. Disabil. **10**(3), 275–287 (2006)
3. Atkinson, D.: Research and empowerment: involving people with learning difficulties in oral and life history research. Disabil. Soc. **19**(7), 691–702 (2004)
4. Bleumers, L., All, A., Mariën, I., Schurmans, D., Van Looy, J., Jacobs, A., Willaert, K., de Grove, F.: State of play of digital games for empowerment and inclusion: a review of the literature and empirical cases. In: EUR 25652 Joint Research Centre Institute for Prospective Technological Studies. Luxembourg: Publications Office of the European Union (2012). doi:10.2791/36295
5. Bretherton, J., Pleace, N.: An Evaluation of the Broadway Skills Exchange Time Bank. Centre for Housing Policy, University of York (2014)
6. Cahn, E.: No More Throw-Away People: The Co-production Imperative. Essential Books, Washington, D.C. (2000)
7. Coleman, R., Clarkson, J., Dong, H., Cassim, J.: Design for Inclusivity: A Practical Guide to Accessible, Innovative and User-Centred Design. Gower Publishing Limited, Hampshire, UK (2012)
8. Cornwall, A., Jewkes, R.: What is participatory research? Soc. Sci. Med. **41**(12), 1667–1676 (1995)
9. Druin, A.: The role of children in the design of new technology. Behav. Inf. Technol. **21**(1), 1–25 (2002)
10. Glynos, J., Speed, E.: Varieties of co-production in public services: time banks in a UK health policy context. Crit. Policy Stud. **6**(4), 402–433 (2012)

11. Hooper, C., Nind, M., Parsons, S.J., Power, A., Collis, A.: Building a social machine: co-designing a TimeBank for inclusive research. In: WebSci 2015, Oxford, UK, 28 June–01 July 2015. doi:10.1145/2786451.2786472

12. Lewis, A., Parsons, S., Robertson, C., Feiler, A., Tarlton, B., Watson, D., Marvin, C.: The role and working of reference, or advisory, groups involving disabled people: reviewing the experiences and implications of three contrasting research projects. Br. J. Spec. Educ. **35**(2), 78–84 (2007)

13. Manning, C.: 'My memory's back!' Inclusive learning disability research using ethics, oral history and digital storytelling. Br. J. Learn. Disabil. **38**(3), 160–167 (2010)

14. Nind, M.: Participatory data analysis: a step too far? Qual. Res. **11**(4), 349–363 (2011)

15. Nind, M.: What is Inclusive Research?. Bloomsbury Academic, London (2014)

16. Nind, M., Armstrong, A., Cansdale, M., Collis, A., Hooper, C., Parsons, S., Power, A.: TimeBanking: Towards a co-produced solution for power and money issues in inclusive research. Int. J. Soc. Res. Methodol. (in press). doi:10.1080/13645579.2016.1179469

17. Parsons, S., Cobb, S.: Who chooses what I need? Child voice and userinvolvement in the development of learning technologies for children with autism. In: EPSRC Observatory for Responsible Innovation in ICT. http://observatory-rri.info/?q=obs-doc/report/case-study/473 (2013). Accessed 22 Jan 2016

18. Parsons, S., Cobb, S.: Reflections on the role of the 'users': challenges in a multi-disciplinary context of learner-centred design for children on the autism spectrum. Int. J. Res. Method Educ. **37**(4), 421–441 (2014)

19. Seyfang, G.: Time banks: rewarding community self-help in the inner city. Commun. Dev. J. **39**(1), 62–71 (2004)

20. Walmsley, J., Johnson, K.: Past, Present, and Futures. Jessica Kingsley Publishers, London (2003)

Implementing UNCRPD – Strategies of Accessibility Promotion and Assistive Technology Transfer in North Rhine-Westphalia

Michael Hubert[1]([✉]), Christian Bühler[1,2], and Wolfgang Schmitz[1]

[1] Research Institute Technology and Disability (FTB) of ESV, Wetter, Germany
mh@ftb-esv.de
[2] Technical University (TU) Dortmund, Dortmund, Germany

Abstract. The UN Convention on the Rights of Persons with Disabilities (UNCRPD) has been statutorily confirmed and recognised by the German Bundestag and Bundesrat without limitation. The resulting obligations have been adopted by the government of North Rhine-Westphalia by means of an action plan called 'One Society for all – NRW Inclusive'. Reflecting the accessibility focus of Article 9 UNCRPD, the 'Agentur Barrierefrei NRW (Accessibility Agency NRW)' covers this field of action comprehensively. Main focuses are the built environment, qualification and sensitisation of decision makers, survey of public buildings, qualification and empowerment of users and there organisations, accessibility in the European context, easy language and Assistive Technology (AT) with its links to accessibility and Universal Design (UD). Actions are widely based on user involvement and participation and produce outcomes within the scope of UNCRPD's general obligations.

Keywords: UNCRPD · Accessibility · Inclusion · Action plan · Assistive technology · Participation

1 Introduction

In Germany the UNITED NATIONS CONVENTION ON THE RIGHTS OF PERSONS WITH DISABILITIES (UNCRPD) has been statutorily confirmed and recognised by the Bundestag and the Bundesrat without limitation. The convention has reemphasized barrier free accessibility to infrastructures, mobility and transportation and to ICT. Underlining its relevance, accessibility is one of the general principles within the philosophy of the UNCRPD lined out in Article 3 [1]. The important role of accessibility and assistive technology (AT) as cross-sectional issues is widely covered by the convention, as well [1]. According to Article 4 UNCRPD's general obligations include measures aiming at e.g.:

- Promotion of technologies that are useful for people with disabilities
- Qualification and awareness raising of experts
- Securing the participation of people with disabilities and their organisations [1]

© Springer International Publishing Switzerland 2016
K. Miesenberger et al. (Eds.): ICCHP 2016, Part I, LNCS 9758, pp. 89–92, 2016.
DOI: 10.1007/978-3-319-41264-1_11

2 Background and Approach

The North Rhine-Westphalian action plan 'Eine Gesellschaft für alle – NRW inklusiv (One Society for all – NRW Inclusive)' [2] enacted in July 2012 and projected until 2020 offers a strategic framework for the implementation of the UNCRPD in NRW, the most populous federal state of Germany with about 18 Million inhabitants.

With this participative approach based on a new culture of inclusive thinking and acting the NRW government intends to join forces with civic society and NGOs expecting to achieve long-term and sustainable social innovation [2]. At the present time important activities by means of social politics and legislation in this context are e.g.:

- Tendering of competence centres for self-determined living
- Preparation of the 'Inklusionsstärkungsgesetz (Inclusion Enforcement Act)'
- Revision of the building legislation

The 'Agentur Barrierefrei NRW (Accessibility Agency NRW)' supports the NRW policy for the implementation of comprehensive accessibility in line with the UNCRPD obligations [2]. In close collaboration with self-help organisations of people with disabilities and networking with actors and decision-makers in public administration, policy and economy the Accessibility Agency NRW provides independent information and a widespread spectrum of counselling services, aiming at the attainment of accessibility and application of AT in various areas of life. Important activities of the Agency are:

- Provision of structured background information e.g. regulations, standards and guidelines via its accessible web portal.
- Qualification and sensitisation of decision-makers by different means. E.g. the operation of revising the building legislation in North Rhine-Westphalia is supported by comments of the Agency on expert level.
- Training and advice for user organisations improving their technical know-how and enabling them to actively participate in the planning process as granted by law.
- A large-scale survey on barrier-free access to public buildings. Accessibility information is provided by an accessible web portal.
- Involvement in the 'EureWelcome' initiative designed to improve the cross-border mobility in the 'Euregio Maas-Rhine' [2].
- Information and consultancy on accessible communication and Easy-to-Read language [3] for the public sector and organisations of persons with disabilities.

3 The Assistive Technology Track

Aiming at comprehensive social inclusion, the assistive technology track of the Accessibility Agency NRW promotes the application of modern technologies by using a tri-focal approach on AT, barrier-free access and Universal Design (UD). To outline certain activities and methodologies, the track can be divided into four major activity lines.

3.1   The Exhibition

Within the exhibition technical solutions and single devices for mobility, everyday life, security and alternating displays are presented complemented by accessible WC showrooms and a fully equipped widely accessible flat. Combinations of solutions from AT, UD and barrier-free access are ready to be demonstrated and tried out. Thus the overall perspective of standardised technology accessible for many users is complemented with individual user perspectives drawn from real life, e.g.:

Accessible bathrooms are equipped with assistive devices for personal care and mobility. Adaptable kitchen facilities are complemented with elements to optimize the contrasts for persons with visual impairments. The accessible entrance of the flat with automatized door drive and dazzle-free illumination can be opened with different kinds of assistive devices. The AAL System based on a KNX-EIB network inside the demonstration flat can be operated either by standard devices or by assistive devices for environmental control.

3.2   Individual Guidance

In terms of individual guidance the Accessibility Agency NRW cultivates a close internal co-operation with a locally operating housing consultation service with overlapping tasks concerning accessible building, options for home adaptation and the application of AT devices.

Individual guidance is mainly concerned with client-specific technical solutions and their financing clarification. The service is requested by people with diverse disabilities, older people or assisting persons. The motives are situated mainly in the participation areas of mobility, communication, learning, work, self-care, habitation and domestic living. Many single case documentations indicate, that the Agency's non-commercial and independent advice that considers activity requests of the users and allows individual trial and adaptation helps people using AT more effectively.

3.3   Information, Training and Instruction

The Agency provides information and advice services for specific target groups coming e.g. from self-help organisations, or have a professional background from services in care, rehabilitation, social support, crafting or AT industry. Besides a program for interested visitor groups the Agency frequently provides training and instruction courses to different AT and accessibility related topics. Highly demanded are training courses for housing consultants where AT innovations are presented.

With the intention of a wider dissemination of the accessibility and social inclusion concerns of the NRW action plan the Agency hosts special exhibitions in line with lectures, discussions and guided tours highlighting specific subjects relevant for the envisaged user groups. These special formats are developed in cooperation with network partners from disability organisations and NGOs in the field.

3.4 Networking

The Agency's staff members are involved in several committees and co-operate in other projects with the professional backgrounds of rehabilitation science and technology. Examples for the Agency's networks in the AT track are:

- Expert committees of the Association of German Engineers (VDI) concerning the accessibility of buildings (VDI 6008)
- Expert committee 'Assistive Technology provision' of the German association for rehabilitation (DVfR)
- A national research network for AT provision
- Expert committee of the German association of occupational therapists (DVE)

On the regional and local level the Agency participates in close networking partnerships with NGOs, organisations of people with disabilities and public authorities.

4 Conclusions

This rather short outline shall illustrate, that the AT track of the Accessibility Agency NRW is an important contribution to the accessibility field of action of the NRW action plan. The outlined activities produce many outcomes and effects within the scope of the above mentioned general obligations of UNCRPD.

The multi-professional approach of an independent competence centre has been found to be advantageous to promote accessibility implementation and AT application. Assigning responsibility not only to the authorities but also to the civil society is effective in terms of awareness raising regarding accessibility and assistive technology needs of the envisaged inclusive society. The unique overall setting of the Accessibility Agency NRW is supposed to be of interest to other federal states, too. The NRW government intends the legal anchoring of the Agency and its functions in the Inclusion Enforcement Act currently being in preparation.

References

1. United Nations: Convention on the Rights of Persons with Disabilities (2006). http://www.un.org/esa/socdev/enable/rights/convtexte.htm. Accessed 30 Jan 2016
2. MAIS NRW: Aktionsplan des Landes "Eine Gesellschaft für alle – NRW inklusiv" (2012). http://www.ab-nrw.de. Accessed 30 Jan 2016
3. Bühler, C., Schmitz, W., Hubert, M.: "The Accessibility Agency" - promoting the development of inclusive environments by mainstreaming accessibility issues. In: Assistive Technology from Adapted Equipment to Inclusive Environments: AAATE 2009, pp. 697–702 (2009)

Developing a Technology-Based Speech Intervention for Acquired Dysarthria

A Psychological Approach

Ute Ritterfeld[1(✉)], Juliane Muehlhaus[1,2], Hendrike Frieg[2], and Kerstin Bilda[2]

[1] Department of Language and Communication,
TU Dortmund, Dortmund, Germany
{ute.ritterfeld, juliane.muehlhaus}@tu-dortmund.de
[2] Department of Applied Health Sciences,
Hochschule fuer Gesundheit, Bochum, Germany
{hendrike.frieg, kerstin.bilda}@hs-gesundheit.de

Abstract. New technology promises high potential for empowerment and training in the health area. Effectiveness of training, however, is based upon realiable and frequent usage of technology. To achieve this goal we propose an approach based upon psychological models of motivation, namely self-determination theory. Using the example of patients with acquired speech motor impairments as dysarthria due to Parkinson's disease, we outline design strategies for tailored and adaptive technology that is embedded in speech therapy and allows for autonomous usage. "ISi-Speech" profits from an inter-disciplinary team of technicians, speech therapists and psychologists who were recently funded by the German ministry of Education and Research to build a digital training system for treatment of dysarthria. End users will be involved into design and formative evaluation processes.

Keywords: Parkinson's disease · Self-determination theory · Technology-based speech therapy

1 Introduction

Language is a key factor for successful communication and participation in society. Speech motor impairments, on the other side, pose a substantial risk for social isolation [1, 2]. Especially in elderly individuals, neurological diseases such as Parkinson's disease or stroke are often associated with speech motor impairments as dysarthria. Although these patients may have access to words and syntax, their abilities to voice and articulate can be severely inhibited. Speaking is strenuous and loses its clarity to be well understood. In many cases of Parkinson's disease, patients lack insight as to how severely their speech is impaired and attribute misunderstanding to other's hearing deficits. This is typically the case in elderly couples. Often, a downward spiral of speaking difficulty resulting in withdrawal from communication and eventually social isolation is initiated. Speech therapy aims to promote communication skills in patients.

K. Miesenberger et al. (Eds.): ICCHP 2016, Part I, LNCS 9758, pp. 93–100, 2016.
DOI: 10.1007/978-3-319-41264-1_12

A therapist selects a set of exercises suitable for the individual patient and works with him/her in a dialogic face-to-face situation. Speech training for patients with acquired neurological impairments includes training of articulation, speech rate, prosody, vocal loudness, respiration, voice, and functional communication. For patients suffering from Parkinson's disease, treatment emphasizes vocal loudness, recalibration of sensori-motor perception and self-cueing to facilitate generalization of treatment effects into functional communication, as exemplified in the evidence-based Lee Silverman Voice Treatment (LSVT®) [3]. In many countries, a limited set of treatment units is funded by the health insurer with the consequence that many patients have only one appointment per week in speech therapy. However, sustainable effects for treatment of dysarthria have primarily been gathered using intensive treatment approaches like LSVT® with at least two to four 60 min sessions a week [3, 4]. Unfortunately, increase of frequency often fails due to a lack in human resources. This is where technology comes into play.

We argue that face-to-face speech therapy can hugely profit from being supplemented with technology-based intervention in order to not only enhance (1) the frequency of training, but also (2) individual tailoring, and (3) highly specific feed-back. As we envision such adaptive technology either to be embedded within a clinical setting or installed at a patient's home, we consider mobile devices ideal. Empowerment and autonomy of patients might be supported, if technologies can be used independently from a therapist [5].

However, in both cases, within therapy or independent usage the speech therapist carries responsibility to select, introduce, and monitor the adequate technology for persistent usage. Yet, information on technology that is both effective and has potential for autonomous use is still sparse. Research and development need to address solutions that will be accepted by therapists as well as by patients. We therefore propose an approach in which technology design and evaluation is based on psychological models [6]. This approach could inform a better understanding of technology-based interventions, their usefulness and their effectiveness.

2   Technology-Based Speech Intervention for Patients with Parkinson's Disease

Recently, German engineers for speech signal processing and informatics, media designers, and researchers from the fields of psychology and speech and language pathology were granted a nationally funded R&D project: 'Individualisierte Spracherkennung in der Rehabilitation fuer Menschen mit Beeintraechtigung in der Sprechverstaendlichkeit' (ISi-Speech) [individual speech recognition in therapy for people with motor speech disorders] (in German). The interdisciplinary team joined efforts to develop a digital training system for patients suffering from Parkinson's disease. The main goal is to develop an automatic speech recognition system applicable to distorted speech integrated in a speech therapy application that carries the motivational potential contributing to frequent and autonomous usage. These challenges shall be met within an elaborate and continuous user driven design exemplifying psychological theories.

2.1   Theory-Based Design: Effective Use of New Technologies

Acceptance of technology in both, patients and therapists, requires an approach that combines attractiveness of the system, intuitive usability, and convincing effectiveness [7]. Taken together, these features heavily influence the two major but rather independent motivational usage components: selection and persistence.

Selection. The selection process determines if and which tool is chosen at a particular time and with a specific goal. The motivation for selection is based on expectancies and previous experiences and – most importantly – on the knowledge about availability of the tool in question. In the case of Parkinson's disease, which mainly affects the elderly, chances are that patients themselves initially have no knowledge about speech training technology available. Consequently, it will be the therapist who decides to use a technology for a certain therapy goal and selects which technology s/he would like to introduce to a specific patient. This can be called external or prescribed selection and has important implications for usage motivation and subsequently for the effectiveness of a treatment. If the therapist is not convinced her/himself about the chosen technology, it will be almost impossible to convince a patient if needed. If, however, the therapist is a strong believer of this treatment approach, s/he still needs to convince the patient. If s/he does not succeed, a patient will at best agree to use the tool for the sake of fulfilling the therapist's expectations. Worse, s/he will respond with reactance. Commitment and compliance will be low to null. The patient will not use the technology prescribed as required. Frustration on both sides, the therapist's and the patient's, are inevitable.

In the medical realm, processes of motivation often do not get sufficient attention. The paradigm of a doctor prescribing a medication and signing a prescription might still result in a patient complying with taking the pills because of the authority of the doctor and comparably low costs for the patients. If a doctor, however, advises to live a different lifestyle, e.g., exercise or eat healthier, compliance is often too low to result in effective changes. Therapists introducing technology to a patient with Parkinson might suggest a tool, initiate, and advice usage, but need to rely on self-sustained continuous training in the patient.

To ensure maximum motivation for usage patients need to be fully informed about the technology, it's assets but also conditions and potential barriers for effectiveness. Transparency of the selection process and consensus in the final decision will help to establish the required foundation for persistent usage.

Persistence. Even consensus about selecting a treatment is not sufficient to ensure its usage. Factual duration of its use and repetition frequency are of utmost importance. This so called persistence is a crucial necessity for effectiveness of the intervention. Persistence relies on different parameters than selection. Especially in the beginning, selection is based upon beliefs or arguments whereas persistence is mainly experience driven. If the usage of a technology system is convincing, a person will continue. In case of negative experiences, such as frustration or boredom, motivation for usage will immediately drop. The main principle for sustained motivation lies in the adequate level of challenge, being neither too high nor too low. Ensuring such an optimal level requires immediate adaptability of the system: not only the system needs to be tailored to different persons, but also to different states within a person. In addition, immediate and specific feed-back makes the difference in keeping motivation for persistent usage high.

Immersion. If selection and persistence in usage are implemented successfully, chances are high that usage elicits the optimal experience in which a user allocates all attention to the system. This is called immersion. Immersion is proposed as an ideal balance between cognitive and emotional engagement through which training and enjoyment are blended for optimal development [8]. Often, such a blending of learning with enjoyment is supposed to be elicited by entertainment features such as colors, pictures or animations. However, these superficial frills do not support immersion, they rather distract from it. Immersion is a state of deep experience which in contrast to superficial endeavors is characterized as being rather immune to distractions. This deep, non-distracted experience is sometimes described as a state of flow [9] in which users even forget about time and place surrounding them. Video games represent the typical paradigm for immersive experiences in technology usage. In the last years, ample researchers attempted to identify the psychological mechanisms of gaming that can be utilized for learning and training, also in the health domain [10, 11].

2.2 Psychological Mechanisms of Immersion and Effectiveness

The role of immersion for effectiveness of technology usage is well explained with psychological theories of motivation such as the self-determination theory (SDT) [12–14]. SDT proposes three conditions for personal growth as the main motor for intrinsic motivation: autonomy, competence and relatedness.

In the last 15 years, research with the perspective of SDT has been applied to the health domain where patients' perception of support for their autonomy, competence and relatedness has been investigated intensively (e.g., [15]; for a summary see [16]). Technology-based interventions have a tremendous potential to facilitate patient's motivation for a sustainable usage [17].

In the case of ISi-Speech we envision to trigger the core elements of SDT in ensuring a patient's autonomy first, with respect for the selection process and second, with self-sustained usage. Regarding the selection process, we already emphasized the importance of consensus between therapist and patient. Within the concept of SDT consensus can only be reached if a person feels free to decline a suggestion or with other words, if s/he experiences autonomy. Autonomy is lost if a patient feels pressured. However, autonomy can still be secured if a patient is not yet convinced to use a tool but willing to try it out. For continuous usage, autonomy emerges with the amount of control a patient can execute. Independence from others to operate a tool plays a key role.

Competence is first defined as a relative rather than absolute value and is hereby experience oriented and not objectively set. The experience of competence requires a comparison with either previous achievements (individual), others (social) or a goal (normative). ISi-Speech attempts to implement all three elements in providing highly specific graphic and acoustic individual feed-back on achievements and previous achievements to conclude about individual improvements. Comparisons with references groups may be presented in a way that demonstrates relative higher competence in the user. For normative evaluations, steps achieved towards a preset and realistically tailored goal will be made transparent.

Connectedness in health intervention technology can facilitate a double path: on one side connectedness between a patient and his/her therapist will ensure a feeling of being guided and supported with expertise, experience, and empathy. Especially in situations of draw backs, failures or doubts a trusting and encouraging connection to the therapist allows to overcome obstacles and keep on track. On the other side, connection to other users may be utilized as a source for feeling embedded. For example, other users may be built into the system as information units for social comparison or, depending on the mode of secure usage, as integrated features for accessing supplemental networking features. In addition, so called para-social propositions to avatars are proven to have a huge potential for the feeling of social inclusion [18]. See Table 1 for some examples how SDT might be implemented into ISi-Speech.

Table 1. Implementing SDT into ISi-Speech

	Goal	Example of SDT application to ISi-Speech
Autonomy	The patient identifies the value and importance of the technology-based intervention.	The therapist introduces ISi-Speech to his/her patient with Parkinson and advices the usage. The patient is convinced that s/he will be better understood when s/he trained at least twice a day with ISi-Speech.
Competence	The patient experienced personal growth by comparing her/his improvement individually, socially or normative.	*Individual*: "Compared to last week, distinctive articulation of p versus b has become 20 % more clearly." *Social*: "Other patients with Parkinson have more difficulties than you in pronouncing p and b clearly." *Normative*: "You mastered the first two steps towards your goal of distinguishing p and b clearly."
Relatedness	Therapist-patient relationship and relationship between users of technology supports the patients' need of being respected and understood as well as feeling social included.	When the patient fails with his/her exercise in ISi-Speech, the therapist supports him/her to follow his/her goal. Both pay attention to the results of two other users that are ranked on the ISi-board by the amount of clearly pronounced words with p they logged over a day.

Most interestingly, SDT can be applied to any personal condition, being oblivious to people's age, skills or other life circumstances. Over the years, research compiled a vast record of empirical evidence on the relevance of autonomy, social interlinking (relatedness), and competence for personal growth. Following this theory, each person can experience autonomy and competence, given a tailored technological approach.

In a recent study Silva, Marques and Teixeira [19] identified two barriers for successful SDT-based interventions: doubts about the application and missing improvement attributed to its usage. This insight emphasizes again the high relevance of attention given to the selection process as well as to the persistent usage enabling feed-back. In Parkinson's disease feed-back is given an additional role as patients are often inadequate in self-perception regarding their speaking. As mentioned above, they have a tendency to falsely attribute problems in communication to others. Feed-back that utilizes play back combined with accurate and specific evaluation of recorded speech will guide towards more adequate self-perception.

ISi-Speech serves as an example for applying psychological theory into designing technology for speech intervention in patients with Parkinson's disease. We propose that incorporation of a sound motivational model will enhance chances for sustainable usage. To ensure adequacy of the motivational model, continuous involvement of end users into the development process is required [20]. We hereby apply a set of standardized questionnaires as well as semi-structured interviews to evaluate each step in the design process with attention to usability and effectiveness. In addition, we envision a formative evaluation process on motivation with monitoring the three STD features perceived autonomy, competence, and connectedness and subsequently the experience of motivation.

3 Summary and Conclusion

In this paper we described how technology-based interventions can be explicitly informed by psychological theories. The principles of SDT such as autonomy, competence, and relatedness can facilitate activity, engagement, social interaction, and scaffolding, all contributing to potential personal growth, also in people with special needs. The incorporation of SDT during development processes of a R&D project such as ISi-Speech promises acceptance and effectiveness of training in the user. We envision to being hereby able to substantially empower patients with Parkinson's disease and contribute to social inclusion. Furthermore, with a user driven approach already implemented in the early stages, we expect to guide the design towards a deeper understanding of patients' needs and experiences with this novel technology-based intervention in Speech and Language Therapy. With ISi-Speech we are not suggesting to make the therapist redundant. Instead, they will be responsible for the selection of a tool and reaching consensus about its usage with a patient. In addition, s/he will have to adjust the system, evaluate usage and modify the system accordingly. Including technology into speech training will hereby change the role of the therapist. We consider this a chance for personal growth for both, the patient and the therapist.

Acknowledgements. The 'ISi-Speech' (grant agreement no. 16SV737/3-7) project is supported by the Federal Ministry of Education and Research under the Program 'IKT 2020 - Research for Innovations'.

References

1. Gage, H., Grainger, L., Ting, S., Williams, P., Chorley, C., Carey, Borg, N., Bryan, K., Castleton, B., Trend, P., Kaye, J., Jordan, J., Wade, D.: Health services and delivery research specialist rehabilitation for people with Parkinson's disease in the community: a randomised controlled trial. NIHR J. Libr., Southampton UK (2014)
2. Schubert, A.: Dysarthrie. Diagnostik-Therapie-Beratung (Dysarthria. Diagnostics-Therapy-Advice). Schulz Kirchner, Idstein (2007)
3. Fox, C., Ebersbach, G., Ramig, L.O., Sapir, S.: LSVT LOUD and LSVT BIG: behavioral treatment programs for speech and body movement in Parkinson Disease. Parkinsons Dis 2012/391946 (2012)
4. Spielman, J., Ramig, L.O., Mahler, L., Halpern, A., Gavin, W.J.: Effects of an extended version of the lee silverman voice treatment on voice and speech in Parkinson's disease. Am. J. Speech Lang. Pathol. **16**, 95–107 (2007)
5. Bilda, K., Muehlhaus, J., Ritterfeld, U. (eds.): Neue Technologien in der Sprachtherapie (New Technologies in Speech and Language Therapy). Thieme, Stuttgart (in press)
6. Ritterfeld, U.: Psychologische Grundlagen (Psychological Principles). In: Bilda, K., Muehlhaus, J., Ritterfeld, U. (eds.) Neue Technologien in der Sprachtherapie (New technologies in Speech and Language Therapy). Thieme, Stuttgart (in press)
7. Vishwanath, A.: The psychology of the diffusion and acceptance of technology. In: Sundar, S.S. (ed.) The Handbook of the Psychology of Communication Technology, pp. 313–331. Wiley, Sussex UK (2015)
8. Ritterfeld, U., Weber, R.: Video games for entertainment and education. In: Vorderer, P., Bryant, J. (eds.) Playing Video Games - Motives, Responses, and Consequences, pp. 399–413. Lawrence Erlbaum, Mahwah NJ (2006)
9. Csikszentmihalyi, M.: Flow: The Psychology of Optimal Experience. Harper and Row, New York NY (1990)
10. Ritterfeld, U.: Von videogames zu health gaming. Eine Einfuehrung (From video games to health games. An introduction). In: Dadaczynski, K., Schiemann, S., Paulus, P. (eds.) Gesundheit spielend foerdern. Potentiale und Herausforderungen von digitalen Spieleanwendungen fuer die Gesundheitsfoerderung und Praevention, pp. 173–190. Beltz Juventa, Weinheim (2016)
11. Ritterfeld, U., Cody, M., Vorderer, P.: Serious Games: Mechanisms and Effects. Routledge, Taylor and Francis, Mahwah NJ (2009)
12. Deci, E.L., Ryan, R.M.: The "what" and the "why" of goal pursuits: human needs and the self-determination of behavior. Psychol. Inq. **11**, 227–268 (2000)
13. Deci, E.L., Ryan, R.M.: Self-determination theory. In: van Lange, P.A.M., Kruglanski, A.W., Higgins, E.T. (eds.) Handbook of Theories of Social Psychology, vol. 1, pp. 416–459. Sage, London (2012)
14. Ryan, R.M., Deci, E.L.: Self-determination theory and the facilitation of intrinsic motivation, social development and well-being. Am. Psychol. **55**, 68–78 (2000)
15. Deci, E.L., Ryan, R.M.: Self-determination theory: a macrotheory of human motivation, development, and health. Can. Psychol. **49**(3), 182–185 (2008)
16. Ng, J.Y.Y., Ntoumanis, N., Thogersen-Ntoumani, C., Deci, E.L., Ryan, R.M., Duda, J.L., Williams, G.C.: Self-determination theory applied to health contexts: a meta-analysis. Perspect. Psychol. Sci. **7**, 325–340 (2012)
17. Ryan, R.M., Patrick, H., Deci, E.L., Williams, G.C.: Facilitating health behaviour change and its maintenance: interventions based on self-determination theory. Health Psychol. Rev. **10**, 2–5 (2008)

18. Yee, N., Bailenson, J.N., Urbanek, M., Chang, F., Merget, D.: The unbearable likeness of being digital: the persistence of nonverbal social norms in online virtual environments. Cyberpsychol. Behav. **10**, 115–121 (2007)
19. Silva, M.N., Marques, M., Teixeira, P.J.: Testing theory in practice: the example of self-determination theory-based interventions. Health Psychol. Rev. **16**, 171–180 (2014)
20. Buehler, C.: Empowered participation of users with disabilities in universal design. Univers. Access Inf. Soc. **1**(2), 85–90 (2014)

Re-thinking Assistive Technology Service Delivery Models in the Light of the UN Convention

Renzo Andrich[(✉)]

Centre for Innovation and Technology Transfer,
IRCCS Fondazione Don Gnocchi, Milan, Italy
renzo.andrich@siva.it

Abstract. This paper offers some reflections on key concepts to be considered when developing policies related to assistive technology provision in the light of the UN Convention. The starting point is the Position Paper issued by AAATE and EASTIN in 2012, which defines the mission of a service delivery system (SDS) as "ensuring that all people with disabilities can access appropriate assistive solutions that are able to support autonomy in their life environment". From the organizational viewpoint, we can identify three main SDS models: the "medical model", the "social model" and the "consumer model". A reasonable criterion for establishing a boundary between products that require medical models and those that don't is that of clinical risk. The more the system moves from a medical to a social or consumer model, the more should it be based on user empowerment approaches. The GATE initiative of the World Health Organization and some national policies (such as the Australian NDIS assistive technology strategy) are firmly built upon user empowerment approaches. End-users education as well as the availability of *"super partes"* assistive technology information (i.e. independent of commercial interest) also plays a fundamental role in user empowerment. The paper offers a quick survey of the main information systems available today worldwide, and presents the latest achievement of today's major information resource, the European Assistive Technology Information Network.

Keywords: Assistive technology · Service delivery systems · UN convention · Information systems

1 Introduction

The purpose of this paper is to offer some reflections on key concepts to be considered when developing policies related to assistive technology provision in the light of the UN Convention [1].

The Position Paper issued by AAATE (the Association for the Advancement of Assistive Technology in Europe) and EASTIN (the European Assistive Technology Information Network) in 2012 [2] indicates a framework for exploiting the role of assistive technology (AT) in supporting care and participation of people with disabilities and elderly people through appropriate service delivery systems (SDS).

© Springer International Publishing Switzerland 2016
K. Miesenberger et al. (Eds.): ICCHP 2016, Part I, LNCS 9758, pp. 101–108, 2016.
DOI: 10.1007/978-3-319-41264-1_13

This document can be considered a milestone for reflections on this issue. It resulted from a large consensus exercise involving experts from all over Europe, discussing on how the rights pointed out by the UN convention in relation to access to AT could be actually implemented in service delivery practice. These rights are explicitly underlined in several articles of the Convention, such as art 4/g (general obligation to *"promote the availability and use of new technologies, including information and communications technologies, mobility aids, devices and assistive technologies, suitable for persons with disabilities, giving priority to technologies at an affordable cost"*); art. 20/b (measures *"facilitating access by persons with disabilities to quality mobility aids, devices, AT and forms of live assistance and intermediaries, including making them available at affordable cost"*); art. 24/3 (measures to make available alternative communication modes and means in education) and art 27/i (measures ensuring *"that reasonable accommodation is provided to persons with disabilities in the workplace"*).

2 The Scope of an AT Service Delivery System

This Position Paper defines the mission of a SDS as *"ensuring that all people with disabilities can access appropriate assistive solutions that are able to support autonomy in their life environment"*.

Two main keywords appear in this definition: assistive solution and autonomy.

The first one - *assistive solution* - suggests a wider view than just focusing on the match between a specific need and an AT product. The match should be sought instead between a person (not only described in terms of abilities Vs disabilities but also of life priorities, personal values, social relationships and environmental contexts) and an assistive solution – intended as a personalized blend of environmental facilitators (including AT products, environmental modifications and personal assistance) that helps overcome disability and enable participation in all aspects of life.

The second keyword - *autonomy* – is defined as *"ability to take control over one's own life, to establish relationships with others and actively participate in society"* [3]. It is a broad concepts related to an empowerment process, in which several contextual factors contribute, such as medical rehabilitation, education, counselling, housing, environmental accessibility, assistive technology and social measures. The concept of autonomy does not apply exclusively to the individual: in certain cases a systemic approach is needed that looks at the whole person's family, for instance by providing assistive solutions tailored to family members' needs to make the burden of assistance sustainable.

Thus the paradigm of the *"4 As"* synthesizes the approach that should inform a SDS: *Assistive technologies + personal Assistance + individual environmental Adaptations = Autonomy*.

Each component of an assistive solution may work as *facilitator* or *barrier*, depending on how well it is implemented and how well it works in combination with the other two factors. Working as facilitator means supporting the person's autonomy, i.e. improving participation in life activities in relation to his/her personal hierarchy of needs. In other words, an assistive solution can be judged as effective if there is evidence that it has improved autonomy, or made it possible to maintain it. Unfortunately, in many EU Countries different agencies are responsible for each component of an assistive solution. For instance, in Italy the National Health Service takes care of assistive technologies, Municipal Social Services provide support for personal assistance, home adaptations can rely on grants provided through other Municipal departments: within this context, building up a consistent and well-coordinated individual assistive solution is often difficult and needs a huge case management work.

The Position Paper also points out that AT service delivery policies should be well coordinated with accessibility policies i.e. those related to infrastructural interventions ensuring that the mainstream environment, products and services are usable by all people, including those with reduced function or who depend on assistive technology. Although *infrastructural accessibility* doesn't fall within the scope of a SDS, it's a prerequisite that should be ensured by all society sectors: indeed even the smartest assistive solution may not work in an inaccessible environment (Fig. 1).

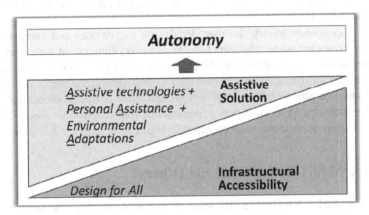

Fig. 1. The add-on effect of assistive solutions (individual intervention) and accessibility (infrastructural intervention) in supporting the person's autonomy.

3 Service Delivery Models

Within today's political climate of budget containment and accountability, calling for evidence-based practice, there is an increasing demand for evidence of cost-effectiveness in any public support system for the users' personal needs [4]. This leads to the question about what would be a cost-effective model that fulfils the rights established by the UN Convention.

Of course there is no single answer, as any SDS is part of a higher-level legislation framework which sets overall policies, approaches and boundaries. However, from the organizational viewpoint, we can identify three main models: the so-called "medical model", the "social model" and the "consumer model".

Within the *medical model* each AT device eligible for public provision is prescribed by qualified professionals under their responsibility. The model is called "medical" due to its similarity to drugs prescription in medical practice, although not in all Countries the authorized prescribers are always physicians (depending on the type of equipment, they may be other health professionals, such as occupational therapists, physiotherapists, nurses etc.). A medical model is usually regulated by a list of products (Registry) or product specifications (Product Categories) eligible for public provision, with or without established prices or reimbursement thresholds. It is worth pointing out that "medical model" is not synonym of "medical approach" or "directive approach": it just indicates an organizational model in which eligibility for reimbursement is decided for each specific device. It is true that professional holds the final decision, however in good practice the selection of the device should be driven by a "partnership approach" even in medical models.

Within the *social* model, the focus is on the whole assistive solution, rather than on specific devices. Once the individual assistive solution has been decided and the budget has been authorized, the choice of the specific devices is quite free, provided that they effectively meet the intended goals. Within a social model, basically any device may be eligible for public provision, unless public procurement policies restrict the range to products meeting certain rules.

Within a *consumer* model, the user decides on the devices and purchases them directly. This does not mean that users have to pay everything out of their pockets (the system may provide financial help through vouchers or cash) nor that they can purchase whatever they wish (financial help is provided against authorized objectives on which the user should be accountable) or that they are left alone in their choices (information and professional support services play a fundamental role in consumer models, in order to empower users to be capable of responsible choices).

4   Is One Model Better Than the Others?

The above-quoted AAATE/EASTIN Position paper alerts that designing a *perfect* service delivery model that fits any national context is not realistic. SDSs should be tailored to national or even regional contexts and need continuous maintenance over time. However "*in working at the improvement of national AT service delivery systems, one should avoid: (1) unrealistic attempts to make a single EU system; (2) making the system too dependent on upper-level political changes; (3) implementing changes that are not adequately supported by knowledge and evidence; (4) reverse back to strict medical approach; (5) lave the user out of the process; (6) increase the gap between those who can afford AT and those who cannot.*"

Therefore there isn't any fixed recipe to decide whether a medical or a social or a consumer model is the most appropriate in given circumstances. It may depend on the *activity context* (daily life, employment, education, leisure etc.), on the *technology domain* (prosthetic/orthotics, daily life equipment, home appliances etc.), on the *professional expertise available*, on *higher-level national regulations* in the health, social, educational or employment sector.

The concept of *clinical risk* [5] may help establish a boundary between products that require medical models and those that don't. A device holding clinical risk may damage the person's health if selected or fitted without appropriate clinical supervision. Tentatively, one could say that *medical models* are appropriate for health-management equipment (products supporting life functions such as e.g. respiratory devices, or preventing complications such as anti-decubitus cushions) or function-oriented equipment (prosthetics, orthotics, footwear, personalized seating systems, hearing aids etc.). Conversely, one could say that *social models* are appropriate for participation-oriented equipment (daily living tools, mobility devices, communication devices, home adaptations, ambient assisted living appliances etc.) where the clinical risk related to wrong choices is less critical; or where the range of equipment that can be considered for the choice is broad and varied, so that there are different alternative ways to build up the assistive solution; and where installation/configuration require technical rather than clinical competencies.

Consumer models could be considered as derived from social models but with more responsibility and decision power shifted to the user. The main advantages of consumer models are that they put the market supply in direct contact with the consumer demand, which is a powerful drive for quality improvement and price reduction; however service delivery systems based on a consumer model can only work if users are empowered to make informed and responsible choices, and to be accountable against the intended objectives. This can be done by providing the user with effective information; by making available *assistive technology information centres* where users can learn about assistive technology in an environment independent of commercial interest; by developing a *partnership attitude* among rehabilitation professionals; by including *empowerment* among the expected outcomes of a rehabilitation, or care, or educational plan; and by enforcing measures to prevent or detect possible non-use or abandonment of the purchased devices.

Informing end-users on the available assistive products and educating them to master their assistive technology is of paramount importance within any model, however especially in social and consumer model. Several EU project, such as ENABLE (www.i-enable.eu) and ENTELIS (www.entelis.net), highlighted that this is particularly true for assistive ICT equipment, as often not only digital skills but also high levels AT competences are needed to bridge the digital divide. On this specific topic the ENTELIS project produced a Position Paper known as "*ENTELIS Manifesto*", including a list of recommendations for all stakeholders involved [6] in policy making, research and development, education and training, and service provision.

A user empowerment perspective is underpinning also the ongoing GATE initiative (Global Collaboration on Assistive Technology) of the World Health Organization [7]. GATE foresees several measures that should be implemented to make AT access a reality, including industrial policies (putting on the market good quality products at reasonable price), research and innovation actions (improving technology or favouring disruptive innovation that may provide new solutions never imagined before) and service delivery policies. One of the expected milestones is the publication of the first *Assistive products Priority List* (APL), i.e. a list of product categories whose access should be guaranteed in all Countries for all persons needing them. The list distinguishes between products that are recommended for provision at *referral level* (i.e. through the intermediation of professional specialists) and those to be provided at *community level* (self purchased or upon advice of general practitioners).

5 User Empowerment: A Keyword for Good Practice

Of course, affirming the above principles is not enough: translating them into national policies and service provision systems is the real challenge.

A remarkable example is offered by the recently-launched Assistive Technology Strategy of the Australian National Disability Insurance Scheme (NDIS) [8]. Its vision statement clearly highlights its empowerment-based approach: *"to build an empowering, sustainable and consistent approach to ensuring NDIS participants have choice in, and access to, individualized assistive technology solutions that enable and enhance their economic and community participation"*. Within this framework three strategic priorities have been identified:

- *"Support and stimulate a vibrant and innovative supply-side market by providing a conduit for innovation and promoting the take-up of technology solutions";*
- *"Support and stimulate informed, active, participant-led demand by empowering participants to choose technology that best supports their needs";*
- *"Deliver a financially robust, sustainable scheme that generates economic and social value with the Agency only intervening to optimize outcomes for participants and economic value for the Scheme".*

Actions are indicated within this framework, and guidelines are provided for professionals assessing assistive solutions. Different assessment models are proposed depending on the user being a "novice" or a "developing" or an "expert" (these terms refer to his or her knowledge and ability to master assistive products), with gradual shift from full professional support to free choice the more the user evolves towards being an expert. It is a quite innovative approach, very consistent with the spirit of the UN Convention.

6 The Role of Assistive Technology Information

The more SDSs evolve towards an empowerment approach, the more AT information system and AT assessment centres play a crucial role in helping the user and his/her family make the most effective choices. AT manufacturers and suppliers often do a great job in providing good-quality information about their products; however we can't avoid that their information be driven by commercial interest. Therefore the availability of super-partes (i.e. independent of commercial interest) information on assistive technology products and solutions is extremely important for the user empowerment and for the effectiveness of a SDS.

Well-established *super-partes* national information systems are publicly available on the Internet in many Countries, such as

- Italy (Portale SIVA: www.portale.siva.it);
- Germany (Rehadat: www.rehadat.de);
- Belgium (Vlibank: www.vlibank.be);
- Denmark (Assistive Technology Data: www.hmi-basen.dk);

- United Kingdom (DLF-data: www.dlf.org.uk, and its related search tools Living Made Easy www.livingmadeeasy.org.uk and Ask Sara www.asksara.org.uk);
- Spain (Catàlogo de Ayudas Técnicas: www.catalogo-ceapat.org);
- France (Handicat: www.handicat.com);
- The Netherlands (Hulpmiddelenwijzer: www.hulpmiddelenwijzer.nl);
- Ireland (AssistIreland: www.assistireland.ie);
- US (Abledata: www.abledata.com);
- Australia (ILC Australia: www.ilcaustralia.org.au and www.ilcnsw.asn.au);
- Brazil (Catalogo Nacional de Productos de TA: http://assistiva.mct.gov.br);
- Argentina (CIAPAT: http://ciapat.org/es/catalogo).

Fig. 2. The new homepage of the EASTIN Portal (www.eastin.eu), in desktop version.

Aggregating all databases into a single global information system has become a realistic prospect today. The most remarkable example is the EASTIN Information system (European Assistive Technology Information Network: www.eastin.eu), which has been re-launched in 2016 in a brand new version with upgraded technology and a multilingual graphic interface that automatically adapts to the user device (Computer, Tablet, Smartphone) (Fig. 2). EASTIN integrates seven out of the above-mentioned national databases and can be searched in 32 languages. It includes tools for other partners to create their own national data base, in case they don't have any yet. The EASTIN network includes partners from almost all EU Countries and has collaboration links with several other Countries globally. Today the EASTIN system provides information on about eighty thousand assistive products available on the European market; it has become the European landmark for AT information, and is currently working towards a global perspective, thus supporting the vision of the GATE initiative of the World Health Organization.

Acknowledgements. This study was partially supported by the Italian Ministry of Health (Current Research Biomedical Programme).

References

1. United Nations Organization: UN Convention on the rights of persons with disabilities. http://www.un.org/disabilities/convention/conventionfull.shtml (2006)
2. Andrich, R., Mathiassen, N.E., Hoogerwerf, E.J., Gelderblom, G.J.: Service delivery systems for assistive technology in Europe: an AAATE/EASTIN position paper. Technol. Disabil. **25**(3), 127–146 (2013)
3. Eustat Consortium: Assistive Technology Education for End-Users: Guidelines for Trainers. European Commission, Milano (1999)
4. Andrich, R., Caracciolo, A.: Analysing the cost of individual assistive technology programmes. Disabil. Rehabil. Assistive Technol. **2**(4), 207–234 (2007)
5. World Health Organization: Patient safety curriculum guide. WHO, Geneve (2011) www.who.int/patientsafety/education/curriculum/en/
6. ENTELIS Consortium: Towards full digital inclusion: the ENTELIS manifesto against the digital divide (2015). www.entelis.net/en/manifesto
7. World Health Organization: The GATE initiative (2015). www.who.int/phi/implementation/assistive_technology/phi_gate/en/
8. National Disability Insurance Scheme: Assistive Technology Strategy (2015). www.ndis.gov.au/about-us/information-publications-and-reports/assistive-technology-strategy

Standards Related to eAccessibility and eInclusion: Dimensions of Interoperability Based on Standards with Respect to eAccessibility and eInclusion

Christian Galinski[1]([⊠]) and Blanca Stella Giraldo Perez[2]

[1] Infoterm, International Information Centre for Terminology, Vienna, Austria
christian.galinski@chello.at
[2] University of Vienna, Vienna, Austria
blancaese@gmail.com

Abstract. There is an affluence of standards (de jure standards as well as de facto standards in the fields covered by eAccessibility and eInclusion) – not to mention legal regulations and guidelines of all sorts. The awareness of the need and importance of standards is comparatively low, because (a) standards often have to be purchased and (b) the information on existing standards is not available in user-friendly form. This paper outlines difficulties and possible solutions concerning the application of pertinent standards from the point of view of the EU project IN LIFE. It further analyses gaps with respect to ICT-supported H-H communication as well as H-M communication, which is an important aspect under the perspective of user empowerment and autonomy.

Keywords: Standards · eAccessibility · eInclusion · EU project IN LIFE · Inter-human communication

1 Introduction

Standards which are referred to in law, in fact, become part of the law. This applies also to standards related to eAccessibility and eInclusion given the fact that:

- All EU Member States have signed the United Nations Convention on the Rights of Persons with Disabilities (CRPD) [1] which came into force in 2008,
- EU joined the CRPD on 22 January 2011 as a regional integration organization,
- Several EU Directives and national laws have implemented the CRPD in 2016.

Therefore, knowledge about standards related to eAccessibility and eInclusion is important for organizations and individuals developing devices and pertinent software (incl. apps and web services), or rendering services to PwD supported by such devices and software. So far, inter-human communication, ICT-supported inter-human communication and the respective content has been rather neglected here.

However, ICTs increasingly rely on reliable structured content to be used across system, language, modality, and other boundaries, which requires the modification or harmonization of existing standards and new – preferably international – standards.

© Springer International Publishing Switzerland 2016
K. Miesenberger et al. (Eds.): ICCHP 2016, Part I, LNCS 9758, pp. 109–112, 2016.
DOI: 10.1007/978-3-319-41264-1_14

The Recommendation on software and content development principles 2010, formulated at the 12th International Conference on Computers Helping People with Special Needs (ICCHP 2010), addresses this situation and was adopted by several committees in the field of standardization [2].

2 State of the Art of Information on Standards Concerning eAccessibility and eInclusion

The EU-Project IN LIFE (INdependent LIving support Functions for the Elderly) [3] revealed that the access to information on standards related to accessibility in general is not easy at all. On the one hand, many standards on general ICT and medical informatics or health informatics also have a bearing on accessibility, especially if they are needed to develop larger technical infrastructures (e.g. for SDS, service delivery systems). On the other hand, IN LIFE identified more than 400 standards dealing with eAccessibility and eInclusion aspects, such as human factors (HF), design for all (DfA) or universal design, and ambient assisted living (AAL). However, there are very few standards on the content of inter-human communication from the point of view of methodology as well as of the respective content resources.

The IN LIFE "Standardization Plan" (SP) has the overall aim to investigate pertinent existing standards and ongoing standardization activities, to identify ongoing standardization activities, where support would be useful, or to initiate new standardization activities, if a gap is identified.

3 Dimensions of Interoperability (IOp)

Not least due to a number of R&D-projects carried out in FP 7 of the EU, standards securing technical interoperability (IOp) for the establishment of and cooperation among the infrastructure(s) of institutions rendering services in the field of accessibility, have led to fairly mature and stable infrastructures. These developed incrementally out of a series of EU projects, whose last one was universAAL (UNIVERsal open platform and reference Specification for Ambient Assisted Living) [4]. The infrastructure of the EU-Project IN LIFE is building up on the above-mentioned results.

Semantic IOp focuses on written (and maybe also spoken) texts, but the communication with or among PwD comprises information in different modalities beyond written and spoken language. So there is a gap here to be closed by standards focusing on inter-human communication in the field of eAccessibility and eInclusion, such as:

- Methodology standards focusing on principles and methods for developing and applying appropriate human communication resources (HCR) for PwD, such as including the specificities of communication with/among PwD in the:
  - description, design, development and management of HCR, e.g. the Concept Coding Framework (CCF) [5], or a standard on "Controlled communication with/among persons with disabilities (PwD)" which would also include behavioral, social, ethical and other aspects,

- description and identification of language varieties, i.e. linguistic variation with-in a language – e.g. for the purpose of developing tools recognizing utterances in spite of speech impairments and providing the necessary output (e.g. in the form of braille or haptic output),
- development of further parts of the OMG standard "The Distributed Ontology Modeling, and Specification Language (DOL)" (EU project OASIS initiated);
• Content standards focusing on the development and management of HCR for PwD based on methodology standards, such as Bliss-Symbols;
• Standards to make ICT (devices, protocols, apps etc.) capable to input, process and output the data of HCR for PwD, including Internet-based technologies.

Most probably, it needs more metamodels and meta-metamodels for making all "terminologies and other language and content resources" interoperable. Under an OWL [6] perspective these data are also referred to as microcontent that can be turned into light-weight ontologies. At highest meta-level DOL is to ensure true semantic IOp.

4   Advantages for Applying Standards and Disadvantages for not Applying Standards

The existence of several hundred standards at international level in a comparatively 'narrow' field, such as eAccessibility and eInclusion indicates that there may be a need for more transparency in order to facilitate the use of these standards – not to mention the need for harmonization efforts. Just the difficulty to find information on such standards can be a risk factor and is not helpful in terms of sustainability.

The high cost of caring for PwD will further increase in line with the ageing of society bringing forth more PwD, and increasingly also persons with multiple disabilities. Standards – especially interoperability standards – are an important factor for securing sustainability which in connection with the caring of PwD can also refer to:

• Affordability of services and tools for individual PwD and their care givers,
• Investment security with respect to the establishment of systems and services for organizations/institutions providing services to PwD and their care givers, as well as to companies developing the respective ICT support tools or services,
• Worthwhile investment by public administration in establishing or reforming their institutions or systems for the caring of PwD.

In IN LIFE deliverable D9.1 it is analyzed to what extent standards are – or may become – legally relevant. Thus, insufficient knowledge about pertinent standards (e.g. due to difficulties to find reliable information) is a risk factor for management and professionals alike, not only from a legal perspective. Wrong decisions can damage the reputation of an organization/institution, or even end up in liability cases. The same refers to corporate social responsibility (CSR), [7] a lack of quality of many semantic interoperability standards and deficiencies of standards for quality assessment of such standards [8]. Besides, conflicting or insufficient standards could create harm to the reputation of standards developing organizations (SDOs).

5 Proposal for a System to Evaluate Standards Dynamically

The database developed in IN LIFE so far is certainly a useful result for the project itself, but data would become outdated already in a few months, as standards are subject to periodic reviews and revisions, or may be withdrawn. Therefore, a continuous updating mechanism would be desirable, e.g. by means of a system for active user participation which for instance would allow to share and compare information on individual standards and related other regulatory documents and evaluate them in a user-driven way, to come up with recommendations for using, extending, revising, withdrawing and merging standards, and to provide weighted keywords on the content of individual standards.

6 Outlook

The world of standardization today is highly complex with many competing or cooperating stakeholders. Joint efforts to make the IN LIFE database of information on standards in the field of eAccessibility and eInclusion accessible and sustainable may be a good basis not only for improving access to standards, but also for harmonizing or aligning pertinent regulations as much as possible or necessary.

Acknowledgments. This paper presents work from the project "INdependent LIving support Functions for the Elderly" (IN LIFE, the EU project No. 643442 under HORIZON 2020, the EU Framework Programme for Research and Innovation) co-financed by the EU Commission.

References

1. United Nations: Convention on the Rights of Persons with Disabilities (2006)
2. MoU/MG: MoU/MG/12 N 476 Rev.1 Recommendation on software and content development principles 2010 (2012)
3. INdependent LIving support Functions for the Elderly (IN LIFE). http://www.inlife-project.eu/
4. UNIVERsal open platform and reference Specification for Ambient Assisted Living (universAAL). http://universaal.sintef9013.com/index.php/en/about/about-background-projects
5. Concept Coding Framework (CCF). http://www.conceptcoding.org/
6. World Wide Web Consortium (W3C): 'OWL 2 Web Ontology Language RDF-Based Semantics (Second Edition)', W3C Recommendation, 11 December 2012 (2012e). http://www.w3.org/TR/owl2-rdf-based-semantics/
7. ISO: ISO 26000:2010 Guidance on social responsibility (2010)
8. Folmer, E.: Quality of semantic standards. Doctoral dissertation, University of Twente, The Netherlands (2012)

Fostering the Development of Inclusively Minded Engineers

Seiichiro Miura[1(✉)], Naohiro Hayashi[1], Sakiko Ogoshi[2],
Hitoshi Nishi[2], Takashi Yoshioka[3], Yutaka Yamaguchi[3],
and Yasuhiro Ogoshi[4]

[1] Mechanical and Control Engineering Advanced Course,
National Institute of College of Technology,
Tokuyama College, Shunan, Yamaguchi, Japan
{miura, m09hayasiln}@tokuyama.ac.jp
[2] Department of Electrical Engineering and Computer Science,
National Institute of Technology, Fukui College, Sabae, Fukui, Japan
{ogoshi, nishi}@fukui-nct.ac.jp
[3] OMRON Kyoto Taiyo Co. Ltd., Kyoto, Japan
{takashi_yoshioka,
yutaka_yamaguchi}@ktaiyo.omron.co.jp
[4] Graduate School of Engineering, University of Fukui, Fukui, Japan
y-ogoshi@u-fukui.ac.jp

Abstract. We developed an internship program with a special subsidiary company in order to educate engineers with an inclusive mind. A participating student has designed and manufactured equipment for workers with disabilities during the internship. We found that the student learned relations between major subjects at engineering and production techniques through interviews. In addition, we also considered the program is related to knowledge management. This suggests that the internship program with a special subsidiary company is one possible way for growing inclusive minded engineers.

Keywords: Educational · Design for engineers · Assistive technology · Knowledge management

1 Introduction

In an increasingly globalized world, we need to realize an inclusive society in which individuals can improve and demonstrate their abilities. For persons with disabilities to demonstrate their abilities, it is necessary to implement systems to support them and fostering scientists and engineers in such fields as welfare and medical care. In the future, we need more diverse support technologies for handicapped persons. This leads hopefully to an economic structure which sustains such personalized support technologies for individual treatment. Therefore, we think that providing opportunities to learn such techniques is important for engineering students, in order to be able to support a person with disabilities. An internship program in companies gives students the chance to get firsthand experience. To educate an engineer with a universal and an inclusive design in mind, a special subsidiary company (SSC) is one of the best companies, because it

© Springer International Publishing Switzerland 2016
K. Miesenberger et al. (Eds.): ICCHP 2016, Part I, LNCS 9758, pp. 113–116, 2016.
DOI: 10.1007/978-3-319-41264-1_15

employs not only many persons with disabilities but also experienced engineers, and has universal design environment. We attempted to establish an internship program as an educational model to foster inclusively minded engineers. By the way, "The National Institute of Technology, Japan", called KOSEN, is a unique educational organization offering a five-year engineering education, admitting 15 years old students [1]. Within the Japanese school system, the KOSEN covers high school level and the first two years of a university. The students generally have equal or higher ability compared with university students, enabling them to receive abroad technical education. What is more, the KOSEN offers an additional two-year course where higher education in engineering in conducted. In present, the number of graduates of engineering is about 10,200, as compared to the 97,500 graduates of total higher engineering education in Japan. In this paper, we introduce our first approach to an education model of the internship program with the company for a sixth grade student. And we also consider its qualitative evaluation with Nonaka's SECI model.

2 Content of the Internship Program with SSC

The special subsidiary company system was established to facilitate the hiring of handicapped people as part of the Welfare Employment System of Japan since 1976. A company having more than 50 employees is required by law to employ at least 2.0 % handicapped persons. Alternatively, the company is allowed to establish a SSC for handicapped persons, employing them at this subsidiary instead at the parent company or corporate group. As of May 2014, there are 391 SSCs in Japan. We collaborated with OMRON KYOTO TAIYO Corporation which established as a joint venture company of OMRON Corporation and the Social Welfare Organization Japan Sun Industries in 1985, allowing our student to participate in the internship. Japan Sun Industries has been providing jobs for people with disabilities by Dr. Yutaka Nakamura since 1965 [2]. OMRON KYOTO TAIYO has 167 employees of which 127 are disabled and produces industrial machinery products such as sockets, sensors, relays, health equipment and PLC power supply units. There is also an Engineering Division (ED) adapting each machine to compensate for lost physical functions of a worker. During a two-month internship, it was required to design and develop a solution for one of the ED's annual improvement projects. While the subject was assigned by the company, the student was expected to independently carry out almost all the design. Of course, a student could consult with a technical director at the ED when necessary. Furthermore, the budget for a two-month internship was less than 100,000 JPY, in addition to using the facilities of OMRON KYOTO TAIYO.

3 Result of Internship Program with SSC

The student who participated as the first in the internship program, tackled with developing a packing case machine that was modified such that a hearing impaired worker would not forget to affix tape to the packing case (Fig. 1). To examine educational effects of the internship, we interviewed the student. It was found that the student acquired tacit knowledge of elements of fluid mechanics, industrial mechanics, mechanical design theory, programming, machining practices, sequence programing, Productive technologies and how to use air cylinders. The greatest insight indicated by the student was the concept of the operator's safety and work environment being the maximum priority. The student also developed the vision of a manufacturing engineer as a person who is helpful to other people. Note that the student learned sign language voluntarily to contact the hearing impaired operator. The student then reported that he felt "joy to work" and "pleasure in helping society" as an engineer. In addition, this program has been also beneficial for the company.

Fig. 1. Packing case machine developed by the student within two months

4   Consideration of the SECI Model at Internship Program

Nonaka's Innovation theory has been implemented by various companies and has had a positive impact [3, 4]. The SECI model maintains that tacit knowledge and explicit knowledge are not separate but mutually complementary entities (Fig. 2). They interact with each other in the creative activities of human beings. An interaction between tacit and explicit is called the knowledge conversion process. This process consists of four stages: socialization, externalization, combination and internalization. We found that the SECI model describes accurately a knowledge-creating system to aid the support of people with disorders. The first stage, Socialization (tacit to tacit), explains social interaction as tacit to tacit knowledge transfer, sharing tacit knowledge face-to-face or through experiences or know-how. At this stage, the student has learned through workers with disabilities and experienced engineers. The second stage, Externalization (tacit to explicit), embed the combined tacit knowledge which enable its communication. At this stage, the student writes daily report during the internship. The third stage, Combination (explicit to explicit), combines different types of explicit knowledge like building prototypes. Explicit knowledge is collected from inside or outside the organization and then combined, edited or processed to form new knowledge. The student reports to other persons, for example at conferences, about what he or she has learned during the internship. The fourth stage, Internalization (explicit to tacit), is realized by learning and doing; on the other hand, explicit knowledge becomes part of an individual's knowledge and will be assets for an organization. The fact that the student has felt "joy to work" and "pleasure in helping societies" when he or she developed assistive equipment, is as such an asset for the SSC. In addition, the student also gets some feedback for himself. Within the KOSEN education, internship programs have been prepared for all students. Eventually, through a phenomenon called "knowledge spiral", knowledge creation and sharing becomes part of the culture of an organization.

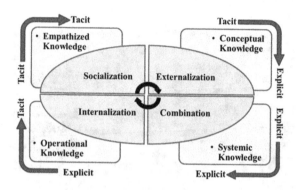

Fig. 2. Schematic of the SECI model

5 Conclusion and Outlook

We introduced an internship program with a special subsidiary company to grow inclusive minded engineers. This has made great contributions to understanding of an inclusive mind for the student. This learning process can apply to the SECI model. The result indicates that the internship program with SSC is one possible way for the students to arise an inclusive mind. In addition, the student and the program give positive influence on SSC. According to the interview survey on the other 10 SSCs, they show interest in our internship program and want to launch it on their own companies. We have been already engaged in developing a quantitative assessment method of the program and expanding the program in cooperation with the SSCs.

References

1. http://www.kosen-k.go.jp/english/education-system.html
2. http://www.taiyonoie.or.jp/english/
3. Nonaka, I., et al.: The Knowledge-Creation Company. Oxford University Press, Oxford (1995)
4. Nonaka, I., Takeuchi, H.: The Knowledge Creating Company: How Japanese Companies Create the Dynamics of Innovation. Oxford University Press, Oxford (1996)

Cloud Computing in European Schools – The Impact on Inclusive Education

Ingo Karl Bosse[✉]

TU Dortmund University, Dortmund, Germany
ingo.bosse@tu-dortmund.de

Abstract. Cloud Computing can be a key driver for innovation and transformation in learning and teaching. The School on the Cloud network, consisting of 57 partners from multiple disciplines in 18 European countries, aims to explore this technology to find new dynamic ways of delivering education. One key result published thus far analyses 59 existing good-practice case studies exploring the impact of the Cloud on personalized learning for pupils with special needs. It also discusses how teachers can use new technologies as a value added component in inclusive education.

Keywords: Inclusive education · E-inclusion · Cloud computing

1 Application Idea

Cloud Computing can be a key driver for innovation and transformation in learning and teaching. The School on the Cloud Network aims to explore new dynamic ways of delivering education. Cooperating across multiple disciplines, its 57 partners from 18 European Countries seek to answer the question of how education should respond to the potential of Cloud-based tools and technologies, and assess their impact on inclusive education. Besides the increasing use of media in classrooms, inclusive education is a global megatrend in the 21st century. Both provide stimulating profound changes for educational institutions. "A key characteristic of 21st century education is that classrooms are more diverse than ever" [1]. Students have very different needs due to their social and cultural backgrounds, their linguistic backgrounds, and their physical and intellectual abilities. Viewing education through the lens of inclusion implies adapting "[f]lexible teaching and learning methods [...] adapted to different needs and learning styles (...) with innovative approaches to teaching aids, and equipment as well as the use of ICTs" [2]. The School on the Cloud Network published 59 existing good-practice case studies [3]. These are analyzed in order to answer the following question: how can cloud-based learning help to create the personalized learning materials that are needed in inclusive classrooms? Drawing on the research's initial results, this article focuses in particular on the use of cloud-based technologies for the purpose of learning.

© Springer International Publishing Switzerland 2016
K. Miesenberger et al. (Eds.): ICCHP 2016, Part I, LNCS 9758, pp. 117–120, 2016.
DOI: 10.1007/978-3-319-41264-1_16

2 Personalized Learning on the Cloud

Due to the diverse needs of pupils with disabilities personalized learning should be central to any approach to teaching and learning. Besides offering the possibility to adjust materials quickly to individual needs, one of the main reasons in favour of using the cloud in schools is its ability to lower costs.

The School on the Cloud Network started to analyse what exactly constitutes personalized learning. Although there are many definitions and interpretations, there is a consensus that personalized learning puts the learner at the centre of any approach to teaching. It actively identifies and adjusts the individual's learning goals and maps out how he/she can access and acquire information. To make this possible, the existing virtual learning environment (VLEs) must be transformed into real personal learning environments.

3 Methodology

The network's first step was to conduct an analysis of European and international literature on personalized learning that also involves cloud based elements. This state-of-the-art analysis was followed by a group discussion and an analysis of 59 case studies compiled by the members of the School on the Cloud Network. The first result produced in the course of this process was a project-related definition of personalized learning.

The basic idea of personalized learning is for learners to exercise ownership, responsibility and control over their experiences, rather than to be constrained by centralized, instructor controlled learning, which is based on the delivery of pre-packaged materials [5, 6]. 'Participation' is the key to understanding personalized learning, as a personal process, in which each participant in any activity is 'constructing' their own version of the process [7]. According to Verpoorten et al. [6] personalized learning relies on three interrelated theories:

- Constructivism: learning as a process in which persons actively construct knowledge, and competences through interacting with their environment
- Reflective thinking: instructional practice should aim learning at the level of understanding and use as well as at meta-levels of learning
- Self-regulated learning focuses on the cognitive and communication processes through which learners control their learning.

It is important that learners do not only have access to materials to read, websites to explore, assignments to complete or tests to perform, but also to tools which allow them to monitor to monitor their progress on these activities. Especially for pupils with special needs, the usability of materials and media is at least as important as their accessibility. Several dimensions are interconnected in the notion of personalized learning experiences. These dimensions can be structured along the following core concepts: ownership, participation, diversity, regulation and reflection. This includes the aspect of critical thinking.

4   Results of the Case Study Analysis from a Special Needs Point of View

The analysis of 59 case studies has identified the cloud as a key driver for change and innovation in (inclusive) education. Beyond this finding, however, many researchers appear to have taken a piecemeal rather than a coordinated approach to studying it in detail. The subjects of the case studies are e-books, e-portfolio, e-content, digital platforms, web-based knowledge sharing, digital repository, use of tablets/BYOD in schools, class management systems, online communities of practice and staff mobility and training. The predominance of e-resources, e-community and device use indicates the need for an effective ecosystem to support teachers and trainers to facilitate personalized learning. The results show that personalized learning, while a widespread idea, is still only rarely considered in combination with special needs education. However, some schools show how to enhance the use of Information and Communication Technologies (ICT) in inclusive classrooms. For example, ICT has been used to create more effective learning paths in a primary school in Italy, to learn sign language with an app in Portugal or design and use a crowdsourcing web map about barriers for persons with physical disabilities as pupils recently demonstrated in Slovenia. These examples show not only how cloud based education can enhance everybody's ability to learn, but also that special education can be a key driver in proliferating cloud related learning.

5   Conclusion

The main conclusion to date can be summarised as follows: in order for personalized learning to come to fruition, students need not only to be able to choose and personalize what tools and content they are going to use, but also to have access to the necessary scaffolding to support their learning [5]. In order to accomplish the educational goals, the ideal approach to teaching and learning is to find the right balance between giving students the choice to meet their needs and preferences whilst maintaining a structured educational framework provided by the teacher.

Though these actions and projects are not all Cloud based, they do imply the use of Cloud tools and resources. The use of Cloud Computing strategies seeks to integrate students with special needs or disadvantaged pupils. Digital-age students want an active learning experience that is social, participatory and supported by rich media. Additionally, there is also a growing need to support and encourage learner control over the whole/entire learning process [8].

According to McLoughlin and Lee [5] many social software tools offer the learner the possibility to organise his/her own learning experience (with monitoring, collaborative working, questioning and self-evaluation, various representations). This gives the learner a sense of autonomy and control over his/her own learning and career planning. To enable this, we need to redesign the existing course managements systems and virtual learning environments as they do not fully use and interate the potential of social media and the knowledge of special needs education.

Yet much more remains to be done going forward. Pedagogic change and a greater personalization of learning are both essential components for student centred, self-regulated, independent and inclusive learning.

References

1. Edyburn, D.L., Edyburn, K.D.: Tools for creating accessible, tiered, and multilingual web-based curricula. Interv. Sch. Clin. **XX**(X), 1–7 (2011)
2. UNESCO: Policy Guidelines on Inclusion in Education. http://unesdoc.unesco.org/images/0017/001778/177849e.pdf
3. Donert, K., Kotsanis, Y. (eds.) Education on the Cloud 2015: State of the Art Case Studies. School on the Cloud Network, Working Group 1, Del. 6.4b (2015). http://schoolonthecloud.eu
4. OECD: Personalising Education, Schooling for Tomorrow. OECD Publishing, Paris (2006). doi:http://dx.doi.org/10.1787/9789264036604-en
5. McLoughlin, C., Lee, M.J.W.: Personalized and self regulated learning in the Web 2.0 era: international exemplars of innovative pedagogy using social software. Aust. J. Educ. Technol. **26**(1), 28–43 (2010)
6. Verpoorten, D., Glahn, C., Kravcik, M., Ternier, S., Specht, M.: Personalisation of learning in virtual learning environments. In: Cress, U., Dimitrova, V., Specht, M. (eds.) EC-TEL 2009. LNCS, vol. 5794, pp. 52–66. Springer, Heidelberg (2009)
7. Ainscow, M.: Responding to the challenge of learner diversity: a briefing paper for the Teaching and Learning in 2020 Review. University of Manchester Faculty of Education (2006)
8. Dron, J.: Designing the undesignable: social software and control. Educ. Technol. Soc. **10**(3), 60–71 (2007). http://www.ifets.info/journals/10_3/5.pdf

Methodology for Universal Design of ITs; Epistemologies Among Norwegian Experts

Miriam Eileen Nes Begnum[(✉)]

Faculty of Computer Science and Media Technology,
NTNU Norwegian University of Science and Technology,
Teknologivn. 22, 2815 Gjøvik, Norway
miriam.begnum@ntnu.no

Abstract. Achieving inclusive eSocieties has prompted a focus on universally designed IT-solutions. One strategy to ensure high quality universal design is identifying methodological best-practices. Literature voice different paradigms and points to diverging user-centeredness. This paper explores strategies and epistemological views employed by Norwegian experts through survey research. Results confirm a user-centered methodological approach is common. Both mechanical worldviews and a no-contact strategy as well as high-contact and involved strategies are identified. The paper discusses methodological traditions in the sample as well as successfulness of survey items.

Keywords: Universal design epistemology · User centered methodology · Design strategies · User involvement · User contact

1 Introduction

Norway has legislated that all public ICT-solutions must be inclusive and universal designed, in order to combat democratic, economical and ethical issues in the expansive self-service eSociety. In addition to determine quality assuring criteria for final solutions, best-practice process criteria could help ensure universal design (UD). British Standard 8878 suggests a user-centred approach to web accessibility [1]. UD processes reported in literature are often user centered, inclusive and iterative. However, even if universal design is viewed as an extension of user-centered approaches there are multiple practiced degrees of user contact, user involvement, user sensitivity and critical thinking in the field [2,3]. The range of user-centeredness and epistemological beliefs varies [4]. This study is a step towards understanding the impact of methodology on universal design quality. The goal of this exploratory study is to gain more insight into how universal design is practiced by Norwegian experts on universal design of ICT. Through survey research the paper explores methodologies strategies, epistemological views and paradigmic stances currently employed.

© Springer International Publishing Switzerland 2016
K. Miesenberger et al. (Eds.): ICCHP 2016, Part I, LNCS 9758, pp. 121–128, 2016.
DOI: 10.1007/978-3-319-41264-1_17

2   Background

Academic approaches for universal design of IT are often user-centered and seem well aligned with ISO 9241-210 [5]. Common methodologies are user-centered design (UCD), inclusive design, user sensitive inclusive design, emphatic design, user involvement and participatory design [4]. At least two epistemological cultures appear to be present in the field, with different philosophical justifications for what one believes is valid knowledge and how it can be aquired. The first epistemological culture seems focused on technology, checklists, standards, automatic tests and inspections [6,7], to view UD as an added constraint and influenced by (post)*positivism* [8]. The second epistemology is positive towards UD, focus on users and includes epistemological reflections linked to *critical*, *interventionistic* and *interpretive* paradigms. The second culture is frequently identified in participatory design (PD), inclusive design (ID) and user-sensitive inclusive design (USID) approaches [9,10].

Methodological approaches seem related to *paradigms*, overarching mindsets including academic culture, ideology, epistemologies and *worldviews*. Different strategies may be applied when faced with real-life challenges such as tight deadlines and limiting resources. One is rationally defining the best way forward within constraints; top-down stepwise and/or empirical, experimental and inductive. Such strategies connects to *mechanical* worldview [8] viewing software engineering as a complex problem to be solved through analytical approach, and *hard systems thinking* where a solution may be considered correct or not-correct based on fulfilling specifications. It appears such views may be tied to a user-centered methodology using *low* user contact and focused on end-result [4].

A second strategy is to actively influence decisions, including altering specifications and constraints. This is an *interventionistic* strategy, tied to a *dialectic* approach where several possible solutions and viewpoints are considered [8]. The expert is again taking on the role of a problem solver, but this time in a more political manner. The typical interventionsitic stand is technology is non-neutral. The focus is not so much on creating a correct solution in relation to specifications, as arriving at a good solution from ethical and socio-technical viewpoints. Such stances seem common within participatory design and user sensitive inclusive design. A third approach is focusing on dialogue in order to come to a mutual agreement, where the goal is to arrive at a solution that fits all stakeholders to the largest extent possible. Such *romantical* views fit with soft system thinking which encourages considerations of different perspectives and negotiations. An *interpretive* (or constructivist) paradigm could be tied to romantical views, opposing the positivist emphasis of facts being facts, instead viewing subjective "truths" as individual explanations of empirical experiences (*relativism*).

3   Research Approach

The study focuses on Norwegian domain experts developing universally designed IT-solutions. Conducting an in-depth interview study prior to a survey in order to better frame the items and focus of a survey was considered. This article focus on five items designed to map epistemologies and methodology. In addition, the survey covers specific methods usage and practices, user groups in focus and map key definitions through a total of 21 items (including background data). The study is approved by the Norwegian Social Science Data Services (NSD).

3.1 Target Group

The target group is identified using a non-probabilistic draw from a not easily well-defined population on the basis of established basic data [11]. A list of domain experts was comprised using the following approach; (1) experts among the members of the recent Norwegian network focusing on Universal Design and ICT, (2) experts among companies sponsoring Oslo Interaction Design Association and (3) experts being referred by identified experts. The experts are selected for their visibility in the field over perceived academic background and area of expertice. The goal was to indentify 30–50 domain experts. The resulting list of survey recipients included 70 experts from 13 enterprises; 8 consultancies, 2 medium-sized companies, 2 smaller R&D companies, 1 non-profit institute and 1 government agency. At least 13 of these are well-known for their expertise. An estimate is that around 20–40 % have a high domain expertise while the majority of around 30–50 % have a fairly high competence. The final sample is considered sufficient for seeking insights over generalizable results, representing major enterprises and institutions in the field.

3.2 Survey Design

In order to explore how user-centered and empathic the experts are the survey asks for degrees of agreement with different strategies. Experts are asked for agreement with the approaches: (A) user-centeredness without direct user contact, (B) user-centeredness with direct user contact (specifying the goal of the user-contact is to deepen knowledge), (C) user-centeredness emphasizing user-involvement (specifying the expert participates in users everyday life), (D) participation design (states users are equal to designers/developers and asked for input throughout the process - typical traits in participatory design) and (E) empathic design (without tying understanding needs to involvement or contact, exemplified as simulating disability or observing use). It was assumed that strategies A to D would be on a scale with increasing level of user contact, from no contact in A to high-contact and involvement in D. The user-centered and empathic strategies are phrased in relation to "my work", thus linked to what the experts *do* and not necessarily what their opinions are. While this may introduce a bias, but it also makes makes the question less provoking and easier to answer. For agreement measures, a 4-point Likert scale was used, forcing the respondents to take a non-neutral stand. The same was also done for exploring agreement with polarized mechanical, romantic and interventionist worldviews and interpretive or positivistic paradigms.

From a theoretical point of view, a negative correlation is expected between mechanical and romantic views, and between interventionistic and loyal beliefs. The experts are further asked about agreement with 6 paradigmic statements. The 1st, 3rd and 5th statements are assumed positivistic and stress the importance of objectiveness, factual findings and precice criteria. The 2nd, 4th and 6th are interpretive and emphasize mutual understanding, collaboration and end-user involvement. The respondents are asked to select whether they prefer qualitative methods providing closeness to users, in-depth understanding and rich insights, or quantitative methods providing overview, validity and representative information. The phrasing of both options are positive and attempted equated for desirability. The relativist stand is phrased as viewing *truths as interpreted and constructed based on interpretations, common perspective needs to be agreed upon.* The opposing stance is *uncovering truths through triangulation, counteracting erroneous perspectives.*

4   Results

4.1   Survey Sample

26 experts (37 %) responded to the survey. Only complete survey responses were allowed. 39 % of the respondents are women and 61 % men, which is considered an equal distribution to the ratio of 37 % women and 63 % men in the target group. Years of experience ranged from 2 to 25 years, with aritmethic mean 7.73 and median 7. This is considered high compared to the age distribution of a majority below 40 years of age. The impression is that many highly experienced experts are responding to the survey. No biases are identified in the respondents compared to the sample. Job titles vary greatly, with 21 unique titles across the 26 respondents. Only 2 titles specify universal design as area of expertice. Most experts report they are interdisciplinary and 73 % work within three areas or more including at least two of the common areas visual design (65 %), programming (65 %), interaction design (85 %) and content production (50 %). 46 % of the respondents have interdisciplinary academic backgrounds, ranging from pedagogics, law and journalism to more traditional development and design disciplines.

4.2   Methodological Strategies

Table 1 shows that experts are fairly divided on a *no-contact* strategy (A) as well as participatory design (D), and seem somewhat partial to high-contact involvement (C). However, they seem to agree with some-contact strategies to understand user needs (73 % for B and 88 % for E). Table 2 shows there are strong correlations between strategies C and D, as well as between disagreeing with A and agreeing with strategies C and D. As expected, strategy E does not significantly correlate with the other strategies, however neither does B. There are no identified background variables influencing strategy responses.

Table 1. Agreement with methodological design strategies

Strategy	Full disagree	Partial disagree	Partial agree	Full agree
A: UCD no contact	35 %	23 %	31 %	11.5 %
B: UCD some contact	11.5 %	15 %	46 %	27 %
C: involved, fairly high c	31 %	27 %	27 %	15 %
D: participatory, high c	27 %	23 %	27 %	23 %
E: empathic design	8 %	4 %	65 %	23 %

Table 2. Correlations between design strategies (Spearman's rho, 2-sided)

	A: no c	C: involved	D: participatory
A: no c.	1	−0.72, Sig. 0.000	−0.65, Sig. 0.000
C: involved	−0.72, Sig. 0.000	1	0.77, Sig. 0.000
D: participatory	−0.65, Sig. 0.000	0.77, Sig. 0.000	1

4.3 Epistemological Stances and Worldviews

61.5 % prefer qualitative methods while 38.5 % prefer quantitative. 27 % align themselves with relativism. Table 3 present the frequencies of agreement with mechanical, romantic and interventionistic views. There is a weak tendency between ethical views, which could indicate a boosting underlying factor (e.g. ethical awareness). There are moderate correlations between romantic and ethical views, but none between mechanical and romantical stances (Table 4). In order to investigate further how the views are distributing themselves in relation to each other and whether they are measuring different views or not, a Principal Component Analysis (PCA) was conducted. PCA was conducted in a purely exploratory fashion, as the data are not continuous or nearly continuous. The findings are interesting: 2 factors can be found, which together accounts for 76 % of the total variance. This indicates that two different worldviews are measured in the item. Those agreeing with mechanical views are the only ones loading Component 2 on 0,945, in addition to loading component 1 on 0,188. The other views are all loading highly in component 1. In other words, this item seems to measure mechanical versus non-mechanical views.

Table 3. Agreement with worldview

Worldview	Fully disagree	Partial disagree	Partial agree	Fully agree
Mechanical	0 %	15 %	42 %	42 %
Romantical	0 %	11.5 %	54 %	35 %
Interventionistic	0 %	27 %	39 %	35 %
Loyal	8 %	34.5 %	38.5 %	19 %

Table 4. Crosstabulations between worldviews (Spearman's rho, 2-tailed)

	Mechanical	Romantical	Interventionistic	Loyal
Mechanical	1	-	-	-
Romantical	-	1	0.468, Sig. 0.016	0.468, Sig. 0.016
Interventionistic	-	0.468, Sig. 0.016	1	0.384, Sig. 0.053
Loyal	-	0.468, Sig. 0.016	0.384, Sig. 0.053	1

4.4   Paradigm Stances

There is a strong correlation between the assumed interpretive 4th and 6th statements on collaboration and involving end-users ($\rho s = 0.66$), but none to the 2nd on mutual understanding (Table 5). There are moderate correlations between objectiveness and precise criteria ($\rho s = 0.0.53$) and precise criteria and finding facts ($\rho s = 0.47$). An exploratory PCA show 3 quite clear components that explain 79 % of variance. The statements load the first two components inconsistingly, but the 2nd statement on mutual understanding is the only strongly loading the last component. Looking *only* at the assumed positivist statements, one component is identified. Looking *only* at the three assumed interpretive statements, two different components are found, where the 2nd loads Component 1 on 0,189 and Component 2 on 0,975, while the other two load Component 1 on 0,912 and 0,884 and Component 2 on 0,04 and $-0, 25$.

Table 5. Agreement with paradigmic stances

Stance - area emphasized	Fully disagree	Partial disagree	Partial agree	Fully agree
1st - Objectiveness	0 %	19 %	46 %	35 %
2nd - Mutual understanding	0 %	4 %	58 %	39 %
3rd - Finding facts	0 %	4 %	35 %	62 %
4th - Collaboration	0 %	0 %	35 %	65 %
5th - Precise criteria	4 %	15 %	27 %	54 %
6th - Involving end-users	0 %	4 %	23 %	73 %

4.5   Methodological Traditions

A moderate correlation ($\rho s = 0.4$) is identified between mechanical views and agreement with a no-contact strategy. Highly significant correlations are found between the 6th stance on end-user involvement and user-involved strategies (strong for C $\rho s = 0.67$, moderate for D $\rho s = 0.42$). Mechanical views correlate negatively to user involvement ($\rho s = -0.41$) and 6th stance ($\rho s = -0.55$), as do the 1st stance on objectiveness to romantical views ($\rho s = -0.50$). The impression is of a connection between mechanical views and a no-contact strategy on one hand, and non-mechanical alignment and user-involved methodologies on the other. Preferring qualitative methods correlates negatively to mechanical (ρs $= -0.48$), no-contact (ρs $= -0.45$) and 1st (ρs $= -0.49$) statements. A crosstabulation shows none preferring qualitative methods fully agree with no-contact strategy A. A majority of the sample agree with strategy E, which correlates moderately to romantical (ρs $= 0.41$) and loyal (ρs $= 0.43$) views. Non-relativist epistemologies correlates moderately to 3rd stance on factual uncovering (ρs $= 0.44$).

5 Discussion

Overall, the sample seems aligned with user-centred principles [5]. There are indications of opposing strategies, but expected correlations between epistemological beliefs and methodological approaches are blurred. Experts seem fairly consistent in expressing adherence to high-contact user-involved strategies versus a no-contact approach throughout survey items. Measuring alignment with mechanical versus no-mechanical views is successful, but separating romantic and interventionistic views is not. The assumed positivistic 1st, 3rd and 5th statements likely measure similar stances, while the 2nd measure something different than the 4th and 6th. It is unknown whether literature based theory is correct in pitting mechanical views against intertwined romantism and interventionism, and positivist against intertwined interpretive and critical. An alternative hypothesis would be that romantical views correlate more with interpretive traditions focused on facilitation, interpretation and cooperation, while e.g. USID and PD belong to critical design and interventionist non-relativistic stances.

There seems to be an acquiescence response related to epistemological views or tacit knowledge instead of conscious epistemological stances, as experts agree with both romantic (89 %), mechanical (85 %) and interventionistic (74 %) views. A redesign could combat effects of items designed equated for desirability. Correlations indicate strategies C and D imply a user-involved style (assumed high-contact) while strategy A measure an opposing no-contact (or low-contact) strategy. Strategy B may be a social desirability bias. Strong relationships between stances on collaboration and end-user involvement may be influenced by the fact that both are highly immersed principles.

A crosstabulating on relativism and quantitative-qualitative preferral shows that the most common category is to prefer qualitative methods and use method triangulation. This indicates pragmatic experts utilizing a wide range of strategies from different epistemological traditions. There are no clear relationship between the background of the experts and their epistemological beliefs. This is not suprising due to the interdisciplinarity of the experts and the low N of the sample. The experts work across disciplines and have backgrounds from several fields, with different individual combinations. The population "experts within universal design of ICTs" is not easily defined. Ensuring validity through sampling is challenging. Filtering items ensuring the experts are in the target population may continue to be necessary. Self-reported expertice in the area may help establish data validity. One could consider adding self-measurement of depth of expertice.

6   Conclusion

There are indications of diverging methodological styles in the Norwegian sample between a mechanical no-contact tradition and user-involved approaches. Some connections are identified between epistemology and methodological alignment, but more varied than theory would suggest. This could be indicative of interdisciplinarity and pragmatism, point to tacit knowledge and aquiescence effects or suggest that theoretical assumptions do not fit real-life practices. Links between methodology and overarching paradigms are still blurred. Compared to investigating epistemology and methodology though literature, this domain expert survey bring new insights that future studies will continue to explore. In addition to improved survey items, an in-depth interview study focused on UD success projects will investigate methodology, constraints, epistemology and interdisciplinarity. Continued work hopes to contribute to exploring relationships between epistemologies, methodologies and UD quality.

Acknowledgments. Thank you to survey respondents, pilot testers and S. McCallum and A. C. Begnum for valuable input in design, analysis and discussions.

References

1. ACCESS 8878: Web Accessibility - Code of Practice. https://www.access8878.co.uk/
2. Newell, A.: Accessible computing - past trends and future suggestions. ACM Trans. Access. Comput. 1(2), 9:1–9:7 (2008)
3. Keates, S., Clarkson, P.J., Harrison, L.A., Robinson, P.: Towards a practical inclusive design approach. In: CUU 2000. ACM (2000)
4. Begnum, M.E.N.: Universal Design Methodologies and Epistemologies (Submitted to Universal Access in the Information Society)
5. ISO 9241–210:2010 Ergonomics of human-system interaction - Part 210: Human-centred design for interactive systems. www.iso.org
6. Wobbrock, J.O., Kane, S.K., Gajos, K.Z., Harada, S., Froehlich, J.: Ability-based design: concepts, principles and examples. ACM Trans. Access. Comput. 3(3), 9:1–9:27 (2011)
7. Horton, D.: Design Education: An interview with Valerie Fletcher. http://rosenfeldmedia.com/a-web-for-everyone/design-education-an-interview-with-valerie-fletcher/
8. Dahlbom, B., Mathiassen, L.: Computers in Context: The Philosophy and Practice of System Design, 1st edn. Wiley-Blackwell, Oxford, UK (1993)
9. Dewsbury, G., Rouncefield, M., Clark, K., Sommerville, I.: Depending on digital design: extending inclusivity. Hous. Stud. 19(5), 811–825 (2004)
10. Massimi, M., Baecker, R.M., Wu, M.: Using participatory activities with seniors to critique, build, and evaluate mobile phones. In: ASSETS 2007, pp. 155–162. ACM (2007)
11. Lazar, J., Jinjuan, H.F., Hochheiser, H.: Research Methods in Human-Computer Interaction. Wiley, London (2010)

Using ICT and Quality of Life: Comparing Persons with and Without Disabilities

Djordje M. Kadijevich[1]([✉]), Gordana Odovic[2], and Dejan Maslikovic[3]

[1] Institute for Educational Research, Dobrinjska 11/III, P.O.B. 546,
11000 Belgrade, Serbia
djkadijevic@ipi.ac.rs
[2] Faculty of Special Education and Rehabilitation, University of Belgrade,
Belgrade, Serbia
gordanaodovic@gmail.com
[3] Art Academy, Alfa BK University, Belgrade, Serbia
maslikovicd@gmail.com

Abstract. Calls to promote greater participations of persons with disabilities in society usually deal with the use of various IC-based technologies. Many of initiatives also deal with the quality of life (QoL) of those persons and discuss possible impacts of ICT use on that quality. By comparing persons with and without disabilities, this study examined the extent to which (1) individuals used IC-based technologies, (2) their QoL was improved due to the use of those technologies, and (3) this use (USE) was related to that QoL improvement (IQoL). It was found that both USE and IQoL were lower for persons with disabilities, and that correlation between USE and IQoL was stronger for those persons. The study examines the role of education and its potential to improve the QoL for persons with disabilities as a result of better use of ICTs.

Keywords: ICT use · Quality of life · Persons with disabilities · Persons without disabilities

1 Introduction

Calls to promote greater participations of persons with disabilities in the society usually deal with the use of various IC-based technologies, such as the Internet, computers, mobile phones, cable TV, and e-government (e.g., [1]). Many of initiatives also deal with the quality of life (QoL) of those persons, and discuss possible impacts of ICT use on that quality (e.g., [2]). Regarding research studies, our literature search evidenced that researchers have usually examined the relationship between the use of particular ICT, and QoL in a general sense (e.g., [3,4]). It is, of course, important to find out whether (and to what extent) the use of one particular IC-based technology would improve the quality of life of persons with disabilities. However, it is equally, or even more important, to find

K. Miesenberger et al. (Eds.): ICCHP 2016, Part I, LNCS 9758, pp. 129–133, 2016.
DOI: 10.1007/978-3-319-41264-1_18

out which of several IC-based technologies have potential to improve the quality of life to a greater extent, which has not been studied in literature to date. By comparing persons with and without disabilities, this study examined to what extent (1) individuals used IC-based technologies, (2) their QoL was improved due to the use of those technologies, and (3) this use (USE) was related to that QoL improvement (IQoL).

2   Method

This study used a convenient sample of 185 participants: 95 had various disabilities (mobility, visual, and hearing impairments), whereas 90 had no disabilities.

Two variables were mainly used, namely ICT use (USE) and QoL improvement due to ICT use (IQoL). Each of these variables was measured by a 5-item instrument which referred to the five IC-based technologies mentioned above. (An IQoL item was "Has the use of Internet improved the quality of your life?"; answer could be "No", "Yes – to a small extent", "Yes – to a moderate extent", or "Yes – to a large extent"; it was numerically expressed as 0, 1, 2, or 3, respectively.) By transforming raw answers into Guttman's [5] image form scores[1], the two measures attained high reliability (Cronbach's alpha: 0.86 for USE, and 0.93 for IQoL). The study also used several background variables (e.g., gender, education, and income), which were of binary nature. The values of all variables were collected using a questionnaire, which was mostly completed in the traditional, paper-and pencil way either by participants themselves or by study assistants when personal response was limited or not possible.

Apart from descriptive analyses (in terms of means and percentages), this study used a number of t-tests for independent samples to compare means of variables in question. To signal the strength of the difference found, the t-test results were coupled with Cohen's d. This strength (or effect size) may be considered small for $d = 0.2$, medium for $d = 0.5$, and large for $d = 0.8$ [6].

3   Results

USE was lower for persons with disabilities (1.67 $vs.$ 1.91; $t = 3.516, df = 183, p = 0.001$; $d = 3.516\sqrt{\frac{1}{95} + \frac{1}{90}} = 0.52$). Regarding the five IC-based technologies, significant differences (with lower values for persons with disabilities) were found for the Internet (1.42 $vs.$ 1.74; $p = 0.000; d = 0.53$), computer (2.10 $vs.$ 2.38; $p = 0.019; d = 0.35$), mobile phone (2.11 $vs.$ 2.43; $p = 0.001; d = 0.51$), and e-government (1.08 $vs.$ 1.25; $p = 0.000; d = 0.57$). No significant differences were found for cable TV (1.64 $vs.$ 1.76; $p = 0.112$).

IQoL was lower for persons with disabilities (1.88 $vs.$ 2.05; $t = 2.010, df = 183, p = 0.046; d = 0.30$). Regarding the five technologies, significant differences (with lower values for persons with disabilities) were found for QoL improvement

---

[1] For details, see www.mi.sanu.ac.rs/~djkadij/zipi03.pdf.

due to the use of Internet (2.21 *vs.* 2.45; $p = 0.034; d = 0.31$), computer (2.16 *vs.* 2.44; $p = 0.008; d = 0.39$), and e-government (1.29 *vs.* 1.46; $p = 0.012; d = 0.37$). No significant differences were found for QoL improvement due to the use of mobile phone (2.16 *vs.* 2.34; $p = 0.090$) or cable TV (1.59 *vs.* 1.57; $p = 0.794$).

The relation between USE and IQoL (measured by Pearson's correlation) was positive for persons with disabilities ($r = 0.77, df = 93, p = 0.000$), as well as for persons without disabilities ($r = 0.58, df = 88, p = 0.000$). Furthermore, this relation was stronger for persons with disabilities ($Z = 2.393, p = 0.017$).

4   Discussion

Having in mind the USE-related and IQoL-related averages reported above, there is a space to improve both USE and IQoL for persons with disabilities, particularly in relation to the use of the Internet, computer, and e-government.[2]

What may a key factor be to improve matters?

An analysis of the contextual variables used, indicated that persons with disabilities had lower education levels (at least a college level degree: 39 % *vs.* 67 %), were less frequently employed (54 % *vs.* 93 %), and had lower income (more than 40,000 RSD $\approx$ 330 EUR: 18 % *vs.* 64 %). As no significant differences were found with respect to gender (females: 43 % *vs.* 57 %; $p = 0.066$), and age (older than 35: 62 % *vs.* 61 %), a key factor for improvement may be education. The relevance of education in building ICT inclusive society has been mentioned in several studies (e.g., [8]). It seems that a person's social status, shaped by his/her education, is related to both the quantity and quality of online activities (e.g., the higher status, the less yet more beneficial use of the Internet [9]).

What may better education improve for persons with disabilities?

An additional analysis regarding the two educational levels evidenced that although no significant differences were found for USE (1.79 *vs.* 1.59; $p = 0.073$) and IQoL (2.02 *vs.* 1.79; $p = 0.078$), there were significant differences (favoring more educated) for the Internet use (1.65 *vs.* 1.28; $p = 0.007; d = 0.58$), computer use (2.32 *vs.* 1.97; $p = 0.033; d = 0.45$), QoL improvement due to the Internet use (2.47 *vs.* 2.05; $p = 0.018; d = 0.51$), and QoL improvement due to computer use (2.43 *vs.* 1.99; $p = 0.006; d = 0.59$). (For persons without disabilities, no significant differences were found for USE and IQoL, as well as for each of their ten indicators.)

What would this better education provide?

Research has evidenced that students with disabilities may (and usually do) lack digital capital (e.g., accredited ICT qualifications, positive encouragements to use technology, appropriate assistive technologies, adapted instruction, appropriate learning materials, or specialized online forums). This lack would prevent or limit their success within their educational environments [10]. It is therefore

---

[2] Regarding e-government, its role in this study was mainly restricted to applying for or obtaining of official documents. As several services in this e-sector require digital signature, appropriate training to deal with this signature may be needed [7].

crucial for educational institutions to identify kinds of digital capital needed by their students with disabilities and provide these students with appropriate digital assets in flexible ways.

This study also evidenced that the relation between USE and IQoL (measured by Pearson's correlation) was stronger for persons with disabilities (0.77 *vs.* 0.58; $Z = 2.393, p = 0.017$), which is a sign that persons with disabilities are in greater need of the use of ICTs to improve the quality of their lives. Clearly, if widely available to persons with disabilities, ICTs could bring many benefits and new opportunities for different aspects of their lives [11], which would indeed improve the quality of their lives.

5   Conclusion

Undoubtedly, investing in better education, providing students with the right kind of digital capital, would result in more use of ICTs. A long-term goal would be to improve the quality of life of persons with disabilities as a result of more use of ICTs. This goal seems attainable because this study showed that, for persons with specific disabilities, there is a high positive correlation between the use of ICTs and the quality of life improvement due to this use. To monitor our progress towards this important goal, a detailed measure of this improvement may be developed and utilized.

Acknowledgements. This work was supported by the Ministry of Education, Science, and Technological Development of the Republic of Serbia (project "Improving the Quality and Accessibility of Education in Modernization Processes in Serbia"), and SAGA and Open Society Fund (project "Role of ICT in Development of an Inclusive Society").

References

1. ITU: The ICT Opportunity for a Disability-Inclusive Development Framework. ITU, Geneva, Switzerland (2013)
2. World Summit on the Information Society: Outcomes Document. ITU, Geneva, Switzerland (2010)
3. Anderson, B.: Social capital, quality of life and ICTs. In: Anderson, B., Brynin, M., Gershuny, J., Raban, Y. (eds.) Information and Communications Technologies in Society: E-Living in a Digital Europe, pp. 163–174. Routledge, Oxford (2007)
4. Gustafson, D.H., et al.: The effect of an information and communication technology (ICT) on older adults' quality of life: study protocol for a randomized control trial. Trials **16**, 191 (2015)
5. Guttman, L.: Image theory for the structure of quantitative variates. Psychometrika **18**(4), 277–296 (1953)
6. Cohen, J.: A power primer. Psychol. Bull. **112**(1), 155–159 (1992)
7. García-Crespo, Á., Paniagua-Martín, F., Colomo-Palacios, R., Gómez-Berbís, J.M.: E-inclusion for people with disabilities in E-government services through accessible multimedia. Int. J. Inf. Syst. Soc. Change **3**(3), 37–51 (2012)

8. Petrie, H., Gallagher, B., Darzentas, J.S.: A critical review of eight years of research on technologies for disabled and older people. In: Miesenberger, K., Fels, D., Archambault, D., Peňáz, P., Zagler, W. (eds.) ICCHP 2014, Part II. LNCS, vol. 8548, pp. 260–266. Springer, Heidelberg (2014)
9. van Deursen, A.J., van Dijk, J.A.: The digital divide shifts to differences in usage. New Media Soc. **16**(3), 507–526 (2014)
10. Seale, J., Georgeson, J., Mamas, C., Swain, J.: Not the right kind of 'digital capital'? An examination of the complex relationship between disabled students, their technologies and higher education institutions. Comput. Educ. **82**(1), 118–128 (2015)
11. Toboso, M.: Rethinking disability in Amartya Sen's approach: ICT and equality of opportunity. Ethics Inf. Technol. **13**(2), 107–118 (2011)

The Use of Working Prototypes for Participatory Design with People with Disabilities

Brandon Haworth, Muhammad Usman, Melanie Baljko$^{(\boxtimes)}$, and Foad Hamidi

Department of Electrical Engineering and Computer Science, York University,
4700 Keele street, Toronto, ON M3J 1P3, Canada
{brandon,usman,mb,fhamidi}@cse.yorku.ca

Abstract. The inclusion of people with disabilities and their circle of stakeholders in the design and deployment of digital assistive technology is increasingly being recognized as important. The Do-It-Yourself Assistive Technology (DIY-AT) approach investigates methodologies and tools to support accessible making practices. In prior work, we successfully used a DIY-AT approach to develop TalkBox, an open-source direct-selection communication board for those with little or no functional verbal communication. In this paper, we describe a follow-up project in which we use TalkBox as a prototyping platform to facilitate co-design and co-fabrication of DIY-AT. We present results from (1) a workshop in which users with disabilities and their parents/caregivers fabricated their own TalkBoxes, and (2) a collaborative co-design session with a non-verbal child and his mother wherein the potential for TalkBox variants led to novel design decisions. We illustrate the outcome of our process by describing the multi-vocabulary variant called Hot Swappable Talk-Box, in which RFID technology is used to afford easy switching among different vocabulary sets.

Keywords: Do-It-Yourself (DIY) · Assistive technology · Participatory design · Open-source hardware · Communication boards · SGDs

1 Introduction

In recent years, Do-It-Yourself (DIY) and Maker approaches to the development of digital assistive technology (AT) have received attention from the research community as having potential to provide users with affordable and customizable solutions [1,5,7]. Additionally, researchers have recognized the importance of developing tools and processes that support user empowerment and skill learning through design [8]. For example, Ladner has pointed out that participating in inclusive AT design activities can have positive psychological impact on users with disabilities [8]. In the project described here, we employed a previously developed DIY-AT prototype called TalkBox [4] to explore these possibilities through a series of structured sessions which empowered users to fabricate and customize their own variations of the system and provide designers with further feedback and input.

© Springer International Publishing Switzerland 2016
K. Miesenberger et al. (Eds.): ICCHP 2016, Part I, LNCS 9758, pp. 134–141, 2016.
DOI: 10.1007/978-3-319-41264-1_19

2   Background: Participatory Design and Assistive Technology

Participatory Design (PD) has long been applied to the development of AT [2,9,10]. In recent years, the emergence of more affordable and easy-to-use technologies has further enabled users with disabilities to design and fabricate their own digital AT systems. For example, Hurst and Tobias presented two DIY-AT case studies [7]. In the first, instructors at an adaptive art class created alternative drawing tools for their students who had motor disabilities in response to inadequate consumer product options. In the second case study, a retired engineer developed a series of open-source AT solutions and, together with a selection of AT designs from other people, made them available on his website.

Despite the immediate possibilities of DIY-AT, researchers identify the ongoing need to investigate tools and processes that make "making accessible" and ways in which barriers of technical expertise and cost can be further mitigated [1,5,6]. In response, and as part of this effort, we developed TalkBox [4]. TalkBox aims to provide a prototyping platform that is relatively easy to use as a tool to facilitate PD activities, and also to provide a way for non-technical users to develop their own digital ATs.

Fig. 1. An initial version of the TalkBox the design [4]

TalkBox, shown in Fig. 1, is an open-source DIY communication-board that combines a capacitive touch sensor with a Raspberry Pi computer to implement a Speech Generation Device (SGD) for non-verbal users [4]. It incorporates a direct-selection, fixed vocabulary set which can be modified, although not "in situ" (i.e., in the middle of a communicative exchange) and, depending on user, possibly requiring assistance. TalkBox was developed using a Participatory Design (PD) methodology in which members of our lab worked closely with a special education teacher to develop and to improve iteratively the design to meet stakeholder needs. In this paper, we use TalkBox as a prototyping tool to facilitate collaborative fabrication sessions and subsequent feedback to extend its functionality by creating an alternative version, "Hot Swappable" TalkBox.

3 Using TalkBox to Facilitate Participatory Design Sessions with Users with Disabilities

The TalkBox has served as a prototyping platform to facilitate two collaborative participatory design sessions with users with disabilities. In these sessions, participants worked collaboratively to guide customizations to fit recipient needs.

3.1 "TalkMake" Workshop

We used TalkBox as the underpinning technology in a Participatory Design workshop, "TalkMake". With this workshop design, our aim was to investigate the degree to which non-technical users with disabilities, their parents/caregivers, and other stakeholders could assemble their own TalkBoxes given a set of documentations, materials, and other supports. Our workshop was designed to be attended by "teams" rather than by individuals: each team was to have, at its core, a maker with a disability and was to be augmented by other stakeholders as needed (e.g., parents, caregivers, special education teachers, educational assistants, etc.). In preparation for the workshop, we developed kits that consisted of all necessary TalkBox components. We also prepared a set of instructions that described the fabrication process in non-technical terms. We tested the instructions in advance of the workshop through a pilot session. We invited members of the "Devices 4 Disabilities" student club at York University to assemble TalkBoxes using the provided documentation and to provide feedback. On the basis of the feedback and on our observations, we further revised the instruction material and the design of the material kits. We also conducted additional sessions to train student volunteers in the fabrication of TalkBoxes.

The "TalkMake" workshop took place during the 2014 Toronto Mini Maker Faire; the venue was a fully accessible public library (Toronto Reference Library). Figure 2 illustrates the workshop in progress. Six teams participated: four teams comprised of users with communication disorders and their parents/caregivers, and two teams comprised of other stakeholders active in the assistive technology community. Volunteer undergraduate students supported the teams during a 2-hour session, in which, they built and customized their own TalkBoxes.

The outcomes of the workshop were positive: six TalkBox units were successfully produced. Afterwards, the participants took the TalkBoxes home. While overall the feedback from the participants was overwhelmingly positive, the participatory session did reveal some limitations in the supportive materials. In particular, the process for the setup and the configuration of vocabularies was identified as challenging. Additionally, certain technology-based steps posed challenges: the use of an external software applications to conduct voice recordings, the need to manage the Raspberry Pis file system, and the limited usability of the companion software. Participant feedback also indicated the need for improved vocabulary functionality. At the conclusion of the Maker Faire event, the TalkBox project was the awarded the 2014 "Bridging the Gap" award, which recognizes contributions toward addressing a real human need [11].

Fig. 2. Participants engaged in the TalkMake workshop

3.2   Collaborative Session with Community Partner

We also employed TalkBox when conducting a collaborative design session with a community partner: a primary caregiver and her 10-year old son, who is on the autism disorder spectrum. In the session, we used TalkBox as a technology probe [3], in order to elicit feedback from these users. The child has experienced communication difficulties which have varied over time from moderate-severe to profound. Several years prior, the child learned to use an iPad tablet as a communication device, but did not retain these skills, possibly due to concomitant seizure disorder. He is presently non-verbal and receiving special services within his elementary school.

His mother, as his advocate, was seeking alternative and simpler options to maintain communication with him. Upon hearing about the TalkBox project from friends who attended the "TalkMake" workshop described above, shesought contact with the research team.

After initial phone conversations, we brought TalkBox to the community partners home and, in a collaborative 45-minute session, brainstormed potential customizations for the child. During the session, the child partner interacted with TalkBox for 20 min and utilized some of the direct selection buttons. The adult partner believed that TalkBox has great potential for use by their son, and indicated a desire to have an even more simplified version, with the vocabulary set reduced down to two choices (i.e., "yes" and "no"). She also identified the desire to potentially "swap in" other vocabulary sets and to subsequently expand the available vocabulary. Other needs identified by the stakeholder included: enhanced protective covering for the TalkBox electronics; further reduction of exposed connections; increased device portability, and reduced size. A possibility that we identified together was the development of a wearable version of TalkBox in which the entire device would hang from a shoulder strap or sling, with a pouch or other alternative design providing the outer protective covering.

4   The Hot Swappable System: Facilitating Assistive Technology Design

Following the workshop and collaborative session, we decided to extend our device design. For the sake of clarity, we denote the initial version as "Alpha" TalkBox. We sought to modify "Alpha" TalkBox so that it could support the possibility to switch from one vocabulary set to another, even while in the middle of a communicative exchange (so-called "hot swappable" vocabularies). This enhanced version was to be called "Hot Swappable" TalkBox.

To accomplish this enhanced functionality, we incorporated a passive RFID system intended for Near Field Communications (NFC). This same technology is used in transit passes in public transportation networks and, more recently, in mobile phones for phone-to-phone data transfer. Such systems are generally low cost (below CAD 30) and are widely available. The system consists of an RFID reader ($\approx$ 4 cm $\times$ 3 cm $\times$ 5 mm) and the use of one or more RFID tags ($\approx$ 3 cm $\times$ 3 cm by 2 mm). We also augmented the TalkBox companion software, as described below.

4.1   Physical Design

The schematics of the Hot Swappable TalkBox and the RFID-enabled vocabulary card are shown in Fig. 3 (left) and (right), respectively.

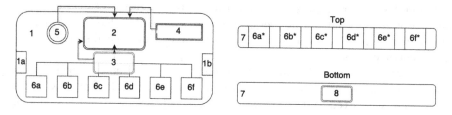

Fig. 3. Schematics of Hot Swappable TalkBox and vocabulary card, with components numerically labelled 1–8. The Hot Swappable TalkBox (left) and the RFID-enabled vocabulary card (right)

The components of Hot Swappable TalkBox, Fig. 3 (left), are as follows: (1) device chassis (typically constructed from paper-faced foam board); (1a) and (1b) mounts for affixing the current vocabulary card (adhesive-backed velcro); (2) a custom 3D-printed case holding the required electronics (a Raspberry Pi, a micro SD card flashed with the on-board TalkBox software, and a MPR121 touch capacitive sensor); (3) the RFID reader module (mounted to the chassis); (4) 5V DC power supply (rechargeable battery); (5) audio output (small rechargeable speaker); (6a–6f) a panel of 6 individual conductive surface buttons (constructed from adhesive-backed aluminum duct tape), connected to component (2) with headered wires. All electronic components are fixed to (1) using velcro.

The components of a RFID-enabled vocabulary card are as follows (numeric labels provided in Fig. 3 (right)): (7) card body (typically constructed from paper-faced foam board, with side-mounted velcro pieces mated to device chassis), (6a*–6f*) labels affixed on the front side of the card body (colour-printed card stock); and (8) the RFID tag affixed to the bottom side of the card body.

A physical instantiation of this design can be seen in Fig. 4. The figure demonstrates that, with this design, the RFID-enabled vocabulary card sits upon the RFID reader (Component 3) and just above the conductive surface buttons (Components 6a–6f). This design allows for easy switching from one vocabulary card to another.

Fig. 4. A Hot Swappable TalkBox design instantiation, with (top image) a 'Basic Needs' vocabulary card in place and (bottom image) with the vocabulary card lifted off and shown upside-down (with the white RFID tag and the black RFID reader revealed).

Once a RFID-enabled vocabulary card is created, it must be further configured. This is accomplished via the TalkBox companion software, which was modified as follows. First, the software allows the user to submit an RFID-enabled vocabulary card for configuration simply by waving it in front of the RFID reader. Each RFID tag is uniquely identified by an ID string. In configuration mode, the user specifies the mapping from each of the 6 touch conductive buttons to specific sounds (sound files of words, phrases, or other vocalizations). The TalkBox companion software allows users to record the vocabulary sounds directly (i.e., without the need of any external software recording tools) or to import them from external libraries.

During operation, the RFID reader automatically detects any RFID-enabled vocabulary card that enters its proximity field. We implemented a card reader processing thread in the on-board TalkBox software. The thread listens for such events and, upon detection, reads and parses the unique RFID ID string and then loads the configured vocabulary set by reassigning the functionality of the conductive touch buttons to the configured vocabulary set.

The on-board TalkBox software was designed to be fault tolerant: if, during the RFID reading process, a problem is encountered, the system responds gracefully. If the system fails to find a vocabulary for the scanned RFID tag ID string, it retains the current settings, meaning that TalkBox leaves the previously mapped vocabulary as-is. This avoids operational failure in the case of unconfigured RFID-enabled vocabulary cards or even 'outside' RFIDs (such as metro or rail passes or other devices which also use NFC RFID cards).

5   Conclusion

In this paper, we situated our present work in our previously-reported project [4], in which we successfully used a DIY-AT approach to develop TalkBox, an open-source communication board for non-verbal individuals. In this follow-up work, we sought to investigate one means to include, to a greater degree, people with disabilities, as well as their teachers, parents, caregivers, and other community members, in the design and deployment of digital assistive technology. This investigation entailed the design and instantiation of the TalkMake workshop. We, along with others, recognize that efforts such as the TalkMake workshop as serving to recognize technology as a process (as opposed to an end-product), and, subsequently, to position key stakeholders within this process. The approach has been made possible, in part, by the rise in maker communities and the upswell of DIY approaches.

The TalkMake workshop generated different types of results. First, we established positive evidence of the viability of the approach of co-fabrication with community members. This demonstrates that knowledge barriers can be effectively circumvented with an appropriately-designed set of materials. Second, and although we did not collect data specifically to capture post-workshop effects, we feel secure in concluding, in a general way, that the workshop accomplished its objective to empower its participants. Third, the workshop spawned, via a subsequent collaborative design session with community partners, an interesting design variant, Hot Swappable TalkBox, which affords the possibility to switch among vocabulary sets during a conversational exchange. So the benefits of approaches such as the TalkMake workshop not only include the adoption of a more empowering framework to technology design, but also the generation of spin-off design variants.

Our future work includes further refinement of the TalkMake workshop (both the instructional materials and the material kits). We are particularly excited by the possibility of employing the recently-released Raspberry Pi Zero model in the place of the Raspberry Pi B+ model, which has the potential to reduce the per-unit cost by half. We plan to continue mounting the TalkMake workshop, both locally and, possibly, in an international setting. Last, we plan to pursue the further iterative development and testing of Hot Swappable TalkBox with our community partner.

Acknowledgements. The authors gratefully acknowledge the valuable contributions of our colleague, Ray Feraday, the many student members of the "Devices 4 Disabilities" student club at York University, and Glenn Barnes, Ontario Coordinator for the Tetra Society of North America. The TalkBox units produced in this project were funded by the Tetra Society of North America and the project was funded, in part, by an internal grant provided by York University.

References

1. Baljko, M., Hamidi, F.: Knowledge co-creation and assistive technology. Sch. Res. Commun. **5**(3), 1–19 (2014). Article ID 0301162
2. Crabtree, A., Hemmings, T., Rodden, T., Cheverst, K., Clarke, K., Dewsbury, G., Hughes, J., Rouncefield, M.: Designing with care: adapting cultural probes to inform design in sensitive settings. In: Proceedings of the 2004 Australasian Conference on Computer-Human Interaction, pp. 4–13 (2004)
3. Dawe, M.: "Let me show you what I want": engaging individuals with cognitive disabilities and their families in design. In: CHI 2007 Extended Abstracts on Human Factors in Computing Systems, pp. 2177–2182. ACM (2007)
4. Hamidi, F., Baljko, M., Kunic, T., Feraday, R.: Do-It-Yourself (DIY) assistive technology: a communication board case study. In: Miesenberger, K., Fels, D., Archambault, D., Peňáz, P., Zagler, W. (eds.) ICCHP 2014, Part II. LNCS, vol. 8548, pp. 287–294. Springer, Heidelberg (2014)
5. Hook, J., Verbaan, S., Durrant, A., Olivier, P., Wright, P.: A study of the challenges related to DIY assistive technology in the context of children with disabilities. In: Proceedings of the 2014 Conference on Designing Interactive Systems, pp. 597–606. ACM (2014)
6. Hurst, A., Kane, S.: Making making accessible. In: Proceedings of the 12th International Conference on Interaction Design and Children, pp. 635–638. ACM (2013)
7. Hurst, A., Tobias, J.: Empowering individuals with Do-It-Yourself assistive technology. In: Proceedings of the 13th International ACM SIGACCESS Conference on Computers and Accessibility, pp. 11–18. ACM (2011)
8. Ladner, R.E.: Design for user empowerment. Interactions **22**(2), 24–29 (2015)
9. Moffatt, K., McGrenere, J., Purves, B., Klawe, M.: The participatory design of a sound and image enhanced daily planner for people with aphasia. In: Proceedings of SIGCHI Conferecne on Human Factors in Computing Systems, pp. 407–414. ACM (2004)
10. Wu, M., Baecker, R., Richards, B.: Participatory design of an orientation aid for amnesics. In: Proceedings of the SIGCHI Conference on Human Factors in Computing Systems, pp. 511–520. ACM (2005)
11. YFile: Lassonde team wins top prize at Toronto Mini Maker Faire (2014). http://bit.ly/1RsPhII. Accessed 9 Dec 2014

Supported Employment –
Electronic Job-Coach (EJO)

Carsten Brausch[1], Christian Bühler[2]([⊠]), Andreas Feldmann[2],
and Miriam Padberg[2]

[1] Landschaftsverband Rheinland, Cologne, Germany
carsten.brausch@lvr.de
[2] Research Cluster Technology for Inclusion and Participation (TIP),
Rehabilitation Technology, TU Dortmund University, Dortmund, Germany
{christian.buehler,andreas.feldmann,miriam.padberg}@tu-dortmund.de

Abstract. Currently there is a lack of software solutions available which
are tailored to the needs of people with acquired brain injuries at the
work place. Therefore, an application for mobile devices called Electronic
Job Coach (EJO) is proposed to support different cognitive challenges
which occur especially during the work like e.g. short term memory which
results in difficulties in remembering the work process or the use of tools.
EJO uses a client server architecture for mobile devices. The first prototype is introduced and a short impression the further work process is
presented. EJO is a joint activity of the technical advisory service of the
LVR - Integrationsamt (Integration Agency - IA) and the TU Dortmund
University.

1 Introduction

1.1 Disability and Work Related Social Services

In Germany vocational participation of people with disabilities is traditionally seen as a very important aspect of social inclusion. Social services provide
advice to employers and employees to create a good match and provide financial support for the appropriate arrangements. In North Rhine-Westfalia the two
"Landschaftsverbände" LVR and LWL play a major role for this services. In this
context supported employment is a concept to facilitate participation of persons
with disability in the first labour market [1]. Besides workplace adaptations,
reorganisation of work and training, assistance at the workplace is provided.

1.2 The Technical Advisory Service of the "LVR - Integrationsamt" (Integration Agency - IA)

The function of the Agency of Labour LVR-IA based on SGB IX (German Social
Legislation Book IX) and reinforced by the UN-CRPD [2] is to facilitate and
sustainably secure the participation of individuals with severe disability at work.

K. Miesenberger et al. (Eds.): ICCHP 2016, Part I, LNCS 9758, pp. 142–149, 2016.
DOI: 10.1007/978-3-319-41264-1_20

It is the goal of LVR-IA to advise and equip people with disabilities at work creating a good match with the work requirements leading to independence at the workplace as far as possible. Therefore, the technical advisory service of LVR-IA constitutes an important advice offering for employers and people with severe disabilities.

The daily experience of technical advisers show that people with cognitive problems e.g. during assembly tasks frequently have to ask colleagues, because they forget the context. This is displeasing and it is often avoided – leading to errors and conflicts. An Electronic Job-Coach could provide the required information context of the task and be a great support in such situations. In this context the services have also the potential to initiate research and development for innovative solutions. The use of modern technology in combination with other measures play an important role. The potential of Information and Communication Technology (ICT) has been employed for workplace adaptation widely and the use of ICT based assistance is another field of interest with great potential of support. The LVR-IA therefore decided to finance and carry out a pilot project in cooperation with TU Dortmund University called "EJO".

1.3   Background and Idea of the Electronic Job-Coach (EJO)

Since a couple of years computer based assistive technology (CB-AT) is used successfully in (tele-)rehabilitation of patients with acquired brain injury [3] as well as supporting daily life activities [4]. However, technology solutions especially to provide people with brain injury to return to the work-place and maintain employment remain scarce [5]. On the other hand often personal assistance is needed. Therefore, many of those people work in sheltered environments and not in the first labour market. Supported employment is a concept which tries to overcome barriers to the first labour market. Often the services are provided during the start phase in a new job. Job-coaches help with the setup, the provisional training and handling of starting problems. However they can't provide continuous assistance at the working place. Here, the idea of the Electronic Job-Coach comes into play: Even if not continuously available at the work place the job-coaches can leave assistance by electronic means and communication options. Modern mobile devices and the great outcome of CB-AT for task scheduling in rehabilitation and daily life activities provide a high assistance potential: applications for mobile devices supporting individuals with ABI in their daily working life, based on the "state of the art" of technology and accessible according to WAI-WCAG [6] and BITV [7].

Therefore the project EJO was started as a pilot project to prove the feasibility of such a concept. Due to the high variety of abilities of persons with acquired brain injury (ABI) a user-centered design is an essential element of the implementation of CB-AT for individuals with ABI [8] and has been adopted in EJO.

2   EJO Approach

2.1   The Target Group – Cognitive Abilities of Individuals with ABI

The functional abilities of persons with ABI are of high variance, both in the degree of severity as well as in the nature of injury. In conformity to [5], the following classification in terms of the ICF [9] with possible effects on cognition performance are typical for persons with ABI:

- Orientation functions (b114), especially orientation to time (b1140) and orientation to place (b1141)
  Persons with ABI often forget appointments or have difficulties in directional orientation leading to misdirection.
- Energy and drive functions (b130), particularly energy level (b1300) and motivation (b1301), also attention functions (b140), particularly sustaining attention (b1400) and shifting attention (b1401)
  A lack of incentive to act, problems in conscious or unconscious driving force for action, a reduction of stamina and a high level of distractibility often leads to inability to take up an activity.
- Memory functions (b144), especially short-term memory (b1440) and retrieval of memory (b1442)
  Individuals with ABI often have difficulties in remembering work processes and learning new contents as well as simply forgetting important information, dates and appointments.
  Mental functions of recalling information like work processes, the functionality and the use of tools, information about a person, as well as problems to express the own thoughts and the ability to promote tools in a different context are characteristics of persons with functional limitations in this field.
- Thought functions (b160), particularly pace of thought (b1600) and form of thought (b1601)
  Individuals with ABI often have a reduced speed of thinking in general, leading to trouble understanding the contents and meanings of other persons and difficulties to express the own thoughts and feelings.
- Higher-level cognitive functions (b164), especially abstraction (b1640), organization and planning (b1641) and time management (b1642)
  Patients with brain injury especially in the frontal lobes of the brain show limitations in decision-making, abstract thinking and carrying out plans.
  They are often unable to use tools in a manner than usual and having a lack in time management, so they cannot estimate the time of an activity. Often an activity is carried out without having necessary materials.
- Mental functions of language (b167), particularly reception of language (b1670) and expression of language (b1671)
  Indicated by a lack of reception and decryption of spoken or written language, persons with ABI often misunderstand explanations and issued instructions.

In order to overcome these limitations several different approaches were developed in the field of CB-AT. In addition to customized calendars and notes, positive feedback, to-do-lists, step-by-step instructions, checklists, voice recorders and reminders, the use of multimedia and indoor-navigation systems are the most successful developments in CB-AT for individuals with ABI [4,10].

2.2 Main Ideas and Key Features of the EJO Prototype

The great outcome of CB-AT in rehabilitation and for activity of daily living was attributable to the adaption to resources and know-how of a user [3]. Hence a user-centered design is an essential element of EJO. In order to adapt EJO to different limitations and requirements different presentations on the graphical user interface and the clear visualisation of multimedia contents are key features of EJO, such as

– graphics, e.g. exploded drawings of structural elements,
– videos, e.g. instruction videos for visualisation of a working process,
– text, e.g. checkpoint-lists, manuals and data sheets of work pieces,
– audio, e.g. important information recorded by the personal job-coach.

Classical CB-AT for rehabilitation like electronic memory aids, personal data assistants and electronic diaries are in use to compensate cognitive impairments like planning and organization during every-day workplace life [4], a main idea of EJO is to furnishing them together in a mobile application and expand the functionality regarding to the needs of an end-user at the respective workplace. To reduce stigmatization no special AT hardware is used: EJO uses commercially available technology with growing popularity as the basis hardware, more precisely smartphones and tablets (Android and iOS).

Based on fundamental concepts and functions of CB-AT, oriented towards applications for scheduling tasks like "Visual Schedule Planner" [11], "First Then Visual Schedule HD" [12] and "Marti" [13], the general requirements and key features of EJO can be summarised as follows:

– barrier-free user interface, this means EJO must follow adjustments in the four principles of accessibility: perceptibility, operability, robustness and understandability.
– multi-modal representation of information,
– intuitive operability and implementation in accordance to developer guidelines of Google and Apple,
– supply of context-sensitive help,
– portability and modular design for use with different mobile devices,
– openness in form of a free available web-service for other applications of co-operation partners,
– usability is ensured for a wide range of users,
– full administrative functionality, i.e. supporting the creation and administration of tasks, user accounts etc.

2.3 Software Architecture and Applied Technology

Figure 1 shows a typical client-server model. The Electronic Job-Coach is used by the employee and job-coach on a smartphone or tablet, which communicates via an internet connection e.g. WiFi with a web-service on the server-side.

This client itself is an Android or iOS application, but is developed with a cross-platform approach. It is not constructed as native application using the specific technology of the mobile platform like the Android or iOS-SDK. Instead the application is based on the Ionic Framework [14], which allows to develop mobile applications with HTML5, CSS3 and JavaScript. This offers the possibility to develop a barrier-free website considering the WAI-WCAG 2.0 and BITV 2.0 as required in Sect. 2.2.

Furthermore Ionic rests upon Cordova [15] and AngularJS [16]. The former allows the application to use native functions of the mobile platform like the camera, vibration, the file system and many more. The latter is a modern JavaScript framework, developed by Google Inc. and based on a model-view-view-model pattern, for constructing the whole application. With the cross-platform approach, it is possible to build the Electronic Job-Coach for the required mobile platforms just with one code base and the same set of skills of the developers. The produced application nearly has the look and feel of a native application, but the content is just wrapped in an operating system specific web-view.

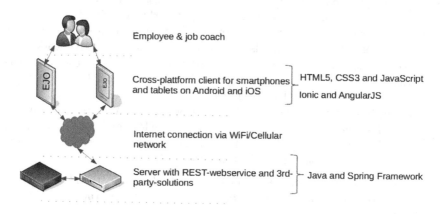

Fig. 1. Overview of the software architecture and applied technology

As mentioned before the client communicates with a web-service. This web-service is based on REST (representational state transfer) [17], which is a programming paradigm for distributed systems and is heavily based on the HTTP-protocol [18]. The delivered information is represented in JSON (JavaScript Object Notation) [19], which perfectly fits to the Java Script framework AngularJS.

The whole concept of the REST-web-service suits the required openness of the whole system (see Sect. 2.2) for other applications. However, the server does not only provide a REST-web-service. With the Java framework Spring [20] this server also allows to integrate third-party solutions of companies, e.g. ERP-systems (enterprise resource planning) [21,22], because Spring and corresponding Spring projects offers a wide range of functionality to establish a data exchange.

3   Current Status and Future Work

To specify user interface demands, mockups for smartphone and tablet were designed. Figure 2 shows on the left side a smartphone mockup showing a certain step of a work procedure A with different types of media for explaining the step in tabs and some control elements at the bottom. The user can choose between a plain text description, a picture, an audio and a video. With the control elements the user is able to (described from left to right) move a step backward, call for help, pause the task or move a step forward. Figure 2 shows on the right side the mockup for the landing page of the tablet. It is an overview of all possible tasks, but sorted by the state of the task which is also indicated by the typical colours of a traffic light system. The view allows the user to retrieve information about a task, start a task or to create a task. The last two actions would result in a different view. After a phase of evaluating the mockups in a team of advisors and member of social services, a first prototype of EJO was implemented and is available for end-users for tablet and mobile. The structure of the functional prototypes in Fig. 3 is similar to mockups shown before. In order to adapt the functionality in accordance to the requirements of an individual end-user, different degrees of complexity of handling the application were implemented. If the overview of the tablet is too complicated the application can be configured only to show the appropriate task or even the appropriate step.

Fig. 2. A mockup of the smartphone for certain step and a mockup of the tablet with an overview for all tasks

Fig. 3. View of step in the smartphone prototype view of landing page in the tablet prototype

It is also possible to display only the media preferred by the user, e.g. if user prefers images the prototype just shows the image and combines this with a short explanation of the step by text-to-speech.

However, detailed tests with end-users are necessary in order to meet the requirements according to the guidelines of user-centered design. The first tests are performed in the context of household service, e.g. the task of setting a table.

After detailed prototype tests and improvement of the prototype, different tasks with various complexity will be added to the EJO system. The development of training concepts is another important issue in the further development of EJO as well as the implementation of administration functions.

3.1 Conclusions

The potential to support people with disabilities by the EJO system has led to high expectations. Yet, the prototypes need to be expanded and evaluated with different tasks. A particular issue is the flexibility and the usability of the system including the administration of the system. The expansion for more individual users and other user groups like persons with mental handicap is a long-term goal.

References

1. Kamp, M., Lynch, C., Haccou, R.: Handbook Supported Employment. World Association for Supported Employment, International Labour Organsiation (2013). http://www.wase.net/handbookSE.pdf
2. United Nations: Conventions on the Rights of Persons with Disabilites and Optional Protocol (2013). http://www.un.org/disabilities/documents/convention/convoptprot-e.pdf
3. Cole, E.: Patient-centered design of cognitive assistive technology for traumatic brain injury telerehabilitation. Synth. Lect. Assistive Rehabilitative Health-Preserving Technol. 2(1), 1–159 (2013). Morgan and Claypool Publishers
4. Rispoli, M., Machalicek, W., Lang, R.: Assistive technology for people with acquired brain injury. In: Lancioni, G.E., Singh, N.N. (eds.) Assistive Technologies for People with Diverse Abilities, pp. 21–52. Springer, New York (2014)
5. Artman, L.K., McMahon, B.T.: Functional limitations in TBI and their relationship to job maintenance following work re-entry. J. Vocat. Rehabil. 39, 13–21 (2013)
6. World Wide Web Consortium: Web Content Accessibility Guidelines (WCAG) 2.0 (2008)
7. Verordnung zur Schaffung barrierefreier Informationstechnik nach dem Behindertengleichstellungsgesetz 2.0 (2011)
8. Cole, E.: Patient-centered design: interface personalization for individuals with brain injury. In: Stephanidis, C. (ed.) Universal Access in HCI, Part II, HCII 2011. LNCS, vol. 6766, pp. 291–300. Springer, Heidelberg (2011)
9. World Health Organisation: International Classification of Functioning (2001). http://www.who.int/classifications/icf/icf_more/en/
10. Scherer, M.: Assistive Technologies and Other Supports for People with Brain Impairment. Springer Publishing Company, New York (2012)
11. Good Karma Applications Inc.: Visual Schedule Planner (2009). http://www.goodkarmaapplications.com/visual-schedule-planner1.html
12. Good Karma Applications Inc.: First Then Visual Schedule HD (2010). http://www.goodkarmaapplications.com/ftvshd-first-then-hd.html
13. Infologique Innovation Inc.: Marti (2011). http://www.marti.mobi
14. Drifty: The Ionic Frontend-Framework (2015). (http://ionicframework.com/)
15. Adobe Systems: Apache Cordova (2015). https://cordova.apache.org/docs/en/latest/guide/overview/
16. Google Inc.: AngularJS. https://angularjs.org/
17. Fielding, R.T., Taylor, R.: Principled design of the modern web architecture. ACM Trans. Internet Technol. (TOIT) 2(2), 115–150 (2002)
18. Fielding, R.T.: Architectural Styles and the Design of Network-Based Software Architecture. Disseration at the University of California, Irvine. Chapter 5 (2000)
19. ECMA International: The JSON Data Interchange Format (2013). http://www.ecma-international.org/publications/files/ECMA-ST/ECMA-404.pdf
20. SpringSource: Spring Framework. https://spring.io/
21. Wylie, L.: A vision of the next-generation MRP II, Gartner Group 40 (1990)
22. Jacobs, F.R.: Enterprise resource planning (ERP) a brief history. J. Oper. Manage. 25(2), 357–363 (2007)

Mobile Apps and Platforms

Mobile Apps and Platforms

Introduction to the Special Thematic Session

Marion Hersh[1(✉)] and Alireza Darvishy[2]

[1] Biomedical Engineering, University of Glasgow, Glasgow G12 8LT, Scotland
marion.hersh@glasgow.ac.uk
[2] Accessibility Lab, Institute for Applied Information Technologies,
Zurich University for Applied Sciences, 8400 Winterthur, Switzerland
dvya@zhaw.ch

Abstract. This short paper presents five papers discussing accessibility, usability and other end-user issues related to mobile apps for disabled people. The papers include experimental investigations, end user-interviews and end-user questionnaires on particular technologies, including new prototypes, and the development of guidelines. End-user groups included frail older people, people with cognitive impairments and visually impaired people. They are introduced by a brief discussion of mobile apps potential, accessibility and usability.

Keywords: Accessibility · Usability · Mobile apps · Design · End-user issues

1 Introduction

Mobile devices are becoming increasingly popular. Mobile phone penetration was on average 111.26 % in Europe in 2007 and smart phone ownership is predicted to be 64.7 % in western Europe in 2017 [1]. Mobile phone ownership is also significant in the majority world (developing) countries. These factors all show the technology's potential, including for mobile assistive devices for disabled and older people. For instance, smart phones have a number of features, including a camera, GPS, accelerometers, magnetometer and gyroscope sensors for localisation, wide bandwidth speaker, high quality directional microphone, 3G, WiFi and Bluetooth and low power consumption, which make them suited to travel, data collection and processing and other assistive applications [2–4]. Mobile devices such as smart phones and tablets are also modern general use products with a positive image [4] unlike the stigma associated with many assistive devices [5].

However, the very factors i.e. very small size and multi-functionality that make mobile devices attractive by making them easily portable and enabling them to be used at any time and place, can lead to accessibility and usability barriers, particularly to disabled and older people. Mobility and small size result in reduced memory and processing speed, and the need for batteries to be regularly recharged [6], and small, relatively difficult to see or feel screens, keyboards and pointers. Screen size has been considered in a disciplinary context [], but not as a wider accessibility issue with implications for use by disabled and older people. Recognition of the importance of user-centred design and awareness of the context of use [7, 8] may be particularly relevant in avoiding accessibility and usability problems for disabled people.

2 Accessibility, Usability and Evaluation Criteria

Operating systems such as iOS and Android offer many built-in accessibility features [9]. There were many different apps, for instance over half a million apps for the iOS Apple operating system in 2011 [10]. There has been some consideration of app accessibility and usability, though mainly for particular applications, such as the usability of mobile passenger information systems [11] or mobile health apps [12], or particular groups of disabled people e.g. aphasic [13] and autistic people [14]. A study of several mobile learning projects [6] identified four main categories of usability issues, which are also relevant to other mobile applications: physical attributes (e.g. size, weight, memory, battery life), content and software applications, network speed and reliability, and the physical environment. Mobile devices are often used in unpredictable real-world circumstances to which participants responded constructively, but not in ways that could easily be fed back to inform the technology design [15].

A list of six criteria for the evaluation of apps has been developed, covering the relevance of the app functionality to the user's needs, feedback, adjustability (personalisation), ease of use, cost and benefits [16]. The other five criteria relate to general evaluation, but the first one is user specific. It also indicates the need for clear information about what the app does to allow users to make informed choices. Detailed recommendations for the development of apps are lacking, but brief recommendations have been provided for user acceptance of advanced traveller information systems, including designing for the 95th or 98th percentile rather than the 'average' user to take the needs of disabled users into account; the use of solutions in different sensory modalities; clear simple designs; direct easy-to-access information systems; and solutions which allow all users to travel more independently and purposefully [17].

3 Session Papers

The session consists of five papers which discuss the accessibility and usability issues of different types of mobile apps for different groups of disabled end-users. The papers include experimental investigations, end user-interviews and end-user questionnaires on particular technologies, including new prototypes, and the development of guidelines. The end-user groups considered include frail older people, people with cognitive impairments and visually impaired people.

Working with frail elderly EVA users to determine ways to support agency in single switch connectivity with mobile technologies; L. Kwok, M. Whitefield, S. Fels-Leung, M. Meza and D.I. Fels, Komodo OpenLabs and Ryerson University, Canada reports interviews with two frail older people on the potential of the Tecla Shield (an assistive technology using a single switch to access touch screens and control smart phones and tablets) to support them. They thought the new version (EVA) might give them increased control over devices and reduce their need for assistance, but were concerned about the size, mounting system, and need for additional learning. The authors plan further user studies to determine whether EVA is usable, can be customised and provides appropriate functions for frail older people, as well as the impact of its use on users' sense of agency, control and well being.

Cognitive accessibility to mobile ICTl: ETSI STF 488, Martin Böcker (BMWi, Germany), Niolaos Floratos, ANEC, Europe, Loïc Martinez (Universidad Politécnica de Madrid, Spain), Mike Pluke (Castle Computing Ltd., UK), Bruno Von Niman (Vonniman Consulting SG, Sweden) and Gill Whitney (Middlesex University, UK) discusses the work of the STF 488 team of experts of the European Telecommunications Standards Institute (ETSI) on determining the user needs of people with cognitive impairments for mobile devices and applications, and producing guidelines for the development of accessible mobile ICT for this group. 28 user needs have been identified, divided into 11 categories, with several categories covering communication of different types, and others decision making, memory and undertaking tasks. The guideline structure follows that of the Europe Standard on accessible ICT. However, there does not seem to have been any direct end-user involvement in the work.

The other three papers concern technology for visually impaired people, namely smartphones, colour detection and smart glasses. Can visually impaired smartphone users correctly manipulate tiny screen keyboards under a screen reader condition? Takashi O-hasia, Takahiro Miura, Masatsugu Sakajiri, Junji ONishi and Tsukasa Ono, Tsukuba University of Technology and University of Tokyo, Japan discusses an investigation of the ability of blind and partially sighted people to find touchscreen buttons for different sizes and numbers of buttons using an experimental touch screen application. Despite significant differences between the responses of blind and partially sighted participants they are not discussed separately. 10 pixels was found to be the minimal acceptable size, with a significant increase in errors for smaller buttons. Inexperienced participants with touch screens found fewer, large buttons easier to use, whereas experienced ones preferred more, smaller buttons as easier to use. Considerable further investigation with larger numbers of end-users is still required.

Towards a natural user interface to support people with visual impairments in detecting colours, Sergio Mascetti, Chiara Rossetti, Andrea Gerino, Christian Bernareggi, Lorenzo Picinali and Alessandra Rizza, Università degli Studi di Milano, Italy and Imperial College, UK presents the preliminary prototype of an app called JustPoint which recognises a ring worn on one finger. This is a preliminary stage in the development of a mobile app which recognises the user's finger and the colour that it is pointing to and describes it to the user. This app is intended to overcome the difficulties experienced by blind users in pointing at the target item when using colour identification apps. However, it may not fully resolve the problem, since it will give the colour of the item the user is pointing at, but this may not be the intended item.

What do low-vision users really want from smart glasses? Faces, text and perhaps no glasses at all, Froide Erika Sadnes, Oslo and Akershus University College of Applied Sciences, Norway reports on a study of the functionality of interest to people with low vision involving three semistructured interviews. Facial recognition followed by text recognition, particularly on moving vehicles, were the most important issues, since they were able to photograph stationary text to enlarge it. There was little interest in smart glasses and augmented vision. However, further research involving a large number of end-users will be required to confirm the results.

References

1. http://www.statista.com/statistics/203722/smartphone-penetration-per-capita-in-western-europe-since-2000/
2. Doughty, K.: SPAs (smart phone applications) - a new form of assistive technology. J. Assist. Technol. **5**(2), 88–94 (2011)
3. Kothari, N., Kannan, B., Glasgow, E.D., Dias, M.B.: Robust indoor localization on a commercial smart phone. Procedia Comput. Sci. **10**, 1114–1120 (2012)
4. Pauca, V.P., Guy, R.T.: Mobile apps for the greater good: a socially relevant approach to software engineering. In: Proceedings of the 43rd ACM Technical Symposium on Computer Science Education, pp. 535–540 (2012)
5. Hersh, M.A.: Deafblind people, stigma and the use of communication and mobility assistive devices. Technol. Disabil. **25**(4), 245–261 (2014)
6. Kukulska-Hulme, A.: Mobile usability in educational contexts: what have we learnt! Int. Rev. Res. Open Distance Learn. 8(2) (2007)
7. Evans, D., Taylor, J.: The role of user scenarios as the central piece of the development jigsaw puzzle. In: Attewell, J., Savill-Smith, C. (eds.) Mobile Learning Anytime Everywhere: Papers from MLEARN 2004 (2005)
8. Malliou, E., Miliarakis, A.: The MOTFAL project. Mobile technologies for ad hoc learning. In: Attewell, J., Savill-Smith, C. (eds.) Mobile Learning Anytime Everywhere: Papers from MLEARN 2004 (2005)
9. Darvishy, A.: Accessibility of mobile platforms. In: Marcus, A. (ed.) DUXU 2014, Part IV. LNCS, vol. 8520, pp. 133–140. Springer, Heidelberg (2014)
10. Walker, H.: Evaluating the effectiveness of apps for mobile devices. J. Spec. Educ. Technol. **26**(4), 59–63 (2011)
11. Beul-Leusmann, S., Samsel, C., Wiederhold, M., Krempels, K.-H., Jakobs, E.-M., Ziefle, M.: Usability evaluation of mobile passenger information systems. In: Marcus, A. (ed.) DUXU 2014, Part I. LNCS, vol. 8517, pp. 217–228. Springer, Heidelberg (2014)
12. Zapata, B.C., Fernández-Alemán, J.L., Idri, A., Toval, A.: Empirical studies on usability of mHealth apps: a systematic literature review. J. Med. Syst. **39**(2), 1–19 (2015)
13. Brandenburg, C., Worrall, L., Rodriguez, A.D., Copland, D.: Mobile computing technology and aphasia. Aphasiology **27**(4), 444–461 (2013)
14. Khan, S., Tahir, M.N., Raza, A.: Usability issues for smartphone users with special needs – Autism. In: IEEE International Conference on Open Source Systems and Technologies, pp. 107–113 (2013)
15. Kukulska-Hulme, A.: Human factors and innovation with mobile devices. In: Hansson, T. (ed.) Handbook of Research on Digital Information Technologies, pp. 392–403. IGI Global, Hershey (2008)
16. Buckler, T., Peterson, M.: Is there an app for that? Developing an evaluation rubric for apps for use with adults with special needs (2012). http://kansasmedicineandscience.kumc.edu/xmlui/bitstream/handle/2271/1095/JBSNR-2012-Buckler-IsThereAnApp.pdf?sequence=1. Accessed 22 Jan 2016
17. Geehan, T., Suen, L.: User acceptance of advanced traveler information systems for elderly and disabled travellers in Canada. In: Proceedings of the IEEE-IEE Vehicle Navigation and Information Systems Conference, pp. 389–392 (1993)

Can Visually Impaired Smartphone Users Correctly Manipulate Tiny Screen Keyboards Under a Screen Reader Condition?

Takashi Ohashi[1]([✉]), Takahiro Miura[2], Masatsugu Sakajiri[1], Junji Onishi[1], and Tsukasa Ono[1]

[1] Faculty of Health Science, Tsukuba University of Technology,
4-12-7 Kasuga, Tsukuba, Ibaraki 305-8521, Japan
`ot153202@cc.k.tsukuba-tech.ac.jp`,
{`sakajiri,ohnishi,ono`}`@cs.k.tsukuba-tech.ac.jp`
[2] Institute of Gerontology, The University of Tokyo,
7-3-1 Hongo, Bunkyo-ku, Tokyo 113-8656, Japan
`miu@iog.u-tokyo.ac.jp`

Abstract. Accessibility functions on touchscreen computers improved user experience of people with visual impairments. Regardless of this situation, they have some problems using touchscreen interfaces including smartphones and tablets. The reason includes the arrangements of accessible objects may differ for visually impaired users because of the manipulations under screen readers are different from those without screen readers, the characteristics of desired object sizes and arrangements on the touchscreen computers for the visually impaired remain unclear. The purpose of this research is to find a way for the visually impaired to accurately and efficiently manipulate the keyboard. This study especially seeks to find the optimum conditions for the number and sizes of buttons (including the area) for the visually impaired. For this purpose, we developed an experimental application.

Keywords: Visually impaired people · Smartphone · Software keyboard · Screen reader

1 Introduction

As touch screens on smart phones and tablets have become more prevalent, increasing number of visually impaired people are using them. Due to the fact that these devices have few hardware switches and tactile feedback, accessibility features are being introduced for the visually impaired. The most common features are VoiceOver [3] for iOS and TalkBack [4] for Android.

Apple also provides an application design guideline for visually impaired iOS users [5]. Applications developed along this guideline are accessible to visually impaired people using VoiceOver. Leporini et al. and Wong et al. reported on the usage situations for Italian and American visually impaired

© Springer International Publishing Switzerland 2016
K. Miesenberger et al. (Eds.): ICCHP 2016, Part I, LNCS 9758, pp. 157–164, 2016.
DOI: 10.1007/978-3-319-41264-1_21

users using VoiceOver, respectively [6,7]. Montague et al. investigated user situations for those with visual and motor impairments [9]. Kane reported preferable gestures in some cases by American visually impaired people [8]. They proposed guidelines for touchscreen interfaces for visually impaired users based on their results. Oliveira et al. presented the different demands about the various text entry methods of touchscreen display in visually impaired people [10]. Miura et al. investigated touchscreen computers usage and interaction situations for the Japanese visually impaired population [11].

Based on the improvements of accessibility functions and the accumulation of user situations, visually impaired persons can comfortably use the accessibility features to operate touch devices. However, totally blind people find it difficult to locate the target object on some screen layouts. Miura et al. studied the time it takes to find a single button that is randomly placed on a screen for different button sizes and placement [1]. The study showed that it took the shortest amount of time to locate the button when it was placed in the center of the touch screen. Miura et al. also reported the time necessary to find a button and the correct response rate when 4, 12, or 20 buttons were randomly placed one-dimensionally and two-dimensionally on a screen [2]. They found that when buttons were randomly placed, more time was required to find the button as the number of buttons increased but the correct response rate did not vary greatly. Our study was conducted on a limited number of buttons but it is inferred that there is a limit on the number of buttons that allow simple usage of touch screens.

At the same time, when people, including the visually impaired, use touch screens, many systematically placed buttons, such as calendars and keyboards, allow users to predict where the buttons are located. Nowadays, when using touch screens to communicate through applications such as LINE or Facebook, keyboard input is essential. Keyboard input requires an accurate and efficient selection of systematically placed buttons.

The purpose of this research is to find a way for the visually impaired to accurately and efficiently manipulate the keyboard. This study especially seeks to find the acceptable and optimum conditions for the number and sizes of buttons (including the area) for the visually impaired. For this purpose, we developed an experimental application.

2   Experimental Method on Suitability of Button Placement

2.1   Participants

Seven visually impaired participants (six males and one female, aged 20 to 22) took part in the experiment. Among the seven participants, four participants were totally blind (with experience using VoiceOver), and three participants had slightly impaired vision (one person had been using VoiceOver for less than a year, and the other person had never used VoiceOver). All of their visual impairments were congenital. Four of them had been using a touch screen for over four years, two of them had used for a year or more and less than two years and one of them had never used one.

2.2 Method

We developed an experimental application for touch screens and studied the button accessibility for the number and size of buttons. Figure 1 shows the application screens for the experiment with the procedures. This application shows the: (1) Startup screen; (2) Input instruction screen; and (3) Input screen respectively. This application was developed on Xcode 6.3 and installed on an Apple iPhone 5s (OS: iOS 7.1).

The procedure was as follows: let the participants sit in a chair; have them hold the experimental terminals in their non-dominant hand; and ask them to use their dominant hand to slide it over the screen and search for the buttons. The experiment prohibited using flick motions to search.

The participants used the experimental application shown on Fig. 1 and repeated the same pattern ten times. There were two placement patterns for each number of buttons, which increased from 12 to 20, 30, and 50 with button sizes set to 100 %, 75 %, 50 %, 25 % and 10 % of the screen area, and repeated the process.

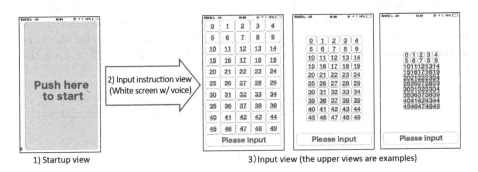

Fig. 1. Overview and flow of experiment application

2.3 Evaluation Items

For the evaluation, the application measured the time it took to find the button after entering the input screen and the correct response rate. We also interviewed the participants on the following items:

Daily Use of Touch Screen Devices: (1) Use. (2) Screen reader use. (3) Vision. (4) Type of devices. (5) Method of use (placing or holding). (6) Hand(s) they use to hold. (7) Frequently used operation motion.

About the Experiment: (1) Placement memory. (2) Learning effect. (3) Increased difficulty with increased number of buttons. (4) Increased difficulty with decreasing sizes of buttons. (5) Button accessibility for each of the 24 items. (6) Button accessibility as the number of buttons increased. (7) Button accessibility as the sizes of buttons decreased.

2.4   Method of Statistical Test

To test the response time and correct response rate in comparing categorical data, we implemented multiple comparisons of the Tukey-Kramer method after a one-way analysis of the variance. We used the single regression analysis to analyze each parameter according to response time when comparing quantitative data such as width and height of buttons, button area on the screen, and the number of buttons. The study also used the Stepwise method to judge a model by AIC multiple regression analysis when calculating the contribution rate of four parameters for response time and correct response rate. The effect size was calculated by Cohen's d. The study defined the significant difference as follows: $|d| < 0.2$: negligible, $|d| < 0.5$: small, $|d| < 0.8$: medium, $|d| > 0.8$: large.

3   Results and Discussion

3.1   Time It Takes to Press the Buttons and Correct Response Rate

Figure 2 shows the time it took to press the buttons. The error bars indicate standard error. It took more time to press the buttons as the number of buttons increased, but the correct response rate did not vary greatly. As for the sizes of buttons, four out of eight items showed that button sizes of 75 % took the least time.

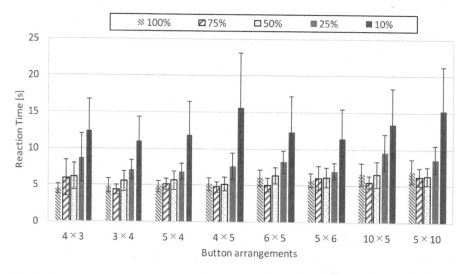

Fig. 2. Reaction time by the number of buttons and button size. The error bars represents standard error

The correct response rate dropped when sizes were at 10 %, but it did not vary considerably from 100 %, 75 %, 50 %, and 25 % where the correct response rate ranged between 92–100 %. When displaying 50 buttons with a size of 25 %, the correct answer rate was 98 %, showing that the rate did not decrease when the sizes of buttons decreased or the number of buttons increased.

However, when repeated enough times, learning effect may increase the correct response rate.

3.2 Results of Statistical Test

The results showed that there was a significant difference in the reaction time and correct response rate ($p < 0.001$) between the totally blind participants and others with slight visual impairments. However, the effect sizes $|d|$ on the correct response rate and the reaction time between the level of impairment are 0.71 (medium) and 0.24 (small), respectively. Regardless of its difference, the study does not discuss the difference between the two groups and uses the data from all participants together in the discussion for considering user interface conditions such as the number of buttons and button allocations.

When the button sizes of 10 % and 25 % were used, input time was greater in statistical significance when compared those of 50 %, 75 % and 100 % (for all conditions, $p < 0.001$, the level of effect $|d|$: 1.07 (large)). In addition, when comparing 10 % and 25 %, input time was greater in statistical significance when using 10 % ($p < 0.001$, $|d|$: 0.77 (medium)). Regarding the correct response rate, only the buttons at 10 % was significantly low to all other conditions (for all conditions, $p < 0.001$, the level of effect $|d|$: 2.20, large).

With regards to the number of buttons, when using 50 buttons, the experiment duration was greater in statistical significance compared to 12, 20 and 30 buttons ($p < 0.05$, $|d|$: 1.80 (large)). Regarding correct response rate, though there was no significant difference in the number of buttons, the rate decreased with the increasing number of buttons ($p > 0.10$, effect size $|d|$: 2.70 (large)).

There was no significant difference in input time for different placement patterns for when the number of buttons was 20, 30, and 50 ($p > 0.10$). On the other hand, when using 12 buttons in a 3×4 placement, there was a tendency for the input time to be significantly greater than with a 4×3 placement ($p = 0.048$). However, their effects were $|d| = 0.15 < 0.20$, which is negligible, so it is hard to state that the difference is significant. Correct response rate did not show statistical significances among all conditions ($p > 0.10$, $|d| < 0.20$ (negligible)).

There was another tendency that, when the size of buttons decreased in height and width (unit: pixel), input time was decreased in statistical significance (single regression analysis, $p < 0.001$). As for the correct response rate, below approximately 10 pixels was the threshold where less than that dramatically lowered the correct response rate. To determine the correlation between a button's height and width, the size of the button panel, and the number of buttons to input time and correct rate, the study used multi-regression analysis by using the Stepwise method with the AIC (Akaike's information criterion) judgement. It showed that the size of the button panel and the number of buttons were more significant than button height and width (significant difference of primary effect: $p < 0.001$). The significant difference was not confirmed in the interactions of these two variables ($p > 0.10$).

These results indicate that the area of the keyboard panel occupying the screen and the button placement within the screen influences the input speed on the VoiceOver keyboard input. However, the keyboard panel size does not show a significant difference, whether it is 50 % height and width or full-size. However, we discovered that, as shown in Fig. 3, button size may also be important to input the keys correctly. The results indicated that it was necessary that button sizes were larger than 10 pixels for the height and width. When either height or width was less than 10 pixels, the correct response rate dropped remarkably.

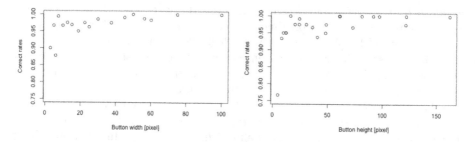

Fig. 3. Correct rates by the width (left) and height (right) of a button

3.3 Interview Results

Experience in Using Touch Screens. All the participants in the experiment had used touch screens before. Two of them were Android users, and four of them were iPhone users. Four of them had used a touch screen for over four years, and two of them had used one for a year or more and less than two years. As for the screen readers, six had used one for over three years, and one had used one for less than a year. Four participants were totally blind, and three participants had partial visual impairments.

All of them normally use the device by holding it in their hands; five of them slide their fingers on the screen and double tap, and two of them flick and double tap.

Response to the Experiment Conditions. In this experiment, because the number of buttons in the same button placement showed in the same order, the questionnaire asked whether participants memorized the button placement or not, and five of them said that they had memorized the button placement. The experiment may also have had a learning effect where all the participants answered that they quickly adapted as more tasks were performed.

The responses to the questions regarding button accessibility depending on the numbers and sizes of buttons were as follows. Participants with less experience in using touch screens responded that the increased number of buttons and smaller sizes of the buttons made it difficult to use; but, on the other hand, three out of the four participants with experience in using touch screens for over three years responded that this made it easier to use. This result indicated that the users can manipulate many buttons with increasingly comfort as their experience under a screen reading increased. In this experiment, the maximum number of buttons was 50 buttons. The question was then asked whether it would be easier to use if the number of buttons increased, and five participants agreed, while one disagreed. To another question asking whether the 25 % size was easy to use, three agreed, two were neutral, and one disagreed. For the 10 % size, all six participants disagreed.

4   Conclusion and Future Work

In this work, we investigated the acceptable conditions for the number and sizes of buttons (including the area) for visually impaired people in a screen reading condition. The results indicate the following:

- Participants performed significantly worse in input time and/or correct response rates in the conditions of button size: 10 % and 25 %, and the number of buttons: 50.
- There was no important difference in input time and correct response for different placement patterns for when all conditions of the number of buttons because there were significances in some conditions but these effect sizes were small or negligible.
- The area of the keyboard panel occupying the screen and the button placement within the screen mainly influence the input speed on the VoiceOver keyboard input.
- It was necessary that button sizes were larger than 10 pixels for the height and width. When either height or width was less than 10 pixels, the correct response rate dropped remarkably.
- Participants with less experience in using touchscreens responded that the increased number of buttons and smaller sizes of the buttons made it difficult to use; but, on the other hand, participants with experience in using touch screens for over three years tended to respond that this made it easier to use.

Our future work includes the similar evaluation to successive button interaction of the button arrangements in this study, implementation of variable sized software keyboard, and implementation and evaluation of tactile feedbacks on the button arrangements.

Acknowledgements. This work was partially supported by JSPS KAKENHI Grant Numbers 26285210, 15K04540, and 15K01015. We are also grateful to the students of the Tsukuba University of Technology for their great help.

References

1. Miura, T., Sakajiri, M., Eljailani, M., Matsuzaka, H., Onishi, J., Ono, T.: Accessible single button characteristics of touchscreen interfaces under screen readers in people with visual impairments. In: Miesenberger, K., Fels, D., Archambault, D., Peňáz, P., Zagler, W. (eds.) ICCHP 2014, Part I. LNCS, vol. 8547, pp. 369–376. Springer, Heidelberg (2014)

2. Miura, T., Ohashi, T., Sakajiri, M., Onishi, J., Ono, T.: Accessible button arrangements of touchscreens for visually impaired users. J. Technol. Persons Disabil. (2016, to appear)

3. Accessibility - iOS - VoiceOver - Apple. http://www.apple.com/accessibility/ios/voiceover/. Accessed 25 Mar 2016

4. Talkback - Google play. https://play.google.com/store/apps/details?id=com.google.android.marvin.talkback. Accessed 25 Mar 2016

5. Apple iOS Human Interface Guidelines. https://developer.apple.com/library/ios/documentation/UserExperience/Conceptual/MobileHIG/. Accessed 25 Mar 2016

6. Leporini, B., Buzzi, M.C., Buzzi, M.: Interacting with mobile devices via voiceover: usability and accessibility issues. In: Proceedings of the 24th Australian Computer-Human Interaction Conference, OzCHI 2012, pp. 339–348. ACM, New York (2012)

7. Wong, M.E., Tan, S.S.K.: Teaching the benefits of smart phone technology to blind consumers: exploring the potential of the iphone. J. Vis. Impair. Blind. **106**, 646–650 (2012)

8. Kane, S.K., Wobbrock, J.O., Ladner, R.E.: Usable gestures for blind people: understanding preference and performance. In: Proceedings of the SIGCHI Conference on Human Factors in Computing Systems, CHI 2011, pp. 413–422. ACM (2011)

9. Montague, K., Hanson, V.L., Cobley, A.: Designing for individuals: usable touchscreen interaction through shared user models. In: The Proceedings of the 14th International ACM SIGACCESS Conference on Computers and Accessibility, ASSETS 2012, pp. 151–158. ACM, New York (2012)

10. Oliveira, J., Guerreiro, T., Nicolau, H., Jorge, J., Gonccalves, D.: Blind people and mobile touch-based text-entry: acknowledging the need for different flavors. In: The Proceedings of the 13th International ACM SIGACCESS Conference on Computers and Accessibility. ASSETS 2011, pp. 179–186. ACM (2011)

11. Miura, T., Sakajiri, M., Matsuzaka, H., Eljailani, M., Kudo, K., Kitamura, N., Onishi, J., Ono, T.: Usage situation changes of touchscreen computers in Japanese visually impaired people: questionnaire surveys in 2011–2013. In: Miesenberger, K., Fels, D., Archambault, D., Peňáz, P., Zagler, W. (eds.) ICCHP 2014, Part I. LNCS, vol. 8547, pp. 360–368. Springer, Heidelberg (2014)

Working with Frail, Elderly EVA Users to Determine Ways to Support Agency in Single Switch Connectivity with Mobile Technologies

Lawrence Kwok[1], Margot Whitfield[2], Sander Fels-Leung[2],
Mauricio Meza[1], and Deborah Fels[2(✉)]

[1] Komodo OpenLabs, Toronto, Canada
lawrence.kwok@gmail.com, mauricio@kmo.do
[2] Ryerson University, Toronto, Canada
{margot.whitfield, sander.felsleung, dfels}@ryerson.ca

Abstract. Older adults, particularly the frail elderly, have limited communication support options other than those that have been designed for those with disabilities. The technologies supporting people with disabilities have traditionally relied on single-purpose, heavy and costly "made for the disabled" systems, most of which are outdated and designed to comply with byzantine funding frameworks instead of being designed around user needs. Some of these devices could be replaced by mobile apps and accessories at lower costs. The Tecla Shield, an assistive technology tool, has been designed to allow single-switch access to mobile devices, but frail elderly users were not considered in its development. The needs of frail elderly people may be considerably different than younger people, because communication and physical access to common devices such as televisions, lights and beds, may be more important to this user population. Two frail elderly people were interviewed about their needs for a device such as the Tecla Shield and how they may see using it within their current environment. These two individuals thought that the new version of the Tecla Shield, called EVA, would enable them to have more direct control over devices that they normally had to ask for assistance to use - enabling them to decide when and where they needed assistance, or not. However, concerns were expressed about the size and mounting system as well as the learning curve.

Keywords: Single switch · Assistive devices · Older technology users · Users with disabilities

1 Introduction

Older adults, particularly the frail elderly, have limited communication support options other than those that have been designed for those with disabilities. The technologies supporting people with disabilities have traditionally relied on single-purpose, heavy and costly "made for the disabled" systems, most of which are outdated and designed

© Springer International Publishing Switzerland 2016
K. Miesenberger et al. (Eds.): ICCHP 2016, Part I, LNCS 9758, pp. 165–170, 2016.
DOI: 10.1007/978-3-319-41264-1_22

to comply with byzantine funding frameworks instead of being designed around user needs. Some of these devices could be replaced by mobile apps and accessories at lower costs. Some single-switch users, however, experience difficulty accessing mobile solutions [4]. The Tecla Shield, an assistive technology tool, has been designed to allow single-switch access to mobile devices, but frail elderly users were not considered in its development. The needs of frail elderly people may be considerably different than younger people, because communication and physical access to common devices such as televisions, lights and beds, may be more important to this user population. In this paper we describe an initial needs analysis with two frail elderly Tecla Shield users and the ensuing development that was carried out to meet their needs. Our research focuses on creating a proof-of-concept system to leverage a state-of-the-art mobile device to provide simple access to communication, environmental controls and cognitive aids for older adults that are dependent on others for activities of daily living and are often in institutional care.

2 Background

There has been some prior work on smartphone application development to support the needs of frail elderly. For example, Medvedev et al. [5] created a Smartphone app that can be used to monitor physiological parameters over time. These measures included ECG, blood pressure, and heart rate. There are numerous other devices designed to monitor and measure various aspects of people's health [7], levels of frailty [3], cognitive states [2], and levels of risk for activities such as falling [9]. However, most of these apps are designed to monitor people rather than allowing them to interact with apps that they would like to use.

Other systems are either specialized devices (e.g., big Launcher http://biglauncher.com/ or ITT Easy5 (www.ahdistribution.com/Easy5_mobile_phone_for_the_elderly.html) or specialized interfaces/software that would alter the default smartphone interface to one that may be better suited to a specific user profile. For example, PhonAge [1] is designed to provide specialized apps for services such as emergency assistance as well as configure and order menus, icons and text displays to suit an older user. All of these solutions and systems are either using the touch screen technology that is part of the smartphone or tablet system or replacing it with other interface components such as physical buttons. What seems to be an important gap is the lack of support to allow users with limited hand control to access touch interface technology. They could then take advantage of mainstream apps and features of smartphone and/or tablets to their benefit or interest, or to have causal agency[1] over their smartphone use.

---

[1] Wehmeyer et al. [8] defines causal agency as "the individual who makes or causes things to happen in his or her life does so with an eye towards causing an effect to accomplish a specific end or to cause or create change" (p. 352).

3 System Description

The Tecla Shield by Komodo Openlab is an assistive device that enables individuals with limited mobility to access touch-screens and control smartphones and tablets (see https://gettecla.com/ for more information on the original Tecla Shield). Komodo has already developed the first two versions of a "switch interface" to access iOS and Android mobile devices (see Fig. 1 for an example setup with one user and iPad tablet running iOS) and has validated the impact and interest of users. Over a ten week period Komodo conducted quality assurance interviews with 24 users, clinicians and resellers of the current market version of Tecla Shield. The interviews generated a list of features and improvements that were desirable for the next Tecla (see Table 1).

Fig. 1. Tecla Shield version 1 single switch control system with iPad tablet and single switch (with permission from Komodo OpenLab)

Table 1. Hardware and software/interface features requested by users

Hardware	Software/interface
• Disambiguate the status lights • Provide a more robust housing for connection to switches • Implement Silent Mode	• Implement a system setup wizard • Develop switch control tutorials • Provide a consistent user experience • Provide customizable menus with redundancies to support basic-to-advanced users • Add connections to environmental controls • Add device switching • Design for independent use and use with assistance

The third version of the Tecla Shield, or EVA, attempts to resolve these identified issues. Also, it will allow frail elderly individuals with mobility impairments to gain access to state-of-the-art mobile devices and be enabled to do the following: communicate through phone, email, sms, and social media; access information (internet, eBooks, magazines, news, maps); and access leisure activities (music, movies) and other functionalities that in the past would require additional dedicated assistive devices (speech generation, camera, remote control). EVA includes device-specific connectivity so that users can select and define accessible switches, and mount and position EVA equipment. The interface is optimized using native Android libraries in a non-standard way in order to translate single-switch user input into wireless communication protocols and to device actions. Figure 2 provides a system level diagram of EVA.

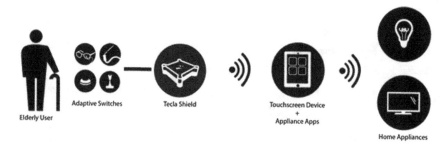

Fig. 2. Tecla EVA system diagram

4 Methodology

4.1 Research Questions

The following research questions will be addressed through this research:

1. What are the unique issues regarding Smartphone use and needs for frail elderly users?
2. What elements are required in order for EVA to meet the needs of frail elderly?

Using the theory of inclusive design [6], two frail elderly users were asked to give feedback regarding the setup of Tecla equipment and the end devices proposed for testing. They each have had over 100 h of use with the current Tecla Shield and were interviewed for about 30 min for their feedback.

5 Results

The first individual was well connected at home with multiple electronic devices in different rooms. She was very accustomed to being independent in some activities and requiring assistance for others. Her cat sometimes managed to disconnect her devices, leaving her stranded and without a way to call for assistance. She saw EVA as potentially being a way to have more direct control over devices/appliances that she would normally only be able to ask for assistance to use. Comments about EVA were that it was potentially interesting for bed use, because there was a greater desire for additional access to surrounding devices from bed using only one switch interface, compared to a wheelchair where different switch interfaces would be accessible in different locations of the house. She also thought that the term, 'agency' is preferred over independence because it means that she has the choice of when to call for assistance; sometimes she wants assistance and other times she does not.

The second user was part of a couple, where one person used the Tecla Shield and the other did not. The Tecla Shield was used mostly for email and Skype. The Tecla user's priority for the new system was to be able to make emergency calls quickly and effortlessly in case her partner had an accident, especially at night or in bed. However, she was concerned about the size of EVA, how and where it would be connected/mounted and how it could be accessed. She believed that the best locations for the system were either on her wheelchair, bed or in her den. Finally, she did not want EVA to be much different from the existing Tecla Shield because she did not want to spend much more time learning yet another technology.

6 Discussion and Impact

For this paper we set out to understand how the Tecla Shield could be developed further to specifically address the needs of frail and elderly users of adaptive switch technology. By combining quality assurance data and personal interviews, we learned that providing access through Tecla Shield to communication technology and basic appliances, such as lighting, potentially addresses the experience of dependence, helplessness and isolation. By designing a system that can sustain and expand user agency, we might be able to help users feel connected, engaged and in control of certain key activities without continually having to ask for assistance or change physical location. As such, EVA will act as a single switch interface that allows users to connect their existing adaptive switches to a single hub, so that they can switch from device to device, and activity to activity without changing physical location or asking for assistance.

The potential impact on design of single switch systems involves ensuring that the system can be easily and seamlessly be integrated with emergency call systems, existing technologies used by the individual and can enable agency by supporting independent use as well as assistance from others when desired. It is important to recognize that single switch users are often surrounded by technology that they are using and want to continue to use (e.g., television, telephones, computers, mobile technologies, etc.). Having to learn complicated new procedures that do not integrate with existing knowledge or technology use is undesirable and not recommended. Finally, support for care-givers, family members and others that interact with the individual is also crucial to the success of single switch design technologies. Developing training materials for care-givers and families, involving them in the integration and learning processes, and providing opportunities for this group of people to take advantage of the technology can also increase the adoption and use of single switch technologies by the single switch user.

Future work involves user studies with frail, elderly users to determine whether EVA meets the usability, customisation and use goals for this user population. In addition, we will study the impact that this technology has on a user's sense of agency, control and well-being.

7 Conclusion

Older adults, particularly the frail elderly, have had few options to support communication other than those that have been designed for others with disabilities. By using an existing assistive technology platform (Tecla Shield) to survey and explore the potential uses for the frail elderly, product development can integrate these uses and expand frail elderly access options to mainstream products.

Acknowledgements. We gratefully acknowledge the Canadian Frailty Network and the Business Innovation Access Program of the Industrial Research Assistance Program of Canada for funding this project. We also thank the single switch contributors to this project for being so generous with their time and effort with assisting in improving the Tecla Shield.

References

1. Abdulrazak, B., Malik, Y., Arab, F., Reid, S.: PhonAge: adapted smartphone for aging population. In: Biswas, J., Kobayashi, H., Wong, L., Abdulrazak, B., Mokhtari, M. (eds.) ICOST 2013. LNCS, vol. 7910, pp. 27–35. Springer, Heidelberg (2013)
2. Brouillette, R.M., Foil, H., Fontenot, S., Correro, A., Allen, R., Martin, C.K., Keller, J.N.: Feasibility, reliability, and validity of a smartphone based application for the assessment of cognitive function in the elderly. PLoS ONE 8(6), e65925 (2013). doi:10.1371/journal.pone.0065925
3. Fontecha, J., Hervás, R., Bravo, J., Navarro, F.J.: A mobile and ubiquitous approach for supporting frailty assessment in elderly people. J. Med. Internet. Res. 15(9), e197 (2013). doi:10.2196/jmir.2529
4. Jones, M., Grogg, K., Anschutz, J., Fierman, R.: A sip-and-puff wireless remote control for the Apple iPod. AT 20(2), 107–110 (2008)
5. Medvedev, O., Kobelev, A., Schookin, S., Jatskovsky, M., Markarian, G., Sergeev, I.: Smartphone-based approach for monitoring vital physiological parameters in humans. In: Magjarevic, R., Nagel, J.H. (eds.) World Congress on Medical Physics and Biomedical Engineering 2006, pp. 4020–4022. Springer, Berlin (2007)
6. Newell, A.F., Gregor, P., Morgan, M., Pullin, G., Macaulay, C.: User-sensitive inclusive design. UAIS 10(3), 235–243 (2011)
7. Rosser, B.A., Eccleston, C.: Smartphone applications for pain management. J. Telemedicine Telecare 7(6), 308–312 (2011)
8. Wehmeyer, M.L.: Beyond self-determination: causal agency theory. J. Dev. Phys. Disabil. 16(4), 337–359 (2004)
9. Yamada, M., Aoyama, T., Okamoto, K., Nagai, K., Tanaka, B., Takemura, T.: Using a smartphone while walking: a measure of dual-tasking ability as a falls risk assessment tool. Age Ageing 1–4 (2011)

Towards a Natural User Interface to Support People with Visual Impairments in Detecting Colors

Sergio Mascetti[1,2(✉)], Chiara Rossetti[1], Andrea Gerino[1,2],
Cristian Bernareggi[1,2], Lorenzo Picinali[3], and Alessandro Rizzi[1]

[1] Department of Computer Science, EveryWare Lab,
Università Degli Studi di Milano, Milano, Italy
sergio.mascetti@unimi.it
[2] EveryWare Technologies, Milano, Italy
[3] Dyson School of Design Engineering, Imperial College London, London, UK

Abstract. A mobile application that detects an item's color is potentially very useful for visually impaired people. However, users could run into difficulties when centering the target item in the mobile device camera field of view. To address this problem, in this contribution we propose a mobile application that detects the color of the item pointed by the user with one finger. In its current version, the application requires the user to wear a marker on the finger used for pointing. A preliminary evaluation conducted with blind users confirms the usefulness of the application, and encourages further development.

Keywords: Blind people · Visual impairments · Mobile device · Smartphones · Color detection · Computer vision

1 Introduction

Research on assistive technologies is currently facing a shift in its main focus; from computer accessibility to real world accessibility through computer. This phenomenon is particularly evident in the field of assistive technologies for people with visual impairment. Nowadays most devices (including mobile ones) are accessible to blind people and people with low vision through well engineered and generally stable commercial applications. There are still some open issues, for example with image exploration, but overall well established interaction paradigms exist to access most interface elements, like buttons, lists, etc. Consider for example accessibility to mobile devices, where VoiceOver and TalkBack (for iOS and Android devices, respectively) make most applications accessible, even if not specifically designed for users with visual impairments.

This situation allows researchers to focus on applications, specifically designed for people with special needs, that ease the access to the real world and provide support in completing everyday activities. Clearly, mobile devices are convenient platforms to support such applications, as they are easier to

© Springer International Publishing Switzerland 2016
K. Miesenberger et al. (Eds.): ICCHP 2016, Part I, LNCS 9758, pp. 171–178, 2016.
DOI: 10.1007/978-3-319-41264-1_23

carry, generally ready for use and they also have sensors (e.g., accelerometer) that are unavailable on traditional devices. There are indeed many commercial applications, as well as research projects, aimed at supporting visually impaired people in their everyday tasks. Among others applications, some support outdoor orientation and independent mobility (commercial applications like *AriadneGPS*[1], *iMove*[2] and many research projects [1–6]), others help recognising objects (like *AudioLabels*[3]) or sources of lights (like the commercial application *LightDetector*[4]).

In this paper we consider the problem of detecting the color of items (e.g. objects, surfaces, etc.) in the real world. There are many applications, already on the market, aimed at supporting this task; the user points the device camera towards the desired item and then the app "reads aloud" the color in the image center or in the point where the user taps[5]. This interaction is suitable for color-blind users and/or for users with residual vision, who can still see shadows and distinguish between objects. However it is ineffective for blind users, who in many cases have problems in pointing the target item.

This contribution presents our ongoing research to address the above problem with a natural user interface aimed at supporting people with visual impairments in discovering the color of real world items. The ultimate goal is to have a software that recognizes a user's finger, detects the color being pointed by the finger and then describes it to the users, either with text to speech or with a sonification approach (i.e., with non-speech audio). The preliminary prototype *JustPoint* presented in this contribution is aimed at evaluating this idea with one simplification: instead of recognizing the actual finger, *JustPoint* recognizes a marker, a sort of ring that the user wears on the distal phalanx (see Fig. 1). The reason for this simplification is that this contribution focuses on the evaluation of system usability and ergonomics. Finger detection will be added as a future work: it is a non-trivial but doable task, as proved by many papers addressing this problem [7,8].

This contribution first describes *JustPoint* (Sect. 3) and then presents the experimental evaluation we conducted to evaluate the prototype effectiveness (Sect. 4). Finally (Sect. 5) we discuss how we intend to address the issues that emerges from the evaluation and to improve current prototype.

2   Related Work

In recent years, different solutions have been investigated to enable people with visual impairments to recognize colors. These solutions can be roughly divided into two categories: those addressed to people with color deficiency and those

---

[1] https://itunes.apple.com/en/app/ariadne-gps/id441063072?mt=8.
[2] https://itunes.apple.com/en/app/imove/id593874954?mt=8.
[3] https://itunes.apple.com/en/app/audiolabels/id496513473.
[4] https://itunes.apple.com/en/app/light-detector/id420929143?mt=8.
[5] Examples are the "See Color" and "ColorVisor" apps, available on the AppStore.

addressed to people who are not able to see colors at all (i.e., totally blind or severely sight impaired people[6]). In the following, the works concerning both categories are examined.

In the first category (i.e., solutions for people with color deficiency), Tanuwidjaja et al. and Popleteev et al. independently propose solutions on wearable smart glasses [9,10]. These solutions automatically adapt the colors in the scene according to the type of color blindness and show the result on the smart glass display with an augmented reality approach. Both solutions cannot be directly applied to support blind people.

Manaf et al. [11] propose a system to support color blind people to detecting colors. One of the system's feature is similar to the one we propose in this contribution: to recognize the color pointed by the fingertip, however the interaction with blind users is not discussed.

Different solutions have been specifically proposed for blind people. Abboud et al. [12] propose EyeMusic, an application that enables the sonification of images captured through a camera. Colors are represented through different musical instruments and color combinations are mapped on a pentatonic music scale. Bologna et al. [13] propose SeeColor, an application aimed at supporting independent mobility. The scene is captured through the camera and most relevant objects are sonified. Colors are mapped into different musical instruments. The focus of these two contribution is on the sonification method to convey image information (including color) rather than on the user-interaction. Both solutions suffer from this limitation: a blind person can run into difficulties when he/she needs to point the camera towards a small target.

Findlater et al. [14] propose a technique for conveying visual information (e.g., color, labels, etc.) on objects that can be touched, capturing images through micro-camers mounted on the fingers. While this solution is promising, it also incurs into two issues. First, it requires specialized hardware, second, since the camera is mounted on the finger it can prevent the finger mobility, if not properly designed.

3   Color Identification with *JustPoint*

JustPoint is a fully functional Android prototype that (1) acquires images from the device camera, (2) detects the marker, (3) computes the "target area" pointed by the user, (4) identifies colors in the target area and (5) provides the result to the user. Figure 1 shows an example image for each of these 5 steps.

1. The image acquisition phase captures images from the camera video stream, using automatic exposure and focus. In our experiments, conducted with a Nexus 5, about 30 frames per seconds can be acquired, while fewer (i.e., about 3) can be processed. Since, at each instant, we want to process the most recent frame, a new frame is acquired only when the previous one has been processed.

---

[6] Henceforth we refer to these people as "blind people" or "blind users".

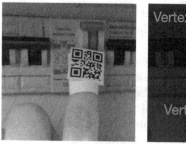
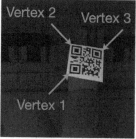

| (a) Image acquisition. | (b) QR-code detection. | (c) Target area extraction. |

| (d) Color detection. | (e) Result is read. |

Fig. 1. Five steps of the color recognition procedure. (Color figure online)

2. In its current version, the marker is a QR-code. To exclude that other QR-codes that appear in the image are erroneously detected as the marker, *JustPoint* verifies that the string encoded in the actual marker matches a predefied string. When detecting the QR code, the position of its vertexes in the image is computed (see Fig. 1(b)).

3. In the third step *JustPoint* extracts the "target area", i.e., the image portion the user is pointing to. Thanks to some evaluations with the final users, we defined this as a circular region, approximately the same size as the finger width (i.e., circle diameter is the same as QR code edge), positioned right after the QR code, along the finger direction (see Fig. 1(c)).

4. The idea to identify colors in the target area is to label each pixel with a color name and then to count the number of pixels for each label. Adopting this approach each color name is associated with its "frequency" i.e., the number of pixels with that color divided by the total number of pixels in the target area. *JustPoint* considers 11 color names, as defined by Berlin and Kay [15]: black, white, grey, red, yellow, green, blue, violet, brown, orange. To assign a color name to each pixel, *JustPoint* adopts a simple and effective solution: the target area is converted in its HSV representation (from RGB) and then threshold values on S and V channels are used to distinguish "black", "white" and "grey" colors. Other colors are distinguished though threshold values on the H channel with the only exception of "orange" and "brown" that are

distinguished also considering the V channel. Note that this coarseness of the color bin division increases the method robustness with respect to device camera gamut shifts.

5. User is informed with a Text To Speech (TTS) synthesizer that reads the name of the colors identified in the target area.

With a standard TalkBack-based interaction, the user can set the "number of colors" preference that represents how many colors, among those with frequency higher than the "min-frequency" threshold, should be read to the user. Consider the example shown in Fig. 1(e). If "number of colors" is set to 1, then "blue" is read, as this color has the highest frequency ($\sim$40 %). If the parameter is set to 2, "blue and grey" is read, as grey is the second color with highest frequency ($\sim$30 %). The same text is read if "number of colors" is set to 3. Indeed, the third color with highest frequency is "brown" ($\sim$15 %), but its frequency is below the "min-frequency" threshold (i.e., below 25 %).

4   System Evaluation

JustPoint was designed with a user centered approach. The development stage was continuously monitored and evaluated by one member of the design team, who is congenitally blind. In addition, we conducted three evaluation sessions with blind subjects; one before the prototype was developed, one with a preliminary prototype and, finally, one with the final version of *JustPoint*.

In the preliminary evaluation we described the idea of the application to two congenitally blind subjects (one 37 years old male, one 37 years old female) and we asked them to point with one hand an object whose color they want to discover. At the same time subjects had to hold the device in the other hand and point the camera towards the object. While doing that, instead of the actual application (which at the time had not been developed yet), subjects were asked to record a video. The result is therefore a set of recordings representing what the camera was pointing at during the simulated use of the application. The test was conducted in a non-supervised environment.

Two main considerations emerged from this evaluation. First, for a blind person it is not trivial to hold the device with one hand and point its camera towards the other hand that is pointing an object. In most cases the two subjects were holding the device very close to the pointing hand, which was out of the camera field of view. The second consideration is that a blind person may not have a clear idea of the environmental light conditions. Indeed, one video was recorded in an almost totally dark room where colors were not perceivable.

Based on the experience of the first evaluation session, we added two functions to the application; first, when the application runs for the first time, it suggests the user to put the device camera right above the pointing finger and than move the camera away. Second, if light is too low *JustPoint* warns the user and turns the flash light on.

The second evaluation session was conducted during the app development stage. It was performed with the two subjects involved in the previous evaluation and by one late-blind subjects (28 years old male) in a supervised environment. Subjects were asked to use the application to detect the color of some objects provided to them. Two main observations arose. Firstly, while the user is trying to point the device in the correct direction, the app does not give any feedback, hence the user does not know if the app is working properly. To fix this problem we added a feature that plays a pure tone sound every 2 s when no QR code is detected. The second observation was that the color detection technique, based on RGB representation at that time, was not accurate enough. Consequently we modified it as described in Sect. 3.

The third evaluation session was conducted with an improved version of *JustPoint* and was aimed at evaluating the usability of the application while identifying the color of different objects. We asked the same blind subjects of the second evaluation session to recognize the color of three sets of objects: books, small toys and liquid in bottles. The three subjects were able to accomplish all tasks successfully. They did not run into difficulty in pointing the camera correctly and this operation generally took about one second, or even less. All subjects independently commented that the application is very useful but that wearing the ring with the QR code is not convenient. In particular one subject noted that she would not always have the ring with her when she would need to recognize a color.

5 Future Work

While the current version of *JustPoint* is still preliminary, its user-centred design highlighted a number of features and its evaluation suggests that it can be practical and useful.

The main limit of *JustPoint*, in its current version, is that it requires the user to wear a marker on the finger. We intend to address this by implementing a finger detection technique.

Considering the user interaction, we intend to investigate the use of wearable devices (like *Google Glass*[7] or *Sony SmartEyeglass*[8]). One research question is whether it is easier to point the target object if the camera is placed on the user's head.

Another important improvement for *JustPoint* is to implement sonification for delivering information about the colors. Sonification could be used as the sole audio feedback method, or in conjunction with speech information. A similar approach has been followed by the same team when working with a navigational task [2]. This will allow the user to distinguish between a continuous range of colors, rather than a discrete one. Furthermore, sonification will allow the transfer of additional information to the user (e.g. colors of the areas surrounding the finger, indications about how to orient the phone in order for the camera to be able to catch the pointing finger, etc.).

---

[7] https://developers.google.com/glass/.

[8] https://developer.sony.com/develop/wearables/smarteyeglass-sdk/.

Finally, the performance of *JustPoint* can be improved by adopting parallel computation (i.e., process more than one frame a given time) and possibly by using the highly parallel GPU architecture to speed up computation.

Acknowledgments. The work of Andrea Gerino, Cristian Bernareggi and Sergio Mascetti was partially supported by grant "fondo supporto alla ricerca 2015" under project "Assistive technologies on mobile devices". The work of Alessandro Rizzi was partially supported by grant "fondo supporto alla ricerca 2015" under project "Discovering Patterns in Multi-Dimensional Data".

References

1. Mascetti, S., Ahmetovic, D., Gerino, A., Bernareggi, C., Busso, M., Rizzi, A.: Robust traffic lights detection on mobile devices for pedestrians with visual impairment. Comput. Vis. Image Underst. (in press)
2. Mascetti, S., Picinali, L., Gerino, A., Ahmetovic, D., Bernareggi, C.: Sonification of guidance data during road crossing for people with visual impairments or blindness. Int. J. Hum.-Comput. Stud. **85**, 16–26 (2015)
3. Ahmetovic, D., Manduchi, R., Coughlan, J., Mascetti, S.: Zebra crossing spotter: automatic population of spatial databases for increased safety of blind travelers. In: Proceedings of the 17th International ACM SIGACCESS Conference on Computers and Accessibility (2015)
4. Manduchi, R., Coughlan, J., Miesenberger, K., Coughlan, J.M., Shen, H.: Crosswatch: a system for providing guidance to visually impaired travelers at traffic intersection. J. Assist. Technol. **7**(2), 131–142 (2013)
5. Hara, K., Azenkot, S., Campbell, M., Bennett, C.L., Le, V., Pannella, S., Moore, R., Minckler, K., Ng, R.H., Froehlich, J.E.: Improving public transit accessibility for blind riders by crowdsourcing bus stop landmark locations with google street view: an extended analysis. ACM Trans. Accessible Comput. (TACCESS) **6**(2) (2015). (5)
6. Brady, E.L., Sato, D., Ruan, C., Takagi, H., Asakawa, C.: Exploring interface design for independent navigation by people with visual impairments. In: Proceedings of the 17th International ACM SIGACCESS Conference on Computers & Accessibility, pp. 387–388. ACM (2015)
7. Baldauf, M., Zambanini, S., Fröhlich, P., Reichl, P.: Markerless visual fingertip detection for natural mobile device interaction. In: Proceedings of the 13th International Conference on Human Computer Interaction with Mobile Devices and Services, pp. 539–544. ACM (2011)
8. Chun, W.H., Höllerer, T.: Real-time hand interaction for augmented reality on mobile phones. In: Proceedings of the 2013 International Conference on Intelligent User Interfaces, pp. 307–314. ACM (2013)
9. Tanuwidjaja, E., Huynh, D., Koa, K., Nguyen, C., Shao, C., Torbett, P., Emmenegger, C., Weibel, N.: Chroma: a wearable augmented-reality solution for color blindness. In: Proceedings of the 2014 ACM International Joint Conference on Pervasive and Ubiquitous Computing, UbiComp 2014, pp. 799–810. ACM, New York (2014)
10. Popleteev, A., Louveton, N., McCall, R.: Colorizer: smart glasses aid for the colorblind. In: Proceedings of the 2015 Workshop on Wearable Systems and Applications, WearSys 2015, pp. 7–8. ACM, New York (2015)

11. Manaf, A.S., Sari, R.F.: Color recognition system with augmented reality concept and finger interaction: case study for color blind aid system. In: 2011 9th International Conference on ICT and Knowledge Engineering (ICT & Knowledge Engineering), pp. 118–123. IEEE (2012)

12. Abboud, S., Hanassy, S., Levy-Tzedek, S., Maidenbaum, S., Amedi, A.: Eyemusic: introducing a visual colorful experience for the blind using auditory sensory substitution. Restorative Neurol. Neurosci. **32**(2), 247–257 (2014)

13. Bologna, G., Gomez, J.D., Pun, T.: Vision substitution experiments with see colOr. In: Ferrández Vicente, J.M., Álvarez Sánchez, J.R., de la Paz López, F., Toledo Moreo, F.J. (eds.) IWINAC 2013, Part I. LNCS, vol. 7930, pp. 83–93. Springer, Heidelberg (2013)

14. Findlater, L., Stearns, L., Du, R., Oh, U., Ross, D., Chellappa, R., Froehlich, J.: Supporting everyday activities for persons with visual impairments through computer vision-augmented touch. In: Proceedings of the 17th International ACM SIGACCESS Conference on Computers & #38; Accessibility, ASSETS 2015, pp. 383–384. ACM, New York (2015)

15. Berlin, B., Kay, P.: Basic Color Terms: Their Universality and Evolution. University of California Press, Berkeley (1991)

Cognitive Accessibility to Mobile ICT

Martin Böcker[1], Nikolaos Floratos[2], Loïc Martínez[3(✉)], Mike Pluke[4],
Bruno Von Niman[5], and Gill Whitney[6]

[1] Dr. Boecker & Dr. Schneider GbR, Munich, Germany
boecker@humanfactors.de
[2] ANEC, Etterbeek, Belgium
nf@cyberall-access.com
[3] Universidad Politécnica de Madrid, Madrid, Spain
loic@fi.upm.es
[4] Castle Consulting Ltd, Ipswitch, UK
Mike.Pluke@castle-consult.com
[5] Vonniman Consulting SG, Stockholm, Nacka, Sweden
bruno@vonniman.com
[6] Middlessex University, London, UK
g.whitney@mdx.ac.uk

Abstract. Persons with cognitive impairments form a diverse group, with limitations in one or more types of mental tasks such as conceptualizing, planning, remembering and understanding numbers and symbols. It has been recognized that current accessibility guidelines provide limited support for these persons and that more work is needed. ETSI has established a team of experts, STF 488, which intends to produce (1) a set of usage needs of persons with cognitive impairments when using mobile devices and applications and (2) a set of guidelines to develop mobile ICT with cognitive accessibility. This paper describes the ongoing work of STF 488, its approach, current results and the future work of the team.

Keywords: Cognitive impairment · Accessibility guidelines · User needs · Mobile ICT

1 Introduction

The concept of cognitive impairment is extremely broad. In general, a person with a cognitive impairment has more difficulties with one or more types of mental tasks than the average person [1]. Braddock et al. describe cognitive impairments as "a substantial limitation in one's capacity to think, including conceptualizing, planning, and sequencing thoughts and actions, remembering, interpreting subtle social cues, and understanding numbers and symbols." [2].

Cognitive impairments can include learning impairments (difficulty to learn in conventional ways), language impairments (difficulty to understand or producing language), or can include some form of ageing-related cognitive impairment (e.g. dementia – including Alzheimer's disease – memory loss, lack of orientation, etc.).

© Springer International Publishing Switzerland 2016
K. Miesenberger et al. (Eds.): ICCHP 2016, Part I, LNCS 9758, pp. 179–186, 2016.
DOI: 10.1007/978-3-319-41264-1_24

Individuals with cognitive impairments can face unique challenges that are often pervasive and changing throughout their lives.

Cognitive impairments are relatively common, affecting between 1–2.5 % of the general population in the Western world [3]. This corresponds to 5–12.5 million people in the EU (European Union) and EFTA (European Free Trade Association). Considering the fact that older people typically present some form of age-related cognitive impairment, this percentage becomes even more significant.

Current trends in mobile Information and Communication Technology (ICT), with devices based on touchscreens with difficult to discover gesture-based interactions, are creating new barriers for persons with cognitive impairments. Guidance is needed to help designers integrate cognitive accessibility into new mobile ICT products and services.

During the past decade, the need to study cognitive impairments and their possible impact on and benefits from ICT has been identified (e.g. during the development of the WCAG 2.0 Recommendations in W3C) and acted upon. The area has been under consideration in numerous European and other research activities (see [4]), some of which have finished or are about to finish. Therefore, the European Commission decided that it was right to support the ETSI (the European Telecommunications Standards Institute [5]) proposal to initiate standardization activities and produce guidance for the accessibility of mobile technologies by persons with cognitive, learning or language impairments. An STF (Specialist Task Force, a team of experts) has been established to perform this work: STF 488 [6].

This paper describes the ongoing work of STF 488, its approach, current results, future work and conclusions.

2 STF 488

STF 488 is a team of 6 experts that was established by ETSI March 2015, with the support of the European Commission [6]. The STF will classify and analyse the needs of persons with limited cognitive, language and learning abilities when using mobile ICT. This includes persons with cognitive impairments and some older people.

The expected result of the work of STF 488 will be two documents:

- A Technical Report (TR 103 349) that will describe the functional needs of persons with limited cognitive, language and learning abilities for an improved user experience when using mobile ICT devices and their related applications.
- An ETSI Guide (EG 203 350) with design guidelines for mobile devices and applications. These design guidelines will enable people with cognitive impairments to obtain the maximum benefit from the use of mobile technology. The recommendations of the ETSI guide will be based on the "Design for All" approach, where possible.

The work of STF488 is expected to finish at the end of year 2016, with the publication of the TR and EG, after approval by the ETSI Technical Committee of Human Factors.

3 Approach of STF Work

STF 488 has agreed on a standards-based approach for defining cognitive impairments, usage needs and guidelines (summarized in Fig. 1).

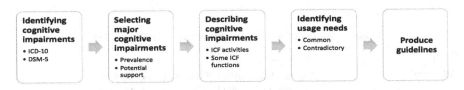

Fig. 1. Summary of the working approach of ETSI STF 488

The group has identified two major sources of information for identifying the major diagnosed cognitive impairments: ICD-10 [7], from the World Health Organization (WHO) and DSM-5 [8], from the American Psychiatric Association (APA). Both documents include information about cognitive impairments, as part of a wider collection of mental and behavioural disorders and impairments.

A subset of diagnosed cognitive impairments has been selected based on two criteria; prevalence (how many individuals have a particular cognitive impairment), and potential support (whether persons having a particular cognitive impairment can use and benefit from mobile technologies, with the support of the required assistive technologies). As a result, several cognitive impairments have been considered: intellectual disabilities (including Down syndrome), dyslexia, attention deficit and hyperactivity disorder (ADHD), autism spectrum disorder and age-related impairments such as dementia (including Alzheimer's disease).

The second step has been to describe these impairments using the vocabulary of ICF-CY, the International classification of functioning, disability and health, children & youth version [9]. The main items that have been used to describe cognitive impairments are activities (execution of tasks or actions by an individual). In some cases the team has agreed to add some body functions (physiological functions of body systems, including psychological functions) that were required to describe some impairments beyond the information provided by activities.

The cognitive-related ICF activities (and some functions) are the basis for identifying usage needs, which describe what users with cognitive impairments need from mobile ICT so that it becomes accessible to them. Section 4 describes the result of the work in usage needs.

The last step in the process is to produce guidelines to support designers and developers in the process of creating mobile devices and applications that can be successfully used by persons with cognitive impairments. Section 5 provides information of the guidelines developed by the team.

4 Usage Needs

The team has identified a set of 28 usage needs, grouped into 11 categories, as listed in Table 1. In TR 103 349, each usage need will have a list of related ICF activities and functions, as well as a mapping to ISO/IEC TR 29138-1 [10], a document that contains user needs for all types of disabilities.

Table 1. Listing of usage needs identified by ETSI STF 488

Category	Usage needs
Attention	• Usage with limited ability to focus attention • Usage with limited ability to direct attention • Usage with limited ability to shift attention
Reading	• Usage with no ability to read • Usage with limited ability to recognize written language • Usage with limited ability to comprehend written language
Writing	• Usage with no ability to write • Usage with limited ability to correctly write words and use punctuation • Usage with limited ability to produce written language
Calculating	• Usage with no ability to calculate • Usage with limited ability to understand simple mathematical concepts
Decision making	• Usage with limited ability to make a choice among options • Usage with limited ability to interpret the effects of choices taken
Undertaking tasks	• Usage with limited ability to initiate a task • Usage with limited ability to organise for a task • Usage with limited ability to carry out a task • Usage with limited ability to complete a task • Usage with limited ability to manage time • Usage with limited ability to adapt to time demands
Receiving speech	• Usage with no ability to receive spoken language. • Usage with limited ability to understand spoken language
Receiving non-verbal messages	• Usage with limited or no ability to understand body gestures • Usage with limited or no ability to understand symbols • Usage with limited or no ability to understand drawings and photographs
Speaking	• Usage with limited or no ability to speak
Producing non-verbal messages	• Usage with limited or no ability to produce gestures
Memory	• Usage with limited ability to recall from short-term memory • Usage with limited long-term memory

The resulting set of usage needs represents a comprehensive description of issues that persons with cognitive impairments may have when using mobile ICT. Most usage needs are applicable to several cognitive impairments.

Table 2 provides one example of a usage need: the case where the user has a limited ability to focus attention on the current task and any external stimuli could cause the user to lose track of the current activity. Each usage need has a short title (for ease of reference), a full title, a text describing the need of the user of mobile ICT and several notes. The first three notes relate the usage need to activities and functions of ICF-CY and to user needs in ISO/IEC TR 29138-1. Then there is a note listing cognitive impairments that are related to the usage need. The fifth note points to other usage needs that may contradict the current one. Finally, notes 6 and onward provide additional explanations for the usage need.

Table 2. An example of usage need: focusing attention

Short title	Focusing attention
Title	Usage with limited ability to focus attention
Usage need	Some users need an environment in which there are no stimuli unrelated to their current task
Notes	NOTE 1 Related ICF activities: d160 Focusing attention NOTE 2 Related ICF functions: b1400 Sustaining attention NOTE 3 Related user need in ISO/IEC TR 29138-1: 7-4 NOTE 4 Related diagnoses of cognitive impairments: ADHD, Dementia (including Alzheimer's disease), Intellectual disabilities (including Down syndrome), Aphasia NOTE 5 This usage need contradicts Shifting Attention - Usage with limited ability to shift attention NOTE 6 The distracting stimulus can be in any modality: visual, auditory, tactile, etc.

In the case of "Focusing attention", Table 2 shows that it is related to attention-related activities and functions from ICF-CY, and that it is related to user need 7-4 of ISO/IEC TR 29138: "the ability to avoid visual or auditory distractions that prevent focusing on a task". Some diagnoses of cognitive impairments that require support for focusing attention are ADHD, dementia, intellectual disabilities and aphasia.

The fifth note explains that this usage needs contradicts "shifting attention", where the users need specific support to shift their attention form one task to the next relevant task. That means that guidelines supporting "focusing attention" can create additional barriers for users that need support for "shifting attention". This is an example of usage needs implying the need for individualization in mobile ICT: the interaction has to be adapted to the abilities of individuals. This is the only way to avoid creating barriers for some user groups while supporting other specific user groups.

The current draft of TR 103 349 links the usage needs to the user needs contained in ISO/IEC TR 29138-1. This international technical report is currently being revised, and it will be based on information presented in another international document: ISO/IEC Guide 71 [11], a guide for standard authors for addressing accessibility for persons with disabilities in future standards. The team of experts recognised this fact and it is probable that future versions of TR 103 349 may relate to ISO/IEC Guide 71 instead of relating to ISO/IEC TR 29138-1.

5   Guidelines

The experts of STF 488 are actively developing guidelines for the accessibility of mobile ICT for persons with cognitive impairments. At the moment of writing, the structure of EG 203 350 is mirroring the structure of EN 301 549, the European Standard on accessible ICT for public procurement [12]. The goal of this approach is to enable using the guidelines for cognitive accessibility to be an input for future updates of EN 301 549. The resulting structure is shown in Table 3. Two clauses have been added to the EG that do not appear in the EN structure: clause 7 to collect a large set of guidelines about the use of language (that apply to both the user interface and the documentation), and clause 14 to collect guidelines that only apply to specific services that provide support for some cognitive impairments.

Table 3. Structure of EG 203 305

Introductory clauses	Introduction 1. Scope 2. References 3. Definitions, symbols and abbreviations 4. Overview 5. General design issues for mobile ICT
Clauses containing guidelines	6. Guidelines applicable to any mobile ICT 7. Guidelines on use of language 8. Guidelines specific to mobile ICT with two-way voice communication 9. Guidelines specific to mobile ICT with media playing and recording capabilities 10. Guidelines specific to hardware of mobile ICT 11. Guidelines specific to mobile Web 12. Guidelines specific to mobile software 13. Guidelines specific to documentation for mobile ICT 14. Support services
Annexes	• List of usage needs • Accessibility principles • Requirements and recommendations in EN 301 549 that provide support for cognitive accessibility

The Guidelines are being collected from existing literature and best practice, or, in the absence of existing recommendations, they are being developed. In addition, the guidance will describe individualization strategies so that the mobile device or application can be personalised to the needs of individual users. As described in the previous section, the individualization is needed because, in some cases, the usage needs of persons with different cognitive impairments are contradictory and cannot be applied following a design for all approach.

Table 4 below shows an example of a current proposed guideline in the current draft of EG 203 350, that applies to any type of mobile ICT. Each guideline will have a title, a provision and several notes. One note will relate each guideline to the usage needs it supports. A second note will point to external sources for the guideline (if applicable). Additional notes and examples will be used to provide explanations and clarifications on the meaning and application of the guidelines.

Table 4. An example of a guideline proposed in the current draft of EG 203 350

Full word labels
The mobile ICT should provide full word labels instead of abbreviations. NOTE 1: Related usage needs: recognize written language, comprehend written language. NOTE 2: Source ETSI EG 202 116 [13].

The guideline in Table 4 says that it is better to provide full word labels, instead of abbreviations. This guideline supports the needs of persons having difficulties to either recognize (e.g. dyslexia) or to comprehend (e.g. intellectual disabilities) written language.

6   Future Work and Conclusions

The work of ETSI STF 488 is ongoing. Public drafts of TR 103 349 [14] and EG 203 350 [15] have been made available recently. Experts in the field will be welcome to review the drafts and provide comments to improve them. In addition, a workshop is being organised in May 2016 to present the drafts and gather comments that will be processed for the final drafts, expected in summer, 2016.

The resulting documents are expected to provide knowledge (the TR) and guidelines (the EG) to improve the cognitive accessibility of mobile ICT. The expected result will be mobile ICT that is easier to use by persons with difficulties to conceptualize, plan, sequencing thoughts and actions, remember, interpret subtle social cues, understand numbers and symbols, learn, read or write, etc.

References

1. Blanck, P.: The struggle for web eQuality by persons with cognitive disabilities. Behav. Sci. Law **32**(1), 4–32 (2014)
2. Braddock, D., Rizzolo, M., Thompson, M., Bell, R.: Emerging technologies and cognitive disability. J. Spec. Educ. Technol. **19**(4), 49–56 (2004)

3. Gillberg, C., Soderstrom, H.: Learning disability. Semin. Lancet **362**(6), 811–821 (2003)
4. ETSI. Terms of Reference - Specialist Task Force STF ZV (TC HF). Recommendations to allow people with cognitive disabilities to exploit the potential of mobile technologies. Version 0.3.1, January 2015. https://portal.etsi.org/stfs/ToR/ToR488v03_HF_EC2014_10_Accessibility_Cognitive.doc
5. ETSI. European Telecommunications Standards Institute. Home page (2016). http://www.etsi.org/
6. ETSI. Specialist Task Force 488: Recommendations to allow people with cognitive disabilities to exploit the potential of mobile technologies. STF 488 homepage (2016). https://portal.etsi.org/STFs/STF_HomePages/STF488/STF488.asp
7. World Health Organization. International Statistical Classification of Diseases and Related Health Problems 10th Revision – ICD-10 Version (2016)
8. American Psychiatric Association. Diagnosis and statistical manual of mental disorders, 5th edn. (2013)
9. World Health Organization. International classification of functioning, disability and health: children and youth version: ICF-CY (2007)
10. ISO/IEC. ISO/IEC TR 29138-1. Information technology – Accessibility considerations for people with disabilities –Part 1: User needs summary (2009)
11. ISO/IEC. ISO/IEC Guide 71: Guide for addressing accessibility in standards, 2nd edn. (2014)
12. CEN, CENELEC, ETSI. EN 301 549. Accessibility requirements suitable for public procurement of ICT products and services in Europe. V1.1.2 (2015)
13. ETSI. ETSI EG 202 116: Human Factors; Guidelines for ICT products and services: "Design for All". European Telecommunication Standards Institute (2009)
14. ETSI. Draft ETSI TR 103 349 V0.0.6. Human Factors (HF); Functional needs of people with cognitive disabilities when using mobile ICT devices for an improved user experience in mobile ICT devices (2016). https://docbox.etsi.org/HF/Open/Latest_Drafts/
15. ETSI. Draft ETSI EG 203 350 V0.0.6. Human Factors (HF); Guidelines for the design of mobile ICT devices and their related applications for people with cognitive disabilities (2016). https://docbox.etsi.org/HF/Open/Latest_Drafts/

What Do Low-Vision Users Really Want from Smart Glasses? Faces, Text and Perhaps No Glasses at All

Frode Eika Sandnes[1,2(✉)]

[1] Department of Computer Science, Faculty of Technology, Art and Design,
Oalo and Akershus University College of Applied Sciences, Oslo, Norway
Frode-Eika.Sandnes@hioa.no
[2] Faculty of Technology, Westerdals Oslo School of Art, Communication
and Technology, Oslo, Norway

Abstract. Recent advances in low cost wearable computers opens up new possibilities for the development of innovative visual aids. A head-mounted display with cameras that capture views of the physical world, a wearable computer can process the image and present an augmented view to the user. Although, some research is reported into the development of such visual prosthetics the functionalities often appear ad-hoc. This study set out to identify what functionality visually impaired users need in various contexts to reduce barriers. Information was gathered via interviews of visually impaired individuals. The results show that recognizing faces and text is the most important functions while the idea of smart glasses where questioned.

Keywords: Universal design · Low vision · Computer-assisted visual aids

1 Introduction

Recent technological developments have opened up new opportunities for providing valuable assistive technologies for disabled individuals. Wearable and mobile computing technologies have become smaller, more powerful and more affordable. General off-the-shelves devices can be applied in various domains through open application programming interfaces. High-speed Internet connectivity gives constant access to vast amounts of information. Tasks requiring heavy processing can be moved to the cloud. Consequently, innovative and exiting new approaches are emerging.

However, the technical focus may divert the attention away from the needs of users. This study addresses the most prominent needs of individuals with low-vision. Semi-structured interviews were used to identify their functional needs. These needs are discussed in relation to the current research on computer-based visual aids. The results suggest that there are gaps between the research and the actual needs.

© Springer International Publishing Switzerland 2016
K. Miesenberger et al. (Eds.): ICCHP 2016, Part I, LNCS 9758, pp. 187–194, 2016.
DOI: 10.1007/978-3-319-41264-1_25

2 Related Work

The idea of smart glasses goes back more than 20 years with the early work of Peli [1] who studied basic image processing for image enhancement. In particular, Peli et al. studied the visually impaired individuals' recognition of faces [2]. Everingham et al. [3] used a technique to identify objects in images and colour these using saturated colours. Users are thus made aware of objects that otherwise are blurred or blend in with the background. Harper [4] explored a head-mounted image magnification device.

More recent works based on state-of-the-art hardware include Zhao et al. [5] who experimented with magnification, contrast enhancement and on-the-fly optical character recognition. A similar attempt was made by Kálmán et al. [6] who addressed automatic light and contrast enhancements and augmented edge enhancement. They also marked pedestrian crossings and performed traffic light detection. Tanuwidjaja et al. [7] implemented a colour adjustment system for Google glass to counterbalance colour-blindness. Google glass has also been used for edge enhancements [8]. Hicks et al. [9] explored a device that exploits partially sighted users peripheral vision and adds depth information to nearby objects by making them brighter.

Lab systems have demonstrated concepts including obstacle detection based on stereoscopic images [10] and radar based indoor navigation [11]. Vision systems without displays have also been explored including Merino-Gracia et al.'s [12] head-mounted camera system for real time text recognition with text-to-speech audio.

Most of the studies on smart glasses seem to be based on assumptions about low vision. Dougherty et al. [13] identified that low-vision devices are not used by the target group. On reason for this abandonment could be that the devices do not match the users' needs. Satgunam et al. [14] studied whether users find contour enhancements useful. They concluded that moderate enhancements may help, but more research is needed. Luo and Peli [15] explored the effectiveness of augmenting large visual fields onto smaller regions for individuals with reduced field of view and reported positive effects. A few documented qualitative studies address the functional needs of individuals with low vision. One of these is Cimarolli et al.'s [16] study of older individuals. They found that the main challenges are connected to transportation, recognizing people in a social settings and psychological issues. This study thus attempted to further identify the functional needs of individuals with low vision as a basis for developing more useful low-vision aids.

3 Method

Three visually impaired academics in their 40 s, 50 s and 70 s, two male and one female, were interviewed using a semi-structured guide. Two of the participants had low and very low vision from birth, respectively. The third participant had uncorrected vision for most of his life, but was diagnosed with retinitis pigmentosa (RT) in his fifties, with a current tunnel field of view of about 1 degree and no colour vision.

The goal of the study was presented to the participants and they were asked to ignore issues related to personal computer use and issues in at home. This is because the both personal computers and the home were considered controllable by the individual. The participants were asked to focus on issues beyond their control. The interviews were conducted in Norwegian and the quotations herein are simplified translations.

4 Results

The interviews revealed three particular problem areas, namely recognizing faces, recognizing text and the stigma of visual aids. These issues and their related coping strategies are discussed in the following sections.

4.1 Recognizing Faces

Recognizing faces emerged as the most emphasized issue. Social interaction depends on knowing with whom one is interacting. The reduced ability to recognize faces often leads to an experience of relational asymmetry where only the non-visually impaired part knows who the other person is. Moreover, the non-visually impaired person may be unaware of the other person's low-vision. Even if they know, they may not realise the consequences. A person who is trained to interact with low-vision individuals may say "Hi, it is John here", while most people may not realize the importance of such cues. This effect may be strengthened by the fact that low-vision individuals' often try to give the other person perceived eye-contract as one learn from an early age that eye contact is key to successful social interaction. This eye contact is often one-directional where the low-vision individual will look in the direction of the voice. This may give a biased impression of the interaction quality.

One participant commented that he had a former career in radio journalism where he listened to and perceived people's voices. He claimed to have trained his listening abilities, by listening to the timbre of the voice, modulations, choice of words and manner of speaking. He was able to identify people he knew directly from their voice, and only on a very few occasions was he unable to determine who the other person was. He also pointed out that he moved slower and used a white cane to signal his low vision, "I do not want people to think I am intoxicated from how I move".

Several examples of challenging situations were mentioned such as meeting with people approaching from afar. To recognize a face the person needs to be at close proximity before the low-vision individual can identify the person. One coping strategy is to recognize the clothes, a distinctive coat, a certain shape handbag or backpack, big hair or the gait of the approaching person and seeing if the person is walking in a path towards oneself. However, this strategy fails completely in situations where the person is wearing something unusual, such as on a special occasion or party. The participant with RP often experienced clearly seeing a nose, an eye or hair colour, but that this was enough.

It is customary to greet another person with a wave of the hand, sometimes combined with a verbal greeting. If there is no verbal greeting the low-vision individual may miss the greeting completely and be completely unaware that they are approaching someone they know. The chance of missing a greeting is more prominent with crowds.

The other person may become insulted and think the low-vision individual is being arrogant. A verbal greeting from afar can also be challenging if the low-vision individual do not recognize the voice of the person. Is the person greeting me? One coping strategy is to respond to all verbal greetings regardless. Responding to greetings intended for others is embarrassing.

An acquaintance may suddenly pop, for example on the tram, with "How are you?" One respondent's copying strategy is simply to respond: "Who are you?" Such responses may be perceived as being impolite and abrupt. Another respondent's coping strategy was to pretend to know the person and use general phrases in the initial part of the discussion before identifying the person. The time to recognize a person depends on how socially close the person is. A friend is often recognized from the voice, overall shape and on the general movement patterns, while remote acquaintances are harder to recognize. "Sometimes I didn't know who I actually spoke to".

Indoor situations present other problems. One of the respondents had to network as part of the job, chat with various people at social gatherings and raise issue with unfamiliar individuals. It is challenging to find people in a dark room full of people. The noise level makes it hard to single out a person based on the voice. The participant which was least affected by low-vision presented the following example of a coping strategy. A seminar with prominent people was preceded by a social reception where the goal was to raise an issue with a politician. The respondent sat at the front during the seminar to make mental notes about the clothes and other distinctive signs. Later, he would stroll around and discretely observe people, listen to voices and circle a few rounds around individuals who matched the descriptions to get a better look at their faces before approaching. The participant found these occasions very stressful and challenging. Another respondent totally rejected the idea of social networking in such settings.

The third participant used such occasions actively as a journalist. He has always found it a challenging with gatherings comprising unfamiliar individuals, irrespective of eyesight. He occasionally still attended such events. However, he did so with hesitation without an accompanying person. His coping strategy was not to approach other people, but rather let people approach him while remaining in one place. He viewed this to be a loss as he is as a curious person who enjoys meeting new people. He cited a leader of an RP-organization who said that her greatest loss having gotten RP is that she no longer can see the reactions on people's faces.

When giving talks, he would point out his low vision so that attendees would know to present themselves when approaching him. This participant also pointed out that the size of a gathering is an issue. Gatherings with up to 16 people were unproblematic, while 100 people are next to impossible.

Challenges with social interaction and recognizing faces were also identified by Cimarolli et al. [16] and the mechanisms of recognizing faces has been addressed in the early work by Peli et al. [2]. Beyond that, the research into face recognition aids is limited. This is a paradox as the face recognition research is vast [17]. Could some of these face-recognition techniques be applied in the realisation of useful aids?

4.2 Recognizing Text

The recognition of text, especially in the context of transportation, came up as the second most important issue. Having the freedom to move around unassisted is essential for leading an independent and dignified life. Non-moving texts were not regarded too problematic by two participants. One coping strategy is to use a smartphone to take pictures of the text and explore a magnification. This strategy works well for information boards and display monitors and small print on products in shops. "You can usually take your time" said one participant.

Large airports were commented as being very easy to navigate – the bigger, the better. The person with RP noted that he rarely did air travels without other people, where "at least one person would have better eye-sight than myself". On the few occasions when travelling alone he would use the guide services offered by the airports. One participant commented that large subway systems such as Paris and London are easier to navigate than the small Oslo subway. The Paris and London subways have colour coded lines and coloured trains matching the lines, while in Oslo the colour coding is not used consistently. All the trains look the same with the same colour scheme.

Information displays on moving vehicles such as busses and subway trains are problematic. It is impossible to see which route number or destination of a bus before it is very close, and if the bus requires the passenger to issue a stop signal it will be too late. As one participant pointed out, "buses and trucks look too similar". Another participant noted that "it is not possible to use the smartphone camera. It is hard to take a clear picture quickly of a rapidly approaching vehicle, and there is simply not enough time to take the picture, pan and zoom-in on the display. The bus will already have passed by."

Several coping strategies were mentioned by the participants. One participant reported that bus stops are increasingly equipped with information signs that mostly solve the problem. These are easier to see and can be read with the smartphone, while less important stops often do not have information boards. Occasionally, the boards do not work. Information boards installed by one bus-operator may not show information about buses from other companies. "The metropolitan buses where I live are displayed on the board, while the airport express is not, since it is operated by a different company. It runs less frequent, and I am very worried about missing it".

Another participant said that the information boards were not useful, and that one strategy was to give a stop signal to all bus-like vehicles, for then to ask the driver. This participant had many experiences of being shouted at by bus drivers. Moreover, some truck drivers had also been angry for being stopped. To overcome this problem the participant had experimented using a white cane as a symbol of visually impairment. However, the white cane had little effect. "I also use the time to guess which bus is arriving, but this is risky since the actual arrival times often deviate from the timetable". Another participant said that the schedule was his only choice when taking the bus without an accompanying person.

Another issue is that of type of bus stop. One participant stated that "I prefer the small bus stops, because the busses always stop in the same location. At big bus stops the bus may stop anywhere depending on the traffic conditions and other buses".

The subway poses similar challenges, but results in different coping strategies. "I board the first train that arrives and then figure out from the information board inside which train I am on. I then change trains at the next station if needed. The subway trains have information signs on the side as well as on the front. The side-signs are easier to read, and I tend to stand at a particular spot on the platform to better see them."

All participants agreed that in-vehicle audio announcements of destinations, and information displays are useful. As one participant said "you really notice the importance of good information boards and audio when travelling to countries without such facilities".

One of the participants relies less on public transport. Instead, he uses a government system where qualifying individuals are allowed a certain number of free taxi journeys. Individuals who find it very hard to use public transport due to disability may apply for this scheme. Obviously, taxis eliminate many of the practical obstacles of getting from one place to another. He also said that he never takes the tram as the main obstacle is to use the automatic ticket vending machines. Taking the train from major train stations however, is less of a problem since they usually have ticket clerks. Likewise, taking buses across the city limits are also ok since drivers sell tickets on-board. It is also hard to pay for the ticket on the airport express train, because it is difficult to find the credit card slot. He pointed out that he needs help finding free seats. However, staff are usually quite happy to assist.

This participant also mentioned problems navigating around a city. "Cities are filled with aggressive drivers that often miscalculate my slow movements". However, his tunnel vision allows him to see the boundary between the pavement and building walls, the street curb and the white zebra crossings, and therefore manages to walk around the city by himself. He navigates by counting streets, and this strategy requires knowledge of the area. "If I lose count, I lose track of where I am. Also, cities do change".

He also noted that it is difficult to enter unfamiliar places as he is unable to read shop signs and find shop entrances. Once inside the problems continue. Often there are stairs going down immediately inside and stairs are difficult with tunnel vision. Finding things inside buildings can be hard without help, for instance finding reception desks in hotels or specific products in a shop.

The issue of transportation has also been identified by Cimarolli et al. [16], and the issue of on-the-fly text recognition devices has been explored by several researchers [5, 12]. The results presented herein support these and similar research efforts. Also, much research have been conducted into the recognition of vehicle licence plates [18, 19]. Could such techniques be applied to aids for low-vision individuals? Although the transportation infrastructure has made enormous advances in terms of assistance to the visually impaired in recent years, the results suggests that there still are some gaps that perhaps could be filled by devices that can help identify arriving vehicles.

4.3   Stigma of Unusual-Looking Equipment

Participants also confirmed the importance of visual aids looking "normal" as there is great stigma connected to "strange-looking" assistive technology. "I do not want to wear ugly things." Recent technology may change this as Google glass, Hololens and Oculus Rift are considered "cool".

The participant with the least reduced vision was quite positive towards the idea of smart glasses, while participants with lower vision preferred audio. "It is very demanding to interpret the visual stimuli as it is, and I would prefer to have information read out such as the name of the person I am looking at or the number of the bus approaching. I do not bother enlarging the text on my phone or use voice over to see who is calling; I am simply answer the phone and ask – who is calling?" These statements suggest that head-mounted real-time text recognition systems with audio feedback [12] may be a step in the right direction.

The participant with tunnel vision declared that he was not too interested in technology. For example, he had not experimented with talking GPS-devices or modern smartphones. He had traditionally not been too concerned with the appearance of things, but that this awareness has grown over the years. "It is strange…after I lost my colour vision I have wanted to wear clothes with bright colours".

5 Conclusions

This study addressed the needs and coping strategies of low-vision individuals. The results indicate that the recognition of faces is the main challenge for low-vision individuals. Next, the recognition of texts on buildings and moving vehicles is the second most important challenge. Future research into visual aids should therefore focus on developing and testing face and text recognition systems in relevant contexts. Another interesting finding revealed by the interview is whether smart glasses are the solution. Perhaps the solution is non-visual? The results lead to the hypothesis that preference for visual versus audio feedback is related to the level and type of reduced vision.

Acknowledgements. The author is grateful to associate professor Siri Kessel for valuable discussions.

References

1. Peli, E.: Image enhancement for the visually impaired – simulations and experimental results. Invest. Ophthalmol. Vis. Sci. **32**, 2337–2350 (1991)
2. Peli, E., Lee, E., Trempe, C., Buzney, S.: Image enhancement for the visually impaired: the effects of enhancement of face recognition. J. Opt. Soc. Am. **11**, 1929–1939 (1994)
3. Everingham, M.R., Thomas, B.T., Troscianko, T.: Head-mounted mobility aid for low vision using scene classification techniques. Int. J. Virtual Reality **3**, 3 (1999)
4. Harper, R., Culham, L., Dickinson, C.: Head mounted video magnification devices for low vision rehabilitation: a comparison with existing technology. Br. J. Ophthalmol. **83**, 495–500 (1999)

5. Zhao, Y., Szpiro, S., Azenkot, S.: ForeSee: a customizable head-mounted vision enhancement system for people with low vision. In: Proceedings of the 17th International ACM SIGACCESS Conference on Computers and Accessibility, pp. 239–249. ACM (2015)
6. Kálmán, V., et al.: Wearable technology to help with visual challenges-two case studies. Stud. Health Technol. Inform. **217**, 526–532 (2015)
7. Tanuwidjaja, E., Huynh, D., Koa, K., Nguyen, C., Shao, C., Torbett, P., Weibel, N.: Chroma: a wearable augmented-reality solution for color blindness. In: Proceedings of the 2014 ACM International Joint Conference on Pervasive and Ubiquitous Computing, pp. 799–810. ACM (2014)
8. Hwang, A.D., Peli, E.: An augmented-reality edge enhancement application for Google Glass. Optom. Vis. Sci. **91**, 1021–1030 (2014)
9. Hicks, S.L., Wilson, I., Muhammed, L., Worsfold, J., Downes, S.M., Kennard, C.: A depth-based head-mounted visual display to aid navigation in partially sighted individuals. PLoS ONE **8**, e67695 (2013)
10. Costa, P., et al.: Obstacle detection using stereo imaging to assist the navigation of visually impaired people. Procedia Comput. Sci. **14**, 83–93 (2012)
11. Gomez, J.V., Sandnes, F.E.: RoboGuideDog: guiding blind users through physical environments with laser range scanners. Procedia Comput. Sci. **14**, 218–225 (2012)
12. Merino-Gracia, C., Lenc, K., Mirmehdi, M.: A head-mounted device for recognizing text in natural scenes. In: Iwamura, M., Shafait, F. (eds.) CBDAR 2011. LNCS, vol. 7139, pp. 29–41. Springer, Heidelberg (2012)
13. Dougherty, B.E., Kehler, K.B., Jamara, R., Patterson, N., Valenti, D., Vera-Diaz, F.A.: Abandonment of low vision devices in an outpatient population. Optom. Vis. Sci. **88**, 1283 (2011)
14. Satgunam, P., Woods, R.L., Luo, G., Bronstad, P.M., Reynolds, Z., Ramachandra, C., Peli, E.: Effects of contour enhancement on low-vision preference and visual search. Optom. Vis. Sci. **89**, E1364 (2012)
15. Luo, G., Peli, E.: Use of an augmented-vision device for visual search by patients with tunnel vision. Invest. Ophthalmol. Vis. Sci. **47**, 4152–4159 (2006)
16. Cimarolli, V.R., Boerner, K., Brennan-Ing, M., Reinhardt, J.P., Horowitz, A.: Challenges faced by older adults with vision loss: a qualitative study with implications for rehabilitation. Clin. Rehabil. **26**, 748–757 (2012)
17. Zhao, W., et al.: Face recognition: a literature survey. ACM Comput. Surv. **35**, 399–458 (2003)
18. Huang, Y.-P., Chang, T.-W., Chen, J.-R., Sandnes, F.E.: A back propagation based real-time license plate recognition system. Int. J. Pattern Recognit. Artif. Intell. **22**, 233–251 (2008)
19. Huang, Y.-P., Chen, C.-H., Chang, Y.-T., Sandnes, F.E.: An intelligent strategy for checking the annual inspection status of motorcycles based on license plate recognition. Expert Syst. Appl. **36**, 9260–9267 (2009)

Accessibility of Web and Graphics

Image Processing and Pattern Recognition Tools for the Automatic Image Transcription

Zehira Haddad$^{(\boxtimes)}$, Yong Chen, and Jaime Lopez Krahe

THIM CHART, Université Paris8, 2 rue de la Liberté, St. Denis, France
{zhaddad-bousseksou, jlk}@univ-paris8.fr

Abstract. The main objective of this work is to automate the conversion process of pedagogical images into information easily understandable by blind people and visually impaired people. This is performed by determining automatically the different areas of interest in the image, then identify each region by assigning it a texture which will be for example transformed in relief. The text present in the image is also detected, recognized and transformed in accessible text (in Braille text or vocal message). The solution that we offer by this work is to provide a tool that tries to find automatically the principal information conveyed by the image and then transmit it to blind people.

Keywords: Image accessibility · Image transcription · Text detection · Image resolution enhancement · Curvelet transform · Stroke Width Transform (SWT) · OCR · Image segmentation

1 Introduction

Image accessibility is an important area of research. Indeed, tactile images are widely used as an efficient accessibility tool to visually impaired people in many domains especially in schools and educational environments. The principal drawback of relief images is that blind people do not know always Braille. Moreover, the interactive map is a fairly simple and convenient way to access information for these people. A type of interactive map combines relief map and voice synthesis [1]. Users explore the relief image with their finger. At the same time a tablet below the image gives vocal explanation which has the same functionality as a legend. Another technique provides a novel opportunity to present an image to blind people; it is the touch screen with electro-vibration feedback [2]. With this electro-vibration feedback technique, we can simulate touch with different textures on the screen. Unfortunately, until now, the tactile image creation is done manually. With a computer, the designers use generally an image editing software to redraw an image from its original version. Given the current scientific research development in pattern recognition and image processing in general, we propose solutions to this problem.

To transcribe an image, two important stages must be realized: (i) the text detection, recognition and transcription in Braille, (ii) the segmentation of the different image areas and the affiliation of textures.

Generally, images like pedagogical images often need to be enlarged and enhanced for better OCR detection. Indeed, OCR does not work with small text and could give

K. Miesenberger et al. (Eds.): ICCHP 2016, Part I, LNCS 9758, pp. 197–203, 2016.
DOI: 10.1007/978-3-319-41264-1_26

very poor results with extended texts of poor quality. For these reason, we propose a new image resolution enhancement method which improves the quality of super resolution image. The classical technique to enlarge an image is interpolation. The classical image interpolation techniques are nearest neighbor interpolation, bilinear interpolation, and bi-cubic interpolation. Furthermore, the wavelet transform has been used successfully in image resolution enhancement and various approaches resulting therefrom [3]. However, all these well-known techniques present some visual drawbacks which are mainly due to the loss on the high image frequency components corresponding to the edges. In fact, we observe a smoothing in the interpolated image. The principal goal of the actual research is to ameliorate the image quality of super resolution by preserving the edge information. In this purpose, we propose a super resolution approach based on Curvelet transform which is dedicated to well representing curves and contours in an image.

Furthermore, the text zone in images transmits very rich and useful information for the image comprehension. But it is very difficult to localize text robustly in images that contain complex backgrounds with compromising edges and curves. Indeed, the application of the OCR directly in an image gives very poor results. The cause is due to the OCR which is generally dedicated for scanned text because it depends strongly on the correct separation of text from the background. Hence, there has been research focusing on the development of text detection methods in image which facilitate the OCR work. When we examine the previous research in this domain, we distinguish three classes of approaches: texture based approaches [4, 5], region based approaches [6, 7] and hybrid approaches [8]. Among these methods some of the most interesting are based on the Stroke Width Transform (SWT) of the image. These methods use image edges and lead the connected components by verifying some conditions on the SWT. The bibliographic study demonstrates clearly that these methods are very efficient compared to others. However, their performance depends strongly on the exact detection of the image edges. For these reasons, we propose a text detection approach based on a combination of Curvelet transform and SWT. Indeed the use of Curvelet transform allows highlighting the curves and well extracting the contours of the image [9], which has the effect of ensuring good text detection via SWT transform and the corresponding rules. Once the text is enhanced and well detected, the use of an OCR allows the transcription.

The second phase is the segmentation in order to differentiate the regions in image. There are generally two types of segmentation approaches: those based on regions and those based on contours. For this work, we opted for a fuzzy approach based on regions [10].

2   Methodology

The proposed approach contains the following stages: image resolution enhancement; text detection, recognition and transcription; image segmentation and post treatment.

2.1   Image Resolution Enhancement

The proposed image resolution enhancement approach firstly consists in decomposing the image by Curvelet transform into different frequency subbands corresponding to different scales and different orientations [9]. Then, we enhance edges present in the different high frequency images of the Curvelet decomposition by using a nonlinear function defining by the following formula:

$$R(i,j) = \begin{cases} G\, x(i,j) \left(1 - \dfrac{|x(i,j)|}{M}\right)^{p} + x(i,j) & x \leq M \\ \\ x & otherwise \end{cases} \tag{1}$$

Where $x(i,j)$ is the input image; M the upper limit of nonlinear enhancement; G the gain factor; p defines the rate of attenuation towards M.

By applying the proposed function, we increase the Curvelet coefficients in order to enhance the edges. After enhancing the edges, the interpolation of image resulting of the Curvelet decomposition is done by applying bicubic interpolation of a certain factor. Finally, this image is fused with the interpolated original image by taking the maximum value component.

2.2   Text Detection, Recognition and Transcription

The main idea of the proposed approach is to combine the Curvelet transform and the SWT in order to propose an efficient text detector. The text detection via SWT is a very interesting approach which has proven its efficiency [7]. The objective of this combination is to take the benefit of Curvelet transform for the curves and edges enhancement. We propose to detect edges by examining the Curvelet coefficients values. These coefficients inform us about how they are aligned in the image. Indeed, more accurately a Curvelet is aligned with a given curve in an image; higher is its coefficient value. Therefore, the approach consists of arranging the coefficients of each subband and applies a thresholding in order to take only the most significant part of them. Thus, we will enhance and extract the edge information. After this, we use the extracted edges for the determination of SWT (Stroke Width Transform). The SWT method determinates the only effective features of text and uses its geometric signature to reject non-text areas. So, this system provides reliable text region detection based on certain rules corresponding to characteristics of text area. For the text recognition step, we use Tesseract OCR.

2.3   Segmentation and Post-treatment

Segmentation is based on new Fuzzy C Means (FCM) approach which uses color, space and spatial information [10]. First, an automatic estimation of the geographic regions number is done by analyzing the color histogram in RGB and HIS spaces. So, we detect the peak number and the pixel point on the peak as the initial clustering number. Then, we use the particle swam optimization algorithm to determine the initial clustering center of FCM [10]. Subsequently, we use the classical FCM segmentation which is based on optimizing a quadratic criterion of classification. There by, we detect automatically each region of the image and in order to make it tactile, we can easily join it a texture that will be transformed in relief. However, we took into account some recommendations related to blind tactile exploration [11]. For example, in order to facilitate the tactile image comprehension by visually blind people, we apply a smoothing and reinforcement of contours corresponding to each textured region via some mathematical morphology methods. Also, we took great care to choose a number of textures well distinguishable.

3   Experimental Results

In the experimental study, we use a database of eight pedagogical images and in order to know if the produced tactile maps are operational by visually blind people, we organized an experimental test on these images with eight blind people.

The following figures present a sample of obtained tactile images. Firstly, images are printed on a multi-layer paper with a normal printer. Then we pass this paper in the oven for heat, which will ultimately produce a relief map where only the black lines will swell with the heat.

We remark that we kept the original text and we transform it in light gray. This is not a problem for blind people because it will not inflate.

Without the availability of the proposed solution, the eight used pedagogical images would have required manual conversion.

During the experimental study, the overall objective is to explore eight relief images in order to understand their content. For this, we worked with eight blind persons.

Each image in relief is presented to an experimenter; we allowed a necessary time to understand the image content. When the experimenter thinks that he was well understood the content after exploring the image, he informs us and at this time, we present him a short questionnaire of four questions on the image content. This questionnaire will therefore be subject to an evaluation on 10 points.

The four questions are asked in order of complexity of understanding (from the easiest to the most difficult).

It was important to make clear to visually impaired experimenters that it is not them who were judged but it's our work on relief images which is judged by them (Figs. 1, 2 and 3).

Figure 4 represents the obtained scores by each participant Pi, and the average score M for each image. So, we can conclude that created relief images by the proposed method are understandable by participants. However, some people perceived certain difficulty to understand some images because they did not know the represented content. For example, a person which does not know the sequence of '4 Seasons' and the relationship with the earth and sun. He will have some difficulties to understand the four different positions of the earth around the sun for the four seasons.

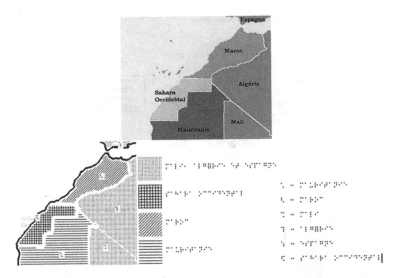

Fig. 1. Geographic tactile image. (Color figure online)

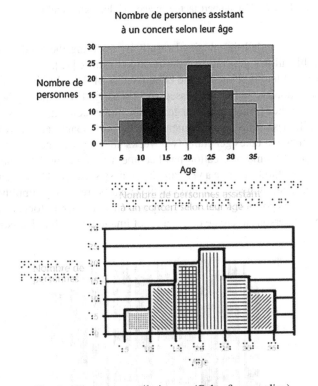

Fig. 2. Histogram tactile image. (Color figure online)

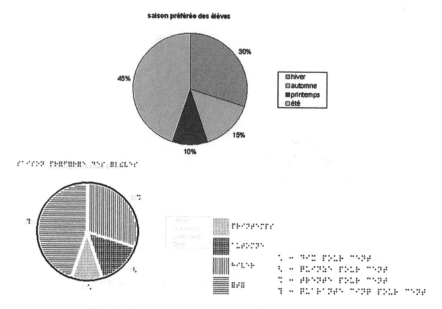

Fig. 3. Camembert tactile image. (Color figure online)

We have also extended the obtained results by applying the Student's t-test with database data; this allows generalizing the obtained results [12].

This treated problem is related to the effectiveness of the relief image creation. We met with transcriptionists and we discussed and exchanged with them. They explained us that to create a relief pedagogical image in educational context, it takes few hours to several days. Likewise, during experimental tests, participants also revealed us that to have a relief image, it takes generally two weeks after that the request have been sent to the creator. So, the time of creation has become a very important issue.

The proposed method can give a very quick and easy solution. The system only takes few minutes to get a relief image. The tasks of the creators are greatly simplified. With the proposed method, it is possible for any ordinary person (a teacher, or for example a family member of a blind person) to create easily a relief image for the blind person.

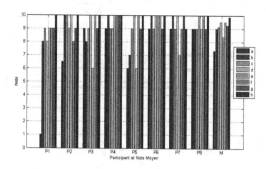

Fig. 4. Scores obtained by participants for each image. (Color figure online)

4 Conclusion

The presented work permits to detect automatically different information in quite simple image (like pedagogical images) in order to make it accessible. This was possible by proposing new image processing approaches adapted to the addressed problem. A tactile exploration of image is also proposed facilitating greatly the purely manual work of transcribers. The obtained results of the experimental study demonstrate the utility of the produced tactile maps for blind people.

As future works, we can extend this work in order to propose an accessibility tool for certain numeric and web images (scanned images or downloaded from internet). We can also easily suppose a system of relief image in tablet with a voice synthesizer or a touch screen with Feedback-electro-vibration.

Acknowledgements. This work was supported by PICRI CARTASAM no. 13020599.

References

1. Brock, A., Truillet, P., Oriola, B., Picard, D., Jouffrais, C.: Design and user satisfaction of interactive maps for visually impaired people. In: Miesenberger, K., Karshmer, A., Penaz, P., Zagler, W. (eds.) ICCHP 2012, Part II. LNCS, vol. 7383, pp. 544–551. Springer, Heidelberg (2012)
2. Bau, O., Poupyrev, I., Israr, A., Harrison, C.: TeslaTouch: electrovibration for touch surfaces. ACM Symposium on User Interface Software and Technology (ACM UIST) (2010)
3. Birare, S.D., Nalbalwar, S.L.: Review on super resolution of images using wavelet transform. Int. J. Eng. Sci. Technol. 2(12), 7363–7371 (2010)
4. Gllavata, J., Ewerth, R., Freisleben, B.: Text detection in images based on unsupervised classification of high-frequency wavelet coefficients. In: 17th International Conference on Pattern Recognition (ICPR 2004), vol. 1, pp. 425–428 (2004)
5. Ye, Q., Huang, Q., Gao, W., Zhao, D.: Fast and robust text detection in images and video frames. Image Vis. Comput. 23(8), 565–576 (2005)
6. Neumann, L., Matas, J.: A method for text localization and recognition in real-world images. In: Proceedings of ACCV, Part IV. LNCS, vol. 6495, pp. 2067–2078 (2010)
7. Epshtein, B., Ofek, E., Wexler, Y.: Detecting text in natural scenes with stroke width transform. In: Proceedings of the CVPR (2010)
8. Pan, Y., Hou, X., Liu, C.: A hybrid approach to detect and localize texts in natural scene images. IEEE Trans. Image Process. 20(3), 800–813 (2011)
9. Candes, E.J., Demanet, L., Donoho, D.L., Ying, L.: Fast discrete curvelet transforms. Multiscale Model. Simul. 5, 861–899 (2006)
10. Ding, Z., Sun, J., Zhang, Y.: FCM image segmentation algorithm based on color space and spatial information. Int. J. Comput. Commun. Eng. 2(1), 48–51 (2013)
11. Wolfe, J., Levi, D., Kluender, K., Bartoshuk, L., Herz, R., Klatzky, R., Lederman, S.J., Merfeld, D.: Sensation and Perception, 3rd edn. Sinauer Associates, Inc., Sunderland (2011)
12. de Winter, J.C.F.: Using the Student's t-test with extremely small sample sizes. Pract. Assess. Res. Eval. 18, 1–12 (2013)

Generating Image Descriptions for SmartArts

Jens Voegler[(⊠)], Julia Krause, and Gerhard Weber

Institute of Applied Computer Science, Technische Universität Dresden,
Dresden, Germany
{jens.voegler,gerhard.weber}@tu-dresden.de,
Julia.Krause5@mailbox.tu-dresden.de

Abstract. Visual information such as SmartArts are often used in presentations and lectures. SmartArts are visual information containing some text and graphical elements. They have to be described verbally to become accessible for visually impaired and blind people. But a manual image description is often not provided or misses information about the pictorial part of SmartArt diagrams. We present a PowerPoint Add-In to create image descriptions semiautomatically. Both a short description and a long description containing details are generated. The author can adjust the generation by modifying a template. In a user evaluation the quality of manually and semi-automatic transcribed images were tested.

Keywords: SmartArt · Alternative description · Images

1 Introduction

Accessible study materials are very important in the educational field. The transcription of these documents is a manual process, in particular for images. Alternative descriptions of images are crucial to provide accessible educational materials for students. In a study on images in web pages, it was shown that short, as well as long descriptions, are essential for understanding information represented in images [6]. Lecture materials for students convey many concepts through graphics and - depending on the domain - also graphical notations. Highly structured textual elements like lists, tables and headings are transcribed straight forward by a human transcriber. The textual elements may be transformed also automatically for some sources, but arbitrary images were excluded from this approach in the past.

SmartArts are a kind of structured images, and commonly utilized to illustrate processes or a relation between elements visually in office software. In many institutions Microsoft® PowerPoint is the main authoring program. We analysed the authoring programs used for lecture materials visited by blind and visually impaired students at TU Dresden during winter term 2015 covering subjects in Psychology, Computer Science and Sociology. The analysis was semiautomatic. A script interpreted metadata of the PDF-files and PowerPoint files were counted manually if no PDF files were available. The results of the analysis are shown in Fig. 1. This figure illustrates that multiple programs and various operating systems are used. The values for the category *others* and *PSscript.dll* are also listed, as they occur frequently in this analysis. These entries

K. Miesenberger et al. (Eds.): ICCHP 2016, Part I, LNCS 9758, pp. 204–211, 2016.
DOI: 10.1007/978-3-319-41264-1_27

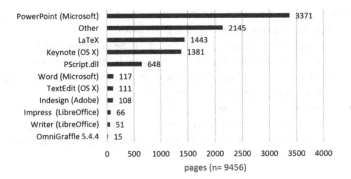

Fig. 1. Used authoring programs/tools

indicate various tools that cannot be named, like the Print2PDF function. All together 52 tools were used for preparing slides.

Microsoft® PowerPoint offers various kinds of SmartArts for well-structured graphical layout-types. For advanced users it is also possible to design and edit the type of a SmartArt.

In this paper we discuss the automatic extraction of textual content of a SmartArt and adding further information for blind and visually impaired users about the layout being used. We propose ensuring all visual information requires twofold alternative descriptions to carefully point out important concepts first and more detailed information afterwards. Steps include (1) the serialisation of the text and (2) the description of the visually represented information. Both types of information form a short and a long image description.

To ensure flexibility and processing of non-standard uses of text and SmartArt a two-step approach for encoding the document structure is helpful. We have identified Markdown for efficient transcription of documents [7] and discuss in the following how to generate image descriptions into Markdown notation.

2   Relevant Works

There are three different approaches to describe visual information. Neural networks and other classifiers enable the generation of image descriptions by using natural language. Neural networks are trained with existing images. New images will be prepared for the analysis by grouping all pixels into regions. After that the regions will be analysed and interpreted. If the neural network is well trained the results will be very good. For the description of SmartArts a neural network appears to be too much overload at this point.

In the second, specific markup languages are defined like PlantUML, BlindUML [5] or GraphViz. For this approach, it is necessary that the readers and authors have to learn the specific language. In addition, an author often has to learn a new workflow because the new markup language requires a new editor. Finally, the reader has to learn the markup language for understanding the descriptions.

Another approach is the manually description by the creator/publisher of the image. Therefor different guidelines and manuals are available. How to describe an image in HTML is explained in [8, 9]. Many programs support the description of images basing on the attribute title and description (see page 57 in [1, 4]).

All three approaches are not really comfortable and easy going. In the following, we propose utilizing an AddIn for PowerPoint for improving the alternative description of graphics and to allow manual modification during the transcription process using Markdown.

3   Markdown

Markdown is the implementation of a simplified, human-readable description language to write markup such as used in HTML. The Markdown syntax cannot be viewed as an HTML replacement, since it covers only parts of the HTML tags. However, using additional HTML markup is supported [2].

3.1   The MarkdownConverter

MarkdownConverter is a new tool to convert PowerPoint presentations into a Markdown document automatically. It was developed as a PowerPoint AddIn and is currently tested during the transcription process of accessible study material at Technical University Dresden. Currently, the following PowerPoint elements are supported: heading, paragraphs, lists, formulas, tables, images and their alternative description, as well as images created by using the free forms of Microsoft®.

After the transcription, the markdown files contains generated text and references to images. Images and grouped image elements are preserved within an accessible document. In particular, grouped image elements are exported as images in the PNG-format[1]. Thus, blind readers have a textual description and visually impaired readers can view the image using appropriate assistive technologies for magnification or improving colour contrast.

Too long and complex alternative descriptions will be stored in a separate file and linked from the main content file. Finally, the processing pipeline continues by converting all the Markdown files to HTML using Matuc[2]. Matuc is a customized converter and is based on Pandoc[3].

---

[1] The development of an SVG is in progress.

[2] https://elvis.inf.tu-dresden.de/wiki/index.php/Matuc (German Website).

[3] http://pandoc.org/index.html.

4   SmartArt Graphics

SmartArts graphics are supported since the PowerPoint Version 2007. Figure 2 shows an example of a SmartArt – a chevron list mirroring a tabular layout. SmartArts are being used to visualize information, a process or relationships. They help the presenter to talk to the audience about complex contents, while a large number of types for SmartArt exist. Additionally, it is possible to extend the SmartArt repository[4].

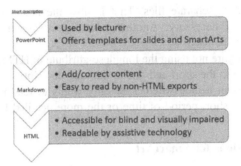

Fig. 2. Example of a SmartArt

SmartArt templates are grouped into lists, process, cycle, hierarchy, relationship, matrix and pyramid. Each template has a unique name and technically, the content of a SmartArt is a nested list [3].

5   Concept of the SmartArt Converter

The SmartArt converter derives two descriptions from each SmartArt graphics basing on a template. Before a semiautomatic description can be generated the author has to write the template description for each SmartArt which is used in the presentation. Due to this template the process is semiautomatic.

In the template the alternative description is composed by using text and by defined placeholders. Once the template descriptions have been entered, they are saved in an XML document and can be arbitrarily accessed and edited. If an already described SmartArt is used in a new presentation, the previously saved template description text will be reused.

The SmartArt converter creates various files (see Fig. 3). All files are saved in the Markdown format and can be converted to HTML by using Matuc (Markdown AGSBS TU Converter). The textual elements of the presentation are saved in the main content file. The short and long descriptions of SmartArt and also the alternative

---

4 https://support.office.com/en-us/article/Create-a-SmartArt-graphic-4c36e284-2b76-400d-99d7-6cf198a33a4b .

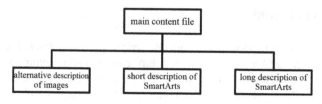

Fig. 3. Generated files

description are saved in separate files. That is how the reader can navigate to the relevant information if necessary. Another advantage of separate files is that the Markdown syntax can be used.

In our approach we are not using the longdesc-attribute of HTML5 [8], because two links are needed – one to the short and one to the long description. So the reader of the transcribed materials can decide whether he only wants to read relevant information during the lecture in a short period of time or the more detailed long description.

5.1 Short Descriptions for SmartArt

A short description contains only a selection of important information such as the name of the SmartArt category as well as the nested list of all elements. Figure 4 (left side) shows the short description of Fig. 2. The main goal is to provide a fast and easy access to the visual shown information.

5.2 Long Description for SmartArt

For a more detailed description, it is necessary to name information like colours, the position and level of the element and the content. Furthermore we provide an introduction, a main part and a description of each list element. The introduction names the category and the name of the SmartArt. In addition, the introduction should inform the reader about size and structure verbally. The main part describes a general outline whereas the focus of the final part lies more on individual content points. Overall our converter provides nine placeholders depending on the category and text category, introduction, main part and description of children.

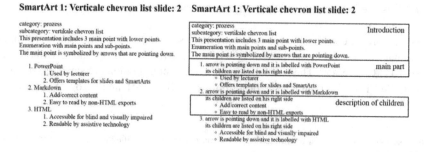

Fig. 4. Short (left) and long description (right)

Figure 4 (right side) shows an example of a long description of the chevron list (see Fig. 2). Currently we support the use of SmartArt templates in the default way only.

6   Evaluation of Semiautomatic Generated Description

The goal of the evaluation is to assess whether semiautomatic generated descriptions contain adequate information to understand the SmartArt from a nonvisual description. For this a selection of five different SmartArt graphics of existing lecture materials was chosen. Each graphic has been described manually by expert transcribers and additionally by our SmartArt converter. In the next step of our evaluation the short description was presented and the subject had to rebuild the SmartArt by using paper shapes and printed labels. Afterwards the long description was presented to the subject and he/she could correct the SmartArt. The same approach was applied to the manual description. Each rebuild SmartArt was documented by taking a picture (see Fig. 5).

The evaluation was recorded by video. During the experiment the subjects were requested to think aloud and reveal their thoughts. After each type of SmartArt the subject rated the long and a short description with the manual one. Before the first SmartArt was shown the subjects were asked whether they read alternative descriptions during their lectures, and in the end it was asked whether they will read the short description during the lecture?

Figure 6 shows that 3 subjects will read the short description during the lecture after explaining the concept of short and long description. Only one subject said she focuses mainly on the lecture. The importance of elements of a SmartArt was also evaluated (see Fig. 7). Information like the colour and background are more unimportant as structure of the description and relation between shapes. The comments during the evaluation point up that an automatic generation has a lack of information, e.g. explaining by using clockwise. This is reflected in the answers to the final question whether they will prefer a generated description instead of a manually one. The answer was no by two subjects, one would prefer the generated description and one did not care about it. Manual descriptions are more concise than the generated ones.

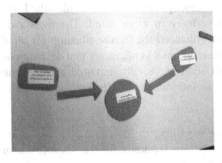

Fig. 5. Result for the long description (left side) and manual description (right side)

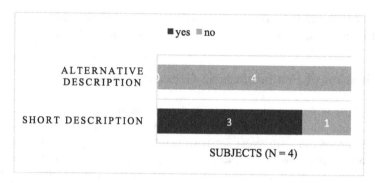

Fig. 6. Use of manual and short description during the lectures (Color figure online)

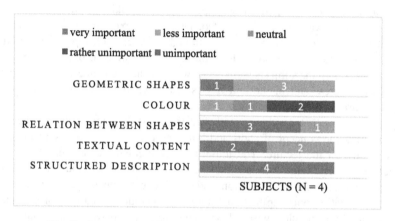

Fig. 7. Importance of SmartArt elements (Color figure online)

7 Summary and Conclusion

Image descriptions sometimes require long descriptions. We have identified the SmartArt graphics features to be described verbally in more detail. The evaluation results have shown that short descriptions can enhanced the lecture situation for blind students. For a better acceptance of the long description it is necessary that descriptions are going to be designed in cooperation with blind or visually impaired person in an iterating process. In addition, a database must be introduced in order to provide already existing SmartArts for other authors.

Acknowledgements. We thank Florian Dietz for supporting the development of the MarkdownConverter for Microsoft PowerPoint and Sebastian Humenda for the development of Matuc.

References

1. Adobe: Creating Accessible Adobe PDF Files - A Guide for Document Authors, March 2016. https://www.adobe.com/enterprise/accessibility/pdfs/acro6_pg_ue.pdf
2. MacFarlane, J.: Retrieved from Pandoc a universal document converter, 23 March 2016. http://pandoc.org/
3. Microsoft: Retrieved from Learn more about SmartArt graphics, January 2016. https://support.office.com/en-us/article/Learn-more-about-SmartArt-graphics-91d1bf9b-8c06-4e21-ad31-f2c21af7d53b
4. Microsoft: Add alternative text to a shape, picture, chart, table, SmartArt graphic, or other object, March 2016. https://support.office.com/en-us/article/Add-alternative-text-to-a-shape-picture-chart-table-SmartArt-graphic-or-other-object-44989b2a-903c-4d9a-b742-6a75b451c669
5. Müller, K.: How to make unified modeling language diagrams accessible for blind students. In: Miesenberger, K., Karshmer, A., Penaz, P., Zagler, W. (eds.) ICCHP 2012, Part I. LNCS, vol. 7382, pp. 186–190. Springer, Heidelberg (2012). doi:10.1007/978-3-642-31522-0_27
6. Petrie, H., Harrison, C., Dev, S.: Describing images on the web: a survey of current practice and prospects for the future. In: Proceedings of Human Computer, pp. 1–10 (2005). http://www.academia.edu/download/30388620/hcii05_alt_text_paper.pdf
7. Voegler, J., Bornschein, J., Weber, G.: Markdown – a simple syntax for transcription of accessible study materials. In: Miesenberger, K., Fels, D., Archambault, D., Peňáz, P., Zagler, W. (eds.) ICCHP 2014, Part I. LNCS, vol. 8547, pp. 545–548. Springer, Heidelberg (2014). doi:10.1007/978-3-319-08596-8_85
8. W3C: Retrieved from HTML5 Image Description Extension (longdesc), 26 February 2015. https://www.w3.org/TR/html-longdesc/
9. W3C: Retrieved from Techniques for WCAG 2.0, March 2016. https://www.w3.org/TR/WCAG20-TECHS/

Mobile Interactive Image Sonification
for the Blind

Torsten Wörtwein[1], Boris Schauerte[1], Karin Müller[2],
and Rainer Stiefelhagen[1,2(✉)]

[1] Computer Vision for Human-Computer Interaction Lab (CVHCI),
Karlsruhe Institute of Technology, Karlsruhe, Germany
rainer.stiefelhagen@kit.edu
[2] Study Centre for the Visually Impaired (SZS), Karlsruhe Institute of Technology,
Karlsruhe, Germany

Abstract. Web-based, mobile sonification offers a highly flexible way
to give blind users access to graphical information and to solve various
everyday as well as job-related tasks. The combination of a touch screen,
image processing, and sonification allows the user to hear the content of
every image region that he or she indicates with his/her finger position
on a tablet or mobile phone. In this paper, we build on and expand
our previous work in this area and evaluate how six blind participants
can perceive mathematical graphs, bar charts, and floor maps with our
sonifications and tactile graphics.

1 Introduction

Nowadays, two common ways of presenting spatial information to blind users are
tactile graphics and sonification. Tactile graphics offer intuitive access to spatial
information for blind people, especially if they have experience with braille. However, in recent years, we can observe that more and more people use electronic
devices and software such as screen readers instead of printed braille to access
text, since especially younger people tend to prefer electronic text on computers. For example, in Britain, it is nowadays assumed that only 15–20 thousand
people use braille out of approximately two million blind and low vision individuals [18]. One major disadvantage of printed braille and tactile graphics is
that they require special hardware such as tactile embossers. These devices are
often complex, only provide help for specific tasks, and are produced in small
numbers, which leads to high costs, low flexibility, and a low availability, since no
blind person wants to carry a costly array of various devices around at all times.
In contrast, smartphones and tablets have become omnipresent, mass produced,
multi-function devices. In other words, they are the digital Swiss Army Knifes
of our era. Astonishingly, despite the fact that blind people are unable to see the
content shown on the touchscreen, smartphones have become an essential tool in
the lives of many blind people. For example, all participants in our evaluation use
their smartphone every day and several of them own tablets and smart watches

K. Miesenberger et al. (Eds.): ICCHP 2016, Part I, LNCS 9758, pp. 212–219, 2016.
DOI: 10.1007/978-3-319-41264-1_28

Fig. 1. Experiment setting: two blind participants equipped with a headphone trying to identify a box plot (left) and a mathematical function plot (right) by moving their finger on the tablet surface

as well. In fact, blind people have become so apt in operating these devices that some apps are exclusively developed for – and even by [6] – blind users.

In our work, we use modern web-technologies to implement an interactive image sonification platform that can be accessed with a web-browser on devices that many blind users use on a daily basis (most importantly, smartphones, tablets and desktop computers). Hence, our system can be used almost everywhere, see Fig. 1 for the minimal setup. Since we can implement various sonification algorithms and switch them depending on the user's context, we can use these sonifications to allow blind users access to a wide variety of information that is typically presented in the form of images (e.g., maps, plans, graphs, or charts). Furthermore, electronic devices allow flexible interaction with the user to adapt to his needs. For example, a tactile graphic does not change once it is printed, whereas an electronic representation allows to change its scale, the level of details, the way of sonification, or even output modalities (e.g., sound, speech, or vibration).

2 Related Work

In recent years, various assistive systems for blind people have been developed (e.g., [2,23,25]) that rely on a variety of different technologies such as, e.g., computer vision [20], crowdsourcing [5], and touchscreens [13,24]. For example, it is possible to use computer vision to detect the walkable area in front of a blind person and then transform the information about obstacles into haptic or auditory feedback to guide a blind user around detected obstacles (see [15,20]). Turning information into auditory signals is called sonification (see [11]; e.g., [1–3,12,17,19,23,25]) and is a very common mean to present visual information such as, e.g., maps to blind people [23]. Sonification systems may use different techniques of sound synthesis, which we can differentiate into two main categories: Entirely synthetic sounds and sounds composed with musical instruments (e.g., piano and guitar sounds) [1,2]. As for sonification for visually impaired people, there also exist two main categories when it comes to image sonification: Low-level sonification of arbitrary images (e.g., [1,2,8]), i.e. sonification of basic

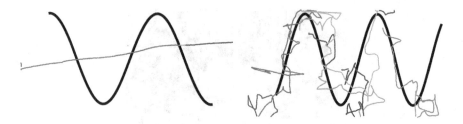

Fig. 2. Finger trajectories with function value sonification (left) and distance sonification (right)

image properties like color [8] and edges [25], and task-specific sonification (*e.g.*, [23]). Furthermore, we have to differentiate between sonification methods that sonify the image as a whole and present it to the user in form of a pre-calculated audio clip (*e.g.*, [16]) and systems that allow user interaction (see, *e.g.*, [10]), *e.g.* by sonifying the image area under the mouse cursor (*e.g.*, [1,25]). Web and mobile technologies have also been explored to assist blind people. Most prominently, Bigham *et al.* incorporate sighted persons ("the crowd") to help blind people find specific objects [4,5] on a picture taken with their iPhone.

3   Interactive Image Sonifications

In the following, we briefly describe the evaluation of several sonification methods for three tasks: mathematical graph identification, proportion estimation in bar charts, and path finding on floor maps.

3.1   Mathematical Graphs: "Identify the Underlying Function of the Presented Graph."

The *distance sonification* sonifies the distance to the plotted function. The frequency becomes lower the closer you are to the function. Hence, it encourages a free exploration of the whole *image*. We used an adapted depth-first-search to calculate the shortest distance to the graph.

Similar to the sonification by Grond *et al.* [9], the *value sonification* sonifies the value of the function at the x-location of the user's finger. Accordingly, the user will hear a high tone, if the function's value is high and vice versa. As a consequence, it is only necessary to move your finger from left to right, see Fig. 2.

The following functions are used: a linear, hyperbolic, parabola, sine, square-root, and an exponential function. The function value is represented by the position of the first non-background pixel per column.

3.2   Bar Charts: "Interpret the Relative Dimensions Between the Bars in a Bar Chart"

The *semantic map sonification* closely resembles a tactile graphic. Each texture is mapped to a different frequency (for the background and for each bar).

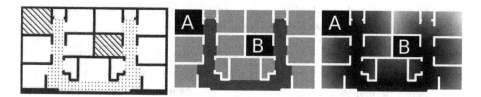

Fig. 3. Floor map as tactile graphic (left) and heat maps of frequencies of the semantic map sonification (middle) as well as the guided sonification (right)

The *value sonification* again sonifies the function value or in other words the height of the bars. Accordingly, the output frequency at an image location corresponds to the height of the bar at this location.

3.3 Floor Maps: "Find the Way Through a Corridor from One Room to Another on a Floor Map"

The *semantic map sonification* again resembles the tactile graphic, see Fig. 3. The source (A) and destination (B) room, corridors, other rooms, and walls are mapped to distinct frequencies. Thus, this sonification denotes the semantic information of a floor map.

To assist the task to find a path from room A to room B, the *guided sonification* guides the user to the destination. Therefore, a path from the source to destination is computed. The further you are away from the path the higher the frequency. Walls are denoted with the highest frequency, while the source and destination room share the lowest frequency. We use an A* algorithm to find the shortest path between the two rooms. Since the shortest path is along the walls and not centered in the corridor, we penalize pixel close to a wall based on a depth-first-search. After we calculated the path, we compute the distance to the path in the same manner as in *distance sonification*.

3.4 Frequency Mapping

All distances and function values are not directly mapped to output frequencies, because a twice as high frequency is not perceived as being twice as high by the human auditory perception. Therefore, we use the Mel transformation [22] to have a meaningful auditory representation. However, too low frequencies are hardly heard, we add a constant offset just before the Mel transformation to have perceivable frequencies. Thereby, we lose absolute relations but equal distances are still perceived equally. Frequencies range from 51.49 Hz (80 Mel) to 254.93 Hz (350 Mel).

4 Experimental Evaluation

We performed experiments with six blind participants. Four of them were female. The average age was 38.2 years ($SD = 8.1$). All participants have normal hearing

Table 1. Average and standard deviation of time required by the participants to complete each task for all evaluated methods (in seconds).

Method/task	Math. Graphs	Bar Charts	Floor Maps
Tactile graphics	9.5 (4.9)	28.8 (12.6)	49.4 (8.6)
Semantic map sonification		98.9 (28.3)	131.1 (80.5)
Value sonification	25.0 (6.7)	49.9 (9.1)	
Distance/guided sonification	106.0 (43.0)		114.5 (70.2)

and use touchscreens on a daily basis. All except one participant have at least passed the German *Abitur* (A-Levels) examinations. Only two participants use tactile graphics on a regular basis (several times a month). The participants did not have any prior training with our sonification system nor were they involved in the development.

To exclude variations due to different hardware and software configurations (*e.g.*, in stimulus size), all participants used the same platform: A first generation Samsung Nexus 10 tablet (10-inch touchscreen) with Android 5.1, AKG K 701 circumaural headphones and Google Chrome 47 as browser, see Fig. 1.

4.1 Evaluation Methodology

All participants answered first a demographics questionnaire. To ensure a reproduction of this experiment, the same instructions were read to all participants. In addition, they received the instructions in Braille without contractions (*i.e.*, *Deutsche Blindenvollschrift*). Our experiment consists of three tasks: mathematical function plots, bar charts, and floor maps. To solve each of them, three methods were evaluated: first using tactile graphics followed by two sonifications in random order. After each method, participants were asked the *After-scenario Questionnaire* (ASQ) on a five-point likert scale (third question is not applicable) to asses the usability of the methods [14]. After completing each task, participants were asked to rank the usability of the three used methods. The overall usability of the system was evaluated after all tasks on the positive *Software Usability Scale* (SUS) [7]. Each task and method had to be solved by several examples (six function plots, three bar charts, and three floor maps). To avoid a learning effect between the methods and to have an equal difficulty for each method, we varied the examples (function plots were scaled, bar charts were permutated, and floor maps were flipped as well as rotated). The order of the examples per method and task was randomized as well as whether and how the example was varied. For all examples, we measured the time to complete the current example and recorded the finger trajectory. In case of function plots, participants were asked to name or precisely describe the function. For bar charts, participants had to count the number of bars, order them by size, and name the size relations relative to the smallest bar (*e.g.*, "the left bar is twice as high as the smallest bar"). Floor maps were evaluated whether they found the destination and whether they were able to describe a valid path between the source and destination room. Since many participants were not familiar with mathematical functions, they were told the name of the function after each tactile example.

Table 2. Average and standard deviation of *ASQ* for all tasks and methods.

Method/task	Math. Graphs	Bar Charts	Floor Maps
Tactile graphics	5.0 (0.0)	4.8 (0.6)	4.3 (0.8)
Semantic map sonification		3.8 (0.8)	3.1 (1.4)
Value sonification	4.0 (0.8)	3.7 (0.6)	
Distance/guided sonification	2.2 (0.9)		2.7 (1.0)

4.2 Results

Tables 1 and 2 summarize the required time and the ASQ. Let us now briefly present our results. If we compare our new sonifications (*i.e.*, graph value, bar value, and guided floor map) to the sonifications that we used in our prior publications (*i.e.*, graph distance, semantic bar map, and semantic floor map), we can see that the users require less time to solve the tasks with our new sonifications. The average task completion time reduced to 25.0 from 106.0, to 49.9 from 98.9, and to 114.5 from 131.1 s for mathematical graph, bar chart, and floor map understanding, respectively. For example, it can easily be seen in Fig. 2 that the value sonification requires only few, simple finger swipes to understand the graph. But, this does not always lead to a higher user satisfaction as measured by the ASQ. The graph value sonification is significantly better for the graph sonification (3.9 on the ASQ scale of 1 to 5) compared to the graph distance sonification (2.2). But, the ASQ score of our new sonifications is lower for the bar chart sonification (3.8 vs 3.7) and the floor map understanding (3.1 vs 2.7).

Compared to the tactile graphics, we still observe a substantial gap in the users' quantitative task performances and subjective ratings. The tactile graphics still perform best in terms of task completion times (9.5, 28.8, and 50.0 s for graphs, bar charts, and floor maps, respectively) and ASQ scores (5.0, 4.8, and 4.3).

Overall, all users rate the intuitiveness of our mobile sonification system as being very high, *i.e.* a 4.0 on the SUS scale of 1 to 5. Furthermore, even though our sonifications differ substantially, the whole system is perceived as being consistent (SUS score of 4.33).

5 Conclusion

We have tested several tasks with various sonification methods and six blind users. We included tactile graphics as a baseline in our evaluation.

218 T. Wörtwein et al.

All our newly introduced sonifications reduced the time that the participants require to interpret mathematical graphs, bar charts, and floor maps. Unfortunately, we observed that lower completion times do not automatically correlate with a higher user satisfaction. Tactile graphics are still preferred over sonification by all but one of our participants. However, the fact that we already have users that prefer our sonification over tactile graphics is extremely promising and encouraging, because we should not forget that our web-based sonification is in an early technological stage and still suffers from technical challenges such as, e.g., the lack of real-time capabilities in modern browsers (see [21]).

Although we use vibration to notify users when they leave the sonified image area, we have not yet used vibration as a distinct information channel, but we plan to do this as part of our future work.

Acknowledgments. We thank Giuseppe Melfi for his help during the experimental evaluation and Gerhard Jaworek for being our voluntary blind user for alpha tests.

References

1. Banf, M., Blanz, V.: A modular computer vision sonification model for the visually impaired. In: Proceedings of the International Conference of Auditory Display (2012)
2. Banf, M., Blanz, V.: Sonification of images for the visually impaired using a multi-level approach. In: Proceedings of the Augmented Human International Conference (2013)
3. Bearman, N., Brown, E.: Who's sonifying data and how are they ng it? A comparison of ICAD and other venues since 2009. In: Proceedings of the International Conference on Auditory Display (2012)
4. Bigham, J.P., Jayant, C., Ji, H., Little, G., Miller, A., Miller, R.C., Miller, R., Tatarowicz, A., White, B., White, S., et al.: VizWiz: nearly real-time answers to visual questions. In: Proceedings of the Annual ACM Symposium on User Interface Software and Technology. pp. 333–342. ACM (2010)
5. Bigham, J.P., Jayant, C., Miller, A., White, B., Yeh, T.: VizWiz: locateit-enabling blind people to locate objects in their environment. In: Proceedings of the Computer Vision and Pattern Recognition Workshops (CVPRW), pp. 65–72 (2010)
6. Blüher, J.: About visorapps (2015). http://en.visorapps.com/about-visorapps/
7. Brooke, J.: SUS - a quick and dirty usability scale. Usability Eval. Ind. **189**, 4–7 (1996)
8. Cavaco, S., Henriques, J.T., Mengucci, M., Correia, N., Medeiros, F.: Color sonification for the visually impaired. Procedia Technol. **9**, 1048–1057 (2013)
9. Grond, F., Droßard, T., Hermann, T.: SonicFunction: experiments with a function browser for the visually impaired. In: Proceedings of the International Conference on Auditory Display. Georgia Institute of Technology (2010)
10. Hermann, T., Hunt, A.: An introduction to interactive sonification. IEEE Multimedia **12**, 20–24 (2005)
11. Hermann, T., Hunt, A., Neuhoff, J.G.: The Sonification Handbook. Logos Verlag, Berlin (2011)

12. Heuten, W., Henze, N., Boll, S.: Interactive exploration of city maps with auditory torches. In: CHI Extended Abstracts on Human Factors in Computing Systems (2007)
13. Klatzky, R., Giudice, N., Bennett, C., Loomis, J.: Touch-screen technology for the dynamic display of 2D spatial information without vision: promise and progress. Multisensory Res. **27**(5–6), 359–378 (2014)
14. Lewis, J.R.: IBM computer usability satisfaction questionnaires: psychometric evaluation and instructions for use. Int. J. Hum. Comput. Interact. **7**(1), 57–78 (1995)
15. Martinez, M., Constantinescu, A., Schauerte, B., Koester, D., Stiefelhagen, R.: Cognitive evaluation of haptic and audio feedback in short range navigation tasks. In: Miesenberger, K., Fels, D., Archambault, D., Peňáz, P., Zagler, W. (eds.) ICCHP 2014, Part II. LNCS, vol. 8548, pp. 128–135. Springer, Heidelberg (2014)
16. Meijer, P.B.: An experimental system for auditory image representations. Trans. Biomed. Eng. **39**(2), 112–121 (1992)
17. Ribeiro, F., Florêncio, D., Chou, P.A., Zhang, Z.: Auditory augmented reality: object sonification for the visually impaired. In: Proceedings of the International Workshop on Multimedia Signal Processing (2012)
18. Rose, D.: Braille is spreading but who's using it? (2013). http://www.bbc.com/news/magazine-16984742. bBCNews
19. Sanchez, J.: Recognizing shapes and gestures using sound as feedback. In: CHI Extended Abstracts on Human Factors in Computing Systems (2010)
20. Schauerte, B., Koester, D., Martinez, M., Stiefelhagen, R.: Way to Go! Detecting Open Areas Ahead of a Walking Person. In: Agapito, L., Bronstein, M.M., Rother, C. (eds.) ECCV 2014 Workshops, Part III. LNCS, vol. 8927, pp. 349–360. Springer, Heidelberg (2015)
21. Schauerte, B., Wörtwein, T., Stiefelhagen, R.: A web-based platform for interactive image sonification. In: Accessible Interaction for Visually Impaired People (2015)
22. Stevens, S.S., Volkmann, J., Newman, E.B.: A scale for the measurement of the psychological magnitude pitch. J. Acoust. Soc. Am. **8**(3), 185–190 (1937)
23. Su, J., Rosenzweig, A., Goel, A., de Lara, E., Truong, K.N.: Timbremap: enabling the visually-impaired to use maps on touch-enabled devices. In: Proceedings of the International Conference on Human Computer Interaction with Mobile Devices and Services (2010)
24. Taibbi, M., Bernareggi, C., Gerino, A., Ahmetovic, D., Mascetti, S.: AudioFunctions: eyes-free exploration of mathematical functions on tablets. In: Miesenberger, K., Fels, D., Archambault, D., Peňáz, P., Zagler, W. (eds.) ICCHP 2014, Part I. LNCS, vol. 8547, pp. 537–544. Springer, Heidelberg (2014)
25. Yoshida, T., Kitani, K.M., Koike, H., Belongie, S., Schlei, K.: EdgeSonic: image feature sonification for the visually impaired. In: Proceedings of the Augmented Human International Conference (2011)

Online Graphics for the Blind: Intermediate Format Generation for Graphic Categories

Roopa Bose[✉] and Helmut Jürgensen

Department of Computer Science, The University of Western Ontario,
London, ON N6A 5B7, Canada
rbose4@uwo.ca, hjj@csd.uwo.ca

Abstract. We describe a general framework for generating tactile and multimodal graphics from various sources. The key module to generate the intermediate format for a specific graphic category is illustrated by example.

Keywords: Tactile graphics · SVG · Graphics for blind

1 A Framework for Multimodal Graphics

We describe part of a system by which blind or visually impaired persons can access graphical information (diagrams, maps etc.) using multimodal displays. Special solutions with respect to the type of graphics or the type of rendering exist (e.g. [4,7,9]). Our framework provides a more general solution. Information – overview and graphical detail – is extracted from the input stream and converted into an intermediate format. It is then classified so as to select and compute the appropriate internal representation and the parameters required for subsequent processing. Next the internal representation is simplified according to its category into a format which is device-independent. Special drivers adapt these data to the respective output modalities.

To create tactile graphics, often a platform has been built to generate specific types of SVG files which are then transformed for the tactile output device (e.g. [1,3,5,6]). In contrast, we focus on extracting and separating information from generic SVG files as found on the WEB into an intermediate format which can then be rendered using an appropriate driver. We plan to extend this approach beyond SVG to other graphics formats at a later stage. Our framework will be developed as a rule based system. Figure 1 shows its block diagram. The general framework has three parts:

- *Base framework:* It creates an XML equivalent of the input document for processing overview information; it separates graphic content from text, extracts metadata, and creates a metadata file in a specific format with the extracted information for future use. The filtering, library, and transformation modules in Fig. 1 form the base framework.

© Springer International Publishing Switzerland 2016
K. Miesenberger et al. (Eds.): ICCHP 2016, Part I, LNCS 9758, pp. 220–223, 2016.
DOI: 10.1007/978-3-319-41264-1_29

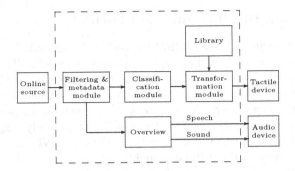

Fig. 1. Block diagram of the framework

- *Classification module:* It separates the graphic content into appropriate categories and the category-dependent relevant information in an intermediate format for further processing like simplification.
- *Overview information processing:* The overview information for the selected graphics is produced from the XML equivalent of the source document and the metadata information file.

In the production of tactile graphics, different kinds of graphics require different kinds of simplification for better understanding [2]. The classification module classifies graphics according to various categories and subcategories. The main categories include those of pictures and of diagrams. The former has portraits, landscapes, maps, paintings etc. as subcategories. In the category diagrams there are subcategories like object-relationship diagrams (e.g. tree diagram), variable-relationship diagrams (e.g. scatter plot), process-relationship diagrams (e.g. flow charts), hybrid diagrams (e.g. data visualization diagrams) etc. The module classifies a given graphics based on the information in the metadata file. This information is either author-provided or derived using machine-learning methods. Once the category and subcategory is determined, information extraction and simplification is performed according to rules for that particular category-subcategory pair. Structural information and data are separated from the graphics source to generate an intermediate format file which also incorporates basic overview information from the XML file and the metadata file. The intermediate format serves the following purposes:

1. The voice or haptic modalities or their combination can be used to deliver structural information and data.
2. Information in the intermediate format is device-independent and is available to the respective drivers for output rendering.
3. Voice synthesisers and AI programs can also use this intermediate format to answer queries asked by a low-vision person using the visual version of the graphics. Also conversation-based user interfaces can benefit from the intermediate format.

2   Generating the Intermediate Format

In this paper, we focus on the classification module. We explain how it generates an intermediate format when the graphic category is known. The development of our framework uses a top-down approach, initially implementing the classification module with rules for a particular category-subcategory pair, that of diagrams and object-relationship. Later rules will be added for other such pairs. Currently the scope is restricted as follows: (1) the module handles only diagrams/object-relationship; (2) the input to the module is restricted to SVG files; (3) category and subcategory information will be available in the metadata file.

Object-relationship diagrams illustrate the interaction or relationship between similar kinds of objects. State diagrams, tree diagrams, node-link diagrams etc. are examples of this class. We briefly explain how our classification module works for an example of object-relationship diagram. SVG is an XML-based markup language for describing two-dimensional graphics. SVG also allows text from any compliant XML namespace. Graphic objects in SVG are created using paths consisting of straight lines and curves (see [8] for details). Diagrams in SVG format are created in various ways. Here, we consider only the skeleton of the SVG file independently of the creation method. are represented in the SVG source as shown below. We only include the source for the parent node and its edge to the node below it. The other nodes and edges are described similarly.

```
<g id=''node1"class=''node">   <title>parent</title>
    <ellipse fill=''none"stroke=''black" cx=''96"
       cy=''-162" rx=''35.6194"ry=''18"/>
    <text text-anchor=''middle"x=''96" y=''-158.3"
       font-family=''Helvetica,sans-Serif" font-size=''14.00">
       parent</text>   </g>
<g id=''edge1" class=''edge">   <title>parenttoelement</title>
    <path fill=''none"stroke=''black"
       d=''M96,-143.697C96,-135.983 96,-126.712 96,-118.112"/>
    <polygon fill=''black"stroke=''black"
       points=''99.5001,-118.104 96,-108.104 92.5001,
       -118.104 99.5001,-118.104"/>   </g>
```

Our algorithm processes this source to extract structural information and data and generates an XML file. The rules to do so for this particular category-subcategory pair are stored in an XML schema file. The XML output has three parts: overview information, structural information and data. Overview information is obtained from the files generated by the base framework. Style information like stroke color, shape of node, etc. is added to the structural information section. The actual information about the root node, its edges and weights, and information about its child node forms the data part. The following steps are carried out in order to generate the XML file from the SVG source.

1. Image width, height and essential coordinates are retrieved.
2. Group elements are processed to find node groups and edge groups. Node groups have circles or ellipses. Edge groups have paths. Directed graphs have polygon elements to show the direction of edges.

3. For the elements in the node group, position, title and structural information like fill, stroke, transform etc. are retrieved.
4. For the edge group, coordinates and directions are determined.
5. In the final stage, XML output is generated by combining all the node-edge information.

The resulting skeletal structure of the XML output looks as follows.

```
<xml>
<overview><parent><element>
  <leftchild> </leftchild> <rightchild> </rightchild>
  </element></parent></overview>
<structuralinfo>
  <node id=0;stroke=black;root= yes;shape=''ellipse">parent</node>
  <edge fill=''none" ...></egde>  ...  </structuralinfo>
<data> <node id=0;isroot=''yes";ischild=''no";isleaf =''no";root=0;
  child=null>parent</node>
  <edge id =1;sourcenode= 0;endnode= 1;  ... ></edge> ... </data>
</xml>
```

In this paper, we discussed the idea of a framework for generating multimodal graphics from various sources. The main parts of the framework and their functions are listed. The key module to generate a device-independent intermediate format is illustrated by example for a specific diagram category.

References

1. Bornschein, J., Prescher, D., Weber, G.: SVGPlott – generating adaptive and accessible audio-tactile function graphs. In: Miesenberger, K., Fels, D., Archambault, D., Peňáz, P., Zagler, W. (eds.) ICCHP 2014, Part I. LNCS, vol. 8547, pp. 588–595. Springer, Heidelberg (2014)
2. Edman, P.K.: Tactile Graphics. American Foundation for the Blind, New York (1992)
3. Goncu, C., Marriott, K.: Tactile chart generation tool. In: Proceedings of the 10th International ACM SIGACCESS Conference on Computers and Accessibility, Assets 2008, pp. 255–256. ACM, New York (2008)
4. HyperBraille®. http://www.hyperbraille.de/
5. Minatani, K.: Proposal for SVG2DOT. In: Sik-Lányi, C., et al. (eds.) Assistive Technology, pp. 506–511. IOS Press, Amsterdam (2015)
6. Rotard, M., Otte, K., Ertl, T.: Exploring scalable vector graphics for visually impaired users. In: Miesenberger, K., Klaus, J., Zagler, W.L., Burger, D. (eds.) ICCHP 2004. LNCS, vol. 3118, pp. 725–730. Springer, Heidelberg (2004)
7. Rotard, M., Taras, C., Ertl, T.: Tactile web browsing for blind people. Multimed. Tools Appl. **37**(1), 53–69 (2008)
8. SVG Working Group: About SVG, 2D graphics in XML. http://www.w3.org/Graphics/SVG/About.html
9. Wang, Z., Xu, X., Li, B.: Bayesian tactile face. In: Proceedings of the CVPR 2008, pp. 1–8. IEEE (2008)

LiveDescribe Web Redefining What and How Entertainment Content Can Be Accessible to Blind and Low Vision Audiences

Margot Whitfield[✉], Raza Mir Ali, and Deborah Fels

Ryerson University, Toronto, Canada
{margot.whitfield,raza.mirali,dfels}@ryerson.ca

Abstract. Post production audio description (AD) has become recognized as a standard accessibility requirement for blind and low vision (B/LV) audiences and their friends and family. Although it is standardized, it is not commonly used due to the intensive effort involved in its creation and the lack of browser-based tools available for its production. In this paper, we will describe a new technology called, LiveDescribe, developed to allow description to be produced within a web browser for online videos such as those on YouTube.

Keywords: Audio description · Blind and low vision · Online accessibility applications · Describers

1 Introduction

Post production audio description (AD) has become recognized as a standard accessibility requirement for blind and low vision (B/LV) audiences and their friends and family [5]. Together, B/LV audiences and their friends and family can enjoy audio visual forms of popular culture, such as online video content. Spoken descriptions of the important visual characteristics in the content, such as action, characters and setting, are used to create a second audio track that is inserted between the original dialogue to represent the original visual content in audio form [5]. Timing, word choice and descriptive precision, given the available non-dialogical space, and expressive delivery are viewed as artistic processes [9] as opposed to a straightforward translation. However, because description is an intensive task [1] and there are few browser-based tools, described content is not commonly available for online video content. In this paper, we will describe a new technology called, LiveDescribe, developed to allow description to be produced within a web browser for online videos such as those on YouTube.

2 Background

Unlike television, web content is regulated provincially (in Canada) using a set of global standards, the World Wide Web Consortium Web Content Accessibility Guide-lines (WCAG) 2.0. However, AD remains excluded (Section 1.2.5) in WCAG 2.0 compliant measures (e.g., see the Accessibility for Ontarians with Disabilities

© Springer International Publishing Switzerland 2016
K. Miesenberger et al. (Eds.): ICCHP 2016, Part I, LNCS 9758, pp. 224–230, 2016.
DOI: 10.1007/978-3-319-41264-1_30

website for more details at http://www.aoda.ca/wcag/). As such, video sharing sites, including YouTube, are left to develop their own software solutions, standards, enforcement and awareness mechanisms for accessibility for B/LV audiences. In terms of other accessibility tools, YouTube provides captioning for people who are Deaf/hard of hearing, using a number of approaches: (1) Instruction for producers; (2) "Community contribution" options for crowdsourcing; and (3) Automatic captioning (see https://goo.gl/U4dLvN for more details). By giving producers/consumers the tools and resources to produce captions, video sharing sites are including their audiences as participants, an important component in YouTube's success [4].

Although post-production AD is cognitively demanding and time consuming, it is also enjoyable [9]. Automating AD tasks (such as AD space detection) should increase efficiencies and reduce production time [1]. As a web-based application, LiveDescribe has reduced the number of tasks (e.g. user no longer have to download and upload video and audio files) and maintains better user-task focus (e.g. users access YouTube videos from the same page rather than switching between pages) from the previous desktop version (outlined in [2]). These modifications should increase the scalability and immediacy of the application, key ingredients to any successful web application [10].

The task of creating web-based multimedia editing tools is complex. LiveDescribe and YouDescribe (VDRDC, 2013) are currently the only known open source and web-based AD software available where AD can be generated from a website directly. While there are other AD software tools (for purchase or free), they must be down-loaded to a computer to be used for AD (for a list see [7]). The AD tracks made with this type of tool must be uploaded to the Internet once they are completed on the computer. Furthermore, other online graphic editor applications such as Moovely (animation/presentation, www.moovly.com), Clker (image, www.clker.com/) and Wevideo (video, www.wevideo.com) exist but do not allow for multi-track audio and are not optimized for AD production.

3 System Design

LiveDescribe is an online AD application that allows users to write, record, edit and view AD YouTube videos in a web browser. The application is designed using an inclusive design strategy where users have been involved from the beginning [9]. The goal is to allow anyone who is interested in creating AD to do so with little knowledge of AD or AD software tools. The user interface is timeline-based, similar to other audio/video editing software and is comprised of generic interactive components including record, pause/play, forward/backward buttons, volume and track sliders, and text-box editor (see Fig. 1). In addition, LiveDescribe automatically detects non-dialogue segments using three signal processing algorithms (zero-crossings, entropy, and root mean square) detecting spaces with an 80–90 % accuracy [2]. These spaces are unmodifiable and represented using coloured blocks (purple) whereas, user-generated descriptions can only be added or deleted and are represented in green boxes (see Fig. 1). The user can type in the text that they want to say using the text box to the left of the waveform tracks. Once a description is recorded, a number-sequenced block is generated on the waveform track with a corresponding text box (to the upper right of the waveform tracks) which can be deleted or edited. The added description palette can be used to add the actual description transcript or used as a label identifier or other explanation of the description added. The user can also add in "extended" descriptions where the video will be stopped in order for the description to play and then begin again after the description has finished. To mark a description as extended, the user can select the extended checkbox (located under the play button).

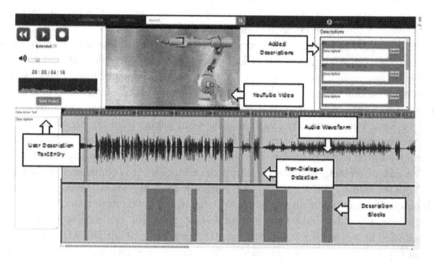

Fig. 1. Editing screen (including YouTube video stream, user description text entry (left of audio tracks), description text box (right of video), control panel (left of video), and audio tracks)

LiveDescribe is hosted on a dedicated website (www.livedescribe.com) allowing it to be used directly on that site. YouTube videos can be directly retrieved to LiveDescribe using its search function, described and then the YouTube video and its corresponding AD are made playable and searchable on the LiveDescribe site. LiveDescribe enables content producers and consumers to create and view videos with AD. Once the AD video is published it can be seen and rated (with a thumbs up or thumbs down) by other users. Similar to YouTube, the LiveDescribe community determines the order of displayed AD videos based on the AD's popularity. Un-described and described videos related to a search are presented to users in two separate columns. Videos with multiple descriptions are listed in ranked order and differentiated by the content creator's username (located under the video title, similar to YouTube).

4 Methodology

Ten amateur describers (five female, five male) were recruited to evaluate the usability of LiveDescribe. Most of the participants (seven) were from a university computer science program. Participants ranged in age between 18 and 29 years. Seven participants highest level of education was high school, two had university degrees and one had a college degree.

Study participants were asked to complete a 22 question pre-study survey (19 forced choice, 5-point Likert scale type, and 3 open-ended questions) that collected demographic data and information about computer skills (operations, multimedia, etc.), multimedia editing experience, television and film viewing length and frequency. Participants were also asked about their knowledge of, opinion of (positive and negative), and experience with developing AD (informal/live and pre-recorded).

Next, participants were provided with a demonstration of the different features of LiveDescribe and the user interface. Following this, participants were asked to create AD which involved watching two existing comedic YouTube videos (4:23 and 4:19 minutes respectively) and then adding description boxes, recording audio, moving and deleting description boxes, and using the web application. Amateur describers were given the option of writing down their descriptions within the software tool or simply recording them aloud as the video played. All participants completed the study in less than one hour.

Participants then completed a 31 question (29 forced choice and 2 open-ended) post-study survey that was based on the SUS instrument [3] modified for LiveDescribe tasks. All sessions were video recorded, and all keystrokes and mouse movements were logged. The data presented in this paper are a preliminary analysis of some of the major themes that appeared in the video data and survey comments. Due to the small number of participants, the 5-point Likert scale responses are condensed into a 3-point Likert scale as described by Jacoby and Matell [6].

5   Results and Discussion

A majority of people found the task of creating descriptions to be "easy" as seen in Fig. 2. When asked about their experience creating description using LiveDescribe, the majority of participants also said it was "good" (see Fig. 2), suggesting participants found it slightly easier to use the software than the task of generating descriptions. Some comments from participants included "clear", "direct", "easy to understand", "user friendly", "simple and intuitive interface" and "fun to use" when asked to describe the "strength of the software or description task". One participant found the "extend option really useful in short videos."

When asked about frequency of creating descriptions using LiveDescribe on YouTube, participants ranged in expected frequency: "often" (2 responses), "sometimes" (2), "once in awhile" (3), "never" (1), and "don't know" (2). When asked to rate the level of difficulty (from "easy" to "difficult") with aspects of description development, participants found the simplest tasks to be those associated with using the software, such as "writing description in the text box", "creating a new description space", "moving descriptions in the timeline", "recording description", "navigating through the video" and "deleting descriptions" (6 to 9 people found these tasks to be "easy").

The most difficult tasks for participants was the actual development of descriptions, including tasks such as "deciding what aspects of the video to describe", "understanding the video material", and "selecting the best word for description" (4 to 6 people found these tasks to be "difficult"). "Matching length of description with

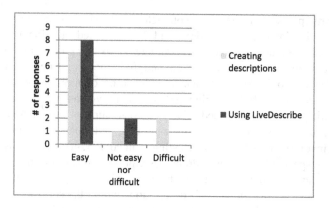

Fig. 2. Number of responses for level of difficulty in creating AD and using LiveDescribe

available space", which can be a difficult task, was considered by the majority (5 participants) to be "neither easy nor difficult." Participants also suggested that they could be incentivized to create descriptions using LiveDescribe if financially compensated.

When asked how easy would it be to use this software 1 day, 1 week, 1 month or 6 months after use, eight respondents said it would be "easy" for all categories indicating the tool use is self-explanatory or easy to retain over time. With respect to their assessment of how sighted and blind users would react to their AD, a greater majority thought that blind users would react more positively than sighted users (see Fig. 3).

When asked about usefulness of the automatic space detection feature and the ability to write out and edit written descriptions users found writing and editing written descriptions to be slightly more useful (see Fig. 4). However, these ratings were provided after only a single use of LiveDescribe and may change over time. As one person mentioned that the LiveDescribe software "takes time to learn and properly use the functions."

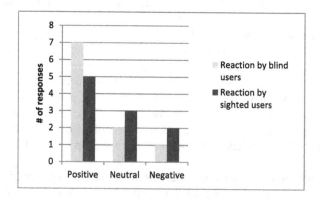

Fig. 3. Rating of reaction by blind or sighted users to AD

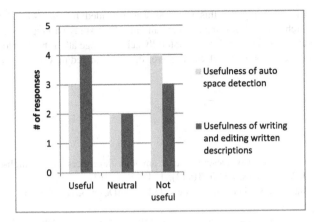

Fig. 4. Rating of usefulness of auto-space detection and written description features of LiveDescribe

Users also commented that they would like to have advanced search options for AD YouTube videos, such as searching for specific words, description styles and languages. They also suggested that it would be useful to have an AD search option in YouTube and be able to upload additional audio tracks within YouTube without having to leave the site. Future iterations of LiveDescribe will consider advanced search options as outlined by users.

6 Impact

As video materials are becoming a prominent method of user-generated web content, particularly through web and social media sites such as YouTube, FaceBook, and Vimeo, having AD is crucial for enabling B/LV users to access to popular culture. However, AD can be difficult, time-consuming and arduous to make for content producers. In addition, there are few incentives, other than good will, to create AD for personal videos posted online. Having a web-based tool that can be used directly in a browsed, that automatically finds spaces to insert AD and that is fun to use may help people willing and interested in creating AD to do so without complicated steps of downloading and uploading content. In addition, it also facilitates multiple users creating AD for the same content which, in turn, provides B/LV viewers with choice – a novel approach to content creation and consumption.

7 Conclusion

Description of online video content by amateurs is difficult though feasible. With minimal training in post-production AD processes and little experience with the LiveDescribe software tool, description is even considered enjoyable for amateurs.

Acknowledgements. Funding for this research was provided by the Natural Sciences and Engineering Research Council of Canada. We thank all of the study participants for their efforts and assistance in this research. Finally, we gratefully acknowledge all of the developers that have been involved in the creation of LiveDescribe over the years including Carmen Branje, Kristian Ott, Valentin Serrago and Davor Kljucevic.

References

1. Branje, C., Fels, I.D.: LiveDescribe: can amateur describers create high-quality audio description? J. Vis. Impair. Blind. **106**(3), 154–165 (2012)
2. Branje, C., Marshall, S., Tyndall, A., Fels, D.I.: LiveDescribe. In: AMCIS 2006, Acapulco (2006)
3. Brooke, J.: SUS: A "quick and dirty" usability scale. In: Jordan, P.W., Thomas, B., Weerdmeester, B.A., McClelland, I.L. (eds.) Usability Evaluation in Industry, pp. 189–194. Taylor & Francis, London (1996)
4. Burgess, J., Green, J.: YouTube: Online Video and Participatory Culture. Wiley, West Sussex (2013)
5. ISO-IEC DTS 20071-21: Information technology – user interface component accessibility - Part 21 (2007): Guidance on audio descriptions. http://www.iso.org/iso/catalogue_detail. htm?csnumber=63061
6. Jacoby, J., Matell, M.S.: Three-point Likert scales are good enough. J. Mark. Res. **8**, 495–500 (1971)
7. Packer, J., Vizenor, K., Miele, J.A.: An overview of video description: history, benefits, and guidelines. J. Vis. Impair. Blind. **109**(2), 83 (2015)
8. Preece, J., Sharp, H., Rogers, Y.: Interaction Design: Beyond Human-Computer Interaction. Wiley, West Sussex (2015)
9. Whitfield, M., Fels, D.I.: Inclusive design, audio description and diversity of theatre experiences. Des. J. **16**(2), 219–238 (2013)
10. Wu, Y., Offutt, J.: Modeling and testing web-based applications. GMU ISE Technical ISE-TR-02-08 (2002)

Insights into Internet Privacy for Visually Impaired and Blind People

Georg Regal[1]([⊠]), Elke Mattheiss[1], Marc Busch[1],
and Manfred Tscheligi[1,2]

[1] AIT Austrian Institute of Technology GmbH,
Giefinggasse 2, 1210 Vienna, Austria
{georg.regal,elke.mattheiss,marc.busch,
manfred.tscheligi}@ait.ac.at
[2] Center for Human-Computer Interaction, University of Salzburg, Sigmund
Haffner Gasse 18, 5020 Salzburg, Austria
manfred.tscheligi@sbg.ac.at

Abstract. Tracking blockers protect from and inform about hidden trackers and services that collect data in the background while the user is surfing the web. However, existing tracking blockers provide information and feedback visually and thus are barely accessible for visually impaired and blind users. In this paper we present insights about privacy concerns of visually impaired Internet users. Moreover we present feedback strategies and guidelines for an accessible tracking blocker developed in a user centered design process. The underlying feedback principles and guidelines can be used for the design of Privacy Enhancing Technology in other domains, and therefore serve as reference for designers and developers.

Keywords: Internet privacy · Visually impaired · Tracking blocker · Feedback · Design guidelines

1 Introduction

Privacy is gaining importance, and concerns regarding Internet privacy and data security are increasing among Internet users. Privacy Enhancing Technology (PET) can not only help to protect the user's privacy but also provide information to the user, which has an educational effect. "Tracking blockers" are one kind of PET protecting and informing about hidden trackers and services that try to collect data in the background while the user is surfing the web. PET can increase awareness and help to gain control. However, existing tools provide information and feedback usually in a visual way and thus are barely accessible for visually impaired and blind (VIB) users.

As Privacy is a right for all users, in this paper we investigate the accessibility of tracking blockers. We present insights about privacy concerns of VIB Internet users as well as feedback strategies and guidelines for an accessible tracking blocker. Although we focus on a tool that prevents tracking and behavioral analysis, the underlying feedback principles also apply to the design of PETs in other domains, where users need to be informed about the privacy state of a webpage.

© Springer International Publishing Switzerland 2016
K. Miesenberger et al. (Eds.): ICCHP 2016, Part I, LNCS 9758, pp. 231–238, 2016.
DOI: 10.1007/978-3-319-41264-1_31

2 Related Work

Despite efforts to raise awareness, a considerable amount of Internet users are unware of risks related to internet security and privacy[1]. There has been a longstanding research in the area of privacy policy interfaces that display settings and preferences regarding personal information, mostly in the context of social media platforms.

Most studies compare different layouts of these privacy policy interfaces [8, 10]. Information about Internet privacy has always been closely connected to Internet security. Most related work focuses on appropriate and understandable warning messages when surfing the internet (e.g. warning for phishing websites) [4, 6, 11]. Most tools focused on visual interaction and cues, exceptions are ambient interaction techniques [9] and the so-called warning glove [13]. A comprehensive collection of best practices and design guidelines for trust indicators (mostly visual cues that guide users in privacy decisions and convey privacy information) can be found in Egelman [5]. A good introduction to "web bugs" and tracking is provided by Dobias [3].

Little research regarding Internet privacy and security in the domain of VIB users focuses on privacy, security and trust of VIB Internet users or the accessibility of specific security features. An analysis of security and privacy challenges for people with disabilities is provided by Hochheiser et al. [7]. Their work provides insights into existing privacy and security concerns and reflections on the concept of universally useable privacy and security. Focus is put on three concrete domains: "Anti-Phishing Tools", "Passwords" and CAPTCHAs.

Research by Buzzi et al. [2] focuses on the area of e-Commerce services, who investigated trust for screen reader users. They evaluated accessibility and perceived trust in the secure transaction for the eBay platform. This work was done as an expert review by the authors (one of them was blind). Their results show that it is crucial to provide security and privacy information accessible to screen reader users. Also security information should be placed in the main part of the UI, so that users can access the information quickly. In later research [1] the authors provide guidelines how to promote trust in e-commerce websites for people with visual disabilities.

A main security-related problem on the Internet for people with visual impairment is the inaccessibility of human-proof tools like CAPTCHAs. Sauer et al. [12] implemented an accessible human-proof tool and evaluated it with five blind users. The proposed solution combines visual and audio CAPTCHAs, in contrast to the current solutions, where audio CAPTCHAS are a distinct system. They posit, that joined CAPTCHAs can be more accessible to visually impaired users and more easily adopted to different languages and cultures.

Besides rare efforts in the area of accessibility and privacy, to the best of our knowledge, there has been no research targeted to the requirements and needs of VIB Internet users regarding accessible tracking blockers so far.

---

[1] https://www.prlog.org/12128262-internet-study-shows-users-are-unaware-of-threats-and-risks.html.

3 Analysis of Privacy Concerns of VIB Users

First we aimed to gathered comprehensive insights into privacy concerns of VIB Internet users.

3.1 Method

To gain deeper insights into the privacy concerns of VIB users we conducted (1) two workshops, (2) an online survey, (3) a tool review of existing tracking blockers and (4) interviews and observations.

First two workshops, with 5 participants each, were conducted. In the first workshop 4 men and 1 woman (mean age = 49.6 years, SD = 12.73), 3 of them blind and 2 severely visually impaired, participated. In the second workshop 3 men and 2 women (mean age = 44.2 years, SD = 11.19), 2 of them blind and 3 severely visually impaired, participated. First, questions related to general privacy concerns, negative experiences while surfing the Internet and strategies or tools to protect privacy were discussed. Second participants formed groups of 3 people and existing threats to privacy were presented, discussed and ranked by the groups according to their severity. The presented threats were Cloud-Storages, Online Shopping, Location-Based Data Analysis, Social Networks, Spyware, Search-History, Tracking and Behavioral Analysis. To underpin the severity ratings in the workshops with more data, we conducted an online survey, which was answered by 23 participants. The threats (the same as used in the workshops) were presented and participants rated the relevance of these threats.

Next four existing tracking blockers, Ghostery[2], Privacy Badger[3], DisconnectMe[4] and Blur[5], were reviewed by the authors regarding accessibility. Subsequently, we conducted a study with 10 participants (7 men, 3 women; mean age = 41.70 years, SD = 7.70, 2 blind, 3 blind without light perception, 2 severely visually impaired, 3 visually impaired). Participants fulfilled defined tasks with Ghostery, the only partly accessible of the before mentioned tools, to get a feeling of the functionality of the tracking blocker. Subsequently a laddering interview was conducted to get insights into the need of specific features of a PET. Therefore we repeatedly asked the participants why a specific feature or characteristic is important to them, until they arrived from consequences of these characteristics to underlying values.

3.2 Results

The conducted expert review revealed that most exiting tools are not accessible. Only the tool Ghostery was considered as partly accessible. However, only the old version of

---

[2] Ghostery: https://www.ghostery.com.

[3] Privacy Badger: https://www.eff.org/de/node/73969.

[4] DisconnectMe: https://disconnect.me.

[5] Blur: https://www.abine.com/index.html.

the menu is accessible by keyboard. Privacy Badger is not accessible by keyboard only. This was also confirmed by the developers on the mailing list, but they stated interest in improving the accessibility. For Disconnect.Me and Blur no information about keyboard accessibility could be found.

In Fig. 1(a) the results of the ranking done in the first workshop are shown, in Fig. 1(b) the answers of the online survey are presented. The workshops and online survey revealed that privacy concerns are indeed relevant to VIB internet users. In the workshop Spyware and Adware was rated as most worrisome by two groups, one group considered Search History and one group considered Location-based Data to be most worrisome. This is also reflected in the online survey. Spyware and Adware was considered to be the second worrisome threat, 11 users totally agreed and 7 users agreed that Spyware and Adware is a worrisome threats. Search History was considered to be the third worrisome threat with 10 users totally agree and 5 users agree. In contrast to the rating in the workshops were Social Networks was seen as a rather low to medium threat, in the online survey Social Networks were the most important threat, with 12 users totally agreed and 6 agreed that Social Networks are a worrisome threat.

Overall Tracking and Behavioral Target Analysis were seen as a medium severe threat by the target group (low to medium positions in the workshop) and most participants selected only "agree" for the statement "I consider this threat to be worrisome". We posit that this is partly due to missing awareness of the possibilities of tracking and behavioral analysis. An accessible PET can help to overcome this by providing appropriate information to the users during browsing the web. This is an important part of PET, as information in the context where a threat is happening can lead to better understanding of this threat.

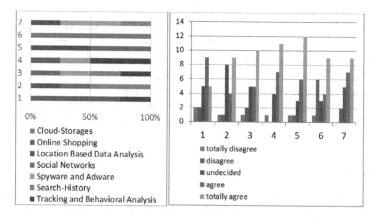

Fig. 1. (a) Rating of threats in the two workshops from 1 "Most worrisome" to 7 "Least worrisome" Fig. 2. (b) Answers in the online survey to the question "I consider this threat to be worrisome" - (1) tracking and behavioral analysis, (2) cloud-storages, (3) search-history, (4) spyware und adware, (5) social networks, (6) online shopping, (7) location-based data analysis (Color figure online)

The evaluation showed that Ghostery is not completely accessible, but participants were able to fulfill the tasks. The qualitative data analysis of the laddering interviews revealed 15 characteristics, 16 consequences and ten values related to PET. The values mentioned by most participants are accessibility (which is not surprising as it is the prerequisite for visually impaired people to use a tool) and privacy protection. However, interestingly also values like control, equality of opportunity, and self-determination play a significant role.

4 Interaction Design for an Accessible Tracking Blocker

Based on the results of the privacy concerns analysis we defined design criteria and developed an HTML prototype of the interaction concept and feedback strategies.

4.1 Method

In two workshops mainly feedback strategies were discussed, which vary between low vision and blind users. In the first workshop 5 blind people participated (3 men, 2 women, mean age = 42.60 years, SD = 9.21, 2 blind without light perception, 3 blind with light perception). In the second workshop 5 visually impaired people participated (4 men and 1 woman, mean-age = 44.00 years, SD = 8.64, 4 severely visually impaired, 1 visually impaired). First users were asked how a tracking blocker should provide feedback about the state of a webpage and participants presented and discussed their ideas. Subsequently ideas for feedback (audio-only in workshop 1, audio and visual in workshop 2) were presented to them and discussed in the group.

Based on the user feedback we selected the most promising ideas and developed interaction concepts and feedback strategies. The interaction concepts and feedback strategies were evaluated in a user study with 17 participants. Each user visited 3 predefined pages (no trackers, little number of trackers, high number of trackers). Feedback and information about each page was provided with the developed interaction prototype and for comparison with the tool Ghostery.

4.2 Interaction Prototype

Users had easy access to quick information and subsequently further details about the trackers, by using keyboard shortcuts. The developed prototype is shown in Fig. 2. To allow for non-visual usage, the prototype can be fully controlled by keyboard, with a simple menu structure and provides appropriate information to the screen reader.

When loading the page (and through a key combination) feedback about the state of the site is provided by a symbol (e.g. Fig. 2a) and a sound. Additionally in a second step a list of trackers (Fig. 2b) can be shown by using a key combination. The menu is designed as a list and thus allows for easy navigation by the arrow keys up and down. Blocking of trackers can be enabled or disabled by pressing the space bar or clicking on the toggle button. Additional information to each tracker can be shown (Fig. 2c) by pressing the right arrow key or clicking on the menu item.

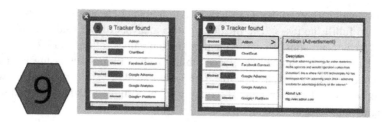

Fig. 2. Interaction prototype (a) example of visual feedback (b) list of trackers (c) additional information about one specific tracker (Color figure online)

4.3 Guidelines for an Accessible Tracking Blocker

Based on the findings of the co-design workshops and the interaction and feedback concept evaluation we deduced several guidelines for designing PET's for VIB, presented in the following.

Control. Guidelines deduced are:

- Users must be able to define if a tracker is blocked or allowed, as users want to use some services (e.g. social media plugins) although privacy concerns exist. Settings should be set globally but must be changeable for specific sites.
- For blocking or allowing trackers the usage of toggle buttons is recommended. The toggle button should provide the state through position and color and must also provide a meaningful description of the state to the screen reader.
- Keyboard operation must be available for all options to allow for quick manipulation and access using keyboard based assistive technology (e.g. screen reader).

Feedback. Guidelines deduced are:

- Participants argued for three levels of feedback (harmless, critical and dangerous).
- Acoustic feedback was preferred by blind participants. A short, concise tune should be played, which informs if a tracker was detected or blocked. The tune must not be too intrusive, and it must be possible to deactivate acoustic feedback in the personalization settings. Feedback should be realized using different sounds (e.g. different instruments). Combinations of tunes (e.g. third, quart) were not sufficient.
- Visual Feedback was preferred by partially sighted participants. Visual feedback can be provided through different symbols. Similar to traffic signs, the symbols suggested and preferred by the users were a circle, a triangle and a hexagon. Visual feedback should be complemented by color, but is important to notice, that color must not be the only distinguishing criterion. Thus the shape plays an important role. Participants argued for three shapes to represent the three feedback states. Visual feedback must provide a sufficient contrast between the feedback and the background. A contrast ratio of 4.5 to 1 is needed to fulfill WCAG guideline 1.4.3.

Personalization. Guidelines deduced are:

- Users must be able to choose the desired feedback modalities. For example acoustic feedback was suggested by blind users, whereas partly sighted users considered it as annoying. Also feedback should be presented on different channels, if desired.
- Users must be able to select the occurrences of warnings. Some users preferred to be warned only on critical and dangerous sites. Other users wanted to get feedback on all sites, to get actively informed that a site is harmless and to get feedback that the tool is working.

Information. Guidelines deduced are:

- Users prefer little automatic information, but the possibility for quick access to further information.
- Information should be available in different languages.
- The automatic feedback must not disrupt the user's workflow. A two stage feedback process was rated positive.
- By using a keyboard shortcut it should be possible to access quick information. By using the same shortcut within a defined time, further detailed information should be provided. Users argued for using the same keyboard shortcut twice (instead of two different shortcuts) as users of assistive technology have already to remember a lot of combinations.
- Users shall be able to choose the keyboard shortcuts, as assistive technology often already "blocks" certain key combinations.

5   Conclusion

In this work we presented insight into privacy concerns of VIB users and guidelines for accessible PET in the domain of tracking blockers. A challenging aspect of the project was the heterogeneous target group. Especially the multiple forms of visual impairment were an influential factor, which resulted in the guidelines for personalization.

This work provides first insights into the design of PET for VIB people in the domain of tracking and behavioral analysis and serves as reference for web designers and developers. Nevertheless researched in design for PET in other domains is still needed and shall be addressed in future work.

Acknowledgements. We would like to thank the Hilfsgemeinschaft (Austrian Association in Support of the Blind and Visually Impaired) for their support. This work has been partly funded within the project BlindFaith funded by the Internet Foundation Austria in the 9th netidee call and within BlindBits, a project conducted in the program Sparkling Science funded by the Austrian Federal Ministry of Science, Research and Economy.

References

1. Akhter, F., Buzzi, M.C., Buzzi, M., Leporini, B.: Conceptual framework: how to engineer online trust for disabled users. In: 2009 IEEE/WIC/ACM International Joint Conference on Web Intelligence and Intelligent Agent Technology, pp. 614–617 (2009)
2. Buzzi, M.C., Buzzi, M., Leporini, B., Akhter, F.: User trust in ecommerce services: perception via screen reader. In: Proceedings - 2009 International Conference on New Trends in Information and Service Science, NISS 2009, pp. 1166–1171. IEEE Computer Society (2009)
3. Dobias, J.: Privacy effects of web bugs amplified by web 2.0. In: Fischer-Hübner, S., Duquenoy, P., Hansen, M., Leenes, R., Zhang, G. (eds.) Privacy and Identity Management for Life. IFIP AICT, vol. 352, pp. 244–257. Springer, Heidelberg (2011)
4. Egelman, S., Cranor, L.F., Hong, J.: You've been warned. In: Proceeding of the Twenty-Sixth Annual CHI Conference on Human Factors in Computing Systems – CHI 2008, pp. 1065–1074. ACM Press (2008)
5. Egelman, S.: Trust me: design patterns for constructing trustworthy trust indicators. Doctoral thesis, School of Computer Science, Carnegie Mellon University (2009)
6. Felt, A.P., Reeder, R.W., Almuhimedi, H., Consolvo, S.: Experimenting at scale with Google Chrome's SSL warning. In: Proceedings of the 32nd Annual ACM Conference on Human Factors in Computing Systems - CHI 2014, pp. 2667–2670. ACM Press (2014)
7. Hochheiser, H., Feng, J., Lazar, J.: Challenges in universally usable privacy and security. In: Symposium on Usable Privacy and Security (SOUPS) 2008 (2008)
8. Lipford, H.R., Watson, J., Whitney, M., Froiland, K., Reeder, R.W.: Visual vs. compact. In: Proceedings of the 28th International Conference on Human Factors in Computing Systems - CHI 2010, pp. 1111–1114. ACM Press (2010)
9. De Luca, A., Frauendienst, B., Maurer, M., et al.: Does MoodyBoard make internet use more secure? In: Proceedings of the 2011 Annual Conference on Human Factors in Computing Systems - CHI 2011, pp. 887–890. ACM Press (2011)
10. McDonald, A.M., Reeder, R.W., Kelley, P.G., Cranor, L.F.: A comparative study of online privacy policies and formats. In: Goldberg, I., Atallah, M.J. (eds.) PETS 2009. LNCS, vol. 5672, pp. 37–55. Springer, Heidelberg (2009)
11. Pemble, M.: Crying 'Havoc', Crying 'Wolf' or Just Howling at the Moon? Netw. Secur. 2001(9), 14–16 (2001)
12. Sauer, G., Holman, J., Lazar, J., Hochheiser, H., Feng, J.: Accessible privacy and security: a universally usable human-interaction proof tool. Univers. Access Inf. Soc. 9(3), 239–248 (2010)
13. Schmuntzsch, U., Sturm, C., Roetting, M.: The warning glove – development and evaluation of a multimodal action-specific warning prototype. Appl. Ergon. 45(5), 1297–1305 (2014)

Understanding How People with Cerebral Palsy Interact with the Web 2.0

Letícia Seixas Pereira[(⊠)] and Dominique Archambault

EA 4004 – CHArt-THIM, Université Paris 8, Paris, France
leticia.seixas-pereira@etud.univ-paris8.fr,
dominique.archambault@univ-paris8.fr

Abstract. As recent studies show, people with disabilities still face several problems when using the web, therefore, even with all the efforts already made, there are yet issues without a clear solution. In this context, this paper presents an empirical study on the identification of navigation barriers by users with cerebral palsy and how some dynamic components, widely used nowadays, can directly influence their online activities.

Keywords: Web accessibility · User evaluation · Cerebral palsy · Web 2.0

1 Introduction

According to World Health Organization, 15 % of world's population have an impairment[1], becoming essential to provide their equally web interaction [1]. Web accessibility aims to enable those users to perceive, understand, navigate and contribute with the web. This task may be difficult for a variety of people with disabilities. The richness of resources provided are frequently not accessible for some of them [2].

HCI researches focusing on methodologies for users with disabilities represent the subject less addressed among them. Works on visual impairment represent the majority of them (25 %) while studies on people with cognitive and physical disabilities are present, each one, in only 9 % [3]. Thus, it is necessary to better understand how those users interact with Rich Internet Applications (RIAs), identify the barriers preventing them to access its content and investigate their common behaviors. Then, it is possible to better follow the problems they face and where to direct research efforts [1].

2 Background

Cerebral palsy (CP) is a brain injury that may cause muscle tightness or spasms, in-voluntary movement and impaired speech. Most of people with CP may present difficulties to use a mouse, using just the keyboard or other kind of adapted device. Regarding web accessibility, research on users with CP is very limited [4]. However, several studies analyzing the navigation of people with other disabilities are available.

---

[1] http://www.who.int/mediacentre/factsheets/fs352/en/.

© Springer International Publishing Switzerland 2016
K. Miesenberger et al. (Eds.): ICCHP 2016, Part I, LNCS 9758, pp. 239–242, 2016.
DOI: 10.1007/978-3-319-41264-1_32

The Disability Rights Commission (RDC) [5], with participation of 50 users with visual, hearing and physically impairments and also with learning disabilities, contributed with an extensive problems list faced by these users, and a set of recommendations and actions to be taken in order to improve web accessibility. Rømen and Svanæs [6], with a research correlating the problems faced by visually impaired, dyslexic and motor impaired users, showed that only the application of W3C guidelines was not enough to address the accessibility needed, i.e., guidelines should be based on empirical data as validated also empirically, reinforcing the need of a user evaluation.

More recently, Power et al. [1] and Giraud et al. [7], used empirical researches to identify interaction strategies and magnify the difference between blind and sighted navigation - emphasizing the difficult faced by visually impaired users when interacting with the web. Even already considering dynamic applications and RIAs environments, they included only users with print disabilities.

However, the web interaction of people with CP may be affected by lack of control and dexterity. They may experience some lack of clarity in navigation mechanisms and the disorganization of page layouts [8]. Those users often require assistance or an alternative resource as the web becomes more complex [9]. While their navigation is not satisfactory due to their impairments, more observation and study are needed.

3   Research Design

3.1   Selection of Participants

According to previous studies [9], five users is enough to find most of the usability issues in a website, so, the evaluations included five participants with different sub-types of CP. First, a profile form was orally applied. Three of our five users were female, two were male, all aged between 30 and 35 years old. They all use the Internet for more than 3 years, but with different levels of experience. Three of them used a track ball and one had a support of a screen reader/speech recognition software.

3.2   Selection of Used Websites

The website selection was made in four steps:

1. Websites Selection: To have a relevant social sample, we used a list provided by Alexa's (http://www.alexa.com) to perform a search identifying the most accessed websites in France.
2. Widgets Identification: Based on Chen et al. [10], the websites provided on Alexa's were analyzed and seven were selected for containing, at least, three of the nine indicated most common used widgets on webpages (auto suggest list, popup content, tabs, carousel, collapsible panels, slideshow, ticker, popup window and customizable content).
3. Websites Evaluation: A WCAG 2.0 semi-automatic evaluation, using Cynthia Says (http://www.cynthiasays.com) tool, was carried out and analyzed for each homepage (Table 1).

Table 1. Evaluation list carried out with selected

	Conformance level	Success criteria violated
Amazon	Fail	21
Yahoo	Fail	20
Le Figaro	Fail	14
Pages Jaunes	Fail	13
Deezer	Fail	9
Voyages SNCF	Fail	12
Booking	Fail	21

3.3 Evaluation Script

The participants were informed about the research details and were presented the tasks to be executed. They were encouraged to use "think aloud" verbal protocol. It was emphasized that, at any moment, they could demand a repetition of the current task, give up or take a break.

Problems the users faced during evaluations, as well as additional comments and reactions, were registered by camcorder and as notes. After each website, they were asked to summarize major difficulties and how they affected task achievement.

4 Results and Conclusions

During evaluations, when asked about their difficulties, two items were constantly reported: information overload – reported as "too much information" and difficulty in locating themselves – reported as being "lost all the time".

Regarding their interaction with dynamic elements during the tasks execution, some recurrent difficulties, in five of the nine found widgets, were highlighted:

- Use the Auto Suggest List, as the visited websites did not present a default behavior between them, they were confused on how to use the search feature;
- Recognize relevant content available through images in Carousel or Slideshow - as some of them identified only the current picture as a content, not interacting with the element or perceiving as list/sequence of information;
- Manage/retake the current task after a Popup Content triggered by an extern event;
- Perceiving the content change in sections displayed by Tabs.

Other components representing an obstacle for tasks execution were:

- Fill form fields containing a short hint (placeholder attribute), as some users tried to erase the default content, often going to previous pages with the backspace key;
- Identify an error message when the page is not updated - by running the research, some users waited for a response and, depending on their resolution, applied zoom on the browser or even their position on the page, the message was not perceived.

All observations were condensed and from that behavioral analysis, we identified common barriers faced by users with cerebral palsy, providing inputs for further studies. As this represents ongoing research, users with different subtypes of CP will be included, as well as other kinds of impairments. Further, a deeper analysis will be conducted to correlate those barriers with WCAG 2.0 and WAI-ARIA.

Acknowledgements. This work was undertaken with support from Coordenação de Aperfeiçoamento de Pessoal de Nível Superior (CAPES), Brazil, grant Doutorado Pleno no Exterior – Proc. BEX 13508/13-0.

References

1. Power, C., Petrie, H., Swallow, D., Murphy, E., Gallagher, B., Velasco, C.A.: Navigating, discovering and exploring the web: strategies used by people with print disabilities on interactive websites. In: Winckler, M. (ed.) INTERACT 2013, Part I. LNCS, vol. 8117, pp. 667–684. Springer, Heidelberg (2013)
2. Harper, S., Chen, A.Q.: Web accessibility guidelines: a lesson from the evolving web. World Wide Web **15**, 61–88 (2012). Springer, US, The Netherlands
3. Petrie, H., Gallagher, B., Darzentas, J.S.: A critical review of eight years of research on technologies for disabled and older people. In: Miesenberger, K., Fels, D., Archambault, D., Peñáz, P., Zagler, W. (eds.) ICCHP 2014, Part II. LNCS, vol. 8548, pp. 260–266. Springer, Heidelberg (2014)
4. Small, J., Schallau, P., Brown, K., Appleyard, R.: Web accessibility for people with cognitive disabilities. In: Proceeding of CHI EA 2005 CHI 2005 Extended Abstracts on Human Factors in Computing Systems, pp. 1793–1796. ACM Press, New York, USA (2005)
5. Disability Rights Commission: The Web: Access and Inclusion for Disabled People. The Stationery Office, London (2004)
6. Rømen, D., Svanæs, D.: Evaluating web site accessibility. In: Proceedings of 5th Nordic Conference on Human-Computer Interaction Building Bridges - NordiCHI 2008, p. 535. ACM Press, New York, USA (2008)
7. Giraud, S., Colombi, T., Russo, A., Thérouanne, P.: Accessibility of rich internet applications for blind people: a study to identify the main problems and solutions. In: Proceedings of 9th ACM SIGCHI, pp. 163–166 (2011)
8. Pérez, J.E., Arrue, M., Valencia, X., Moreno, L.: Exploratory study of web navigation strategies for users with physical disabilities. In: Proceedings of W4A 2014, pp. 1–4. ACM Press, New York, USA (2014)
9. Nielsen, J.: Why You Only Need to Test with 5 Users. http://www.nngroup.com/articles/why-you-only-need-to-test-with-5-users/
10. Chen, A.Q., Harper, S., Lunn, D., Brown, A.: Widget identification: a high-level approach to accessibility. World Wide Web **16**, 73–89 (2013)

Developing a Framework for Localised Web Accessibility Guidelines for University Websites in Saudi Arabia

Asmaa Alayed(✉), Mike Wald, and E.A. Draffan

School of Electronics and Computer Science, University of Southampton,
Southampton, UK
{asialg14,mw,ead}@ecs.soton.ac.uk

Abstract. This paper presents a new framework for localised web accessibility guidelines for university websites in Saudi Arabia. The main purpose of this framework is to provide the basis for the development of localised guidelines. Applying these localised guidelines on Arabic websites would enhance their accessibility for Arab people with disabilities. The development process of the new framework is described in detail. This process involved three phases, determination, synthesis and specification phases. The proposed framework comprises six main components; web accessibility, genre-specific cultural markers, costs, user diversity, Internet infrastructure and technology variety.

Keywords: Web accessibility guidelines · Localisation · Culture · Disability · Saudi Arabia · University websites

1 Introduction

People with disabilities in Saudi Arabia were estimated to be more than 700,000 in 2015[1] which constitutes over 7 % of Saudi citizens. Among those disabled, there are individuals who have an interest in accessing the content of university websites for different reasons. For instance, to apply for a university degree or to find information about the university and courses. Therefore, there is a pressing need for proper web accessibility guidelines in order not to exclude people with disabilities from obtaining the benefits of accessing university websites [1].

Web accessibility guidelines such as Web Content Accessibility Guidelines (WCAG 2.0) [2] that are developed in Western countries (North America and Western Europe) are used by some Arabic developers when developing Arabic websites [3]. However, some of the success criteria or the guidelines do not fit all cultures and all languages. Applying the WCAG 2.0 guidelines to Arabic websites would raise more accessibility issues and require different success criteria and possibly even techniques to maintain accessibility levels. This problem has been reported by a number of researchers, as they suggest the importance of adapting the accessibility guidelines to the Arabic context [4, 5, 8]. The current paper seeks to contribute to this body of

---

[1] http://rs.ksu.edu.sa/82739.html
http://www.alriyadh.com/104799 .

© Springer International Publishing Switzerland 2016
K. Miesenberger et al. (Eds.): ICCHP 2016, Part I, LNCS 9758, pp. 243–250, 2016.
DOI: 10.1007/978-3-319-41264-1_33

knowledge by developing a new framework to localise accessibility guidelines for university websites in Saudi Arabia.

In this paper, related work is discussed in Sect. 2. Section 3 explains the development process of the new framework. The proposed framework with its components is described in Sect. 4. Section 5 concludes with a summary of the paper.

2   Related Work

To the best of the researchers' knowledge and based on the literature review, limited studies on web accessibility of the Arabic websites have been found. The main focus of these studies such as [1, 5–8], is on evaluating web accessibility of e-government websites in a number of Arabic countries. Among those studies, [1] was the only one found to assess the accessibility of university websites in Saudi Arabia, however, it focuses on the English versions of these websites not the Arabic ones. There has been a consensus on the low accessibility levels of the examined websites and a lack of awareness of its impact on people with disabilities. Moreover, the issue of localisation to the Arabic context and its influence on accessibility has not been investigated by these studies.

This paper aims to address this gap by providing a better understanding of Arab people and their their approach to web based information and their preferences as to how it is presented This understanding and other accessibility related issues have been developed into a framework to localise accessibility guidelines. To make this research more achievable, the study is focuses on one Arabic country, which is Saudi Arabia and one website genre which is university websites.

3   Developing a New Framework for Localised Web Accessibility Guidelines for University Websites in Saudi Arabia

The framework has been developed by investigating the literature in a number of research areas. These areas comprise: web accessibility as the main area, with different guidelines that contribute to accessibility, and also cultural, technical and financial aspects and their impact on accessibility guidelines. Each one of these areas has contributed to the development of the framework. The framework has been developed in three main phases:

3.1   Phase One

The purpose for the first phase was mainly to determine, from literature, the components and aspects that need to be considered when localising web accessibility guidelines. This determination phase involved the following steps:

1. Identification and review of the literature concerned with web accessibility and localisation.
2. Identification of the components that need consideration in the localisation process.
3. Exclusion of the components that are not relevant to building localised web accessibility guidelines, such as accessibility of web authoring tools.
4. Categorisation of the components based on their meaning and scope.

The first phase resulted in the identification of seven components; namely web accessibility, cultural markers, genre markers, costs, user diversity, Internet infrastructure and technology variety.

3.2 Phase Two

In the second phase, the components and all of their subcomponents and elements identified in Phase One were synthesised to form the framework for localised web accessibility guidelines. This phase involved the following steps:

1. Extraction of any duplication among the components, subcomponents and elements.
2. Synthesis of the components that have duplicated subcomponents and elements.

Two components were synthesised in this phase and made one component which became genre-specific cultural markers.

3.3 Phase Three

As this research investigates the localisation in a Saudi context, some of the identified components in Phase Two needed more specification in the third phase.

1. Review of the literature concerned with localisation for Saudi Arabia.
2. Identification of the components that may challenge or facilitate the localisation for a Saudi context and specifically university websites.
3. Detailed specification of culturally related components and their subcomponents.

One component with its subcomponents was specified in detail in this phase: genre-specific cultural markers.

4 Proposed Framework

Figure 1 shows the proposed framework with all of its components and subcomponents.

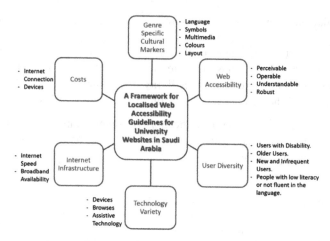

Fig. 1. A new framework for localised web accessibility guidelines for university websites in Saudi Arabia

4.1 Genre Specific Cultural Markers

Cultural markers are interface elements and features that are acceptable and preferred within a particular cultural group [9]. Genre specific cultural markers are elements and features of a specific website genre for a particular cultural group [9]. This component comprises 5 subcomponents as described below.

Language. As the official language in Saudi Arabia is Arabic, a brief explanation of the features of this language and how it is different from English is provided. Arabic is spoken as a first language by over 200 million people, mostly in the Middle East and North Africa, and was ranked fourth language in the world in terms of the number of native speakers[2].

- **Direction of Reading and Writing**: Arabic is considered as a Semitic and bi-directional language because the script is read and written from right to left, whereas numerals are read from left to right [10, 11].
- **Uni-Case Language:** no upper or lower case variations in Arabic.
- **Formation of the Letters:** Each letter may have two to four different forms depending on its position in the word. Arabic letters consist of 17 base letters. The remaining letters are made up by the addition of dots that can vary in number and position. As a consequence, distinguishing these letters could add to the difficulties faced by Arabic readers [11].
- **Cursive Form and Spaces:** Arabic script is written in a cursive style with the letters being joined to each other by ligatures. Of the 28 letters, only 22 are two way connectors, while the remaining six letters cannot be joined as they are one way connecting letters. For this reason, an Arabic word may have one or more spaces

---

[2] http://www.ethnologue.com/statistics/size .

within the same word depending on how many of these letters are used in the word [12]. These spaces together with the fact that Arabic is a uni-case language can cause a problem in identifying the boundaries of the words in Arabic script, especially for poor or beginner readers.

- **Diacritical Marks:** In Arabic, diacritical marks (small diagonal marks above or below letters) are used to represent short vowels and help readers in pronunciation [12, 13]. Reading accuracy in Arabic requires the vowelising of word endings according to their grammatical function in the sentence (for example, subject or object), which needs a high level or linguistic skills comprising phonological and syntactical processing [13]. However, websites that have content in this type of orthography are very limited [14].

- **Homographic Language:** A huge number of Arabic words appear as non-vowelised, when appearing out of context, are homographic [12]. This means homographic words can carry more than one pronunciation and meaning, which causes semantic and phonological ambiguity. In this case, the context is needed to ensure the correct reading for these words.

- **Gender-Specific Language:** Arabic is a gender specific language, resulting in some spoken and written words having a different form based on their male or female type. Sometimes, diacritics are needed in text to differentiate between genders [15].

- **Font Type, Size and Text Emphasis:** to achieve more clarity in the presented Arabic text, [14] recommended paying attention to the font type, size and the emphasis of the text. The fonts that have flowing cursive form with full and deep curves and straight and vertical uprights are much clearer than angular types. The recommended text size was in the range of 16-20pt, which is why Arabic script usually appears in larger sizes than English, in print and electronic form.

- **Alignment of Text:** The Arabic justification of text alignment should be right justified or fully justified. Fully justified text was not considered as a problem because in Arabic, words can be stretched to fill the width of the line instead of introducing inconsistent spaces between words as in English [16].

- **Diglossic Language:** Arabic is highly diglossic [10], which means Arab people use a localised form of spoken Arabic in their homes and neighbourhoods, a language totally different from Modern Standard Arabic (MSA). This linguistic phenomenon is called diglossia [17].

- **Long Sentences:** [14] agreed that shorter sentences are easier to read and understand. However, the nature of Arabic allows for longer sentences that span many lines, in contrast to English.

Symbols. Some symbols are strongly culture-defined because what they represent is not available in another country. Using inappropriate symbols that the user cannot recognise or with which they identify therefore reduces the accessibility of the web product. Moreover, the use of certain symbols, icons, or images may be offensive or even against the law in some countries [3].

Multimedia. The use of multimedia in a website would differ from one culture to another [18, 19]. According to [20], Saudi users prefer to have more images and less text compared with Western countries who prefer more text and fewer images. For designing Arabic websites it is important to choose pictures that do not have an impact on a conservative society [21].

Due to the fact that some people in Saudi Arabia do not listen to music and believe it is forbidden from a religious point of view depending on how conservative they are, if a Saudi user navigates a website that presents a video with music in the background, for example, he might not continue watching it and consequently quit the website. Although, this is not the case for all Arab users, as they differ in their beliefs and traditions, an appropriate way to deal with such a situation is needed, and this is not found in the existing guidelines. So, besides providing text alternatives for the video, the developers would provide a hint for people that there is music in the video, and/or provide another version of the video without music if they prefer no music ([22] discusses the issue of music in Islam).

Colours. Colours are related to emotional and cultural associations and can have an influence on users from different cultural backgrounds [9]. Colours might produce varying emotional reactions that can impact accessibility.

Layout. Page layout refers to the display layout that guides scanning information and reflects the logical flow of task [18, 19]. Appropriate menu design and layout would give a website's users with a contextual and structural model for understanding and accessing information [18]. Page orientation differs from culture to another due to text direction, for example, for right to left Arabic text the side menu will change in direction to be on the right [9].

4.2   Other Framework Components

- Web Accessibility: This component focus on making websites perceivable, operable, understandable and robust [2]. So, people with disabilities can perceive, understand, navigate, and interact with the web, and that they can contribute to the web [23].
- User Diversity: Users with disabilities, older users, new and infrequent users and people with low literacy or those not fluent in the language [2, 23] should be considered when aiming to develop an accessible websites.
- Technology Variety: A broad range of hardware and software needs to be supported [24]. Moreover, the use of different assistive technologies, which are used by people with special needs, should be taken into account.
- Internet Infrastructure: Internet speed and broadband availability in the country could affect the ability to connect to the web which may also influence accessibility of the web content [25].
- Costs: Users could be prevented from accessing the Internet and surfing the Web due to the high costs of devices and Internet connection [26, 27].

5 Conclusion and Future Work

This paper presented the process of developing a framework for localised web accessibility guidelines for university websites in Saudi Arabia. The resultant framework consisted of six main components which are relevant to the process that could offer those with disabilities more equitable access.

After developing the framework, the next immediate task will be to carry out an expert evaluation study to investigate the agreement among a number of experts on its components. The purpose of this activity is to confirm the framework and explore other additional components. The expert review will be conducted by interviewing a panel of native Arabic speakers. The experts will be either developers of university websites in Saudi Arabia or researchers in the area of web accessibility.

The framework will be endorsed having received confirmation from the experts that it would provide the basis for the development of localised guidelines.

References

1. Masood, M., Rana, F.M., Rana, U.: Evaluating web accessibility of university web sites in the kingdom of Saudi Arabia. Int. J. Technol. Knowl. Soc. 7(3), 1–15 (2011)
2. Web Content Accessibility Guidelines (WCAG 2.0). https://www.w3.org/TR/WCAG20/
3. Al-Badi, A.: A framework for designing usable localised websites. Ph.D. thesis, School of Computing Science, University of East Anglia (2005)
4. Al-Khalifa, H.S.: Exploring the accessibility of Saudi Arabia e-government websites: preliminary results. In: ICEGOV, Proceedings of the 4th International Conference on Theory and Practice of Electronic Governance, Beijing, China, pp. 274–278 (2010)
5. Abanumy, A., Al-Badi, A., Mayhew, P.: E-government website accessibility: in-depth evaluation of Saudi Arabia and Oman. Electron. J. E-Gov. 3(3), 99–106 (2005)
6. Khan, M.A., Buragga, K.A.: Effectiveness of accessibility and usability of government websites in Saudi Arabia. Can. J. Pure Appl. Sci. 4(2), 1227–1231 (2010)
7. Mourad, M.B.A., Kamoun, F.: Accessibility evaluation of Dubai e-government websites: findings and implications. J. E-Gov. Stud. Best Pract. 2013, 1–15 (2013)
8. Al-Faries, A., Al-Khalifa, H.S., Al-Razgan, M.S., Al-Duwais, M.: Evaluating the accessibility and usability of top Saudi e-government services. In: Proceedings of the 7th International Conference on Theory and Practice of Electronic Governance, ICEGOV 2013, pp. 60–63. ACM, New York, NY, USA (2013)
9. Barber, W., Badre, A.: Culturability: the merging of culture and usability. In: Proceedings of the 4th Conference on Human Factors and the Web, vol. 7, no. 4, pp. 1–10 (1998)
10. AlGhanem, R., Kearns, D.M.: Orthographic, phonological, and morphological skills and children's word reading in Arabic: a literature review. Read. Res. Q. 50(1), 83–109 (2015)
11. Mahfoudhi, A., Everatt, J., Elbeheri, G.: Introduction to the special issue on literacy in Arabic. Read. Writ. 24(9), 1011–1018 (2011)
12. Elbeheri, G.: Dyslexia in Egypt. In: The International Book of Dyslexia: A Guide to Practice and Resources, pp. 79–85 (2005)
13. Abu-Rabia, S., Abu-Rahmoun, N.: The role of phonology and morphology in the development of basic reading skills of dyslexic and normal native Arabic readers. Creat. Educ. 3, 1259–1268 (2012)

14. Al-Wabil, A., Zaphiris, P., Wilson, S.: Web design for dyslexics: accessibility of Arabic content. In: Miesenberger, K., Klaus, J., Zagler, W.L., Karshmer, A.I. (eds.) ICCHP 2006. LNCS, vol. 4061, pp. 817–822. Springer, Heidelberg (2006)

15. Rowais, F.A., Wald, M., Wills, G.: An Arabic framework for dyslexia training tools. In: 1st International Conference on Technology for Helping People with Special Needs (ICTHP), pp. 63–68 (2013)

16. Benatia, M.J.E., Elyaakoubi, M., Lazrek, A.: Arabic text justification. TUGboat 27(2), 137–146 (2006)

17. Ferguson, C.A.: Diglossia. Word. Language and Social Context, pp. 232–251 (1959)

18. Cyr, D., Trevor-Smith, H.: Localization of web design: an empirical comparison of German, Japanese, and United States web site characteristics. J. Am. Soc. Inform. Sci. Technol. 55 (13), 1199–1208 (2004)

19. Sun, H.: Building a culturally-competent corporate web site: an exploratory study of cultural markers in multilingual web design. In: Proceedings of the 19th Annual international Conference on Computer Documentation, pp. 95–102. ACM (2001)

20. Almakky, H., Sahandi, R., Taylor, J.: The effect of culture on user interface design of social media. A case study on preferences of Saudi Arabian on the Arabic user interface of Facebook. Int. J. Soc. Educ. Econ. Manag. Eng. 9(1), 107–111 (2015)

21. Al-Sedrani, A., Al-Khalifa, H.: Design considerations for the localization of Arabic e-commerce websites. In: Seventh International Conference on Digital Information Management (ICDIM), pp. 331–335 (2012)

22. Otterbeck, J., Ackfeldt, A.: Music and Islam. Contemp. Islam 6(3), 227–233 (2012)

23. Henry, S.L.: Understanding web accessibility. In: Web Accessibility, pp. 1–51. Apress (2006)

24. Shneiderman, B.: Universal usability. Commun. ACM 43(5), 84–91 (2000)

25. Aleid, F., Rogerson, S., Fairweather, B.: Factors affecting consumers adoption of e-commerce in Saudi Arabia from a consumers perspective. In: IADIS International Conference E-commerce, pp. 11–18 (2009)

26. Alrawabdeh, W.: Internet and the Arab world: understanding the key issues and overcoming the barriers. Int. Arab J. Inf. Technol. 6(1), 27–32 (2009)

27. Sait, S.M., Al-Tawil, K.M., Sanaullah, S., Faheemuddin, M.: Impact of internet usage in Saudi Arabia: a social perspective. IJITWE 2(2), 81–115 (2007)

Towards Accessible Innovative Assessment Items

Eric G. Hansen[⊠], Carlos Cavalie, Teresa King, Mark T. Hakkinen,
Jason J. White, and Jennifer Grant

Educational Testing Service, Princeton, NJ, USA
{ehansen, ccavalie, tking, mhakkinen,
jjwhite, jgrant}@ets.org

Abstract. Educational assessment represents a huge challenge for accessibility, and the use of highly visual assessment tasks that rely on idiosyncratic interactions that may be unfamiliar to test takers further increases that challenge. The authors describe a prototype innovative mathematics item and an initial evaluation of its usability for diverse audiences, including individuals with visual and other disabilities. The study illustrates the use of technical standards for developing accessible innovative assessment items and illustrates the challenges of meeting diverse access needs.

Keywords: Assessment · Testing · Disabilities

1 State of the Art

There is increasing use in education of assessment items (questions) that are innovative in the sense of going beyond a simple, single-selection multiple choice format, such as use of interactivity, novel response format or use of media (graphics, audio, video, animation). Some strategies exist for making these innovative items accessible to visually disabled populations. For example, items that contain graphics may be made more accessible using text description and tactile graphics or perhaps audio-tactile graphics [1, 2]. However, when graphical materials are interactive and change dynamically, additional solutions are called for. This paper describes some approaches to accessibility that are needed when traditional approaches are inadequate. We explore these in the context of an interactive mathematics item that presents several accessibility challenges.

This study makes several contributions to the fields of education and accessibility. First, it illustrates an innovative use of technical standards to make interactive graphical objects more accessible. Second, it underscores the importance of involving assessment developers (for example, to help define the construct being assessed and help write instructions for interactive objects). Third, it demonstrates the value of using a broader set of users, both with and without disabilities, to evaluate the accessibility and usability of novel interactive components.

A variety of recent technical standards may be helpful in designing and developing accessible innovative items. For example, the Web Content Accessibility Guidelines (WCAG) of the World Wide Web Consortium (W3C) provides a general framework

© Springer International Publishing Switzerland 2016
K. Miesenberger et al. (Eds.): ICCHP 2016, Part I, LNCS 9758, pp. 251–258, 2016.
DOI: 10.1007/978-3-319-41264-1_34

for accessibility of Web-based systems [3]. Furthermore, the W3C's Web Accessibility Initiative Accessible Rich Internet Applications (WAI-ARIA) technology [4] is often needed in order to make interactive Web-based user interfaces accessible. Our approach in the current effort is to apply WAI-ARIA and other technologies to establish best practices for designing and developing accessible innovative assessment items.

2   Methodology

Our basic strategy for this study was to examine diverse users interacting with an innovative item as a way to identify usability and accessibility issues. Among the users were individuals with and without disabilities. We used relatively simple mathematics content involving the addition of fractions in order to improve the likelihood that problems in using the math item were due to usability problems rather than the difficulty of the content.

2.1   Participants

Our sample of participants consisted of 10 individuals with experience in disability issues and/or usability issues. Six participants had a diagnosed disability. Three (all with low vision) were in grades 9 to 11; all others were adults. The most common disability status reported by participants was "none" (n = 4) followed by "low vision" (n = 3), "blind" (n = 2), and "learning disability" (n = 1). Nine participants had either represented a specific disability of interest to this study or reported expert level knowledge in at least one disability. One participant with no reported disability was a usability expert for general audiences. When asked about their preferred assistive technology (AT) usage, the two participants who were blind cited JAWS (Freedom Scientific) and one of them also cited braille – both refreshable and hardcopy. The three participants with low vision all reported using ZoomText (Ai Squared) enlargement software.

2.2   Delivery Platform

The study utilized a recent version of the Google Chrome browser running on the Microsoft Windows 7 platform, with test sessions conducted on either a laptop or desktop personal computer. One or more participants used screen enlargement (ZoomText) and screen readers (NVDA from NV Access, and JAWS). Item content was accessed from a remote server, or if connectivity was not available, via a local server on a personal computer.

2.3   The Fraction Model Item

The fraction model item used in the study is shown in Fig. 1a. The item essentially consisted of a stem (textual prompt presented to the test taker) plus the "fraction model object." Following is the text of the stem of the item.

"Alice ate 1/4 of a pizza. Brandon ate 3/8 of the same pizza. What fraction of the pizza was eaten by Alice and Brandon? Represent your answer on the fraction model below.

Use the arrow buttons to divide the circle into more or fewer parts. Then shade the fraction model by selecting the parts".

Figure 1a shows the fraction model item used in this study. The item is essentially a fraction-addition question with a fraction model object for recording one's answer.

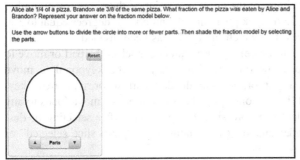 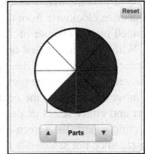

Fig. 1. (a) On left is an image of the item screen. (b) On the right is an enlarged image of the fraction model object showing five of the eight "pizza slices" selected, representing the fraction "five-eighths."

The Fraction Model Object. As shown above, the fraction model object appears visually within the item, positioned visually just below the stem. When delivered to a user as part of an assessment, the fraction model object allows the user to (a) divide an object (circle or rectangle) into a number of equal sized parts and then (b) select the number of parts. The number of parts selected from the available number of equal-sized parts thus constitutes a fraction. The test taker uses the "increment" (up arrow) button to increase the number of parts into which the geometric object is divided and a "decrement" (down arrow) button to decrease the number of parts. A "reset" button allows the taker to quickly deselect any parts that have been selected and reset the number of parts to the default number (in this case, 2). The object's interface is fully keyboard operable by using the tab, enter, and up and down arrow keys.

Screen Reader Operation of the Fraction Model Object. This section describes the interaction for a screen reader user who is blind and is using the keyboard. Keyboard operability would also be helpful to some fully sighted individuals, notably individuals with physical (motor) disabilities. Having heard the stem, the user of a screen reader can press tab, which changes the software's focus to the fraction model object. The following description pertains to the NVDA screen reader; voicing may be slightly different if using another screen reader.

Focus goes first to the reset button, and the user hears, "Reset circle to two parts." By tabbing again, focus goes to the right half of the circle, which is highlighted in yellow, and the user hears, "Pizza circle containing selectable parts list. Pizza slice not selected, 1 of 2." By tabbing again, focus goes to the increment button, which is announced as "increase number of parts button." Tabbing again gives focus to the decrement button, which is announced as the "decrease number of parts button." Tabbing again returns focus to the reset button, thus returning to the beginning of the tab order for the fraction model object.

Once the user has divided the circle into the desired number of parts (using the up and down arrow buttons in the user interface), he or she uses the tab key to cycle back to the "first" of the parts of the circle. The first part has its left boundary on the line from the center of the circle to the 12 o'clock position on the circle and its opposite boundary on the line from the center of the circle to a point on the circle some number of degrees clockwise from the 12 o'clock position – the number of degrees equal to 360 divided by the number of slices into which the circle has been divided.

With the focus on that first part (slice), the user can either select the part or move to another part by using the up arrow (or left arrow) key on the keyboard to move counterclockwise to the previous part or, by using the down arrow (or right arrow) key, to move clockwise to the next (i.e., second) part. Thus, the user can move focus to any part and either select or deselect it by pressing the space bar. After selecting or deselecting a part, the screen reader announces its status (e.g., "pizza slice selected" or "pizza slice not selected").

While one or more parts have been selected, if the user changes the number of parts (via the increment or decrement button), then any selected parts (slices) are automatically deselected. Once the desired number of parts (pizza slices) has been selected, the work for that item is done. In an operational test item, the user would generally then navigate to the "next" button to continue to the next item, but there was no "next" button in this prototype.

Technologies Used in the Item. An earlier version of the item, which was designed to be keyboard operable, used HTML, Cascading Style Sheets (CSS), JavaScript, and Scalable Vector Graphics (SVG) technologies. During the current study, we further enhanced the item using Accessible Rich Internet Applications (WAI-ARIA) attributes to make it compatible with screen reader software. While it is common to use WAI-ARIA attributes with HTML, we used WAI-ARIA attributes within the SVG content (i.e., the fraction model object). Specifically, we assigned the fraction model an ARIA role of "listbox," with "aria-multiselectable" set to "true" to enable the user to select more than one slice simultaneously. Each slice was accordingly given an ARIA option role, and the "aria-selected" state was updated by JavaScript code in response to the user's actions. This kind of usage of WAI-ARIA attributes within SVG is relatively uncommon in web development because support for WAI-ARIA in SVG contexts has only recently become available in web browsers and screen readers. Currently, support for use of WAI-ARIA attributes varies by the combination of screen reader and web browser that is used.

Other Instruments Used in the Data Collection. Other key instruments included a background interview, user usability problem severity ratings, and post-item questions. The background interview included questions about the participant's disability status and use of assistive technologies. Participants were asked to rate the severity of usability problems encountered in the session according to the following scale [5]:

(1) Minor: Causes some hesitation or slight irritation. (2) Moderate: Causes occasional task failure for some users; causes delays and moderate irritation. (3) Critical: Leads to task failure; causes user extreme irritation. Post-item questions were asked, such as "Overall, how difficult or easy was it to use this item? (1 = very difficult; 7 = very easy)" and "What are your highest priority improvements for this item?"

2.4   Session

Each participant underwent an individualized session with one or more researchers present. The participant accessed the prototype interactive item via a web browser and assistive technology (if needed). Participants were asked to attempt to answer the item correctly but were also told that the purpose of the study was not to evaluate their content knowledge. Participants encountered the item without any practice items or detailed instructions. Thus, it is believed that when answering questions about usability, participants were rating, at least in part, the ease of learning to use the item, as well as the ease of using the item.

3   Results

Half of the participants used an assistive technology such as screen enlargement (ZoomText) (n = 3) and screen readers (NVDA, JAWS) (n = 2); the remaining used no assistive technology. While most participants appeared to find the fraction model item rather usable, all participants identified areas for improvements. Particularly, there tended to be gaps in understanding what the item expected from individuals with visual disabilities.

3.1   Overall Ease of Use

We asked participants to provide an overall rating of the difficulty/ease of using the fraction model on a scale of 1 to 7 with "1" signifying "very difficult" and 7 signifying "very easy." Two of the nine individuals who provided a rating rated the fraction model as 7 ("very easy") and two others rated it as 1 ("very difficult").

3.2   Severity of Usability Problems

When participants identified usability problems in the fraction model they were asked to also provide a rating of the problem on a 3 point scale (3 = "critical"; 2 = "moderate"; 1 = "minor"). Participants identified and rated 26 usability problems – 11 rated as critical, 13 as moderate, and 2 as minor. (An additional 8 problems were unrated for severity due to lack of time.) Blindness ("blind") was the area of experience with the highest number of problems (n = 15) and the largest number of critical problems (n = 8). Furthermore, a nondisabled usability expert was the one person who identified the largest number of problems (n = 8).

3.3   Types of Usability Issues

A variety of usability issues or problems were noted. Several of these, including some considered by users as most severe, might be addressed at least partially through improved instructions. Following are the majority of the issues noted.

1. Unclear reference to "arrows." Several individuals with visual disabilities were confused as to whether the arrows for increasing or decreasing the number of parts were onscreen or on the keyboard. (They were onscreen arrows.) This was also a notable problem for the low vision participants, probably because the onscreen arrows below the fraction model were off-screen due to use of screen magnification.
2. Unclear meaning of "fraction model." The use of the term "fraction model" in the stem of the item led to some confusion. One participant suggested that the fraction model object should be labeled as such to clarify what the stem was referring to.
3. Unclear possibility of selecting more than one slice. It was not intuitive to all users that they could select more than one slice. The screen reader announcement of the presence of a "list box" confused at least one user, who indicated that, "The pizza is labeled as a list box, but it isn't. I think a checkbox would work better than the list box being used currently. I would know that I could choose more than one."
4. Lack of count of slices. Two users wanted feedback (e.g., a display) showing the number of equal sized slices into which the pizza had been divided.
5. Lack of submit button. One participant with low vision was confused by the lack of a submit button. (Because the absence of a submit button was an artifact of this being a prototype, this is arguably not a usability problem per se.)
6. Poor visual contrast. One user with low vision wanted better visual contrast for the reset button.
7. Controls not visible when using enlargement. One user with low vision noted that the arrows for the fraction model were off screen at first (rated as a moderate problem).
8. Location of controls. The usability expert suggested that arrow buttons should be moved up next to the reset button. It would place all the fraction model controls in one location and closer to the question referring to them. (This was from the usability expert.)
9. Line length too long. One participant suggested that the line length was too long.
10. Space bar did not work. One participant wanted to use the space bar to select the slice (rather than having to use only the enter key).
11. Line indicating the active slice is confusing. One nondisabled participant with expertise in learning disabilities indicated that the light blue line to indicate the active slice was confusing. (This line is visible on the fifth "slice" in Fig. 1a).

3.4   Things Liked

When asked about things that they liked (usability positives), results were obtained from 7 participants as follows. (Due to time constraints, not all participants were asked.) (1) Clear screen, beautiful layout, soothing color scheme. (2) Nice to have reset button. (3) The pie was helpful. (4) A lot of white space is good. Selecting slices is intuitive. (5) I liked visualization – the model. (6) I liked that selected pieces of the fraction turn dark blue. (7) I also like that the model is present because it makes it easier to work out the fraction.

4 Discussion

Many participants appeared to find the fraction model item rather usable, yet a number of areas for improvement were cited, several of which might be addressed through better instructions. The study would have benefited from involvement of an assessment developer (e.g., item writer) who could help provide those instructions without undermining measurement of the skills targeted for measurement.

4.1 Recommendations

Putting the results of this study into a larger frame, following are recommendations for individuals seeking to develop innovative assessment items that are accessible to individuals with disabilities.

1. Use a methodology such as Evidence Centered Design [6, 7] to reason about accessibility in the context of the validity of the assessment results.
2. Develop items from the earliest stages (i.e., from scratch) to be compatible with all modern standards-based browsers and diverse assistive technologies.
3. Use realistic assessment contexts to examine the usability of innovative accessibility features.
4. Use multidisciplinary teams. In aggregate, the team designing and developing innovative assessment items should have expertise not only in accessibility and software development, but also content (e.g., math) assessment expertise.
5. Use existing technical standards such as WAI-ARIA for improving the accessibility of innovative items.
6. Involve assessment developers in prototyping. This can help ensure that content is appropriate, that instructions are adequate, and that the intended purpose of an item is understood by all team participants.
7. Conduct usability studies with diverse users. Involve users with disabilities, and, as appropriate, without disabilities.
8. Ensure that usability study participants have practice and familiarization opportunities that are consistent with the format and the focus of the study.
9. Collaborate with others to improve technical standards for accessibility to support requirements identified in the assessment context.

10. Consider providing additional information (beyond the instructions) for individuals with visual disabilities, which may help them quickly orient to the layout and components of an item, information that might be obtained at a glance by sighted test takers.
11. Consider the possibility that some items (e.g., especially highly visual or interactive ones) might not be amenable to being made accessible to some audiences. Where that occurs, it may be necessary either to forego use of that item or to develop an alternate item that is accessible.

References

1. Gardner, J.A., Bulatov, V., Stowell, H.: The ViewPlus IVEO technology for universally usable graphical information. In: Proceedings of 2005 CSUN International Conference on Technology and People with Disabilities (2005)
2. Hansen, E.G., Shute, V.J., Landau, S.: An assessment-for-learning system in mathematics for individuals with visual impairments. J. Vis. Impair. Blind. **104**(5), 275 (2010)
3. Caldwell, B., Cooper, M., Reid, L.G., Vanderheiden, G. (eds.): Web Content Accessibility guidelines 2.0 (2008). http://www.w3.org/TR/WCAG20/
4. Craig, J., Cooper, M. (eds.): Accessible Rich Internet Applications (WAI-ARIA) 1.0. W3C Recommendation (2014). http://www.w3.org/TR/2014/REC-wai-aria-20140320/
5. Suaro, J.: Rating the Severity of Usability Problems (2013). http://www.measuringu.com/blog/rating-severity.php
6. Mislevy, R.J., Steinberg, L.S., Almond, R.G.: On the Structure of Educational Assessments. Meas.: Interdiscip. Res. Perspect. **1**(1), 3–62 (2005)
7. Hansen, E.G., Mislevy, R.J.: Accessibility of computer-based testing for individuals with disabilities and English language learners within a validity framework. In: Hricko, M., Howell, S. (eds.) Online Assessment and Measurement: Foundation, Challenges, and Issues. Idea Group Publishing, Inc., Hershey, PA (2005)

Web Page Clustering for More Efficient Website Accessibility Evaluations

Justyna Mucha[1], Mikael Snaprud[1,2(✉)], and Annika Nietzio[3]

[1] Universitet i Agder, Grimstad, Norway
justyna.mucha@uia.no
[2] Tingtun AS, Lillesand, Norway
mikael.snaprud@tingtun.no
[3] Forschungsinstitut Technologie Und Behinderung (FTB) der Evangelischen
Stiftung Volmarstein, Ruhr, Germany
eiii@ftb-esv.de

Abstract. Despite advances in the legal framework to assure web accessibility people with disabilities still find barriers hindering websites access. The European Internet Inclusion Initiative (EIII) has delivered methods and tools to carry out large scale evaluations of websites. The tools have been used to carry out 180 million tests on $540,000$ web pages to check 1065 websites at a rate of about 7 sites per hour. This paper outlines an approach to reduce the number of web pages needed to compute accessibility scores. The suggested approach relies on machine learning to cluster the web pages according to the barriers detected and to select representative pages for the score calculation. Analysis of the experimental results has confirmed the validity of the accessibility test result as a new feature for clustering web pages, which is planned to be implemented in the EIII website checker tools.

Keywords: Web accessibility · Clustering · EIII · Evaluation · Enhancement

1 Introduction

With a continuous increase in the number of websites, an automatic and efficient evaluation approach is strongly desirable. Moreover, in some cases the process of sampling may not support the overall aim of assessing the whole website. Therefore a more focused way of selecting individual pages would improve the quality of the analysis.

Monitoring of large numbers of pages on many websites is a computationally intensive task. Important bottlenecks are the crawling of websites, where idle time between each page is needed so that the checked site is not overloaded, and the processing of numerous tests on each page. High computational costs leave room for checker optimization. In most cases websites contain pages that use similar templates and differ only in their content. Many web accessibility issues are caused by the structure, i.e. the template, of the web page. The actual content of the page has little influence on these issues.

© Springer International Publishing Switzerland 2016
K. Miesenberger et al. (Eds.): ICCHP 2016, Part I, LNCS 9758, pp. 259–266, 2016.
DOI: 10.1007/978-3-319-41264-1_35

The study described in this paper uses the checker tools developed by the EIII. The tests are based on the Web Content Accessibility Guidelines (WCAG) 2.0 and can identify areas that violate accessibility regulations.

2 Related Work

Several approaches have been proposed to reduce the number of web pages needed to compute a representative score for a website. According to Chakrabarti and Mehta [1], web pages can be grouped together on the basis of Document Object Model (DOM) similarities, provided relevant elements of DOM are under inspection. In the domain of web accessibility, Harper et al. [2] propose a DOM Block Clustering on relevant DOM elements where two pages are considered to belong to the same demographics if their sequence of elements in the DOM is the same. With application of the method 0.14 % of the pages could bring the coverage of 80 % of a site. Earlier on, similar attempts were carried out to cluster web pages on their structure with a sample from a dataset by Crescenzi et al. [3]. Brajnik et al. [4] have gone one step further and additionally examined 13 sampling methods of choosing cluster representatives and their impact on web accessibility evaluations.

The idea of web page clustering based on Unified Resource Locator (URL) was introduced by Hernández et al. [5]. Notably this approach does not require downloading the page before checking since the clustering is based only on external properties. The solution to the sampling suggested by Zhang et al. [9] is based on URL clustering to enable fast web accessibility evaluation. Looking for common patterns in URLs is meant to assure scalability allowing for an efficient evaluation of the large websites.

A more detailed discussion of sampling approaches and web accessibility metrics can be found in a report published by the EIII [10]. The current EIII approach is based on uniform random sampling of 600 pages—or less if the website is smaller.

3 The Proposed Approach

In order to enhance the evaluation process, it is proposed to apply clustering to group together similar pages in terms of the web accessibility barriers they contain. Clustering as an unsupervised method of machine learning aims to infer common patterns from the members of the analyzed dataset and group them with regard to these patterns. No prior, external information is provided what kind of patterns can be found. An array of test results representing an accessibility profile of each page is used to cluster them.

In our approach web page clustering is based on the outcome of accessibility evaluations, which resulted from checking HTML structure and DOM elements. Moreover, in this study, an extended approach has been chosen. Web pages are evaluated *after* the application of JavaScript and CSS code, which influences the HTML structure and DOM elements.

4 Implemented Solution

Each of the web pages has been modelled in a numeric way as a vector of accessibility test results that were produced during the accessibility evaluation by the EIII accessibility checking tool.

The data obtained from the accessibility evaluation tool is provided as a matrix M of dimensions $n \times f$, where n = number of pages to cluster (sample size); f = number of the web page attributes (number of different tests applied on the website multiplied by 3, the number of possible test outcomes: *fail, pass, verify*).

Each matrix element M_{ij} represents a total number of test results t_j of a particular outcome type on a page p_i. $M_{ij} \in \mathbb{N}_0$ since 0 value indicates that the particular test outcomes did not occur on the page even if the test was applied. An upper bound of the codomain is not set.

Website s has been transformed into a dataset Q. A single page p_i from Q is represented as a vector $\mathbf{v}_i$.

$$\mathbf{v}_i = \begin{bmatrix} M_{i1} \\ M_{i2} \\ \vdots \\ M_{if} \end{bmatrix}_{i \times f} \tag{1}$$

Web pages with similar accessibility test results are clustered together.

In our study, various ways of clustering web pages and their impact on the accessibility scores have been explored. Four different clustering approaches, have been designed and implemented to compare their relevance and to analyze them. The selected methods of cluster analysis techniques are classic hierarchical agglomerative clustering (HAC), the more complex one involving dimensionality reduction with PCA application (HCPC), model-based clustering technique (MB) and finally K-Means partitioning clustering method that have comprised together a diverse suit of clustering approaches. Algorithmic details on each of the methods can be found in [6,7]. In the implemented solution, the barriers found on one, randomly selected web page from each cluster have been used to compute a representative score for the overall website.

5 Results

The sample size can be reduced by calculating the accessibility score for the whole website only on representative web pages extracted from each identified cluster. The research has shown that by incorporating the clustering into the evaluation procedure a reduction in the number of web pages needed to calculate the accessibility score is attainable. Table 1 presents the achieved reduction ranging from 70.6 % to 99.8 % compared to the current EIII implementation. Less pages are required to determinate the accessibility issues. The initial experiments have shown that the accessibility scores are similar to the current ones from EIII and that they also seem independent of the number of identified clusters.

Table 1. Reduction of the sample size with a novel approach compared to the current EIII implementation. The table gives a website number, *No* - for short reference, *URL* - for the website, *EIII pages* - number of pages used in current EIII approach and *Novel approach pages* - for the number of pages needed with the novel approach to assess the accessibility of the website.

No	URL	EIII pages	Novel approach pages
W_1	www.leitir.is	34	10
W_2	www.namsskogan.kommune.no	62	8
W_3	www.frogn.kommune.no	297	7
W_4	www.digitalqatar.qa	601	6

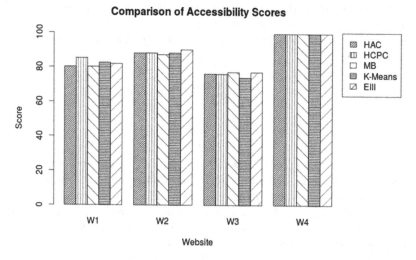

Fig. 1. Comparison of the accessibility scores of the studied websites computed by different clustering methods. The dataset labels correspond to the websites in Table 1.

The methods have been applied on a testing set of four websites, varying in size and origin. The relation between the accessibility score computed solely on cluster representatives and the EIII current score for the four evaluated websites has been depicted in the Fig. 1. The analysis has shown that the novel evaluation scores were very similar to those currently computed by the EIII tool. Most similar accessibility scores were obtained with use of the K-Means clustering method. From the algorithmic perspective, the K-Means method has a linear time complexity and a small space needed for the observations and centroids.

As a side effect, the novel approach can identify CMS templates implemented on the website. This allows for a more targeted repair and contributes to a faster and more efficient way of fixing the accessibility barriers.

5.1   Overview of the Website Templates

The factual indicator of the goodness of the proposed approach can be expressed as well as a study of the real templates discovered on the websites in the clustering process. In other words, how the clusters correspond to the templates used on the websites. The arrays of web accessibility violations and the degree of the recurrence were the subject of the examination.

Each website was analyzed after clustering with the K-Means approach. From each cluster, a sample of random pages was selected. The sample size varied between the websites due to the website size and the cluster size. If a cluster contained fewer members than the sample size, the whole cluster was analyzed. The URLs, EIII accessibility score and the distribution of the accessibility barriers were taken into consideration.

Table 2 presents the overview of the findings for 2 exemplary clusters from website W_4. Web pages in the same clusters have either the same accessibility scores or nearly the same. The same suite of the accessibility tests was applied during the checking process. Mostly, the number of test instances was alike. Some outliers can be also found, e.g. in cluster number 1, where one of the cluster members has an abnormal (in terms of the cluster tendency) number of barriers described with test *F89*. A detailed description of *F89* and the other tests carried out by the EIII tool can be found in [11]. The analysis of the URLs in the clusters is summarized in the Table 3. The clustering approach identified different types of pages: the first cluster covers pages with a blog structure presenting several news items, while the second cluster identified the author pages of the website.

Table 2. Overview of the templates found in W_4 together with the EIII accessibility scores relating to the examined web page. Maximum 5 were randomly selected from each cluster. The URLs of the cluster representatives can be found in a Table 3.

C_i	EIII score	Barriers
1	99.33	SC4-1-1-id: (1), H91: (4), F89: (7), H64(3), H44 (1)
	99.35	SC4-1-1-id: (1), H91: (4), F89: (16), H64(6), H44 (1)
	99.44	SC4-1-1-id: (1), H91: (4), F89: (7), H64(6), H44 (1)
	99.49	SC4-1-1-id: (1), H91: (4), F89: (7), H64(6), H44 (1)
	99.46	SC4-1-1-id: (1), H91: (4), F89: (7), H64(6), H44 (1)
2	99.30	SC4-1-1-id: (1), H91: (4), F89: (7), H44 (1)
	99.38	SC4-1-1-id: (1), H91: (4), F89: (7), H44 (1)
	99.38	SC4-1-1-id: (1), H91: (4), F89: (7), H44 (1)
	99.38	SC4-1-1-id: (1), H91: (4), F89: (7), H44 (1)
	99.38	SC4-1-1-id: (1), H91: (4), F89: (7), H44 (1)

Table 3. Overview of the distribution and similarity of URLs in the clusters found in W_4. The EIII accessibility scores are provided for reference.

C_i	EIII score	URL
1	99.33	http://www.digitalqatar.qa/category/%D8%A7%D9%84%D8%B3%D8%B1%D9%82%D8%A9-%D8%A7%D9%84%D8%A3%A9
	99.35	http://www.digitalqatar.qa/en/page/58/
	99.44	http://www.digitalqatar.qa/en/category/technology/page/22/
	99.49	http://www.digitalqatar.qa/en/tag/mena/
	99.46	http://www.digitalqatar.qa/en/tag/twitter/page/7/
2	99.30	http://www.digitalqatar.qa/author/dalabdulla
	99.38	http://www.digitalqatar.qa/en/author/bwesolowski/page/8/
	99.38	http://www.digitalqatar.qa/en/author/asharma/page/6/
	99.38	http://www.digitalqatar.qa/en/author/kalmaadeed/
	99.38	http://www.digitalqatar.qa/en/author/talthani/

6   Discussion

The goal of the study has been to examine the impact of the clustering on the accessibility score computation and to validate the accessibility test result as a clustering feature. In addition to that, a point of interest has been set to assess how well the new approach performs compared to the method currently implemented in the EIII project, which does not involve any clustering technique. The credibility and goodness of the novel solution have been investigated. The clustering properties of the accessibility test results have been analyzed.

The analysis showed that the clustering of web pages allows for finding the true patterns of the accessibility issues. All of this points to the fact, that understanding the accessibility issues of a single page p from a cluster C_i can expose the barriers that all of the cluster members share. Taking this one step further, disclosing the particular barriers on one page allows for a more efficient way of fixing the accessibility problems on the website by pointing to the cluster members and the elements that violate accessibility. Noteworthy, the proposed method also removes the bias caused by websites with a large number of similar pages, such as error pages or calendar pages, which can dominate the score and conceal problems in other parts of the web site. With a clustering approach those pages are separated from the rest of the domain. Pages with error messages such as invalid links, can also become grouped in one cluster.

A comparison with the two related clustering approaches based on URLs [8,9] and based on DOM Block clustering [2] indicates that the approach outlined here is more likely to arrive at more relevant clusters. Several cases where URLs of very different appearance are indeed referring to very similar pages have been observed. The DOM can be changed by the JavaScript application and therefore the clustering should be carried out after this application to assure that the clustering as far as possible is carried out on the content as perceived by the user. That has not been done in [2].

In the first phase of the project a number of the accessibility tests have been applied on the websites. The dimensionality of the datasets, regarded as the number of tests performed on a particular website, is not fixed. As the number of accessibility tests gets higher, the computational costs of the clustering operations may increase.

There is also involved some level of uncertainty. It appears to be improbable to envisage the number of existing patterns on the website since no information about the website is provided. The presented approach requires additional pre-computation to be conducted before the actual clustering. In order to determine the optimal number of clusters on a website, a few cluster validation methods needed to be applied. For instance with K-Means clustering, the Elbow Method, the Silhouette and the Gap Statistic method were used to decide how many clusters can be extracted from the dataset. Additionally the degree of similarity between two pages seems to be a subjective matter. The minimal threshold of the similarity cannot be decided unless by a human.

7   Outlook

The study has laid a basis for an important enhancement of the current EIII accessibility evaluation. In an iterative process of downloading, and testing, the web pages can be clustered one by one until the cut-off conditions are fulfilled, e.g. a sufficient amount of clusters or similarity threshold between consecutive results is reached. Then a sample of pages can be retrieved from each cluster. The final accessibility score of the website can be calculated on a subset of cluster members.

With a growing number of people accessing the Internet from mobile devices, accessibility becomes crucial also for this use for all user groups. In most cases, users with disabilities may encounter similar barriers when browsing the Internet on mobile phones or tablets as they would using computers. To cater for the mobile access considerations there are several design guidelines and collections of best practices available like those from IBM or the BBC listed by the W3C Mobile Accessibility Task Force [12]. The approach indicated in this paper can already be used to evaluate mobile content on websites by configuring the crawler to retrieve pages prepared for mobile access.

To refine the evaluation for mobile access we would like to explore further tests tailored to the distinctive functions of mobile devices, such as navigation with a smaller screen, changing screen orientation or variants of interaction not using a mouse etc. See also [13]. As a result, the novel approach involving web page clustering may contribute to the improvement of the web accessibility on mobile devices.

Another area of improvement is the addition of further tests in EIII. It would be interesting to investigate how these test influence the results of the clustering.

It may be the case that only some tests suffice to cluster web pages. Test that do not provide additional information for the clustering could be removed from the dataset representation to improve the performance of the clustering computation.

Acknowledgements. The EIII project (http://eiii.eu) was co-funded by the European Commission under FP7 Project no.: 609667. The results presented in this paper build on the outcomes of several previous projects and the collaboration of the EIII team with researchers, practitioners and users.

References

1. Chakrabarti, D., Mehta, R.: The paths more taken: matching DOM trees to search logs for accurate webpage clustering. In: Proceedings of the 19th International Conference on World Wide Web, pp. 211–220. ACM (2010)
2. Harper, S., Moon, A.A., Vigo, M., Brajnik, G., Yesilada, Y.: DOM block clustering for enhanced sampling and evaluation. In: Proceedings of the 12th Web for All Conference, Florence, Italy, pp. 15:1–15:10. ACM (2015)
3. Crescenzi, V., Merialdo, P., Missier, P.: Clustering web pages based on their structure. Elsevier Sci. Publishers B.V. Data Knowl. Eng. **54**, 279–299 (2004)
4. Brajnik, G., Mulas, A., Pitton, C.: Effects of sampling methods on web accessibility evaluations. In: Proceedings of the 9th International ACM SIGACCESS Conference on Computers and Accessibility, Tempe, Arizona, USA, pp. 59–66. ACM (2007)
5. Hernández, I., Rivero, C.R., Ruiz, D., Corchuelo, R.: CALA: an unsupervised URL-based web page classification system. Elsevier Sci. Publishers B.V. Know.-Based Syst. **57**, 168–180 (2014)
6. Alpaydin, E.: Introduction to Machine Learning. Adaptive Computation and Machine Learning. MIT Press, Cambridge (2014). icchp: fraley02
7. Fraley, C., Raftery, A.E.: Model-based clustering, discriminant analysis, and density estimation. J. Am. Stat. Assoc. **97**(458), 611–631 (2002)
8. Hernández, I., Rivero, C.R., Ruiz, D., Corchuelo, R.: A statistical approach to URL-based web page clustering. In: Proceedings of the 21st International Conference on World Wide Web, WWW 2012 Companion, Lyon, France, pp. 525–526. ACM (2012)
9. Zhang, M., Wang, C., Bu, J., Yu, Z., Zhou, Y., Chen, C.: A sampling method based on URL clustering for fast web accessibility evaluation. Zhejiang Univ. Press Front. Inf. Technol. Electron. Eng. **16**, 449–456 (2015)
10. Nietzio, A., Berker, F.: D4.1 Integration Methodology (EIII project final report) (2015). https://box.tingtun.no/d/75ca8eab85/files/?p=/EIII-submitted-deliverables/D4.1-Integration-Methodology-v1.0.pdf. Accessed 15 Mar 2016
11. European Internet Inclusion Initiative (EIII): EIII Page Checker HTML Tests (2016). http://checkers.eiii.eu/en/tests/. Accessed 10 Mar 2016
12. Web Content Accessibility Guidelines Working Group (WCAG WG) and the User Agent Accessibility Guidelines Working Group (UAWG): Mobile Accessibility Task Force (Mobile A11Y TF) (2014). https://www.w3.org/WAI/GL/mobile-a11y-tf/. Accessed 23 Mar 2016
13. Mobile Accessibility Task Force (Mobile A11Y TF): Mobile Accessibility: How WCAG 2.0 and Other W3C/WAI Guidelines Apply to Mobile (2016). http://w3c.github.io/Mobile-A11y-TF-Note/. Accessed 23 Mar 2016

Ambient Assisted Living (AAL) for Aging and Disability

SEAMPAT

An ICT Platform for Medication Reconciliation with Active Patient Involvement

Valéry Ramon[1(✉)], Ravi Ramdoyal[1], Sophie Marien[3],
Arnaud Michot[1], Jimmy Nsenga[1], Gustavo Ospina[1], Fabian Steels[1],
Quentin Boucher[4], Delphine Legrand[3], Christine Burnet[5],
Perrine Vanmerbeek[5], and Anne Spinewine[2,3]

[1] Centre d'Excellence en Technologies de l'Information et de la Communication
(CETIC), Charleroi, Belgium
{valery.ramon, ravi.ramdoyal, arnaud.michot,
jimmy.nsenga, gustavo.ospina, fabian.steels}@cetic.be
[2] Louvain Drug Research Institute,
Clinical Pharmacy Research Group (UCL/LDRI/CLIP),
Université catholique de Louvain, Louvain-la-Neuve, Belgium
anne.spinewine@uclouvain.be
[3] CHU UCL Namur, Pharmacy Department,
Université catholique de Louvain, Yvoir, Belgium
{sophie.marien, delphine.legrand,
anne.spinewine}@uclouvain.be
[4] Research Centre in Information System Engineering (UNamur/PReCISE),
Université de Namur, Namur, Belgium
quentin.boucher@unamur.be
[5] Research Centre in Information, Law and Society (UNamur/CRIDS),
Université de Namur, Namur, Belgium
{christine.burnet, perrine.vanmerbeek}@unamur.be

Abstract. The transitions across different health care settings, in particular home and hospital, may be critical regarding the continuity of patient's medication. Some of the medication discrepancies occurring during these transitions can potentially be harmful to patient's health and therefore lead to increased use of healthcare resources and increased costs. The goal of SEAMPAT is to define, implement and evaluate an ICT-based medication reconciliation (MedRec) process in which the patient is actively involved in providing information about his/her current medications. MedRec is the formal and collaborative process of obtaining and verifying a complete and accurate list of patient's current medications.

Keywords: ICT-based medication reconciliation · Continuity of care · Patient empowerment · User-centred design · Multi-disciplinary approach

K. Miesenberger et al. (Eds.): ICCHP 2016, Part I, LNCS 9758, pp. 269–276, 2016.
DOI: 10.1007/978-3-319-41264-1_36

1 Introduction

The transitions across different health care settings, notably home and hospital, may be critical regarding the continuity of patient's medication. Some of the medication discrepancies occurring during these transitions are intentional and justified by the patient's clinical condition. Other ones are not and result from either imprecise information about current medications (indication, dose regimen,...) or from unintentional information loss. These can potentially be harmful to patient's health (leading to extended hospital stay, early readmission, unplanned visits to the emergency department or even death) and therefore lead to increased use of healthcare resources and increased costs.

To obtain a complete and accurate list of all current medications, patient engagement is increasingly recognized as a key determinant. However, limited work addressed the value of patient empowerment and the benefit of using information and communication technologies (ICT) in this process.

The goal of SEAMPAT is to define, implement and evaluate an ICT-based medication reconciliation (MedRec) process in which the patient is actively involved in providing information about his/her current medications. MedRec is the formal and collaborative process of obtaining and verifying a complete and accurate list of patient's current medications. It aims at ensuring that no medication was added, omitted or modified by inadvertence during the transitions across multiple care settings. SEAMPAT develops a proof-of-concept prototype made of two web applications: one for patients, usable at home or at hospital, and one for healthcare professionals (HCPs) (physicians, pharmacists) to help them perform MedRec. These two applications will be interconnected through the Walloon Regional eHealth network of Belgium (Réseau Santé Wallon).

This paper mainly focuses on the patient's application which is at a more advanced stage of development.

2 State of the Art in This Area

Firstly, a literature review was performed, mainly in the PubMed bibliographic database, in order to identify existing ICT tools that support patient empowerment/engagement for MedRec. It was completed by a search for patents in FamPat and Espacenet patent international databases. Several interesting tools were found. They allow the patients to validate their medications and give additional information about these medications. These most relevant tools in the context of SEAMPAT are:

- The Colorado Care Tablet (CCT) [1, 2] was iteratively designed using a participatory approach with patients aged 65 and above. It has a user-friendly interface. The application offers different functionalities such as encoding medications, accessing to information about medications (i.e. adverse events), preparing an appointment, etc. The researchers also provided some design guidelines useful for patient application developers.
- The Automated Patient History Intake Device (APHID) [3–5] was first elaborated for patients scheduled for an outpatient consultation. Usability and satisfaction were

evaluated and patients' feedback was collected to improve the tool. This one appeared to be easy to use for the patients. A randomized controlled trial is ongoing.

- The Interactive Patient Medication List [6] enables patients to document their medication intake based on a consolidated medication list. It also offers additional functionalities: access to all medication sources available on the health network and identification of the differences, adherence evaluation, ordering in advance medication at the pharmacy, etc. According to the inventor of this patent, the tool is not yet implemented but has already been discussed in focus groups with HCPs.

- The Patient Gateway Medication Module [7, 8] is a patient portal designed to improve the accuracy of medication lists within the electronic health record. The patient validates his medications and can add other information related to medication adherence, allergies, side effects and indication. A set of usability tests were done to iteratively refine the tool.

In parallel, a literature search was performed, again in PubMed, to identify factors influencing patient participation in approaches to improve quality and safety of healthcare. Based on twelve relevant articles (systematic reviews, narrative reviews and qualitative studies), a table was built with facilitators and barriers to patient's participation. Finally, a systematic review of tools for HCPs that fully support MedRec was also conducted. However, it is not detailed here since this paper mainly focuses on patient's side.

Considering all those references, SEAMPAT innovates by providing the first ICT tool exploiting such a large set of patient medication sources to perform MedRec. As further explained later in this paper, these sources come from both inside and outside hospital and include the patient's input on an equal footing with HCPs sources. It is also the only tool accessible to the patient from home.

3 Methodology Used

Firstly, a literature review and a search for patents were performed, as described above. In parallel, ten focus groups were organized with patients and HCPs. They were composed of two to eight people with the same profile (patients, hospital pharmacists and community pharmacists, general practitioners and specialist physicians). The goal was to explore their experience about medication discrepancies as well as their fears, needs and expectations of an ICT solution for MedRec in which the patient is actively engaged.

Relying on all information collected from the literature review and through those focus groups, a requirement specifications document has been elaborated and reviewed with all project associated stakeholders (i.e. members of the advisory board and representatives of the different institutions supporting the project). This document has then been used as a basis for the specification and design of the patient's application. The project stakeholders were again closely associated to the definition of the detailed architecture of the application, including its external interfaces and the format of the data flows. The data structures have been defined based on the Belgian standard KMEHR [9] used for the exchange of structured health information.

Based on the conclusions obtained in the literature review and also on discussions with some medical experts supporting the project, three target patient groups were selected for the evaluation phases: pulmonary transplanted patients, patients visiting their general practitioner at least once a month and patients hospitalized for a scheduled surgery. The focus is on patients at risk of discrepancies. All patients will take at least 5 medications, and at least half of the patients will be older than 65.

As far as the user interfaces are concerned, they are designed using the following methodology:

- by taking into account the ten major usability principles synthesized from recommendations from usability experts (such as [10, 11]) and existing standards (such as ISO 9241, ISO 14915 and AFNOR Z67-133.1);
- by considering the closest applications found in the literature search, namely the CCT of Siek and the APHID of Lesselroth et al.;
- and, very importantly, with an iterative approach actively involving the final users, based on the user-centred design presented in [12]. Bearing in mind the users' profile and context, it notably consists in associating the users throughout the development lifecycle, studying their behaviours and reactions and progressively refining the system based on their regular feedback. This leads to user interfaces which are more efficient, more user-friendly and satisfactory for their users while favoring the adoption of the final system.

In this iterative process, it was decided to foresee three main iterations, the first two ones being already accomplished at this time:

- Static prototype (mock-ups): its objective was to evaluate the content rather than the form (relevance of the presented information, understandability of the considered flows and interactions, high-level structuration of the screens). The evaluation was performed through discussion groups with 15 users in total (5 users per target group) and via a satisfaction questionnaire. The user interfaces were adapted following to the users' feedback.
- Interactive prototype with fake data: the objective of this second prototype was to put the users in a more realistic situation, allowing them to navigate through the different screens, in order to observe their take up of the application and identify problematic interactions. Due to external constraints, fake medication data were used. The evaluation, involving 30 users in total (10 users per target group), was performed through usability sessions guided by a reference scenario (add, modify, delete medications) and with a satisfaction questionnaire. Again, the user interfaces have been modified after those sessions.
- Dynamic prototype with real data: the objective of this third stage is to offer to the users an entirely functional prototype connected to their real medication data in order to make the final adjustments. The evaluation, which has not started yet, will involve 45 to 60 users (15 to 20 per target group) and last a few months.

In parallel to the medical and technical works, a juridical analysis identifies the applicable laws or regulations which can lead to constraints or guidelines to the elaboration of the SEAMPAT tools. It also cares about the formalities necessary to the evaluation phase (e.g. declaration to ethical committee, patient and HCP informed consent forms). An analysis of the social acceptability of the project is also performed by an anthropologist to understand how the MedRec process actually satisfies a social need.

4   Research and Development Work - Results

Two web applications (using HTML5/Javascript technologies) are being proto-typed and interconnected through the Réseau Santé Wallon (RSW):

- An application for the patients, usable on desktop, laptop or tablet at home or in the hospital: it will allow the patients to consult and report the list of their current medications starting from the data communicated by healthcare professionals (HCPs) in primary as well as secondary care (pharmacists, physicians including both general practitioners and specialists) on the RSW. The patients will report whether they take each medication listed, how (dose regimen) and possibly for what purpose (indication) and who advices it (name of prescriber). They can also mention additional medications. The information will be made available to HCPs through the RSW. The patients will be encouraged to update their medication list before any visit to a doctor.
- An application for HCPs to support the MedRec process: for a given patient, it will highlight the medication discrepancies between the medication list a HCP has in his/her electronic patient record, the patient's list and the medications reported by other HCPs. Thanks to this information, the HCP will perform medication reconciliation and update his/her own list. The reconciled list will be made available to other HPCs and to the patient through the RSW. The application will be integrated as an additional module in the medical software commonly used by the HCP. Be-cause at a lower stage of development (its specifications are coming to an end), it is less discussed in this paper.

A conceptual scheme of the SEAMPAT system is shown in Fig. 1. This system is protected by high security mechanisms. Patient's authentication is performed with the Belgian electronic identity (eID) card and its associated PIN code. Data transfers over Internet only occur through secure connections (https, VPN IPsec tunnel) and data themselves are encrypted before their transfer (double encryption). Only patients who gave their consent for registration to the RSW are able to use the application. The juridical work identified the major applicable laws. They concern health data protection, the patient's rights (a.o. the right to be informed) and the exercise of regulated health professions. These texts provided various guidelines which were integrated into the architecture of the solution. Access rights to medication data available on the RSW follow the rules defined in the Privacy Policy of RSW, established from this legal framework.

A screenshot of the main screen of the patient's application is shown on Fig. 2. For each proposed medication, the patient is helped by a picture of the box and is invited to select one of the following choices:

- "Yes, as indicated": if he/she takes it exactly as indicated.
- "Yes, but differently": if he/she takes it with a different dosage regimen. Then, in one additional pop-up (not shown on Fig. 2), he/she can give additional precisions.
- "No, I'm not/not any more": if he/she is not taking it or not taking it any more.
- "Maybe. I'm not sure": if he/she no longer knows whether or not he/she takes it.

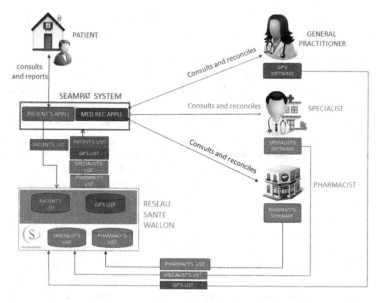

Fig. 1. Conceptual scheme of the SEAMPAT solution

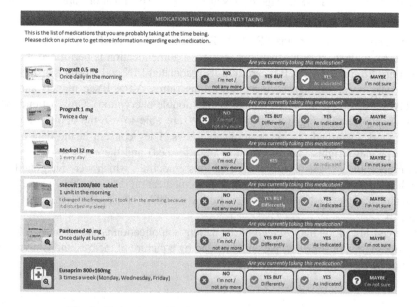

Fig. 2. Patient's application – screenshot of the main screen

At this stage of the project, as mentioned earlier, two successive versions of the patient's application have already been developed and evaluated. The main outcomes from the two evaluation phases are the following. First, most patients agreed or even strongly agreed that the user interface was easy to use and that the application may help reduce medication errors thanks to a better communication between patients and HCPs. Besides, the observations of the patients' interactions with the application and the analysis of the satisfaction questionnaire led to several adjustments whose main ones are: (1) the possibility for the patient to mention extra information (medication indication, reason for stopping medication, name of the prescribing doctor), (2) a simplification of the overall user interaction process (a read-only mode, without possibility for the patient to edit the medication list, has been removed), (3) a better placement, size and/or emphasis of some buttons or icons, (4) an improvement in the contrast of colours.

Taking into account all patients' feedback collected so far, the application is now being enhanced to connect to the patients' real medication data available on the RSW.

5 Scientific and Practical Impact

As already said above, unintentional medication discrepancies can potentially be harmful to patient's health (leading to extended hospital stay, early readmission, unplanned visits to the emergency department or even death) and therefore lead to increased use of healthcare resources and increased costs. The scientific literature claims that at least one potentially harmful discrepancy appears for 45 % of patients. Moreover, 27 % of prescription errors at hospital are due to an incomplete medication history at hospital admission. Also, 25 % of hospital readmissions are due to poor communication relating to medication at hospital discharge. MedRec is one of the five priority axes of the World Health Organization (WHO) (High 5 s project: http://www.high5s.org). It is also a usual requirement for hospital accreditation.

The project results may contribute to improve the quality of healthcare of Walloon patients, in particular older people and/or polymedicated chronic patients. They may also benefit the project stakeholders and companies developing medical software applications for patients, hospitals and physicians in private practice.

6 Conclusion and Future Work

So far, the vast majority of patients involved in the project have shown tremendous enthusiasm and interest and are willing to continue to work with us. Their constructive feedback enabled to refine already twice the patient's application. The prototype is now being connected to the patients' real medication data available on the RSW. In about two months, it will be evaluated with 45 to 60 voluntary patients, 15 to 20 per target group. The application for HPCs, whose specifications are coming to an end, should also be developed and evaluated with potential users in the next few months.

Acknowledgments. The authors gratefully acknowledge the Walloon Region of Belgium for its financial support of the SEAMPAT project (Grant no. 1318069). SEAMPAT is an ongoing three-year (2014–2017) collaborative research project funded by the Walloon Region of Belgium. The multi-disciplinary partnership includes medical experts (physicians, pharmacists) as well as experts in ICT, experts in law and in anthropology. The research work is guided by an advisory board gathering a broad panel of stakeholders. It is also supported by the Réseau Santé Wallon, a medical software provider, a university hospital and a major Belgian health mutuality insurance.

References

1. Siek, K.A., Khan, D.U., Ross, S.E., Haverhals, L.M., Meyers, J., Cali, S.R.: Designing a personal health application for older adults to manage medications: a comprehensive case study. J. Med. Syst. **35**(5), 1099–1121 (2011). doi:10.1007/s10916-011-9719-9
2. Ross, S.E., Johnson, K.B., Siek, K.A., Gordon, J.S., Khan, D.U., Haverhals, L.M.: Two complementary personal medication management applications developed on a common platform: case report. J. Med. Internet Res. **13**(3), e45 (2011). doi:10.2196/jmir.1815
3. Lesselroth, B.J., Felder, R.S., Adams, S.M., Cauthers, P.D., Dorr, D.A., Wong, G.J., et al.: Design and implementation of a medication reconciliation kiosk: the Automated Patient History Intake Device (APHID). J. Am. Med. Inform. Assoc.: JAMIA **16**(3), 300–304 (2009). doi:10.1197/jamia.M2642
4. Lesselroth, B., Felder, R., Adams, S., Cauthers, P., Wong, G.J.: System and method for automated patient history intake. Patent Application Publication (2014)
5. Lesselroth, B.J., Dorr, D.A., Adams, K., Church, V., Adams, S., Mazur, D., et al.: Medication review software to improve the accuracy of outpatient medication histories: protocol for a randomized controlled trial. Hum. Fact. Ergon. Manuf. Serv. Ind. **22**(1), 72–86 (2012). doi:10.1002/hfm.20287
6. Tripoli, L.C.: Interactive patient medication list. Patent Application Publication (2013)
7. Schnipper, J.L., Gandhi, T.K., Wald, J.S., Grant, R.W., Poon, E.G., Volk, L.A., et al.: Design and implementation of a web-based patient portal linked to an electronic health record designed to improve medication safety: the Patient Gateway medications module. Inform. Prim. Care **16**(2), 147–155 (2008)
8. Schnipper, J.L., Gandhi, T.K., Wald, J.S., Grant, R.W., Poon, E.G., Volk, L.A., et al.: Effects of an online personal health record on medication accuracy and safety: a cluster - randomized trial. J. Am. Med. Inform. Assoc.: JAMIA **19**(5), 728–734 (2012). doi:10.1136/amiajnl-2011-000723
9. Kind Messages For Electronic Healthcare Record - Belgian implementation standard. https://www.ehealth.fgov.be/standards/kmehr/
10. Shneiderman, B., Plaisant, C.: Designing the User Interface: Strategies for Effective Human-Computer Interaction. Pearson, New York (2009)
11. Tognazzini: First Principles of Interaction Design (Revised & Expanded) (2014). http://asktog.com/atc/principles-of-interaction-design/
12. Gould, J.D., Lewis, C.: Designing for usability: key principles and what designers think. Commun. ACM **28**(3), 300–311 (1985)

BRELOMATE - A Distributed, Multi-device Platform for Online Information, Communication and Gaming Services Among the Elderly

Jakob Doppler[1]($\boxtimes$), Sabine Sommer[2], Christian Gradl[1],
and Gernot Rottermanner[1]

[1] Institute for Creative Media Technologies, St. Pölten UAS, Austria
jakob.doppler@fhstp.ac.at
[2] Ilse Arlt Institute on Social Inclusion Research, St. Pölten UAS, Austria

Abstract. While inexpensive mobile devices and services become the primary means of online communication the elderly are prevented from participating due to technical difficulties and common barriers. Among the older users communication and entertainment are considered key aspects to alleviate loneliness. Elderly people are at high risk of facing social isolation with rising age. This article proposes a distributed, multi-device platform called BRELOMATE to promote social participation and online communication. Firstly the system architecture and a prototypical gaming service with integrated video-conferencing are presented. Secondly the user centered design process and the results of a first user study are shown.

Keywords: Multi-device · Social isolation · Tablet · TV · Online communication · Gaming · Videoconferencing · Teleparticipation

1 Introduction

Elderly people are at high risk of facing social isolation with rising age. Studies show that over 17 % of people aged 80+ are affected due to the loss of life partner and friends, sudden changes of living arrangements, and a general mobility declines [2]. Thus, fostering social participation and communication is a major concern to maintain autonomy and independence of the elderly in the ageing society. Research shows that information and communication technology (ICT) may help to ease social isolation of elderly people [2]. The fast growth of miniaturized and inexpensive devices and mobile services become the primary means of information access and online communication. However technical difficulties and common barriers such as complex interaction metaphors, high information density and poor usability prevent older people with low media literacy from using these services [3].

Whereas there is a strong evidence to the benefits of affordable and accessible social media and online services for the elderly the leading IT industry

© Springer International Publishing Switzerland 2016
K. Miesenberger et al. (Eds.): ICCHP 2016, Part I, LNCS 9758, pp. 277–280, 2016.
DOI: 10.1007/978-3-319-41264-1_37

shows no economic interest in developing inclusive solutions for a growing target group. This might be due to the fact that compared to the middle-aged populations elderly require customizable solutions based on their education, previous media and technology experience and interest. Additionally multi-modal ICT products for the elderly are either designed for a special purpose (e.g.healthcare, monitoring & alarm) or limited in their functionality.

This article aims to: (1) present the architecture of a distributed BRELO-MATE platform and its multi-device interaction concept, (2) discuss the user centered design (UCD) process involving the elderly throughout all phases and elaborate on the on first user study results of the turn-based gaming service *Schnapsen* with integrated video-conferencing, and (3) give an outlook on the next steps of the UCD process and the ongoing platform development.

2   Platform Architecture

The main goal of the BRELOMATE platform was to design and develop a distributed information, communication and gaming platform. We facilitated a multi-device approach that consists of affordable and potentially available ICT in private households such as a TV and maybe even internet and a tablet. Each household is required to have a tablet that acts as a second screen control interface that locally connects to an set-top box for visualization and audio/video interaction on the TV (see Fig. 1). Both devices combined define the client setup that communicates to the BRELOMATE server and third-party frameworks such as the WebRTC[1] platform OpenTok for integrated and inter-operable video-conferencing.

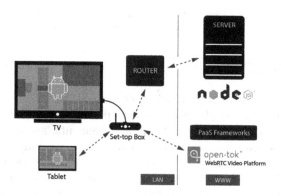

Fig. 1. Architecture of the BRELOMATE platform showing the local client and the internet server

The hardware and the software of the client has to meet minimal requirements: We use any tablet running on minimum Android 4.4.3 and the Orbsmart

---

[1] WebRTC is a W3C real-time communication standard https://webrtc.org/.

S82² (quad-core CPU 1.8 GHz, octa core GPU Mali-450/OpenGL ES2.0 support/Android 5.1) as a set-top box for sufficient multimedia processing power. We developed a first gaming service on Android based on the turn-based card game *Schnapsen* popular in German speaking countries. Figure 2 shows the user interface of the tablet and the set-top box during early prototype user tests. The tablet interface shows one players' hand. The set-top box visualizes the shared table game elements like the deck of cards and two video elements from the integrated web camera and the other players video stream.

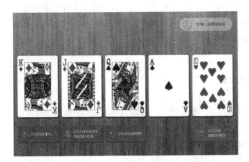

Fig. 2. Test setting at the universities' usability lab showing the user interfaces of tablet and the complementary set-top box during a user test with the turn-based card game *Schnapsen.* Tablet control UI (left) and Set-top box visualization UI (right)

3 User Centered Design Process and Results

From early on we involved different groups of elderly users starting with the requirement analysis & design phase to the iterative prototyping and testing phase. We defined a series of focus groups and user tests throughout the course of one and a half years to evaluate our hypothesis on key issues of user interaction and experience. Initially learning that entertainment and communication were considered key aspects of digital technologies also for the elderly, we investigated if video-conferencing and gaming could be a playful approach to foster inclusion and social networking. The results of an initial user study with pen and paper prototypes and mockups showed that they prefer a tablet-based solution over tangible interfaces such as NFC-based playing cards [1]. A first user study with an early prototype of BRELOMATE (7 female and 8 male, age: 72 ± 11 yrs) revealed that even with little to no initial explanations the seniors were able to use the platform and play the game *Schnapsen.* Two identical setups were set up at the usability lab of the university (see Fig. 2) and the private homes of two participants at a remote location.

---

² Orbsmart Android-based set-top box http://www.orbsmart.com/products/orbsmart-s82/.

Continuing with our user-driven approach in December 2015 we encouraged a group of seniors (7 female and 3 male, age: 68 ± 7 yrs) to share their ideas on detailed scenarios and task performance. As an example one scenario involved the statement: *I get an invitation by another person to play a card game with them.* The users unanimously agreed that an easy and intuitive navigation was of major concern. The tablet should work as a "remote control for the TV" and switching between all relevant information, eg. incoming calls or gaming invitations, should only pop up on the tablet screen with visual (eg. blinking) or audible hints. They came up with a list of important information of the personal profile that includes the (full) name and the city as mandatory fields. Additionally, other personal information such as the profile picture, online status should not be available to other participants on default.

4   Conclusion and Future Work

With BRELOMATE we managed to design, develop and test a distributed, multi-device platform for information, communication and gaming. Results showed that even the first-time tablet users were playfully introduced to second-screen gaming. They quickly engaged in real-time video conversation as shown in tests that lasted more than 30 min.

While usability is a very relevant aspect for all further developments, it should also be noted that self-determination also seems to be a key factor for our target group. Whether is concerns privacy issues like sharing personal information to actively accepting or declining gaming invitations or being able to add other features (internet browser, different games), this request for self-determination shouldn't be overlooked in the further development of the BRELOMATE platform.

Acknowledgements. The authors would like to thank all focus group participants. This work is supported under grant agreement No. 5629694 (BRELOMATE 2) from The Austrian Research Promotion Agency.

References

1. Doppler, J., Rottermanner, G., Sommer, S., Pflegerl, J., Judmaier, P.: Design and evaluation of a second screen communication and gaming platform for fostering teleparticipation of the socially isolated elderly. In: Wichert, R., Klausing, H. (eds.) Ambient Assisted Living, vol. Ambient. Springer International Publishing, Frankfurt (2016)
2. Eiffe, F.F.: Soziale Lage lterer Menschen in sterreich. Technical report, Band 11, Bundesministerium fr Arbeit, Soziales und Konsumentenschutz, Wien (2012)
3. Nef, T., Ganea, R.L., Mri, R.M., Mosimann, U.P.: Social networking sites and older users - a systematic review. Int. Psychoger./IPA **25**(7), 1041–1053 (2013)

Electronic Medication Dispensers Finding the Right Users – A Pilot Study in a Norwegian Municipality Home Care Service

Ingrid S. Svagård$^{(\boxtimes)}$ and Elin S. Boysen

Department of Instrumentation, SINTEF ICT, Pb. 124 Blindern, 0314 Oslo, Norway
{Ingrid.Svagard,ElinSundby.Boysen}@sintef.no

Abstract. This paper presents the reports on a pilot study in Norway where electronic medication dispensers were tested by 16 elderly users, exploring the effects for both end users and the care service. There were large variations in the users' individual perceptions of the dispenser. Persons with reduced eyesight or manual dexterity reported great personal benefits and increased feeling of independence and dignity. On the other hand, several patients stopped using the dispenser due to either cognitive challenges and/or feelings of insecurity. The home care service using electronic medication dispensers must take great care in finding the right users to increase probability of success, both for the user and the service.

Keywords: Electronic medication dispenser · Home care service

1 Background/Problem

Medication adherence – the extent to which patients take medication as prescribed by their doctors – is critical for optimal benefit from drug therapy. Many users need help with the medication from nurse home visits. This can be due to challenges such as reduced dexterity in the hands/fingers, reduced eye-sight, reduction of cognitive abilities (e.g. dementia) or general frailty.

However, the medication service faces three important challenges: *(i)* Some users can have up to 6 nurse visits a day only for receiving medicine. This is not always appreciated by the user, who prefers to be more self-reliant. *(ii)* The medication service is extremely resource intensive for the municipality, and *(iii)* it is one of the home care services most ridden with (registered) deviations/errors, mostly due to the challenge for the care personnel to time the home visits with the exact administered time for medication. This calls for a radical change in how medication services are organized and carried out by municipal health care services.

This short paper reports on a pilot study in Norway where electronic medication dispensers were tested by 16 elderly users, and explores the effects for both end users and the care service. The pilot was carried out as a research and innovation project in collaboration between the home care services of Bærum municipality, the technology provider Dignio and the research organization SINTEF during 2014 and 2015.

© Springer International Publishing Switzerland 2016
K. Miesenberger et al. (Eds.): ICCHP 2016, Part I, LNCS 9758, pp. 281–284, 2016.
DOI: 10.1007/978-3-319-41264-1_38

2 State of the Art

Adherence to long-term therapy for chronic illnesses in developed countries averages only 50 % [5]. Means to improve adherence varies from the simplest alarm clocks to mobile phone apps [2] to remember timing, and dosette boxes or multi dose packaging to administer the right dose. However, these means do not ensure that the user actually takes the prescribed medicine. Monitoring devices for medicine administration have become common after 2005 with suggested devices such as smart medical refrigerator [1] and other mobile home-based devices for management of medication [3].

The idea behind electronic medication dispensers is that the devices combine timely reminders and correct dosage. Also, the lack of medicine intake at a certain time can result in warning messages to the user, health personnel and/or relatives. In a randomised controlled trial Vervloet et al. [6] investigated the impact of an additional reminder in form of an SMS message to the user if the medicine had not been taken. Their results showed a significant increase in adherence compared to users with medications dispensers without reminders or users with no medication dispenser. However, as Wetzels et al. [7] point out, the management of a chronic disease should be personalized because the person is ultimately responsible for the success of the intervention. Thus, a medication device poorly fitted to personal needs will give little or no effect. Further, as discussed in [8], the work of medication is not just about timing. It also consists of synchronization with meals, being in the same location as the medicines and in a social setting where the administration of medication feels socially acceptable for the patient. This can not be fully compensated by a medication dispenser.

3 Methodology

The users in the pilot study were recruited by health personnel at two different service units. Inclusion criteria were that the user was already receiving or was about to begin receiving home visits by the municipal care service for aid with medication. In addition, the user must show personal interest in trying the dispenser. Persons with dementia were not included in the pilot study. All users were informed orally and in writing, and they all signed a consent form for participation in the project. An interview with each user was conducted to establish a baseline for all users. A follow-up interview was carried out after 3 months or if the service was ended (for various reasons). The 16 users that were included in the study were women and men between 68 and 96 years of age, with health challenges related to paralysis, finger dexterity, sight reduction and light forms of cognitive reduction. Interviews were also conducted with the health personnel that took part in the pilot.

The dispenser was of type "Pilly", a "carousell" type dispenser where the dosages of pills are put in separate, closed compartments. "Pilly" registers that the pills are taken when the device is turned around to empty the pills in the hand. Alternatively it is used with a separate tilt function with handle that empties the pills into a bowl.

4   Results

There were large variations in the users' individual perceptions of the dispenser. Out of 16 users, 9 liked the dispenser and felt comfortable using it. Persons with reduced manual dexterity or reduced eyesight, and no or very light cognitive dysfunction, reported great personal benefits. These users reported increased feeling of independence and dignity. The tilt function of the dispenser that poured the pills into a bowl enabled them to take the medicine on their own. They reported great joy and pride that they now managed to be self-reliant. Users with a previously active lifestyle underlined the usefulness in that they could bring the dispenser out of the home and no longer had to sit at home waiting for help to take their medicine. They loved how this gave them a great sense of freedom. This group of users also reported that they enjoyed the independence in the reduced number of home visits. A Parkinson patient was particularly thrilled of the increased privacy the dispenser provided him: *"Now I can sit in my underwear and take my medicine"*, referring to feeling of intrusion of having "strangers" coming into his home. He also reflected that his health improved, due to the regular intake of medicine. In fact; a two-week stay in a nursing home for "rehabilitation" left him in a worse state of health . The personnel there preferred to administer the medicine to him themselves, resulting in delays that had clearly negative consequence for his health.

The care service administration benefited as the number of home visits could be reduced. They also anticipated fewer health-related follow-up calls for some of these users, as the timely medication would leave them in more stable health.

For seven users, the use of the dispenser had to be stopped altogether. There seemed to be two main reasons for this: *(i)* cognitive challenges and *(ii)* feelings of insecurity. Persons with some reduction of their cognitive abilities were easily stressed by the sound-signal and found it difficult to understand the basic concept of the dispenser, for example that the pill compartments are supposed to be "locked" at all times except at predefined medication-times. The result was often rough handling of the dispenser, (e.g. shaking or using sharp objects to try and "open it"). A common challenge, for all users, was that large tablets had a higher risk of getting stuck in the small pill compartments. A little gentle poking with e.g. a tooth pick would normally loosen the pills. For the cognitively challenged, this was extra stressful, and often resulted in shaking of the device, which again led to errors and error signals. This is compliant with findings in an earlier study [4] which underlines that for some users, a device that fails to perform exactly as shown leads to a high level of panic, and requires immediate response. The perception that it does not work will not be changed by any rational arguments, and removal of the dispenser is usually requested. For one user in our pilot, it became clear to the care personnel after many weeks, that all the user's reported problems with the device really stemmed from insecurity in losing the daily visits from care personnel. All the users who had problems in adapting to using the dispenser and felt uncomfortable using it, required many unplanned visits for "error handling" and reassuring. Thus, for these users, the potential gain of reduced home visits by the care service effectively vanished.

Another interesting finding from the pilot, for all user groups, is that the sound signals that the device will sound when it is time for medication should be used with care. The continuous sound signals seems to induce stress in many users and were also to some extent superfluous; keeping the time for medication was not the main problem for many of the elderly that took part in the pilot.

5 Conclusion

The pilot study supports previous studies reporting that medical dispensers can be a great aid for medication adherence, for the right users. The study underlines the need to have a clear understanding of the prerequisites for gain, both for the individual user and the care service: For persons that value independence and have the mental capabilities to understand how to interact with the device, the device will benefit both the user – in greater feeling of independence and self-reliance, and the service - in reduced home visits. The health potential is also significant. Timely adherence of medication can greatly affect the users' health. This will have positive consequences for both the users (improved quality of life), and the service (reduced health-related follow-ups and administrative work due to medication deviations). However, for persons with reduced cognitive abilities, even slight benefits are less assured. Introduction of new and unknown technology to this user group may induce stress, both for the user and, as a consequence, for the care service, with an increase in unplanned home visits. Introduction of the technology at an earlier time would probably be helpful. General familiarity with technology is also anticipated to increase with future generations of elderly.

Based on the results of the pilot study, Bærum municipality has developed a specific user mapping form to help the care personnel identify the "right" users, to increase probability of success, both for the user and the service.

References

1. Kuwik, P., et al.: The smart medical refrigerator. IEEE Potentials **24**(1), 42–45 (2005)
2. Mei-Ying, W., et al.: Wedjat: a mobile phone based medicine in-take reminder and monitor. In: 9th IEEE International Conference on Bioinformatics and BioEngineering, BIBE 2009, pp. 423–430 (2009)
3. Nugent, C., et al.: Can technology improve compliance to medication. In: From Smart Homes to Smart Care: ICOST 2005. IOS Press (2005)
4. Ross, P., et al.: Interim report on the evaluation of the introduction of telecare by Portsmouth City Council (2009)
5. Sabaté, E.: Adherence to Long-Term Therapies: Evidence for Action. World Health Organization, Geneva (2003)
6. Vervloet, M., et al.: SMS reminders improve adherence to oral medication in type 2 diabetes patients who are real time electronically monitored. Int. J. Med. Inform. **81**, 594–604 (2012)
7. Wetzels, G., et al.: All that glisters is not gold: a comparison of electronic monitoring versus filled prescriptions - an observational study. BMC Health Serv. Res. **6**, 8 (2006)
8. Wolters, M.: The minimal effective dose of reminder technology. In: CHI 2014 Extended Abstracts on Human Factors in Computing Systems (2014)

Multidimensional Observation Methodology for the Elderly in an Ambient Digital Environment

Adrien Van den Bossche[1], Eric Campo[2], Jenny Duchier[3],
Elizabeth Bougeois[4], Mathilde Blanc Machado[1], Thierry Val[1],
Frédéric Vella[1], and Nadine Vigouroux[1(✉)]

[1] IRIT-CNRS, Université de Toulouse, CNRS, UPS, UT2J, Toulouse, France
{vandenbo,thierry.val}@univ-tlse2.fr,
{Mathilde.Blanc-Machado,vella,vigourou}@irit.fr
[2] LAAS-CNRS, Université de Toulouse, CNRS, UT2J, Toulouse, France
eric.campo@univ-tlse2.fr
[3] INSERM, UMR 1027, Université de Toulouse, UPS, Toulouse, France
jenny.duchier@inserm.fr
[4] LERASS, Université de Toulouse, UT2J, Toulouse, France
elizabeth.bougeois@univ-tlse2.fr

Abstract. This paper proposes a new methodological approach for a better understanding of the needs of elderly people the use of the technology in the use of technologies in an ambient. This methodology is based on the implementation of a multidimensional observation tool mixing ethnographic observation of actions and interviews with a multitechnological infrastructure in a Living Lab. Some preliminary results are presented with the participation of 14 seniors.

Keywords: Ambient digital environment · Multidimensional observation · Elderly people · Living lab

1 Introduction

Ambient Assisted Living (AAL) aims to provide assistive solutions for old people with a wide range of physical and cognitive challenges. Many efforts have been made to increase accessibility to these assistive technologies for older people but the solutions are not yet at the appointment in particular due to the lack of study of the real needs and a clear definition of the elderly profiles (dependent, frail, socially isolated, digital exclusion, etc. [1]). Some specific characteristics prevent or put a brake on the access to these new technologies. The behavior and interaction modes of these people in the use and access to these technologies are not fully understood because of the many influencing factors. Several challenges of the ambient intelligence [2] are to be overcome. Although several innovative technologies have been developed, there is still a strong need to research exploring new design of interaction as well as wireless network tools [3].

K. Miesenberger et al. (Eds.): ICCHP 2016, Part I, LNCS 9758, pp. 285–292, 2016.
DOI: 10.1007/978-3-319-41264-1_39

A significant challenge when studying technologies within the True Life Lab concept [4] is the ambient living where the research is carried out to inform about the acceptability of future innovative technologies or services.

Designing these future technologies can be complicated even if there are ways of including the participant to imagine current uses and interactions: these technologies are new and their potential uses by the participants are yet unknown. Also, the integration of technologies and services in an ambient intelligence must be thought as a whole in a user-centered approach in this double dimension: use and "Usability". A digital environment must be defined as sensitive, responsive and adaptive to the changeable needs of its inhabitants [5]. Moreover, Sun et al. [6] claim that participant involvement is a "key ingredient towards effective AAL, which not only saves social resources but also has positive influence on the psychological health of the elderly people".

Numeric ambient platforms are essential to understand better how information and communication technologies (ICT) can enable to help people in daily activities and to maintain them in their environment as long as possible.

Even though a lot of research has been published about the monitoring of activities in a home dedicated to experimental studies, including wireless sensors [7] or cameras that allow activities extracted from sensors and matched with video observations, these approaches are not sufficient to address the challenges of AAL [2].

That is why complementary methods and tools from social sciences and information and communication technologies need to be merged to explore and analyze behavior of participants with these innovative technologies to design, adapt them, based on related ICT experiences and socio-cultural profiles. It is also important to consider how a new numeric ambient technology including several intuitive interactions based on gesture, tactile and speech (Fig. 1) could fit the profile of the participant.

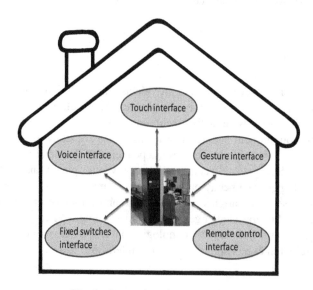

Fig. 1. Interactions in a smart home

Therefore, a methodology [8] mixing ethnographic observation [9] of actions and interviews [10] needs to be investigated. This innovating methodology must take into account several restraints, for instance that the elderly people could not endure a long experimentation time and could be stressed by the numeric ambient environment.

This paper describes a methodology based on the implementation of a multidimensional observation tool mixing ethnographic observation of actions and interviews, with a multitechnological infrastructure in a living lab. Some preliminary validation results are shown.

The paper is organized as follows: Sect. 2 describes the method and observation tools. Section 3 presents the research protocol. Section 4 gives the preliminary results. Section 5 gives a first discussion. Section 6 concludes the paper.

2 Method and Observation Tools

This section aims to present the method and tools developed in a multidimensional platform and the transdisciplinary protocol used for the experimentation.

2.1 Ethnography and Communication Sciences

The social sciences process of the study is inductive, based on grounded theories, and centred on the uses, practices and representations of a person testing a technological environment. The association of ethnography and communication enables us to gather data about what people do and how, in order to understand why they do so. The analysis of the qualitative data is focused both on the actions performed by elderly people and their behaviour during the observation stage, and on their discourse about their experiment, during the interviews. This analysis thus gives comprehensive elements of the way elderly people consider the use of ambient technologies dedicated to palliate the loss of autonomy.

2.2 Observation Platform Architecture

A monitoring tool has been set up, to assess, from an objective and multidimensional way, the behaviour of people in a semi controlled environment. The test environment MIB (smart home of Blagnac technological Institute) [11] is fully automated and proposes different modalities of interaction (speech, tactile, fixed switches interfaces) between the inhabitant and his habitat to allow monitoring, control, information exchange.

The observation platform (Fig. 2) is made from an audio and video network with IP-cameras and microphones, and several communication technologies such as KNX (classical home automation bus), Ivy [12, 13] (bus-software used commonly used in the Human Computer Interaction context. Here, it is used to manage the Text-To-Speech system), WiNo [3] (Wireless Node) and web-based (HTTP, HTTPS) devices such as tablets or proprietary sensors (bed presence, moving sensors, etc.) and actuators (lights, bed, height adjustable sink and cupboard in the kitchen, etc.).

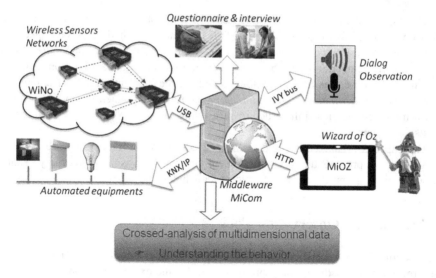

Fig. 2. Observation platform architecture

The various technologies induce a heterogeneity that is close to a real-life situation and needs an important interoperability. To solve the interoperability difficulty, a specific lightweight Middleware "MiCom" has been developed. MiCom enables connections with various technologies and proposes a HTTP-based command set to interact with sensors and actuators, regardless of the communication technology. Every device of the environment can be managed by calling HTTP URLs. Thus, the development of software components such as home automation controllers or Wizard of Oz, to simulate dialog between the inhabitant and the smart home, is easier and more effective.

The MiOZ interactive system is a Wizard of Oz platform. It was designated to simulate the spoken dialogue management between the inhabitant and the smart home. It can send and receive orders and feedbacks to sensors, actuators... regardless of the communication technology available in the smart home of Blagnac technological Institute. Thanks to this system, the experimenter can track the participant's actions, interact with him/her when it is necessary and simulate the smart home voice by means of a text-to-speech system.

2.3   Towards a Transdisciplinary Research Protocol

The transdisciplinary dimension of this approach leaded to the construction of a peculiar research protocol, within which quantitative and technical data and qualitative analysis are interconnected. A cross-analysis of the results must allow assessment of the contribution of digital technologies in the improvement of living conditions and strengthening autonomy at home. Table 1 summarizes the different tools implemented in the observation platform.

Table 1. Methods and tools used

Tools	Information collected
Questionnaires	Sociological profile, potential impairments, interest and use of technologies, expectations
Video observation	Monitoring of human behavior in an automated environment (smart home)
Dialogue recording	Dialogue between participant and digital environment
Semi-structured post experimentation interviews	Interviews about expectations and new visions about technologies
Log file	Data of sensor, tactile interaction

3   Research Protocol

The people recruited to participate to this project are aged of 60 years and more, retired and voluntary. No selection is made concerning cognitive diseases. According to the charter of use of personal data, the participants have to sign a consent letter to prove that they agree with the study and the use of their data that are backed up anonymously. Up to three participants are called on a half day during which researchers accompany them. First, they have to answer a questionnaire to determine their socio-cultural profile, their use of ICT or their intention of using new technologies and their projections about aging. Then, they attend a presentation on the different technologies and services offered by the smart home and, individually, they are asked to use freely this controlled housing for a limited duration of ten minutes in accordance with the protocol. The only instruction for the test is to simulate the usual scenario of their awakening as they realize it every morning, that's to say to carry out the same activities and to replicate their habits as when they wake up in the morning in their home. In this way, they can use classic switches to act on home equipment and/or tactile interface on tablets, to perform the same actions as conventional switches, and/or voice control of the MIB. No example of voice interaction is specified to participants; the aim how people speak to a simulated intelligence to act on their habitat. After the test in the smart home, they are interviewed by researchers in human and social sciences who have observed them during the scenario in the MIB, in order to understand their behavior during the testing and discuss about their feelings and projection in the use of ambient technologies. For this, we have tried out the protocol with 14 participants (5 men and 9 women).

4   Preliminary Results

All data (text messages of the smart home, information from sensors, tactile interaction log and speech) of the participant are saved in a secured database. These data will be matched with the observations.

The 14 people enjoy the experiment. At the beginning of the pre-testing phase, women mainly, showed little anxiety. However, most of the participants found that the smart home was "amazing", or "magic". The participants appreciate the vocal interaction, which seems to be their favourite tool, because it gives both additional sensitivity and extra soul to a technological environment. The participants living by themselves qualify their satisfaction in terms of "humanity of the smart home voice". They think that, with such a tool, one can feel less lonely. They say that the voice is warm, friendly, hearty. The technologies tested during the experiment often appear to the participants as a means of independence and a way to avoid going to a nursing home. However, some of them criticize those technologies because they think that these kinds of equipment might make one lazy; they also express the fact that they want to remain "master at home". Some participants found that this environment was too "medicalized", others wonder about the system reliability or costs at home. However, this cost is never precisely expressed; it is imagined and constitutes a representation which leads to detachment from technologies at home.

Even though the participants declare themselves as "concerned" and "convinced" by the smart home, they also say that they don't need it immediately but in the future. Some of them clearly express their difficulty to project themselves into the loss of autonomy. They do not seem to anticipate their future, except those who already have the experience of a member of the family who suffers or suffered any kind of illness.

This may be analyzed as ambivalence, or reluctance about palliative technologies as far as free and independent aging is concerned.

During the interviews, some participants have a contradictory discourse, compared to their behaviour during the experiment, such as, for instance, being very keen about the voice control and not using it at all. However, this experience has changed positively their perception of new technologies.

As far as installing a technological device at home is concerned, there is a significant difference between owners and tenants of their home: tenants are not interested, as they either can't invest, or their home is not suitable for installation, or they know that they will have to leave it for a nursing home if they become dependent.

5 Discussion

After this pre-testing phase, the methodology and tools have been adjusted. It appeared necessary to focus more on the participants, from an ethical concern, in order to prevent stress and anxiety. The presentation of the smart home was first quick and standardized, it is now longer and more humanized, incarnated: a technical researcher of the team shows the different equipment and explains their use.

An appropriation phase of the different interaction modes –switches, tactile tablet, speech input and speech synthesis– has been added: each participant individually learns and tests them, with the eventual help of a researcher. Some speech messages have been redefined in order to increase their intelligibility and their understanding (better taking into account of the limits of the synthetic voice, such as lack of links between words, bad pronunciation, and use of synonymous) by the inhabitants. New contextualized messages were also added to give greater flexibility and natural to the dialogue.

The immersion in a technological environment is thus facilitated; the participants are ready to realize the scenario described in Sect. 3.

The data of home automation equipment –sensors, roller blinds, motorized furniture, lights– correlated with observations allow us to track all displacements and activities realized by each participant during the scenario. Some motion sensors have been repositioned in the apartment to improve the acquisition of data.

6   Conclusion

This paper proposes a new methodological approach for a better understanding of the needs of elderly people and the use of the technology in an ambient digital environment. This approach is based on the implementation of a multidimensional observation tool. The participants were immersed in an ambient environment in which they could understand and use different technologies to control it: voice, tactile, switches. They were able to perceive how technologies could help them, anticipate the occurrence of a possible impairment or loss of autonomy and thus enable them to stay in their homes. The first analyzes show that the projection into the future is not so obvious. Technological and methodological adjustments were made for a better understanding of the potential uses of ambient technologies elderly people express. The explanation of the technology used was also more detailed.

The next step is to carry on the experiments with 150 people who will try out the different interaction modes proposed. This next phase will enable us to consider different profiles or ideal-types of inhabitants or mode of connected settlements.

Acknowledgments. This work is partially funded by the MSH-T of Toulouse and AG2R La Mondiale Insurance group.

References

1. Chappell, N.L., Cooke, H.A.: Age related disabilities - aging and quality of life. In: Stone, J. H., Blouin, M (eds.) International Encyclopedia of Rehabilitation (2010). http://cirrie. buffalo.edu/encyclopedia/en/article/189/
2. Coughlan, T., Mackley, K.L., Brown, M., Martindale, S., Schlögl, S., Mallaband, B., Arnott, J.: Current issues and future directions in methods for studying technology in the home. Psychology J. **11**(2), 159–184 (2013)
3. Van den Bossche, A., Dalce, R., Val, T.: OpenWiNo: an open hardware and software framework for fast-prototyping in the IoT. In: International Conference on Telecommunications, Thessaloniki, IEEExplore digital library (electronic support), 16–18 May 2016
4. Vigouroux, N., Rumeau, P., Boudet, B., Vella, F., Salvodelli, M.: Wellfar-e-link®: true life lab testing of a homecare communication tool, In: Non-pharmacological Therapies in Dementia, vol. 3, no. 2, pp. 133–142. Nova Science Publishers (2015)

5. Bierhoff, I., van Berlo, A., Abascal, J., et al.: Chapter 3. Smart home environment. In: Roe, P.R.W. (ed.) Towards an Inclusive Future: Impact and Wider Potential of Information and Communication Technologies, pp. 110–156 (2007)

6. Sun, H., De Florio, V., Gui, N., Blondia, C.: The missing ones: key ingredients towards effective ambient assisted living systems. J. Ambient Intell. Smart Environ. Arch. **2**(2), 109–120 (2010)

7. Suryadevara, N.K., Gaddam A., Rayudu, R.K., Mukhopadhyay, S.C.: Wireless sensors network based safe home to care elderly people: behaviour detection. In: Proceedings of Eurosensors XXV, pp. 96–99, 4–7 September 2011, Athens, Greece

8. de Olivier Sardan, J.-P.: Epistemology, Fieldwork, and Anthropology. Palgrave MacMillan, Basingstoke (2015)

9. Goffman, E.: The interaction order. Am. Sociol. Rev. **48**, 1–17 (1983)

10. Corbin, J., Strauss, A.L.: Basics of Qualitative Research: Techniques and Procedures for developing Grounded Theory, 4th edn. San Jose State University, Sage, San Jose (2015)

11. Campo, E., Daran, X., Redon, L.: Une maison intelligente au carrefour des sciences technologiques et des sciences humaines. In: 2nd International Conference sur l'accessibilité et les systèmes de suppléance aux personnes en situation de handicap, pp. 33–42, Paris, France (2011)

12. Buisson, M., Bustico, A., Chatty, S., Colin, F.R, Jestin, Y., Maury, S., Mertz, C., Truillet, P.: Ivy: Un bus logiciel au service du développement de prototypes de systèmes interactifs. In: IHM 2002, Poitiers, 26 November 2002–29 November 2002, pp. 223–226. ACM Press (2002)

13. IVY's web site. http://www.eei.cena.fr/products/ivy. Accessed Feb 2016

An Exploratory Framework Assessing Intrinsic and Extrinsic Motivators Related to Mobile Device Applications and Attributes for the Canadian Seniors

Susan E. Reid[1], Bessam Abdulrazak[2(✉)], and Monica Alas[1]

[1] Bishop's University, Lennoxville, QC, Canada
sreid@ubishops.ca
[2] Université de Sherbrooke, Sherbrooke, QC, Canada
bessam.abdulrazak@usherbrooke.ca

Abstract. This study provides a first exploratory analysis, based on a survey of 103 seniors aged 65–95, to assess the needs/motives which are important to examine in further empirical research and in the development of mobile devices and apps for seniors. Results showed that seniors have intrinsic and extrinsic needs/motives that need to be taken into consideration when conceptualizing mobile attributes/apps to assist seniors. 'Three Tiers of Priority' specific to mobile attributes were uncovered through this research.

Keywords: Mobile devices · Intrinsic motivators · Extrinsic motivators · Seniors

1 Introduction

People aged 65 and over (seniors) suffer from added limitations associated with the aging process [19]. The number of people 65 + worldwide is expected to jump from 390 to 800 million by 2025 [22]. Such changes will have major implications for society including the cost of adapting new practices to better serve this segment [19]. That said, the literature demonstrates that benefits are perceived by seniors who, regardless of their physiological and psychological states, adapt to their new realities. Positive psychological and physical outcomes are generally associated with the ability of seniors to remain autonomous and socially active in their communities. In other words, there are benefits that come from what is known as 'active aging' [17]. Most seniors (e.g., >90 % of Canadian) live independently in their communities. Recent research has demonstrated that mobile devices, such as smartphones, are able to provide support to seniors in terms of managing their daily activities, boosting their social participation [1], reducing dependence on caregivers and improving security [14]. Seniors also exhibit the highest Internet use growth rates.

Seniors are becoming a large and promising market segment in many areas but they are as yet underrepresented in mobile commerce [8]. Developers of mobile applications (apps) need to understand the needs of and factors influencing this segment, such as the perception of and willingness-to-adopt mobile applications as independent participants

© Springer International Publishing Switzerland 2016
K. Miesenberger et al. (Eds.): ICCHP 2016, Part I, LNCS 9758, pp. 293–301, 2016.
DOI: 10.1007/978-3-319-41264-1_40

in a digital-society [10]. As such, this research focuses on uncovering the attitudes towards and interests of seniors with respect to mobile applications and the mobile devices on which they are installed.

2 Literature Review

During the past few years, several mobile tools and social apps have emerged to assist seniors with their health, digital literacy and web-service accessibility [10, 16]. Yet, the pervasive technology literature makes it clear that current solutions, including apps and interfaces, have not been designed with senior's needs in mind [1, 11, 17].

Uses and gratifications for individuals using new media (U&G theory) are determined by how the audience (seniors) views their needs or wants, social and psychological makeup, and media attributes [11]. Quality of Life researchers use a different lens to focus on the functionalities and apps which can satisfy needs of seniors [16, 20]. Other scholars have based their work on the Technology Acceptance Model (TAM) applied to the context of the adoption of mobile phones [4, 12] and its extensions such as TAM3 or UTAUT [15]. Researchers have also examined the adoption and diffusion process using attributes that define innovation, word-of-mouth, and economic factors [7]. Other studies have focused on usability problems related to the design of devices and the complexity of interfaces [15]. To our knowledge, limited research has been done on seniors' attitudes and perceptions of mobile apps and attributes of the mobile devices. As such, our research offers an exploratory study of these issues based on the marketing literature, examining the motivations driving consumers to seek new products. Several researchers have developed shopping typologies to capture motivational differences by consumer type [3, 4, 16], some focused on economic and social motivations [2], while others include factors such as price, convenience, and involvement [21]. Recently, these have included extrinsic (i.e., functional needs), intrinsic factors (i.e., non-functional needs) [5] and personal motives [13] that incite consumers' shopping decisions. Our research [21] has focused on shopping typologies which specify senior shoppers: the 'functionalist' who wants to get in and out of the store as quickly as possible, the 'social shopper' who is primarily motivated by the social aspects of shopping and the 'experiential shopper' motivated by the experience with products, promotions and store environment [18]. Functionalist and social shoppers showed lower adoption rates of mobile devices and services, however, adoption can be encouraged through simplification of services, lowering prices and education [18]. As such, the Smartphone user interface should be tailored to the various needs of seniors in order to promote 'Willingness-To-Adopt' the technology [1].

3 Propositions

The aim of this study is to explore the motives of senior consumers' interests in regards to mobile apps and attributes through the formulation of three propositions:

1. **Proposition P1a-b:** Seniors have different motives, (a) functional (e.g., navigation, price coverage) and (b) non-functional (e.g., social experience, experiential seeking) influencing their interest levels in using mobile applications. The literature suggests that different motives govern user needs to acquire new products. Hence, this proposition investigates different types of extrinsic (functional) and intrinsic (non-functional) motives influencing seniors' use of mobile applications.

2. **Proposition P2a-b-c:** Seniors have different motives, such as (a) functional, (b) non-functional and (c) value-added influencing their interest in mobile device attributes. Studies have demonstrated that perceived value [7] and perceived ease of use [12] of new products affect the purchase behavior intent of mobile health services of seniors [6]. In this study, we propose that seniors have different motives, (a) extrinsic, (b) intrinsic and (c) value-added which affect their interest levels in mobile attributes.

3. **Proposition P3:** There are differences within the senior segment, based on health and level of autonomy, related to their interest in mobile apps and attributes. The shopping typology by Reid [18] demonstrated that health issues mitigate seniors' adoption of mobile devices. We therefore propose that seniors have different levels of interest in in mobile apps contingent upon their level of autonomy.

4 Methodology

A quantitative assessment of the interest and willingness of seniors (65+) to use mobile devices was performed using a focus group of 9 pre-test participants, followed by a survey of 103 participants. Respondents were grouped into 4 usage categories running a spectrum from "I do not use a mobile device" to "I am already using a mobile device." The measures for 33 applications and 34 attributes were developed by using 7-point, Likert self-report scales (1 'strongly disagree'/7 'strongly agree'). For instance, some questions are related to the applications that seniors are using or would like to use (e.g., bus schedule, weather forecast, list and information for grocery and pharmacy, to-do lists). Other questions are related to phone attributes/qualities (e.g., good quality, perceived value, easy to use, easy to buy, number of keystrokes to perform an activity). Respondents were classified according to various demographics and health indicators. To validate our first and second propositions, we used an ANOVA statistical comparison. Chi-square analysis was used to verify our third proposition, which aims at capturing whether interest in mobile apps is related to seniors' level of autonomy.

5 Results

Our research sample was comprised of 103 participants: 68 female/35 male. Income levels ranged from <$10,000 to >$40,000. Respondents were between 65–95 years of age (Table 1). Lastly, 86.4 % (89 participants) had their driver's license.

Table 1. Age distribution of participants

65-< 70	70-< 75	75-< 80	80-< 85	85-< 90	90-< 95	95+
35 (33.98 %)	29 (28.16 %)	21 (20.39 %)	13 (12.62 %)	4 (3.9 %)	1 (0.9 %)	0 (0 %)

Proposition 1 applies a frequency tabulation exercise to investigate the main motivations underlying the types of mobile apps currently used by seniors. Table 2 shows the use of mobile apps is driven by three main motives: social, informal/amusement and functional. The first application category regroups 'Social' motive/ apps (Average mean A $A\bar{x} = 5.24$) and is part of 'non-functional' motives. It includes apps such as contact list, social planner to stay in touch with family and friends and phone calls as a means to socialize with people. Secondly, seniors are using apps that enable them to 'staying informed and amused' ($A\bar{x} = 3.75$) with the sur-roundings and environment, also considered 'non-functional'. These apps are driven by the motive of staying on top of the news, reminders for activities, weather forecast, daily routine planner and having social function suggestions and access to music. The third category corresponds to a more 'practical' and 'functional' motive/type of apps ($A\bar{x} = 2.94$). These include apps conceived to create 'to-do' lists, reminders for taking medications and meal planners.

Table 2. Applications already used by seniors

App used	Frequency	Description	Mean	Type of apps
1	15	Contact list	$\bar{x} = 5.2407$	Social motive/apps
2	14	Social planner (staying in touch with family and friends)		
3	13	Phone calls		
1	9	News/reminders for activities	$\bar{x} = 3.7582$	Informatioal and amusement motive/apps
2	8	Weather forecast/daily routine planner and schedule		
3	6	Finding places/social function suggestions and reminders/music		
1	5	Finding things/objects/reminders for taking medication/other to-do lists	$\bar{x} = 2.9429$	Practical motive/apps
2	4	Meal planner/recipes		
3	3	Exercise planner		

This preliminary tabulation analysis provides early support for the proposition (P1a-b) that seniors have different motives influencing their current mobile apps use. We used ANOVA analysis to validate whether these motives were statistically distinct.

Results confirm social motive is statistically different from the informational and amusement motive (p-val = .046 < α) as well as from the functional motive (p-val = .002 < α). However, the informational and amusement motive is not significantly different from the practical motive (p-val = 1.000 > α). Further, the tabulation of the mobile apps that seniors are interested in using, but do not currently use, also revealed three main motivations (Table 3). These include extrinsic motives ($A\bar{x}$ = 4.30), intrinsic motives ($A\bar{x}$ = 3.12) and utilitarian motives ($A\bar{x}$ = 2.38). The first set is a combination of 'extrinsic motive/apps' as they involve reaching out to the external environment. They include apps for navigation to find objects, phone calls, contact list, weather forecast, social planner and music. The second set is called 'intrinsic motive/ apps' as they involve doing things for oneself. These include apps for staying abreast with the news, ability to navigate for finding things/objects and reminder for activities. The third set is a 'utilitarian motive/apps'. These consist of apps designed to provide seniors with a tool to facilitate their shopping experience through grocery list, planners to alleviate their daily routine and schedule, and provide them assistance through other to-do lists. The ANOVA results reveal the extrinsic motive is statistically different from the intrinsic motive (p-val = .044 < α) and from the utilitarian motive (p-val = .001 < α). The intrinsic motive, however, did not produce a significant result to confirm its means is different from the utilitarian motive (p-val = .415 > α). P1 is supported.

Table 3. Level of interest in new applications

App.	Freq.	Description	Mean	T. Apps
1	20	Finding places	$\bar{x} = 4.3000$	Extrinsic motives/apps
2	19	Phone calls		
3	16	Contact list		
4	14	Weather forecast/social planner (staying in touch with family and friends)		
5	12	Music		
1	10	News	$\bar{x} = 3.1154$	Intrinsic motives/apps
2	7	Finding things/objects/reminders for activities		
1	6	Grocery list/daily routine planner and schedule/translation	$\bar{x} = 2.3768$	Utilitarian motives/apps
2	5	Other to-do lists/healthcare management/social function suggestions and reminders/community events		
3	4	Grocery information (for availability and location of specific products/for pricing and or promotional information)/instruction on how to take medicine or potential side-effects/meal planner/recipes/speech to text		

Proposition 2 suggests seniors have different motives that influence their interest levels when it comes to mobile attributes. The frequency tabulation exercise generated three underlying motives. These encompass an 'ease of use' motive ($A\bar{x} = 6.58$), a 'value' motive ($A\bar{x} = 6.11$) and a 'functional' motive ($A\bar{x} = 5.70$). The primary requirement that seniors are looking for are easy to use attributes of phones, whether meaning easy to understand, ability to start quickly, easy user guide or long battery life. The secondary phone attributes requirements are related to 'value' whether it is the perceived value (benefits to costs), the warranty, access to Internet or low price for service. The tertiary requirements relate to 'functions' like lightweight, bright screen, not many keystrokes to perform action, large screen, large keys and solid keys. The ANOVA results show that all three motives/needs categories are distinctively different from one another. The ease of use motive is significantly different from the value motive (p-val = .012 < α) and the functional motive (p-val = .000 < α). The value motive is also statistically different than the functional motive (p-val = .059 < α). P2 is therefore supported (Table 4).

Table 4. The three tiers of priorities

App.	Freq.	Description	Mean	T. Need
1	53	Easy to use	$\bar{x} = 6.5786$	Primary need: ease of use motive
2	52	Good quality		
3	50	Able to start using it quickly		
4	49	Easy to understand/easy user guide		
5	46	Long battery life		
1	45	Perceived value (i.e., good quality at a reasonable price)	$\bar{x} = 6.1127$	Secondary need: value motive
2	41	Warranty		
3	40	Access to internet		
4	39	Low price for service (data: i.e., internet services)		
1	38	Lightweight	$\bar{x} = 5.6987$	Third need: functional motive
2	37	Not many keystrokes to perform an activity/low price for service (voice: i.e., phone services)		
3	36	Bright screen/solid feeling keys		
4	34	Messaging capabilities		
5	33	Large screen/large keys		
6	31	Alert to third party in case of emergency (e.g., being lost or non-response)		
7	30	Thin shape/built-in camera/low price for device		

Proposition 3 aims at measuring whether interest in mobile apps is related to the level of autonomy (i.e., having a drivers license) experienced by seniors. We tested this by using the Chi-square test analysis. Results show that interest in mobile devices is in fact dependent on level of autonomy (Pearson $\chi2 = 0.047 < \alpha$). P3 is therefore supported. It is also evidenced that seniors who have to rely on others for their transportation care are the ones who see the greatest value in using a mobile device (std. residual = 2.1). This brings even more weight to the importance of developing mobile apps that meet seniors needs and requirements (e.g., attributes), with the purpose of helping seniors through aging well and reducing their dependence on caregivers.

6 Conclusion and Future Studies

The three propositions we put forward in the study presented in this paper provide a first exploratory analysis to enable consideration of which needs/ motives are important to examine in further empirical research. Our results also provide important evidence to be used in the development of mobile devices and apps for the ever-growing senior segment. Based on the results of this study, we know that there are primary needs that seniors have in terms intrinsic and extrinsic motives. These needs have to be further explored and utilized in the conceptualization of mobile attributes and apps in order to provide resources to assist seniors with aging well. There seems to be a general need tendency towards attributes that ensure a proper 'ease of use' (e.g., easy to use, good quality, able to start quickly, easy to understand), provide 'value' (e.g., good quality at a reasonable price, warranty, access to Internet) and has a good array of 'functional' features (e.g., lightweight, not many keystrokes to perform an activity, bright screen, solid feeling keys).

This study also confirms that interest in mobile applications is linked to level of autonomy experienced by seniors. This is a crucial finding when considering that 90 % of senior people live independently and want to remain in their homes in conjunction with the projected growth of this consumer segment to reach 800 million by 2025 [22]. It is precisely during the senior years that ICT offers relevant opportunities for improvement of psychological processes, social aspects and issues that are related to dependency [9]. This study also affirms that seniors aged between 80 and 85 have very specific needs and interests in terms of mobile functions and applications.

Certain limitations confine this research. Expanding the sample size to have a more even distribution across the age brackets and demographics could provide more detailed understanding. Adding a description for each type of application would have ensured the same level of comprehension about each of the applications. Future studies might potentially examine whether seniors' perceived interests in mobile applications and attributes vary if they are living at home or in a senior residence.

Acknowledgments. The authors would like to acknowledge the generous financial support of the FQRNT (INTER), the University of Sherbrooke and Bishop's University, as well as the volunteer assistance of Lizzy Fontana and Mary Jean Reid.

References

1. Abdulrazak, B., Malik, Y., Arab, F., Reid, S.: PhonAge: adapted smartphone for aging population. In: Biswas, J., Kobayashi, H., Wong, L., Abdulrazak, B., Mokhtari, M. (eds.) ICOST 2013. LNCS, vol. 7910, pp. 27–35. Springer, Heidelberg (2013)
2. Angell, R., Megicks, P., Memery, J., Heffernan, T., Howell, K.: Understanding the older shopper: a behavioural typology. J. Retail. Consum. Serv. **19**, 259–269 (2012)
3. Arnold, M.J., Reynolds, K.E.: Hedonic shopping motivations. J. Retail. **79**, 77–95 (2003)
4. van Biljon, J., Renaud, K.: A qualitative study of the applicability of technology acceptance models to senior mobile phone users. In: Multimodal Human Computer Interaction and Pervasive Services, pp. 1–18. IGI Global (2009). ISBN 978-1-60566-386-9
5. Deci, E.L., Ryan, R.M.: The " what " and " why " of goal pursuits: human needs and the self-determination of behavior. Psychol. Inq. **11**, 227–268 (2000)
6. Deng, Z., Mo, X., Liu, S.: Comparison of the middle-aged and older users' adoption of mobile health services in China. Int. J. Med. Inform. **83**, 210–224 (2014)
7. Ferreira, K.D., Lee, C.G.: An integrated two-stage diffusion of innovation model with market segmented learning. Technol. Forecast. Soc. Change. **88**, 189–201 (2014)
8. Gurtner, S., Reinhardt, R., Soyez, K.: Designing mobile business applications for different age groups. Technol. Forecast. Soc. Change. **88**, 177–188 (2014)
9. Llorente-Barroso, C., Viñarás-Abad, M., Sánchez-Valle, M.: Internet and the elderly: enhancing active ageing. Comunicar **23**(45), 29–36 (2015)
10. Luna-García, H., Mendoza-González, R., Álvarez-Rodríguez, F.-J.: Design patterns to enhance accessibility and use of social applications for older adults. Media Educ. Res. J. **45**, 85–93 (2015)
11. Magsamen-Conrad, K., Dowd, J., Abuljadail, M., Alsulaiman, S., Shareefi, A.: Life-span differences in the uses and gratifications of tablets: implications for older adults. Comput. Human Behav. **52**, 96–106 (2015)
12. Mallenius, S., Rossi, M., Tuunainen, V.K.: Factors affecting the adoption and use of mobile devices and services by elderly people–results from a pilot study. In: 6th Annual Mobile Round Table, vol. 31, p. 12, Los Angeles (2007)
13. Megicks, P., Memery, J., Williams, J.: Influences on ethical and socially responsible shopping: evidence from the UK grocery sector. J. Mark. Manag. **24**, 637–659 (2008)
14. Ni, Q., Hernando, A.B.G., de la Cruz, I.P.: The elderly's independent living in smart homes: a characterization of activities and sensing infrastructure survey to facilitate services development. Sensors 2015 **15**, 11312–11362 (2015)
15. Petrovčič, A., Fortunati, L., Vehovar, V., Kavčič, M., Dolnicar, V.: Mobile phone communication in social support networks of older adults in Slovenia. Telemat. Inform. **32**, 642–655 (2015)
16. Plaza, I., Martín, L., Martin, S., Medrano, C.: Mobile applications in an aging society: status and trends. J. Syst. Softw. **84**, 1977–1988 (2011)
17. Reid, S.E., Abdulrazak, B., Alas, M., Bibeau, J.: Pervasive mobile services for active aging: an exploratory investigation into the relationship between willingness-to-adopt mobile devices and shopping experience. In: Chang, C.K., Chiari, L., Cao, Yu., Jin, H., Mokhtari, M., Aloulou, H. (eds.) ICOST 2016. LNCS, vol. 9677, pp. 211–221. Springer, Heidelberg (2016). doi:10.1007/978-3-319-39601-9_19
18. Reid, S.: Mobile assistive services for active aging: Technology for age friendly cities. Presented at the Townshipper's Association, Sherbrooke, QC, Canada
19. Saracchini, R., Catalina, C., Bordoni, L.: A mobile augmented reality assistive technology for the elderly. Media Educ. Res. J. **23**(45), 65–73 (2015)

20. Schulz, R., Beach, S.R., Matthews, J.T., Courtney, K., Dabbs, A.D., Mecca, L.P.: Willingness to pay for quality of life technologies to enhance independent functioning among baby boomers and the elderly adults. Gerontologist **54**, 363–374 (2014)
21. Williams, R.H., Painter, J.J., Nicholas, H.R.: A policy-oriented typology of grocery shoppers. J. Retail. **54**, 27–34 (1978)
22. World Health Organization: World Health Report 2013: Research for universal health coverage. Switzerland, Geneva (2013)

One Size Does Not Fit All

Design and Implementation Considerations When Introducing Touch Based Infotainment Systems to Nursing Home Residents

Øystein Dale[(✉)], Elin Sundby Boysen, and Ingrid Svagård

SINTEF, Oslo, Norway
{Oystein.Dale,ElinSundby.Boysen,
Ingrid.Svagard}@sintef.no

Abstract. Bedside patient infotainment touch screens provide access to a range of information, communication and entertainment services. This paper explores pertinent design and implementation considerations when introducing such infotainment terminals in nursing homes. Given the high prevalence of dementia in nursing home populations, special importance is placed on the needs and requirements of persons with dementia. In the paper, findings from an evaluation of the introduction of an infotainment system in two nursing homes is presented, discussed and contrasted with literature on dementia-friendly design of ICT.

Keywords: Usability · Accessibility · Dementia · ICT · Infotainment terminals

1 Introduction

The use of bedside patient infotainment touch screens providing access to a range of information, communication and entertainment services is commonplace in hospitals, but rare in nursing homes (NH). NH populations have become increasingly older and frailer [1, 2]. In Norway up to 80 % of NH residents suffer from dementia [3]. Dementia is a clinical syndrome caused by underlying illnesses, adversely affecting cognitive function and independent living skills [4]. In 2010 worldwide prevalence of dementia was 35.6 million, and by 2050 it is estimated that 115.4 million will be living with dementia [4]. Dementia adversely affects a person's ability to use information and communication technology (ICT) [5]. As a result, resident-targeted ICT in NH needs to be usable and accessible for persons with dementia (PwD).

This paper explores pertinent design and implementation considerations when introducing touch based infotainment terminals in NH with special importance placed on the needs of PwD. This is done by discussing and contrasting findings from an evaluation of the introduction such a system in two NH in Norway with findings from literature.

K. Miesenberger et al. (Eds.): ICCHP 2016, Part I, LNCS 9758, pp. 302–309, 2016.
DOI: 10.1007/978-3-319-41264-1_41

2 Brief Description of System and the Evaluation Conducted

Touch-based infotainment screens were installed in resident rooms in two NH in Norway late 2013. The approximately 170 IP-based screens measure 18.5 in./5 kg, and are wall mounted with an adjustable arm (Fig. 1). All had identical hardware, Linux software, and user interface (UI) with limited possibilities for individualisation.

Fig. 1. Side-view of screen with adjustable arm, and screenshots of menus (SINTEF/NESK).

The all-touch operated screens provide access to entertainment such as TV, radio and video-on-demand, Internet-based services such as Skype and Flickr, access to NH information such as meal menus, activities etc. The UI consists of a home screen with six main options with grid based sub-menus, e.g., Entertainment, Applications, NH information etc. and a shortcut bar to popular services (see Fig. 1). The services are presented in a web browser, in proprietary UIs, and in UIs from third party providers. The screens replaced the prior TV service to the residents' rooms.

SINTEF conducted an independent evaluation of the system one year post-implementation (Q2 2015). The purpose was to acquire knowledge about the user experiences that could be used to improve existing and future features and services. The evaluation focused on the experiences by residents, their next-of-kin (NoK), and staff. Emphasis was on actual usage, usability and ease of use, perceived usefulness, and issues relating to the introduction of the system and follow-up. This paper presents, describes and discusses the infotainment system as it appeared at the time of the evaluation. Subsequent improvements have been made to the system.

The introduction of the touch screens was part of a greater strategy that also involved providing staff with a number of digital tools and services through the screens, e.g. electronic patient journal and clinical support tools etc. These were not implemented at the time of the evaluation. Their use goes beyond the scope of this paper.

3 State of the Art

ICT is used by NH residents for a variety of purposes, but there is little knowledge about the feasibility of using computer activities with PwD in NH settings [7]. There are a number of R&D-efforts describing the use of touch screens with a personalised and simplified UI for PwD [8–11]. Of particular interest are the CIRCA, Companion and MemoryBox devices which have a similar form factor to the evaluated system, and share some of its features and services [8–10]. These systems have shown to have several possible benefits for PwD and their carers, such as positively affecting symptoms, autonomy and wellbeing for PwD, provide respite for carers, and act as a platform for shared activity [8–10]. We were unable to identify literature that specifically focused on the use of touch-based infotainment systems in NH settings.

The need for simple and user-friendly ICT UIs for PwD is well established, but there has in recent years been little published research focusing exclusively on ensuring dementia-friendly interfaces [6]. It is important to consider both personalisation of the UI, and mechanisms that further user acceptance [6]. Further, flexible interfaces that can be adapted over time to the changing needs of the PwD are deemed important [6]. PwD should take part in all phases of the development [12]. Appropriate training, support, and follow up are important [13, 14].

In short, special care needs to be taken to design dementia-friendly ICT. The amount of research on what constitutes dementia-friendly design of ICT is limited. There is some research on the use of touch screens for PwD. There is little research on the use of touch-based dementia-friendly infotainment systems in NH settings.

4 Methodology of the Evaluation

A number of research modalities and methods were used in data collection for the evaluation. These were:

- Six residents and their NoK (N = 12) took part in qualitative interviews (30–90 min) relating to their experience with the touch screens. Residents were also observed while operating the system. To be included residents had to regularly use the screens either independently and/or with their NoK, staff or others, and be able to give informed consent.
- Two 90 min qualitative group interviews were conducted with nursing and care staff at both NHs relating to their own experience with using the system, as well as their experience with the residents using the touch screens (N = 12).
- An Internet-based survey distributed by e-mail was conducted with the residents' NoK about their own, and their impressions of their resident's experience with the touch screens (response rate 35 %, N = 52).

In addition system server log data on usage (time used/type of service) for one month was analysed. Literature was acquired through searches in peer reviewed literature databases, and general searches on the Internet.

5 Results from the Evaluation

The residents and their NoK use the touch screens mainly for watching TV. This was not surprising as the screens had replaced the prior TV service. On average, the TV feature is used around two hours per screen daily. We assume there are large individual differences. The screens are also used for listening to the radio, and for web services. These features are utilised far less than the TV feature (see Fig. 2). The survey data from the NoK, and interviews with residents confirms that TV and radio are the most widely used services. On average, web services are accessed five hours per month per screen. Popular web services are movies, streaming TV and watching YouTube. Web services are mainly used by NoK or staff together with the residents. Both the residents interviewed and the majority of the NoK who responded in the survey, state that they are satisfied with the services available on the screens.

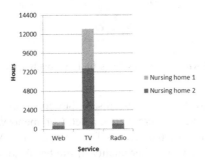

Fig. 2. Total hours of use for touch screen content for month of May 2015. Data from Lincor.

Staff uses web services such as music and YouTube as shared entertainment whilst conducting physical care in the resident rooms. They also use YouTube, music and photos for reminiscing activities with the residents. According to the NoK survey respondents, the majority of the residents require assistance operating the screens. There is little evidence to support much independent use of web services by the residents. A number of residents reportedly do not use the touch screens.

Almost two thirds of the NoK who responded to the relevant survey question report that they did not think the residents find the screens easy to use (see Fig. 3). Concrete challenges mentioned includes dealing with the number of choices provided, navigating the menus, and the physical operation of the touch screen. Reasons given for the challenges encountered include diminished cognitive abilities and impaired motor function, vision and hearing, as well as lacking ICT experience. Notably, all six residents interviewed reported that they did not find the screens difficult to operate. Observation of them operating the screens showed, however, that they either had difficulties operating the screens independently, or that they did not always chose the most efficient way of navigating the UI.

Several NoK called for a simplified and flexible system. One suggestion was: "It is important to limit the number of touches necessary to get to what the user is interested in". Another NoK suggested that: "The screen should have a very simple starting page with large coloured fields with different colours and motifs in which the user have, for instance, three options. These could be TV, radio, and personal photos".

Staff reported that they found the system easy to operate, and survey data showed that NoK also found the touch screens easy to use (see Fig. 4). One exception being log on routines to web services such as the video-on-demand service Skype and Flickr, that were deemed cumbersome. A new log in was required every time a service was accessed. It was stated by some of the NoK that the procedure made it almost impossible for the residents to access these services independently.

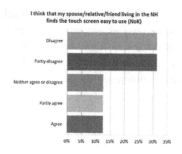

Fig. 3. NoK appraisal of whether the residents find the touch screens easy to use (N = 16).

Both the residents and staff interviewed said they found the screens useful. Several of the staff reported that screens were a great asset. Comments were made by both staff and NoK on the usefulness of the screens for the residents. A staff member offered about a client that: "I perceive that her quality of life has become totally different after she started watching TV. She used to have a TV she did not use, but this [the screen] she uses". One visitor/friend states that: "The screen is very important for my client because she is totally bedbound. She is mentally alert and interested in [TV] programs on society and news. The screen keeps her alive". The NoK were more reserved, and were split in their views on the usefulness of the system from their own perspective. All groups reported that additional training would be beneficial.

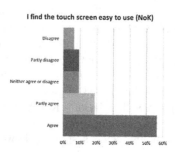

Fig. 4. NoKs appraisal on whether they find the touch screens easy to use (N = 32).

6   Discussion Including Contributions to the Field

Although, care had been taken to simplify the UI of the touch screens to achieve ease of use for all including PwD, the findings in the evaluation indicate that this was only partly achieved. Below we discuss and contrast selected findings from the evaluation with recommendations from literature so that others can learn from our experiences.

According to literature, dementia-friendly ICT should ideally:

- Be the result of involvement of PwD in all development phases [12].
- Have a UI which is simple, and easy to operate [5, 6].

- Allow for personalisation and individualisation, and be flexible and adaptable [6].
- Promote user acceptance [6], and be integrated in to the daily life of the PwD [11].
- Include appropriate training, support and follow up [13, 14].

It should be noted that this list is not exhaustive. Adhering to these criteria does not guarantee that ICT can be mastered by PwD, but increases the likelihood of a match between user requirements and the solution being implemented. We will now deal with these criteria in terms of how they were met in the evaluation.

Reportedly, PwD and proxies were consulted to some extent in the design of the system. Partial involvement is often the case in such projects [12]. Their involvement should not only be limited to ensuring an appropriate design of the UI, but also involve which services to be included and other principal decisions pertaining to the solution.

Several factors may make the UI of the infotainments screens somewhat complicated to use. First, the design and UI is not consistent. Some screen menus are tile/grid based whereas other services are accessed through a web browser, proprietary, or through third-party UIs. This may be confusing for the user as the UI and interaction required is context sensitive. Nevertheless, the use of a web browser interface and third-party apps does potentially enable access to a vast number of services. These might otherwise not have been available, or required a great deal of development if one should access them from a totally self-developed and modified UI.

Second, there are a number of choices in the menu system (up to 10 plus a shortcut bar), and three menu levels. This may represent too much information to process, and means that a service such as accessing the TV feature may require up to four presses/touches on the screen. Third, the log in routine to certain web services may complicate usage. The latter is an example of the difficulty of balancing usability and accessibility needs with privacy and security issues.

The standard infotainment screen set up at the time of the evaluation offered few opportunities for personalisation or individualisation. It was possible to change the system language and add input peripherals. The number and types of services were the same for all. This "one-size-fits-all" approach is a drawback, as one can to a very limited extent adjust the system to match the needs, requirements and preferences of the individual PwD. This may also adversely impact user acceptance, as acceptance of technology starts with identifying needs and personalising functions of the technology to the PwD [11]. There are a number of benefits from an operational and maintenance perspective having a standard set up, but the heterogeneous needs in NH populations suggests a more flexible approach.

Gradual integration of ICT into daily life of the PwD is important for user acceptance [11]. The screens were used by staff and residents together for a number of different activities, e.g. for entertainment, reminiscing, relaxation, to provide conversation topics, and others. Both NHs had a strategy and wish to incorporate the screens in their everyday routines and activities. Despite this, usage appeared to be more ad hoc rather than a planned, organised and concerted effort to incorporate the screens into the daily lives of the residents, and the activities at the NHs. This may have impacted on user acceptance and usage levels.

[11] point out that usage of new technology by PwD may be influenced by spousal support. A number of the NoK seemed to be sceptical to the use of the infotainment

screen by the PwD. This may have influenced some of the residents' willingness to try the screens. Further, our interview and survey data indicate that the residents' old age and lack of prior exposure to ICT made them less likely to adopt screen usage.

Appropriate training and follow up is important for the successful use and implementation of ICT for PwD [13, 14]. Group training was offered to staff and NoK, whereas residents were provided with one-to-one instruction. All groups reported that additional training would be useful. Training should be part of a larger comprehensive implementation strategy linked to the integration of the screens in everyday life at the NH. Further, time should be allocated to staff to allow for the ongoing support to the residents when using the screens. Lack of time for staff to provide ongoing support was an issue raised by all three user groups.

7 Conclusion and Planned Activities

Following the evaluation, a number of improvements have been made to the screens to simplify use. The study shows that TV is the most popular service, and that other services are used far less. It may be TV is the main service the residents prefer to use, and that they opt not to try other services. This view was confirmed by the interviewed residents. Also, the limited joint use of other services on the screens by residents and their next-of-kin need not be a reflection on the system as such, but simply that they wish to spend their shared time pursuing non-screen activities. Future more technology savvy nursing home generations, may have different preferences.

The number and types of services that infotainment systems can contain is virtually limitless. Given the special user interface needs of nursing home populations, it is essential to provide modified solutions which provide selected services and functionalities in a manner usable and accessible to persons with dementia. This can best be achieved through adopting an universal and user centred design approach, allow for personalisation and flexibility, promote user acceptance, by providing adequate and appropriate training and follow up for all stakeholders, and integration into the daily services and activities at the nursing homes. We are considering further R&D activities focusing on staff usage of the touch screens.

Acknowledgements. The authors would like to thank the informants, the Nursing Home Division at the Municipality of Oslo, NESK, and Lincor for their contribution to the evaluation. The work was funded by the Regional Research Funds Hovedstaden.

References

1. Den norske legeforening: Flere leger i sykehjemmene. Policynotat nr., August 2012. http://legeforeningen.no/PageFiles/103783/Flere%20leger%20i%20sykehjemmene.pdf
2. Sahyoun, N.R., Pratt, L.A., Lentzner, H., Dey, A., Robinson, K.N.: The changing profile of nursing home residents: 1985–1997. Aging Trends **4**, 1–8 (2001)

3. Selbaek, G., Kirkevold, Ø., Engedal, K.: The prevalence of psychiatric symptoms and behavioural disturbances and the use of psychotropic drugs in Norwegian nursing homes. Int. J. Geriatr. Psychiatry **22**, 843–849 (2007)

4. Prince, M., Bryce, R., Albanese, E., Wimo, A., Ribeiro, W., Ferri, C.P.: The global prevalence of dementia: a systematic review and metaanalysis. Alzheimers Dement. **9**, 63–75 (2013)

5. Ancient, C., Good, A.: Issues with designing dementia-friendly interfaces. In: Stephanidis, C. (ed.) HCII 2013, Part I. CCIS, vol. 373, pp. 192–196. Springer, Heidelberg (2013)

6. Ancient, C., Good, A.: Considering people living with dementia when designing interfaces. In: Marcus, A. (ed.) DUXU 2014, Part IV. LNCS, vol. 8520, pp. 113–123. Springer, Heidelberg (2014)

7. Sunghee, H.T., Beck, C., Hong, S.H.: Feasibility of providing computer activities for nursing home residents with dementia. Nonpharmacol. Ther. Dement. **3**, 1–10 (2013)

8. Astell, A., Ellis, M., Bernardi, L., Alm, N., Dye, R., Gowans, G., Campbell, J.: Developing technology to support the relationship between people with dementia and caregivers. In: Proceedings of the 22nd Conference of Alzheimer's Disease International, Berlin, pp. 30–33 (2007)

9. Kerssens, C., Kumar, R., Adams, A.E., Knott, C.C., Matalenas, L., Sanford, J.A., Rogers, W.A.: Personalized technology to support older adults with and without cognitive impairment living at home. Am. J. Alzheimers Dis. Other Demen. **30**, 85–97 (2015)

10. Davison, T.E., Nayer, K., Coxon, S., de Bono, A., Eppingstall, B., Jeon, Y.H., van der Ploeg, E.S., O'Connor, D.W.: A personalized multimedia device to treat agitated behavior and improve mood in people with dementia: a pilot study. Geriatr. Nurs. **37**, 25–29 (2016)

11. Karlsson, E., Axelsson, K., Zingmark, K., Sävenstedt, S.: The challenge of coming to terms with the use of a new digital assistive device: a case study of two persons with mild dementia. Open Nurs. J. **5**, 102–110 (2011)

12. Spana, M., Hettinga, M., Vernooij-Dassen, M., Eefsting, J., Smits, C.: Involving people with dementia in the development of supportive IT applications: a systematic review. Ageing Res. Rev. **12**, 535–551 (2013)

13. Social Care Institute for Excellence: Using ICT in activities for people with dementia: a short guide for social care providers. http://www.scie.org.uk

14. Alzheimer's Society: Dementia-friendly technology. A charter that helps every person with dementia benefit from technology that meets their needs, London, UK (2014). https://www.alzheimers.org.uk/site/scripts/download_info.php?fileID=2256

Support Services for Informal Caregivers: Survey with Providers in Austria

Susanne Hensely-Schinkinger[✉]

Multidisciplinary Design Group, Institute for Design and Assessment of Technology,
Vienna University of Technology, Vienna, Austria
susanne.hensely-schinkinger@tuwien.ac.at

Abstract. Support services with informal caregivers as primary target group can reduce the burden caused by the care work. But at the moment the offer in Austria is underdeveloped and underutilized due to problems on the side of the providers and on the side of the informal caregivers. After doing expert interviews, a questionnaire was created and distributed to providers in Austria. It focused on current offers of support services and their acceptance, marketing activities, future of the overall offer in Austria and ICT usage. This paper presents the results of the questionnaire and also compares it to former studies done in this area.

Keywords: Support service · Informal care · Provider · Survey

1 Introduction

A permanent help and care that is unpaid, not based on a contractual basis and done by persons who do not possess any training certificate in this area is called "informal care" [1]. In Austria, 80 % of all care is provided by informal caregivers [2].

Doing the care work as an informal caregiver lead to physical load and emotional stress [2]. This can be evident as mental overload, hopelessness, back pain, etc. [3]. The level of burden can increase when the informal caregiver is still having a paid job next to the care work or is also elderly and has own health problems [4]. Due to these facts, the group of informal caregivers is named our society's "hidden patients" [5].

To reduce this burden, a number of support services are offered in Austria with informal caregivers as primary target group. Individual advising, self-help groups, training seminars etc. [6]. But the offer of such services is underdeveloped in Austria and just suffices at the moment because many persons who would need it are not making use of them [2]. Reasons for this non-take-up differ from underestimation of care work to refusal from care receiver to a lack of knowledge [7].

These barriers exist both on the side of the providers of support services but also on the side of the informal caregivers. The possibility of using information and communication technologies (ICT) in the implementation of support services should be considered to reduce stumbling blocks like problems with distance or mobility, missing temporal flexibility for provision of services, still remaining anonymous etc.

© Springer International Publishing Switzerland 2016
K. Miesenberger et al. (Eds.): ICCHP 2016, Part I, LNCS 9758, pp. 310–313, 2016.
DOI: 10.1007/978-3-319-41264-1_42

2   Related Research

A number of research studies have addressed support services with informal caregivers as primary target group [2, 8, 9]. The offers range from individual advising, via self-help groups through to trainings. Existing services are poorly used because of missing information and not fitting the needs. The most used services are categorized as "information supply" but still too less. The target group still missing support regarding psychological help, financial support, and care training.

The interview study with providers in the City of Vienna showed that several types of support services with different foci are offered at the moment [10]. Training seminars and individual advising are used the most. Although some efforts have been done in this regard, more temporal and local flexibility is needed. Different types of informal caregivers and different ways of communication have to be taken into regard.

ICT-supported services contain much potential to develop innovative offers and reduce informal caregivers' burden [11, 12]. Although some studies evaluated various kinds of solutions like websites offering content from experts and peers or social media technologies for linking informal caregivers with each others [13, 14], still scant knowledge about how to effectively implement such solutions is available. In this regard, it is very important to tailor technology-based support services to the individual needs of the heterogeneous group of informal caregivers [12].

The situation in Austria can be compared to several other European countries [15]. Informal care support is most elaborated in Germany and Austria. The proportion of people in Sweden, Germany, Austria, Spain and Italy using informal care exceeds the proportion of people using formal care. The City of Vienna provides the second largest number of care allowance recipients compared to the other Austrian federal states and is first placed in numbers like health care professionals doing this work, etc. [16].

3   Methodology

Based on expert interviews with representatives from institutions being the biggest provider of support services for informal caregivers in the City of Vienna [10], a questionnaire was elaborated and distributed to other providers located in Austria. 27 institutions, from single-person businesses via interest groups through to big established companies in the social sector, were addressed via mail. Between July and September 2015, 23 questionnaires were filled in – 15 of them with valid answers.

The questionnaire consisted of 5 closed and 22 open questions around current offers and their acceptance, marketing activities, future of the overall offer and ICT usage. The open ones were analyzed with the qualitative content analysis (QCA).

4   Results

The analysis of the data regarding current offers of support services for informal caregivers as the primary target group shows that two thirds of all participants are providing advising. Almost half of the participants are offering self-help groups with an expert leading or just as a regulars' table. Also training seminars and lectures to a variable extent are offered currently by almost half of the participants. Only 4 out of 15 participants said that they are offering hourly care or a combination of services.

When it comes to the acceptance of support services, the data shows different experiences between the participants. Some stated individual advising as well accepted whereas other mentioned the opposite. Also services like hourly care and training seminars are used with varying popularity. Only when it comes to group meetings or self-help groups, the majority of the participants are in agreement that they are underutilized. The main reason that were mentioned by 11 out of 15 participants why support services in general are not used although they are needed is shame about the care situation and its aspects. But also time, missing information and mobility were named as a barrier by around one third of all participants.

When it comes to awareness, more than half of the participants were sure that their current offers are well known among the group of informal caregivers. The other participants were aware that they are doing too little marketing due to restrictions in time, personnel and financial resources. Some of the participants also complained about a missing service point for informal caregivers and that informal caregivers have to be proactive to get to know institutions offering support services for them.

With 13 out of 15 participants, the majority would support the usage of ICT to improve support services for informal caregivers. Half of them mainly argued that the upcoming generations of informal caregivers are more open to such technologies and will therefore also use them in the context of informal care. The second most common argument for using ICT in support services is that problems like distance, limited mobility, response time, time coordination and also shame can be potentially reduced. Those participants who were not supporting ICT usage argued that it couldn't be a replacement for a face-to-face contact. In general, more than half of the participants stated that ICT usage makes most sense in individual advising, seminars and experience exchange. But therefore, the framework conditions regarding personnel, technology, time and finance need to be defined. Almost half of the participants reported that they are already using ICT in their currently offered services. Most of them are using it for individual advising via mail. The overall experience with ICT usage is positive – some participants pointed out that it is easier and allows faster response.

5 Conclusion and Future Work

Although the sample of this study looks quite small, it can be considered acceptable when it is compared to the available population of the target group in Austria.

Advising is the most used service but the acceptance of training seminars differs between the interview study [10] and the results of the questionnaire. Combination of services is still underdeveloped and needs enlargement. A central contact point needs to be established. The providers are aware that integration of ICT in support services is needed for the upcoming generation and can reduce some of the barriers. An appropriate framework regarding personnel, time and finance must be defined.

A second questionnaire will be applied to the target group of informal caregivers to analyze their opinion on the status quo. The comparison of both questionnaires will lead to suggestions for targeted enhancement – with a focus on ICT usage.

References

1. Hörl, J., Kolland, F., Majce, G.: Hochaltrigkeit in Österreich: Eine Bestandsaufnahme. Bundesministerium für Arbeit, Soziales und Konsumentenschutz, Vienna (2008)
2. Pochobradsky, E., Bergmann, F., Brix-Samoylenko, H., Erfkamp, H., Laub, R.: Situation pflegender Angehöriger. ÖBIG, Vienna (2005)
3. Winkler, I., Kilian, R., Matschinger, H., Angermeyer, M.C.: Lebensqualität älterer pflegender Angehöriger von Demenzkranken. Z. Gerontpsychol. Psychiatr. 19, 17–24 (2006)
4. Bischofsberger, I., Lademann, J., Radvanszky, A.: "work & care" – Erwerbstätigkeit und Pflege vereinbaren: Literaturstudie zu Herausforderungen für pflegende Angehörige, Betriebe und professionelle Pflege. Pflege 22, 277–286 (2009)
5. Emlet, C.A.: Assessing the informal caregiver: team member or hidden patient? Home Care Provid. 1, 255–262 (1996)
6. Schalek, K., Boschert, S.: Wissenswertes für pflegende Angehörige. Caritas Österreich, Vienna (2013)
7. Lamura, G., Mnich, E., Wojszel, B., Nolan, M., Krevers, B., Mestheneos, L., Döhner, H.: Erfahrungen von pflegenden Angehörigen älterer Menschen in Europa bei der Inanspruchnahme von Unterstützungsleistungen. Z. Gerontol. Geriatr. 39, 429–442 (2006)
8. Schneider, U., Trukeschitz, B., Mühlmann, R., Jung, R., Ponocny, I., Katzlinger, M., Österle, A.: Wiener Studie zur informellen Pflege und Betreuung älterer Menschen 2008 (Vienna Informal Carer Study - VIC2008). Forschungsinstitut für Altersökonomie der WU Wien, Vienna (2009)
9. Trukeschitz, B., Michalitsch, V.: "Wo der Schuh drückt" - Stellungnahmen und Verbesserungsvorschläge pflegender Angehöriger zu Betreuungs- und Pflegedienstleistungen in Wien. Forschungsinstitut für Altersökonomie der WU Wien, Vienna (2011)
10. Hensely-Schinkinger, S.: Support services for informal caregivers: first results of expert interviews with providers in the City of Vienna. Stud. Health Technol. Inform. 217, 852–856 (2015)
11. Barbabella, F., Lamura, G., Schmidt, A.E.: Potenzial und Verbreitung von IKT zur Unterstützung pflegender Angehöriger. Soziale Sicherheit CHSS, Switzerland (2013)
12. Lopez-Hartmann, M., Wens, J., Verhoeven, V., Remmen, R.: The effect of caregiver support interventions for informal caregivers of community-dwelling frail elderly: a systematic review. Int. J. Integr. Care 12, e133 (2012)
13. Stewart, J.: ICT's for informal care givers. Gerontechnology 11, 392 (2012)
14. Pagán-Ortiz, M.E., Cortés, D.E., Rudloff, N., Weitzmann, P., Levkoff, S.: Use of an online community to provide support to caregivers of people with dementia. J. Gerontol. Soc. Work 57, 694–709 (2014)
15. Suanet, B., van Groenou, M.B., van Tilburg, T.: Informal and formal home-care use among older adults in Europe: can cross-national differences be explained by societal context and composition? Ageing Soc. 32, 491–515 (2012)
16. Statistik Austria. http://www.statistik.at

AAL-Case Management

A Key to Successful Service Provision

Sabine Katzmaier[✉]

Johannes Kepler University, Altenberger Straße 69, 4040 Linz, Austria
sabinekatzmaier@hotmail.com

Abstract. The technical development of IT-based products for aged people under the term Ambient Assisted Living (AAL) has been heavily researched over the recent years. However, implementation lags behind. Among others there is demand for assistance and guidance of the aged people in form of a Case Management system. In course of a qualitative study design recommendations have been developed which should find consideration when implementing the AAL-Case Management.

Keywords: Ambient Assisted Living · Case management · Service provision

1 The Research Idea

AAL applies to IT-based products and systems serving assistance to elderly persons. The objective is to increase quality of life and to assist in dealing with daily life and routine [1]. The technical development of innovations in the field of AAL is highly advanced. However, the implementation of the concept and greater application of the IT-based products are lagging behind [2]. The difficulties in introducing AAL can be traced back to a lack in service orientation and insufficient organization of associated services [2–4]. There is repeated demand for implementation of Case Management for the field of AAL – this to ensure the assistance and guidance of the aged people respective to AAL [5–7].

Case Management represents a method of social work supporting people in compensating their deficits [8] by initiating formal and informal support. The assistance takes place as process which is divided and structured into several consecutive phases [9]. This study on hand refers to the breakdown of the Case Management Processes into the following seven phases [10]. The Outreaching/Case Finding/Intaking phase describes the process of establishing contact between client and Case Management. Assessment covers the situation of the client as basis for the phase of Planning Assistance to determine the objectives and concrete support measures. In course of Contract Management contact to and between the respectively involved service providers is established. As these measures are implemented, these are analyzed by Case Management in course of the Monitoring/Assisting Observation phase and if necessary modified. The degree of satisfaction of the clients is determined by Evaluation. Evaluative Follow-Up serves for verifying the effectivity of the measures. The Case Managers support their clients throughout the whole process.

K. Miesenberger et al. (Eds.): ICCHP 2016, Part I, LNCS 9758, pp. 314–317, 2016.
DOI: 10.1007/978-3-319-41264-1_43

In course of the Regio13-funded research project INVERSIA and subsequent doctorate the demand for AAL-Case Management represented the primary object of research. The prime objective was to develop recommendations for the design of the Case Management phases in the field of AAL to contribute to successful service provision.

2 Methodology

A qualitative study based upon Grounded Theory by Glaser and Strauss [11], was conducted. The experience of practitioners in AAL and case management as well as the special fields of assistive technologies, appliances and home environment counseling - which exhibit contextual overlaps with AAL - have been gathered and compiled between fall 2010 and spring 2015. In the terms of Triangulation [12] different qualitative assessment methods were combined. In addition to an explorative interview, an expert interview and six problem oriented interviews, four focus groups with four respectively three times with two participants were conducted. In total 18 experts were interviewed. Three of these were additionally accompanied in their practical activities in course of a participatory observation. The analysis of the empirical research as well as the findings of literature research provide the basis for deriving the design recommendations for AAL case management.

3 Empirical Results

In the following, the findings of the empirical survey with respect to the phases of the Case Management are outlined. For the phase of Outreaching/Case Finding/Intaking the facilitators - such as relatives or service providers of social or health care - assume a significant position. In rare occasions the people concerned seek counsel or assistance proactively. At the beginning of counsel or assistance the assessments to determine the starting point of all interview partners are performed. The assessments are consistently considered important and stated as basis for the further planning. The orientation of actions along the requirements of the clients in course of the Assistance Planning phase is stated as the vital success factor. Counseling with respect to funding of the planned and frequently cost-intensive measures appears to be equally important. The interview partners report that in course of Contract Management it is frequently possible to establish access to cost-effective local alternatives for conducting and implementing the plans. In course of Monitoring/Assisting Observation the necessity for observation of the needs of the clients is emphasized. On occasion changes of the client's health situation makes rapid customization of the measures necessary. In addition extensive enrollments of the clients and their surroundings are stated as success factor for later application of aids, auxiliary equipment and assistive technologies. Evaluation of the consultancy services is in part neglected by the interview partners. However, the interview partners which report of systematic evaluation can derive essential conclusions for improving the process. Evaluative Follow-Up is not performed by any of the interview partners.

The Case Management process of the individual clients is followed with varying intensity by the interview partners. In part the counseling of the client ends after planning is completed. For these cases, implementation is sole responsibility of the clients and their relatives.

4 Discussion

From the empirical results and the literature the design recommendations were derived. These are structured according to the phases of Case Management as follows. For the Outreaching/Case Finding/Intaking phase it can be assumed that the facilitators represent an essential factor for establishing initial contact. It appears important to comprehensively inform, make aware and brief the employees in health and social care about the - to a wide extent - unknown field of AAL and further about the promise of AAL-Case Management. In course of the Assessment phase it is possible to resort to existing standardized instruments from health care. For acceptance of the - currently - rather unknown AAL-Tools the comprehensive inclusion of relatives and additional service providers seems necessary at this stage of the process. In course of Planning Assistance the combination of AAL-products and services offered by different service providers takes place. Close cooperation of all involved parties can be considered a factor for success. An addition, the topics of funding and options for testing the AAL products should be provided for. Contract Management is the point of concrete interconnection of all participants. Close counsel by the AAL-Case Management is very important in face of the complexity and novelty of the AAL-Tools. In the Monitoring/Assisting Observation phase the AAL-Case Managers should give attention to comprehensive enrollment of the involved parties, provide personal and personalized support options as well as monitor assembly, installation and adaptation of the AAL products. The findings in literature as well as the positive experience in empirical analysis very strongly indicated that Evaluations should be conducted systematically. Also performing Evaluating Follow-Up after a certain period of time might positively contribute to assessing sustainability of the AAL Case Management and AAL Tools.

Comprehensive and integrated counseling and assistance of the clients by AAL-Case Managers appears sensible as the implementation of AAL – in tendency – requires a high number of participants and comprehensive knowledge of the fields of social and health care as well as technology are indispensable. Due the complexity in AAL the termination of assistance after completion of planning is not recommended. Instead, the full process should be dealt with by both clients and AAL-Case Manager to ensure successful provision of service.

5 Contributions to the Field and Conclusions

Based upon the design recommendations ten quintessential demands of the AAL Case Management were derived. From the perspective of the clients these are as follows:

- My needs are in the focus.
- The Case Manager considers himself comprehensively responsible for me.

- I am assisted throughout the whole process.
- The Case Manager records what I actually need.
- The Case Management is not limited to AAL. I am also offered other appliances and service which support and facilitate me in living as self-dependently as possible.
- The Case Manager has full overview of possible offers and services.
- The Case Manager seek to find a simple and cost-efficient solution which suits me.
- I receive advice independent of economic interests of the Case Management.
- I receive proven products and I can test the products myself prior to purchase.
- In case of questions I can turn to a familiar person.

The ten stated requirements could find application as trend-setting guidelines for developing services of a concrete AAL Case Management.

References

1. Bundesministerium für Bildung und Forschung. http://www.aal-deutschland.de
2. Georgieff, P.: Ambient Assisted Living: Marktpotentiale IT-unterstützter Pflege für ein selbstbestimmtes Altern. FAZIT-Schriftenreihe, MFG Stiftung, Baden-Württemberg (2004)
3. Gersch, M.: Tragfähige (?) Geschäftsmodelle im Bereich "E-Health@Home". E-Health@Home Tagung, Duisburg (2009)
4. Liesenfeld, J., Loss, K.: Geschäftsmodelle für Dienstleistungen im Bereich der Telemedizin und E-Health@home. 3. Deutscher AAL-Kongress, Berlin (2010)
5. Prilla, M., Rascher, I.: AAL? Lieber nicht! Eine praktische Betrachtung von Barrieren des Transfers von AAL-Lösungen in den Markt und ihrer Überwindung. 5. Deutscher AAL-Kongress, Berlin (2012)
6. Hastedt, I.: Geschäftsmodellentwicklung im Projekt 'Lange selbstbestimmt zu Hause leben durch situative Assistenzsysteme und bedarfsgerechte Dienstleistungen für pflegende Angehörige'. 5. Deutscher AAL-Kongress, Berlin (2012)
7. Hartmann, A., Vollmer, E.: Das AAL-Projekt WohnSelbst: Erfahrungen und neue Wege. 5. Deutscher AAL-Kongress, Berlin (2012)
8. Kleve, H.: Case management. In: Kleve, H., Haye, B., Hampe-Grosser, A., Müller, M. (eds.) Systemisches Case Management, pp. 40–56. Carl-Auer-Systeme, Heidelberg (2006)
9. Ewers, M.: Das anglo-amerikanische case management. In: Ewers, M. (ed.) Case Management in Theorie und Praxis, pp. 53–90. Huber, Bern (2005)
10. Wissert, M.: Tools und Werkzeuge beim case management. Case Manag. 3, 43–46 (2006)
11. Glaser, B., Strauss, A.: Grounded Theory: Strategien qualitativer Forschung. Huber Verlag, Bern (1998)
12. Flick, U.: Triangulation. VS Verlag für Sozialwissenschaften, Wiesbaden (2008)

What People with Dementia Want: Designing MARIO an Acceptable Robot Companion

Dympna Casey[1(✉)], Heike Felzmann[1], Geoff Pegman[2],
Christos Kouroupetroglou[3], Kathy Murphy[1],
Adamantios Koumpis[4], and Sally Whelan[1]

[1] School of Nursing & Midwifery National University of Ireland,
Galway, Ireland
{dympna.casey,Heike.Felzmann,kathy.murphy,
sally.whelan}@nuigalway.ie
[2] RU Robots, Manchester M28 1WF, UK
geoff.pegman@rurobots.co.uk
[3] CARETTA NET, Ethn. Antistaseos 32, Ampelokipi,
Thessaloniki 56334, Greece
chris.kourou@caretta-net.gr
[4] University of Passau, Innstraße 41, 94032 Passau, Germany
Adamantios.Koumpis@uni-passau.de

Abstract. Companion robots designed for PWD need to be customised to meet individual needs if they are to be perceived as useful and acceptable. This paper presents a brief review of the literature on the usefulness of robots for people with dementia; it also includes an overview of the ethical considerations that inform robot development and a description of a qualitative study which describes how people with dementia and other key stakeholders helped to design and shape this robot. An overview of the unique aspect of the MARIO robot and the scientific impact of this work is also presented.

Keywords: Companion robots · People with dementia · User led design

1 The R&D or Application Idea

The number of people with dementia is expected to double every 20 years to 66 million by 2030 and 115 million by 2050 [1]. More than a third of people with dementia have reported loneliness [2]. Robots have the potential to combat the devastating impact of loneliness in people with dementia by improving mood, quality of life [3] and reduce social isolation by facilitating people with dementia (PWD) to maintain social contacts. However companion robots designed for PWD need to be customised to meet individual needs if they are to be perceived as useful and acceptable. It is imperative therefore that technologists and robot developers talk and listen to what people with dementia and their carers say about having a companion robot and what it is they would like a robot companion to be able to do for them. However there is little reported in the literature as to how this can be done and what it is people with dementia would like to see in a robot companion.

© Springer International Publishing Switzerland 2016
K. Miesenberger et al. (Eds.): ICCHP 2016, Part I, LNCS 9758, pp. 318–325, 2016.
DOI: 10.1007/978-3-319-41264-1_44

2 State of the Art

Dautenhahn (2007) defines companion robots as being useful and possessing social intelligence and skills which enable them to interact with people in a socially acceptable manner [4].

2.1 Use of Social Robots for PWD

Paro, a seal-like robot, and other zoomorphic robots have built on the success of animal therapy and been successfully used to facilitate therapeutic work with PWD, to enhance social interactions and reduce social isolation [5–9]. Robotic animals can be more acceptable than real animals for reasons of safety, hygiene, and being hypoallergenic. Paro has been the most widely studied zoomorphic robot adopted into practice. Other zoomorphic robots include Pleo, a dinosaur, and Aibo, a robotic dog. Studies reveal positive attitudes towards robotic dogs [10]. In one small short term study in an American residential home, Aibo was found to stimulate more social interaction than a real dog [11].

Robotic dolls are an alternative to zoomorphic robots for use with PWD who may have negative feelings towards animal robots. The robotic doll Babyloid was compared with Paro in terms of acceptability, with older people (n = 29) living in a Japanese nursing home [12]. Both robots were rated highly for acceptability but Paro was preferred. A humanoid socially intelligent robot providing a music based game has also been used for cognitive therapy [13]. This robot provides PWD with verbal and non-verbal feedback aiming to stimulate concentration on a game. It was tested with older people with cognitive impairment (n = 9) residing in a senior living care facility. All participants responded to the music provided by the robot. Those with the more severe dementia responded for relatively less time and one responded after 6 months. Two people with mild dementia enjoyed the game, but six with severe dementia did not respond to it.

Robots are also being developed to improve contact between PWD living in residential care and their families. Giraff, a mobile telepresence robot with internet connectivity and skype, was assessed for feasibility with PWD (n = 6) through observing them making 6 calls during a 6 week period [14]. Semi-structured interviews were also conducted. PWD were able to recognise the telepresence robot as a representation of their family member. In addition participants' emotional response and engagement improved and they found Giraff enjoyable to use and it improved their social connectedness.

2.2 Perceived Usefulness (PU)

In order to be accepted, social robots need to be perceived by users as useful and relevant to their current unmet needs [15–19]. A mismatch between needs and the solutions offered by robots are a barrier to acceptance and robot adoption. Hawkey et al. (2005) found carers and PWD disagreed as to what they wanted from a robotic device designed to help deal with repeated questioning. PWD wanted information about future events long before they were due to occur whereas carers wanted information given half hour or less before an event [20].

In order to identify robots as useful, unmet needs have to be perceived [16]. In addition carers and PWD have different unmet needs and can envisage robot uses differently [21, 22].

2.3   Perceived Ease of Use (PEOU)

PEOU is important as evidence suggests carers accept robots or reject them on the basis of whether or not they are usable for PWD. Some carer relatives consider PWD will not be able to use robots due to their cognitive deficits [17, 23]. Kerssens et al. (2015) conducted a small study with PWD (n = 7) and their life partner carers to test the feasibility and acceptability of using Companion, a touch screen technology to deliver psychosocial interventions. A life story interview was completed with both the carer and PWD and the robot was then personalised with participants' own photographs, videos and messages from people they trusted [24]. Over a 3 week period participants used Companion. Carers also selected between one and four symptoms to be targeted as goals for intervention. Other measures recorded included the PWD and carer's expectation of the technology and Davis [25] scales of PEOU and PU. Post intervention results revealed that Companion was easy to use, and it significantly facilitated meaningful positive engagement and simplified the carers' daily lives.

3   Ethical Considerations

The use of care robots is considered ethically contentious for a potentially vulnerable group like persons with dementia. The Care Centred Value Sensitive Design (CCVSD) approach for care robots aims to address these concerns by ensuring both at the design and implementation stage that robots do not endanger and where possible enhance the realisation of ethically valuable forms of care [26, 27].

In the MARIO project, an extensive ethical framework was developed at the outset to analyse the potential ethical challenges. The framework was informed by the ethical literature, stakeholder perspectives, and consultation with academic experts, formal carers and persons with dementia. This framework underpinned the development of a set of ethics checklists which specify expectations of good ethical practice, drawing on core ethical principles and concepts in healthcare ethics, research ethics and value sensitive design (VSD). Particularly prominent ethical challenges in relation to the use of care robots include the following:

1. The nature of care and replacement of human care: There are significant concerns that the use of robots may contribute to a reductive understanding of the nature of care, reducing it to the effective and safe performance of specific tasks, without consideration of the importance of the interpersonal experience of care for both carer and care recipient [28–30].

2. User autonomy: Design decisions determine whether robots are likely to diminish or enhance a user's autonomy [26, 31]. Paternalistic restrictions on users' activities by the robot are ethically problematic, although they can be justifiable under certain circumstances [28].

3. Dignity and deception: Some care robots are considered to negatively affect users' dignity through infantilisation [32, 33]. However robots could be designed to potentially show more respect and patient behaviour toward users than is sometimes possible with human carers [32].

4. Attachment to and dependency on the robot: Robot users may get emotionally attached to their robots. While such attachment is desirable for increasing robot acceptance, it also has the potential to be emotionally harmful [29, 33]. A phased withdrawal protocol will be implemented with MARIO to avoid abrupt withdrawal. Care also will to be taken to ensure that the robot does not deskill users.

5. Risk and safety considerations: Robots that engage in autonomous physical action raise safety concerns, by potentially creating obstacles or acting in unpredictable ways.

6. Privacy and data protection: Robots whose functionalities include capturing user information raise significant privacy and data protection issues.

7. Informed consent: Given the cognitive impairments associated with dementia, particular care needs to be taken that such communication takes place when the person is able to engage with the information, that the information is adapted to their information processing abilities and that no pressure is put on users if they have misgivings about participating. Full ethical approval will be obtained in advance of MARIO arriving in any pilot site.

4 Methodology Used

The MARIO project aims to address the difficult challenges of loneliness, isolation and dementia in older persons through companion/service robots. The aim of this small qualitative study reported here was to identify the elements of importance to end users, in particular people with dementia that would make MARIO acceptable to them and more likely that they would engage and interact with it. A descriptive qualitative methodology and semi structured interviews were used to collect the data. Focus group interviews were conducted and involved people with mild to moderate dementia (n = 22) and nursing staff (n = 49) in long stay care residential nursing homes in Ireland and their relatives (n = 6). The CORTE framework [34] was used to guide the interviews with people with dementia. This guide consists of four main areas; gaining COnsent, maximizing Responses, Telling the story, and Ending on a high (CORTE guide). This process maximizes the meaningful involvement of persons with dementia, ensuring that their voices are heard and to the fore. Qualitative content analysis was used to analyse the data. Ethical approval was obtained from the University Ethics Committee.

5 R&D Work and Results

The findings from people with dementia and health care staff reveal that similar to some of the findings from the literature, acceptance is influenced by a variety of factors including the ability of MARIO to have a friendly face; to be able to customize MARIO's appearance e.g. putting a shirt on MARIO; to speak slowly and loudly; to know them as a person knowing their likes and dislikes, to be useful, to be able to play their favorite music, or read them a book, show them a movie, to connect them to their families and friends e.g. via Skype; to be able to locate keys or handbags, to remind them when to take their medications, remind them of important events and appointments; that MARIO would have access to their life story, their interests and hobbies and use this information to foster conversations and reminisce about events that they could remember more easily. People with dementia and health care staff were all receptive to the idea of having MARIO as a companion robot and the need for MARIO to be able to prompt, guide and support the person with dementia as their memory failed was considered crucial. The findings from this work are now being used to guide technologists to ensure that the MARIO robot has the functionalities that best meet the needs of the key stakeholders, making it more likely to be acceptable and that the resultant robot is truly a user led initiative.

6 The Unique Aspects of the MARIO Robot System

MARIO combines a range of functionalities which both make it a unique robot system but also one that is uniquely able to provide support to PWD, their caregivers and related healthcare professionals. At its heart, MARIO aims to provide cognitive support to PWD, rather than the physical support of many other assistive and companion robots. The key functionalities currently under development that in combination provide these unique capabilities are outlined below:

1. Speech as a primary mode of interaction: Like several companion robots (e.g. Blue Frog Robotics's Buddy and Aldebaran's Pepper) MARIO communicates primarily through speech allowing non-contact and at a distance interaction.
2. Entertainment functions: As with several home oriented companion robots, MARIO is equipped with entertainment functions for PWD in the form of games, music, audio books and videos. However, unlike most systems, these entertainment functions may be configured by the primary care-giver to be personalised to the needs of the individual PWD. A unique capability of MARIO will be the ability to engage the PWD in reminiscing about their past as well as people and places with emotional significance.
3. Information provision: Several guide robots (e.g. WeRobots Autonomous Guides or Engineered Arts Robothespian) are designed to provide people with information about their immediate surroundings and directions. MARIO combines these functions with functions more normally found on hand held devices, such as calendar reminders, medication reminders, personal and factual information (contacts; day of the week) and information about the location of places and objects in order to be an information resource for the PWD.

4. Social connectedness: There are several virtual presence robots (e.g. Giraff Technologies' Giraff, RP-VITA from iRobot and InTouch Health, or Revolve Robotics Kubi). However, MARIO uses mobile telepresence to enable the PWD to maintain and extend social contact by embedding the capability within a social networking system designed for PWD.

5. Adapting responses to the user's emotional state: Many robots, mainly designed to resemble animals, aim to have an emotional contact with the user (e.g. Intelligent Systems' PARO or Hasbro's companion pets). MARIO, however, does not specifically aim to engender emotional attachment but rather to try and assess the emotional state of the PWD in order to modify the nature and content of the dialogue to facilitate understanding.

6. Health monitoring: As with MARIO, several developmental companion robots (e.g. the EC Framework 7 Accompany project) have as part of their function the monitoring of the person and collection of health data. MARIO takes this a stage further and undertakes formal assessments in terms of undertaking parts of the Comprehensive Geriatric Assessment (CGA) in order to assist healthcare professionals and to provide an ongoing assessment of the PWD's capabilities.

7 The Scientific and Practical Impact or Contributions to the Field

This paper demonstrates that people with dementia have the capacity to voice their needs and wants in terms of robot companions. The methodology described here will help researchers and technologists to ensure that the social companion robots they develop are more likely to be acceptable to people with dementia and best meet their needs.

8 Conclusion and Planned Activities

The findings, from the aforementioned qualitative work are currently being used to help ensure that MARIO is fit for purpose. The first pilot and iteration of MARIO will commence in September 2016, only then will the acceptability of MARIO as a companion robot be known.

Acknowledgements. The research leading to these results has received funding from the European Union Horizons 2020 – the Framework Programme for Research and Innovation (2014–2020) under grant agreement 643808 Project MARIO "Managing active and healthy aging with use of caring service robots".

References

1. Prince, M., Guerchet, M., Prina, M.: Policy Brief for Heads of Government. The Global Impact of Dementia 2013–2050. In: Alzheimer's Disease International, London (2013)
2. Kane, M., Cook, L.: Dementia 2013 The Hidden Voice of Loneliness. In: Alzheimer's Society, London (2013)
3. Moyle, W., Cooke, M., Beattie, E., Jones, C., Klein, B., Cook, G., Gray, C.: Exploring the effect of companion robots on emotional expression in older adults with dementia. A pilot randomized controlled trial. J. Geriatr. Nurs. **39**, 46–53 (2013)
4. Dautenhahn, K., Woods, S., Kaouri, C., Walter, M., Koay, K., Werry, I.: What is a robot companion – friend, assistant or butler. In: International Conference on Intelligent Robots and System, IROS, Edmonton, Canada (2005)
5. Chang, W.L., Sabanovic, S., Huber, L.: Use of seal-like robot PARO in sensory group therapy for older adults with dementia. In: Proceedings of the 8th ACM/LEEE International Conference on Human-Robot Interaction, pp. 101–102. IEEE Press (2013)
6. Klein, B., Cook, G.: Emotional robotics in elder care – a comparison of findings in the UK and Germany. In: Ge, S.S., Khatib, O., Cabibihan, J.-J., Simmons, R., Williams, M.-A. (eds.) ICSR 2012. LNCS, vol. 7621, pp. 108–117. Springer, Heidelberg (2012)
7. Sung, H.C., Chang, S.M., Chin, M.Y., Lee, W.L.: Robot-assisted therapy for improving social interactions and activity participation among institutionalized older adults. A pilot study. Asia-Pac. Psychiatry **7**, 1–5 (2015)
8. Takayanagi, K., Kirita, T., Shibata, T.: Comparison of verbal and emotional responses of elderly people with mild/moderate dementia and those with severe dementia in responses to seal robot. PARO. Front. Aging Neurosci. **6**(257), 1–5 (2014)
9. Wada, K., Shibata, T., Kawaguchi, Y.: Long-term robot therapy in a health service facility for the aged - a case study for 5 years. In: 11th IEEE International Conference on Rehabilitation Robotics, 1 and 2, pp. 1084–1087 (2009)
10. Marx, M.S., Cohen-Mansfield, J., Regier, N.G., Dakheel-Ali, M., Srihari, A., Thein, K.: The impact of different dog-related stimuli on engagement of persons with dementia. Am. J. Alzheimers Dis. Dement. **25**, 37–45 (2010)
11. Kramer, S.C., Friedmann, E., Bernstein, P.L.: Comparison of the effect of human interaction, animal-assisted therapy, and AIBO-assisted therapy on long-term care residents with dementia. Anthrozoos **22**, 43–57 (2009)
12. Furuta, Y., Kanoh, M., Shimizu, T., Shimizu, M., Makamuara, T.: Subjective evaluation of use of Babyloid for doll therapy. In: IEEE World Congress on Computational Intelligence, WCCI, Brisbane Australia (2012)
13. Tapus, A., Vieru, A.-M.: Robot cognitive stimulation for the elderly. In: Ferrández Vicente, J.M., Álvarez Sánchez, J.R., de la Paz López, F., Toledo Moreo, F. (eds.) IWINAC 2013, Part I. LNCS, vol. 7930, pp. 94–102. Springer, Heidelberg (2013)
14. Moyle, W., Jones, C., Cooke, M., O'Dwyer, S., Sung, B., Drummond, S.: Connecting the person with dementia and family, a feasibility study of a telepresence robot. BMC Geriatr. **14**, 7 (2014)
15. de Graaf, M., Allouch, S., Klamer, T.: Sharing a life with Harvey: exploring the acceptance of and relationship-building with a social robot. Comput. Hum. Behav. **43**, 1–14 (2015)
16. Stafford, R.: The contribution of people's attitudes and perceptions to the acceptance of eldercare robots. The University of Auckland (2013)
17. Pino, M., Boulay, M., Jouen, F., Rigaud, A.S.: "Are we ready for robots that care for us?" Attitudes and opinions of older adults toward socially assistive robots. Front. Aging Neurosci. **7**(141), 1–15 (2015)

18. Mitzner, T.L., Chen, T.L., Kemp, C.C., Rogers, W.A.: Identifying the potential for robotics to assist older adults in different living environments. Int. J. Soc. Robot. 6(2), 213–227 (2014)
19. Heerink, M., Krose, B., Evers, V., Wielinga, B.: Assessing acceptance of assistive social agent technology by older adults: the Almere model. Int. J. Soc. Robot. 2, 361–375 (2010)
20. Hawkey, K., Inkpen, K., Rockwood, K., McAllister, M, Slonim, J.: Requirements gathering with Alzheimer,s patients and caregivers. In: 7th International ACM SIGAACCESS Conference on Computers and Accessibility, pp. 142–149. ACM, Baltimore, USA (2005)
21. Saaskilahti, K., Kangaskorte, R., Pieska, S., Jauhiainen, J., Luimula, M.: Needs and user acceptance of older adults for mobile service robot. In: 21st IEEE International Symposium on Robot and Human Interactive Communication, RO-MAN, pp. 559–564. Institute of Electrical and Electronics Engineers Inc., Paris, France (2012)
22. Broadbent, R., Tamagawa, N., Kerse, B., Knock, A.: Retirement home staff and residents' preferences for healthcare robots. In: 18th IEEE International Symposium on Robot and Human Communication, pp, 645–650. IEEE (2009)
23. Frennert, S., Eftring, H., Östlund, B.: Older people's involvement in the development of a social assistive robot. In: Herrmann, G., Pearson, M.J., Lenz, A., Bremner, P., Spiers, A., Leonards, U. (eds.) ICSR 2013. LNCS, vol. 8239, pp. 8–18. Springer, Heidelberg (2013)
24. Kerssens, C., Kumar, R., Adams, A.E., Knott, C.C., Matalenas, L., Sanford, J.A., Rogers, W.A.: Personalized technology to support older adults with and without cognitive impairment living at home. Am. J. Alzheimer Dis. Dement. 30, 85–97 (2015)
25. Davis, F., Bagozzi, R., Warshaw, P.: User acceptance of computer technology. A comparison of two theoretical models. Manag. Sci. 35, 982–1003 (1989)
26. van Wynsberghe, A.: Healthcare Robots: Ethics, Design, and Implementation. Routledge, London (2015)
27. van Wynsberghe, A.: Designing robots for care: care centered value-sensitive design. Sci. Eng. Ethics 19, 407–433 (2013)
28. Sorell, T., Draper, H.: Robot carers, ethics, and older people. Ethics Inf. Technol. 16, 183–195 (2014)
29. Sparrow, R., Sparrow, L.: In the hands of machines? The future of aged care. Mind. Mach. 16, 141–161 (2006)
30. Vallor, S.: Carebots and caregivers: sustaining the ethical ideal of care in the twenty-first century. Philos. Technol. 24, 251–268 (2011)
31. Pearson, Y., Borenstein, J.: Creating "companions" for children: the ethics of designing esthetic features for robots. AI & Soc. 29, 23–31 (2014)
32. Sharkey, A.: Robots and human dignity: a consideration of the effects of robot care on the dignity of older people. Ethics Inf. Technol. 16, 63–75 (2014)
33. Sharkey, A., Sharkey, N.: Granny and the robots: ethical issues in robot care for the elderly. Ethics Inf. Technol. 14, 27–40 (2012)
34. Murphy, K., Jordan, F., Hunter, A., Cooney, A., Casey, D.: Articulating the strategies for maximising the inclusion of people with dementia in qualitative research studies. Dement. Int. J. Soc. Res. Pract. 14, 800–824 (2015)

The EnrichMe Project

A Robotic Solution for Independence and Active Aging of Elderly People with MCI

Claudia Salatino[1(✉)], Valerio Gower[1], Meftah Ghrissi[2], Adriana Tapus[3],
Katarzyna Wieczorowska-Tobis[4], Aleksandra Suwalska[4], Paolo Barattini[5],
Roberto Rosso[6], Giulia Munaro[6], Nicola Bellotto[7], and Herjan van den Heuvel[8]

[1] IRCCS Fondazione Don Carlo Gnocchi Onlus, Milan, Italy
{csalatino,vgower}@dongnocchi.it
[2] Robosoft Services Robots, Bidart, France
meftah.ghrissi@robosoft.com
[3] U2IS, ENSTA ParisTech, Université Paris-Saclay, Palaiseau cedex, France
adriana.tapus@ensta-paristech.fr
[4] Uniwersytet Medyczny Im Karola Marcinkowskiego w Poznaniu, Poznan, Poland
kwt@tobis.pl, asuwalska@gmail.com
[5] Kontor 46, Turin, Italy
paolo.barattini@kontor46.eu
[6] Elettronica Bio Medicale, Foligno (PG), Italy
{rosso,munaro}@tesan.it
[7] University of Lincoln, Lincoln, UK
nbellotto@lincoln.ac.uk
[8] Stichting Smart Homes, Eindhoven, Netherlands
herjan.heuvel@gmail.com

Abstract. Mild cognitive impairment (MCI) is a state related to ageing, and sometimes evolves to dementia. As there is no pharmacological treatment for MCI, a non-pharmacological approach is very important. The use of Information and Communication Technologies (ICT) in care and assistance services for elderly people increases their chances of prolonging independence thanks to better cognitive efficiency. Robots are seen to have the potential to support the care and independence of elderly people. The project ENRICHME (funded by the EU H2020 Programme) focuses on developing and testing technologies for supporting elderly people with MCI in their living environment for a long time. This paper describes the results of the activities conducted during the first year of the ENRICHME project, in particular the definition of user needs and requirements and the resulting system architecture.

Keywords: Robotics · AAL · User requirements · Residential care · Long term human robot interaction · Gerontology · Non-invasive physiological monitoring

© Springer International Publishing Switzerland 2016
K. Miesenberger et al. (Eds.): ICCHP 2016, Part I, LNCS 9758, pp. 326–334, 2016.
DOI: 10.1007/978-3-319-41264-1_45

1   Introduction

The population of the western countries is ageing. Age-related changes in mental and physical abilities can make living independently at home challenging or even impossible for the elderly. Mild cognitive impairment (MCI) is a state related to ageing, and sometimes evolves to dementia. A subgroup of people with MCI will not develop dementia and will not experience the deterioration of cognitive functions over time. As there is no pharmacological treatment for MCI, a non-pharmacological approach is very important [1]. These measures include lifestyle changes, such as diet modification and smoking cessation, and an increase of intellectual, physical and social activities [2]. The use of Information and Communication Technologies (ICT) in care and assistance services for elderly people increases chances of prolonging independence thanks to better cognitive efficiency [3]. Moreover Tapus et al. [4] showed that an in-home socially assistive robotic agent can improve the ability of the patient to function at home and within society. Over the past decades, many robots for the elderly have been developed, aiming to support a range of different activities of elderly people: robots are seen to have the potential to support the care and independence of elderly people [5]. An interesting systematic review [6] recently investigated robots being developed to support the elderly in their independent living and categorized these robots based on their Technology Readiness Level (TRL). Only a few projects including mobile autonomous robot companions operating in real life have been implemented in Europe so far. Additionally, only some of them have been designed for users with cognitive impairment.

The project ENRICHME "Enabling Robot and assisted living environment for Independent Care and Health Monitoring of the Elderly" (www.enrichme.eu, funded by the EU H2020 Programme) among other research works on the same topic focuses on testing technologies for supporting elderly people with MCI particularly in their living environment and for a long time. It tackles the progressive decline of cognitive capacity in the ageing population developing an integrated platform with a mobile service robot for long-term human monitoring and interaction, which helps the elderly person to remain independent and active for longer by enriching his/her day-to-day experiences at home. The key research questions of ENRICHME are the following:

- Which are the best robotic and AAL services enabling older people with Mild Cognitive Impairments (MCI) to remain independent and safe?
- How can we provide experimental long-term evidence demonstrating that robotic and AAL services are effective to prolong the independent living of the elderly at home and in community dwellings?
- How can we provide experimental long-term evidence demonstrating that older people and caregivers accept robotic and AAL systems?

The ENRICHME robotic solution will be based upon an existing robotic platform: the Kompaï robot [7] developed by one of the project partners: Robosoft. This paper describes the results of the first year activities of the ENRICHME project, in particular the definition of user needs and requirements and the resulting system architecture.

2 The ENRICHME Approach

The ENRICHME project is aimed at developing and testing a novel coupling of a socially intelligent robot with unobtrusive and unencumbering activity tracking devices that, together, provide real-time, adaptive and readable feedback to users. Novel context-aware Human Robot Interaction (HRI) will provide tools for cognitive stimulation and social inclusion, which improve over time by learning from and adapting to the state of the user. A professional infrastructure of networked care will widen the social sphere of intervention in support of elderly and caregivers. An iterative design process goes through the duration of the whole project for the collection of user requirements, verification of the developed system and validation in collaboration with end-users (elderly, formal and informal care personnel, family members, etc.) to guarantee the adherence of the project to real world situations and settings.

2.1 Evaluation of User Needs and Requirements

Since the evaluation of robot-related needs and requirements of elderly individuals is a complex task, it is crucial to combine different methods to increase the validity of the results. A mixed method, with quantitative-qualitative evaluations has been used to analyse the robot-related aspects of everyday life, so that the strengths of each are emphasized [8]. The objective was to assess whether ENRICHME concept in the whole and its functional requirements could be acceptable for potential users, to which extent, and if additional requirements were needed. To measure subjects preferences about system functionalities and characteristics, quantitative evaluations were needed; in order to give the respondents the opportunity to be proactive, the evaluation was designed to survey their free thoughts.

Based on the literature review and the expertise of the ENRICHME project partners [9, 10], the Users' Needs, Requirements and Abilities Questionnaire (UNRAQ) was developed [3]. The UNRAQ is composed of four parts. Part 1, the introductory part of the questionnaire characterizes the responders. Part 2 concerns the appearance of the robot and the willingness of the participant to own one. Part 3 includes a list of statements to which the participant is asked to express his/her level of agreement-disagreement. These statements pertain to four areas: the interaction with the robot, the role of the robot, some social aspects, and the assistive role. Answers are structured using a 5-point Likert scale. The final part 4 of UNRAQ is the creativity box. UNRAQ was developed in English and then localized into the other five languages of the ENRICHME consortium (French, Greek, Italian, Dutch, and Polish). Pictures of the Kompaï robot were shown to the end-users before the survey, in order to give them a more realistic image of the robot concept.

A focus group discussion was chosen as the qualitative method to elicit user needs and requirements. The focus group interviews were organised on the basis of a detailed script prepared for this purpose. The script was written in English and translated into Greek, Italian, and Polish to be used in each country. The script included an introduction and a warm-up exercise to elicit a discussion about the attitude of the participants towards new technologies. The main part of the focus group interview started with the presentation of short videos about the robots. The discussion that followed had two sections focused on two scenarios created by the consortium partners describing a typical daily routine of two potential users of the ENRICHME system.

For both interviews and focus groups, the inclusion criteria for elderly individuals were the following: being aged 65 years and older, being able to understand and answer the questionnaire or to take part in the focus group; researchers also tried to include the same number of women and men within the sample. Caregivers were both informal [those who take care of someone with no professional background in care] and formal caregivers [those who are professionally prepared to provide care]. Respondents were recruited among those who were interested in sharing their opinions regarding the use of robots to assist elderly persons living at home and who accepted to take part in the study. The participants were selected in senior clubs, care centres, out-patients' clinics. The inclusion was based on their informed consent to participate. As a whole 327 individuals in all 6 countries of the ENRICHME consortium were involved; 126 participants were elderly (mean age 75.3) and 201 were caregivers.

3   Results

3.1   Definition of User Needs and Requirements

In the following, the results of the initial evaluation phase through UNRAQ and focus groups are summarized.

Three quarters of the participants accepted the appearance of the robot. Half of the participants would like to have a robot at home, and as many as two thirds would like to use it. In the entire analysed group just one quarter of participants thought that the elderly were ready to operate the robot and able to cope with this task. Half of the participants thought that the elderly wanted to increase their knowledge about the robots so as to be able to operate them (Fig. 1). A vast majority (nearly 100 %) of participants thought that robots would make the life of the elderly easier.

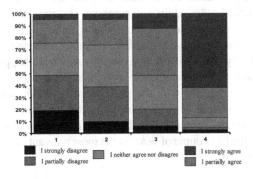

Fig. 1. Detailed opinions of participants related to the following statements: 1. The elderly are prepared to interact with a robot, 2. The elderly are able to manage with the robot, 3. The elderly want to increase their knowledge about the robots to be able to operate them, 4. The robot should instruct the elderly person what to do in the case of problem with its operation

In the opinion of the elderly and their caregivers, an important function of the robot is monitoring the safety of the home, a significant majority (approximately 95 %) of participants also wanted the robot to monitor the state of health of the elderly, and call for help whenever necessary. A little over half of participants thought that the elderly persons should have control over the robot. The elderly want to be able to decide whether or not to use the robot at a given time; however, focus groups participants stressed that the robot should call the medical staff in emergency situations without following the owner's orders. There was also considerable acceptance of the fact that the robot could detain a lot of information about the user (social, medical, and other).

Opinions that the robot could decrease the sense of loneliness and improve the mood of the elderly person were basically positive. However, participants also stated the obvious, i.e. that a robot would never replace another human being. Approximately three quarters of elderly participants reported that the robot could encourage the elderly to enhance their contacts with friends. Nearly 90 % of the participants expected that the robot should have entertainment functions. Around 70 % of the participants thought that the robot should detect the owner's mood (facial expression). Here, doubts mostly pertained to the fact that facial expression is insufficient for reliable determination of the mood.

3.2   Personas, Scenarios & Use Cases

Personas, scenarios and use cases methodology [11] has been and will be used throughout the duration of the project. Personas and scenarios presented within project proposal were defined according to the analysis of typical use cases in each country and considering those people who may have more benefits from ENRICHME experience in terms of improvement of quality of life, with some input from real-world experiences provided by the clinical partners of the project.

Personas and scenarios have been updated following the latest insights from interviews and focus groups. Figure 2 shows an example of persona. Ranking of functional and non-functional requirements was calculated on the base of percentage of agreement expressed by interviewed older adults and caregivers through UNRAQ questionnaire. Monitoring health status, reminding important tasks (i.e. taking medications), management of high risk and emergency situations are the most accepted functionalities. One of the worries of elderly people is the potential for accidents happening at home; for both elderly participants and the caregivers, social functions seem less important for the studied end-users in comparison with the assistive roles, confirming findings of Ezer et al. [12] and Faucounau et al. [13]. A selection of top-rated functional and non-functional requirements was then compared with the results of requirements and evaluation studies performed in the last couple of years in the most relevant EU projects with actual robotics and AAL systems.

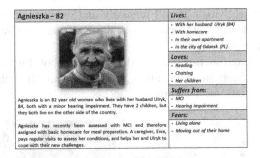

Agnieszka – 82		Lives:
		- With her husband Ulryk (84)
		- With homecare
		- In their own apartment
		- In the city of Gdansk (PL)
		Loves:
		- Reading
		- Chatting
		- Her children
		Suffers from:
Agnieszka is an 82 year old woman who lives with her husband Ulryk, 84, both with a minor hearing impairment. They have 2 children, but they both live on the other side of the country.		- MCI
		- Hearing impairment
		Fears:
Agnieszka has recently been assessed with MCI and therefore assigned with basic homecare for meal preparation. A caregiver, Ewa, pays regular visits to assess her conditions, and helps her and Ulryk to cope with their new challenges.		- Living alone
		- Moving out of their home

Fig. 2. Exemplification of a persona description

Updated personas, scenarios and requirements were used to elaborate seven use cases: 1: Games & Entertainment; 2: Time Management; 3: Social Contact; 4: Medication & Nutrition; 5: Health Monitoring; 6: Comfort at Home; 7: Anomaly Detection. The results obtained by this stage generated specific requirements and concrete use cases, enabling designers and technologists to start with the development phase of the ENRICHME concept.

3.3   The ENRICHME Architecture

Socially intelligent robots are those capable of exhibiting natural-appearing social qualities. This poses a lot of new challenges because the robot must operate in open and unconstrained environments and interact with users who are not technicians. In ENRICHME, an existing interactive service robot is integrated within an assistive living environment and upgraded with the necessary capabilities and technical features to support the independent living of elders. The system will help formal and informal caregivers, as well as medical providers, to monitor and support the elderly at home, in particular those with MCI.

The ENRICHME system has three different levels of intelligence: robot, ambient, and social (Fig. 3).

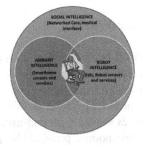

Fig. 3. ENRICHME intelligence

The integrated robot and AAL services will facilitate cognitive capability preservation through reminiscence and biography tools, long-term social interaction and promotion of leisure activities. It will regularly and unobtrusively monitor relevant physiological parameters, motion activities, and other behaviours (e.g., vocal), which are indicative of the person's state.

Some of the existing functionalities of the Kompaï robot (Fig. 4) are autonomous navigation, voice synthesis and recognition, security systems (like obstacles detection, automatic stop on contact, etc.), and internet access.

Fig. 4. Kompaï robot in its previous and current versions

In ENRICHME, this platform is going to be enhanced and customized with new equipment and functionalities: non-invasive sensors for physiological monitoring, advanced vocal and visual interaction capabilities, new software for safe navigation in home environments, learning and adaptation of cognitive capabilities to the user's preferences and needs over time for long term interaction.

The assisted living environment provides complementary sensors and actuators to: localize and monitor human's and robot's activities, reduce the risk of hazards, trigger alerts in case of anomaly detection or in case of erratic human behaviour. An RFID ecosystem is deployed tagging objects, furniture and appliances of particular interest for the everyday life of the user, and equipping the robot with an RFID reader for object localization and identification.

The ENRICHME platform for Networked Care is a visualization interface that will be accessed by the medical personnel to monitor data made available by the robot and the smart home environment and processed by the federated servers.

4   Conclusions and Future Work

The work done until now provided the consortium with the necessary information to confirm and refine the system functionalities and to proceed in their development to be ready for the next evaluation steps. As the second evaluation step, the acceptability, usability and learnability of the proposed system and services, and of the multi-modal human-robot interaction will be evaluated with end users and their caregivers; these tests will be held in two AAL test homes, provided by project partners SMH in the Netherlands and FDG in Italy [14]. The purpose of these tests is to identify overall usability and user-experience flaws, and to improve the actual ENRICHME services, before going for the long-term user studies in peoples' own homes. Following some system improvements, 9 ENRICHME systems will be delivered for the 12 months testing in elderly house facilities. Each testing site, LACE in Lincolnshire, UK, PUMS in Poznan, Poland, AKTIOS in Agia Paraskevi, Greece, will be equipped with 3 systems. Each of the three systems will be assigned for 4 months to a certain elderly person who lives independently within an elderly facility or at her/his own home.

Acknowledgements. The ENRICHME project is funded by European Commission's Horizon 2020 Programme (Grant agreement #643691C). The authors are especially grateful to all persons who accepted to be interviewed and provided valuable information.

References

1. Horr, T., Messinger-Rapport, B., Pillai, J.A.: Systematic review of strengths and limitations of randomized controlled trials for non-pharmacological interventions in mild cognitive impairment: focus on Alzheimer's disease. J. Nutr. Health & Aging **19**(2), 141–153 (2015). doi:10.1007/s12603-014-0565-6
2. Eshkoor, S.A., Hamid, T.A., Mun, C.Y., Ng, C.K.: Mild cognitive impairment and its management in older people. Clin. Interv. Aging **10**, 687 (2015). doi:10.2147/CIA.S73922
3. Cylkowska-Nowak, M., Tobis, S., Salatino, C., Tapus, A., Suwalska, A.: The robot in elderly care. In: Proceedings of SGEM 2015 Conference on Psychology & Psychiatry, Sociology and Health Care, pp. 1007–1014 (2015)
4. Tapus, A., Țăpuș, C., Matarić, M.J.: The use of socially assistive robots in the design of intelligent cognitive therapies for people with dementia. In: IEEE International Conference on Rehabilitation Robotics, ICORR 2009, pp. 924–929. IEEE, June 2009
5. Bekey, G.A.: Co-existing with Robots. In: 2006 IEEE/RSJ International Conference on Intelligent Robots and Systems, pp. nil33–nil33. IEEE, October 2006
6. Bedaf, S., Gelderblom, G.J., De Witte, L.: Overview and categorization of robots supporting independent living of elderly people: what activities do they support and how far have they developed. Assist. Technol. **27**(2), 88–100 (2015). doi:10.1080/10400435.2014.978916
7. http://www.robosoft.com/robotic-solutions/healthcare/kompai/index.html
8. Tashakkoro, A., Teddlie, C.: Handbook of Mixed Methods in Social and Behavioral Research. SAGE Publications, Thousand Oaks (2003)
9. Pigini, L., Facal, D., Blasi, L., Andrich, R.: Service robots in elderly care at home: users' needs and perceptions as a basis for concept development. Technol. Disabil. **24**, 303–311 (2012). doi:10.3233/TAD-120361
10. Schroeter, C., Mueller, S., Volkhardt, M., Einhorn, E., Huijnen, C., van den Heuvel, H., Gross, H.M.: Realization and user evaluation of a companion robot for people with mild cognitive impairments. In: 2013 IEEE International Conference on Robotics and Automation (ICRA), pp. 1153–1159. IEEE, May 2013. doi:10.1109/ICRA.2013.6630717
11. Lidwell, W., Holden, K., Butler, J.: Universal Principles of Design, p. 182. Rockport Publishers, Beverly (2010). ISBN 978-1-61058-065-6
12. Ezer, N., Fisk, A.D., Rogers, W.A.: More than a servant: self-reported willingness of younger and older adults to having a robot perform interactive and critical tasks in the home. Proc. Hum. Factors Ergon. Soc. Ann. Meet. **53**, 136–140 (2009). doi:10.1518/107118109X12524441079382

13. Faucounau, V., Wu, Y., Boulay, M., Maestrutti, M., Rigaud, A., the QuoVADis project: Caregivers' requirements for inhome robotic agent for supporting community-living elderly subjects with cognitive impairment. Technol. Health Care **17**, 33–40 (2009). doi:10.3233/THC-2009-0537

14. Andrich, R., Gower, V., Caracciolo, A., Di Rienzo, M.: The DAT project: a smart home environment for people with disabilities. In: Miesenberger, K., Klaus, J., Zagler, W.L., Karshmer, A.I. (eds.) Computers Helping People with Special Needs. Lecture Notes in Computer Science, vol. 4061, pp. 492–499. Springer, Heidelberg (2006)

Walking Aid Identification Using Wearables

Thomas Moder$^{(\boxtimes)}$, Karin Wisiol, and Manfred Wieser

Working Group Navigation of the Institute of Geodesy,
Graz University of Technology, NAWI Graz, Graz, Austria
{thomas.moder,karin.wisiol,manfred.wieser}@tugraz.at

Abstract. The distribution of wrist-worn wearable devices grows rapidly, also among aging people. Within such wearables, inertial sensors are incorporated and may be used, next to their intended purpose, for identifying the currently used walking aid of the senior. After detecting whether the user is moving or not moving, a machine learning approach can be used to identify the currently used walking aid using acceleration and angular rate features. To overcome the wearable attitude uncertainty, the computed features are based on the normalized measurements of the three sensor axes, and they overlap at approximately 0.25 s. The defined walking aids for this approach include standing, walking normal, use of a walking cane and the use of a walker or a wheelchair. A ten-fold cross validation with the labelled training data delivers recall values of 98 % for a window size of 2.56 s. When predicting the currently used walking aid in real time, blunders may occur in the classification. Such blunders can additionally be overcome by the modelling of the probability of the transition between the use of one walking aid to the use of another. The determination of the used walking aid in real time delivers 97 % correctly identified walking aids within defined test scenarios. The identification of the currently used walking aid is mainly used as input parameter for positioning or routing applications, e.g., planning a path which is walkable with the currently used walking aid.

Keywords: Walking aids · Wearables · Motion recognition

1 Introduction

The wearable electronics market is rapidly growing, and the main share by far belongs to wrist worn devices like smartwatches and fitness bands [1]. Next to that, many seniors are already used to wearing emergency wristbands, usually for safety applications to, for example, execute emergency calls directly. Within state-of-the-art wearable electronics, sensors for communication next to acceleration and angular rate sensors are already present and may be used, next to their intended purpose, for a walking mode identification of seniors. With a prior moving or non-moving detection, it is possible to identify the used walking aid of a pedestrian, based on wrist-worn inertial sensors by machine learning techniques. If the used walking aid of a senior can be detected robustly, it may be a valuable parameter for safety or navigation applications.

© Springer International Publishing Switzerland 2016
K. Miesenberger et al. (Eds.): ICCHP 2016, Part I, LNCS 9758, pp. 335–341, 2016.
DOI: 10.1007/978-3-319-41264-1_46

2   State-of-the-Art

Human motions may be definied as locomotions, daily activities, multimodal motions or equivalents. State-of-the-art surveys exist and are thoroughly discussed in [2]. Generally, human motion recognition can be done with visual systems, physiological sensors or inertial sensors. Originally, inertial sensors were mounted on body parts which receive high impacts from locomotion, like directly on the foot or at the waist. This has evolved to human motion recognition, based on inertial sensors, also with wearable devices, see [3]. The precision and robustness achievable is directly correlated to the defined motions and input features. [4] shows the identification of locomotion modes with hand-held devices based on pattern recognition with inertial sensors. However, for seniors a specific walking aid identification, based on wearable sensors was not conducted so far.

3   Methdodology

The approach for identifying walking aids is tackled in two steps. Firstly, a moving or non-moving detection is carried out and secondly, if moving is detected, the motion recognition for walking aid identification is conducted. It is important that contrary sensors of the wearable device are used for both steps to not correlate both approaches, which possibly leads to unstable behavior. See Fig. 1 for the basic system design of a walking aid identification using wearable sensors.

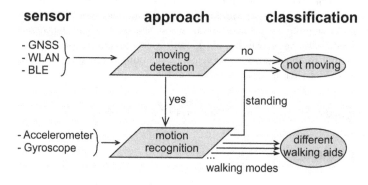

Fig. 1. System design

For the moving or non-moving detection, outdoors and indoors may be differentiated. Outdoors, the Global Navigation Satellite Systems (GNSS) may be used. The velocity information calculated out of the Doppler measurements from the satellite signals is robust enough for a moving or non-moving detection, though its accuracy is directly dependent on the used GNSS chip, which varies between wearables. Depending on the accuracy of the used GNSS sensor, the threshold for the moving or non-moving detection has to be adapted.

Indoors, GNSS signals are not available due to the obvious signal path loss through building structures. However, all state-of-the art wearables either have WLAN or Bluetooth Low Energy (BLE) front-ends for connecting to other devices. Additionally, in almost every building, WLAN or Bluetooth beacons are pinging and are therefore measureable with the wearable device. The measurement receivable within the application programming interface is the Received Signal Strength Indicator (RSSI), which is directly correlated to the distance. A statistical test based on the standard deviation of the received WLAN or Bluetooth RSSI can differ moving from non-moving for indoor scenarios.

When moving is detected based on GNSS, WLAN, or Bluetooth, a motion recognition based on the inertial sensors of the wearable device is realized with a machine learning approach. Inertial sensors include at least the acceleration sensor and, if available, additionally the angular rate sensor of the wearable. The feature computation for the machine learning is based on moving windows, overlapping at approximately 0.25 s, and focuses on norm features of the accelerometer and the gyroscope. In Fig. 2, the defined walking aids which may be identified using wearable sensors, e.g. smartwatch or fitness tracker wristbands (red bar), are shown. In this paper the definition includes standing during phases of rest or transitions between walking aids as well as the walking modes walking normal, use of a walking cane, use of a walker or a wheelchair.

walking normal   walking cane   walker   wheelchair

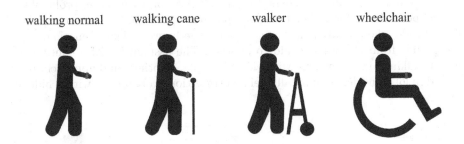

Fig. 2. Walking aid definition (Color figure online)

4   Results

Within first tests, training data was accumulated with all walking aids with four different persons, two males and two females. The machine learning classification was evaluated using seven acceleration as well as seven gyroscope features to achieve a low computational performance of the classification. In Table 1, the recall values of the ten-fold cross validation are shown for different window sizes. The recall values represent a theoretical measure, calculated out of the labelled training data, and represent the probability of correctly identified samples. The accuracy with which the walking aids can be detected is always $> 90\%$, with an average recall rate of about 94 % for a window size of 1.28 s and 98 % for a window size of 2.56 s.

Table 1. Recall values [%] of walking aid identification

Window size [s]	Weighted average	Standing	Walking normal	Walking cane	Walker	Wheel-chair
1.28	94.3	95.2	96.7	92.5	97.0	90.2
2.56	98.1	96.8	99.3	97.3	99.0	97.3
5.12	99.6	98.6	100.0	99.7	99.9	99.0

The classification based on the sample data obviously works more precisely with an increased window size. However, the drawback of long window sizes is the time delay of at least half the window size which occurs while predicting the walking aid identification.

In Fig. 3, a prediction of a test trajectory of a person using two walking aids is shown. The test trajectory starts with the person standing for 10 s, then walking with a walking cane until 85 s, standing again for 10 s, using a walker until 170 s and standing until the end of the time series. Multiple test runs for predictions with similar results were conducted. The prediction of the motions after the classification generally matches the labelled ground truth, though obvious blunders are present.

To eliminate possible blunders, the introduction of a transition probability, like proposed in [5] for locomotions, is a possible approach. A transition probability tackles the probabilistic chance of a change between defined motions, e.g. the change from one walking aid to another. The assumption of a continuous use of walking aids is realistic with elderly people. Another valid approach, presented in [6], considers empirically defined transition probabilities with a hidden

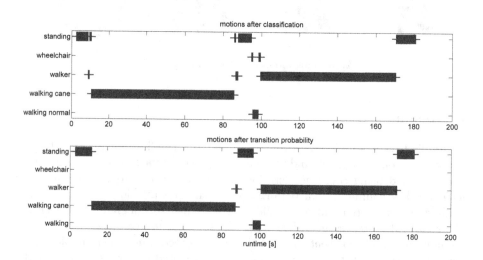

Fig. 3. Walking aid prediction

Markov process directly during classification, though an empirical definition of the transitions between the use of walking aids would be necessary. The prediction of the motions after applying a transition probability according to [5] is shown in the lower plot of Fig. 3. Out of more than 700 samples, 20 samples do not accord to the used walking aid. This equates to roughly 97 % accuracy compared to ground truth observations for the short test trajectory.

Finally, the generated subject-independent model was used to predict the used walking aid of actual seniors, wearing a wearable sensor. Within the environment of the assisted living facility in Eggersdorf, tests with three seniors either using walkers or a walking cane were carried out. The identification of the actual used walking aid with seniors is reliable, when the walking aid is used for a certain time and the window size of the prediction could be chosen accordingly.

5 Scientific and Practical Impact

The main benefit of walking aid identification, using a wearable sensor, is that it can be used as parameter for safety or navigation applications. In positioning approaches like pedestrian dead reckoning or position filtering, the currently used walking aid may be used as input for increasing the positioning accuracy. For example, in [7], the implementation of detected locomotions into building layouts for indoor positioning is proven. As shown in Fig. 4, the modelling of probabilities according to the currently used walking aid based on a building layout is easily realizable. While the weight, according to the building layout with the use of a walker, is low on stairs, medium on stair ramps which may be overcome with a walker, it is modeled high on level surfaces. This information may then be used as map-based weight within a particle filter process for positioning.

Fig. 4. Walking probability with use of a walker (Color figure online)

Within navigation algorithms, specific walking aids may be used as input for route planning, e.g., planning a path just along walkable ways with the currently used walking aid. Details about possible navigation applications with user-specific route planning are, e.g., presented in [8]. It is, e.g., possible to compute the used weight under consideration of the currently used walking aid as input for shortest-path routing problems. Therefore, edges within a routable graph may receive a weight for each walking aid, e.g., a level walkway might receive high weights for all walking aids while stairs would receive low weights for walkers and wheelchairs. Within the shortest-path computation, these weights can be used as a factor with the distance or time parameter or used within a multi-criteria route optimization [9]. Next to that, the use of the information of the used walking aid may directly be applied in the guidance process of a navigation system.

6   Conclusion

Within this paper, we show the possibility of walking aid identification with cheap, universally available devices (wearables) already usable for seniors. As usable walking aids, normal walking, the use of a walking cane, and the use of a walker or wheelchair are defined. Features computed out of the acceleration, angular rate and pressure rate sensors are used within a basic machine learning approach to detect the currently used walking aid in real time.

First tests show recall rates of $> 94\,\%$, if a general distinction between moving and non-moving is detected in advance. The hit rate of the identification of the currently used walking aid may even be increased by the introduction of a transition probability. Such a walking aid identification could potentially be of great practical benefit as an input parameter in health monitoring or navigation applications, especially for seniors.

Acknowledgments. Part of this work was performed in the frame of the Austrian research promotion program *benefit* as a feasibility study, funded by the Federal Ministry for Transport, Innovation and Technology via the Austrian Research Promotion Agency, project number 846215.

The authors would like to thank the assisted living facility in Eggersdorf for their voluntary support and help during this research as well as their residents for participating in locomotion experiments and providing feedback.

References

1. Intelligence, B.I.: The Werarables report: growth trends, consumer attitudes, and why smartwatches will dominate (2015). http://uk.businessinsider.com/the-werable-computing-market-report-2014-10?r=US&IR=T. 21 May 2015
2. Lara, D.O., Labrador, M.A.: A survey on human activity recognition using wearable sensors. IEEE Commun. Surv. Tutor. **15**(3), 1192–1209 (2013). Q3 2013
3. Labrador, M.A., Yejas, O.D.L.: Human Activity Recognition - Using Wearable Sensors and Smartphones. CRC Press, Boca Raton (2014)

4. Susi, M.: Gait analysis for pedestrian navigation using MEMS handheld devices, thesis. Department of Geomatics Engineering, Calgary, Canada (2012)
5. Moder, T., Wisiol, K., Hafner, P., Wieser, M.: Smartphone-based indoor positioning utilizing motion recognition. In: International Conference on Indoor Positioning and Indoor Navigation, Banff, Alberta, Canada (2015)
6. Bobokov, D., Grimm, F., Steinbach, E., Hilsenbeck, S., Schroth, G.: Activity recognition on handheld devices for pedestrian indoor navigation. In: International Conference on Indoor Positioning and Indoor Navigation, Banff, Alberta, Canada (2015)
7. Hafner, P., Moder, T., Wisiol, K., Wieser, M.: Indoor positioning based on bayes filtering using map information. In: IFAC Conference on Embedded Systems, Computer Intelligence and Telematics, Maribor, Slovenia (2015)
8. Pressl, B., Mader, C., Wieser, M.: User-specific web-based route planning. In: Miesenberger, K., Klaus, J., Zagler, W., Karshmer, A. (eds.) ICCHP 2010, Part 1. LNCS, vol. 6179, pp. 280–287. Springer, Heidelberg (2010)
9. Pressl, B.: Knowledge-based route planning: data modelling and multi-criteria time-constrained route optimization for people with disabilities. Dissertation. Graz University of Technology, Graz, Austria (2012)

How Can We Develop AAC for Dementia?

John L. Arnott[✉] and Norman Alm

School of Science & Engineering: Computing,
University of Dundee, Dundee, DD1 4HN, UK
{jarnott,nalm}@computing.dundee.ac.uk

Abstract. Augmentative and alternative communication (AAC) methods are used to support people who have communication problems. Attempts have been made to apply AAC to assist the communication of people with cognitive impairments, including people with dementia. Two systems, CIRCA and Talking Mats, took as their starting points different types of communication situation which are problematic with dementia. Both systems have proved to be of benefit to user populations, encouraging further exploration in the field. Such exploration is likely to be gradual and incremental, given the nature of the challenges involved, building on retained capabilities of persons with dementia. There are implications for approaches to system design and development, including the software engineering of new systems.

Keywords: AAC · Augmentative communication · Dementia · Older people

1 The Rise of Dementia

Dementia is a progressive neurological deterioration that at present cannot be prevented or reversed. It is a condition associated primarily with ageing. As the population of older adults grows worldwide, the number of people with dementia will increase proportionally. This number is predicted to rise from 25 million in 2000 to 63 million by 2030 and to 114 million by 2050 [26].

Dementia's most characteristic result is degradation of working (short-term) memory. This creates difficulty in recalling and discussing recent events. However, memories of events from earlier in the person's life, especially childhood and early adulthood, can still be relatively intact. As the illness progresses, all aspects of cognitive function are involved, including language production, judgment and problem solving [8]. This progressive deterioration means that people with dementia become increasingly reliant on family or professional caregivers for meeting all of their needs.

2 The Potential of ICT Support for People with Dementia

While pharmacological treatments for dementia are being developed, their impact is limited so far, and there is an urgent need for non-pharmacological treatments to meet the social and emotional needs of people with dementia and their carers [22, 25].

K. Miesenberger et al. (Eds.): ICCHP 2016, Part I, LNCS 9758, pp. 342–349, 2016.
DOI: 10.1007/978-3-319-41264-1_47

Developments must take account of the needs, abilities and desires of the intended users, especially in respect of the cognitive impairments of people with dementia, which can interfere both with their ability to participate in the development process and their ability to use new technology once it is created [4].

One particularly challenging aspect of coping with dementia is the deterioration in the ability to communicate. This can be frustrating and disempowering for people with dementia and distressing for family and carers they are trying to communicate with. Developing interventions to support communication and maintain relationships between people with the cognitive disability of dementia and those who care for them is a growing social and healthcare priority.

3 Applying Existing AAC Structures to Support Communication in Dementia

Augmentative and alternative communication (AAC) as a field has, for many years, been developing both technological and non-technological systems to support the communication of people who have communication problems [7, 23]. AAC users with physical impairments include people with cerebral palsy from birth and people with acquired conditions such as motor neurone disease. Some attempts have been made to apply AAC systems for people with cognitive impairments, such as aphasia [14], and interactional difficulties such as autism [18]. Attempts have also been made to apply some of the techniques and technologies of AAC to try to assist the communication of people with dementia.

Egan et al. [12] conducted a systematic review of studies on techniques to improve communications between caregivers and persons with dementia and found that the strongest support was for the use of memory aids combined with caregiver training. The field was said to need more thorough investigation through high-quality randomized controlled trials (RCTs), existing trials being relatively uncommon. An RCT by Bourgeois et al. [9] found that participants with dementia using memory aids made significantly more utterances and had more informative interactions with their caregivers, where the caregivers had first been given relevant communication training.

Bourgeois et al. [10] reported that non-electronic or low-tech AAC approaches have been used by speech–language pathologists to support communication and social interaction for people with dementia. Elsewhere it was reported that verbal conversation could be improved with AAC communication boards if relevant training was first given to participants [16]. High-tech AAC can be problematic however; it was found [15] for example that pre-programmed digital voice output in devices proved distracting to participants with moderate dementia and reduced their conversational performance compared to devices without digital voice output. Fried-Oken et al. [17] also reviewed AAC-supported communication for patients with neurodegenerative disease, including Alzheimer's disease (AD), observing that "Communication supports, including high-tech, low-tech, and no-tech approaches, should be tailored to the specific needs and abilities of each person, and should be modified throughout disease progression".

Ekström et al. [13] described a single-case study of a person with dementia using a personalized AAC application on a tablet computer during interaction with her husband. She required considerable support from her husband in using the tablet and while there was more interaction occurring when the tablet was in use, there was no evidence of the tablet supporting communicative initiatives for the person with dementia. The study concluded that a personalized communication application on a tablet may encourage communication for people with dementia, but pointed also to a need for further investigation.

Efforts to apply existing AAC methods and technologies to the problem of communication for people with dementia which assume that relatively simple adaptations may be sufficient could be underestimating the magnitude of the cognitive challenges that a system appropriate for dementia must address.

4 Developing New Structures Based on the Experience of Dementia

In addition to investigating ways in which existing AAC systems might be adapted to help people with dementia, research has also been undertaken into focussing on specific communication problem areas with dementia, and devising ways of ameliorating these specific difficulties. The hope here is that eventually, a large suite of such tools might be able to offer people with dementia a much fuller communication experience than they currently have. Two systems which have hitherto been developed took as their starting points two different types of communication situation which are problematic with dementia: free-flowing conversation and expressing an opinion. In each case the developers devised a scaffolding for the communication based on what the person with dementia was still capable of.

5 Supporting Free-Flowing Conversation Through Reminiscence

CIRCA is a multimedia computer system developed to make possible again free-flowing conversation between people with dementia and caregivers [1–5]. The system is based on presenting reminiscence materials from a wide range of archives. Reminiscence provides an opportunity for people with dementia to speak about memories from earlier in their lives, which are often well-preserved, despite the lack of working (short-term) memory. Engaging in reminiscence is considered to contribute to well-being and to provide a positive activity for people with dementia [11].

5.1 Flexibility and Dynamic Linking with Hypermedia

CIRCA uses reminiscence materials in a hypermedia format to address the memory and conversation maintenance problems experienced by people with dementia. Two features of hypermedia make it particularly suitable for people with dementia. First is its inherent flexibility. Users of the computer have the freedom to move between interconnected but individual items as they choose. This is beneficial for people with memory loss as it does not put any penalty on 'losing the place' in the system. Whatever place the user is in is the right place to be, and exploring and 'getting lost' are actively encouraged as strategies to enjoy experiencing the material. Secondly, hypermedia provides the opportunity to link items from a range of media in a dynamic way. Text, photographs, graphics, sound recordings and film recordings can be seamlessly intertwined to present an inviting and lively activity for people with dementia and caregivers to explore and discuss together (Fig. 1).

Fig. 1. CIRCA prompting discussion through the display of generic reminiscence material

5.2   Outcomes with CIRCA

In controlled trials CIRCA was shown to support an engaging conversation maintenance activity which was not replicated in traditional reminiscence sessions. There were notable differences between the two session types in the verbal and nonverbal behaviour of both parties. In traditional reminiscence sessions the caregivers worked very hard to keep the interaction going, particularly by asking lots of questions. These were typically closed questions (e.g. "Did you used to do that?" "Do you remember those?"), which did not encourage either initiation or choosing by people with dementia. Caregivers reported in interviews after the two reminiscence activities that they found the traditional sessions much more demanding and that twenty minutes felt like a long time. By contrast they found it relatively easy to facilitate a shared interaction using CIRCA [5].

Lower levels of initiation were recorded for people with dementia in the traditional sessions compared to CIRCA sessions. Measures of non-verbal behaviour such as attention to the task and mutual laughter showed similar results, with sessions with CIRCA being more effective than traditional reminiscence sessions.

The success of CIRCA for people with dementia may reflect that it focusses on one cognitive task that they can still perform: using their long-term memory to tell stories based on events from their past. An interesting aspect of CIRCA is that it prompts these memories by means of generic reminiscence material. It was found that using personal material was not necessary [6]. The sheer size of the collection of generic material ensured that there was always something to talk about.

6   Supporting the Expression of Opinions and Views

Talking Mats is a communication framework which can help people with dementia (and other communication difficulties) to express their views and opinions [19–21]. The system uses a mat, such as a doormat or carpet tile, to which symbols and pictures can be attached by hook and loop tape. A touch-screen tablet-based version is also available. Symbols representing emotions are placed along the top to form a visual rating scale. The emotions can be as simple as 'positive', 'neutral' and 'negative' or more detailed, depending on the user. A relevant topic is discussed and a symbol representing it is placed at the bottom of the mat. As the session progresses the user expresses their views by placing pictures representing various aspects of the topic on the mat, grouping them underneath the appropriate rating symbols. The process is engaging and empowering, and the result is a vivid pictorial representation, in some detail, of the person's views (Fig. 2).

Fig. 2.   An example of a Talking Mat (left) and one under construction (right). (Symbols © Adam Murphy and owned by Talking Mats Ltd.)

6.1   Outcomes with Talking Mats

Talking Mats has been found to be successful in a number of ways with people who have dementia. The quality of communication was analysed with Talking Mats compared to structured and unstructured conversation [20]. Sessions were recorded and studied for evidence of effectiveness, perseveration, and distractibility. Conversations using Talking Mats lasted longer than ordinary conversations; they were more effective for people with dementia than both unstructured (ordinary) or structured conversations. Improvements were evident in the participants' understanding, engagement, and ability to keep on track and make their views understood. The reliability of information provided was enhanced. The amount of time spent 'on-task' – e.g. making eye contact and engaging actively in conversation – increased when using Talking Mats, and participants were less frequently distracted. Instances of repetitive behaviour such as repeating words, phrases, ideas or actions were reduced.

Although people with dementia and their family carers both felt more involved in discussions when using Talking Mats, the increased feeling of involvement was significantly higher for the family carers, who repeatedly reported feeling 'listened to' by the person with dementia and felt that their loved one could actually 'see' their point of view. One carer said: "It never seems like he is listening to me. With this I can make him sit down and look at symbols and get him to understand what I am trying to say."

The success of Talking Mats for people with dementia may be that it 'externalises' cognitive processes in a simple and easy to understand way. The layout of pictures in front of the person acts both as a reminder of what the person has already said and an emerging easy-to-read picture of what their views and opinions are.

7 Discussion

7.1 Further Exploration of AAC in Dementia

Developing communication support systems for people with dementia is an important priority. So far, some low-tech AAC systems have proved to be of benefit, but high-tech AAC systems seem to be too confusing for people with dementia to understand and to operate. The best way forward may be to start with the capabilities of the person with dementia, and build from there, always keeping in mind that the user-interface to any communication system will need to be extremely simple, however complex the functioning is 'behind the scenes'. The CIRCA system was built on the ability of the person with dementia still to draw on their long-term memory. The Talking Mats approach provides them with a simple and easy to understand layout, and a procedure that does not require their working memory to be employed. It is noteworthy that both CIRCA and Talking Mats involve the other person in the conversation (conversation partner) actually helping to sustain it, but with considerably less effort than is normally required. The structure which the two systems offer takes much of the burden from the conversation partner, and allows them to join in a mutually satisfying interaction where the control of the person with dementia is maximised.

A strategy for further exploration of AAC in dementia would thus be to build on the capabilities retained by persons with dementia, using AAC methods and technologies to gradually augment these capabilities, while focussing carefully on the user experiences of the persons with dementia and their conversation partners. Progress is likely to be gradual and incremental as the challenges are great, but some encouragement can be taken from previous outcomes.

7.2 Implications for Software Engineering of AAC Systems for Dementia

From the standpoint of Software Engineering, a particularly challenging aspect for new developments in this field is eliciting requirements. Standard practice is to derive user requirements from conversations and structured interactions, such as questionnaires, with potential users. In the case of people with dementia this is likely to be of limited assistance. Deriving requirements from carers is possible, both as surrogate users and as participants themselves in communications with the person who has dementia. Projects, however, can be built on an evidence base derived not from interviews or questionnaires, but from direct observation of users interacting with an evolving series of prototypes. Where necessary, this can involve video-recording, transcribing, and coding sessions to enable a very fine-grained analysis of the interaction [2, 4]. It is widely accepted that user involvement in the design process and understanding the user is highly desirable [24]. In the case of people with dementia, for reasons set out above, we would say it is essential.

8 Conclusion

Supporting communication for people with dementia is a growing priority, given the increasing number of people so affected. Applying existing AAC systems with some modification may not be sufficient to meet the challenges inherent with the users' lack of short-term memory and other cognitive challenges. Developing new systems which build on their remaining cognitive abilities may be a more fruitful approach.

References

1. Alm, N., Astell, A., Ellis, M., Dye, R., Gowans, G., Campbell, J.: A cognitive prosthesis and communication support for people with dementia. Neuropsychol. Rehabil. **14**(1–2), 117–134 (2004)
2. Alm, N., Dye, R., Gowans, G., Campbell, J., Astell, A., Ellis, M.: A communication support system for older people with dementia. IEEE Comput. **40**(5), 35–41 (2007)
3. Astell, A.J., Ellis, M.P., Alm, N., Dye, R., Campbell, J., Gowans, G.: Facilitating communication in dementia with multimedia technology. Brain Lang. **91**(1), 80–81 (2004)
4. Astell, A., Alm, N., Gowans, G., Ellis, M., Dye, R., Vaughan, P.: Involving older people with dementia and their carers in designing computer based support systems: some methodological considerations. Univ. Access Inf. Soc. **8**(1), 49–58 (2009)
5. Astell, A., Ellis, M., Bernardi, L., Alm, N., Dye, R., Gowans, G., Campbell, J.: Using a touch screen computer to support relationships between people with dementia and caregivers. Interact. Comput. **22**(4), 267–275 (2010)
6. Astell, A., Ellis, M., Alm, N., Dye, R., Gowans, G.: Stimulating people with dementia to reminisce using personal and generic photographs. Int. J. Comput. Healthc. **1**(2), 177–198 (2010)
7. Beukelman, D.R., Mirenda, P.: Augmentative and Alternative Communication: Supporting Children & Adults with Complex Communication Needs. Paul H. Brookes Publishing Co., Baltimore (2013)
8. Bird, T., Miller, B.: Alzheimer's disease and other dementias. In: Hauser, S., Josephson, S. (eds.) Harrison's Neurology in Clinical Medicine, pp. 298–319. McGraw-Hill, New York (2010)
9. Bourgeois, M.S., Dijkstra, K., Burgio, L., Allen-Burge, R.: Memory aids as an augmentative and alternative communication strategy for nursing home residents with dementia. Augment. Altern. Commun. **17**(3), 196–210 (2001)
10. Bourgeois, M., Fried-Oken, M., Rowland, C.: AAC strategies and tools for persons with dementia. ASHA Lead. **15**, 8–11 (2010)
11. Brooker, D., Duce, L.: Wellbeing and activity in dementia: a comparison of group reminiscence therapy, structured goal-directed group activity and unstructured time. Aging Ment. Health **4**(4), 354–358 (2000)

12. Egan, M., Bérubé, D., Racine, G., Leonard, C., Rochon, E.: Methods to enhance verbal communication between individuals with Alzheimer's disease and their formal and informal caregivers: a systematic review. Int. J. Alzheimer's Dis. **2010** (2010). Article ID 906818
13. Ekström, A., Ferm, U., Samuelsson, C.: Digital communication support and Alzheimer's disease. Dementia, 6 December 2015. Article: 1471301215615456
14. Fox, L., Fried-Oken, M.: AAC aphasiology: partnership for future research. Augment. Altern. Commun. **12**(4), 257–271 (1996)
15. Fried-Oken, M., Rowland, C., Baker, G., Dixon, M., Mills, C., Schultz, D., Oken, B.: The effect of voice output on AAC-supported conversations of persons with Alzheimer's disease. ACM Trans. Access. Comput. **1**(3), 15 (2009)
16. Fried-Oken, M., Rowland, C., Daniels, D., Dixon, M., Fuller, B., Mills, C., Noethe, G., Small, J., Still, K., Oken, B.: AAC to support conversation in persons with moderate Alz-heimer's disease. Augment. Altern. Commun. **28**(4), 219–231 (2012)
17. Fried-Oken, M., Mooney, A., Peters, B.: Supporting communication for patients with neurodegenerative disease. NeuroRehabilitation **37**, 69–87 (2015)
18. Mirenda, P., Iacono, T. (eds.): Autism Spectrum Disorders and AAC. Brooks Publishing Company, Baltimore (2009)
19. Murphy, J., Gray, C., Cox, S.: Communication and Dementia: How Talking Mats Can Help People with Dementia to Express Themselves. Joseph Rowntree Foundation, London (2007)
20. Murphy, J., Gray, C.M., Cox, S., van Achterberg, T., Wyke, S.: The effectiveness of the Talking Mats framework with people with dementia. Dement. Int. J. Soc. Res. Pract. **9**(4), 454–472 (2010)
21. Murphy, J., Oliver, T.: The use of Talking Mats to support people with dementia and their carers to make decisions together. Health Soc. Care Community **21**(2), 171–180 (2013)
22. National Institute for Health and Clinical Excellence: NICE clinical guideline 42: Dementia: Supporting people with dementia and their carers in health and social care. NICE, London (2006)
23. Newell, A.F., Arnott, J.L., Cairns, A.Y., Ricketts, I.W., Gregor, P.: Intelligent systems for speech and language impaired people: A portfolio of research. In: Edwards, A.D.N. (ed.) Extra-Ordinary Human-Computer Interaction: Interfaces for Users with Disabilities, pp. 83–101. Cambridge University Press, Cambridge (1995)
24. Rogers, Y., Sharp, H., Preece, J.: Interaction Design, pp. 326–328. Wiley, Chichester (2011)
25. Sink, K., Holden, K., Yaffe, K.: Pharmacological treatment of neuropsychiatric symptoms of dementia: a review of the evidence. J. Am. Med. Assoc. **293**(5), 596–608 (2005)
26. Wimo, A., Winblad, B., Aguero-Torres, H., von Strauss, E.: The magnitude of dementia occurrence in the world. Alzheimer Dis. Assoc. Disord. **17**, 63–67 (2003)

The Impact of PDF/UA
on Accessible PDF

The Impact of PDF/UA on Accessible PDF

Introduction to the Special Thematic Session

Olaf Drümmer[(✉)]

callas software GmbH/axaio software GmbH, Berlin, Germany

Abstract. This STS aims to present an overview of the progress made with regard to accessible PDF in the context of the PDF/UA standard. The four years between publication of PDF/UA in July 2012 and the ICCHP 2016 conference encompass a time period long enough to provide worthwhile insights about recent developments. Papers range from survey based overview information, and findings around improved tooling, to a glimpse into the future by looking at research on providing access to structurally or graphically rich content without having to rely on alternate descriptions or alternate representations.

Keywords: PDF · Tagged PDF · PDF/UA · ISO 14289 · Graphs · Charts · Formulas · Audio · Sound · Print disability · Screen reader · SVG · HTML · EPUB · Document accessibility · Alternate description · Alternate representation · Remediation · Algorithm

1 Introduction to This Special Thematic Session (STS)

The PDF/UA standard for accessible PDF documents, and for tools and assistive technologies (AT) for accessing PDF/UA documents, has been published by ISO as ISO 14289-1 in July 2012. Those who developed the PDF/UA standard envision a much improved landscape for accessibility of PDF documents. This applies to both the creation and the consumption of accessible PDF documents.

PDF/UA regulates how content – graphics, text, multimedia, annotations, form fields – is to be included in a PDF file in order to be considered accessible. While leaving implementation details – how content components are technically incorporated in the PDF file, or how assistive technology takes advantage of accessible content in PDF/UA documents – to solution developers, it provides a clearly defined benchmark: a first in the field of accessible PDF documents.

According to early adopters – most notably software developers who already ship or have at least announced PDF/UA enabled tools or solutions – the wait shouldn't be long until those interested in accessible PDF find a much more workable eco-system. Tools are being democratized, such that not only specialists but in principle every document creator can save their documents to accessible PDF at any time. At least one screen reader developer – NV Access to be precise – has already enhanced support for accessible PDF in their NVDA screen reader on the background of PDF/UA, which for example supports access to complex tables.

At the same time it was clear from the beginning that extensive education will be necessary to nudge document producers and consumers towards adoption of PDF/UA. The fact that Germany (in 2014, in the form of a translated version of the standard) and the USA (in March 2016) have adopted PDF/UA as national standards will definitely have its effect. In addition, PDF/UA is being considered for inclusion in the upcoming section 508 refresh of the Access Board in the USA. And last but not least it still has to be proven that PDF/UA really does work in reality as advertised, and does work well.

This STS aims to present an overview of the progress made for accessible PDF in the context of the PDF/UA standard. The four years between publication of PDF/UA and the ICCHP 2016 conference encompass a time period long enough to provide reports about developments in the various fields discussed above.

2   Areas Covered by This Special Thematic Session (STS)

Yoshiaki Tani presents a paper – prepared together with Takuya Takaira and Akio Fujiyoshi – on Sound-Embedded PDF aiming to help Elementary School Students with Print Disabilities accessing text books. While this concept might also be feasible and worthwhile independent of tagged PDF or PDF/UA, full integration with PDF/UA regulated syntax provides for a degree of accessibility that goes substantially beyond a simple interactive audio enrichment to PDF files.

For many problems there is a general choice of either removing the problem or finding a solution for the problem. Australia seems to be leaning towards removing the problem of insufficient access to PDF files by recommending or even requiring not to use PDF at all for communication and publication purposes, or at least to provide more accessible alternatives in all cases. Driven by the insight that especially the now ubiquitous adoption and use of mobile devices hasn't provided a more accessible PDF experience to users with or without disabilities alike, Gian Wild discusses a number of actual or supposed strengths of PDF over other content formats, and aims to help decision makers make up their mind regarding preferable content formats in the light of the degree of accessibility that these formats can provide.

Alireza Darvishy shares recent developments and findings on Automatic Paragraph Detection for Accessible PDF Documents. This paper is rooted in ongoing work at the ZHAW (Zurich University of Applied Sciences) on providing readily available tools for deriving PDF/UA files from existing office documents. The current work of the group around Alireza Darvishy focuses on a new algorithm for the automatic detection and tagging of paragraphs in PDF documents. Using this algorithm, remediation of existing PDF documents can be carried out much more efficiently and with a lower error rate – a much needed effect given the number of existing PDF documents that have not already been created in an accessible fashion.

Reports on the current state of affairs regarding the use of PDF by people with disabilities are often based on anecdotal evidence, rough estimates or even just personal opinion. Karen McCall decided to address this unsatisfactory situation and in early 2016 carried out an extensive survey among people with disabilities, targeting aspects – in addition to the usual demographic data – such as whether PDF is consumed at work, or for education or leisure, user experience when accessing PDF, or quality of support by existing PDF readers and assistive technology.

Going beyond what is available or supported today, several groups of researchers have recently explored possibilities how to make rich graphical content more accessible, leaving behind the limitations of either providing alternative descriptions or alternative presentations for content that otherwise is not generally accessible. Substantial progress in this field has been presented at a workshop early 2016 in Japan – The 3rd International Workshop on "Digitization and E-Inclusion in Mathematics and Science 2016" (DEIMS2016) – by groups of researchers around Volker Sorge, Fumiyasu Sato and Siddhartha Gupta. In summer 2015 a group of students from the Johannes Kepler University in Linz, Austria – Markus Weninger, Gerald Ortner and Tobias Morowinger – studied how graphs – such as pie charts, bar charts, scatter plots and so forth – can be made fully and inherently accessible in an automated fashion without having to revert to alternative descriptions or alternative representations. In their project Accessible Scalable Vector Graphics (ASVG): Use of intention trees for accessible charts the team chose SVG – an XML syntax which is based on the same graphic model as PDF – for ease of coding. Their findings nonetheless are applicable not just to PDF and SVG, but also to HTML and EPUB.

References

1. Sorge, V.: Assistive technologies for STEM subjects – from Bitmap graphics to fully accessible chemical diagrams. In: Proceedings from the 3rd International Workshop on "Digitization and E-Inclusion in Mathematics and Science 2016" (DEIMS2016), 4–6 February 2016, Shonan Village Center, Kanagawa, Japan (2016)
2. Sato, F., Fujiyoshi, A.: Recognition of condensed structural formulas of chemical compounds using a formal grammar. In: Proceedings from the 3rd International Workshop on "Digitization and E-Inclusion in Mathematics and Science 2016" (DEIMS2016), 4–6 February 2016, Shonan Village Center, Kanagawa, Japan (2016)
3. Gupta, S., Belani, M.V., Kaushal, D., Balakrishnan, M.: Microsoft excel charts accessibility: an affordable and effective solution. In: Proceedings from the 3rd International Workshop on "Digitization and E-Inclusion in Mathematics and Science 2016" (DEIMS2016), 4–6 February 2016, Shonan Village Center, Kanagawa, Japan (2016)
4. Weninger, M., Ortner, G., Hahn, T., Drümmer, O., Miesenberger, K.: ASVG – accessible scalable vector graphics: intention trees to make charts more accessible and usable. J. Assist. Technol. 9(4), 239–246 (2015)

Are PDFs an Accessible Solution?

Gian Wild[1(✉)] and Daniel Craddock[2]

[1] AccessibilityOz, Melbourne, VIC, Australia
gian@accessibilityoz.com
[2] Department of Justice, Consumer Affairs Victoria, Melbourne, VIC, Australia
daniel.craddock@justice.vic.gov.au

Abstract. PDFs are everywhere on the web, and with the advent of the PDF Techniques for the W3C Web Content Accessibility Guidelines, Version 2.0, the general public could be led to believe that PDF is an accessible technology. But is it an appropriate accessible solution for content? In a study conducted by Consumer Affairs Victoria, overwhelmingly people chose web pages to view their content, instead of PDFs. When given a choice, 99.6 % of users choose a web page instead of a PDF to view information.

Keywords: Accessibility · PDF · Adobe Acrobat · WCAG 2.0 · PDF/UA · HTML · Document accessibility · Tagged PDF · Web Content Accessibility Guidelines

1 Introduction

With millions of PDFs on the web [1], the accessibility compliance of this document format is of the utmost importance. Whereas it is generally accepted that HTML can be made fully accessible [2], the accessibility compliance of PDFs is a more controversial issue.

1.1 About Web Accessibility

Web accessibility is about making sure web sites, web applications and mobile apps (including PDFs) are accessible to people with disabilities. There are four groups of people assisted by an accessible site: people with cognitive disabilities; people with vision impairments; people with physical disabilities; and people with hearing impairments. The estimate of people with disabilities in the US varies between 40 million [3] and 57 million Americans [4]. This is a conservative estimate.

W3C Web Content Accessibility Guidelines, Version 2.0. Web accessibility of web sites is best achieved by following the Web Content Accessibility Guidelines, Version 2.0. The World Wide Web Consortium (W3C) has worked in the area of web accessibility since 1998 and they have developed a set of recommendations called the W3C Web Content Accessibility Guidelines, which have been endorsed around the world.

© Springer International Publishing Switzerland 2016
K. Miesenberger et al. (Eds.): ICCHP 2016, Part I, LNCS 9758, pp. 355–358, 2016.
DOI: 10.1007/978-3-319-41264-1_48

The W3C states that "following these guidelines will make content accessible to a wider range of people with disabilities, including blindness and low vision, deafness and hearing loss, learning disabilities, cognitive limitations, limited movement, speech disabilities, photosensitivity and combinations of these" [2].

The W3C Web Content Accessibility Guidelines, Version 2.0, contain specific techniques for providing accessibility features within PDF.

1.2 About Adobe PDF

Adobe was founded in 1982 [5]. In 1993 Adobe released Acrobat 1.0 [6]. The PDF format was invented by John Warnock [6], one of the founders of Adobe, who envisioned a paperless office where graphics-heavy documents could be sent to different computers and completely retain their original look [7].

Adobe introduced tagging in 2001 in Version 5.05 [8] which allowed assistive technologies to determine information about the contents of the PDF, just as they do with web pages.

Tagging in PDFs. PDF is based on Postscript, a programming language used to develop vector graphics. However, PDF, like Postscript, is reliant on generating a raster image – which ensures it looks the same across different systems [6]. This is the major problem with PDF: the content is a generated image. Affixing tags to features such as headings is complicated by the fact that tags are being added to sections of an image, not parts of text, such as with a webpage. This leads to one of the more problematic issues with PDF: the difficulty and unreliability in the tagging process [9]. Tagging cannot be done automatically and always includes an element of manual work which can be very time-consuming [9].

2   Methodology: Testing the Popularity of PDFs Compared to Web Pages

In 2011 the Department of Primary Industries decided to remove all the PDFs in their web site and replace them with web pages [10]. This resulted in a 38 % page view increase; an additional 1.6 million page views of the web site [10].

As a result of this, Consumer Affairs Victoria web site began running a study of the popularity of PDFs compared to web pages. In a number of articles web users are given a choice: view the web page or download the PDF.

3   Results

The results are staggering. When the study first began in 2013, the average number of pageviews for the PDF was 831 individual pageviews; compared to the average number of pageviews for the web page which was 109,157. This means, when given a choice, 99.3 % of users chose the web page rather than the PDF.

Over the subsequent two years, the percentage of people choosing web pages has only increased. In the latest statistics, in 2015, 99.6 % of users chose the web page. That means only 0.4 % of users chose to download a PDF when given a choice; for every PDF download there were 227 views of the web page. And we're not talking small numbers here, in 2015 there were 2.4 million page views, and during the same period there were only 10,000 PDF downloads.

4 Why Do People Use PDF?

There are a lot of reasons why people use PDFs, and in many cases valid arguments can be made against the use of PDFs for content.

4.1 Security

People always talk about how secure PDF is, but it isn't really any more secure than any other document format. It's pretty easy to break into a secure PDF file, or at least recreate it. And there is one web format that is much more secure than PDF: your web site. Someone has to hack your server in order to change that.

4.2 Brand

People always talk about how the brand of an organisation is important and fill annual reports with "hero images" of people walking by the beach or sitting at a café. It's supposed to make the people reading the annual report feel good about the company. But think about the brand of your organisation when someone is standing at the traffic lights trying to download the PDF of your store opening hours or of your delivery menu? It might be a beautiful PDF, but your customers won't care if it takes three minutes to download.

4.3 Print Versions

People always say that others want print versions… print versions of brochures, annual reports, fees, maps etc. Well providing these items as PDFs just passes the cost of printing on to your customers. And did you know that ink costs more than bottled water? More than crude oil? More than perfume? More than human blood? [11].

4.4 It's Easy

People always say creating a PDF is easy. It's easy *because the information is created in another application first*. No one created a PDF in Adobe Acrobat. No designer or technical writer boots up Adobe Acrobat in the morning to get started on their work. Instead, they are working in another application, such as InDesign or Word and then printing to PDF. The content is created in another format first – so maybe you should be providing that format to your customers.

5   Conclusion

PDFs are not an appropriate accessible solution; overwhelmingly people choose web pages over PDFs. In addition to this, the many reasons why PDFs apparently must be used can be easily negated.

References

1. How many PDF files are there in the world? https://www.quora.com/How-many-pdf-files-are-there-in-the-world
2. World Wide Web Consortium: Web Content Accessibility Guidelines (WCAG) 2.0. https://www.w3.org/TR/WCAG20/
3. Houtenville, A.J., Brucker, D., Lauer, E.: Annual Compendium of Disability Statistics: 2014. Institute on Disability, University of New Hampshire, Durham (2014)
4. Brault, M.W.: Americans with disabilities: 2010. Curr. Popul. Rep. **7**, 1–131 (2012)
5. Adobe – 25th Anniversary Newsletter. https://www.adobe.com/aboutadobe/history/newsletter/
6. The PDF, a brief history of the universal file format. http://www.investintech.com/resources/articles/pdffilehistory/
7. The history of PDF I How the file format and Acrobat evolved. http://www.prepressure.com/pdf/basics/history
8. PDFs and accessibility. http://usability.com.au/2004/05/pdfs-and-accessibility/
9. Darvishy, A., Hutter, H.-P., Horvath, A., Dorigo, M.: A flexible software architecture concept for the creation of accessible PDF documents. In: Miesenberger, K., Klaus, J., Zagler, W., Karshmer, A. (eds.) ICCHP 2010, Part 1. LNCS, vol. 6179, pp. 47–52. Springer, Heidelberg (2010)
10. Case study: Unlock valuable content trapped in PDFs I Briarbird. http://briarbird.com/archives/case-study-unlock-valuable-content-trapped-in-pdfs/
11. Ink Costs More Than Human Blood I Visual.ly, http://visual.ly/ink-costs-more-human-blood

A Simple Viewer and Editor of Sound-Embedded PDF for Elementary School Students with Print Disabilities

Yoshiaki Tani[1(✉)], Takuya Takaira[1], and Akio Fujiyoshi[2]

[1] Graduate School of Science and Engineering, Ibaraki University,
Hitachi, Ibaraki, Japan
{15nm7201,15nm716f}@vc.ibaraki.ac.jp
[2] Faculty of Engineering, Ibaraki University, Hitachi, Ibaraki, Japan
akio.fujiyoshi.cs@ibaraki.ac.jp

Abstract. This paper introduce is a simple viewer and editor of sound-embedded PDF that is suitable for elementary school students with print disabilities. These days, a lot of teaching materials are created in PDF. For student with print disabilities, the use of sound-embedded PDF was proposed. However, the production of documents in sound-embedded PDF was difficult for most teachers and students because complex tasks with expensive application software were necessary. Therefore, a simple viewer and editor of sound-embedded PDF was developed.

Keywords: PDF · Accessibility · Teaching materials · Sound-embedded PDF · Print disabilities

1 Introduction

Recently, a lot of electronic documents are published in PDF. PDF is the most widely used format for fixed-layout digital documents such as textbooks, magazines, and picture books. It is difficult for people with print disabilities to use a PDF file without audio support. Accessible PDF [1] helps them to read a PDF file by a screen reader. The correct order of sentences for reading out is specified in accessible PDF. PDF/UA is the international standard of the accessible PDF technology. Accessible PDF is quite available in Europe and the United States. However, documents in Japanese language are difficult for a screen reader to read out correctly because of multiple readings of kanji characters and the weakness of word dividers of Japanese writings. Thus a screen reader often misread Japanese documents. This problem is a very important matter for textbooks for children.

For textbooks for students with print disabilities, the use of "Sound-Embedded PDF" was proposed [2] (Fig. 1). Sound-embedded PDF is PDF with embedded sound files corresponding to the text. A sound-embedded PDF file can be used with a general PDF viewer such as Adobe Acrobat Reader on Windows 7 (or higher) and Mac OS X. If a part of text is clicked on the screen, then

K. Miesenberger et al. (Eds.): ICCHP 2016, Part I, LNCS 9758, pp. 359–366, 2016.
DOI: 10.1007/978-3-319-41264-1_49

Fig. 1. Sound-embedded PDF textbook

the selected text is highlighted and the corresponding embedded sound is reproduced. We think sound-embedded PDF can help students with print disabilities
for reading and understanding documents in textbooks. However, the production
of sound-embedded PDF textbooks is difficult for most teachers and students
because complex tasks with expensive application software such as Adobe Illustrator [6], Adobe Acrobat Pro [7] and JUST PDF [8] are necessary.

This paper introduces a simple viewer and editor of sound-embedded PDF
that is suitable for elementary school students with print disabilities. The viewer
and editor can be used without expensive application software. It is designed so
that teachers and students can record their voice and reproduce the sound on
PDF intuitively. Teachers can make teaching materials with their narration, and
students can return them with their answering voice.

2   PDF

Portable Document Format (PDF) is a standard file format used to present a
digital document independent of application software, hardware, and operating
systems [3]. Currently, PDF is one of the open standards maintained by the
International Organization for Standardization (ISO). PDF can contain additional contents such as links, buttons, audio and video. In addition, PDF/A-3
(ISO 19005-3:2012) [4] allows us to embed any types of files into a PDF file.

2.1 Accessibility of PDF Document

PDF can use simple assistive functions of viewers such as scaling and black-and-white reversal. To make PDF more accessible PDF was developed. Accessible PDF is tagged PDF for logical reading order and semantics.

PDF/Universal Accessibility (PDF/UA) is the international standard format for accessible PDF technology (ISO 14289-1) [5]. PDF/UA ensures accessibility for people with disabilities who use assistive technology such as screen readers, screen magnifiers, joysticks and other technologies to navigate and read electronic content.

2.2 Sound-Embedded PDF

Documents in Japanese language are difficult for a screen reader to read out correctly because of multiple readings of kanji characters and the weakness of word dividers of Japanese writings. Thus PDF with embedded sound files was proposed [2].

There are the following two ways to embed sound files into a PDF file.

1. Embedding sound files as attachments, and
2. Embedding sound files as multimedia objects.

The first way is easier. Embedding sound files can be done with Adobe Acrobat Reader. Adobe Acrobat and Acrobat Pro are not necessary. To embed a sound file, choose "Record audio" or "Attach file" in "Comment tool." "Record audio" arrows us to recode voice directly with the microphone of a device (Fig. 2(1)). A pre-recorded sound files in WAVE format can also be attached. "Attach file" is used to attach any types of media files including MP3 format. Embedded sound files are displayed by icons on PDF document (Fig. 2(2)).

(1)   (2)

Fig. 2. (1) Sound recorder, and (2) icons of embedded sound files

The other way is not so easy. Though Adobe Acrobat Reader can reproduce embedded sound of multimedia objects, Adobe Acrobat Pro is necessary to embed sound files as multimedia objects.

2.3   How to Create Sound-Embedded PDF with Highlight Function

Highlight function can be realized with multimedia objects in a PDF file. To create sound-embedded PDF with highlight function, Adobe Illustrator [6], Adobe Acrobat Pro [7] and JUST PDF [8] are necessary. The creation of sound-embedded PDF can be done in the following three steps:

1. Preparing layers,
2. Embedding sound files, and
3. Setting actions.

Preparing layers is necessary for the highlight action. Translucent rectangular objects are used to highlight text. The translucent rectangular objects are arranged on a different layer for each part of a text. Layers and translucent rectangular objects are made by Illustrator.

In order to embed sound files as multimedia objects into a PDF file, we use JUST PDF. JUST PDF has a sound tool that can make a button object with an embedded sound file. The buttons can be transparent so that they don't change the look of a document. When a button object is clicked, the embedded sound file can be reproduced.

To set actions, we use Adobe Acrobat Pro. The highlight function using layers made by Illustrator is realized as actions of button objects. Figure 3 shows the multimedia properties of a button where actions are set.

2.4   Evaluation of Sound-Embedded PDF with Highlight Function

The usability of sound-embedded PDF was checked by asking three dyslexic elementary school students. They are in the 5th grade and have difficulty of reading. A tablet PC, Surface Pro 3 (Microsoft Corporation, Windows 8.1) was prepared. Sound-embedded PDF of a part of textbooks in Japanese language published by Mitumura Tosho Publishing Co.,Ltd was installed on the PC. Adobe Acrobat Reader DC was used to read the PDF. One week after they started using sound-embedded PDF, they were asked about the following questions:

1. Could you read displayed sentences easily?
2. Could you change pages easily?
3. Could you select sentence easily?
4. How do you think the highlight function?

The answer of each question was chosen from "very easy", "easy", "fair", "difficult" and "very difficult." For question 1, two students answered "easy" and one "fair." For question 2, all three answered "very easy." For question 3, two students answered "very easy" and one "easy." For question 4, all three answered "very good."

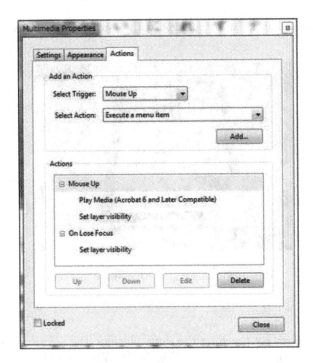

Fig. 3. Multimedia properties

The results of evaluation revealed that the highlight function is very effective for elementary school students with print disabilities.

3   Simple Viewer and Editor of Sound-Embedded PDF

Adobe Acrobat Reader is not suitable for elementary school students with developmental disabilities because it is not so simple and too much functions. Thus we developed a simple viewer and editor of sound-embedded PDF that are suitable for elementary school students with print disabilities. It is designed so that teachers and students can record their voice and reproduce the sound on PDF intuitively. It has only indispensable functions in a classroom use. Complicated tasks and expensive application software are not necessary any more.

The simple viewer and editor is developed on Java with JavaFX and Apache PDFBox [11]. Apache PDFBox library is an open source Java tool for working with PDF documents. PDFBox is used to get page images from a PDF file and to embed sound files and icon images. Since the application is developed on Java, it runs on multi-platforms: Windows, Mac OS X and Linux.

The simple viewer and editor of sound-embedded PDF supports the following functions on the screen of a tablet:

Turning Pages: Pages can be changed with a swipe motion (Fig. 4).

Fig. 4. Turning page with a swipe motion

Recording Voice: By touching the same place on the screen for a while, the function of recording voice is invoked (Fig. 5(1)). When voice is recorded, an icon appears on the screen (Fig. 5(2)).

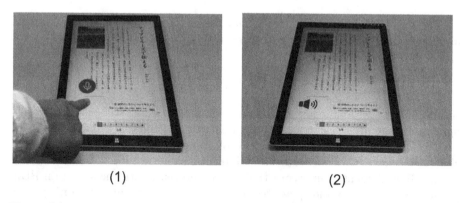

(1)   (2)

Fig. 5. (1) Recording voice and (2) an icon of recorded sound appearing on the screen

Reproducing Sound: By touching an icon of recorded voice, the sound is reproduced (Fig. 6(1)).

Changing Icon: An icon of recorded voice can be changed by touching the icon for a while (Fig. 6(2)).

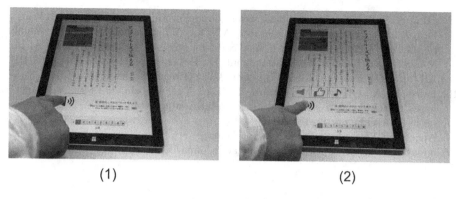

Fig. 6. (1) Reproducing sound and (2) changing an icon of recorded sound

Magnification: The screen can be magnified up with a pinch-in motion.

Black-and-White Reversal: The black-and-white reversal function is supported.

4   Conclusion and Future Work

A simple viewer and editor of sound-embedded PDF was developed for elementary school students with print disabilities. The viewer and editor is designed so that teachers and students can record their voice and reproduce the sound on PDF intuitively. Complicated tasks and expensive application software are not necessary any more to create sound-embedded PDF.

We plan to implement the highlight function on the simple viewer and editor. It is also planned to evaluate the simple viewer and editor by asking dyslexic elementary school students to use it.

The system will be released on the website of our laboratory [12].

Acknowledgements. This work was partially supported by JSPS KAKENHI Grant Number 26282044.

References

1. PDF Association. http://www.pdfa.org/
2. Tani, Y., Takaira, T., Fujiyoshi, A.: Trial production of sound-embedded accessible PDF. In: The Proceedings of DEIMS 2016 (2016)
3. Adobe PDF. https://acrobat.adobe.com/us/en/products/about-adobe-pdf.html
4. ISO 19005-3:2012. http://www.iso.org/iso/catalogue_detail.htm?csnumber=57229
5. ISO 14289-1:2012. http://www.iso.org/iso/catalogue_detail.htm?csnumber=54564
6. Adobe Illustrator CC. http://www.adobe.com/products/illustrator.html
7. Adobe Acrobat DC. https://acrobat.adobe.com/us/en/acrobat.html

8. JUST PDF 3. https://www.justsystems.com/jp/products/justpdf/feature4.html
9. Fujiyoshi, A., Fujiyoshi, M., Ohsawa, A., Ota, Y.: Development of multimodal textbooks with invisible 2-dimensional codes for students with print disabilities. In: Miesenberger, K., Fels, D., Archambault, D., Peňáz, P., Zagler, W. (eds.) ICCHP 2014, Part II. LNCS, vol. 8548, pp. 331–337. Springer, Heidelberg (2014)
10. Fujiyoshi, A., Ohsawa, A., Takaira, T., Tani, Y., Fujiyoshi, M., Ota, Y.: Paper-based textbooks with audio support for print-disabled students. In: The Proceedings of AAATE, pp. 11–18 (2015)
11. Apache PDFBox. https://pdfbox.apache.org/
12. onpariPDF. http://apricot.cis.ibaraki.ac.jp/onpariPDF

Automatic Paragraph Detection for Accessible PDF Documents

Alireza Darvishy[✉], Mark Nevill, and Hans-Peter Hutter

InIT Institute of Applied Information Technology,
ZHAW Zurich University of Applied Sciences, Winterthur, Switzerland
alireza.darvishy@zhaw.ch

Abstract. This paper describes a new algorithm for the automatic detection and tagging of paragraphs in PDF documents. This is an important feature of the PDF Accessibility Validation Engine (PAVE) [1] which is an open-source web application for the analysis and semi-automatic correction of accessibility issues in PDF documents. The tool is currently used by a large number of users, and their feedback is collected and evaluated. The evaluation so far revealed some major usability issues mainly due to the missing paragraph detection functionality. After an introduction in PDF accessibility this paper discusses the current usability issues with PAVE and describes the newly proposed algorithm to alleviate them. A first evaluation and conclusion of the results will be provided in the final paper.

Keywords: Accessible PDF · Tagged PDF · Visual implement · Algorithm · Screen readers · Document accessibility

1 Introduction

Modern assistive technologies improve the ability for people with disability to work effectively with current software. People with impaired vision specifically face the challenge that information is commonly presented visually on a screen. Screen readers [2] are used in such situations to render the content of the screen using speech synthesis or braille output devices.

To allow users to navigate software interfaces and documents, screen readers must expose structural information to the user. For documents, a screen reader will provide key combinations that enumerate headings, figures or other elements. Listening to these items provides the user with an overview of the document, and selecting an item makes the screen reader navigate to the specific item and read the text of the document out aloud starting from that position.

Some document formats have all content embedded in the kind of structural information needed by screen readers. The PDF format, however, is primarily designed to allow precise visual positioning of elements within a document, but these elements do not have any information about their structural relationship to other elements in the document. In order to introduce this kind of structural information the PDF format allows a tree of structural information separate to the content. This structural information, however, may be absent or incomplete depending on the software that generated the PDF file.

© Springer International Publishing Switzerland 2016
K. Miesenberger et al. (Eds.): ICCHP 2016, Part I, LNCS 9758, pp. 367–372, 2016.
DOI: 10.1007/978-3-319-41264-1_50

There are a number of tools available to create accessible PDF documents [3], but PAVE [1] is the only available open source web based application for validating and fixing accessibility issues directly in the PDF files. It has been awarded with the first price at 2014's Conference on Computers Helping People with Disabilities (ICCHP) [4]. It performs automatic fixes for some accessibility issues, while providing an interactive interface for fixing others manually. The most common kind of manual fix necessary is annotating (tagging) the elements of the PDF file with the structural in-formation described above. In a pilot period this tool was used by a large number of users, their feedback was collected and evaluated. The evaluation revealed some major usability issues described in the next section.

2   Usability Challenges with PAVE

In a PDF file, a sequence of characters with uniform formatting and positioned on the same line usually form a single textual element, although in some cases each individual character is such an element. A document will therefore have at least one separate element per line, and often many more. When no structural information is present, this leads to hundreds of elements in a single page that need be annotated, and thousands in a whole document. Users of PAVE have reported that the editing phase is overwhelming due to the often long list of individual items that need fixing. As shown in the screenshot below, all text elements that are not annotated with structural information are individually displayed as "issues" (Fig. 1).

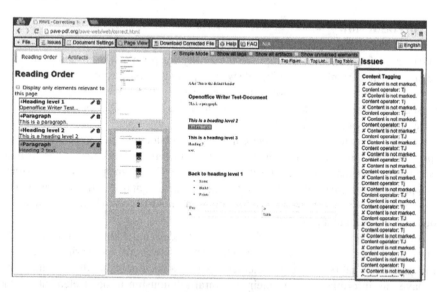

Fig. 1. In the page editing phase, the user is presented with a long list of technical issues that has often been reported as overwhelming.

3   Usability Improvement of PAVE

The main objective for improvements of the usability of PAVE is to reduce the number of actions a user must take to fix a document, and thereby reducing the time spent on each document. The most common action that has to be performed is the grouping of regular text elements into paragraphs. We have therefore implemented an algorithm to automatically perform such grouping wherever blocks of text follow standard layout patterns.

3.1   Automatic Tagging of Paragraph Elements

First, we must determine the text elements that should be considered. Our goal is to tag paragraphs of body text, while requiring the user to tag elements that require additional information such as headings and figures. We determine body text by examining the distribution of element heights; we assume body text constitutes a majority of the elements in the document. Any elements that exceed the median element height with a small error margin are ignored.

We then group text elements into blocks based on interstitial whitespace (Fig. 2). To do this, we first use a vertical line sweep to find potentially overlapping lines. For any potential overlap, we check if there is an actual overlap (allowing for a small margin). If an overlap is present, we mark the elements as part of the same text block.

Fig. 2. Grouping of text elements into blocks based on spatial proximity.

Paragraphs must be created in the correct order, so that the screen reader reads them in order. Before creating the paragraphs we therefore establish an order between text blocks. Ordering by a single coordinate may produce wrong results, e.g. in the case of multiple columns. Based on [5], we instead use the XY-Cut algorithm from [6] to determine an order of the text blocks (Fig. 3).

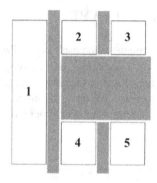

Fig. 3. The reading order of the detected blocks inferred by the XY-cut algorithm.

Within each text block, we use left and right justification as cues to indicate the start and ends of paragraphs (Fig. 4) [7]. We determine if shared left or right edges exists by calculating the median of the start and end positions of the lines in the block, and testing if the majority of the lines are close to the calculated value. If a suitable left edge is found, any lines that do not start on the left edge are the beginning of a paragraph.

Fig. 4. Left and right justification are used as cues for detecting paragraph starts and ends.

4   Evaluation

The above example shows a page of a technical paper. The paper did not have any tags when uploaded, and was automatically tagged using the algorithm described. In Fig. 5, we see that all regular paragraphs of an entire page were tagged in order (marked green), while the remaining elements (marked red: figure, caption and headings) are left to the user as they require additional semantic annotation (heading level, figure caption and alternative text). In Fig. 6, the paragraphs and ordering have been manually highlighted. We see that the ordering correctly follows the two columns, and the one paragraph spanning the columns is combined to a single paragraph.

Fig. 5. The result of the analysis by our tool for a two-column document. Green parts denote the successfully detected paragraphs. Red parts denote text blocks that are left to the user by our tool such as figures or headings (Color figure online).

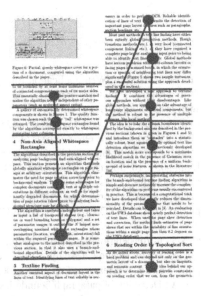

Fig. 6. The reading order as inferred by our tool.

With this new paragraph detection algorithm one kind of tagging issue that may well occur a hundred times in one document can now be solved automatically. In the document used in Figs. 5 and 6, the automatic tagging algorithm reduced the number of elements requiring user action from 679 to 214. This algorithm has therefore a huge potential impact on the efficiency of the tagging of PDF documents with PAVE.

In order to evaluate the efficiency gain of the paragraph detection algorithm and the effect of the other usability improvements implemented in the new version of PAVE extended usability tests with real users are being performed in the next weeks. We will monitor user interactions with the service in the background to measure the number of accessibility issues and the time spent to fix all issues in the document. With structured feedback questionnaires we will elicit the impact on user confidence and satisfaction. In order to set the feedback in place a large number of users will test the application for 4 weeks intensively. The users will report their feedback using structured feedback forms. The results will be discussed in a focus group with users. These steps are carried out within the next few weeks.

5   Conclusion

There are millions of PDF documents available on the internet. Most of them are not accessible for people with a visual impairment. PAVE facilitates analysing and fixing accessibility issues directly in PDF documents in an easy and intuitive way. A first pilot phase showed some major usability challenges mainly due to a missing paragraph detection algorithm. A new algorithm for detecting paragraphs was implemented within PAVE and is currently being tested with a set of different PDF documents and with real users.

References

1. Darvishy, A., Hutter, H.-P., Mannhart, O.: Web application for analysis, manipulation and generation of accessible PDF documents. In: Stephanidis, C. (ed.) UAHCI 2011. LNCS, vol. 6768, pp. 121–128. Springer, Heidelberg (2011)
2. Screen readers. http://www.freedomscientific.com/Products/Blindness/JAWS
3. Darvishy, A., Hutter, H.-P.: Comparison of the effectiveness of different accessibility plugins based on important accessibility criteria. In: Stephanidis, C., Antona, M. (eds.) UAHCI 2013, Part III. LNCS, vol. 8011, pp. 305–310. Springer, Heidelberg (2013)
4. SS12 EU 2014 Finals and Winners. http://ss12.info/Europe/
5. Déjean, H., Meunier, J.-L.: A system for converting PDF documents into structured XML format. In: Bunke, H., Spitz, A. (eds.) DAS 2006. LNCS, vol. 3872, pp. 129–140. Springer, Heidelberg (2006)
6. Meunier, J.-L.: Optimized XY-cut for determining a page reading order. In: Proceedings of the Eighth International Conference on Document Analysis and Recognition (ICDAR 2005), pp. 347–351. IEEE Computer Society, Washington, DC, USA (2005)
7. Chu, Y., Adachi, J., Takasu, A.: Detection of paragraph boundaries in complex page layouts for electronic documents. In: Information Processing Society of Japan (IPSJ) (2012)

PDF/UA and the User Experience Survey

Karen McCall[✉]

Karlen Communications, Paris, Ontario, Canada
info@karlencommunications.com

Abstract. The first iteration of the PDF and the User Experience Survey provides an insight into the user experience of people with disabilities who use adaptive technology on a variety of devices and platforms to access PDF or Portable Document Format content. The goal of this ongoing research is to provide progressive baselines of data which in turn support developers and researchers in designing and implementing tools necessary to ensure access to accessible PDF/ UA conforming documents, PDF/UA conforming viewers/readers and PDF/UA conforming adaptive technology. The underlying premise is to support the advancement and implementation of PDF/UA or ISO 14289.

Keywords: PDF/UA · Strategy · Training · Procurement · Development cycle

1 Background

For many years, those of us working in the field of accessible document design and the accessibility of digital content have heard anecdotal horror stories from people with disabilities who use adaptive technology to access PDF documents about the inaccessibility of the format and the perceived lack of attention that developers of the PDF conversion tools, developers of the PDF readers/viewers, developers of the adaptive technology, developers of the authoring tools and document authors themselves pay to the accessibility of the PDF documents produced.

While those of us researching and developing tools to bridge the gap between document authors, authoring tools, conversion applications, PDF/UA conformance "and the user, new this," this is the first qualitative data based on the user experience we have. The *PDF and the User Experience Survey* provides data needed to research collaboratively and advocate for the implementation and integration of PDF/UA into the global document authoring and conversion ecosystem.

2 Survey Structure

The survey has three parts: demographic information, information on devices and software used to access PDF along with estimates of how many PDF documents are accessed for work, home, education and leisure, and their knowledge of PDF/UA and what benefits it has for them.

© Springer International Publishing Switzerland 2016
K. Miesenberger et al. (Eds.): ICCHP 2016, Part I, LNCS 9758, pp. 373–376, 2016.
DOI: 10.1007/978-3-319-41264-1_51

A Total of 146 surveys were completed [1]. Many of the results confirm what "we know" but other results indicate a high level of exclusion that currently exists in areas of employment, education and quality of life (home and leisure).

97 % of participants stated that they access PDF documents for work with 82 % stating that they access PDF documents for home and 98 % stating that they access PDF documents for education. These are three critical areas of one's life with a significant barrier to information. When this is combined with the data from the survey indicating that 62 % of participants are accessing PDF documents on a daily basis, the "digital divide" increases.

What may be surprising is the number of types of devices and software/tools that are being used to access PDF documents. On Windows, OSX/IOS and Android devices, the majority of adaptive technology used are screen readers. The surprise is in the data collected for the other types of devices and software used to access PDF documents. Many participants are taking PDF documents out of a traditional PDF viewer/reader into applications that currently do not support access to structured documents such as Voice Dream Reader and the Victor reader Stream (Fig. 1).

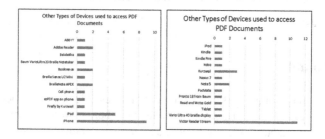

Fig. 1. Other types of tools used to access PDF documents by those with disabilities.

3   User Experience

People with disabilities are using many types of tools to access PDF yet the frustration level is palpable. Frustrations identified were a lack of tagged PDF, an inability to navigate the content of a PDF document, the unreliability of the viewer/reader, long loading times, not being warned that a link leads to a PDF document, constant crashing of the document, adaptive technology not being able to work with the PDF document or viewer/reader, an inability to save forms, no structure, no logical layout and that when reading a PDF document, focus jumps around the document in no logical order. The complete list of comments for these questions are in the survey report [1]. This is a summary of the comments.

When asked to identify what does work when accessing PDF documents, the responses were overwhelming in stating that if a PDF document is well tagged, even tables can be read through row and column, navigation is "quick and efficient," access to complex tables (for example, for health coverage information) is easy (the word "pleasure" was used for this comment), loading of documents is usually fast and "user guides and manuals" are laid out logically.

4   The Current State of Conversion Tools and PDF/UA

While there are several tools available to assist document authors to create more accessible PDF documents [2] as well as companies to assist in creating and implementing strategies and policies for ensuring that PDF content is more accessible [3] there is still a plethora of PDF content that exists and is not accessible. The focus of research and development appears to be on current document authors while the area of remediating existing PDF or PDF from scanned images of content represents an equal challenge in terms of remediation and PDF/UA conformance.

Part of the problem in remediating PDF documents has been a lack of an international standard. While those of us who have been working in the field for many years may "know" what an accessible PDF is, often the interpretation has been up to document remediators, individual departments and organizations. Even with the implementation of PDF/UA, it is identified by many as a "technical specification" which may create a barrier that it is too complicated for document authors.

Even with tools such as axesPDF [4] and the CommonLook Office Global Access [5] remediation tools, there is a perceived steep learning curve requiring a significant investment in training. With focus on new documents, similar tools are needed for legacy documents that must be accessible and conform to PDF/UA.

45 % of participants in the PDF and the User Experience Survey have heard about PDF/UA but the comments indicate that there is confusion about its implementation. The comments reflect an attitude of the standard being too technical and not clearly defining what it means to the end-user when implemented. Other comments indicate that it is difficult to find information or developers who are actively working to implement the specifications in authoring tools used by document authors or in applications or affordable add-ins to applications used to remediate untagged PDF documents.

To summarize the comments on the benefits of PDF/UA and accessible PDF, many felt that "PDF documents are beyond salvaging", that "like WAI/WCAG the standard is a double-edged sword", that if implemented, PDF UA would make accessing and reading PDF documents easier and many harbor a hope that PDF documents will get the attention to accessibility that they need.

5   Summary

The PDF and the User Experience Survey provides original qualitative evidence and data supporting the need to research and develop tools that provide seamless conversion to PDF/UA conforming documents for both current document authors and those remediating legacy documents.

It is clear from the responses to the survey that the people who will be affected by the implementation of PDF/UA do not understand how its implementation will affect their ability to access PDF-based content in a consistent manner with consistent expectations. It is critical that the person accessing PDF documents using adaptive technology be able to clearly and concisely advocate for the implementation of PDF/UA in order for PDF/UA to be a successful international standard.

It is clear from the survey results that the frustrations are prevalent for anyone who accesses PDF documents using adaptive technology with the current state of PDF document accessibility, viewer/reader accessibility and the ability of adaptive technology to leverage the benefits of PDF/UA or accessible PDF documents.

It is clear that for many people with disabilities, they feel that the only way to access content of PDF documents, which are supposed to be "portable" is to take the content out of the PDF format and save it into a format that supports "portable" access to content (for example, Voice Dream Reader, a BrailleNote, PacMate or the Victor Reader Stream).

Those of us working in the areas of research, development and on the PDF and PDF/UA standards must be more visible in the community of users to help "translate" the technical specifications into plain language and real life scenarios so that people with disabilities using adaptive technology to access PDF documents can begin to advocate with us for its implementation as part of legislation, policy and development.

We must demystify the conversion process to PDF/UA conformance so that "the person in the cubicle tasked with ensuring PDF accessibility" has a working knowledge of what they are doing. While a model of outsourcing PDF/UA conformance will work for high volumes of front-facing public documents, there are PDF documents with a short shelf life that departments and organizations need to make accessible in a timely manner (for example sale flyers, lunch specials and internal event flyers).

References

1. McCall, K.: PDF and the User Experience Survey. Karlen Communications - Karen McCall, London (2015). ISBN 978-0-9868085-7-9
2. Spencer, A., McCall, K.: A strategic approach to document accessibility: integrating PDF/UA into your electronic content. In: Miesenberger, K., Fels, D., Archambault, D., Peňáz, P., Zagler, W. (eds.) ICCHP 2014, Part I. LNCS, vol. 8547, pp. 202–204. Springer, Heidelberg (2014)
3. Bianchetti, R., Erle, M., Hofer, S.: Mainstreaming the creation of accessible PDF documents by a rule-based transformation from Word to PDF. In: Miesenberger, K., Karshmer, A., Penaz, P., Zagler, W. (eds.) ICCHP 2012, Part I. LNCS, vol. 7382, pp. 595–601. Springer, Heidelberg (2012)
4. CommonLook PDF Global Access, CommonLook, NetCentric. http://commonlook.com/accessibility-software/commonlook-pdf/
5. McCall, K.: Legislation and standards of accessibility versus intelligent design. In: Proceedings of the Conference Universal Learning Design, Paris 2014, pp. 77–82. Masaryk University, Brno (2014). ISBN 978-80-210-6882-7

Standards, Tools and Procedures in Accessible eBook Production

Standards, Tools and Procedures in Accessible eBook Production

Introduction to the Special Thematic Session

Reinhard Ruemer[1](✉), Georgios Kouroupetroglou[2],
Tomas Murillo-Morales[3], and Klaus Miesenberger[3]

[1] BookAccess, Linz, Austria
reinhard.ruemer@bookaccess.at
[2] National and Kapodistrian University of Athens, Athens, Greece
koupe@di.uoa.gr
[3] Johannes Kepler University, Linz, Austria
{Tomas.Murillo_Morales,Klaus.Miesenberger}@jku.at

Abstract. This Special Thematic Session (STS) on Standards, Tools and Procedures in Accessible eBook Productions intends to give insight into the State-of-the-Art procedures and tools in Accessible eBook Production and also to get to present some best-practice examples first hand. Fields that are tackled by this Special Thematic Session are: Audiobook Production, Accessible Graphics and Figures, Mathematics and automated Braille production, workflow and concrete production tools and practices.

Keywords: Accessible ebooks · Tools · Procedures · Accessible documents · Mathematics · Graphics · Figures · TTS

1 Introduction

The accessible eBook production process is a very diverse process which requires many different steps and procedures:

- The source: from which the production starts vary from an actual printed book to a file from a common word-processing application or a PDF, up to a file in a Desk-top Publishing Tool (DTP), such as InDesign or Quark Xpress.
- The conversion: Addressing complexity e.g. linear access of non-linear materials (vision) and better readability (cognition). Books may consist of different levels of complexity, beginning from novels to complex structures of workbooks with many graphics, mathematical formulas or scientific symbols for school pupils or students, including also books with multilingual text.
- The Presentation: Personalized access including issues like haptic or audio presentation.
- The workflow: Efficient production of accessible and personalized materials, including standards (e.g. DAISY, EPUB), legislation, involving publishers and authors, management, user involvement and delivery services.

- All the above mentioned steps demand more and intense R&D to make the process of eBook production more efficient and the products better accessible and usable.

2 Session Goal

In this Session we will get to see very interesting results of research done in the field of accessible eBook Production. The goal is to get insight into the State-of-the-Art procedures and tools and also to get to know some best-practice examples first hand

3 Session Overview

Collins et al. describe in their paper a complete workflow developed and created with-in the Reading Involves Shared Experience (RISE) project. This joint venture project between Swarthmore College and Gallaudet University aimed at developing a workflow to create and produce children's eBooks with text and sign language videos. The workflow implemented, uses commercial software tools as well as open source soft-ware and free web based services. The project also implemented a content delivery framework in which the RISE eBooks are shared.

Pino et al. are presenting a Web-based Information System for the Workflow Management and Delivery of Accessible eBooks. With the implementation of this Information System at the University of Athens, the whole process of providing study materials for disabled students with was transformed from a mostly offline/manual workflow to an Information System driven online process. This includes the following steps: Users and Requests Management, Digital Content Management and Delivery System. As a result, the time between a student requesting material and the delivery of it could be reduced dramatically. The system also supports a wide range of document formats.

In their presentation, Takaira et al. from the Ibaraki University, they will present a Unified Production System for Various Types of Accessible Textbooks, namely multimodal Textbooks, Sound-Embedded PDF Textbooks and Audio Textbooks with augmented reality Technology. These book types were developed for use in ordinary classrooms hence their appearance is almost similar to regular books or PDFs. Also the effectiveness of the production process itself has been increase with this tool by a considerable amount.

Fume et al. have developed a Text To Speech (TTS) based DAISY content creation Tool called DaisyRings. This web application provides a transliteration system that can convert plain text to DAISY content including formatted HTML and audio data using TTS technology. In over two years this tool has been used by over 1000 individuals and nearly 50 different groups including public library staff. In their paper, Fume et al. present the practical evaluation of this tool, e.g. like how the system has been used, and they will also show the effectiveness of their proposed method for the creation of TTS based DAISY books.

Murillo-Morales et al. will present the upgrade of their LaTeX to Braille conversion System used for educational materials in Austria. This revamped version makes use of state-of-the-art technologies and techniques for automatic Braille document generation, including math and other non-linear information widely used in educational materials especially school books in primary and secondary education in Austria.

John Gardner will give an overview on the new version of the ViewPlus IVEO audio/touch technology tackling the issue of access to figures for blind persons. In practice figures are potentially very accessible to a wide variety of students with print disabilities through a combination of tactile and audio description, but audio-tactile technology has been labour-intensive and often difficult to use. The ViewPlus IVEO software could be a major step in the evolution of audio/touch toward a future in which figures can be universally accessible to everybody.

4 Conclusion

Within this session very interesting research results and tools have been introduced for the production of accessible eBooks. We saw, that through information systems be it desktop software or web based systems and through automatization not only the process of creating accessible eBooks but also the quality of those books can be improved. Many organizations have implemented their own production process workflow. This Session gave insight in detail in some of them. This insight can be the base for further development of a universal accessible eBook production process or for specific organizations to extend or adapt their production process using some of the best practices/tools presented in this session.

Development of a Unified Production System for Various Types of Accessible Textbooks

Takuya Takaira[1]([⊠]), Yoshiaki Tani[1], and Akio Fujiyoshi[2]

[1] Graduate School of Science and Engineering, Ibaraki University,
Hitachi, Ibaraki, Japan
{15nm716f,15nm7201}@vc.ibaraki.ac.jp
[2] Faculty of Engineering, Ibaraki University, Hitachi, Ibaraki, Japan
akio.fujiyoshi.cs@vc.ibaraki.ac.jp

Abstract. This paper presents a unified production system for various types of accessible textbooks. For students with print disabilities, it is important that various types of accessible textbooks should be available so that students can choose one as appropriate. The unified production system enables us to prepare production master data of several types of accessible textbooks at a time.

Keywords: Accessible textbooks · Print disabilities · Multimodal textbooks · Sound-embedded PDF

1 Introduction

Textbooks are considered to be the primary teaching instruments that are necessary to guarantee the quality of education. For students with print disabilities, it is important that various types of accessible textbooks should be available so that students can choose one as appropriate. In Japan, large print textbooks and DAISY textbooks have been available for students with print disabilities in compulsory education. Recently, textbook publishing companies started producing large print textbooks by themselves at their expense. The quality of large print textbooks is very improved. DAISY (Digital Audio Accessible Information System) is a world standard of accessible books for people with print disabilities [1]. A number of textbooks are translated into DAISY by the efforts of volunteers. Many students with print disabilities in special supported classrooms use either large print textbooks or DAISY textbooks. However, the number of students in ordinary classrooms who use these textbooks is very few.

As new types of accessible textbooks suitable for use in ordinary classrooms, the authors have developed three kinds of textbooks with audio support: Multimodal textbooks [2,3], Sound-embedded PDF textbooks [4], and Audio textbooks with AR technology. Multimodal textbooks are paper-based textbooks with audio support utilizing invisible 2-dimensional codes and digital audio players with a 2-dimensional code scanner. Because invisible 2-dimensional codes are printed overlappingly on normal characters of regular textbooks, the look

K. Miesenberger et al. (Eds.): ICCHP 2016, Part I, LNCS 9758, pp. 381–388, 2016.
DOI: 10.1007/978-3-319-41264-1_52

of multimodal textbooks is almost the same as regular textbooks. When a 2-dimensional code is scanned, the corresponding speech sound is reproduced. Sound-embedded PDF textbooks are digital interactive textbooks that run on PDF viewers such as Adobe Acrobat Reader. When a text is tapped on the screen, the text is highlighted and the corresponding speech sound is reproduced. Audio textbooks with AR technology are one of augmented reality applications on a regular textbook. When a page of a regular textbook is captured by a camera of a tablet, and some part of the textbook on the screen is pointed, the corresponding speech sound is reproduced.

In order to ease the production of various types of accessible textbooks for students with print disabilities, a unified production system was developed. The information of the structure of a document is essential for the production of each type of accessible textbooks. By Japanese "Barrier-free textbook law", we can obtain PDF data of regular textbooks from textbook publishing companies. From a PDF file of a textbook, the unified production system automatically recognizes the layout of the textbook. Since the PDF file of a textbook only contains the information of characters, lines, and pictures, the structure of a document such as headings, paragraphs, and sentences has to be recognized.

The unified production system outputs production master data of the three kinds of textbooks with audio support. Since the unified production system was developed, the cost of production of accessible textbooks was much reduced. In addition, the number of mistakes was much decreased.

2   Unified Production System for Accessible Textbooks

The unified production system (Fig. 1) is an application software developed on Java with standard widget toolkit (SWT). It runs on multi-platforms: Windows and OS X. Apache PDFbox [5] is used to obtain character information and page images from a PDF file. The table 1 shows the system requirements.

Table 1. System requirements

Operating system	Windows 7 or later OS X 10.9 or later
Display resolution	XGA 1024 × 768 (Full HD 1900 × 1080 recommended)

The system was originally developed for the production of multimodal textbooks. Since the production master data of multimodal textbooks contains enough information to produce accessible textbooks in other formats, the system was extended.

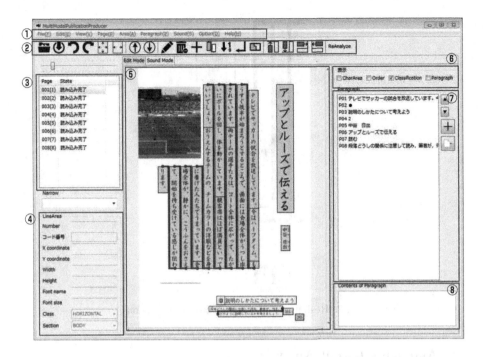

Fig. 1. Screenshot of the unified production system

2.1   Usage of the Unified Production System

The system is designed so that average PC users can use it smoothly. It has the following features:

- Major functions can be accessed by pushing icons on the tool bar (area 2 of Fig. 1).
- At the center, a page image of a PDF file is shown (area 5 of Fig. 1). The scale is adjustable with the scalebar. Pages are selectable from the list (area 3 of Fig. 1).
- Lines in a page are editable. Each line has the information of characters composing it. They can be combined and connected to form a "sentence". Creation of a new line and resize of a line can be done with mouse operations (Fig. 2).
- A set of sentences form a paragraph. Paragraphs are editable (area 7 of Fig. 1).
- Speech sound files can be assigned to each sentence with drag and drop operations. Sound formats, wave and mp3 are supported. Speech sound files are combined automatically when more than 2 files are assigned to the same line. The assignment of speech sound files can be checked on the system.

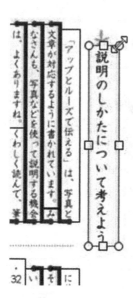

Fig. 2. Resizing a line with a mouse operation

2.2 Automatic Layout Analysis

The system automatically analyzes the layout of a PDF file. The analysis is done in the following steps:

1. The system uses Apache PDFbox to obtain character information from a PDF files. The information of font name, font size, position, size of bounding-box and order of characters are obtained.
2. A sequence of characters with the same font name and the same font size are combined and connected if they don't contain a full stop character at the middle. The combined charters form sentence Full stop characters are chosen from '.', ':', ';' , ',', '?', '!', '' and ''.
3. A class is automatically assigned to each sentence. A class is chosen from "HEAD", "BODY", "NOTE", "LIST" and "AUXILIARY" by font size and position in a page.
4. A sequence of sentences in the same class are combined if an indentation dose not exist between lines. They form a "paragraph".

2.3 Creating Production Master Data with the System

Production master data are created by the following directions.

1. Choose an input PDF file.
2. The system automatically analyzes the layout of the PDF file. The results of analysis are displayed on the center of the window.

3. Errors of the automatic analysis can be corrected by users with the editor of the system. It is easy because of the simple interface of the editor.
4. The system outputs a manuscript for reading the document. The script will be transferred to volunteers or a speech synthesizer.
5. Assignment of sound files to sentences can be done by drug and drop operations. Users can check the assigned sound.
6. By choosing a type of accessible textbooks, the system outputs a production master data.

3   New Types of Accessible Textbooks

As new types of accessible textbooks suitable for use in ordinary classrooms, three kinds of textbooks with audio support were developed.

It is desirable that each student with print disabilities can choose an appropriate one from large print textbooks, DAISY textbooks, and these 3 kinds of accessible textbooks.

3.1   Multimodal Textbooks

Multimodal textbooks (Fig. 3) are paper-based textbooks with audio support. Invisible 2-dimensional codes are printed overlappingly on normal characters of regular textbooks. When a 2-dimensional code is scanned, the corresponding speech sound is reproduced. We think multimodal textbooks are best in ordinary classrooms because the paper textbook looks the same as a regular textbook, the price of a digital audio player is reasonable (about 30 euro), and the digital audio player is small and can be used with a headphone.

Since sight and hearing help each other, students can read the textbooks easily and correctly.

Fig. 3. Multimodal textbooks

386   T. Takaira et al.

3.2 Sound-Embedded PDF Textbooks

PDF is a standard file format used to present document independent of application software, hardware, and operating systems [6]. Sound-embedded PDF textbooks (Fig. 4) are PDF documents with embedded sounds that run on a PDF viewers such as Adobe Acrobat Reader [7]. Digital interactive functions of PDF such as highlight, reflow, black and white reversal are also available in sound-embedded PDF. A computer or tablet with PDF viewer is necessary to use sound-embedded PDF textbooks.

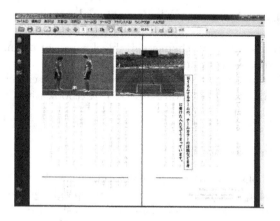

Fig. 4. Sound-embedded PDF textbooks

3.3 Audio Textbook with AR Technology

Audio textbooks with AR technology (Fig. 5) are one of augmented reality applications on a regular textbook. The application was developed for Android platform. When images of a page of a regular textbook captured by the camera of a tablet device are converted into a feature vector, the page number of the images is identified by comparing the feature vector to vectors in the feature space of the page images of the textbook.

Some part of the textbook on the screen is pointed, the corresponding speech sound is reproduced. A tablet device with a camera or smartphone is necessary to use audio textbook with AR technology. A regular textbook is also necessary. This textbook is suitable for temporary use.

4 Effectiveness of the Unified Production System

Before the development of the unified production system, the production of multimodal textbooks was done with Garyotensei (Apollo Japan Co., Ltd). Garyotensei is an image editing software for 2-dimensional code patterns. Its usage is like a bitmap editor such as Microsoft Paint, which is used with a lot of mouse operations.

Fig. 5. Audio textbooks with AR technology

In order to evaluate the unified production system, we compare the time needed to produce dot patters of 2-dimensional codes for a collection of pages from textbooks with our system to the time needed with Garyotensei. The collection consists of 6 pages; story, expository writing, work, Kanji table, discussion and essay from textbooks in Japanese language for elementary school published by Mitsumura Tosho publishing Co., Ltd. The number of pages, characters and sentences of the collections of pages are shown in Table 2.

Table 2. Number of pages, characters, sentences

Number of pages	Number of characters	Number of sentences
6	2108	177

For experimental subjects, 3 university students are employed. They are asked to create dot patters of collection of the pages by the different ways. The one way is using Garyotensei and the other is using the unified production system.

The result is shown in Table 3. The time needed with the unified production system is about one-third of the time needed with Garyotensei.

Table 3. Result of experiment

Subject	Garyotensei	Unified production system
Subject A	22 min 45 s	7 min 55 s
Subject B	31 min 55 s	10 min 30 s
Subject C	24 min 10 s	9 min 41 s

5 Conclusion

A unified production system was developed for efficient production of 3 new kinds of textbooks with audio support. The cost of preparation of production master data of these new textbooks was much reduced with the system. In addition, the number of mistakes was much decreased.

It is planned to extend the function of the unified production system so that it can output production master data in DAISY and accessible PDF [8].

The system will be released on the website of our laboratory [9].

Acknowledgement. This work was partially supported by JSPS KAKENHI Grant Number 26282044.

References

1. DAISY. http://www.daisy.org/
2. Fujiyoshi, A., Fujiyoshi, M., Ohsawa, A., Ota, Y.: Development of multimodal textbooks with invisible 2-dimensional codes for students with print disabilities. In: Miesenberger, K., Fels, D., Archambault, D., Peňáz, P., Zagler, W. (eds.) ICCHP 2014, Part II. LNCS, vol. 8548, pp. 331–337. Springer, Heidelberg (2014)
3. Fujiyoshi, A., Ohsawa, A., Takaira, T., Tani, Y., Fujiyoshi, M., Ota, Y.: Paper-based textbooks with audio support for print-disabled students. In: The Proceedings of AAATE 2015, pp. 11–18 (2015)
4. Tani, Y., Takaira, T., Fujiyoshi, A.: Trial production of sound-embedded accessible PDF. In: The proceedings of DEIMS 2016 (2016)
5. Apache PDFbox. https://pdfbox.apache.org/
6. Adobe Systems Incorporated. PDF Reference, 6th edn. version 1.23. http://www.adobe.com/content/dam/Adobe/en/devnet/acrobat/pdfs/pdf_reference_1-7.pdf
7. Adobe Acrobat Reader. https://acrobat.adobe.com/jp/ja/products/pdf-reader.html
8. PDF Association. http://www.pdfa.org
9. Multimodal Publication Producer. http://apricot.cis.ibaraki.ac.jp/Multimodal PublicationProducer

RISE eBooks: Leveraging Off-the-Shelf Software Components in Support of Deaf Literacy

Riley Collins[1], Gene Mirus[2], and Donna Jo Napoli[1(✉)]

[1] Swarthmore College, Swarthmore, PA, USA
riley3.collins@gmail.com, dnapoli1@swarthmore.edu
[2] Gallaudet University, Washington, D.C., USA
gene.mirus@gallaudet.edu

Abstract. The RISE bimodal-bilingual eBooks project is a joint initiative of Gallaudet University and Swarthmore College in the United States aimed to promote shared reading activities between hearing adults and their deaf children, although the format may welcome users from a broader spectrum. It produces ebooks, typically using published picture books as a base, and adding sign language videos, where the countries and languages involved right now number a dozen, but the global interest is growing steadily. The project has developed a workflow that is easily implementable using commercial off-the-shelf software, or open source alternatives, with an aim of making the production of bimodal-bilingual ebooks both readily accessible and efficient.

Keywords: Deaf children · Literacy · ebooks · Sign languages

1 Introduction: Background and Rationale

Literacy allows us to process a complex of knowledge in a variety of media: oral, manual-visual, or print. When we listen to a story (told ritualistically, so that it is (nearly) the same every time, or more individualistically), or watch one (signed ritualistically or individualistically), or read one, we process multiple things. First, there is the primary information of who did what to whom, when, where, why, and how. But second, is more subtle information, what we here call secondary, such as what the unstated motives were for this behavior and what the likely impact is on the affected parties. Secondary information enriches primary information, allowing us to feel empathy, make inferences and, therefore, predictions, and comprehend the story's relevance to our own lives, which may be distant from the lives of the story characters. Secondary information is what makes us care about stories.

In a sense, all information that is imparted from one person to another forms a story, though the majority of these stories are of a minimal sort. This is why journalists talk about the "feature story" of the day, whether it be about a scientific discovery, a medical alert, a military debacle. We organize information, fiction or nonfiction, around that set of primary information factors, and we rely on our audience understanding the secondary information factors to get the full import of what we are trying to convey. Again, it is

K. Miesenberger et al. (Eds.): ICCHP 2016, Part I, LNCS 9758, pp. 389–396, 2016.
DOI: 10.1007/978-3-319-41264-1_53

the secondary information that makes the audience care about the news; it clarifies the import of the news and makes it profound for them.

All this means that literacy is essential to people partaking fully of their own humanity. Further, print literacy is necessary to gaining information beyond that conveyed by those people we have immediate access to orally or visually, thus being print-literate is critical in modern society. Gaining print literacy, however, can be difficult. For hearing people of ordinary intelligence and without relevant disabilities, difficulty in gaining print literacy may be relative to the deep (i.e., opaque) or shallow (i.e., transparent) nature of the orthography: learning to read in character systems that have little to no correspondence between symbol and sound (for example, Chinese characters as used for Mandarin and many other languages) is far more difficult than learning to read in alphabetic systems, particularly those with a close correspondence between symbol and sound (for example, the Roman alphabet as used for Spanish and Italian, which have close to one-to-one correspondences across-the-board, in contrast to its use for French and English, which have multiple many-to-one correspondences).

For deaf people, difficulty in gaining print literacy has more sources. For one, all orthographies are deep to the deaf. This is obviously true for the deaf person who has little to no access to sound (although signing deaf people use phonological information from sign in reading alphabetic script [1]). However, even deaf people with assistive technology that allows some access to sound have difficulties learning to read (where the child with a hearing aid fares better than one with a cochlear implant [2]). For another, the majority of deaf children do not acquire a first language in the ordinary way – i.e., simply by being surrounded by users of an accessible language, without explicit instruction. Instead, they may be surrounded by spoken language they find inaccessible and not have adequate exposure to a sign language to acquire it well. Researchers point to lack of a firm foundation in a first language as a culprit in the fact that deaf children lag behind hearing peers in print literacy [3].

A third possible contributor to difficulty in gaining print literacy may lie in lack of early exposure to stories. Repeatedly, research on print literacy concludes that shared reading activities (SRAs) when a child is small are important to whether that child will become skilled at reading ([4] and many earlier works). Enjoyable language interaction and play over a story (such as open-ended questions like "What would you do next if you were that bunny?") are critical to understanding not just the primary information, but, especially, the secondary information of the story. Through this language interaction, children come to see books as fun and worth the effort of learning to read. This is why scholars strongly recommend SRAs for deaf children [5].

But it is also why we should strongly recommend visual storytelling. Deaf children learn best when their visual attention is captured [6]. Deaf parents know this instinctively, and when they engage in SRAs with their deaf children, they retell (parts of) the story in sign, often embellishing or orienting the story to entice their own child, as well as employ a range of methods to focus the child's attention [7].

Given all the above, it should come as no surprise that deaf children who sign well have superior print literacy achievement to those who don't [8–14].

Therefore, in an effort to enhance deaf children's literacy skills, we set out to produce materials to encourage SRAs at home with preschoolers, helping to develop the needed visual literacy skills to support later print literacy skills through spurring language interaction that supports understanding of primary and secondary information. Since the huge majority of deaf children are born to hearing parents, many face challenges in acquiring the shared experiences that provide developmental advantages.

2   RISE eBooks

The RISE (Reading Involves Shared Experience) eBooks project was founded as a joint venture between Swarthmore College and Gallaudet University. RISE produces entertaining bilingual-bimodal ebooks, in a sign language and in the text of the ambient spoken language, that are accessible to both deaf children and their (typically hearing) parents, with an aim towards encouraging enjoyable SRAs. The books are drawn from a variety of sources including the public domain (mostly classic books but also a few newer books), and agreements involving the kind permission of Penguin Random House and National Geographic Books (NG), as well as the kind permission of individual children's authors and illustrators. The association with NG has allowed the inclusion of nonfiction ebooks. All the ebooks are prepared for publication through the project's workflow and then published for free on the Internet [15].

2.1   Characteristics of Other Digital Products with Similar Aims

Gallaudet University's Science of Learning Center's project "Visual Language and Visual Learning" (VL2) has produced six ebooks, with original stories in commercial application form [16], using an in-house developed framework [17]. The aim is explicit reading instruction – so the SRA has a pedagogical focus. They use ASL, are marketed for the 5 year old and up, and sold at a reasonable price.

The SMARTSign Center for Accessible Technology in Sign produces a collection of tools that allow readers to access in ASL videos of words, phrases, sentences, and whole pages from popular books. The videos are provided by members of the public, and reviewed by an editorial board to ensure quality. While their tools are free, they are intended to be used in tandem with a copy of the physical book [18].

Additionally, videobooks in various sign languages have been appearing on the Internet increasingly over the past decade [19]. Typically, the stories are original and offered at minor cost. They include text, illustrations, and signing.

2.2   Characteristics of RISE EBooks

RISE ebooks are not explicitly pedagogical. While the sign video on a given page corresponds to the text, the correspondence is loose. Signers cover the information in the text in a manner appropriate to the visual-learning needs of the deaf child; it makes use of the visual vernacular common to sign stories [20], thus giving the children a tradition that is their heritage by virtue of being deaf. The signers, thus, have considerable creative freedom. All are deaf students and signing is their most comfortable means of communication. They are guided by two professors: Gene Mirus, a former member of the

National Theater of the Deaf, and Donna Jo Napoli, a children's author. The signing is energetic and enthusiastic, allowing many points from which parent and child can initiate conversation of a factual and an inferential nature.

The signers' creative energy may have an effect on the children. In observations of children using the ebooks in a school setting in autumns 2013 and 2014 [21], and in a pilot study of their use in school and home in autumn 2014 [22], deaf children mimicked the videos starting as early as the second viewing. Then they re-told the stories to others, varying them to make their feelings about the plot obvious and to add details that personalized the stories. Most important, they had fun, claiming ownership of the ability to tell the stories in a sign language. Thus the ebooks led to complex language interactions about both the primary and secondary information in the stories.

Further, because almost all our ebooks use a picture book produced by a publishing house, the stories and illustrations have been "vetted" for quality. With respect to books for which the copyright has expired, this means the children are introduced to classics that are part of their heritage by virtue of living in a given country. It further means that parents might well be faced with stories they loved as a child and want to share with their children. So parent interest is a given, and that means parents might watch the videos with more concentration, so that their own signing skills improve. This is important, since everyone in the family needs signing skills to interact with the deaf child in a way that promotes the child's overall linguistic abilities and supports the child's psychological needs of being accepted as a deaf person who can interact with family members in all the ordinary ways that family members interact [23].

3   Work Flow

The RISE project's workflow keeps two constraints in mind: ease of use by nontechnical project members, and assurance of clear, accessible representation of text and sign within ebooks. The software in each step is usually interchangeable with at least one other, and the project has utilized commercial software and open-source alternatives. This makes production feasible for groups without access to funds for traditional commercial solutions to the different tasks required by the workflow. In the following workflow description, closed and open-source options are represented. A large part of the workflow is parallelizable, as the signing and text portions of the ebooks can be prepared separately until late in the process. This is convenient as it allows for remote collaboration between teams of producers and signers, a quality that has allowed the RISE project to collaborate with individuals and teams from around the world.

3.1   Text and Video Preparation, and Audio Narration

Ebooks begin the process as a PDF document provided by the book's publishing house or, for older public-domain books, from high quality scans of the physical texts. The PDF is then broken into pages and the pages are reduced to their constituent stylistic elements (text, illustrations) using a standard photo editing suite, either Adobe Photoshop or the GNU Image Manipulation Program (GIMP). Once the PDF has been processed, the resulting files are ready to be used to construct the ebook template.

For each page in the book, a video is prepared on a green screen by a signer. The files are then edited with a video editing suite, Adobe Premiere, Apple's Final Cut Pro, or the open-source Blender, and prepared for the ebook template by replacing the green screen with an appropriate background to match the aesthetic of a given book.

Although the primary audience of the RISE project is deaf children and their hearing parents, each page has associated audio narration in order to make the ebooks accessible to the largest audience possible. This way a deaf person (adult or child) can share the book with a non-reading hearing person. Further, this makes the ebooks more useful to hearing children with special needs who can benefit from exposure to sign languages, including children with autism.

3.2 Template Construction

Once the text and sign files are processed, if this is the first time a particular PDF has been used to make an ebook, we build a template in two formats, ebook and online book. The template is a standardized layout for the placement of text and videos that can be used for any subsequent languages the story will be prepared in.

The ebook template is built in Apple's iBooks Author program, the only available and free program when the RISE project began. It abstracts much of the technical challenge of incorporating videos into an ebook format. The downside to this format is that ebooks made with iBooks Author can be viewed only on certain devices within the Apple family – a regrettable limitation, given expense and availability.

In contrast, the online template is a Google Drive Presentation (GDP), which offers two benefits. First, stories can play on devices beyond the Apple family; anyone with Internet access (at home, or in libraries, schools, or other institutions) can view them. Second, this format allows sharing stories with groups, including classroom settings utilizing modern teaching aids such as a Smart Board. This means that children in a deaf school can enjoy the experience together. Most deaf children in developed countries, however, are mainstreamed, and for the mainstreamed child, the GDP has two additional advantages. First, deaf children can use the same educational material as hearing peers, enjoying the contents together. This is significant in that it removes from the teacher the responsibility of finding materials that include the deaf child – a responsibility not all teachers reliably assume [24]. Second, deaf children can delight at finding themselves in the far too atypical position of having a linguistic advantage over their hearing classmates in that they can teach signs to hearing children who take an interest in the book. Both advantages can help with social integration, one of the major problems for deaf children in mainstream settings [25].

Layout of the template is influenced by two main factors: respect for the original layout, and attention to making visually prominent both languages (sign and text).

For books not in the public domain, templates adhere strictly to the layout of the print book. This adherence required the development of several strategies for inserting videos into pages. The first is utilizing existing blank space in the original layout – simple if there is enough space. A more labor-intensive strategy is to insert the signer into an illustration on the page. The green screen behind the signer is edited so that the signer appears as part of the illustration. When there is not enough blank space or insertion of a video would compromise illustrations and/or text, we utilize a "push button." This is a widget at the top of a page; when pressed it expands to a page-sized video of the signers with the full page (text and illustrations) mapped behind them. Thus readers can enjoy the text and illustration before seeing the video superimposed.

For books in the public domain, liberties can be taken with design, allowing show-casing the signer to enhance narrative and/or telling. One ebook has experimented with a different format. Instead of static text with a video that requires a click to play, both video and text require a button to be pressed for viewing, whether together or inde-pendently. Other books have enhancements to original illustrations in the form of animation, while still others have signers interacting with illustrations.

Once a template is set, a video version of the text is prepared as a final alternate format. The video is produced from the iBooks version of the text, and is made accessible over the Internet. In addition, the video format has been used to experiment with an alternative approach to designing the books. Instead of fitting the video inside pre-existing text and illustrations of a traditional book layout, the alternate format fits text and illustrations into a video of the signer. While this requires more time to produce, it provides another engaging reading experience for deaf children and their parents.

3.3   Revisions and Publishing

The first draft of the ebook is produced in the iBooks format, through collaboration between student signer and student producer/editor. The signer is responsible for the telling of the content. The producer is responsible for formatting and film editing. Both collaborate on every decision. Each pair is coupled with another pair, into teams of 4 people. All four people give feedback on the first draft. The professors also give feedback at every stage, as do other people involved in the education of deaf children.

The second draft is tested on families with deaf children and deaf schools, where observation and feedback lead to further improvements. The third drafts are published and distributed free. Ebooks are available in the iBooks store through Apple, and the GDP and video formats can be downloaded from our website at Gallaudet University.

For legal reasons, books under copyright are not available on the iBooks store, and are instead provided through a content delivery system implemented using Google Drive's API. This provides RISE an easy method for sharing templates with teams, domestic and abroad, interested in producing an ebook and allows partial tracking of how many downloads are done by families or classrooms that have a deaf individual.

4   Reach

Over the three years that the RISE project has been active, more than 6,000 copies of the ebooks have been downloaded through the iTunes store. Since January 2016, a website hosted at Gallaudet University has made available our full range of stories so far (and announces several in progress). The project has produced ebooks in American, Korean, Nepali, Fiji, Japanese, and Brazilian sign languages with the appropriate written text; additional ones in German, Irish, Greek, Saudi Arabian, Swedish, and Italian sign languages with the appropriate written text are in production.

5 Future Work

The project will continue to provide ebooks with stories and non-fiction works for deaf children of all signing abilities. There are presently hundreds of thousands of picture books for hearing children in the USA and only dozens of bilingual-bimodal ebooks for deaf children. The disparity in other countries is also drastic. We hope to change this not simply by adding more stories, but by making available an online manual for producing these ebooks and by teaching deaf children how to tell stories in the visual vernacular, so that we help create new generations of ebook producers.

With respect to more technical aspects, our next step is deployment of a framework to automate the RISE workflow to the greatest possible degree. Optimally we will be able to input edited video along with the appropriate template to automatically produce ebooks on all our supported platforms with no additional work. We also hope to offer an application on Android devices, as they represent a large portion of the market share globally and are more prevalent than Apple devices in developing markets. https://www.gallaudet.edu/american-sign-language-and-deaf-studies/bilingual-bimodal-ebooks.html.

References

1. Holmer, E., Heimann, M., Rudner, M.: Evidence of an association between sign language phonological awareness and word reading in deaf and hard-of-hearing children. Res. Dev. Disabil. **48**, 145–159 (2016). doi:10.1016/j.ridd.2015.10.008
2. Harris, M., Terlektsi, E.: Reading and spelling abilities of deaf adolescents with cochlear implants and hearing aids. J. Deaf Stud. Deaf Edu. **16**, 24–34 (2011). doi:10.1093/deafed/enq031
3. Hoffmeister, R.J., Caldwell-Harris, C.L.: Acquiring English as a second language via print: the task for deaf children. Cognition **132**, 229–242 (2014). doi:10.1016/j.cognition.2014.03.014
4. Skwarchuk, S.-L., Sowinski, C., LeFevre, J.-A.: Formal and informal home learning activities in relation to children's early numeracy and literacy skills: the development of a home numeracy model. J. Exp. Child Psychol. **121**, 63–84 (2014). doi:10.1016/j.jecp.2013.11.006
5. Sullivan, S., Oakhill, J.: Components of story comprehension and strategies to support them in hearing and deaf or hard of hearing readers. Top Lang. Disord. **35**, 133–143 (2015)
6. Dye, M.W.G., Hauser, P.C., Bavelier, D.: Visual attention in deaf children and adults. In: Marschark, M., Hauser, P.C. (eds.) Deaf Cognition: Foundations and Outcomes, pp. 250–263. Oxford University Press, Oxford (2008)
7. Berke, M.: Reading books with young deaf children: strategies for mediating between American Sign Language and English. J. Deaf Stud. Deaf Edu. **18**, 299–311 (2013). doi:10.1093/deafed/ent001

8. Clark, M.D., Hauser, P.C., Miller, P., Kargin, T., Rathmann, C., Guldenoglu, B., Kubus, O., Spurgeon, E., Israel, E.: The importance of early sign language acquisition for deaf readers. Reading Writ. Q. **32**, 127–151 (2016). doi:10.1080/10573569.2013.878123

9. Schick, B.: The development of American Sign Language and manually coded English systems. In: Marschark, M., Spencer, P. (eds.) The Handbook of Deaf Studies, Language, and Education, pp. 219–231. Oxford University Press, Oxford (2003)

10. Paul, P.: Processes and components of reading. In: Marschark, M., Spencer, P. (eds.) The Handbook of Deaf Studies, Language, and Education, pp. 97–109. Oxford University Press, Oxford (2003)

11. Mayer, C., Akamatsu, T.: Bilingualism and literacy. In: Marschark, M., Spencer, P. (eds.) The Handbook of Deaf Studies, Language, and Education, pp. 136–150. Oxford University Press, Oxford (2003)

12. Padden, C., Ramsey, C.: American Sign Language and reading ability in deaf children. In: Chamberlain, C., Morford, J., Mayberry, R. (eds.) Language Acquisition by Eye, pp. 165–189. Erlbaum, Mahwah (2000)

13. Strong, M., Prinz, P.: Is American Sign Language skill related to English literacy? In: Chamberlain, C., Morford, J., Mayberry, R. (eds.) Language Acquisition by Eye, pp. 131–142. Erlbaum, Mahwah (2000)

14. Hoffmeister, R.J.: A piece of the puzzle: ASL and reading comprehension in deaf children. In: Chamberlain, C., Morford, J., Mayberry, R. (eds.) Language Acquisition by Eye, pp. 143–163. Erlbaum, Mahwah (2000)

15. Rise eBooks. http://www.gallaudet.edu/american-signlanguage-and-deaf-studies/bilingual-bimodal-ebooks.html

16. Vl2 storybook app. http://vl2storybookapps.com/

17. Malzkuhn, M.A., Herzig, M.P.: Bilingual storybook app designed for deaf and hard of hearing children based on research principles. Int. J. Adv. Comput. Sci. **3**, 631–635 (2013)

18. Center for Accessible Technology in Sign. Smartsign. http://cats.gatech.edu/content/smartsign

19. Napoli, D.J., Mirus, G.: Shared reading activities: a recommendation for deaf children. Glob. J. Spec. Educ. Serv. **3**, 38–42 (2015)

20. Cook, P.: Visual vernacular. In: Bauman, H.-D., Nelson, J., Rose, H. (eds.) Signing the Body Poetic. University of California Press, Berkeley/Los Angeles (2006). Clip 5.5

21. Mirus, G., Napoli, D.J.: Fun and language interaction: bimodal-bilingual ebooks. Presented at the 22nd International Congress on the Education of the Deaf, 6–9 July 2015, Athens, Greece. Available upon request to the authors

22. Omardeen, R.: A preliminary look into the efficacy of bilingual ASL-English ebooks. Senior thesis. Swarthmore College (2015). Available in Linguistics Department website on http://www.swarthmore.edu

23. Fellinger, J., Holzinger, D., Sattel, H., Laucht, M., Goldberg, D.: Correlates of mental health disorders among children with hearing impairments. Dev. Med. Child Neurol. **51**, 635–641 (2009). doi:10.1111/j.1469-8749.2008.03218.x

24. Vermeulen, J.A., Denessen, E.J.P.G., Knoors, H.E.T.: Mainstream teachers about including deaf or hard of hearing students. Teach. Teach. Educ. **28**, 174–181 (2012). doi:10.1016/j.tate.2011.09.007

25. Wauters, L.N., Knoors, H.E.T.: Social integration of deaf children in inclusive settings. J. Deaf Stud. Deaf Edu. **13**, 21–36 (2008). doi:10.1093/deafed/enm028

A LaTeX to Braille Conversion Tool for Creating Accessible Schoolbooks in Austria

Tomás Murillo-Morales[1(✉)], Klaus Miesenberger[1], and Reinhard Ruemer[2]

[1] Johannes Kepler University, Linz, Austria
{Tomas.Murillo_Morales,Klaus.Miesenberger}@jku.at
[2] BookAccess, Linz, Austria
reinhard.ruemer@bookaccess.at

Abstract. We introduce an upgrade of the LaBraDoor (LaTeX to Braille Door) system, a tool that allows textbooks to be automatically converted from their TeX source into an accessible equivalent in Braille. The revamped version makes use of state-of-the-art technologies and techniques for automatic Braille document generation, including math and other non-linear information widely used in educational materials.

Keywords: Document conversion · Braille · TeX · Accessible textbook · Parsing

1 Introduction

Primary and secondary schools in Austria generally make heavy use of textbooks that support teaching and help students better understand the concepts being taught as well as practicing them. Therefore it is of vital importance that these books are made accessible to visually impaired and blind students. When the contents of the book are purely textual, an electronic version of the print book might suffice, as it can be read aloud by text-to-speech software. However, in most cases textbooks contain information that relies on some kind of visual processing for its proper understanding, such as tables, mathematical formulas, chemical notation and geometrical figures. In these cases, Braille transcripts of the books are of great help for blind students, who can understand the contents of those elements that otherwise would have to be skipped, albeit with certain limitations (e.g. complex diagrams and maps are hard to represent in Braille).

The use of Braille books is nowadays commonplace in Austrian schools with blind pupils. Braille books are converted from their print counterparts, written in a reasonable subset of LaTeX by following a set of guidelines. LaTeX was chosen as the book format because of its excellent typesetting quality, especially when rendering mathematical formulae, and its widespread use in mathematical and scientific publications [1].

In this paper we introduce a modern approach for automatically transforming textbooks from their LaTeX source into their equivalent Braille representation, including tables, one- and two-dimensional math, and other non-linear information.

© Springer International Publishing Switzerland 2016
K. Miesenberger et al. (Eds.): ICCHP 2016, Part I, LNCS 9758, pp. 397–400, 2016.
DOI: 10.1007/978-3-319-41264-1_54

2   State of the Art

Instructional materials are converted into Braille worldwide by the use of Braille translation software and Braille embossers [2]. These programs recognize a variety of digital text formats which are converted to Braille characters in the user-specified language. Some well-known examples include the Duxbury Braille Translator (DBT), Braille 2000 and the Hagener Braille Software (HBS). However, among these only DBT allows LaTeX as the input format, probably due to the fact that parsing full-featured TeX documents cannot be performed in a reliable way. This does not mean that we must discard it as a suitable input format though, as parsers for practical subsets of LaTeX can be implemented [3]. In any case, the presence of customized LaTeX commands (for instance, for placing 2D math blocks) does not allow us to directly use any of the aforementioned tools.

A tool for automatic conversion of documents written in (a subset of) LaTeX into Braille, LABRADOOR [4], was developed at the Institute Integrated Study of the Johannes Kepler University. This system has since been dated by more powerful, flexible tools such as HBS for Braille document creation or the MathML notation for math representation, which feature more flexible configuration settings and output formats. An upgrade of the old LABRADOOR system was then required.

As HBS takes care of many steps in Braille output generation (inserting page breaks, inserting the correct page numbering on the braille output, correct hyphenation of the text, text alignment, etc.) and it was being used already in other areas at our institute, we decided a LaTeX to HBS conversion would fit our needs best.

3   LaBraDoor - LaTeX to Braille Door

The newly implemented LaTeX-to-Braille Door, LaBraDoor, acts as a black box that, given a document written in LaTeX following the layout guidelines for textbooks used in Austrian schools [5], generates a file in the HBS intermediate format that can be later on converted into a Braille document with a great degree of customization. The workflow of the implemented system can be seen on Fig. 1.

The conversion process is a multistep procedure that makes use of several libraries, techniques and intermediate file formats. From the moment a LaTeX source file is prepared by the teacher until the Braille book is ready, the following steps take place:

1. LaBraDoor tokenizes and parses the original document and generates a parse tree (PT) of its contents. A grammar for the ANTLR language recognition tool [6] has been implemented that covers the TeX syntax as given by the authoring layout guidelines. These guidelines [5] indicate authors the subset of LaTeX commands that LaBraDoor supports. These include chapters and sections, tables, math formulae, lists, footnotes, page numbering, and many others. Besides these, customized commands specific for educational contents have been included. For example, the 'add' block commands let teachers define 2-dimensional addition or subtraction problems.

2. The PT then goes through a preprocessing phase in which all the mathematical formulae, elements of the table of contents, footnotes and other bits of data are individually fetched. This process is separated from the grammar definition itself by the implementation of a tree visitor in Java, which helps keeping coupling between components as loose as possible.

3. The mathematical formulae are converted into their Marburg notation Braille counterparts in a two-step process. First, an equivalent MathML representation of the LaTeX formula is created with the SnuggleTeX library [7]. This MathML formula is then converted into Marburg braille with the use of the UMCL command line interface [8]. This has to be done in a preprocessing phase as we cannot infer the length of a Marburg formula from its LaTeX equivalent.

4. Once the formulae have been converted and all relevant data from the preprocessing phase has been gathered, a new TeX file is created with all formulae translated into Marburg and the required placeholders set into place. As an example, the place where the Table of Contents will be generated in the following step is marked by a particular TeX command.

5. A new PT is generated and visited, reusing the grammar of the first step but implementing a new tree visitor, which generates the equivalent HBS command for each of the LaTeX commands found within the document. All text is accordingly modified to comply with the HBS format except the Marburg formulae, which are left as-is and later on interpreted as plain text, as they are already print-ready. The output of this process is a file written in the HBS document description language (which is part of the HBS document conversion suite) [9].

6. Finally, the user can run the HBS software suite [9] to generate high quality braille printouts. Headings, paragraphs, footnotes, margins, spelling, numbering, etc. can be highly customized and printed into several output formats. It is also worth noting

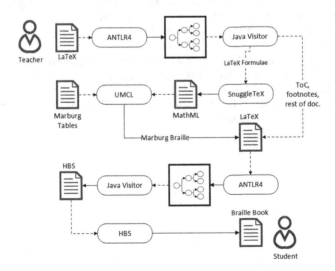

Fig. 1. LaBraDoor – general workflow

that LaBraDoor and HBS can be configured to generate output in electronic text form as well.

4 Conclusion

LaBraDoor, in conjunction with HBS, allows schools teachers in Austria to convert LaTeX documents into high quality braille printouts or electronic documents that blind and visually impaired students can read. The previous, monolithic version of LABRA-DOOR has been fully revamped. Output customization is now extremely high thanks to the use of state-of-the-art formats (MathML for math and HBS for document description). This lets us tackle new requests made by teachers or students in a quick, efficient way, without the need of understanding and modifying the code of the previous tool for each new request.

References

1. Lamport, L.: LaTeX – A Document Preparation System. Addisson-Wesley, Reading (1983)
2. Mulloy, A.M., Gevarter, C., Hopkins, M., Sutherland, K.S., Ramdoss, S.T.: Assistive technology for students with visual impairments and blindness. In: Assistive Technologies for People with Diverse Abilities, pp. 113–156. Springer, New York (2014)
3. Erdweg, S.T., Ostermann, K.: Featherweight Tex and parser correctness. In: Malloy, B., Staab, S., Brand, M. (eds.) SLE 2010. LNCS, vol. 6563, pp. 397–416. Springer, Heidelberg (2011)
4. Batušic M., Miesenberger, K., Stöger B.: LaBraDoor, a contribution to making Mathematics Accessible for the Blind. In: Edwards, A., Arato, A., Zagler, W. (eds.) Proceedings of 6th International Conference on Computers Helping People with Special Needs, ICCHP 1998, Oldenbourg, Wien, München (1998)
5. Ahrer, E.: Richtlinien für das Layout von Schulbüchern für Mathematik, Physik und Chemie für blinde und sehschwache Schüler an Österreichs Schulen. Institut Integriert Studieren, Verein BookAccess, Johannes Kepler Universität, Linz (2013)
6. Parr, T.J., Quong, R.W.: ANTLR: a predicated-LL (k) parser generator. Softw.: Pract. Exp. **25**(7), 789–810 (1995)
7. McKain, D.: SnuggleTeX (2011). http://www2.ph.ed.ac.uk/snuggletex/
8. Archambault, D., Guyon, F.: UMCL transcription tools: universal maths conversion library. Assist. Technol. Res. Ser. **29**, 416–423 (2011)
9. Trothe-Voß, A.: Das Hagener Braille-Software-System (HBS) (2015). https://www.fernuni-hagen.de/at-medien/11_braille.shtml/

Practical Evaluation of DaisyRings: Text-to-Speech-Based DAISY Content Creation System

Kosei Fume[✉], Yuka Kuroda, Taira Ashikawa, and Masahiro Morita

Corporate Research & Development Center, Toshiba Corporation,
1, Komukai-Toshiba-cho, Saiwai-ku, Kawasaki, Kanagawa 212-8582, Japan
{kosei.fume,yuka.kuroda,taira.ashikawa,masahiro.morita}@toshiba.co.jp

Abstract. The Digital Accessible Information System (DAISY) content is gradually gaining popularity among the visually impaired, according to "The Act on the Elimination of Discrimination against Persons with Disabilities" enforced in Japan since April 2016. However, compilation of DAISY-formatted e-books, generally undertaken by volunteers, is time-consuming, and forces users to wait a long time for the delivery of such books, which they might want to read as soon as possible. Therefore, we attempted to improve this situation by providing a text-to-speech (TTS)-based DAISY content creation tool to volunteers. To practically evaluate our concept, we ran a web application site from Fall 2013 to the end of 2015. The site provides a transliteration system that converts plain text to DAISY content, including formatted HTML and audio data, by using TTS technology. The results of the practical evaluation were demonstrated in this study, and show the effectiveness of our proposal method.

Keywords: Transliteration · Text-to-speech · DAISY · Visual disability · Dyslexia

1 Introduction

An audiobook is a form of a book that a visually impaired person or literacy-disabled person can enjoy. It is a recording of a human voice on a tape or CD. In some cases, contents containing text and index information in the form of digital accessible information system (DAISY) and synchronized with a play functionality is compiled using recorded voice. These audiobook CDs and tapes are created by volunteers at a braille library or other public libraries [9]. Contrastively, text-to-speech (TTS) technology is used to read out the text data in some e-book devices and applications; for example, a web document is automatically read by using a screen reader.

DaisyRings[TM] is a trademark of Toshiba Corporation.

© Springer International Publishing Switzerland 2016
K. Miesenberger et al. (Eds.): ICCHP 2016, Part I, LNCS 9758, pp. 401–408, 2016.
DOI: 10.1007/978-3-319-41264-1_55

2   Background

Generally, reading or literal mistakes are not expected with published books. However, achieving 100 % accurate reading is expensive.

In contrast, TTS is a reasonably inexpensive support tool [2,7]. However, it causes reading failures because of the appearance of unknown words, such as new word heteronyms and fluctuations of accent positions. Many of the DAISY creation system support functionalities for recording and manual content authoring. Recently, many tools and plugins have become available for DAISY content creation [4,6,12]. However, the present methods are insufficient for end-users. In general, compiling a DAISY book takes at least two or three months, up to a maximum of one year from receipt of a request to the delivery of the DAISY content (Fig. 1). Recently, several products have been released that exploit TTS functions [14].

However, most of them are standalone applications for Windows PCs; therefore, a volunteer group must pay the license fees for all the members that use the applications. In addition to the cost problems, there are other problems such as difficulty in sharing the created contents and common modifications among group members.

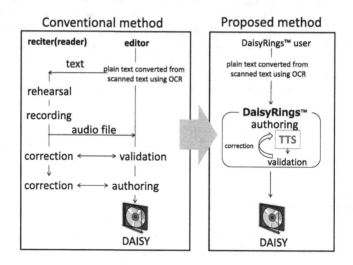

Fig. 1. Transliteration process

3   Previous Work

3.1   Immediacy Prioritized Approach

Considering the need for quick reporting, exploiting TTS in reading applications and devices is a practical method for visually impaired and for people with reading disabilities [2,7]. To make the content more accessible, an interactive approach that targets graphics information is proposed by [3]. [10,16] focuses on the document logical structure approaches are done, and [13] proposes a real-time document-handling approach and skimming approach for information acquisition [1]. Another proposal to improve accessibility for dyslexics is made by [11], who presents layout guidelines for online text.

3.2 Accuracy Prioritized Approach

At the same time, other approaches that involve adding metadata or annotation to contents in advance serve as helpful reading guidelines. A few useful metadata editing or annotation applications [6,12,14] are already in the market. Many tools and plugins for DAISY content creation have recently been made available, such as those described in [4,5]. Using "Daisy pipeline", users are able to convert various documents to a DAISY related format. The "Producer" [14] supports time-consuming and corporative workflow of creating DAISY contents.

4 Limitations

Although various support tools can be used, transliteration still requires considerable money and time. For example, although the task of transliteration of a book is assigned to one volunteer group with several members, it is said to take two or three months, and may take one year to complete.

In contrast, if TTS is used, users can enjoy any text-based content, such as an audiobook, immediately. However, TTS inevitably makes misreadings and improper pauses. In addition, ambiguity in readings of Kanji characters cannot be eliminated. For example, whether "I-CHI-BA" or "SHI-JO" is difficult to determine. Further, TTS cannot correctly read a new word, which is not in the dictionary. There is similar ambiguity in accent. For example, it is difficult to determine the appropriate accent, unless you know whether it is used for "bridge" or "chopsticks". Therefore, from the accessibility point of view, it can be said that only the text information is insufficient.

5 Overview of DaisyRings

5.1 Concept

On the basis of the aforementioned situation, we developed a system that facilitates creation of DAISY-formatted e-books [8]. With this system, you can easily create DAISY e-books by using TTS functions, even if you do not know any phonetic symbols of TTS and any structure notation of HTML and SMIL files.

The use of TTS solves the problem of considerable time required for compiling DAISY content because of the necessity of recording human voice. This is solved by two methods: A correction method, which a beginner can easily use to correct pause, reading, and accent errors: and control symbols, especially designed for TTS, which can be used by experts to correct these errors more specifically.

5.2   System Overview and Details

Transliteration is divided four processes as follows:

1. Extract text information from a book.
2. Generate TTS readings.
3. Synchronize reading and text information.
4. Convert and merge working data to a specified e-book format.

In these processes, DaisyRings are supported from steps 2 to 4. The following information details the working of steps:

– Upload input text.
– Check the reading and accent by playing.
– Correct the reading and accent by using a ruby-type graphical user interface (GUI).
– Insert and delete the pause information.
– Add DAISY headings and page information.
– Build a book.

DaisyRings is a web application that supports these processes. Users can use these functions only to login from Internet browsers.

The details of our system are described in the following text. The main feature is an editing function and TTS-incorporated GUI. In particular, by using the ruby-based reading correction UI shown in Fig. 2, you can correct the misreadings. After changing the input mode from plain text to ruby-format by using a toggle key, you can provide text information to correct mispronunciations or misaccentuations. In general, text information provided through a ruby GUI is read or described with Hiragana or Katakana. We expanded this notation, and therefore our system can accept Kanji or accent symbols from the ruby-formatted input. Further, our system supports the insertion of three types of pauses with simple key combinations. According to our previous survey, one of the most frequently corrected data types is pause-related data.

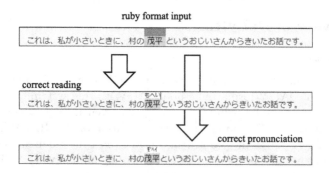

Fig. 2. Ruby-based reading correction UI

This system also supports easy pause insertion and deletion functions. In addition, DAISY-specialized XML elements and attributes, such as "Heading Levels," "Page Marking," and "Groups," are easy to embed as document logical structures by selecting from a drop-down menu. This metadata-adding operation does not require any special skills and knowledge, such as XML or DTD specifications.

6   Experiments and Results

6.1   Log Analysis Based on Site Operations

To test the applicability of the experimental system, the system was operated from Fall 2013 to the end of 2015. To verify our concept, we built the web application and published it free to limited groups, such as public library staff, educational staff, and volunteer groups, in Japan.

During this period, 1029 people from 48 organizations used the system, and we observed 17,021 login events and 4722 user document uploads. The organizations with the highest frequency use are public libraries and facilities that support people with disabilities. In addition, as training materials for DAISY creation, it was also used in college classrooms in a librarian program. For 4722 user documents, the average document length was 289.5 lines and average user uploads were 5.3 documents (maximum 323).

Table 1. Types of evaluation documents and average working time

Document types	Number of documents	Average line numbers (lines)	Average playing time (min)
Flow-type	6	517.50	61.5
Stock-type	3	119.67	12.11
Archive-type	4	154.50	18.5

According to system log analysis, a user takes 238 actions per document on average. These actions include text editing, ruby editing, pause insertion, playing reading sound, menu selection, and exporting DAISY contents. For actual working time analysis, we randomly picked 13 documents that were edited and had completed DAISY content outputs provided by staff of the public library and facility supporting people with disabilities.

Table 1 displays the types of the 13 documents considered in this study. Because the target documents were actual documents provided by the users, the number of documents varies among the document types.

The flow-type information compares the playback and editing times, and shows that playback time is approximately 95 % of the editing time. The editing time is shorter than playback time. The person is reading, because it is impossible

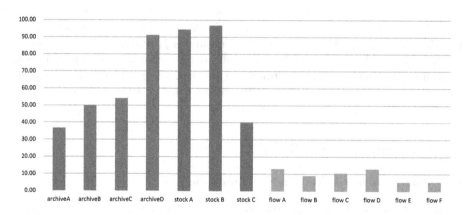

Fig. 3. Editing working time (per 10 lines) (Color figure online)

to create in a time shorter than the playback time, using a transliteration support system has a considerable effect on users. The stock-type information is 6.87 times the playback time. The archive-type information depends on the editing and is 6.35 times the time. The average of all documents and 4.72 times, which is a slightly longer time than in the previous preliminary experiments.

Figure 3 shows the average editing and audio playback times for text containing 10 sentences. The editing time includes time required for editing and correcting of the reading, accent, and text.

6.2 Difference Between Transliteration and Editing Time

We also evaluated system usability by differentiating skills between experienced and novice users.

We first gathered two groups of workers who were paid small amounts of money to complete small tasks. One group contained experienced transliteration users, and the other contained users with no experience in transliteration but with basic PC skills to use the Word processing software. All the members have no experience in using the system. Before task execution, all the workers received an approximately 30 min course on the system use. The task was to transliterate a press release contained 1072 Japanese characters. This transliteration task contained correct readings, accents, and pause information.

Table 2. Working analysis for the same target document

	Editing ruby (times)	Editing pause (times)	Working time (sec)	Playing time (sec)	Working/playing time ratio
Experienced user (9 users)	3.22	3.44	946.78	194.00	4.91
Novice user (10 users)	6.70	22.00	1487.10	199.10	7.50
Total (19 users)	5.05	13.21	1231.16	196.68	6.27

The results are shown in Table 2. The experienced users took less time to edit by reducing repetitive processes and, overall, took a shorter working time.

6.3   Discussion

The experimental results reveal the cost and its tendency to the quality of target document according to the DAISY creation of each document type. In the archive-type information, because reducing the audio playback time is crucial, supporting the playback function and playback effectively increased the working speed. The stock-type information results show that the editing and playback times are almost equal. According to these results, the accuracy of the language analysis in estimating reading, accent, accent, and automatic insertion of pauses is insufficient. According to the flow-type information results, creating DAISY content consumes less time than the playback time, thus verifying the effect of the transliteration support system. However, this can be possible because the number of editing views greatly exceeded, and there are many places where the text does not seem to be read only by looking at it. Thus, it is necessary to improve the natural language analysis modules to achieve more accurate reading and accentuating.

The difference in user skills was seen in the apparent working time. Because the experienced users can easily imagine the work, it is presumed that they reduce wasteful repetitive tasks. However, even experienced users showed a necessity of working time, which was 4.91 times the playback time. Therefore, it is necessary to improve the system performance and basic language analysis, and further improve of the user interface.

7   Conclusions

We developed a TTS-based transliteration system, and a service site was published for Japanese transliteration groups and related members for free of charge from Fall 2013 to the end of 2015. Through this practical experiment, we believe that our concept was proved by the cooperation of the people and the support of many stakeholders. From the trial version, we have completed the transition to the retail version [15]. We will continue to develop and improve the system to meet newly obtained user needs, while watching usage and trends in the transliteration community.

Finally, we would like to thank all the DaisyRings users.

References

1. Ahmed, F., Borodin, Y., Puzis, Y., Ramakrishnan, I.V.: Why read if you can skim: towards enabling faster screen reading. In: Proceedings of the International Cross-Disciplinary Conference on Web Accessibility. W4A 2012, pp. 39:1–39:10. ACM, New York (2012)
2. Apple: VoiceOver. http://www.apple.com/accessibility/

3. Carberry, S., Elzer Schwartz, S., Mccoy, K., Demir, S., Wu, P., Greenbacker, C., Chester, D., Schwartz, E., Oliver, D., Moraes, P.: Access to multimodal articles for individuals with sight impairments. ACM Trans. Interact. Intell. Syst. **2**(4), 21:1–21:49 (2013)
4. DAISY Consortium: DAISY Pipeline. http://www.daisy.org/project/pipeline
5. Daniel, W.: Daisy Tobi: an extensible software tool to author next-generation accessible publications. In: The DAISY International Technical Conference (2009)
6. Dolphin Computer Access: Dolphin Publisher. http://www.yourdolphin.com/products.asp
7. Freedom Scientific: JAWS. http://www.freedomscientific.com/Products/Blindness/JAWS
8. Fume, K., Kuroda, Y., Ashikawa, T., Mizuoka, Y., Morita, M.: TTS-based DAISY content creation system: implementation and evaluation of DaisyRings^{TM}. In: Miesenberger, K., Fels, D., Archambault, D., Peňáz, P., Zagler, W. (eds.) ICCHP 2014, Part I. LNCS, vol. 8547, pp. 69–76. Springer, Heidelberg (2014)
9. Japanese Braille Library: SAPIE. https://sapie.or.jp
10. Miyashita, H., Sato, D., Takagi, H., Asakawa, C.: Aibrowser for multimedia: introducing multimedia content accessibility for visually impaired users. In: Proceedings of the 9th International ACM SIGACCESS Conference on Computers and Accessibility, Assets 2007, pp. 91–98. ACM, New York (2007)
11. Rello, L., Kanvinde, G., Baeza-Yates, R.: Layout guidelines for web text and a web service to improve accessibility for dyslexics. In: Proceedings of the International Cross-Disciplinary Conference on Web Accessibility, W4A 2012, pp. 36:1–36:9. ACM, New York (2012)
12. Science Accesibility Net: ChattyInfty. www.sciaccess.net/jp/ChattyInfty/
13. Shaik, A.S., Hossain, G., Yeasin, M.: Design, development and performance evaluation of reconfigured mobile Android phone for people who are blind or visually impaired. In: Proceedings of the 28th ACM International Conference on Design of Communication, SIGDOC 2010, pp. 159–166. ACM, New York (2010)
14. Shinano-kenshi: Producer. http://www.plextalk.com/jp/products/producer
15. TOSHIBA: Transliteration Editor DaisyRings^{TM}. https://www.toshiba.co.jp/cl/pro/recaius/lineupdaisyrings.html
16. Yu, C.H., Miller, R.C.: Enhancing mobile browsing and reading. In: CHI 2011 Extended Abstracts on Human Factors in Computing Systems, CHI EA 2011, pp. 1783–1788. ACM, New York (2011)

HERMOPHILOS: A Web-Based Information System for the Workflow Management and Delivery of Accessible eTextbooks

Alexandros Pino, Georgios Kouroupetroglou[✉], and Paraskevi Riga

Department of Informatics and Telecommunications,
National and Kapodistrian University of Athens, Athens, Greece
{pino,koupe,p.riga}@di.uoa.gr

Abstract. In this work we present the functional specifications, architecture and implementation of the HERMOPHILOS web-based system developed to auto-mate and accelerate the accessible eTextbooks' production, workflow management, and delivery in an a higher education environment. We describe the redesign of the relative manual procedures and we show how HERMOPHILOS makes things easier and faster for the print-disabled students, as well as for the personnel involved. The web services of HERMOPHILOS include user sign up, user authen-tication, user rights management, students' accessible textbooks re-quests, digital textbook requests to publishers, requests' progress monitoring, original digital text-book copy submission, scanning, OCR, version and archive management, copy-right protection, distribution, and digital content usage statistics. Implementation specifications included support for all browsers, operating systems, and mobile devices, accessible user interfaces (WCAG 2.0 AA), and advanced encryption and security policies. The HERMOPHILOS system sup-ports multiple formats for eTextbooks: plain text (.txt), rich text (.rtf), accessible markup (.xml, .xhtml, and .html), large print (.doc), audio books (.mp3), DAISY 2&3 (text only or full text - full audio), Braille (.brf or .brl), MS-Word (.docx), portable document format (.pdf) and LaTex (.tex). Paperwork was dramatically reduced, and the need for students' visits to the accessibility office was eliminated. The results show that, compared to the traditional procedure, the HERMOPHILOS workflow manage-ment system reduced the overall production and delivery time by 47 %.

Keywords: Accessibility · eTextbook · Accessible books

1 Introduction

Accessible digital textbooks production and distribution is one of the core services that the Accessibility Unit[1] of the University of Athens has undertaken to benefit students with print-disabilities [1]. This service supplies accessible eTextbooks mainly to students who are blind or with low vision, those with upper limbs motion disability resulting in inability to manually handle printed books, and students with dyslexia.

---

[1] University of Athens Accessibility Unit - http://access.uoa.gr/.

© Springer International Publishing Switzerland 2016
K. Miesenberger et al. (Eds.): ICCHP 2016, Part I, LNCS 9758, pp. 409–416, 2016.
DOI: 10.1007/978-3-319-41264-1_56

Although the Unit's experts and personnel lived up to the increasing requests for new accessible eTextbooks for some years, the man-hours needed to meet the overwhelming production requirements have surpassed their potential. A new web-based Information Technology (IT) system has been recently designed and developed in order to automate and accelerate the accessible eTextbooks' production, workflow management, and delivery. In this work we present the functional specifications, architecture and implementation of this new system entitled HERMOPHILOS[2] and report on the qualitative and quantitative improvements that it offered.

First, we describe the traditional procedure of accessible eTextbook request, production, and delivery by all stakeholders, namely the disabled students, the Accessibility Unit's personnel, and the textbook publishers. In the next section, we present the state of the art in the development of accessible eTextbooks in higher education. Then, we will present the new IT system that aims to automate and accelerate the procedure, with its two subsystems, the "Users and Requests Management Subsystem", and the "Digital Content Management Subsystem". Moreover, in the same section, we describe the services that HERMOPHILOS provides. In the next section, we will describe the accessible formats that HERMOPHILOS supports. We will conclude with the results section, showing how the new web-based information system for the workflow management and delivery of accessible eTextbooks improved the efficiency of the traditional eTextbook services provided by the Accessibility Unit.

2 State of the Art

Nowadays, there is a wide range of methodologies for the development of accessible eTextbooks in higher education. Some of them are based on user-centric approaches. These methodologies do not just highlight the individual stents' needs with regards to skills and abilities, but also take into account localization issues in terms of language and cultural differences [2]. On the other hand, the provision of educational material in alternate formats for students with print-based disabilities is challenging and often time-consuming, expensive, and requires special knowledge and training of staff [3].

Legislation, universal guidelines [4] and universal standards [5] play an important role in providing accessible learning material provision (in either traditional or e-learning settings) within a higher education institution. University libraries or accessibility units/disability services offices undertake the role for the production and delivery of accessible eTextbooks [6]. Many libraries [7] or academic accessibility units, like the Institute Integriert Studieren, Johannes Kepler University Linz[3] or the Teiresias Support Centre for Students with Special Needs, Masaryk University[4] are doing an excellent job, but standards of provision of accessible eTextbooks vary from place to place even in

[2] Digital Services of Accessible Academic Textbooks for Students with Disabilities, http://ermofilos.uoa.gr/.
[3] Institute Integriert Studieren, Johannes Kepler University Linz, http://www.jku.at/iis/.
[4] Teiresias Support Centre for Students with Special Needs, Masaryk University, https://www.teiresias.muni.cz/.

the same country. eTextbooks in academic libraries often require new workflows from inquire to access [8].

Related research and development projects which address the challenges faced in providing access to the scientific and technical literature [9] or service solutions [3] are of special interest. Finally, copyright protection of eTextbooks in connection with the disability rights is another challenging issue [10] that varies across countries.

3   The Traditional Procedure

The traditional service followed by the Accessibility Unit of the University of Athens, before HERMOPHILOS was introduced, comprised the following steps:

1. A student who had a disability was registered in the Accessibility Unit's records after filling a form, stating his or her needs, and especially pointing out his or her print-disability.
2. The student applied for accessible textbooks each semester.
3. The Accessibility Unit contacted the publishers and asked for the requested books that are normally distributed in printed format, to be delivered in digital format, as dictated by law. At this point the main difficulties occurred due to the facts that many books were too old and not available in digital format, or that the publishing software that was used to create the digital format did not take into account that Greek font encoding would probably be read by a screen reader; so the printed output would be perfect but the lack of correct encoding would render this document unusable to assistive technology (AT).
4. The processing of the document followed. This step varied according to the nature of the digital document sent by the publisher (if any). In the worst, but the very likely scenario of having just the printed book to work with, the processing involved: scanning; optical character recognition; error correction; image description; math and science transcription; tactile figures creation; accessible document assembly.
5. For copyright protection, the document was password-locked for each student individually. Furthermore, the student signed a legal document that made very clear this digital material was not for sharing. The publisher received a copy of this signed statement, clarifying that the student would use the digital book only for his or her own needs and not distribute it to anyone else.
6. For copyright protection, the document was password-locked for each student individually. Furthermore, the student signed a legal document that made very clear this digital material was not for sharing. The publisher also received a copy of this signed statement clarifying that h or she would use the digital book only for his or her own needs and not distribute it to anyone else.
7. The next step of the procedure was the delivery of the accessible digital textbook to the student. This required the student to come to the Accessibility Unit premises in order to receive the material in a CD and sign all the paperwork. This was also a way to make sure that the same person who applied will receive the book, and no copyright-protected content would leak. Such a possibility would jeopardize the cooperation with the publishers.

8. Finally, the publisher should be notified about the book delivery and receive the signed forms.

4 The HERMOPHILOS System

Many of the aforementioned steps should be made online and new hardware and software was needed, and this was the aim of the new IT system. It includes a server with a high-speed network and internet connection to host all information, online content, website, services, and software. Additionally, a large page color laser printer, a Braille embosser, a tactile graphics printer, a book cutter, a large page scanner, and format conversion software help to enrich the offered accessible media and formats, and speed tasks up. HERMOPHILOS gave the opportunity to redesign some of the procedures and rethink of ways to make things easier and faster for students as well as for the Accessibility Unit personnel. Procedures and actions were rendered as Web Services which will be summarized, along with the issues that they address. For organizational reasons, the system was partitioned into two subsystems. Figures 1 and 2 illustrate the environment and architecture of the new system.

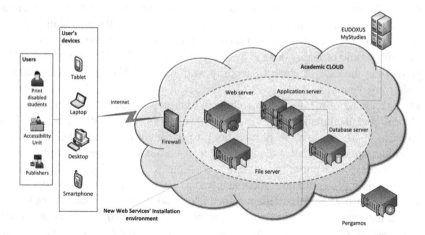

Fig. 1. Web services deployment and operation environment of ERMOPHILOS

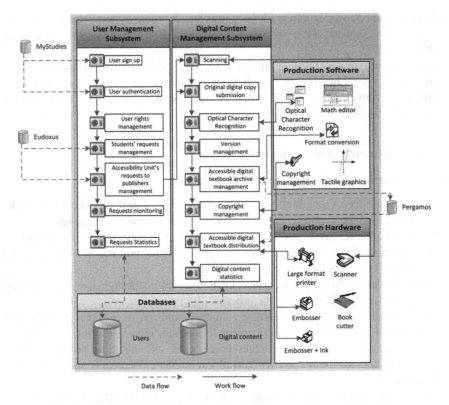

Fig. 2. HERMOPHILOS' functional architecture, workflow, and dataflow

4.1 Users and Requests Management Subsystem

The first subsystem of HERMOPHILOS comprises the following Internet services:

- User sign up service: Three main user groups are using the web services, namely students, publishers, and the Accessibility Unit personnel. Students can use the same credentials they use for all other online University services like MyStudies (the secretariats' system where students declare the courses they will take) and Eudoxus (where students register their preferred books for each course).
- User authentication service: Only the print disabled students are entitled to the accessible digital textbooks and the web services, so this service ensures that only accredited students, personnel, and publishers will access the system.
- User rights management service: A general administrator (a member of the Accessibility Unit staff) manages all user rights for all three user groups.
- Students' accessible textbooks request service: All new requests are made online now, and no physical presence of the student at the Accessibility Unit's office is required.

- Digital textbook requests to publishers' service: A secure system for electronically sending new requests for textbooks to the publishers now automates and speeds up this procedure.
- Requests' progress monitoring service: Both students' requests to Accessibility Unit and the Unit's applications to the publishers are monitored and displayed online.
- Requests' statistics service: All stages of the procedure are logged and executive reports are offered in real time.

4.2 Digital Content Management Subsystem

The second subsystem provides the following Internet services:

- Scanning service: A new high-resolution scanner with a page feeder came with the IT system, and the scanning and storing process can be managed remotely.
- Original digital textbook copy submission service: This service is for the publishers that no longer have to send large files on CDs and normal post just to have an official receipt on paper proving that they fulfilled a request.
- Optical Character Recognition service: OCR now runs on the high-speed server using several processors accelerating the process.
- Version management service: Many volunteers and the Accessibility Unit's staff contribute to OCR correction, document formatting, image description, math and science transcription, tactile graphics preparation, etc. All these produce a huge amount of data and numerous versions of intermediate documents managed online by administrators.
- Accessible formats archive management service: HERMOPHILOS supports the creation of multiple accessible formats: plain text (.txt), rich text (.rtf), accessible markup (.xml, .xhtml, and .html), large print (.doc), audio books (.mp3), DAISY 2&3 (text only or full text-full audio), Braille (.brf or .brl), MS-Word (.docx), portable document format (.pdf) and LaTex (.tex). The required storing capacity is offered by the repository Pergamos provided by the central University digital library system.
- Copyright management service: Digital IDs, electronic signatures, and water-marks are produced and managed centrally, offering a high degree of security and confidence to all stakeholders.
- Accessible digital textbooks distribution service: As soon as the preferred accessible format is ready the student is informed that he or she can immediately download it.
- Digital content usage statistics service: File transfer reports and upload/download statistics are offered by HERMOPHILOS for all stages of preparation and distribution of the digital content.

4.3 Implementation Specifications

The Web Services' deployment and operation environment of HERMOPHILOS is described and illustrated along with its functional architecture, workflow, and dataflow in Figs. 1 and 2. HERMOPHILOS was implemented complying with a set of basic specifications:

- All popular web browsers are supported by HERMOPHILOS (e.g., Internet Explorer, Mozilla Firefox, Google Chrome, Safari, etc.). The latest versions of these web browsers deliver the web interface correctly independently of the platform (i.e., Microsoft Windows, Linux based operating systems, Mac OS X, etc.).
- Web browsers built in portable devices (smartphones, tablets, etc.), and the corresponding operating systems are supported without any information loss for the end user.
- The web interface complies with WAI's WCAG 2.0, and achieves AA level certification. User profiles that specify the interaction with the system and the content presentation style are supported.
- Encryption and security policy is applied during data manipulation, especially when data is routed through the Internet, as well as on the data centers.

5 Results

After statistical analysis, we show that with the traditional manual procedure a student would wait for 45 days in average from request to delivery. This period was reduced to 21 days with the HERMOPHILOS workflow management and delivery system. Various aspects of the new system contributed to this result; for example, the Version Management Web Service made the assignment of editing and correction tasks to multiple editors who work in parallel, easy and manageable, reducing the textbook processing time by 40 %. The new web services such as Sign up, Request submission and monitoring, Authentication, Textbook Submission and Delivery dramatically reduced paperwork, as well as eliminated the need for students' visits to the Accessibility Unit's office. Making all those procedures online reduced movement and communications time overhead by 60 %. The production hardware accelerated book cutting, scanning, OCR, storing, and embossing/printing tasks by 75 % overall.

6 Conclusion

We presented the functional specifications, architecture and implementation of the HERMOPHILOS web-based system developed to automate and accelerate the accessible eTextbooks' production, workflow management, and delivery in a university environment. It includes: (a) the Users and Requests Management Subsystem (targeting the disabled students, publishers of textbooks, and the Accessibility Unit personnel) and (b) the Digital Content Management Subsystem. The HERMOPHILOS system supports the following formats for eTextbooks: plain text (.txt), rich text (.rtf), accessible markup (.xml, .xhtml, and .html), large print (.doc), audio books (.mp3), DAISY 2&3 (text only or full text - full audio), Braille (.brf or .brl), MS-Word (.docx), portable document format (.pdf) and LaTex (.tex). With the traditional procedure, a student would wait for 45 days in average from request to delivery of a new accessible eTextbook. This period was reduced to 21 days with the HERMOPHILOS workflow management and delivery system.

Acknowledgements. This research has been partially co-financed by the European Union (European Social Fund—ESF) and Greek national funds through the Operational Program "Digital Convergence" of the National Strategic Reference Frame-work (NSRF), Research Funding Project 'Accessible Academic Textbooks' eServices for Students with Disabilities" MIS 304140. The publication of this work has been funded by the National and Kapodistrian University of Athens.

References

1. Kouroupetroglou, G., Pino, A., Kacorri, H.: A model of accessibility services provision for students with disabilities in higher education. In: Universal Learning Design International Conference, pp. 23–33. Masaryk University, Brno (2011)
2. Draffan, E.A.: Developing accessible teaching and learning materials within a user centred design framework. In: Miesenberger, K., et al. (eds.) ICCHP 2014. LNCS, vol. 8548, pp. 540–542. Springer, Heidelberg (2014)
3. Christensen, L.B., Keegan, S.J., Stevns, T.: SCRIBE: a model for implementing robobraille in a higher education institution. In: Miesenberger, K., Karshmer, A., Penaz, P., Zagler, W. (eds.) ICCHP 2012, Part I. LNCS, vol. 7382, pp. 77–83. Springer, Heidelberg (2012)
4. Seale, J.: E-learning and Disability in Higher Education: Accessibility Theory and Practice, 2nd edn. Taylor & Francis, London (2014)
5. Crombie, D., Lenoir, R., McKenzie, N., Calvo, F.M.: Identifying trends in accessible content processing. In: Digital Spectrum: Integrating Technology and Culture - Supplement to the Proceedings of the 10th International Conference on Electronic Publishing, pp. 113–121. ELPUB, Bansko, Bulgaria (2006)
6. Eskay, N., Chima, J.N.: Library and information service delivery for the blind and physically challenged in University of Nigeria Nsukka library. Eur. Acad. Res. 1(5), 625–635 (2013)
7. Freeman, M.: "Taking six steps" to reading: improving public library services for people with sight loss in the UK through staff development and reader engagement. Paper presented at: IFLA WLIC 2015. World Library and Information Congress of the International Federation of Library Associations, Cape Town, South Africa (2015)
8. Beisler, A., Kurt, L.: E-book workflow from inquiry to access: facing the challenges to implementing e-book access at the University of Nevada, Reno. Collab. Librariansh. 4(3), 96–116 (2012)
9. Bernier, A., Burger, D.: AcceSciTech: a global approach to make scientific and technical literature accessible. In: Stephanidis, C., Antona, M. (eds.) UAHCI 2013, Part III. LNCS, vol. 8011, pp. 283–290. Springer, Heidelberg (2013)
10. Harpur, P.D., Suzor, N.P.: Copyright protections and disability rights: turning the page to a new international paradigm. Univ. NSW Law J. 36(3), 745–778 (2013)

Universally Accessible Figures

John A. Gardner[✉]

ViewPlus Technologies, Inc., Corvallis, OR, USA
john.gardner@viewplus.com

Abstract. Figures are an essential part of scientific literature, but students with severe print disabilities do not presently have good access to figures. Most figures are "made accessible" by a written or audio description. Tactile representations can make figures accessible, but tactile figures must have braille labels, but relatively few blind people read braille and only a small percentage of blind braille readers can read tactile graphics. Figures are potentially very accessible to a wide variety of students with print disabilities through a combination of tactile and audio description, but audio-tactile technology has been labor-intensive and often difficult to use. A new version of the ViewPlus IVEO audio/touch technology could be a major step in the evolution of audio/touch toward a future in which figures can be universally accessible to everybody. The audio/touch method and the improvements being introduced in the new IVEO version are discussed in this paper.

Keywords: Universally accessible figures · Audio-tactile · SVG · IVEO · Tactile image simplification

1 Introduction

Specialists in the field of information accessibility use many formats, including braille, PDF, html+MathML, EPUB/DAISY, or MS Word to make information accessible to students with disabilities. Formats may differ, but there is general agreement that text, tables, and math and chemistry equations can be made accessible to nearly anyone. There is no such general agreement that it is possible to make figures excellently accessible to everyone. This article discusses the author's conviction that figures can also be made accessible for everybody and innovations that are designed to do just that.

1.1 Accessibility of Figures Today

Although figures are ubiquitous in scientific literature, most people with severe print disabilities have little or no access to the information conveyed by figures. The most common method of "making figures accessible" today is by having a sighted person describe the figure. This is true even though every scientist understands that a word description is not an adequate way to convey the information in a scientific figure.

Tactile figures can provide much better access to people who have learned to read them. Unfortunately, very few people can understand a tactile figure of any complexity.

© Springer International Publishing Switzerland 2016
K. Miesenberger et al. (Eds.): ICCHP 2016, Part I, LNCS 9758, pp. 417–420, 2016.
DOI: 10.1007/978-3-319-41264-1_57

Even most good braille readers have difficulty understanding tactile figures, and anybody who does not read braille fluently has little or no chance of understanding a tactile figure. Sighted children begin learning to understand visual images the day they are born, but blind children seldom have tactile images much less any assistance in understanding them. So it is not surprising that so few blind people learn to understand tactile images.

It has been understood since the pioneering work of Parkes [7] that tactile images are far easier to understand if the figures are accompanied by audio feedback. Parkes' Nomad talking tablet was introduced by the American Printing House and drew considerable praise, but it was very expensive and difficult to use. In addition, creation of both content and the tactile copies were laborious and very expensive. It was a technology ahead of its time and was eventually withdrawn from the market.

In subsequent years, a number of "talking tablets" have been introduced. Loetzsch [5, 6] created and marketed a successful curriculum for health professionals in Germany, and Landau's [3, 4] tablet has been used with proprietary content in several educational settings and is currently being used for a number of specialized tasks such as museum guides. The ViewPlus IVEO technology [1, 2] was introduced in 2005 as a more general figure-access technology. It has been used in varied settings but mostly in elementary special education settings and at a few universities.

1.2   The Audio-Tactile Method

The requirements for audio-tactile access are a tactile copy of the figure, a computer file with information keyed to location on the figure, some type of hardware device that communicates position on the figure to the computer, and a computer application that provides speech and/or braille information to the user. For all commercially-available audio-touch systems, the hardware has always been a touch-sensitive tablet. In order to resolve small objects, a high resolution, relatively expensive tablet is necessary. These typically cost $500 or more. Other details differ among the various systems. The View-Plus IVEO technology uses the open standard, Scalable Vector Graphics (SVG), as its file format. Other systems use proprietary formats.

2   The ViewPlus IVEO Audio-Touch Technology

The new IVEO technology, currently in beta test, is a descendent of earlier IVEO software and hardware. It has been enhanced considerably based on feedback from users. In particular, the system should be considerably more usable than previous versions. If so, IVEO could finally be approaching the long-sought goal of a technology that makes graphics accessible to everybody.

IVEO includes two authoring/conversion applications, Creator and Transformer Pro, and the IVEO Player end-user application. A touchpad is still available, and a new digital pen option is being introduced to fill needs of a variety of users.

IVEO Creator is a descendant of previous IVEO authoring/conversion software. It can be used to create simple IVEO SVG graphics, but it is largely used with pre-existing SVG files to improve the tactile image and to add the meta-information that end users hear when objects or text labels are selected on the tactile copy. The tactile image is created by printing the SVG image with a ViewPlus embosser. Colored regions are embossed by default in a tactile gray scale in which light colors are represented by small dots and dark colors by large dots. Users have a number of printer property options including ability to substitute tactile patterns for color.

Transformer Pro is used to convert bit map graphics to IVEO SVG, add meta-information, and create a separate tactile image. The latter functionality provides all the options available in Creator but also includes several powerful new processing options for simplifying the tactile image. A typical example is illustrated in Figs. 1 and 2.

Fig. 1. US map clip art (Color figure online)

Fig. 2. US map embossed view with no simplification. Boundaries between the states are difficult to distinguish tactually (left) and US Map embossed view with no fill and enhanced lines. Boundaries are easily distinguishable tactually (right)

Slider bars control "simplification" and degree of fill. There are options for substituting automatic or user-definable tactile patterns for colors as well. Simplification includes edge detection and various other techniques that enhance the tactile image. A user can also erase or create tactile features that do not affect the visual image. The tactile image is embossed, and if printed on a ViewPlus printer/embosser, the visual image is printed unchanged. Transformer Pro makes it quick and easy to convert even very complex images to IVEO SVG format excellently accessible by blind people as well as a variety of other severely print-impaired users. Finally, this application also permits one to convert text to braille and/or add braille labels. Braille is generally not used for audio-tactile images because braille is normally much too large to include, and most users do not read braille. But if one wishes to make free-standing tactile copy, Transformer Pro is a convenient tool for doing so.

A new digital pen has been introduced as an alternative to the touchpad. It uses an infra-red sender/receiver device that detects the position of the pen. A pen-follower option in IVEO Player permits the user to hear text and object titles as the pen is moved. More information is obtained by clicking.

3   Conclusions

IVEO is a commercial product to be used today to make graphical information accessible. But it is also an excellent research tool. IVEO permits users to have a great deal of freedom in deciding how much/little information to include in image and graphical object titles and descriptions. It permits more than two levels of information, and it permits great flexibility in simplifying the visual image when creating the tactile image. But ViewPlus does not have the resources to make exhaustive studies of how to optimize these parameters, nor is it ultimately the right organization to do such research. This type of optimization should be done by an independent organization, not the manufacturer of the product. ViewPlus encourages such research and will be happy to be a supportive partner.

References

1. Gardner, J., Stowell, H., Bulatov, V.: The viewplus IVEO scalable vector graphics technology for universally usable complex information. In: Proceedings of the 11th International Conference on Human Computer Interaction, "Universal Access in HCI", Las Vegas, Nevada, USA, vol. 8, 22–27 July 2005. ISBN 0-8058-5807-5. http://www.viewplus.com/about/abstracts/05hcibulatov.html
2. Gardner, J.: Can mainstream graphics be accessible? Int. Technol. Disabil. J. **14**(1) (2014). http://itd.athenpro.org/volume14/number1/gardner.html
3. Landau, S.: Use of the talking tactile tablet in mathematics testing. J. Vis. Impairment Blindness **97**, 85–96 (2003)
4. Landau (see company). http://TactileGraphics.com
5. Loetzsch, J.: Computer-aided access to tactile graphics for the blind. In: Zagler, W., Bushy, G., Wagner, R. (eds.) Computers for Handicapped Persons, 4th International Conference ICCHP 1994, vol. 860, pp. 575–851. Springer, Heidelberg (1994)
6. Loetzsch, J., Roedig, G.: Interactive tactile media in training visually handicapped people. In: Burger, D. (ed.) New Technologies in the Education of the Visually Handicapped - Colloque INSERM, vol. 237, pp. 155–160. John Libbey Publishing Ltd., New Barnet, UK (1996)
7. Parkes, D.: Nomad: an audio-tactile tool for the acquisition, use and management of spatially distributed information by partially sighted and blind persons. In: Tatham, A.F., Dodds, A.G. (eds.) Proceedings of Second International Symposium on Maps and Graphics for Visually Handicapped People, King's College, University of London, pp. 24–29 (1988)

Accessible eLearning - eLearning for Accessibility/AT

Accessible eLearning - eLearning for Accessibility/AT

Introduction to the Special Thematic Session

E.A. Draffan[1(✉)] and Peter Heumader[2]

[1] Faculty of Physical Sciences and Engineering, University of Southampton, Southampton, UK
[2] Institut Integriert Studieren, Johannes Kepler University, Linz, Austria

Abstract. Massive open online courses (MOOCS) and open educational resources (OER) are currently rising in popularity with millions of global learners and teachers taking advantage of a huge amount of free or low-cost online course. Such eLearning platforms are considered good choices to improve one's education as they offer courses which can increase specialist knowledge in many ways. In this special thematic session, we are going to investigate the current state of eLearning in terms of accessibility and usability for people with disabilities.

Keywords: Accessibility · Elearning · Moocs · OER · WCAG

1 Introduction

Teaching and learning strategies increasingly employ Information and Communication Technologies (ICT) which have been shown to play an important role in what has become a global education market [1]. Yet it is often felt they are still failing to reach their potential, despite increased awareness raising and teacher training. Research has shown that there may be countless reasons for this failure, including the terminology that surrounds eLearning technology use within the classroom [2]. Such terms as 'distance learning', 'blended learning', 'mobile learning' and 'Massive Open Online Courses (MOOCS)' can further complicate the understanding of the various delivery systems, especially when they become part of the 'flipped classroom' [3] with the inclusion of online interactive multimedia elements as part of a planned course along with the challenges of personal devices and the use of social media [4].

Where there have been positive drives to include these types of learning there has always been the potential to enhance digital accessibility for the inclusion and participation of learners and teachers with disabilities. Compared to classic learning systems, eLearning can provide a number of advantages for people with disabilities [7] namely:

- Flexibility and additivity: eLearning can support a range of learning styles and learning rates. Digitized information can be easier to access when offered in multiple formats to suit user needs.

- Access to inclusive and equitable education: Accessible eLearning provides people with disabilities a platform that allows them to work and study without encountering barriers to teaching and learning resources.
- Access to learning experience: Access to specialist notations and concepts supported by the use of assistive technologies or other types of technologies such as virtual laboratories. These allow those with certain disabilities to experiment without having to use standard laboratory equipment.
- Empowerment: Accessible inclusive eLearning can enhance the level of freedom and independence for students with disabilities.

Integrating accessibility into eLearning systems is a key requirement to make opportunities and chances provided by these types of online services available for everyone, including those with disabilities.

However, for most of today's eLearning platforms, there still remains the need for potential barriers to access to be removed. In particular issues with the compatibility of systems and services can make it hard for content providers to include multiple formats that provide alternatives for learners accessing the materials. The online video player that has inaccessible controls in one browser but works in another or content that has been saved in an e-book format that can only be read using a certain mobile application and does not include easy navigational elements. These are challenges that have yet to be adequately addressed by standards and guidelines such as W3C Web Content Accessibility Guidelines 2.0 [5] in particular for those who have cognitive and learning disabilities.

Recent studies have also shown that even popular MOOC platforms do not fulfill the requirements in terms of accessibility. A heuristic evaluation of ten courses of one of the major MOOC platforms with respect to WCAG 2.0 showed that all the courses failed to be conform to Level A. This is the easiest conformance level in the WCAG 2.0 to achieve, guarding the absolute minimum of accessibility that is needed for a site to be accessible [8].

In recent years the increase of educational courses hosted online has been exponential with the introduction of Open Educational Resources (OER) allowing a wider community to access knowledge and mix and match content knowing that sharing is encouraged through Creative Commons licensing agreements and Open Source Learning Management Systems. MOOCs have also embraced the concept of sharing with an increasingly global audience taking part in the largely free online courses. The huge numbers of attendees who have varying degrees of technological skills and different access requirements need new pedagogical approaches to ensure successful outcomes [6]. Those presenting the courses set up a series of activities delivered over a period of weeks often with short videos, online articles, slides and downloadable documents plus quizzes to test learning. Learners can interact peer to peer or with experts supporting the courses. These interactions take place via forums, online discussions and even other external communication systems and social media.

2 Overview

The challenges of teaching differently and making eLearning (in whatever form) accessible and easy to use with ICT and assistive technologies (AT) will be discussed in this special thematic session. There will be presentations that offer a wide range of innovative ideas introducing:

- Teaching Accessibility with Personas
- A Scenario-based approach to enhance open learning through accessibility
- Learning through Videos: Are Disabled Students using good Note-taking Strategies?
- How Accessible are MOOCs to the Elderly?
- The European Computer Driving Licence: 15 years later
- A personal reflection on developing a digital accessibility MOOC compared to developing a traditional course.

References

1. Sarkar, S.: The role of information and communication technology (ICT) in higher education for the 21st century. Science **1**(1), 30–41 (2012)
2. Livingstone, S.: Critical reflections on the benefits of ICT in education. Oxf. Rev. Educ. **38**(1), 9–24 (2012)
3. Bergmann, J., Sams, A.: Flip your classroom: Reach every student in every class every day. International Society for Technology in Education (2012)
4. Gikas, J., Grant, M.M.: Mobile computing devices in higher education: student perspectives on learning with cellphones, smartphones & social media. Internet High. Educ. **19**, 18–26 (2013)
5. W3C Web Content Accessibility Guidelines (WCAG 2.0) (2008). http://www.w3.org/TR/WCAG/. Accessed 31 March 2016
6. Leire, C., McCormick, K., Richter, J.L., Arnfalk, P., Rodhe, H.: Online teaching going massive: input and outcomes. J. Clean. Prod. (2015)
7. Seale, J.K.: E-learning and Disability in Higher Education: Accessibility Research and Practice. Taylor & Francis (2013). Promote freedom, independence and individualized learning for students with disabilities
8. Miesenberger, K., Fels, D., Archambault, D., Penaz, P., Zagler, W. (eds.): ICCHP 2014. LNCS, vol. 8548. Springer, Switzerland (2014)

A Personal Reflection on Developing a Digital Accessibility MOOC Compared to Developing a Traditional Course

Mike Wald[✉]

ECS, University of Southampton, Southampton, UK
m.wald@soton.ac.uk

Abstract. This paper presents a personal reflection on developing a 'Digital Accessibility' MOOC as part of the Erasmus+ MOOCAP project and comparing the process to developing a traditional course on the same topic. The few people who currently teach about accessibility on expensive face to face courses at a few universities are currently only reaching a very small number of people whereas many tens of thousands can learn through a MOOC.

Keywords: Digital · Accessibility · MOOC · Reflection

1 Introduction

There are various types of MOOCs[1] but they are all online courses freely available to anyone and have too many learners for a teacher to be able to interact with or assess individually. Therefore to retain students, engagement needs to be enhanced by inter-student interactions facilitated by educators and moderators and features such as Peer Review, liking and following posts. While there are a few online courses teaching accessibility and some publications describing the technical aspects of developing a MOOC there does not appear to be a publication reflecting on the issues and differences encountered by an academic member of staff. This paper fills this gap in the literature through a personal reflection on developing a 'Digital Accessibility' MOOC as part of the MOOCAP project[2] and comparing it to developing a traditional course on the same topic.

2 Digital Accessibility MOOC

There are many resources describing what a MOOC is[3], the benefits of a MOOC[4], the history of MOOCs[5], the technical aspects of creating a MOOC[6], handbooks on how to

---

[1] http://donaldclarkplanb.blogspot.co.uk/2013/04/moocs-taxonomy-of-8-types-of-mooc.html.
[2] http://gpii.eu/moocap/.
[3] https://www.youtube.com/watch?v=eW3gMGqcZQc.
[4] https://www.youtube.com/watch?v=rYwTA5RA9eU.
[5] https://www.insidehighered.com/blogs/hack-higher-education/top-ed-tech-trends-2012-moocs.
[6] http://universityofreddit.com/class/67829/how-to-make-a-mooc.

© Springer International Publishing Switzerland 2016
K. Miesenberger et al. (Eds.): ICCHP 2016, Part I, LNCS 9758, pp. 425–428, 2016.
DOI: 10.1007/978-3-319-41264-1_58

create a MOOC [1] or the costs and benefits of developing a MOOC [2]. Draffan et al. [3] have described the practical process involved in developing the Digital Accessibility MOOCAP project MOOC currently being developed by 8 partners from 7 European countries with Erasmus+[7] funding. Recent research has shown that many MOOC platforms had accessibility issues [4, 5] and it is very important that the platform and content selected for our MOOC is as accessible as possible. All partners have had extensive experience running their own conventional courses at their own institutions that teach various aspects of digital accessibility through face to face lectures, seminars, workshops, assessments as well as providing some online material. Very few of the professors in the project consortium however had previous experience of participating in a MOOC which makes it difficult to take the MOOC student experience into account when developing a MOOC. In contrast when developing and teaching face to face courses at university, professors are generally still using very similar teaching methods to those they experienced themselves as university students and so it is easier for them to design and develop and teach such traditional courses. Over the past 2 years I have enrolled in about 30 MOOCs on 7 different platforms to experience a MOOC from a student's perspective and other MOOCAP project partners were encouraged to enroll on at least one MOOC so they could also gain similar experience. Also very few of the professors had experience of developing courses with other partners from other institutions and countries or of running purely online courses and only one Partner University had previous experience of developing and running MOOCs. One of the most important issues for a MOOC is how to get very busy people to agree give up their valuable time to participate as learners as when people pay nothing they feel they have nothing to lose if they don't participate. A large proportion of the people who enroll on MOOCs do not even start and every week a large percentage of the learners drop out with less than 7 % on average completing the MOOC [6]. A participant of a face to face course has to plan when to make time in their busy schedule to participate, however for a MOOC they need to be very motivated and engaged to make it a priority over their many other interests and commitments. All the information we provide in the MOOC is also being made available as Open Educational Resources (OER) and so we must provide more than just information to engage students in the MOOC.

Unlike a conventional class we can't engage participants through real time interaction (questions, answers, debate, eye contact, facial expressions etc.) between teacher and student or students and other students. A teacher learns the ability to judge the pace of their class from the reactions and body language of their students and can slow down or speed up as required to ensure students understand the concepts presented. That may be one reason why, while students can remain engaged with a teacher in a class for many tens of minutes, research has shown that to engage students in a MOOC most videos should last about 6 min [7]. To create such short engaging and informative videos involves careful editing rather than simply recording normal class presentations. In my traditional course when I teach about making videos accessible I show a video in class without any sound or captions and then show it again with captions and then show it again without any picture or audio description and then finally with audio description

---

[7] http://erasmus-plus.ro/.

and then discuss with the class the issues involved in making videos accessible. This can take about 25 min of class time. When developing the content to teach about this topic in the MOOC it was decided for copyright reasons we would need to script and film our own video content and add a narration and motion graphics and also employ and film a sign language interpreter to demonstrate on-screen signing. The resulting video was 7 min and 31 s long and took many hours to script, film and create but provided an enhanced learning experience compared to simply watching the much longer recording of my class presentation. In my traditional course I typically invite external guest lecturers, rearranging the schedule and order of teaching of topics to fit in with their availability. For the MOOC we filmed the guest lecturers answering questions and then edited their answers to fit the most appropriate place in the MOOC. A teacher can set and mark coursework or exams to assess individual learners' understanding whereas a learner's understanding on a MOOC is normally assessed only through multiple choice questions or automated peer review where learners provide feedback on each other's work. Multiple choice questions can also be used to engage learners and stimulate thought and introduce new material through the answers. To help participants engage actively in the MOOC we pose questions and invite them to complete surveys and publish answers and present current issues and the state of the art as well as carry out tasks and share their findings. Every MOOCAP professor had their own preferred approach to teaching and for pragmatic reasons it was agreed to split the 5 weeks of the Digital Accessibility MOOC into topics. This inevitably required compromise and negotiation, as did agreement on the title 'Digital Accessibility'. We developed user stories about 9 typical disabled people to help engage participants and tie the separate weeks together to show the barriers and solutions in work, learning, leisure, daily activities and travelling. One challenging question we pose in our MOOC is "Why should we care about Accessibility?" as every learner can contribute something to this discussion without having great expertise in the topic. Copyright of images has not been seen as a serious issue by teachers who regularly copy and paste images found on the web into their presentations they show to their classes. Universities who have not been involved with putting resources on MOOC platforms appear to not have involved their legal departments in ensuring that all Open Education Resources produced by members of their staff have obtained the required copyright clearance. A few MOOCAP partners preferred their material only to be available for non-commercial use through Attribution-NonCommercial-ShareAlike CC BY-NC-SA while the majority of partners wanted the materials to also be available for commercial use through the Attribution-ShareAlike CC BY-SA. The MOOC platform also required the resources to have the CC BY-SA license as although MOOCs were free, participants could buy certificates and because of this requirement one partner decided to leave the consortium.

3   Conclusion and Planned Activities

Collaborating with professors in universities in many countries to design and develop a course on Digital Accessibility can be frustrating as compromises need to be made but it is stimulating as it encourages expert discussions and valuable as it provides the

ECDL® PD: 15 Years Later

Andrea Petz(✉) and Klaus Miesenberger

Institute Integriert Studieren, University of Linz, Linz, Austria
{andrea.petz,klaus.miesenberger}@jku.at

Abstract. The EU funded pilot project (funding scheme "Leonardo da Vinci", fostering lifelong learning and promoting further vocational education) ECDL® PD (ECDL® for People with Disabilities) was carried out from 2001–2004. It aimed at adapting the widespread and renowned ECDL® certificate (European Computer Driving License) to the needs of people with disabilities. This adaptation of a mainstream standard certificate was meant to support people with disabilities and other people at a disadvantage (e.g. older people, people with weak social or educational background, or people from minorities or immigrant groups not ready for using their second/new mother tongue at a satisfying level) and to foster their chances at the labor market. What remained from this work? Is ECDL® the ultima ratio for including people at risk of exclusion or with fewer opportunities into the labor market and into society or is it a certificate amongst others without reaching its full potential?

Keywords: ICT · Assistive Technologies · People with Disabilities · Inclusion · People with fewer Opportunities · Certificate · Standard · Sustainability · Labor Market · ECDL® · ICDL®

1 Introduction

The well-known certificate ECDL® enables proficient use of Information and Communication Technologies (ICT) and empowers individuals, organizations and society, through development, promotion, and delivery of quality certification programs throughout the world [1].

Due to its independence from software and organization, the process of obtaining this certificate is best suitable to be adapted to the needs of people with disabilities and to avoid/overcome technological or organizational barriers. By evaluating and adapting curricula, syllabi and exams (without changing the level); developing training and information materials and co-operating with ECDL® Foundation a more powerful tool for the vocational integration throughout Europe was in reach [2].

Today, in 2016, a closer look on what happened in those 15 years (seen from social aspects concerning integration and inclusion as well as from a technological and pedagogical viewpoint) is possible and needed, starting with this activity and a range of follow up work done in European and (inter)national research and development.

K. Miesenberger et al. (Eds.): ICCHP 2016, Part I, LNCS 9758, pp. 429–436, 2016.
DOI: 10.1007/978-3-319-41264-1_59

2   The Certificate, Its Development and Its Advantages

In fall 2001, ECDL® Foundation launched "ECDL® Advanced" in Denmark, Ireland and Austria. "ECDL® Advanced" is a developed version of the classic ECDL®/ICDL®, aiming at establishing a standard in advanced computer knowledge. Seven years before, when the standard ECDL® was developed, no one would have thought about that - or about 1,8 mio. participants in 60 countries worldwide by 2001 [1, 7].

ECDL® Foundation and its partners work to promote a pan-European certificate of industry-standard computing skills. It is set to become the most widespread qualification in the field of work-related computer use, partly because it is targeted at the full spectrum of the population, and partly because of the support and monitoring of the organizations behind it [2].

Technological development lead to changes in how, where and with what ICT is used. The human computer interface changed from command line based manipulation over WIMP and SILK and many other steps to touch devices in diverse sizes for diverse use cases. The emerging task for the accessibility community now is to "interface the new interfaces" and to have in mind new ways of learning, education (e.g. online learning and MOOCs) and target groups/learners that were not even thought of when installing the first structures and materials for making the ECDL® accessible.

The development and publication of "Information for All", the "European Standards for making information easy to read and understand", produced in the framework of the EU funded project "Pathways to adult education for people with intellectual disabilities" and research on usability and learnability of information and text documents lead to additional knowledge and possibilities – especially in the field of curricula, learning materials and exams – but were and are also asking for consideration, implementation and adaptation/restructuring but also new potential users (with individual needs and abilities) not on the screen before.

These "new knowledge", combined with "low-threshold" technology (smartphones, tablets) and use paradigms, again, can be used for including people with disabilities and/ or fewer opportunities into education and employment and finally into our "knowledge society 2.0" but at the same time can build up unsurmountable barriers if not accessible or usable, so flexible standards, rules and guidelines are key [4–6].

Certificates aiming to establish a standard in computer knowledge must adapt to this knowledge, must bridge the gap between needs and possibilities and build a stable yet flexible basis without falling behind or weakening the standard aspect nor the importance of a certificate [3, 7].

ECDL®/ICDL® grew and developed - in 2016 ECDL® was used by "14 million people, in 41 languages, across 150 countries, through a network of over 24,000 test centers. The certification programs are designed to be accessible to all citizens, irre-spective of age, gender, status, ability, or race" [1, 9] - the whole system is a complex network with responsibilities and dependencies, synchronized tasks, curricula and tests that have to be adapted, maintained, tested and rolled out regularly worldwide to ensure a common standard for both, institutions demanding an evidence based certificate in computer knowledge, and the people taking the tests - asking for a useful resource for their personal development and career [8].

3 Dealing with Changes in ICT, AT and Reality

Starting with piloting research and developments in 2001, the original materials, documents and results of ECDL® PD are of course outdated but were a first starting point evaluating how to ensure an accessible ECDL®. While the project faced issues like "Are blind people able to draw a circle with a computer and change its color?", the question today - following OCG (Austrian Computer Society), one of the former ECDL® PD partners representing ECDL® Foundation in Austria - is "Do *people* need to be able to draw a circle with a computer and change its color?".

3.1 Syllabi, Teaching and Training Materials, Tasks and Questions

ECDL® PD was designed to work for four target groups:

- Blind and Partially Sighted
- Deaf and Hard of Hearing people
- People with Cognitive Disability
- People with Mobility Disability

For every target group, the existing public ECDL® materials (Syllabi as well as demonstrator exams) were analyzed for potential accessibility and usability issues. In parallel, guidelines and workflows for designing accessible and usable syllabi and exams were created to keep the findings sustainable also after the project's lifecycle.

A set of demonstrator training materials (digital e.g. as .ppt and printable as .doc) for every target group was developed – following the ECDL® curriculum and the exam tasks in the so called MQTB (Manual Question and Test Base) and were – besides basic accessibility considerations including e.g. structuring and legibility criteria (fonts, typesetting, contrast, flexibility in presentation,…) tweaked for servicing "specific needs" arising from a disability.

In order not to weaken the standard ECDL®, the quantity and quality of tasks and questions remained more or less the same and there is only ONE pool of questions and tasks from which the formal ECDL® exam is compiled independent from a possible disability of the candidate - so questions and tasks were not changed or rewritten *especially for* people with disabilities, but by adapting/creating teaching and training materials and giving examples and clues on how to solve everyday tasks on the computer, the competence level of the candidates should become high enough to deal with mainstream tasks and questions. Also today, the quantitative and qualitative level of ECDL® is the same for all candidates and the findings of the project led to a general adaptation of the exams towards usability, legibility and understandability what lead to a higher quality for all users, not only those with a disability.

Blind and Partially Sighted People. Training materials contained alternative descriptions for images and pictures/charts, extensively implemented shortcuts and hotkeys and the learners were trained to fulfil the tasks via menus and dialogue boxes (as the possibly shorter way with "buttons" was not – fully – accessible). The exam conditions were adapted, e.g. instead of drawing circles in presentations, the candidates were asked to fully describe how to draw a circle in order to guarantee that they can use their knowledge in everyday situations by guiding a sighted person. For exams, people brought their own IT/AT – first and foremost because screenreader software as well as Braille Displays are expensive devices and mainstream test centers would not be capable to provide and maintain state-of-the-art AT. Additionally, exams and materials were checked for accessibility and optimized for being used with TTS/headphones and braille displays only and in combination.

Deaf and Hard of Hearing People. Training Materials were designed in easier language and contained how-to video-like sequences. Single sign language videos were planned and implemented as a test. The production of the whole set of materials in sign language was not possible within the project's duration and funding. Teaching and training materials were implemented for using buttons and for easy to find and retrieve strategies instead of the "blind friendly way" via menus and direct input of commands via keyboard. The exams were adapted, e.g. where feasible and allowed, sign language interpreters were available to help with communicating and asking questions/getting instructions.

Additionally, adaptations of tasks and the restructuring/rewriting in simplified language lead to a better usability and more successful exams but at the same time to discussions on supposed changes in quality/quantity of the exams. After tests, it became obvious, that the "restructured" materials - designed to fit the "specific needs" of deaf and hard of hearing people (as well as basic needs of people with learning disability) - were of benefit also for mainstream exams: the "old" texts lead to misunderstandings and a bias (from high complexity and weak structuring - see example in Fig. 1), especially in the translated MQTB versions in national languages (from English) where the translation influenced the usability of tasks and descriptions profoundly.

Task 23, Demo-Test 5.1 Databases

Original:	Adapted version:
Compile a report implementing table calories by using the fields group_no, kcal_per_100g and product, grouped by group_no sorted in ascending order by kcal_per_100g. Compute the means for kcal_per_100g for this report. Save the report as average_calories.	Compile a report implementing table calories. Use the fields: - group_no - kcal_per_100g - product Group by group_no Sort ascending by kcal_per_100g Compute the means for kcal_per_100g Save the report as average_calories

Fig. 1. Comparison between original and adapted version of an ECDL® MQTB item with the original on the left and the adapted version – consisting of the same words and with only a different structure on the right (translated from German version).

People with Cognitive Disabilities. These materials were checked for structure, legibility and usability out of materials for deaf persons except for sign language video implementation. No formal "Easy-to-Read" paradigms, rules or guidelines were used or implemented at that time. Descriptions were for using the different software products via buttons instead of menus and/or shortcuts.

People with Mobility Disability. The research done for this specific target group was meant for people with a manipulation disability (including people with motor/mobility disability) benefitting from alternative input/point and click devices. The materials were designed for getting the best possible results with the least typing/clicking effort, what means that buttons and the way via menus and shortcuts/hotkeys or keyboard input was mixed. In the exam situation, it was foreseen that people are able to communicate via AAC tools/devices, bring their specific Assistive Technology (joysticks, buttons, sipp/puff devices – everything they would also use on their usual workplace) and also get assistance with handling the hardware (it was necessary for the exam to enter a floppy disk or exchange floppy disks, take paper out of a printer etc.).

3.2 Accompanying Materials

As the ECDL® scheme foresees the implementation of a widespread network of independent ECDL® test centers (where candidates take the exams), expertise in servicing and dealing with people with disabilities or knowledge in AT and how to setup and combine them with the ICT on site cannot be supposed. To guarantee at least a workflow and knowledge of some basic facts in case a candidate with a disability gets in touch, accompanying materials for test centers as well as teaching and training centers and their staff members in task of servicing them were designed.

These "accompanying materials" introduced basic facts on disability, on people with disabilities (code of conduct – like), computer usage by people with disabilities as well as possible adaptations/assistive technology (AT) needed to efficiently use Hard- and Software and where to get information and support in case of questions/problems not foreseen in the materials and consisted of the following items:

- Background information for all target groups
- Checklists and workflows (administrative tasks/servicing people with disabilities)
- Lists with expert organizations/umbrella organizations for people with disabilities in all major cities and further internet resources
- Best practice examples and
- Case studies of test centers already working with people with disabilities

The idea to develop a quality sign for indicating that a specific test or training center is especially suitable for servicing people with disabilities including all standardization and evaluation criteria was dropped.

As ECDL® Foundation was a leading partner in this project, the transfer of these findings and research results, strategies and frameworks into the extensive and worldwide active ECDL®/ICDL® network was guaranteed. Additionally, the administration of all ECDL® related activities (Syllabus creation, MQTB building and the development of criteria for becoming a test center) is worldwide managed centrally by ECDL® Foundation and all structures and materials are transferred to one specific main partner in every country participating in ECDL®/ICDL® for e.g. translation and implementation what guarantees reliability and validity of the needed results before rolling them out to all partner institutions in a specific country.

3.3   Follow-Up Activities

The advancements in ICT/AT, that lead to more accessibility of hard- and software for example through implementing basic tools for accessibility directly into the OS, as well as the success of ECDL® PD and the developed structures and materials encouraged new research and development activities, e.g. ECDL® bf – "ECDL® barrierefrei" (ECDL® without barriers), that worked at national level (Austria and German speaking countries). Partners in this project were the biggest Austrian provider of ECDL® teaching and training materials and Microsoft Austria who also sponsored the activities.

ECDL bf. The idea of ECDL bf was to create "an interactive multimedia teaching and training system without barriers to enable people with disabilities to pass the recognized IT certificate ECDL and thereby foster their integration into the labour market by being able to prove their IT – competencies doubtlessly", and thereby reach the goals [10]:

- Adaptation and/or creation of an accessible multimedia teaching and training environment to include people with specific needs into training activities
- Valorization of this teaching and training activities by following the strict and recognized ECDL quality assurance guidelines and thereby
- Foster the vocational integration of people with specific needs.

ECDL® bf guaranteed and implemented the same interface and look for all users, independent from a possible disability and form of disability. Thus enabled teachers and trainers to instantly check and recognize what participants do, how they deal with the tool and if there are problems. Screenreader users had an interface that looked perfectly the same, but functions, that were not feasible were unavailable and did not result in a lot of tabbing when looking for a specific interaction element. Furthermore, we implemented an extensive set of shortcuts for available interactions (see Fig. 2).

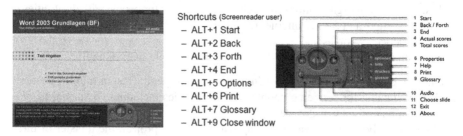

Fig. 2. ECDL bf graphical user interface: overall (left), navigation for screenreader users (middle) and navigation/handling for non screenreader users.

There was a parallel language version in profoundly simpler language. Also the text shown (additionally to the audio output as well as the language level of the audio output) was adapted to a simplified language level, the audio output was a bit slower and read by a female professional speaker. The alternative, male spoken "mainstream" language option (easily to toggle, even in between reading) was necessary because the provider of the teaching and training materials was afraid of losing clients that "might feel offended by the easy (language) level of the materials".

Tests with target group users as well as mainstream users of all age groups, gender and professions showed very quickly that – especially when more complex things were explained – ALL users switched to the simpler version and stayed there as long as needed. Furthermore they stated that they felt very comfortable with the fact that they are able to switch to the easier level whenever needed. Due to financial reasons (the translation into the alternative language level as well as the additional speaker were extremely cost demanding and only sponsored in this first version), this optimal paradigm was not implemented when changing to the new ECDL® syllabus version.

3.4 Back to the Future

Today, ECDL®/ICDL® is available in many countries and many types (e.g. ECDL® advanced with more in depth knowledge and competences) and with adapted Syllabi/ Questions and tasks. But the basic principles of accessible strategies and simplified/ better structured Questions/tasks in exams stayed. Teaching and training materials are available printed and online (also as MOOCs) but the accessibility depends on the provider of these materials. Specialized courses for our "old target groups" with specialized materials are available throughout the ECDL® universe, but there is no longer the "one fits it all" system design that was rated and evaluated best in tests within ECDL® bf.

4 Conclusion

In this paper, we presented 15 years development of accessibility in ECDL®/ICDL®. Whereas the certificate itself and its structures can (at least in Austria resp. Europe) be evaluated as accessible and feasible to include people with fewer opportunities into education and vocation. The accessibility of teaching and learning materials/courses depend also today on the knowledge and commitment of its providers. ECDL®/ICDL® is most prominently used and promoted in secondary education and as basic education for people with disabilities who want to enter office jobs. Other mainstream clients rely more on other, alternative certificates to proof their professional (IT) knowledge.

Acknowledgements. We thank the ECDL® Foundation and the Austrian Computer Society (responsible for ECDL® in Austria) for their support.

References

1. ECDL® Foundation. http://www.ecdl.com/. Accessed Jan 2016
2. Miesenberger, K.: ECDL-PD European computer driving licence for people with disabilities. In: Vollmar, R., Wagner, R. (eds.) Computers Helping People with Special Needs, ICCHP 2000. OCG, vol. 788, pp. 465–472. Oldenbourg, München (2000)
3. Petz, A., Miesenberger, K.: ECDL PD - using a well known standard to lift barriers on the labour market. In: Miesenberger, K., Klaus, J., Zagler, W.L. (eds.) ICCHP 2002. LNCS, vol. 2398, pp. 723–730. Springer, Heidelberg (2002)
4. Lunde, M., Tollefsen, M.: Many ways to ECDL. In: Miesenberger, K., Klaus, J., Zagler, W.L. (eds.) ICCHP 2002. LNCS, vol. 2398, pp. 734–737. Springer, Heidelberg (2002)
5. Tollefsen, M., Lunde, M.: ECDL for visually impaired persons: learning materials, individual training, and distance education. In: Miesenberger, K., Klaus, J., Zagler, W.L. (eds.) ICCHP 2002. LNCS, vol. 2398, pp. 715–722. Springer, Heidelberg (2002)
6. Petz, A.: KISS - keep it short and simple? In: Miesenberger, K., Klaus, J., Zagler, W.L. (eds.) ICCHP 2002. LNCS, vol. 2398, pp. 731–734. Springer, Heidelberg (2002)
7. Carpenter, D., Dolan, D., Leahy, D., Sherwood-Smith, M.: ECDL/ICDL: a global computer literacy initiative. In: 16th IFIP Congress (ICEUT2000), Educational Uses of Information and Communication Technologies, Beijing, China, August 2000
8. Miesenberger, K., Morandell, M.M., Petz, A., Leahy, D.: ECDL-PD: international co-operation to keep the syllabus and MQTB open for everybody. In: Miesenberger, K., Klaus, J., Zagler, W.L., Burger, D. (eds.) ICCHP 2004. LNCS, vol. 3118, pp. 164–170. Springer, Heidelberg (2004)
9. Leahy, D., Dolan, D.: Making an international certificate accessible. In: Miesenberger, K., Klaus, J., Zagler, W.L., Karshmer, A.I. (eds.) ICCHP 2008. LNCS, vol. 5105, pp. 1313–1320. Springer, Heidelberg (2008)
10. Petz, A., Miesenberger, K.: ECDL bf: equal opportunities through equal access to an ECDL e-learning solution. In: Miesenberger, K., Klaus, J., Zagler, W.L., Karshmer, A.I. (eds.) ICCHP 2006. LNCS, vol. 4061, pp. 560–567. Springer, Heidelberg (2006)

How Accessible Are MOOCs to the Elderly?

A Case Study on a MOOC Demo Course

Way Kiat Bong and Weiqin Chen[✉]

Oslo and Akershus University College of Applied Sciences, St. Olavs Plass
POB 4, 0130 Oslo, Norway
{Way.Bong,Weiqin.Chen}@hioa.no

Abstract. Literature has shown that learning, including eLearning and distance education, plays an important role in promoting well-being among the elderly. Currently elderly participants constitute less than 10 % of MOOC participants and very limited research has been conducted on the accessibility of MOOCs for elderly users. This paper presents the findings from a case study focusing on the accessibility of a MOOC demo course for the elderly. Different accessibility issues were found from automated testing and user testing. Although the elderly participants expressed general positive attitude towards using MOOCs to learn new knowledge, it is important for MOOC providers to address the accessibility issues and make their courses accessible to elderly users.

Keywords: MOOC · Accessibility · Elderly · e-Learning · User tests · WCAG

1 Introduction

The number of elderly people is increasing every year. As of today, elderly people constitute a big part of the world population and elderly population is likely to increase over the next three decades [1]. Literature has shown that learning, including eLearning and distance education, plays an important role in promoting well-being among the elderly [2–4].

MOOC (Massive Open Online Course) provides open and online learning environments and have great potential to educate large amount of people in a flexible way that meets the needs of today's learners for an increasingly complex world [5]. As of August 2015, edX, a non-profit and open source MOOC provider has more than 5 million students and offers more than 650 courses in variety of subjects such as business and management, computer science, biology and life sciences [6].

Currently elderly participants constitute less than 10 % of MOOC participants [7]. Research focusing on MOOCs and elderly people are very limited. In this research, we aim to understand the accessibility of MOOCs to the elderly by carrying out a case study on the "edX: DemoX.1 Demo Course". We have conducted user testing with six elderly people in addition to the automated testing based on Web Content Accessibility Guidelines (WCAG 2.0).

© Springer International Publishing Switzerland 2016
K. Miesenberger et al. (Eds.): ICCHP 2016, Part I, LNCS 9758, pp. 437–444, 2016.
DOI: 10.1007/978-3-319-41264-1_60

2 Related Work

Al-Mouh and colleagues evaluated courses in Coursera from two perspectives: users and experts [8]. For user perspectives, they tested with the assistance of screen readers. They concluded that Coursera still had accessibility issues to screen readers' users, thus failed to comply WCAG 2.0 guidelines. For expert perspectives, they conducted heuristic evaluation using ten courses and the outcome indicated the courses' failure to conform to all priority levels (A, AA and AAA).

Instead of evaluating courses, Bohnsack and Puhl [9] evaluated the MOOC providers. They adopted protocol observation while conducting user testing with blind test person rather than opting for W3C guidelines and recommendations for accessibility. They chose Udacity, Coursera, edX, OpenCourseWorld and Iversity. edX was found to be the only MOOC platform accessible with their real-life test-configurations for blind users.

A case study was conducted by Iniesto and colleagues to analyze the degree of accessibility of two MOOC providers: UNED COMA (Universidad Nacional de Educacion a Distancia) and UAb iMOOC (Universidade Aberta) [10]. eXaminator was used to give a score between 1 and 10 that indicated the accessibility of the tested pages while aDesigner was used as a disability simulator so that designers could ensure the web pages were accessible and usable to users with particular disabilities such as blind and reduced vision. None of the MOOC platforms was found to achieve reasonable score that could indicate that they are accessible and understandable to the users.

MOOCs are seen as a good alternative for people who have difficulties to go to school, or attend courses [5, 11, 12]. They have great potentials for the active learning and well-being of elderly people. Sanchez-Gordon and Luján-Mora [13] was the only research we have found focusing on MOOC accessibility for the elderly. They selected five courses from Coursera to conduct accessibility evaluation for elderly users. They first identified web accessibility requirements based on principles in WCAG 2.0 and WAI-AGE. They then performed heuristic testing. Similar to other research on accessibility, Sanchez-Gordon and Luján-Mora found out that all five examined courses have accessibility issues that need to be addressed. In addition, they also argued that WCAG 2.0 success criteria are insufficient as accessibility requirement for the elderly people.

3 Method

For people lack of experience with e-learning platforms or MOOCs, "edX: DemoX.1 Demo Course" gives a clear walkthrough for MOOCs on edX platform. This course shows the users how to take a course, from learning, doing assignment to taking a final exam on edX.

In the first step of the research, we conducted an automated accessibility testing on this demo course using AChecker for conformance with WCAG 2.0 Level A, AA and AAA. We tested all pages from the four main tabs (Home, Course, Discussion, and Progress) in the demo course (Fig. 1a).

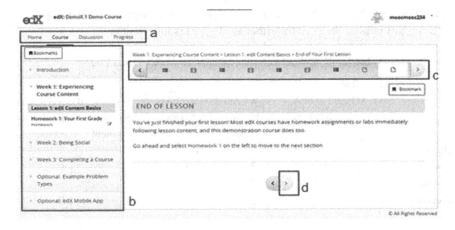

Fig. 1. Main interface of the demo course (a) four main tabs, (b) side bar, (c) progress tab bar, and (d) next button

In the second step, we conducted user testing of the demo course with six elderly users (P1 to P6) aged above 60 who have no experience with MOOCs. All of them are already retired but they still work in small amount from time to time to keep themselves busy. Their computer literacy ranges widely from experience users (using computer daily) to novice (never used computer or visited websites before). They were asked to enroll and complete the course. During the user testing, we observed how they interacted with the course content and took note on the accessibility issues. Interview was conducted after the testing to clarify the accessibility issues identified from the observation and gain deeper understanding of these issues.

4   Result & Discussion

4.1   Automated Testing

Even though there are multiple steps in the progress bar in each lesson (Fig. 1c), the lesson page was only tested once as the web page URL remains the same despite of different contents in different steps. AChecker identifies the accessibility issues and reports them into three main groups, which are known problem, likely problem and potential problems. The results from the automated testing of the demo course using AChecker are presented in Table 1 where we report only the known and likely problems.

As shown in Table 1, even though there is no known problem at WCAG 2.0 level A, the demo course has known problems at both Level AA and Level AAA. Complying with minimum Level AA for web pages is already specified in laws and regulations in countries such as Norway and Australia.

The three known problems for Level AA and Level AAA detected by AChecker are actually the same in all pages: element i (italic) being used and AChecker suggested replacing them with 'em' or 'strong'. Since results for all web pages in tabs Course,

Discussion and Progress have the same results even though the contents are very different, this implies the need to further verify the testing results.

Table 1. AChecker test results for edX: DemoX.1 Demo Course

	Guidelines					
	WCAG 2.0 Level A		WCAG 2.0 Level AA		WCAG 2.0 Level AAA	
	Known problem	Likely problem	Known problem	Likely problem	Known problem	Likely problem
Home	0	0	3	1	3	1
Course	0	0	3	0	3	0
Discussion	0	0	3	0	3	0
Progress	0	0	3	0	3	0

4.2 User Testing

None of the elderly participants managed to go through all lessons and assignments in the course. The user testing discovered many accessibility issues in the course in edX, beyond the problems found in the automated testing. We can categorize the accessibilities issues into two main groups, which are interface design related and course content related.

Interface Design Related Issues. Several of the elderly had problems with buttons. For example, some of them clicked on 'SHOW ANSWER' button while they only intended to check if their answer was correct (Fig. 2). It could be because that the labels for these two buttons were not clear to them and/or they were placed too close to each other, as commented by P1 "I understand what they mean, but maybe they are so close to one another and they mean nearly the same to me".

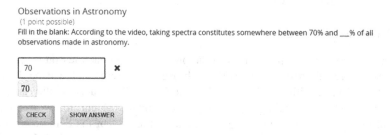

Fig. 2. 'CHECK' and 'SHOW ANSWER' buttons in assignment in demo course

All of them had difficulties moving to next lesson or assignment listed on the side bar. The participants assumed that the next button in the lesson page (Fig. 1d) would take them to the next lesson or assignment. However, the next button only took them to the next step in the lesson or assignment. When they reached the end of the lesson or assignment, the next button was disabled (Fig. 1d). The participants could not figure out how to move to next lesson or assignment. They became very confused, so they just clicked randomly on the items on the side bar.

Most of the participants had problems when attending the assignments about electronic circuit. One of them accidentally enlarged the circuit when he tried to scroll the page using mouse scroll wheel. After the circuit was enlarged, he could not find a way to proceed with the assignment. There was no indication that he had enlarged the circuit so he was not aware about what he could do next.

The drag and drop feature for circuit components posed some challenges for the participants as well. Two of them tried to select the components and draw them on the circuits. However, they did not know that they had to actually drag and drop the components in order to draw them on the circuits. The rest of them were very confused as they did not know where to start.

Another interface issue with the demo course is the amount of information being placed in a single web page. Sometimes the participants were distracted from performing the task at hand as they thought the other information in the same page was related to what they were doing. Most of the time they were trying to read or look at the contents below the videos while videos were playing at the same time. They were distracted and some of them just skipped the videos as they thought the videos were not important or not relevant to the text below.

Most of them also purposely skipped lessons or steps since they could click directly at the side bar on the left (Fig. 1b) and progress tab on the top (Fig. 1c). They also skipped part of the videos since they could click on the video progress bar. When clarifying the reason they skipped the contents or videos, most of them answered that they felt that the contents were very straightforward so they did not really need to go through them.

Furthermore, it was problematic for the elderly users when the interface did not react in the way they should. For instance, at the drag and drop assignment (Fig. 3), no correct answers were shown when the participants clicked on either 'SHOW ANSWER' (Fig. 3a) or 'HIDE ANSWER' (Fig. 3b). The participants found it confusing and were demotivated when the demo course had errors that they did not anticipate.

Course Content Related Issues. Course content is another aspect that creates barrier for the elderly participants. In the same circuit assignments as previous mentioned, none of the participants managed to complete them because of the lack of domain knowledge. The same thing happened when they were facing other course contents that were too technical to them, for instance periodic table of elements. They chose to skip the topics when they realized that the contents were not applicable to them or seemed uninteresting to them.

Through observation, some of the participants showed very little self-confidence when taking the demo course. Apart from their low computer literacy, this could also be because the course content itself is too technical. The participants commented that topics such as periodic table of elements and electronic circuit were beyond their interest and knowledge, and they should not be used in a demo course.

Besides, many wordings in the course content appeared to be boring and too technical to the elderly participants. They did not seem to have the patience to read through the text and comparing with text, they were actually more interested in watching the videos and answering the questions in assignments.

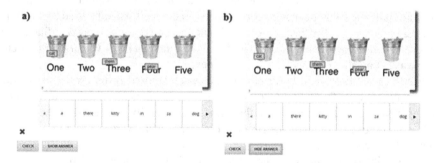

Fig. 3. (a) 'SHOW ANSWER' and (b) 'HIDE ANSWER' in drag and drop assignment

Providing wrong answer in the demo course assignment caused confusion to the elderly participants as well. One of the multiple choice questions asked "which of the following countries has the largest population?" and four choices were given. However, after participants submitted their answer and checked if the answer was correct, the results showed two correct answers instead of one.

Discussion was perceived as unimportant by most of the participants. They did not like to mix their social lives with this new learning platform, as they are either not active in any social media platforms so they are not interested, or they prefer to have some privacy between what they do online at social sites and learning sites. It is likely that they did not fully understand the purpose of the discussion; therefore they did not see the importance of it in the course.

Recommendations. The participants have shown general positive attitude towards using MOOCs to "learn something new and useful". However, there are still participants such as P2 who questioned about his willingness to spend his time in MOOCs since he met so many difficulties caused by accessibilities issues when taking the demo course.

Summarizing the results of user testing with interviews, we proposed a numbers of recommendations to improve the demo course. Some of the recommendations are already specified in WCAG 2.0 guidelines. Others are

- Interface should be simple, organized and informative while icons should be intuitive [3]. The placement of 'CHECK' and 'SHOW ANSWER' buttons should not be grouped together. 'CHECK' button can be placed at left hand side under the blank column to insert answer, while 'SHOW ANSWER' can be placed at right hand side. The word 'CHECK' and 'SHOW ANSWER' should be rephrased to 'CHECK MY ANSWER' and 'SHOW CORRECT ANSWER' to provide clearer definition to the users. Colors could also be added to make clearer distinction between the two.
- Web page should indicate what the user has done or is doing. For example, an icon can be placed to indicate the electronic circuit drawing has been enlarged (WCAG 2.0 Guidelines 2.4 Provide ways to help users navigate, find content, and determine where they are).

- The next button should help users to navigate from one lesson or assignment to next lesson or assignment. It shall not be limited to only navigating the steps in progress bar (WCAG 2.0 Guidelines 3.2 Make Web pages appear and operate in predictable ways).
- The context content should be kept short and simple to retain the users' interest and attention (WCAG 2.0 Guideline 3.1 Make text content readable and understandable).
- The tutorial for specific assignment should be placed at the respective course itself to provide context-sensitive help. The users should be able to access the tutorial when they need it, and not during the demo course as the course content might not be usable to them.
- The course needs to be thoroughly checked to ensure there are no wrong answers or misleading information that might upset and discourage the users.
- The assignments like STEM problems are too technical and they should be removed from the demo course.
- Some basic personalization features should be provided to address the elderly users' needs, such as bigger font size and stronger color contrast.

5   Conclusion and Future Work

In this paper we have reported our study on the accessibility of the edX demo course for elderly people. Through this research we have gained deeper insights about MOOC for elderly, from their attitudes of using MOOCs to accessibility problems that they faced. The automated testing evaluated the conformance of the demo course to WCAG 2.0 at level A, AA and AAA while user testing with interviews identified accessibility issues that were not discovered by the automated testing.

The user testing had only six elderly participants. Choice of course and MOOC platform was also restricted to the "edX: DemoX.1 Demo Course". In the future, we plan to include more elderly and more variety of courses and platforms. Even though the demo course provides a strong justification for this research as it is likely where the edX users start with edX, it is still important to evaluate courses in which the elderly users are genuinely interested.

Furthermore, we performed automated accessibility testing using only AChecker. In the future we plan to perform more automated accessibility testing using different evaluation tools in order to compare the results among evaluation tools and thus increase the reliability of the data [14]. Heuristic evaluation will also be conducted in addition to validate the results from automated testing.

None of our elderly participants managed to complete all lessons and assignments in the demo course. However, they have shown positive attitude towards using MOOCs to gain more knowledge at their free time. It is therefore important for MOOC providers to make their courses interesting and accessible to elderly users. We see the potential of MOOCs where elderly can benefit from learning something new and usable at their own pace. By conducting the study, we hope to inspire more research focusing on accessibility of MOOCs and platforms and contribute to making them more accessible to elderly users.

References

1. Lutz, W., Sanderson, W., Scherbov, S.: The coming acceleration of global population ageing. Nature **451**(7179), 716–719 (2008)
2. Way Kiat, B., Weiqin, C.: Mobile instant messaging for the elderly. Procedia Comput. Sci. **67**, 28–37 (2015). Elsevier
3. Teixeira, V., Pires, C., Pinto, F., et al.: Towards elderly social integration using a multi-modal human-computer interface. In: AAL 2012, Vilamoura (2012)
4. Githens, R.P.: Older adults and e-learning. Q. Rev. Distance Educ. **8**(4), 329–338 (2007)
5. Jansen, D., Schuwer, R.: Institutional MOOC strategies in Europe. In: EADTU (2015)
6. edX on Twitter. http://t.co/LF92R8DWku
7. edX. https://www.edx.org/about-us
8. Al-Mouh, N.A., Al-Khalifa, A.S., Al-Khalifa, H.S.: A first look into MOOCs accessibility. In: Miesenberger, K., Fels, D., Archambault, D., Peňáz, P., Zagler, W. (eds.) ICCHP 2014, Part I. LNCS, vol. 8547, pp. 145–152. Springer, Heidelberg (2014)
9. Bohnsack, M., Puhl, S.: Accessibility of MOOCs. In: Miesenberger, K., Fels, D., Archambault, D., Peňáz, P., Zagler, W. (eds.) ICCHP 2014, Part I. LNCS, vol. 8547, pp. 141–144. Springer, Heidelberg (2014)
10. Iniesto, F., Rodrigo, C., Moreira Teixeira, A.: Accessibility analysis in MOOC platforms. A case study: UNED COMA and UAb iMOOC. In: CAFVIR 2014, pp. 545–550. University of Alcalá (2014)
11. Alario-Hoyos, C., Perez-Sanagustin, M., Kloos, C.D., et al: Recommendations for the design and deployment of MOOCs: insights about the MOOC digital education of the future deployed in MiríadaX. In: TEEM 2014, pp. 403–408. ACM (2014)
12. Hew, K.F., Cheung, W.S.: Students' and instructors' use of massive open online courses (MOOCs): motivations and challenges. Educ. Res. Rev. **12**, 45–58 (2014). Elsevier
13. Sanchez-Gordon, S., Luján-Mora, S.: Web accessibility of MOOCs for elderly students. In: International Conference on ITHET 2013, pp. 1–6. IEEE (2013)
14. Vigo, M., Brown, J., Conway, V.: Benchmarking web accessibility evaluation tools: measuring the harm of sole reliance on automated tests. In: W4A 2013, p. 1. ACM (2013)

OLA! A Scenario-Based Approach to Enhance Open Learning Through Accessibility

Tim Coughlan[1], Alejandro Rodriguez-Ascaso[2], Francisco Iniesto[1(✉)], and Anne Jelfs[1]

[1] Institute of Educational Technology, The Open University,
Milton Keynes, UK
{tim.coughlan, francisco.iniesto,
anne.jelfs}@open.ac.uk
[2] aDeNu Research Group,
Department of Artificial Intelligence, Computer Science School,
Universidad Nacional de Educación a Distancia (UNED), Madrid, Spain
arascaso@dia.uned.es

Abstract. Open Educational Resources (OER) and Massive Open Online Courses (MOOC) have not developed with an inherent capacity to attend to the needs of disabled students. In our research, we aim to understand the social, contextual and organisational issues behind these inadequacies. Through this, interventions and best practices can be developed to improve the situation.

Keywords: OER · MOOC · Accessibility · Disability

1 Introduction and Related Work

Open Educational Resources (OER) and Massive Open Online Courses (MOOCs) offer new opportunities for learners who face limitations of cost, time or distance, entry requirements, or gender. However, this new educational paradigm has not developed with an inherent capacity to attend to the needs of disabled students [1]. This poses a serious problem to its foundation principles of being open to all. Accessibility in open online learning is particularly important since distance education in general attracts more disabled students than traditional education, and this trend is emphasised further in open education. For example Law et al. [2] indicate that while 12 % of students of the Open University in the UK (OU) are disabled (8 % in the rest of UK universities), 16 % of the users of open resources published by the OU (via iTunesU, YouTube and OpenLearn) declared a disability. Open Learning and Accessibility (OLA!) constitutes a strategic challenge for both the OU and the Universidad Nacional de Educación a Distancia (UNED), two of the largest universities in Europe. Both institutions are very active in the production of OER and MOOCs, and have a strong commitment to diversity and equality in education.

Recent research has revealed a lack of support for disabled students in open learning, in terms of poor compliance of platforms and contents with web accessibility standards [3–6], lack of information about accessibility preferences of students, barriers

K. Miesenberger et al. (Eds.): ICCHP 2016, Part I, LNCS 9758, pp. 445–452, 2016.
DOI: 10.1007/978-3-319-41264-1_61

of e-commerce or biometric techniques, or of third party software or social networks, which are used as part of the learning activities.

Given the instability and innovation that characterises open online learning, we avoid a narrow conception of the relevant forms of learning. Our focus is therefore defined to be self-directed learning with open materials. This encompasses MOOCs, OERs, or other structures where the learner has little to no individual human support for their learning. This is in contrast to situations with expectations for individual support to make adjustments, access support services, and to tutor the student.

To advance support for disabled students in these situations, it is necessary to un-pack the specific issues presented in the creation of accessible open learning, while at the same time, taking into account previous research on the accessibility of online and distance learning in general. For example, the EU4ALL project produced a comprehensive list of key requirements for supporting accessibility in further and higher education (HE), reported by Power et al. [7].

In our research, we aim to understand the social, contextual and organisational issues behind these inadequacies, and how the requirements to support learners with disabilities in open learning differ from those devised for other learning situations. Through this, interventions and best practices can be developed to improve the situation. In this paper, we describe a process of engaging stakeholders with scenarios of e-learning originally developed for the EU4ALL project, leading us to revised scenarios to illustrate open online learning specifically, this highlights emerging themes that distinguish the accessibility issues which emerge specifically in open learning.

2 Methodology and Materials

Understanding complex socio-technical processes, such as those involved in the creation of accessible open learning, is a challenge to which qualitative and design-based research methods are well suited, due to the 'wicked problems' faced, that cannot easily be reduced into components [8], and the socially-constructed nature of work, roles, and organisations. Scenarios [9] are a design-based research tool in which narratives of potential user interactions with systems become a basis for discussion with stakeholders, including the development of alternatives in which different events or systems impact upon proceedings. Through capturing and analysing qualitative data drawn from scenario-based interviews with a diverse group of stakeholders, our aim is twofold: (1) to develop an understanding of key themes, (2) to elicit descriptions of existing organisational approaches as well as potential best practices and high-level requirements.

The set of scenarios used as a starting point for this research was published in Rodriguez-Ascaso and Boticario [10]. These are an evolution of the scenarios produced within the EU4ALL project, which were created in an extensive user requirements elicitation process, and were used at different stages of the project to illustrate how stakeholders interacted with the EU4ALL services, or to inform the design of the tasks to be undertaken at UNED's pilot site, with more than one hundred users involved [11]. Scenarios encompass students, who are supported to express their accessibility needs and their feedback through the system; lecturers, who are supported in producing accessible materials, as well and in supervising course's accessibility against the needs of the registered cohort of students; disability officers who support students by assessing their needs, and serve as a liaison between students and other university professionals to remove accessibility barriers; transformation officers who work on the adaptation of materials, in co-ordination with lecturers, and librarians; librarians that manage the learning materials and their accessibility metadata in electronic repositories [12].

The EU4ALL scenarios then went through a process of adaptation, based in a re-view of open learning and accessibility literature that identified common practices in open online learning platforms (first in [10], and then in our OLA! Project). The current scenarios we are using in our on-going research aim to illustrate 5 topics of open learning, namely: the contexts in which students learn; their processes of finding and selecting open learning resources; administrative activities such as joining or paying for courses; processes of communication and collaboration during learning; and the content and activities included in courses, including assessments.

For example, scenarios 1, 2, and 3 are included below:

1. After years away from formal education, and an increasing desire to change their current work and lifestyle, a person becomes interested in learning online. At home there is a personal computer (or tablet, or a mobile phone, or a combination of them), connected to the Internet, with one or more assistive technologies installed, such as a screen reader, a magnifier screen, a speech recognizer, a keyboard or mouse emulator, etc.
2. They begin by searching online for resources about the subject of their interest. This leads them to various MOOCs and OER provided by different universities, and hosted on different platforms. The available information on a particular course usually consists of a video and/or text with a summary of the objectives and learning activities, duration, date of commencement of the next edition of the course, comments by former students, etc.
3. Once a student has chosen a course, (s)he goes through the registration process. Within that process, the student is required to enter certain personal information into the system. Some courses may offer some kind of official recognition of the student's participation. The recognition process may include some kind of identity verification (e.g., webcam pictures, trial period, etc.). Acquiring certain certificates may require a previous payment via credit card, PayPal, etc. On completion, the university behind one of the MOOCs sends an email that suggests that she could sign up for the formal courses they offer. She is interested in this as a next step. Based on her experiences with the MOOC, she feels that she could now manage to study for a degree in the subject at this institution.

Through semi-structured interviews based around these scenarios, conducted with the creators and users of open online learning, we elicit their perspectives on the roles, expectations, and organisational processes in performing work to create accessible open online learning, and the barriers that lead to low levels of accessibility.

As a means to clarify whether the scenarios are relevant and accurate, we first ask participants to rewrite the scenario from their own perspective. When the participants are staff members, we then ask them if and how the scenario is relevant to their own job role, and whether they think there are ways in which this role could be refined to provide better support to the learner in this scenario. When interviewing learners, the questions instead discuss whether they could describe their own experience of such a situation and whether and how there is anything that could further satisfy their needs. This process is repeated for each of the five scenarios.

To conduct a collaborative process of thematic analysis, and produce a coding scheme for the interview data, the four members of the research team met to review all the notes taken from the conducted interviews, and created a structure of themes, through which responses could be assigned and the data can be summarised.

3   Findings

So far, 12 participants have contributed to our work: 2× lecturers who are teaching subjects on accessibility of online learning, 2× specialists on accessibility of online learning, 2× consultants in online learning design and analytics, a disabled student, a disability officer, a specialist on the development of learning objects, a member of the technical staff of a centre offering MOOCs and OERs, a manager of a learning institutions, a manager of an open learning institution, and a producer of OERs, MOOCs and other forms of open online learning activity. All interviewees have studied or worked at the OU or UNED, and have previous experience with open learning.

3.1   Evolution of the Scenarios

The initial set of EU4ALL scenarios illustrated the accessibility aspects of online HE as implemented in the project's services. For instance, one of the scenarios described the initial interactions of David, a new student with low vision, with the UNED virtual learning environment (VLE). Within his registration process, he was asked to fill-in a questionnaire in the VLE about his preferences to access learning content and about the assistive products he may use in daily study activities. Also, this scenario described details about the assistive products and accommodations David used (i.e., Screen Magnifier and DAISY). Furthermore, the student was offered the possibility of being personally assessed by UNED professional experts in accessibility.

After the literature review, the EU4ALL scenarios were adapted to the open learning context of the OLA! Project. With regards to the scenario above, we did not find evidence of open learning platforms gathering accessibility preferences or needs of students at all. Also, it does not appear feasible for open learning institutions to offer professional and personalised assessment of students' accessibility needs. Hence, these two support resources were not included in scenarios used here.

Furthermore, we decided to avoid biasing the participant's response to the accessibility aspects of open learning, at least at the beginning of her/his response. Therefore, we eliminated most of the contents that were specific to accessibility (except for generic support products in scenario 1 "Student's context"). Should the interviewee not address accessibility at all, we would then ask her/him specifically about this topic.

As the scenarios were refined based on a literature review, it is pertinent to explore the responses of the interviewees in terms of how they find the scenario as realistic or valid for their own work. For instance, our original scenario 3 ("Administrative and e-commerce activities") mimicked formal procedures in HE, and expected that accreditation of the MOOC learning would be an important outcome, however this was queried: Low percentages of MOOC learners were actually taking up accreditation, and MOOCs were alternatively viewed by both organisations as a means to get learners interested in registering for formal, paid for courses. Thus an additional area for investigation raised by these responses is whether the platforms and activities used in open learning provide an authentic proxy for those of formal courses, even when the same institutions are involved. Interviewees expressed concerns in relation to this including a lack of information about the accessibility of specific learning activities, and the potential for bad experiences in open learning to damage wider confidence or interest in formal learning. This links to our discussion of student experience below.

3.2 Emerging Themes

In this section, we provide a sample of themes emerging from the analysis of the interview data, which are specific to open learning.

Student Experience. This is key in learning of all kinds, but given that in open learning the learner has limited individual institutional support, aspects such as interest, motivation, stress, coping strategies, and expectations emerged in the interviews in specific ways. For example, in response to scenario 2 (finding and selecting open resources) a blind student described how he reviewed course content and how compatible the course was with his own availability (duration, assignments), etc. When the interviewer noted that he was not addressing the accessibility topic at all, he replied "you are completely right, it is important to me but I never take it into account. I take for granted that courses are not accessible, but in case a course is attractive, I will enrol in it, and fend for myself, even if I needed to ask for help to people I live with". Next, the student reported stress when using the website and the eLearning platform of an on-line institution, because of the accessibility problems that affected key activities, such as the registration process and the navigation through the course's contents. In some cases he needed to rely on someone else to sort these problems out.

Responsiveness. This theme was added to address institutional commitments to accessibility in open learning. At the beginning of our study, it was apparent that neither open learning institutions, nor the students making use of them, had established any mutual understanding of the expected levels of commitment to accessibility. However an OU manager noted that, by early 2015, advocates for the deaf filed federal lawsuits against Harvard and M.I.T., citing violations of antidiscrimination laws by failing to provide closed captioning [13]. This ended with a settlement of the Justice Department with edX Inc. to make its website, course creation platform and mobile applications accessible under ADA, including WCAG 2.0 conformance within 18 months. This may influence other institutions and countries in terms of legislation and policy on the accessibility of open learning. It is clear that fixing accessibility issues requires the investment of institutional resources. A MOOC and OER producer stated: "During a MOOC course, we might receive 300 IT support requests, most of them about accessibility, navigation, awareness, how to get through, download, etc. The platform and its resources should be clearer for the students, but this would require more time, more resources, which are currently limited". A further avenue to improve responsiveness mentioned by interviewees was the potential to create communities around the open resources that could respond to accessibility needs.

Content Re-use: Open learning materials are commonly licenced for remixing and re-use by others. This can involve adapting sub-sections of content, and combining content from different sources [14]. A consultant on online learning design and analytics noted that "there are more eBooks now, and some of them have a reuse policy. In case the staff in charge of a course want to use only a subsection of an eBook, they check that when it stands alone it is still understandable. Then, the targeted content is repackaged and made available through the course platform". The potential to reuse content is at the core of the open education movement. It has potential to improve accessibility by supporting anyone to adapt content, yet it also raises concerns that as parts of a resource are reused, prior work to make the content accessible could be lost.

4 Discussion

Although the accessibility of open learning have been sparsely addressed [15, 16], stakeholders taking part in our interviews confirm the importance of this issue in terms of learner experience, and of efficient provision of a high-quality service (e.g. dealing with large numbers of IT support requests). Accessibility should therefore be considered when evaluating services and in reference models of open learning.

As with other forms of computer-mediated learning, accessibility in open learning depends mainly on an institutional agenda of inclusiveness, rather than on the availability of any single technology. A suitable agenda would influence policies providing the appropriate planning, as well as the necessary human and material resources. However, we have identified challenges that are specific to open learning. These present new technical and organisational challenges:

With regards to the re-use of educational resources across platforms and networks, even if the original resources were produced with all the required accessibility features, is it possible to transport or adapt these features in a remixed resource "out-of-the-box"? The latter means that appropriate standards, technologies and procedures for handling accessibility metadata for both the original and the re-used/re-mixed objects are in place within the platforms, which is not always the case [17].

It is also recognised that the forms of human support that provide responsiveness to accessibility issues in formal study are rarely provided for in open learning. Free or low-cost models in open learning are on the one hand an opportunity for widening access to education, but they often result in a lack of resources to support this access.

As open learning can be used to provide a taster of an institution or subject, or of online learning itself to a person with disabilities who may be interested in formal study, how is this experience reflective of relevant formal learning? Can well-designed open learning facilitate skills and confidence building, given the restrictions on human support mentioned above?

5   Conclusions and Future Work

In the present document we have described the process through which a set of scenarios are used to illustrate and explore issues of accessibility in open online learning, and to identify emerging themes that are specific to this context. The aim is to understand the issues behind the current inadequacies open learning has for disabled students, so that interventions and best practices can be developed.

The current sample has limitations in terms of the coverage of on only two HE institutions that share some similarities (e.g. a distance-learning approach and a focus on inclusivity). The organisational aspects may differ for other providers of open learning. To date we have primarily explored the perceptions of staff, rather of than the learners themselves. The project continues, and our focus is now to interview a diverse sample of learners and to broaden the sample of staff to cover other open learning institutions. Furthermore, the scenario-based approach is useful to identify current challenges and practices, and naturally leads to envisaging and discussing potential solutions. The use of further participatory and user-centred design methods, combined with appropriate learning analytics techniques, will support a continued grounding of this research in the practices and needs of stakeholders.

Acknowledgement. We would like to thank "The Leverhulme Trust" Open World Learning (OWL) programme for its support.

References

1. McAndrew, T., Gruszczynska, A.: Accessibility challenges and techniques for open educational resources (ACTOER). Final report, JISC TechDis (2013)
2. Law, P., Perryman, L.A., Law, A.: Open educational resources for all? Comparing user motivations and characteristics across The Open University's iTunes U channel and Open-Learn platform. Open and Flexible Higher Education Conference 2013, pp. 204–219. European Association of Distance Teaching Universities (EADTU) (2013)
3. Sanchez-Gordon, S., Luján-Mora, S.: Web accessibility of MOOC for elderly students. In: Proceedings of the International Conference on Information Technology Based Higher Education and Training (ITHET), pp. 1–6. IEEE (2013)
4. Al-Mouh, N.A., Al-Khalifa, A.S., Al-Khalifa, H.S.: A first look into MOOCs accessibility. In: Miesenberger, K., Fels, D., Archambault, D., Peňáz, P., Zagler, W. (eds.) ICCHP 2014, Part I. LNCS, vol. 8547, pp. 145–152. Springer, Heidelberg (2014)
5. Bohnsack, M., Puhl, S.: Accessibility of MOOCs. In: Miesenberger, K., Fels, D., Archambault, D., Peňáz, P., Zagler, W. (eds.) ICCHP 2014, Part I. LNCS, vol. 8547, pp. 141–144. Springer, Heidelberg (2014)
6. Iniesto, F., Rodrigo, C., Moreira Teixeira, A.: Accessibility analysis in MOOC platforms. A case study : UNED COMA and UAb iMOOC. In: V Congreso Internacional sobre Calidad y Accesibilidad de la Formación Virtual (CAFVIR 2014), pp. 545–550 (2014)
7. Power, C., Petrie, H., Swallow, D.: D1.3.6 final revision of the functional user requirements for accessibility in education. In: EU4ALL (2011)

8. Zimmerman, J., Forlizzi, J., Evenson, S.: Research through design as a method for interaction design research in HCI. In: Proceedings of the SIGCHI Conference on Human Factors in Computing Systems, pp. 493–502. ACM (2007)

9. Rosson, M.B., Carroll, J. M.: Scenario-based usability engineering. In: Proceedings of the 4th Conference on Designing Interactive Systems: Processes, Practices, Methods, and Techniques. ACM (2002)

10. Rodriguez-Ascaso, A., González Boticario, J.: Accesibilidad y MOOC: Hacia una perspectiva integral. RIED: Revista Iberoamericana de Educación a Distancia 18(2), 61–85 (2015)

11. Boticario, J., Rodriguez-Ascaso, A., Santos, O.C., Raffenne, E., Montandon, L., Roldán, D., Buendía, F.: Accessible lifelong learning at higher education: outcomes and lessons learned at two different pilot sites in the EU4ALL project. J. UCS 18(1), 62–85 (2012)

12. Rodriguez-Ascaso, A., Boticario, J.G., Finat, C., del Campo, E., Saneiro, M., Alcocer, E., Gutiérrez y Restrepo, E., Mazzone, E.: Inclusive scenarios to evaluate an open and standards-based framework that supports accessibility and personalisation at higher education. In: Stephanidis, C. (ed.) Universal Access in HCI, Part IV, HCII 2011. LNCS, vol. 6768, pp. 612–621. Springer, Heidelberg (2011)

13. Lewin, T.: Harvard and M.I.T. Are Sued Over Lack of Closed Captions. The New York Times, 12 February 2015

14. Coughlan, T., Pitt, R., McAndrew, P.: Building open bridges: collaborative remixing and reuse of open educational resources across organisations. In: Proceedings of the SIGCHI Conference on Human Factors in Computing Systems, pp. 991–1000. ACM (2013)

15. Breslow, L., Pritchard, D.E., DeBoer, J., Stump, G.S., Ho, A.D., Seaton, D.T.: Studying learning in the worldwide classroom: research into edX's first MOOC. Res. Pract. Assess. 8, 13–25 (2013)

16. McAuley, A., Stewart, B., Siemens, G., Cormier, D.: The MOOC model for digital practice. In: elearn Space (2010)

17. Allen, E., Seaman, J.: Opening the curriculum: open education resources in U.S. higher education. Babeson Survey Research Group (2014)

Teaching Accessibility with Personas

Claudia Loitsch[(✉)], Gerhard Weber, and Jens Voegler

Institute for Applied Computer Science, Human-Computer-Interaction,
Technische Universität Dresden, Dresden, Germany
{Claudia.Loitsch,Gerhard.Weber,Jens.Voegler}@tu-dresden.de

Abstract. Personas are widely applied in Human-computer interaction and beneficial to understand the target users of a product. We use personas in the MOOCAP project to impart knowledge on Digital Accessibility. This paper presents selected course material of the MOOC Digital Accessibility. The proposed educational concept uses personas repetitively to build foundations of knowledge on accessibility. Additionally, an evaluation of the course material is presented.

Keywords: Personas · MOOCs · Teaching accessibility · Universal design

1 Introduction

There are many efforts to push the development of accessible information technologies ahead, for instance, by providing user interface designer and programmers with authoring tools [19] or infrastructures [20] to produce accessible solutions. Validating web accessibility is also widely tool-supported [15], even for mobile devices [11]. However, despite increasing numbers of tools and frameworks, the lack of expertise in accessibility development is still a main barrier to create technologies for everyone. Awareness and understanding of user needs, interaction and adaptation strategies, accessibility principles as well as solution concepts need further increased and passed on to the community and society to act inclusively. That implies to build foundations of knowledge on accessibility in higher education [7,21] and to provide experiences amongst educators such as in [13]. Online resources, such as the 'Interaction Sandbox' [17], additionally help to gain familiarity with users and disabilities. Educational concepts such as Massive Open Online Courses (MOOCs) are promising in this regard, in particular to attract a large audience. However, the *how to teach accessibility* and *how to promote accessible design* is not sufficiently investigated. The challenge that needs to be taken is to find effective ways to sensitize understanding about diverse needs of people with disabilities or elderly, technological barriers of the daily life and available solutions, e.g., assistive technologies or built-in access features. We argue, imparting guidelines, testing procedures, tools and technologies how to implement accessible user interfaces is crucial, but what you need to start with is to talk about the users. One way in this regard is to use personas.

© Springer International Publishing Switzerland 2016
K. Miesenberger et al. (Eds.): ICCHP 2016, Part I, LNCS 9758, pp. 453–460, 2016.
DOI: 10.1007/978-3-319-41264-1_62

It has been shown, applying the concept of personas in education is effective to get students engaged in designing user interfaces [12]. In this paper, we describe the design of the MOOC *Digital Accessibility* and how personas are included to support teaching accessibility. Additionally, we present the evaluation of the proposed educational concept.

2   Personas and Accessibility

Personas are fictional characters describing a particular customer segment [6]. Instead of talking impersonal and anonymously about the target group, personas help designers, developers and customers to create empathy with the end user and put themselves in a user's way of thinking. That is achieved by giving a persona a name, a picture and describing characteristic, background, desire or a typical day. Additionally, personas used in the field accessibility describe perceptual and motoric capabilities, interaction strategies with information technologies, barriers, or are even supported by design considerations. For instance, the *World Accessibility Initiative* (WAI) have been creating a collection of stories how people with disabilities use the web [3]. In addition to the actual persona, relations to the type of disability, as well as accessibility principles are given. Pilgrim [16] follows an educational concept to impart 25 tips how to make a web site accessible in 30 days by applying personas that have various combinations of physical and mental disabilities and difficulties in reading web sites. In the AEGIS project, seventeen personas were created based on a field study. These personas cover the use of technologies and adaptation strategies of people with disabilities amongst mobile, desktop, and rich internet applications [1]. The AEGIS personas were used to derive accessible interaction models [5] and enable developers to perform an accessibility assessment that focuses on the specific Persona [14]. Personas are constantly used as their application is beneficial in all phases of developing software, for instance, during user analysis [10], development or testing [9]. Investigations were also made in how to create personas with disabilities [18]. In summary, there is a general consensus in research, education and industry, personas are useful to impart accessibility knowledge, increase awareness of technological barriers and allow to talk about the target user in a personal and illustrative way. However, the dichotomy in learning a user requirement from a persona versus understanding how barriers affect a large variety of different users is at the core of this work.

3   MOOCAP

MOOCs for Accessibility Partnership (MOOCAP) is a pan-european project on educating accessible design in ICT [8]. A Massive Open Online Course (MOOC) is being developed and will be hosted by FutureLearn[1]. In addition, the materials are published as Open Educational Resources (OERs). The first developed course

---

[1] https://www.futurelearn.com/.

is on *Digital Accessibility* and imparts introductory knowledge on the topics: needs of people with disabilities and elderly, accessibility of desktop PCs, mobile devices, web, and everyday technologies within 5 course weeks. Each week is subdivided into around 20 learning units that are either an article to read, a video to watch (e.g. interviews with people with disabilities, screen casts of using apps, etc.), a quiz or a discussion where participants have to contribute to a specific topic. A learning unit should not take longer than 6 min to deal with. A distinctive feature is, the learning material is build around 9 day-in-the-life stories[2] that were developed during the project [2]. The day-in-the-life stories were created to help thinking about user requirements of people with disabilities when developing ICT solutions. They are introduced in the first week and are used repetitively during all course weeks.

3.1   An Indicative Example of the Course Material

This section presents an excerpt of learning units that belong to the week *Mobile Accessibility* of the MOOCAP course Digital Accessibility. The materials are available as OERs[3]. The goal of this week is to impart knowledge on how people with disabilities use mobile devices and apps, which barriers they face and what developers can do to build solutions for them. The first unit is an article explaining potential barriers on mobile phones. On the one hand, it is described how Carol (MOOCAP day-in-the-life story), who is blind, uses the touch-screen of her new smart phone. On the other hand, difficulties in using the touch-screens, faced by Marry (MOOCAP day-in-the-life story) who has arthritis, are illustrated. In the second unit, a blind and a physically impaired person explain their usage of a smart phone in a video. In the third unit, learners are asked to report on their own experiences, problems they know, and suggestions by referring a MOOCAP day-in-the-life story or creating a new ad hoc persona. Contrary to the original approach of creating personas based on field research, ad hoc personas are used in practice [4]. The goal of this activity is to encourage learners to look at the accessibility options on their mobile phone and to strengthen to think about user requirements and various technological barriers. In the subsequent learning units, specific challenges that people with disabilities face in their daily life are treated from a developer point of view and exemplary solutions are given. Firstly, finding a yellow pepper amongst a mix by a blind person is illustrated by introducing a colour scanner app (interview with the blind developer of the app and screen cast). Afterwards, outdoor navigation challenges are targeted by demonstrating a way-finding app for blind people (interview with the blind developer of the app). The next unit focuses on multimedia on mobile devises. In the last unit learners are asked to discuss what could make developers more aware of barriers, again by creating a ad hoc persona.

---

[2] The MOOCAP day-in-the-life stories have strong similarities with personas. They were created on the basis of extensive experience with these types of people and not on the basis of a field research. For that reason, the term personas is avoided.

[3] https://drive.google.com/drive/folders/0B7yTykBzKH4fdGNQY0JhNEtCRzg.

4   Evaluation of the Course and the Use of Personas

The aforementioned course material was evaluated with regard to understanding, scope, and presentation. Additionally, we wanted to know, how students assess the use of personas in our course. The evaluation was conducted during a regular seminar of the lecture series *Accessible Documents* which is offered at the Faculty of Computer Science of the University of Technology Dresden. In total, 50 students are registered for this lecture series and 20–30 students usually complete the accompanying seminar in which practical tasks, such as programming accessible applications or carrying out accessibility tests, are conducted. We set our students the task to complete the presented online course as one of the practical seminar tasks. Altogether, the students had 2 weeks to complete the online course.

Material and Method. We transferred the represented course material and the MOOCAP day-in-the-life stories to our local Moodle as we use this platform on a regular basis in our lectures. The seminar was conducted online and no face-to-face classroom activities took place during the two seminar weeks. The students had to work through the following 8 learning units independently (see also Sect. 3.1):

1. Read the *MOOCAP day-in-the-life stories.*
2. Read the article *Potential barriers on mobile devices* which describes challenges of people with disabilities when interacting with smartphones by referring to 2 MOOCAP day-in-the-life stories.
3. Watch the video *What are you using a smartphone for* in which two people with disabilities explain their experiences with their mobile devices.
4. Create a ad hoc persona (as forum arcticle) and report on accessibility issues you or an acquaintance may face on mobile devices. Name features offered by a concrete mobile device to overcome the barrier.
5. Watch the first video in the series *Everyday activities of people with disabilities* in which the blind developer of the app ColourVisor explain how an app help to negotiate the daily hurdle of not seeing colours.
6. Watch the second video in the series *Everyday activities of people with disabilities* in which the blind developer of the app WalkerGuide explain how independent mobility of blind people can be supported by an mobile app.
7. Read the article *Multimedia on mobile devices* which explains further barriers by referring again to 3 MOOCAP day-in-the-life stories.
8. Create a ad hoc persona (as forum article) and report on what might help to engage developers in accessibility.

After the completion of the course, the students were requested to fill out a questionnaire in which we asked to assess the quality of the course material and the use of personas. The questionnaire contained 11 questions. First, the participants were asked to assess their knowledge with regard to e-learning, development of accessible applications, accessibility guidelines, requirements of people with disabilities, and personas. Afterwards, 3 questions were asked to assess whether the aim to impart requirements of people with disabilities was achieved as well as the representation and the scope of course material. The last 3 questions concerned the use of personas. In particular, we asked whether the applied day-in-the-life stories helped to better understand barriers and requirements of people with disabilities as well as to put themselves better in a person needs. Furthermore, we asked the participants to assess whether the task to create individual ad hoc personas was easy to carry out. A Likert scale with 5 items (strongly agree, agree, neither agree nor disagree (neutral), disagree, strongly disagree) was employed for all questions. Additionally, the participants could give remarks for each question.

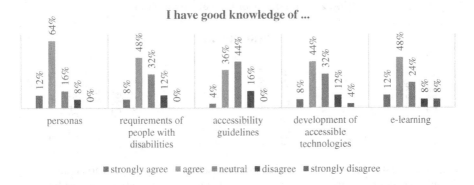

Fig. 1. Knowledge of the participants. Amount of selected items per question in percentage, N = 25 (Color figure online)

Participants. 25 participants completed the course. All participants were students in computer science and aged between 21 and 31 years. Overall, good knowledge (items according to question *"I have good knowledge of ... "* were answered with either strongly agree or agree) of e-learning concepts, the development of accessible technologies, requirements of people with disabilities and personas was reported by more than 50 % of the participants Fig. 1.

Results. The results of the evaluation with regard to the course material are presented in Fig. 2. 96 % of the participants stated, the course imparted needs of people with disabilities when using mobile devices (sum of strongly agree and agree). 80 % of the participants share the opinion that the course material was presented in a way that makes the subject come alive (sum of items strongly agree and agree). 60 % assessed the course material as appropriate to the scope of the seminar. The results of the evaluation with regard to the use of Personas are presented in Fig. 3. 92 % of the participants agreed, personas helped to understand barriers and requirements of users and 96 % stated, personas help to put themselves better in a person. Concerning the creative task to describe own experiences in form of ad hoc personas, 40 % indicated that it was easy to carry out.

The course material ...

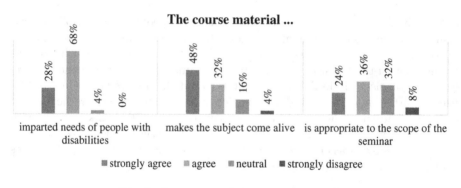

Fig. 2. Assessment of the course material.

Personas ...

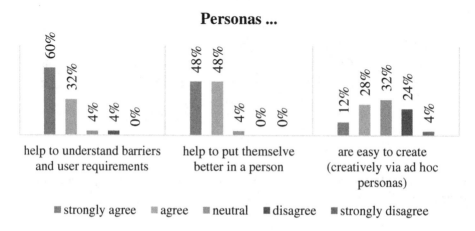

Fig. 3. Assessment of the use of personas.

Discussion. The results show an overall positive feedback according to the course content and the use of personas in teaching. In particular, the videos which where used in conjunction with personas where explicitly mentioned by the participants to be especially helpful. For instance, one user stated that *instead of textual description of a persona, I would have preferred also videos of the persona itself, not only about application scenarios.* In contrary to the positive feedback on the overall course material, applying knowledge of specific barriers and needs to a variety of different users (which was tested in two learning units where we set the task to create ad hoc personas based on own experiences) was more challenging for the participants. 60 % of the participants answered the question *Personas are easy to create* neutral or disagreed). Nevertheless, number and diversity of the created ad hoc personas indicate, this approach is effective to get students think more serious about accessibility and to train the adaptivity of foundational knowledge. In total, 51 ad hoc personas were created during the course (27 describing accessibility issues of people with disabilities and 24 describing developer perspectives). 8 of the created ad hoc personas refer to impairments that were not introduced during the course. For instance, multiple sclerosis, anosmia, dysmelia (hand deformity), or amyotrophic lateral sclerosis (ALS) as well as potential barriers were described and discussed during the online course.

5   Summary and Conclusion

The paper presents an evaluation that shows, personas are appreciated by students in higher education and help to understand demands of people with disabilities on technology. Although textual descriptions of personas are appropriate representations, video personas were mentioned to be more vivid to learn from users. Furthermore, developing ad hoc personas help to adopt how barriers affect a large variety of users. To conclude, we propose to use personas intensely in higher education but also in MOOCs as they are a good communication channel to increase awareness and to overcome the still existing problem of the knowledge gap on accessibility to develop inclusively.

Acknowledgements. Results presented in this paper have been researched within the MOOCAP project which is funded by the ERASMUS+ grant program of the European Union under grant no. 2014-1-DE01-KA203-000679 (MOOC Accessibility Partnership), through the German Academic Exchange Service (DAAD).

References

1. AEGIS Personas Ressource. http://www.aegis-project.eu/index.php?option=com_content&view=article&id=63&Itemid=53
2. MOOCAP day-in-the-life stories Ressource. http://gpii.eu/moocap/?page_id=33
3. Abou-Zahra, S.: How People with Disabilities Use the Web. Draft Updated 1, August 2012. http://www.w3.org/WAI/intro/people-use-web/Overview
4. Chang, Y.N., Lim, Y.K., Stolterman, E.: Personas: from theory to practices. In: Proceedings of the 5th Nordic Conference on Human-Computer Interaction: Building Bridges, pp. 439–442. ACM (2008)
5. Colven, D., et al.: AEGIS Models of User, User Interface and Action (D1.3.2) (2008). http://www.aegis-project.eu/index.php?option=com_content&view=article&id=12&Itemid=31
6. Cooper, A.: The Inmates Are Running the Asylum. Macmillan Publishing Co., Inc., Indianapolis (1999)
7. Fuertes, J.L., Gonzalez, A.L., Martinez, L.: Including accessibility in higher education curricula for ICT. Proc. Comput. Sci. **14**, 382–390 (2012). Proceedings of the 4th International Conference on Software Development for Enhancing Accessibility and Fighting Info-exclusion (DSAI 2012)
8. Gilligan, J., Chen, W., Kelle, S., Darzentas, J.: Mooca: massive open online course for accessibility. In: Universal Design in Education Conference, Theme 1: Delivering Universal Design in Technical Subjects. Dublin Institute of Technology (2015)
9. Henka, A., Zimmermann, G.: Persona based accessibility testing. In: Stephanidis, C. (ed.) HCI 2014, Part II. CCIS, vol. 435, pp. 226–231. Springer, Heidelberg (2014)

10. Henry, S.L.: Just Ask: Integrating Accessibility Throughout Design. Lulu.com (2007)
11. IBM: Mobile Accessibility Checker: (2015). http://www-03.ibm.com/able/accessibility_research_projects/mobile_accessibility_checker.html
12. Jones, M.C., Floyd, I.R., Twidale, M.B.: Teaching design with personas. In: Proceedings of the International Conference of Human Computer Interaction Educators (2008)
13. Keates, S.: Teaching the next generation of universal access designers: a case study. In: Stephanidis, C. (ed.) Universal Access in HCI, Part I, HCII 2011. LNCS, vol. 6765, pp. 70–79. Springer, Heidelberg (2011)
14. Oikonomou, T., Kaklanis, N., Votis, K., Tzovaras, D.: An accessibility assessment framework for improving designers experience in web applications. In: Stephanidis, C. (ed.) Universal Access in HCI, Part I, HCII 2011. LNCS, vol. 6765, pp. 258–266. Springer, Heidelberg (2011)
15. Paternò, F., Schiavone, A.G.: The role of tool support in public policies and accessibility. Interactions 22(3), 60–63 (2015)
16. Pilgrim, M.: Dive Into Accessibility. 30 days to a more accessible web site (2002). http://www.diveintoaccessibility.info
17. Rughiniş, C., Rughiniş, R.: 'In My Shoes' interaction sandbox for a quest of accessible design: teaching sighted students accessible design for blind people. In: Stephanidis, C., Antona, M. (eds.) UAHCI 2014, Part I. LNCS, vol. 8513, pp. 64–74. Springer, Heidelberg (2014)
18. Schulz, T., Skeide Fuglerud, K.: Creating personas with disabilities. In: Miesenberger, K., Karshmer, A., Penaz, P., Zagler, W. (eds.) ICCHP 2012, Part II. LNCS, vol. 7383, pp. 145–152. Springer, Heidelberg (2012)
19. Treviranus, J.: Authoring tools. In: Harper, S., Yesilada, Y. (eds.) WebAccessibility: A Foundation for Research. Springer, Hamburg (2008)
20. Vanderheiden, G.C., Treviranus, J., Gemou, M., Bekiaris, E., Markus, K., Clark, C., Basman, A.: The evolving global public inclusive infrastructure (GPII). In: Stephanidis, C., Antona, M. (eds.) UAHCI 2013, Part I. LNCS, vol. 8009, pp. 107–116. Springer, Heidelberg (2013)
21. Weber, G., Abascal, J.: People with disabilities: materials for teaching accessibility and design for all. In: Miesenberger, K., Klaus, J., Zagler, W.L., Karshmer, A.I. (eds.) ICCHP 2006. LNCS, vol. 4061, pp. 337–340. Springer, Heidelberg (2006)

Learning Through Videos: Are Disabled Students Using Good Note-Taking Strategies?

Abi James[(✉)], E.A. Draffan, and Mike Wald

WAIS, ECS, University of Southampton, Southampton, UK
a.james@soton.ac.uk, {ead,mw}@ecs.soton.ac.uk

Abstract. The importance of note-taking in face to face teaching and learning situations is well understood in terms of successful outcomes for the majority of students. Outcomes from interactions with online learning and the use of videos as a way of revising has been less well researched, in particular with disabled students. This paper aims to introduce the notion that not all disabled students who could use technology to support note taking necessarily find it effective although they prefer to listen and watch videos. A small survey provides an indication that students may not necessarily be making the best use of their technologies or have access to alternative ways of viewing online learning materials. Where there are options to view videos using lecture capture systems; time constraints and the quality of the videos prove to be further barriers, rather than providing a successful outcome. Despite the possibility of multi-modal/multi-channel approaches there also remains very little research on the subject in particular when using more recent Massive Open Online Courses (MOOCs). There are, however, indications that with the increased use of transcriptions and graphical tools, these options could offer good note-taking strategies as part of a more inclusive approach for all students.

Keywords: Videos · Note taking · Graphical tools · Disabled students · Dyslexia

1 Introduction

One of the most important strategies that students develop for learning is the ability to take notes from educational resources. Research has shown that students who are able to take extensive and accurate notes while learning are likely to achieve higher grades [1]. Note-taking can prove to be a particular barrier for disabled students who may have print impairments. While some students with disability may face physical or sensory difficulties in terms of independently capturing notes, others may struggle to concentrate or process information. For example, Boyle [2] identified that students with Learning Disabilities such as dyslexia were likely to miss important points in multiple sections of a lecture. They tended to record fewer points, make incorrect points or record nothing at all. Common adjustments for disabled students have either focused on human-aid such as scribes, translators and transcribers or personal devices for assisting with capturing notes (e.g. audio recorders, smart-pens). But, for students studying in traditional face to face teaching sessions, note-taking remains a challenge [3] and it is a

© Springer International Publishing Switzerland 2016
K. Miesenberger et al. (Eds.): ICCHP 2016, Part I, LNCS 9758, pp. 461–467, 2016.
DOI: 10.1007/978-3-319-41264-1_63

concern that this may also be true when disabled students are presented with videos or other multi-modal online lecture systems such as those offered in MOOCs or distance learning courses.

This paper will examine the evidence behind such claims and consider whether the tools to aid disabled students make notes match their requirements when using online courses. In lectures if poor note-taking is a barrier to learning for disabled students, is e-learning providing the right solutions or causing further stumbling blocks.

2   The Importance of Note-Taking While Studying

Note-taking is considered the process of summarizing information in a systematic way. For learning to occur it requires the student to actively listen or read information while connecting and relating this new information to ideas they already know [4]. Making notes during a lecture is considered to be more cognitively demanding than playing chess [5] as students are required to "attend, store, and manipulate information selected from the lecture simultaneously, while also transcribing ideas just presented and processed" [6]. Studies have shown that the amount of information a student is able to capture while taking notes and how they structure their notes affects their quality [7] and the quality of the notes is a predictor of test performance whether they study their notes or not [8, 9].

However, there is some differing evidence about whether using a computer to type notes is more effective than a more traditional hand-written approach. For example, for those with poor working memory, typing may offer a better solution [10, 11] but for others the process of handwriting increases levels of recall [12]. Bui et al., and others [10–12] also found that when the traditional note-taking approach of summarizing information in hand-written notes was deployed, the students working memory ability predicted the quality of the notes (as defined by the number of important points captured by the student). This would account for the difficulties with note-taking reported by students who have problems with processing information or concentrating (such as those with dyslexia, mental health, learning, and communication difficulties).

Students with sensory or physical impairments which impact on note-taking could experience a similar working memory burden due to the additional effort involved with capturing the information being shared by the instructor. Bui and Myerson [11] also found that a technology based note-taking approach – that of attempting to transcribe the speaker through typed notes – was independent of the student's working memory abilities and as effective at producing high-quality notes for those who are proficient typists.

3   Multimedia E-Learning

Video is increasingly playing a role as a medium for delivering learning resources [13] whether as part of a distance learning provision or supporting face to face delivery. MOOCs and online content creating tools combine video resources with reading materials and discussion forums [14]. Although research has shown that recordings used in this way should be short and informal [15], they still pose an extra demand on the learner to extract information both from the visual aspect of the video and the auditory output. There may be the functional accessibility barrier to video players with perhaps limited keyboard access for those who are unable to use the mouse or use a screen reader. There may also be content barriers related to the audio and visual elements that need to be captioned, audio described and/or have the provision of a written transcription. These issues can all be overcome with some forethought by offering accessible players and alternative formats [16].

Distance and online learning has often been considered a more accessible approach to learning for those students with disabilities who struggle to attend or follow face to face courses. Providing online videos of lectures through lecture capture systems has become more common-place within post-secondary and Higher Education (HE) sectors. This investment has been justified by some as a way of improving access for those who have a disability or struggle to attend lectures [17].

The link between lecture capture and improved student performance is still unclear [18]. The ability to pause, rewind and revisit video content should reduce the processing requirement for the student, compared to face-to-face lectures. Recently developed video players allow for video clips to tagged and bookmarked where key points need to be remembered. Furthermore, MOOCs and lecture capture platforms may provide the facility for students to take text notes while watching a video; time-stamping the notes to allow the student to return to a particular point in the recording. Registered students on MOOCs may also have the chance to return to the course at any time in order to revisit content to enhance overlearning and revision for examinations etc.

Vajoczki et al. [19] investigating the principles of Universal Design and the use of lecture capture stated that the majority of students with disabilities reported it met their accommodation needs, however it appears that this was primarily due to its ability to address issues of non-attendance. It is also well known that unless there is 'universal access' to video content [20] those students who have sensory impairments may not be able to make the most of these resources. A lack of quality captioning and audio descriptions can render a video useless to those with hearing and visual impairments. The positive impact on being able to control the video may also be lost for those with motor and dexterity difficulties.

Little work has been undertaken to understand how students take notes from video resources or whether any particular aspects of the design of the features aids learning. Dunn [21] reported that students were unsure how to take notes from online course materials and did not know whether their strategies were effective. Few studies have looked at the potential impact on disabled students of short or long videos embedded within other learning materials. However, Leadbeater et al. [18] found that students with dyslexia were part of a cohort of students who accessed videos the most. The authors went on to report on a further research study that compared the effectiveness of revision from students' own notes, a video recording of a lecture or a textbook [22]. They compared the results of students with dyslexia to those without dyslexia (neurotypical). Students' test results when revising from the students' own notes provided the smallest improvement for both groups. Neurotypical students performed equally well if they revised from a lecture recording or textbook and better than when revising from their own notes. Dyslexic students performed similarly to their neurotypical peers when revising from a textbook but attained lower scores when revising from a video recording.

Despite the lack of studies in this area, there are indications that although disabled students may prefer to use video resources, (in particular those with specific learning difficulties/dyslexia), they may not be able to reap the benefits from these resources based on their own expectations, skills and abilities and those of the instructors.

4   Investigating Disabled Students Note-Taking Preferences

4.1   Method

A survey was undertaken in order to establish how disabled students (n = 60) in higher education were using technology to take notes and which strategies they found most effective. The disabled students had access to computers and appropriate assistive technologies along with training in their use through the Disabled Students' Allowances [23] or institutional provision. The students were using all forms of learning materials in their daily studies but were most used to taking notes whilst listening to lectures and operating in tutorials or classroom/lab situations. The students were asked to comment on their use of videos but there was an understanding that online learning was only offered as an adjunct to face to face teaching methods. Participants were asked to rank their confidence with note-taking and to rate the effectiveness of various note-taking approaches.

The survey was presented online and publicized through HE staff related online forums. The staff then contacted the disabled students of which 45 % had dyslexia or other Specific Learning Difficulty, 25 % physical difficulties or chronic health conditions, 22 % had a mental health condition, 7 % had sensory impairments and 3 % had social and communication needs. Two students mentioned the fact that they had a hearing impairment but were able to use audio recordings. Two Likert scales were offered using a one to five rating for evaluating frequency and effectiveness of note-taking. The chance to comment was encouraged throughout.

4.2   Results

The initial results from this very small scale study highlighted the issues discussed in this paper with over half the students reporting moderate, low or no confidence in their note-taking abilities (56 %) even though they had access to additional support and assistive technologies when taking notes. As can be seen from the figure below (Fig. 1) despite the wide availability of technology, the most frequently used approach to note-taking remained the use of pen and paper. However, only 56.6 % found this approach to be effective, the lowest percentage of all the strategies surveyed for their effectiveness. The next most used strategy reported by 55.0 % of students was the creation of mind/concepts maps, either on paper or using technology. Of those students that used mind/concept mapping, 75.8 % stated that it was an effective strategy.

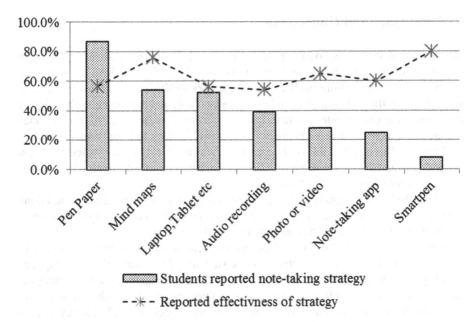

Fig. 1. Reported use and effectiveness of note-taking strategies by disabled students.

It should be noted that typing was used by 53.3 % of the students, but only 56.3 % of this group reported that it was an effective strategy. A few students took photos or used video capture (28.3 %) and some also used dedicated note-taking apps (25.0 %). These tended to be more successful approaches for this group of students with 64.7 % of those using photos or video capture and 60 % of those using note-taking apps rating them effective.

It appeared that only 26 % of the students had access to video recordings and all reported satisfaction with these strategies. But further analysis of the comments revealed that the strategy of reviewing videos as a revision technique was not as effective as the students first thought. The comments included such statements as "watching videos can make note taking more time consuming" and "effectiveness of the video very much depends on the production quality". Production quality was mentioned by Guo et al. [15] as being an issue for all students and is reflected in terms of engagement. As a disabled student (who completed the survey) commented "the effectiveness of video[s] very much depends on the production quality. Clear audio, in focus speaker, close enough to make out etc." 14 % of those accessing videos also noted limited access to transcripts but this may be an awareness issue as much as a need, in terms of transcript availability. A hearing impaired student who also had specific learning difficulties commented on the use of video capture saying "that it was very effective but she rarely had access to captions or transcripts."

5   Discussion and Conclusion

The number of students who took part in this study is low so generalization of any of the results should be undertaken with caution, but the authors believe the outcomes highlight issues that require further research. It appears that currently there is a mismatch between the tools disabled students have available and the strategies they deploy when accessing online video content. Disabled students' preferences for online video resources and perceived benefits are not necessarily leading to improvements in their performance. Not only has this study gone some way to illustrate these issues but recent research [20] and the survey results also indicate that extracting information from multimedia resources remains a challenge.

Given the positive results and marked preference for visual/graphical note-taking tools it is remarkable these strategies have yet to be embraced as part of the support mechanisms offered by MOOCs and other online learning systems.

Furthermore, there is the potential impact of synchronized transcripts with text highlighting, annotation and/or captions for these students. While transcripts and captions are often considered necessary for students with hearing impairments, the synchronization of the text with audio and annotations enables students to use dual channels for processing information in order to increase processing capacity [24, 25]. However, there remains the issue of introducing both students and lecturers to the idea that a range of technology based note-taking tools needs to be offered to students with disabilities. It should also be noted that there may be some trialling and training involved to find the best individual match of note-taking tools and their features to gain the best outcomes.

As the boundaries between video, multimedia e-text and other online learning resources become increasingly blurred, it is important that developers of learning content and digital delivery systems consider both the usability and efficacy of these tools for the wider disabled student community, not just those requiring access through well-known assistive technologies such as text to speech and screen reading.

References

1. Kiewra, K.A.: Investigating notetaking and review: a depth of processing alternative. Educ. Psychol. **20**(1), 23–32 (1985)
2. Boyle, J.R.: Note-taking and secondary students with learning disabilities: challenges and solutions. Learn. Disabil. Res. Pract. **27**(2), 90–101 (2012)
3. Hanafin, J., Shevlin, M., Kenny, M., McNeela, E.: Including young people with disabilities: assessment challenges in higher education. High. Educ. **54**, 435–448 (2007)
4. O'Hara, S.: Improving Your Study Skills: Study Smart, Study Less. Houghton Mifflin Harcourt, Boston (2005)
5. Piolat, A., Olive, T., Kellogg, R.T.: Cognitive effort during note taking. Appl. Cogn. Psychol. **19**(3), 291–312 (2005)
6. Kiewra, K.A., Benton, S.L.: The effects of higher-order review questions with feedback on achievement among learners who take notes or receive the instructor's notes. Hum. Learn. J. Pract. Res. Appl. **4**, 225–231 (1985)
7. Peverly, S.T., Ramaswamy, V., Brown, C., Sumowski, J., Alidoost, M., Garner, J.: What predicts skill in lecture note taking? J. Educ. Psychol. **99**(1), 167 (2007)

8. Kiewra, K.A., Benton, S.L.: The relationship between information-processing ability and notetaking. Contemp. Educ. Psychol. **13**(1), 33–44 (1988)

9. Fisher, J.L., Harris, M.B.: Effect of note taking and review on recall. J. Educ. Psychol. **65**(3), 321 (1973)

10. Bui, D.C., Myerson, J., Hale, S.: Note-taking with computers: exploring alternative strategies for improved recall. J. Educ. Psychol. **105**(2), 299 (2013)

11. Bui, D.C., Myerson, J.: The role of working memory abilities in lecture note-taking. Learn. Individ. Differ. **33**, 12–22 (2014)

12. Mueller, P.A., Oppenheimer, D.M.: The pen is mightier than the keyboard advantages of longhand over laptop note taking. Psychol. Sci. **25**(6), 1159–1168 (2014)

13. Johnson, L., Adams, S., Cummins, M.: NMC Horizon Report: 2013 Higher, Education edn. The New Media Consortium, Austin (2013)

14. Auer, S., Khalili, A., Tarasowa, D.: Crowd-sourced Open Courseware Authoring with SlideWiki. org iJET 8(1): 62–63 (2013)

15. Guo, P.J., Kim, J., Rubin, R.: How video production affects student engagement: an empirical study of MOOC videos. In: Proceedings of the First ACM Conference on Learning@ Scale Conference, pp. 41–50. ACM (2014)

16. Draffan, E.A., James, A., Wald, M., Dickens, K.: MOOCs - the web science experience. In: Proceedings of the W3C Accessible e-Learning Symposium, December 2013 (2013)

17. Taplin, R.H., Kerr, R., Brown, A.M.: Opportunity costs associated with the provision of student services: a case study of web-based lecture technology. High. Educ. **68**(1), 15–28 (2014)

18. Leadbeater, W., Shuttleworth, T., Couperthwaite, J., Nightingale, K.P.: Evaluating the use and impact of lecture recording in undergraduates: evidence for distinct approaches by different groups of students. Comput. Educ. **61**, 185–192 (2013)

19. Vajoczki, S., Watt, S., Fenton, N., Tarkowski, J., Voros, G., Vine, M.M.: Lecture capture: an effective tool for universal instructional design? Can. J. High. Educ. **44**(2), 1–29 (2014)

20. Burgstahler, S.: Opening doors or slamming them shut? online learning practices and students with disabilities. Soc. Incl. **3**(6) (2015)

21. Dunn, K.G.: The challenges of launching a MOOC and reusing that material in a blended campus class. In: Proceedings of the Canadian Engineering Education Association (2015)

22. Leadbeater, W., Anderson, V., Onens, S., Nightingale, K.P.: Supplementary lecture recording. A stepping stone to inclusion? In: Presentation to the ADSHE Conference, June 2014 (2014)

23. Department for Business, Innovation and Skill: Disabled Students Allowances (DSAs) (2016). https://www.gov.uk/disabled-students-allowances-dsas/overview. Accessed Jan 2016

24. Mayer, R.E., Moreno, R.: Nine ways to reduce cognitive load in multimedia learning. Educ. Psychol. **38**(1), 43–52 (2003)

25. Wald, M.: Synote: accessible and assistive technology enhancing learning for all students. In: Miesenberger, K., Klaus, J., Zagler, W., Karshmer, A. (eds.) Computers Helping People with Special Needs. Lecture Notes in Computer Science, vol. 6180, pp. 177–184. Springer, Heidelberg (2010)

Inclusive Settings, Pedagogies and Approaches in ICT-Based Learning for Disabled and Non-disabled People

Inclusive Settings, Pedagogies and Approaches in ICT Based Learning for Disabled and Non-disabled People

Introduction to the Special Thematic Session

Marion Hersh[(✉)]

Biomedical Engineering, University of Glasgow, Glasgow G12 8LT, Scotland
marion.hersh@glasgow.ac.uk

Abstract. This short paper introduces four very different papers on the use of learning technologies to support inclusive learning. It presents a brief overview of the Entelis Network which is supporting the session. It is introduced by a brief discussion of the barriers still experienced by many disabled people to education and employment and the potential of learning technologies to overcome some of these barriers.

Keywords: Learning technologies · Inclusion · Disability · Entelis network

1 Introduction

Education is both of great value in itself and essential for accessing other opportunities, such as employment. It also increases the contribution people are able to make to society. While access to education should be considered a basic right, many disabled people still experience barriers to obtaining an education and employment and are in an enforced state of dependence, rather than being able to earn their own living and contribute to society.

Disabled people are still seriously underrepresented in both further and higher education, though their numbers are increasing [1]. Participation in higher education is potentially empowering to all students, but disabled students still experience a number of barriers to learning and participation and obtain poorer degree classifications despite having comparable entry qualifications [2]. They also have lower average qualifications than the population as a whole [3] and considerably lower rates of employment. For instance, a 2001 survey for the European Blind Union found unemployment rates for blind people ranging from 55 % in Finland to 87 % in Poland [4]. Only an estimated 12 % of 'higher functioning' autistic people are in paid employment [5] and only 25 % of young autistic adults have any education or training after school [6]. Their employment rates in science, technology, engineering and mathematics are particularly low, with barriers resulting from the lack of meaningful access to learning materials and technologies. Disabled people earn significantly less than non-disabled people, with about half of them having incomes below the 'official' poverty line of less than half the national average wage and disabled women particularly disadvantaged [7].

They also are under-represented in professional and managerial occupations and disproportionately congregated in semi- and unskilled occupations although they have 'moved up' the occupational class structure since the mid-1980s [7].

2 The Potential of Learning Technologies

Overcoming these barriers will require a combination of different approaches, which target the underlying structural and collective issues [8]. The focus in this session is the use of learning technologies. Education has always used technology, from a stick for scraping letters and diagrams in the earth or sand onwards. However, the range, diversity and different media in which educational technologies can be developed are many times greater now than at any time in the past. Developments in ICT have the potential to transform teaching and learning. Existing innovative application areas include mobile learning e.g. [9, 10], microlearning [11] games based learning e.g. [12].

It is important that learning technologies are used in ways that increase opportunities for disabled people rather than create barriers or a new digital divide. ICT both has potential advantages for disabled learners and raises issues of the accessibility and usability of these technologies [12] and their match to the particular needs and learning styles of specific groups of disabled people. Accessibility is about the environmental characteristics of the system input and output which either enable or prevent particular groups of users from using the system, whereas usability is the ability of the system to carry out the intended function(s) when used by particular groups of users [13]. Thus, some (groups of) disabled people may require existing learning technologies to be modified or to use assistive technologies to access them and engage in learning tasks [14, 15].

3 The Entelis Network

The session is supported by the Entelis Network (http://www.entelis.net/). It was set up with funding from the Lifelong Learning Programme of the European Commission with the aim of contributing to bridging the digital divide in Europe and worldwide through activities to support the acquisition of digital skills and the effective use of assistive technology. The project's networking activities focus on knowledge exchange and supporting policies to encourage the effective use of assistive technology and learning technologies to overcome some of the barriers to participation in education experienced by disabled people. Specific initiatives have included living labs, the active participation of end-users and knowledge sharing events such as seminars, project development workshops and policy development studies. Project stakeholders cover a wide range of individuals and organisations, including disabled people of all ages, their assistants and carers, educational organisations, researchers, policy makers and assistive technology developers and suppliers.

4   Session Papers

The session consists of four papers which use different learning technologies to support inclusive learning for different user groups. Haptic models of arrays through 3D printing for computer science education by Nicola Papazafiropolos, L. Fanucci, B. Leporini, S. Pelagatti and R. Roncella, Università di Pisa and ISTI CNR, Pisa, Italy, involves the use of 3D printed haptic representations to support blind students learning about computer science data structures and algorithms. A simple, but general framework was presented for use with both visually impaired and sighted students. The model has been evaluated by small numbers of sighted and blind students who found that the approach helped them learn about arrays and sorting algorithms. Further tests with sighted students showed that they were able to describe the algorithms in their own words and carry out the given tasks. The authors plan to carry out more extensive tests and adapt the approach to graphs and trees.

Tablets are a popular technology which is increasingly being used in education. This raises issues of whether tablets do indeed have educational benefits and appropriate ways of using them to ensure that they do improve educational outcomes. Efficacy of tablets for students with learning difficulties studying concepts in geometry, Betty Shrieber, Kibbutzim College of Education Technology and Arts, Israel, examines these and related issues through a study collecting both quantitative and qualitative data on the use of tablets to support learning geometry with three students performing below the class average level. Outcomes were positive with regard to improvement in performance and student enjoyment. There were also indications that the multi-sensory approach made understanding difficult subject matter easier and that the apps introduced a 'play' element to learning. However, further studies will be required with larger numbers of students.

Using biometrics to support affective elearning for users with special needs, Ian Pitt, Katie Crowley, University College Cork, and Tracey Mehigan, Trinity College Dublin, Ireland, discusses the use of sensors to obtain data on learners' emotions and behaviour to assess individual learning styles and support the development of more affective and effective learning systems. The paper presents a comparative study of the emotive elements of learning of dyslexic and non-disabled students obtained from biometric data. While there is some potential in using this type of data to help learners determine the circumstances in which they learn best and realise how much their concentration is reduced when they text in class, there are also very serious associated ethics, privacy and data management issues. This relates both to who will have access to the data and how it will be used.

Designing effective learning technologies for autistic people, Marion Hersh, University of Glasgow, Scotland investigates the current state of the art in the area of learning technologies for autistic people. The focus to date has been on technologies for autistic children with little aimed at adults and therapeutic e.g. emotion recognition rather than academic or wider learning. The paper discusses autism in terms of the social model of disability and neurodiversity rather than the more common deficit approach. Recommendations include the needs for a focus on strengths rather than deficits in learning technology design, technologies designed for adults and technologies with a focus on academic and wider learning rather than therapy, as well as the development of technologies with easy customisation features to allow adaptation to the user, particularly with regard to sensory issues and special interests. There is also a need for the development of methodologies for involving autistic children and adults in the design of learning (and other) technologies.

References

1. Konur, O.: Teaching disabled students in higher education. Teach. High. Educ. **11**(3), 351–363 (2006)
2. Fuller, M., Bradley, A., Healey, M.: Incorporating disabled students within an inclusive higher education environment. Disabil. Soc. **19**(5), 455–468 (2004)
3. Knapp, M., Perkins, M., Beecham, J., Dhanasiri, S., Rustin, C.: Transition pathways for young people with complex disabilities: exploring the economic consequences. Child Care Health Dev. **34**(4), 512–520 (2008)
4. EBU. Survey on the Employment of Blind and Partially Sighted People in Europe. European Blind Union (2001). http://ww.euroblind.org/fichiersGB/surveymb.htm
5. Barnard, J., et al.: Ignored or Ineligible? The Reality for Adults with Autistic Spectrum Disorders. National Autistic Society, London (2001)
6. Touhig, L.: Proposed Changes to the Special Educational Needs (SEN) System. http://www.autism.org.uk/news-and-events/news-from-the-nas/changes-to-sen.aspx. Accessed 1 Aug 2013
7. Burchardt, T.: Enduring Economic Exclusion: Disabled People, Income and Work. Joseph Rowntree Foundation, York (2000)
8. Yates, S., Roulstone, A.: Social policy and transitions to training and work for disabled young people in the United Kingdom. Disabil. Soc. **28**(4), 456–470 (2013)
9. Kukulska-Hulme, A., Traxler, J. (eds.): Mobile Learning: Handbook for Educators & Trainers. Routledge, Abingdon (2008)
10. Motiwalla, L.F.: Mobile learning: a framework and evaluation. Comput. Educ. **49**(3), 581–596 (2007)
11. Hug, T.: Didactics of Microlearning: Concepts, Discourses and Examples. Waxmann Verlag, Münster (2007)
12. Hersh, M.A., Leporini, B.: Accessibility and usability of educational games. In: Gonzalez, C. (ed.) Student Usability in Educational Software and Games, pp. 1–40. Hershey, IGI Global (2012)
13. Federici, S., et al.: Checking an integrated model of web accessibility and usability evaluation for disabled people. Disabil. Rehabil. **27**(13), 781–790 (2005)
14. Day, S.L., Edwards, B.D.: Assistive technology for postsecondary students with learning disabilities. J. Learn. Disabil. **29**(5), 486–492 (1996)
15. Edyburn, D.L.: Assistive technology and mild disabilities. Spec. Educ. Technol. Pract. **8**(4), 18–28 (2006)

Designing Effective Learning Technologies for Autistic People

Marion Hersh[(✉)]

Biomedical Engineering, University of Glasgow, Glasgow, G12 8LT, UK
marion.hersh@glasgow.ac.uk

Abstract. The paper investigates the current state of provision of learning technologies for autistic people and makes recommendations for the design of new technologies and the need for further research. The work is introduced by a discussion of autism from the perspective of the social model of disability. Enduser involvement is obtained from interviews with autistic women and surveys of Polish teachers, therapists and psychologists working with autistic students, and teachers and parents on accessible and usable educational games.

Keywords: Learning technologies · Autism · Recommendations · Design

1 Introduction and End-User Involvement

The paper aims to investigate the existing state of the art in the provision of learning technologies for autistic people and make recommendations for the design of new learning technologies and the need for further research. There has been a significant increase in the number of children obtaining autism spectrum diagnoses [1], with an average of one in 68 eight year olds in the USA found to be autistic in 2010 [2], making it increasingly important that there is appropriate educational provision and support, including well-designed learning technologies, for them. However, learning should not end with compulsory education, giving rise to a need for learning technologies which are appropriate for autistic adults. The term autistic will be used to indicate anyone on the autistic spectrum, including those with Asperger's syndrome.

End-user involvement that informed the work included interviews with autistic women in France, Germany, Poland and the UK carried out as part of an ongoing research project using various methods to take into account their communication preferences, including face to face, written and phone interviews. The main focus was education and employment, but a wide range of other topics was covered, including thought processes, communication, sensory issues and support needs. 120 responses were obtained to a survey of Polish teachers, therapists, psychologists and other educational professionals working with autistic students [3]. It covered training, the presence of additional teachers, communication approaches with non-verbal students, what they considered important, difficulties and suggestions for good practice amongst other topics. A survey of computer based games included relevant responses from the mother

© Springer International Publishing Switzerland 2016
K. Miesenberger et al. (Eds.): ICCHP 2016, Part I, LNCS 9758, pp. 475–482, 2016.
DOI: 10.1007/978-3-319-41264-1_64

of an autistic home-educated teenager and two teachers [4]. The author also used reflection and insights based on her own experiences as an autistic.

2   What Is Autism?

The commonly used definitions are deficit based. This is disempowering to autistic people and not very useful for technology design. An alternative approach involves definitions based on the social model of disability [5, 6] which considers disability to be due to the infrastructural, attitudinal and social barriers experienced by people with particular impairments and neurodiversity. This is related to differences between human brains and minds, leading to differences in neurocognitive functioning [7].

As a result autistic and non-autistic (neurotypical) people generally behave in significantly different ways. In particular, neurotypicals use spoken language, facial expressions and body language to communicate, whereas not all autistics use spoken language. Those who do frequently speak more precisely and literally than neurotypicals, generally rely on verbal content for information and do not understand and may not use body language and facial expressions. Autistic people also have varying needs for social interaction, with some of them avoiding it and my interviews with autistic women indicating that even desired social contact can be very tiring or even exhausting. Neurotypicals frequently use small talk, banter and a variety of social rituals, whereas autistics generally want to get to the point. The interest of the conversation or activity topic seems more important to autistics. Some autistics have fairly narrowly defined special interests, but others are interested in and enjoy conversing on a range of topics. A number of autistic women, in particular, have learnt to simulate neurotypical small talk, sometimes through the use of rule based systems. However, interaction of this type can be exhausting without providing any satisfaction. Many autistic women are good at mimicking neurotypical behaviour, but may pay a heavy price for this ability, in one case subsequently being barely able to leave the house.

Some autistics are fascinated by particular sensations, but many autistics find noise, smells, lights and/or other visual stimuli that neurotypicals may not even notice overwhelming and a cause of very great stress. An appropriate analogy could be being beaten over the head. Some autistics try to calm themselves with 'stimming' movements. Twiddling pens, glasses and hair and swinging legs seem to be socially acceptable, but autistic stimming movements are frequently considered unacceptable. Particularly for autistic children exposure to unpleasant and excessive sensory stimulation can lead to aggression, self-harm and other behaviours considered challenging. The Polish teachers and therapists generally recognised the reasons for such behaviour and tried to adapt environments, made more difficult by their lack of resources and training [3]. To exclude sensory overstimulation autistics may withdraw into themselves and to some extent cut themselves off from the outside world. This withdrawal and the high percentage of incomprehsible (to autistics) information may give them less access to information and knowledge about the world than neurotypicals. A suggested analogy is reading the words of a comic book without seeing the pictures. It is possible to follow the story, but a lot of information is missing. The author's experience and interviews also indicate that logic may be more important for autistics, making neurotypical behaviour frequently incomprehensible, as it often seems illogical.

Only an estimated 12 % of 'higher functioning' individuals are in paid employment and 15 % of young autistic adults in full time employment, participation in postsecondary education is low compared to other disability groups and only 25 % of young autistic adults have any education or training after school [8–10]. Even very highly qualified autistic individuals may experience hiring or workplace discrimination [11]. The extent of the barriers autistic people experience is often misunderstood, particularly if they seem to be coping. For instance, two Dephi panellists considered the autistic person depicted in a scenario to be only 'mildly disabled... high functioning)' [12], as though autistic people need to be totally 'non-functional' to obtain technological or other support. The unhelpful stereotype that all autistic people have significant cognitive impairments means that autistic people with an education, a job and/or a relationship are often assumed to be neurotypical. Their strengths may be downplayed and reinterpreted as deficits. For instance, their abilities in block design tests have been interpreted as weak central coherence (an inability to 'see the big picture') [13].

3   Learning Technologies and Involving Autistics in Design

Computer technologies have been used with autistic students at least since the 1970s [14], and technological developments since then provide a very wide range of possibilities. However, the overwhelming majority of the technologies developed for autistic people are aimed at children, though extension to adults may be possible in some cases. The educational applications are frequently autism specific 'therapeutic' applications rather than academic and general education. These applications include learning emotions [15, 16], improving social skills [17–20], communication [21, 22], independence [23] and modifying behaviour [24]. The rarer general education applications are most commonly literacy e.g. [25–27], though numeracy [28, 29], vocational [23] and practical skills, such as first aid [30], have also been considered.

Technology approaches include video self-modelling on an iPad [28, 29], animated characters [20], virtual reality or environments [16, 17, 31], video clips [22], multimedia e.g. [27], smart phones (apps) e.g. [15, 21, 32], mobile technologies e.g. [33], websites and web-based applications [21, 34], tablet apps e.g. [19], serious/educational games [30, 35], iPods and iPads [36], computer assisted learning [37] and robots [38]. Virtual environments allow autistic people to participate in role play in safe realistic 3D settings that depict social scenarios in an enjoyable way [36].

Studies have found that autistic students may experience particular barriers to learning [39–41] and significant benefits from the use of certain types of electronic communication and interaction [42–44]. Specific examples include the use of mobile e-learning to utilise persuasion techniques with autistic teenagers [45], iOS devices to deliver basic skills teaching via an adapted interface [46], cameras and e-learning software to aid facial social-emotional recognition [47], educational games to enable students with Asperger's syndrome to explore, learn about and participate in meaningful social interaction and collaboration [35], and virtual worlds to create learning scenarios that would be difficult in face to face settings [4, 48–50]. Computer use by autistic students has also been shown to improve concentration and fine motor skills, give generalization to related activities and reduce agitation and self-stimulating and repetitive behaviours [51].

While not specifically about learning technology, AASPIRE provides an interesting model of collaboration between academic researchers and autistic self-advocates, with both groups participating equally in grant proposals, research projects and publications [52]. Otherwise, the focus seems to be on autistic children, with caregivers sometimes used as proxies for non-verbal children [53] rather than working out how best to obtain input from the child, and other types of end-users frequently having a greater involvement than autistic children. Participatory and human centred design projects have involved autistic children in various ways, including as informants at design workshops to inform the look and feel of a virtual environment, formative evaluation studies of the observation of their interaction with simple story boards [54] and participation in single and collaborative design sessions, including generating their own design ideas with one-to-one support if needed [55]. 'High-functioning' autistic teenagers have been used as consultants [56]. There has been limited work examining design issues and the accessibility and usability of learning technologies for autistic people. The extended version of the cultural model of assistive technology design with the four (cultural) elements of language, diversity, lifestyle and cost and the design elements of appearance, characteristics, interface design and usability [57] has potential, particularly if the cultural elements are applied to autistic people.

4 Discussion, Conclusions, and Recommendations

4.1 Discussion

All individuals have strengths and weaknesses. Well designed technological interventions aim to draw on strengths and work round weaknesses. However, many learning technologies for autistic people focus on areas of weakness, such as learning to decipher emotions from facial expressions. A more appropriate approach might be a technologically supported system for learning to apply logical reasoning to analysing behaviour, possibly in the form of a rule based system with its degree of complexity adopted to the user's age and cognitive abilities. Some typical (though not universal) autistic strengths [58–60] are listed below. How they manifest in a given individual will depend on various factors, including their general and cognitive abilities:

1. **Cognitive Processing Abilities**
   a. An ability to focus on and notice detail.
   b. Unusual thought patterns and an ability to make unusual and exciting connections.
   c. Strong abstract visual-spatial reasoning abilities.
2. **Other Characteristics**
   a. Curiosity, intellectual honesty and a willingness to ask critical questions.
   b. Strong memorisation abilities.

   c. An affinity for structure, order and routine.

   d. Rich vocabularies and good powers of expression (Asperger's syndrome).

3. **Special Interests**
   a. Strong, sometimes niche interests & the ability to be really passionate about them.
   b. The ability to focus effectively and work diligently for a potentially very extended period on topics of interest.
   c. The ability to obtain very detailed & extensive information about topics of interest.

4.2 Conclusions and Recommendations

Although space considerations have prevented an in-depth review of learning technologies for autistic people, the following preliminary conclusions can be drawn. Most learning technologies for autistic people have been developed for children and have therapeutic rather than academic or wider learning applications. There have been a few attempts to involve autistic children in the participatory design of learning technologies, but their role has generally been limited and other end-users, such as teachers, have been prioritised. These comments and the previous discussion lead to the following recommendations:

1. **General:**
   (a) A focus on strengths rather than 'deficits' in learning technology design.
   (b) Recognition of the diversity of autistic people.
   (c) The need for learning technologies for adults, as well as technologies that can be used as learners progress through their education.
   (d) Universal design approaches and design approaches which take account of demographic factors, including gender (and the increasing evidence of significant gender based differences between autistic people), culture and age.
   (e) Technologies focusing on academic and wider learning rather than therapy.

2. **Customisation and Use of Interests:**
   (a) Technologies and devices which are easily customisable so they can be adapted to the needs of the particular learner, particularly with regards to sensory issues, avoiding overstimulation and using their particular interests.
   (b) Guidelines and on-line case studies on how best to use special interests to increase motivation and encourage learning.

3. **Participatory Design:**
   (a) Involvement of autistic people in the development of new learning technologies using methods which are appropriate to age, cognitive abilities and sensory issues; and avoid restrictive assumptions or unnecessarily oversimplifying procedures.
   (b) Minimisation of the need for interaction, particularly with new/unknown people, in the design process e.g. a trusted person as an intermediary between each autistic person and the design team, online interaction and/or all communication in writing.
   (c) The development of techniques to stimulate the generation of design ideas.

4. Further Research:

(a) In-depth evaluation of existing learning technologies for autistic people and design for all learning technologies.

(b) Surveys of the learning technology requirements of autistic people.

(c) Development of improved methodologies for involving autistic people in participatory design e.g. using the AASPIRE approach of co-research between autistic self-advocates and academic researchers, and its extension to children.

Acknowledgements. Thanks to the autistic women who participated in interviews & the teachers, other education professionals and parents who completed questionnaires.

References

1. Loiacono, V., Valenti, V.: General education teachers need to be prepared to co-teach the increasing number of children with autism. Int. J. Spec. Educ. **25**(3), 24–32 (2010)
2. Baio, J.: Prevalence of autism spectrum disorder among children aged 8 years. Centers Dis. Control Prev. Surveill. Summ. **63**(2), 1 (2014)
3. Hersh, M.A.: Improving Educational Experiences for Autistic Children and Young People. http://web.eng.gla.ac.uk/assistive/pages/publications.php
4. Hersh, M.A., Leporini, B.: Accessibility and usability of educational games. In: Gonzalez, C. (ed.) Student Usability in Educational Software and Games, pp. 1–40. IGI Global, Pennsylvania (2012)
5. Johnstone, D.: An Introduction to Disability Studies. David Fulton Publishers Ltd, Abingdon (2001)
6. Swain, J., French, S., Cameron, C.: Controversial Issues in a Disabling Society. Open University Press, Buckingham (2003)
7. Fenton, A., Krahn, T.: Autism, neurodiversity and equality beyond the 'Normal'. J. Ethics Mental Health **2**(2), 2 (2009)
8. Barnard, J., et al.: Ignored or Ineligible? The Reality for Adults with Autistic Spectrum Disorders. National Autistic Society, London (2001)
9. Wei, X., et al.: Science, technology, engineering and mathematics (STEM) participation. J. Autism Dev. Disord. **43**(7), 1539–1546 (2012)
10. Touhig, L.: Proposed Changes to the Special Educational Needs (SEN) System. http://www.autism.org.uk/news-and-events/news-from-the-nas/changes-to-sen.aspx. Accessed 1 Aug 2013
11. Paradiz, V.: Autism, Identity and Employment, Transcending the Obstacles of the Working World, 1st edn. Autism Advocate, London (2009)
12. Francis, P., Mellor, D., Firth, L.: Techniques and recommendations for the inclusion of users with autism in the design. Assist. Technol. **21**(2), 57–68 (2009)
13. Shah, A., Frith, U.: Why do autistic individuals show superior performance on the block design task? J. Child Psychol. Psychiatry **34**(8), 1351–1364 (1993)
14. Panyan, M.V.: Computer technology for autistic students. J. Autism Dev. Disord. **14**(4), 375–382 (1984)
15. Gay, V., Leijdekkers, P.: Design of emotion-aware mobile apps for autistic children. Health Technol. **4**(1), 21–26 (2014)
16. Moore, D., Cheng, Y., McGrath, P., Powell, N.J.: Collaborative virtual environment technology. Focus Autism Other Dev. Disabil. **20**(4), 231–243 (2005)

17. Cheng, Y., Ye, J.: Exploring the social competence of students with autism spectrum conditions. Comput. Educ. **54**(4), 1068–1077 (2010)
18. Davis, M., Dautenhahn, K., Nehaniv, C.L., Powell, S.D.: The narrative construction of our (social) world. Univ. Access Inf. Soc. **6**(2), 145–157 (2007)
19. Hourcade, J.P., et al.: Evaluation of tablet apps to encourage social interaction in children. In: Proceedings of the SIGCHI Conference Human Factors in Comput. Systems, pp. 3197–3206 (2013)
20. Tartaro, A., Cassell, J.: Using Virtual Peer Technology as an Intervention for Children with Autism, vol. 231, p. 62. Wiley, Chichester (2007)
21. De Leo, G., Gonzales, C.H., Battagiri, P., Leroy, G.: A smart-phone application and a companion website. J. Med. Syst. **35**(4), 703–711 (2011)
22. Shane, H.C., et al.: Applying technology to visually support language and communication. J. Autism Dev. Disord. **42**(6), 1228–1235 (2012)
23. Odom, S.L., Thompson, J.L., Hedges, S., Boyd, B.A., et al.: Technology-aided interventions and instruction. J. Autism Dev. Disord. **45**(12), 3805–3819 (2015)
24. Neely, L., Rispoli, M., Camargo, S., Davis, H., Boles, M.: The effect of instructional use of an Ipad®. Res. Autism Spectr. Disord. **7**(4), 509–516 (2013)
25. Blischak, D.M., Schlosser, R.W.: Use of technology to support independent spelling by students with autism. Top. Lang. Disord. **23**(4), 293–304 (2003)
26. Pennington, R.C.: Computer-assisted instruction for teaching academic skills. Focus Autism Other Dev. Disabil. **25**(4), 239–248 (2010)
27. Tjus, T., Heimann, M., Nelson, K.E.: Gains in literacy through the use of a specially developed multimedia computer strategy. Autism **2**(2), 139–156 (1998)
28. Burton, C.E., Anderson, D.H., Prater, M.A., Dyches, T.T.: Video self-modeling on an iPad. Focus Autism Other Dev. Disabil. **20**(10), 1–11 (2013)
29. Jowett, E.L., Moore, D.W., Anderson, A.: Using an iPad-based video modelling package to teach numeracy skills. Dev. Neurorehabilitation **15**(4), 304–312 (2012)
30. De Urturi, Z.S., Zorrilla, A.M., Zapirain, B.G.: Serious game based on first aid education. In: 16th IEEE International Conference on Computer Games, pp. 223–227 (2011)
31. Strickland, D., Marcus, L.M., Mesibov, G.B., Hogan, K.: Two case studies using virtual reality as a learning tool. J. Autism Dev. Disord. **26**(6), 651–665 (1996)
32. Mintz, J., Branch, C., March, C., Lerman, S.: Key factors mediating the use of a mobile technology tool. Comput. Educ. **58**(1), 53–62 (2012)
33. Ayres, K.M., Mechling, L., Sansosti, F.J.: The use of mobile technologies to assist with life skills/independence. Psychol. Sch. **50**(3), 259–271 (2013)
34. Tsiopela, D., Jimoyiannis, A.: Pre-vocational skills laboratory. Procedia Comput. Sci. **27**, 207–217 (2014)
35. Loeppky, S.: Gaming and Students with Asperger's Syndrome. http://www.usask.ca/education/coursework/802papers/loeppky/loeppky.pdf. Accessed 4 Jul 2011
36. Boucenna, S., Narzisi, A., Tilmont, E., Muratori, F., Pioggia, G., et al.: Interactive technologies for autistic children. Cogn. Comput. **6**(4), 722–740 (2014)
37. Fletcher-Watson, S.: A targeted review of computer-assisted learning for people with autism spectrum disorder. Rev. J. Autism Dev. Disord. **1**(2), 87–100 (2014)
38. Hersh, M.A.: Overcoming barriers and increasing independence-service robots for elderly and disabled people. Int. J. Adv. Robot. Syst **12** (2015). DOI:10.5772/59230
39. Cain, K., Bignell, S.: Reading and listening comprehension and their relation to inattention and hyperactivity. Br. J. Educ. Psychol. **84**, 108–124 (2014)
40. Davis, M.: Virtual ed. targets rise of autism. Educ. Week Spec. Rep. (2011)

41. Mirenda, P., Wilk, D., Carson, P.: A retrospective analysis of technology use patterns of students with autism over a five-year period. J. Spec. Ed. Tech. **15**(3), 5–16 (2000)
42. Banister, P.: Society's autism e-learning wins gold. Psychologist **25**(12), 923 (2012)
43. Grynszpan, O., Martin, J.-C., Nadel, J.: Multimedia interfaces for users with high functioning autism. Int. J. Hum.-Comput. Stud. **66**(8), 628–639 (2008)
44. Soar, S., Ryan, S., Salisbury, H.: Using patients' experiences in e-learning design. Clin. Teach. **11**, 80–83 (2014)
45. Øhrstrøm, P.: Helping autism-diagnosed teenagers navigate and develop socially. Int. Rev. Res. Open Distance Learn. **12**(4), 54–71 (2011)
46. Fernández-López, A., et al.: Mobile learning technology based on IOS devices to support students with special education needs. Comput. Educ. **61**, 77–90 (2013)
47. Madsen, M. et al.: Technology for just-in-time in-situ learning of facial affect. In: Proceedings of the 10th International ACM SIGACCESS Conference, pp 19–26 (2008)
48. Ball, S., Pearce, R.: Learning scenarios and workspaces with virtual worlds. In: Kingsley, J., Wankel, C. (eds.) Second Life in Higher Education. Kingsley International School (2009)
49. Herrera, G., Jordan, R., Vera, L.: Abstract concept and imagination teaching through virtual reality. Technol. Disabil. **18**, 173–180 (2006)
50. Stendal, K., Balandin, S., Molka-Danielson, J.: Virtual worlds: a new opportunity for people with lifelong disability? J. Intellect. Dev. Disabil. **36**(1), 80–83 (2011)
51. Jordan, R.: Computer assisted education for individuals with autism. In: Autisme France 3rd International Conference, Nice (1995)
52. Nicolaidis, C., Raymaker, D., McDonald, K., Dern, S., Ashkenazy, E., Boisclair, C., et al.: Collaboration strategies in nontraditional community-based participatory research partnerships. Prog. Commun. Health Partnersh. **5**(2), 143–150 (2011)
53. Sampath, H., Agarwal, R., Indurkhya, B.: Assistive technology for children with autism. In: Proceedings of the 11th Asia Pacific Conference on Computer Human Interaction, pp. 325–333 (2013)
54. Keay-Bright, W.: The reactive colours project. Des. Princ. Pract. **1**(2), 7–16 (2007)
55. Parsons, S., Cobb, S.: Reflections on the role of the 'users'. Int. J. Res. Method Educ. **37**(4), 421–441 (2014)
56. Porayska-Pomsta, K., Frauenberger, C., Pain, H., Rajendran, G., Smith, T., et al.: Developing technology for autism. Pers. Ubiquit. Comput. **16**(2), 117–127 (2012)
57. Moktar, M.N. et al.: Extending cultural model of assistive technology design for autism treatment. In: IEEE International Symposium on Robotics and Manufacturing Automation, pp. 172–175 (2014)
58. Barry, M., Pitt, I.: Interaction design: a multidimensional approach for learners with autism. In: Proceedings of the 2006 Conference on Interaction Design and Children, pp. 33–36 (2006)
59. Remy, C., Seaman, P.: Evolving from disability to diversity: how to better serve high-functioning autistic students. Ref. User Serv. Q. **54**(1), 24 (2014)
60. Stevenson, J.L., Gernsbacher, M.A.: Abstract spatial reasoning as an autistic strength. PLoS ONE **8**(3), e59329 (2013)

Efficacy of Tablets for Students with Learning Difficulties Studying Concepts in Geometry

Betty Shrieber[(⊠)] and David Eldar

Kibbutzim College of Education Technology and the Arts, Tel Aviv, Israel
Betty.shrieber@smkb.ac.il

Abstract. The study goal was an investigation into the efficacy of tablets as teaching tools for students with learning difficulties attempting to study concepts in geometry. The study includes three students studying in a fifth grade regular class, whose achievements in geometry fell below class average. The quantitative analysis was based on Single Subject Design that was based on Multiple Baseline Design. Findings indicates a rise in achievements in each student as they began using tablets. Analyzing of multiple baseline data reveals a great degree of baseline variation without tablets, and more moderate and stable variation during intervention. The use of tablets allowed the students accessibility to challenging material, and to initiate each class differently.

Keywords: Learning difficulties · Tablets · Apps · Geometry · Initialization · Single-Subject design · Multiple baseline design

1 Introduction

This study investigates the efficacy of tablets as teaching tools for students with learning difficulties who are attempting to study concepts in geometry. The use of tablet PCs and other tablet technologies in educational settings has increased tremendously over the past decade, and these tools could potentially be very effective for students with learning difficulties. Learning difficulty is not a cause but rather a result of one factor or another [1]. Whereas learning disabilities have a neurological basis, learning difficulties may be caused by a lack of opportunity, incorrect instruction, cultural factors, impoverished or chaotic living environments, or disruptive behaviors [2]. Students with learning difficulties require more intensive, small-group, or one-on-one instruction to make progress in skill acquisition [3]. This need is more urgent for students in late elementary school and higher levels [4].

In recent years, tablets have become an increasingly popular choice in classrooms of every level and field of study. The use of such devices easily focuses the attention of both students and teachers. Tablets can create interaction with content on a personal level and enable real-time monitoring of learning [6]. However, the way in which tablets are used in classes requires a great deal of forethought to ensure this technology does in fact improve teaching outcomes.

© Springer International Publishing Switzerland 2016
K. Miesenberger et al. (Eds.): ICCHP 2016, Part I, LNCS 9758, pp. 483–486, 2016.
DOI: 10.1007/978-3-319-41264-1_65

2 Methodology

2.1 Study Participants and Methods

The participants were three fifth-grade students studying in a regular class. Their achievements in geometry fell below the class average.

This study conducted a single-subject design analysis. Each individual is separately exposed to a series of lessons under control conditions and a series of lessons under experimental conditions [7]. Comparisons are usually made using graphical techniques that examine the performance of each participant [8].

The study control was based on multiple baseline design, which is proven for when the experimenter is assured that the treatment variable is effective when a change in rate appears after its application. The rate of concurrent (untreated) behaviors should remain relatively constant, so that changes that occur can be reliably associated with intervention [9].

2.2 Study Tools and Procedure

Throughout the study, data were gathered for each of the three students. These included (A) student grades, which were scored using mini-test assessments at the end of each class, as well as a final assessment score for final evaluation of all material studied during all 12 lessons; (B) opinions and thoughts regarding the use of tablets based on interviews conducted during and after the intervention; and (C) student reactions to class activities based on tape recordings.

The study comprised 12 one-on-one meetings focusing on a geometry curriculum for sixth grade. The objectives of the study lessons were identical to curriculum objectives. The materials during the study lessons were either traditional during the baseline (books, worksheets, and demonstration aids such as playdough, building blocks, etc.), or using a tablet with applications (TinyTap and more) during the intervention lessons.

3 Findings

Table 1 presents the average scores for all participants during the baseline phase, intervention phase, and final test. The learning process indicates an increase in achievements by each student as they began using tablets. Scores averaged 80–90, in contrast to the much lower scores when using traditional teaching aids (57–60). All three students received high scores (85–95) in the final test. The analysis of multiple baseline data included three main parameters: (A) level, which refers to the average rate of performance during a phase; (B) trend (slope); and (C) variability [10]. Figure 1 presents a visual comparison between the baseline phase (without tablets) and the intervention phase (with tablets). It also includes the final test grades of all three participates. The figure shows that the average rate of baseline performance is lower than that during the intervention for the three participants. Also, the changes in levels for students D and O occurred immediately after the change in phases, and there was no overlap between the phases. For student A, there was an increasing trend during the baseline phase that showed improvement in his grade score without the tablet.

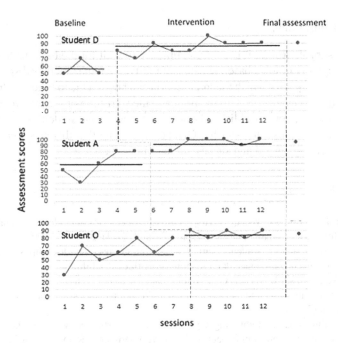

Fig. 1. Multiple baseline design for 3 participants in geometry classes with and without tablets.

However, multiple baseline analysis reveals a great degree of baseline variation without tablets, along with more moderate and stable variation during intervention. Until lesson 8, while students D and A show improvement and stability in variation throughout the intervention phase, student O continues in the baseline phase. It is clear that this baseline graph is characterized by unstable variation, while great improvement occurs in performance with great stability in the graph variation.

4   Summary and Conclusions

The findings indicate that multisensorial learning using tablets allowed these students to understand the subject matter better, which had been difficult for them previously. Having struggled with geometry classes, they showed no stability in scores without tablets (with outcomes improving and deteriorating alternately). Tablets then helped them to improve outcomes in identifying and measuring geometric shapes, and their scores stabilized. The final test also indicates better assimilation of the topics studied.

One of the major difficulties of people with executive function disabilities is the initialization of tasks [11]. Students with learning difficulties have a hard time in initiating challenging tasks that seem too complicated or boring. The use of tablets made challenging material accessible for the students and allowed them to initiate each class differently. Pressing the app icons instigated immediate reaction as the students followed instructions and thus prevented difficulties in task initiation.

4.1 Study Limitations

1. In single-subject design, it is common practice to wait for the baseline to stabilize: "The first quality of ideal baseline data is stability, meaning that they display limited variability" [10], after which the intervention can begin. Due to time constraints, we decided in advance to speed up the pace and the start time of the intervention.
2. The personal relations established between the teacher and students during individualized classes is also noteworthy. One could assume that this was a contributing factor in creating a good and successful learning experience.

References

1. Morgan, P.L., Farkas, G., Wu, Q.: Five-year growth trajectories of kindergarten children with learning difficulties in mathematics. J. Learn. Disabil. **42**(4), 21–306 (2009)
2. Learning, S.: Teaching students with reading difficulties and disabilities: a guide for educators. www.education.gov.sk.ca/reading-difficulties-disabilities
3. Buffum, A., Mattos, M., Weber, C.: Pyramid response to intervention. In: RTI, Professional Learning Communities, and How to Respond When Kids Don't Learn. Solution Tree, Bloomington (2009)
4. Fuchs, D., Fuchs, L.S.: Rethinking service delivery for students with significant learning problems developing and implementing intensive instruction. Rem. Special Educ. (2014). doi:0741932514558337
5. Ochsendorf, R: What Have We Funded? A Summary of Mathematics Research. The National Center for Special Education Research. https://ies.ed.gov/ncser/pdf/Math_2015.pdf
6. Frey, N., Fisher, D., Gonzalez, A.: Teaching with Tablets: How do I integrate tablets with effective instruction?. (ASCD Arias) ASCD, Alexandria (2013)
7. Haas, M.: Teaching methods for secondary algebra: A meta-analysis of findings. NASSP Bull. **89**(642), 24–46 (2005)
8. Horner, R.H., Carr, E.G., Halle, J., McGee, G., Odom, S., Wolery, M.: The use of single-subject research to identify evidence-based practice in special education. Except. Child. **71**(2), 165–179 (2005)
9. Barlow, D.H., Nock, M.: Single case experimental designs: Strategies for studying behavior for change, 3rd edn, pp. 209–251. Pergamon, New York (2008)
10. Byiers, B.J., Reichle, J., Symons, F.J.: Single-subject experimental design for evidence-based practice. Am. J. Speech-Lang. Pathol. **21**(4), 397–414 (2012)
11. Gioia, G., Ispuith, P., Guy, S., Kenwirthy, L.: BRIEF: Behavior Rating Inventory of Executive Function – Professional Manual. Psychological Assessment Resources Inc. (PAR), Lutz (2002)

Using Biometrics to Support Affective eLearning for Users with Special Needs

Ian Pitt[1][✉], Tracey Mehigan[1], and Katie Crowley[2]

[1] University College Cork, Cork, Ireland
ianp@cs.ucc.ie, tracey.mehigan@ucc.ie
[2] Trinity College Dublin, Dublin, Ireland
k.crowley@tcd.ie

Abstract. This paper concerns the use of biometric technology as a means to improve delivery of eLearning material to learners with special needs. We discuss the current state of research and the potential offered by recent advances in and commercialisation of biometric technologies. We then present an ongoing study that examines the application of some of these technologies in learner-assessment of special needs students.

Keywords: Affective computing · Biometrics · eLearning · Learners with special needs

1 Background

1.1 Affective Computing

Affective computing concerns the development of systems that can recognise, interpret and respond to human emotion, thus allowing the creation of applications that support more effective human-machine communication or (when used as a mediating technology) human-human-communication.

Affective computing uses sensors to gather data of the type humans use to identify emotions in others. The sensors used include video cameras to capture facial expressions, posture, gestures, etc., microphones to capture speech, and various other sensors to capture physiological data such as skin temperature, galvanic resistance, pulse-rate, etc. The data gathered is then analysed to identify affective states. For example, speech affect recognisers measure features of speech such as pitch, volume and speed, and use this data along with the linguistic content of the speech to infer the emotional state of the user.

Research has shown that affect plays a key role in our understanding of phenomena such as attention, memory and aesthetics, and helps us gauge the levels of enjoyment, engagement and frustration that the user experiences. By understanding how a user responds both physically and emotionally, it is possible to develop systems that are more intelligent, adaptive and robust and ultimately more useful. In eLearning applications, for example, affective computing techniques could be used to adjust the presentation style of a teaching package depending upon the learner's emotional state (bored, engaged, frustrated, etc.).

© Springer International Publishing Switzerland 2016
K. Miesenberger et al. (Eds.): ICCHP 2016, Part I, LNCS 9758, pp. 487–490, 2016.
DOI: 10.1007/978-3-319-41264-1_66

1.2 Affective Computing and Users with Special Needs

The ability to analyse emotional state offers additional potential to those with special needs. It is widely recognised that, whilst language is an important primary communication channel, a large percentage of the information we receive is communicated non-verbally. Mehrabian [1], for example, argues that only 7 % of a message between two people is communicated verbally, whilst 38 % is communicated through prosody and 55 % through body-language. Someone with a sensory impairment may be unable to access one of the communication channels and thus lose a large percentage of the transmitted message, while those with developmental, learning, anxiety or intellectual impairments may be unable to interpret and respond to emotional stimuli. For example, it has been variously found that people with autism spectrum disorders have more difficulty in recognising faces and facial expressions than non-autistic peers, and also have more difficulty in analysing prosodic features of speech to identify emotion.

The technologies used to assess affective state can be broadly categorised as Behavioural and Psychophysiological. Behavioural data includes facial expressions, postures, gestures, etc., and paralinguistic features of speech. Psychophysiological data includes heart-rate, galvanic skin response (GSR) and electro-encephalographic (EEG) data. Most practical systems have traditionally relied mainly on behavioural data, while the collection of psychophysiological data has been largely confined to laboratory settings because of its reliance on expensive and bulky equipment.

However, this situation is changing rapidly as biometric technologies become cheaper and more widely available. Eye-trackers and simplified EEG headsets are now available as accessories for smart-phones at prices that make them suitable for use in a range of educational settings, and many people now own fitness monitors that monitor heart-rate, etc. In addition, there are several sensor technologies that are not widely used in affective computing but offer considerable potential. For example, almost all smart-phones and tablets are fitted with accelerometers and gyroscopes which can be used to analyse a range of user movements, including (e.g.) gestures. Our own research [2–4] has demonstrated useful correlations between analysis of accelerometer data and various user characteristics commonly categorised as learning style. Current technologies allow for minimally-invasive measures of mental states reflecting attention, engagement and focus, as well as emotional states relating to stress response, valence and frustration.

2   Affective Computing and Inclusive eLearning Environments

The ability to gather such data opens up the possibility of creating eLearning environments that are truly inclusive, adapting to the needs of individual learners with a wide range of educational needs, including many currently regarded as special needs. What's more, it is becoming increasingly possible to do this without using specialist hardware. This fosters inclusion, accommodating users with special needs without requiring them to purchase or use assistive technology aids that set them apart from other users.

The Maple model [5] can be applied in generic eLearning environments to automatically assess an individual's learning style based on his/her interaction with particular learning objects. MAPLE uses a database of learning objects whose sequence, presentation modality, etc., can be tailored to learner's needs through the use of templates. Depending upon their learning-styles, individuals may be influenced in different ways and to varying degrees by the presentation modality (visual/verbal, 2D/3D, ordering of material), the perceived opinions of teachers and peers (time pressure/competitive pressure) and testing (most test paradigms favour verbal/sequential learners). The model is based on the Felder-Silverman model [6] which can be associated with aspects of varying learner-style and personality models.

Assessment of learning style is made through the use of sensor devices which measure factors such as the relative amount of time spent on scrolling, pointing and/or selection operations. This removes the need to use questionnaires (paper-based or online) to assess learning style. This eliminates the stress and inconvenience associated with traditional assessment techniques, and is particularly suitable for use as an assessment tool for those with special needs.

Previous work has shown that certain user-styles are found more commonly among certain groups of special needs learners [7]. However, little work has been carried out to assess whether learning style differences can be applied to special needs students in the same manner as mainstream students.

3   Current Work

In a pilot study conducted by the authors [8], special needs students' attention levels were measured against mainstream students when (a) completing a questionnaire and (b) using automated methods of learner style measurement. The paper-based assessment involved completion of a Felder-Silverman learning-styles questionnaire. The analysis of applied effort, etc., was based around measurements taken with a NeuroSky Brain-Computer Interface (BCI), a lightweight, non-intrusive EEG headset. Previous studies (e.g., [9]) have shown that this device can be used to gauge the effort a subject devotes to a task (attention) and the extent to which the subject is stressed by the task (meditation - high levels indicate low stress and vice versa).

The subjects were required to play a game for ten minutes whilst wearing the BCI. The aim was not to assess their performance at the game but to obtain reliable base-line EEG scores. On completion of the game they were asked to complete the paper-based questionnaire. No time-limit was imposed for completion of the questionnaire. The signals obtained from the headset during completion of the questionnaire were gathered and stored for analysis. Video recordings were also made so as to provide back-up information that could be used to resolve any anomalies in the results.

The results showed that dyslexic students took a longer period of time to complete the questionnaire than the mainstream learner and displayed a higher overall attention level. There was little agreement between the paper-based and automated assessment of each subject's Learning Style, but this was to be expected given the small sample size.

We are now extending this study. We are using a larger student sample, and gathering eye-tracking data as well as EEG data. The eye tracking data allows us to identify the focus of the user's visual attention when completing the questionnaire while also allowing us to measure pupil dilation, gaze trajectories and other metrics reflective of the affective state of the students, allowing for the subsequent assessment of the attentional states of the students. The ability to measure such data will allow us to obtain a perspective on the emotive elements associated with the process of such tasks by dyslexic learners as compared to their mainstream counterparts. In this way we hope to compare the effectiveness of paper-based and automated assessment techniques in assessing the learning styles of mainstream and dyslexic learners, and also to compare the way in which each group is affected by the task.

References

1. Mehrabian, A.: Silent Messages: Implicit Communication of Emotions and Attitudes, 2nd edn. Wadsworth, Belmont (1981). ISBN 0-534-00910-7
2. Mehigan, T., Pitt, I.J.: Individual Learner Styles Inference for the Development of Adaptive Mobile Learning Systems. In: Guy, R. (ed.) Mobile Learning: Pilot Projects and Initiatives, pp. 167–184. Informing Science Press, Santa Rosa (2010). ISBN 1-932886-31-1
3. Mehigan, T.J., Pitt, I.J.: Learning on the move: harnessing accelerometer devices to detect learner styles for mobile learning. In: Proceedings of the Irish Human-Computer Interaction Conference, Cork Institute of Technology, Ireland, 8–9 September 2011
4. Mehigan, T.J., Pitt, I.J.: Detecting learning-style through biometric technology for mobile GBL. Int. J. Game-Based Learn. **2**, 55–74 (2012). ISSN 2155-68492
5. Mehigan, T.J., Pitt, I.J.: Intelligent mobile learning systems for learners with style. In: Tjondronegoro, D. (ed.) Tools for Mobile Multimedia Programming and Development, pp. 131–149. Hershey, IGI Global (2013). ISBN 978-1-4666-4054-2
6. Felder, R.M., Silverman, L.K.: Learning and teaching styles in engineering education. J. Eng. Educ. **78**(7), 674–681 (1988). ISSN 1069-4730
7. Scarborough, H.: Predicting the future achievement of second graders with reading disabilities: contributions of phonemic awareness, verbal memory, rapid naming, and IQ. Ann. Dyslexia **48**, 115–136 (1998)
8. Pitt, I.J., Mehigan, T.J., Crowley, E.K.: Tailoring content to individual needs through analysis of learning-style, In: International Conference on Using New Technologies for Inclusive Learning, Glasgow, UK (2013). http://www.i-enable.eu/?q=node/4
9. Crowley, E.K., Sliney, A., Pitt, I.J., Murphy, D.: Capturing And using emotion-based BCI signals in experiments: how subject's effort can influence results. In: Proceedings of the 25th British Computer Society Conference on Human Computer Interaction, Newcastle-upon-Tyne, UK, 4–8th July 2011

Haptic Models of Arrays Through 3D Printing for Computer Science Education

Nicola Papazafiropulos[1]([⊠]), Luca Fanucci[1], Barbara Leporini[2],
Susanna Pelagatti[3], and Roberto Roncella[1]

[1] Dipartimento di Ingegneria dell'Informazione, Università di Pisa, Pisa, Italy
nicola.papazafiropulos@for.unipi.it
[2] ISTI CNR, Pisa, Italy
[3] Dipartimento di Informatica, Università di Pisa, Pisa, Italy

Abstract. Computer science is taught as a regular subject in the school systems of many countries. Most tools used to teach main topics of computer science curricula, such as data structures and algorithms, are visually oriented. Our work aims to assist visually impaired students to understand fundamental data structures and algorithms through 3D printed haptic models. We developed a simple but general method that can be used by the teacher to introduce data structures and algorithmic thinking to both visual impaired and sighted students in inclusive classes. We evaluated our models for teaching one-dimensional arrays to both visual impaired and sighted students.

Keywords: Haptic models · Blind users · Visually impaired · Inclusive education · Accessibility · 3D printing · Data structures · Arrays

1 Introduction

Computer science is taught as a regular subject in the school systems of many countries. The Convention on the Rights of Persons with Disabilities demands that all states ensure inclusive education at all levels [25]. Even if computer science is a common subject for high school students with disabilities [9], most tools used to teach data structures, algorithmic thinking and basic programming are visually oriented and thus not suitable for blind students.

Assistive technologies allow visually impaired people to access information; however giving only the opportunity to access digital content might be not enough for a fully inclusive education. Paradoxically, students may perceive that assistive technologies place them in an atypical educational situation [22]. Therefore, their technical aids, special education teachers or different teaching concepts could cause them discomfort, by feeling different [6].

For this reason, any educational accessible tool that can be used with both sighted and visually impaired students merits to be investigated, since it can help them to fit in with their classmates and letting them feel "like everyone else".

In computer science, data structures and algorithms are fundamental topics. Most teachers use diagrams, sketches, graphics or animations when introducing them to help students to "visualise" data structures and the behaviour of algorithms. Common

© Springer International Publishing Switzerland 2016
K. Miesenberger et al. (Eds.): ICCHP 2016, Part I, LNCS 9758, pp. 491–498, 2016.
DOI: 10.1007/978-3-319-41264-1_67

assistive technologies, such as braille printers or screen readers, cannot reproduce the same effectiveness gained through the immediacy of an animation.

For these reasons, Capovilla et al. [7] proposed an inclusive teaching method using LEGOTM to introduce algorithmic thinking. They pointed out the importance of an inclusive approach and they developed an approach to teach visually impaired students basic algorithmic thinking that can also be used with sighted students, because it addresses yet another sense. Their haptic model, made of LEGO bricks, were used to teach algorithmic thinking, by recreating the initial situation and the steps leading to the solution. This can represent a first step as a haptic-based approach in computer science, which encourages to further investigate in this direction.

The contribution of our work is a general methodology to teach both data structures and algorithmic concepts to visually impaired students via haptic models. We propose representing data structures through three-dimensional geometrical objects, realized through 3D printing, that can model their most important characteristics. As stated by Hurst and Kane [11] there is great potential in developing accessible tools through 3D printers and other rapid prototyping hardware. This happens not only because they are affordable and easy to learn but also for the possible interactions with online communities. Buehler et al. [4] uncovered that a minority population of designers with disabilities share their 3D printable assistive technologies through Internet.

Our solution intends to exploit 3D printing for reproducing haptic models in computer science. Teachers can use these proposed tactile models to introduce data structures and algorithmic thinking to both visually impaired and sighted students. As an example of our proposal, we present models for one-dimensional and two-dimensional arrays. Our case study is aimed at showing how 3D printing can be used for an inclusive education in computer science.

The structure of the paper is as follows: Sect. 2 describes the background and the related work in the field, Sect. 3 introduces the proposed methodology, Sect. 4 presents the design and the development of our haptic models and describes how they have been employed and evaluated, while Sect. 5 concludes the paper and states the future works.

2 Background and Related Work

Several applications and plug-ins have been proposed for printing content into braille format [3, 27]. Unfortunately, when considering graphics and figures, specific skills are requested to prepare the content before printing it. In addition, figures may be too poor to be able to reproduce complex concepts via braille printers. For instance, Califf et al. [6] observed that even over-sized braille paper could accommodate only small trees and they were not a suitable solution for tree rotations and graphs. Also Braier et al. [2] found that use of braille-based output devices and printing concepts is limited, especially in the case of table-based data. Since, as previously stated, haptic perception allows together a fast overview of and deeper insight into the data, they developed a haptic 3D surface representation of classic diagrams and charts, such as bar graphs and pie charts. Finally, they proposed a model for German schools that includes a 3D printing approach to help integrate students with visual impairments.

There are several examples of using 3D printing in education for visually impaired students. 3D printing has been used by providing them with tactile representations of visual information, and by enabling them to create and adapt their own assistive devices [12]. 3D printing has been used as well as a way of meaningful communication among blind and non-blind students [15]. Buehler et al. found that 3D printing also encourages STEM engagement, besides supporting the creation of educational aids and customized adaptive devices [5].

Lumi Industries is releasing a software that translates text into braille code, creating the 3D model of a 'solid braille label' as a STL file [17], but in our experience, if the file is printed with low-cost fused filament fabrication 3D printers, the label may be unreadable.

LibraryLyna is a project that aims to host the largest collection of high quality educational 3D models to support learning by the blind and the visually impaired. This project provides printable 3D models for different disciplines: chemistry, biology and mathematics. Unfortunately, informatics and computer science are not included [16].

Kostakis et al. [15] examined how technological capabilities of open source 3D printing could serve as a tool for learning and communication. They created an experimental educational scenario focused on 3D design and printing in two high schools in Ioannina, Greece: 33 students were tasked to produce creative artefacts that carried messages in braille. Their experience was positive and led them to suppose that 3D printing can electrify various literacies and creative capacities and can be a way of communication and collaboration amongst blind and non-blind students.

Dickson presented three case studies in which three-dimensional models were used to teach mathematics to visually impaired and blind people [8]. 3D printing has been applied also in teaching mathematics and physics [20], astronomy [28], chemistry [13, 21, 23, 24], geoscience [10] and design concepts [19].

In computer science, however, to the best of our knowledge, approaches similar to ours were rarely proposed. Kane and Bigham [14] used, as we do, 3D printing to teach programming but in their work 3D printing was only a way to let visually impaired students to tactile-visualize the output of the Ruby programs they wrote. We used 3D printing to build assistive devices that teachers can exploit to explain concepts and students can use to reproduce algorithms for a better comprehension.

Indeed, given the excellent results of 3D printing in teaching other subjects, haptic models can be very promising also in computer science education. Furthermore, via 3D printing it is possible to create haptic models similar to those developed by other means and validated by other authors [7, 26]. 3D printing would made similar models replicable all over the world, without any manual or technical skill, just sharing STLs and using 3D printers to build them.

As stated by Másilko and Pecl [18], blind people often prefer reading graphs in a tactile form in relation of the spatial arrangement of nodes and edges, but they cannot modify them due to the limits of the current technologies. As described by Francioni and Smith [9] most haptic models allow only a static representation that cannot describe dynamic behaviour. In this perspective, we intend to consider this important aspect in our study. With 3D printing it is possible to overcome these issues by modelling structures that can be handled in a dynamic way.

3   Methodology

In this section we present a study proposed to model a haptic prototype designed for representing data arrays.

Some existing tools and toys can be used to create haptic models of abstract structures and to simulate algorithms and processes: magnetic toys, LEGO bricks, abacuses and similar. In fact, at many special schools for the blind, such tools have been used for many years to teach the blind mathematical concepts. As previously stated, we can find some examples of this in the literature.

Our goal is to use 3D printing to produce tangible visualisations of abstract data structures as arrays, following systematic rules that allows to model the most important characteristics of these data structures.

High school teachers often teach arrays by comparing them with a sort of container, in which data can be stored. We consider this case, by modelling arrays as flat parallelepipeds with holes that can hold three-dimensional structures that represent data. These parallelepipeds are 1 cm high, 4 cm wide and their length is variable, depending on the number of cells.

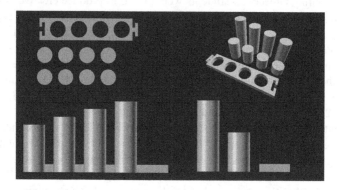

Fig. 1.   Blender model of a 4-cell array with four cells and 8 cylinders representing data.

In our case study we focused on arrays of basic numerical types. We chose to represent numeric data through cylinders with different heights proportional to the numerical value. Arrays have been modelled as flat parallelepipeds with circular holes in witch cylinders can fit (see Fig. 1).

The proposed model was used to explain, to both sighted and visually impaired students, sorting and searching algorithms working on arrays.

These haptic models are designed for being used in inclusive classes, both by blind and sighted students, as they can provide concrete examples to understand complex theoretical structures, since using hands can help students to think during interaction with computational objects [1]. Our 3D printed tools are supposed to support all students in understand the given problem: when the initial situation has been reproduced, each step of the algorithm can be explained by moving and switching the cylinders. When a student has understood the algorithm concepts, he should be able to apply them to the tool, by moving the cylinders and reproducing each step of the algorithms.

We use different shapes to model different types of data. In particular, we used different hole shapes (circular, triangle, square, etc.) in the parallelepipeds for different array types, which can be clearly detected by touch.

Fig. 2. 8-cell sorted array, obtained by joining two 3D printed bases

Commercial 3D printers have print area limitations. To build arrays longer than the printing area, we can link together several bases, by means of joints, thus obtaining arrays of different sizes (see Fig. 2).

Moreover, the same joints can be used to obtain 2D arrays, connecting in parallel two or more bases.

4   Development and Evaluation

The proposed models are so simple to allow even a high school students to develop them, just after a brief introduction of the main 3D printing concepts. Therefore, we involved some sighted students of I.S.I. Fermi, a high school set in Lucca. After a short course on the 3D modelling software Blender, the students of I.S.I. Fermi modelled and printed some of our models. This is an example of how students with a properly supervision can create by themselves the haptic models that will be used during the lessons, with significant benefits in terms of motivation and integration.

In order to understand if our proposal could be a potential solution for an inclusive lesson, we tested the haptic models with both visually impaired and sighted users. Three blind users took part in our study. Firstly, the blind author of this work had a key role in the design process regarding especially the usability of the 3D printed tools. Next, the haptic models have been evaluated with two other visually impaired users. To the first user, totally blind since birth, we presented the model explaining how it was built, what it is represent and how it have to be used. After that, we introduced a sorted array as an array in which cylinders are ordered from the shortest to the highest. Then we swapped the cylinders into a random order and we gave user the constraints: cylinders can only been swapped and cannot be put outside the array. User was asked to think how the cylinders could be moved in order to solve the sorting problem. We then present a simple sorting algorithm (bubble sort algorithm) and we asked the user to solve the sorting problem with a bigger array.

The second user was visually impaired and slightly intellectual developmentally delayed. He is a student of a vocational high school, in which computer science is not a study subject. Since he did not have any programming background, we just presented a brief introduction to basic algorithmic thinking without explaining data structures and IT topics. Also in this case, the user was able to work with the haptic model with no difficulty, and he was able to solve the given tasks. We taught him to sort cylinders with the bubble sort algorithm, by showing several times how the algorithm works on the haptic model. After some initial mistakes, user could follow perfectly all algorithm's steps on an 8-cell array model.

Another possible application of our 3D printed models is in the "educational games" field, which can involve both sighted and visually impaired students. In order to test our model prototype, we evaluated an easy educational game with sighted students of I.S.I. Fermi that printed some models. The game was quite elementary: the teacher created an initial situation by randomly inserting cylinders in the array models. Then the students had to compute the minimum number of switching to reach the sorted situation. The first who claimed the right solution had to show the class how to order the cylinders step by step.

5 Conclusions

This paper describes a new approach in teaching computer science via haptic objects, based on the use of 3D printed models. In particular, we developed a simple but general way to represent data structures, i.e. haptic models for reproducing arrays and their application to algorithms. A short evaluation conducted with both visually impaired and sighted students was successful and encouraged us to better investigate the benefits of using 3D printers in this field. Indeed, the blind users who participated to the experiment declared that haptic models made it easier the understanding of arrays and sorting algorithms much easier. Moreover, educational games tested with sighted students showed how our haptic models can be suitable to teach basic algorithmic thinking to both blind and sighted students: everyone was able to accomplish the given tasks and to repeat the algorithms steps by themselves. Thus, since this method can be used to teach both visually impaired and sighted students, it could be successfully used in inclusive classes as well.

The major limitation of our experiment is the small sample size of test groups. However, the focus of our research was to examine if the proposed teaching method could be feasible. Moreover, our method can be easily replicated, since it relies on a few very simple tools that can be built via 3D printing. Our haptic models are simple enough to be built by students and we suggest to let students to develop their tools: students of I.S.I. Fermi were highly motivating in using the tools they had made, even in elementary tasks, such as swapping cylinders. Anyway, STLs of our models could be shared in order to allow anybody to use them without the need of modelling them.

In the future, we plan to evaluate our method in a realistic case study with inclusive mainstream classes. We also plan to adapt it to other data structures, such as graphs and trees in order to cover all topics of high school computer science curriculum.

Acknowledgements. We would like to thank I.S.I. Fermi, I.S.I. Pertini, U.S.P. Lucca and FabLab Toscana for their support in developing the proposed models.

References

1. Antle, A.N., Droumeva, M., Ha, D.: Thinking with hands: an embodied approach to the analysis of children's interaction with computational objects. In: CHI 2009 Extended Abstracts on Human Factors in Computing Systems, pp. 4027–4032 (2009)
2. Braier, J., Lattenkamp, K., Räthel, B., Schering, S., Wojatzki, M., Weyers, B.: Haptic 3D surface representation of table-based data for people with visual impairments. ACM Trans. Access. Comput. (TACCESS) **6**(1), 1–35 (2015)
3. Braille Translation Software. http://www.indexbraille.com/en-us/support/braille-editors
4. Buehler, E., Easley, W., McDonald, S., Comrie, N., Hurst, A.: Inclusion and education: 3D printing for integrated classrooms. In: Proceedings of the 17th International ACM SIGACCESS Conference on Computers and Accessibility (ASSETS 2015), pp. 281–290 (2015)
5. Buehler, E., Kane, S.K., Hurst, A.: ABC and 3D: opportunities and obstacles to 3D printing in special education environments. In: Proceedings of the 16th International ACM SIGACCESS Conference on Computers, pp. 106–114 (2014)
6. Califf, M.E., Goodwin, M.M., Brownell, J.: Helping him see: guiding a visually impaired student through the computer science curriculum. In: Proceedings of the 39th SIGCSE Technical Symposium on Computer Science Education, pp. 444–448 (2008)
7. Capovilla, D., Krugel, J., Hubwieser, P.: Teaching algorithmic thinking using haptic models for visually impaired students. In: Learning and Teaching in Computing and Engineering (LaTiCE), pp. 167–171 (2013)
8. Dickson, S.: Creating tactile captions in three-dimensional computer-aided design and manufacturing. Rapid Prototyp. J. **11**(5), 293–297 (2005)
9. Francioni, J.M., Smith, A.C.: Computer science accessibility for students with visual disabilities. In: Proceedings of the 33rd SIGCSE Technical Symposium on Computer Science Education, pp. 91–95 (2002)
10. Horowitz, S.S., Schultz, P.H.: Printing space: using 3D printing of digital terrain models in geosciences education and research. J. Geosci. Educ. **62**(1), 138–145 (2014)
11. Hurst, A., Kane, S.: Making "making" accessible. In: Proceedings of the 12th International Conference on Interaction Design and Children (IDC 2013), pp. 635–638 (2013)
12. Jafri, R., Ali, S.A.: Utilizing 3D printing to assist the blind. In: 2015 International Conference on Health Informatics and Medical Systems (HIMS 2015), pp. 55–61 (2015)
13. Kaliakin, D.S., Zaari, R.R., Varganov, S.A.: 3D printed potential and free energy surfaces for teaching fundamental concepts in physical chemistry. J. Chem. Educ. **92**(12), 2106–2112 (2015)
14. Kane, S.K., Bigham, J.P.: Tracking @stemxcomet: teaching programming to blind students via 3D printing, crisis management, and Twitter. In: Proceedings of the 45th ACM Technical Symposium on Computer Science Education, pp. 247–252 (2014)
15. Kostakis, V., Niaros, V., Giotitsas, C.: Open source 3D printing as a means of learning: an educational experiment in two high schools in Greece. Telematics Inform. **32**(1), 118–128 (2014)
16. Librarylyna. http://www.librarylyna.com/
17. Lumi Industries Text to 3D Braille Converter. http://www.lumindustries.com/lumi-industries-cares

18. Másilko, L., Pecl, J.: Making graph theory algorithms accessible to blind students. In: Miesenberger, K., Fels, D., Archambault, D., Peňáz, P., Zagler, W. (eds.) ICCHP 2014, Part I. LNCS, vol. 8547, pp. 549–556. Springer, Heidelberg (2014)
19. McDonald, S., Dutterer, J., Abdolrahmani, A., Kane, S.K., Hurst, A.: Tactile aids for visually impaired graphical design education. In: Proceedings of the 16th International ACM SIGACCESS Conference on Computers and Accessibility, pp. 275–276 (2014)
20. Mikulowski, D., Brzostek-Pawlowska, J.: Problems encountered in technical education of the blind, and related aids: virtual cubarythms and 3D drawings. In: IEEE Global Engineering Education Conference, EDUCON 6826223, pp. 995–998 (2014)
21. Robertson, M.J., Jorgensen, W.L.: Illustrating concepts in physical organic chemistry with 3D printed orbitals. J. Chem. Educ. 92(12), 2113–2116 (2015)
22. Rodney, P.: Does inclusion of visually impaired students work? - What are the pitfalls of inclusion? ICEVI Eur. Newslett. Issue 48 17(3), 13–14 (2011)
23. Rossi, S., Benaglia, M., Brenna, D., Porta, R., Orlandi, M.: Three dimensional (3D) printing: a straightforward, user-friendly protocol to convert virtual chemical models to real-life objects. J. Chem. Educ. 92(8), 1398–1401 (2015)
24. Scalfani, V.F., Vaid, T.P.: 3D printed molecules and extended solid models for teaching symmetry and point groups. J. Chem. Educ. 91(8), 1174–1180 (2014)
25. UN General Assembly: Convention on the rights of persons with disabilities: resolution/adopted by the general assembly, 24 January 2007, A/RES/61/106. http://www.refworld.org/docid/45f973632.html. Accessed 31 Jan 2016
26. Vita, A.C., Kataoka, V.Y.: Blind students' learning of probability through the use of a tactile model. Stat. Educ. Res. J. 13(2), 148–163 (2014)
27. Wintalbra. http://www.spazioausili.net/wintalbra
28. Yajima, M., Toshimitsu, Y., Tetsuya, W.: Tactile star wheel for visually impaired observers. In: Proceedings of the Conference Universal Learning Design, Paris, 2014, pp. 21–24. Masaryk University Brno (2014). ISBN 978-80-210-6882-7

Digital Games Accessibility

Design of a Curriculum Framework for Raising Awareness of Game Accessibility

Thomas Westin[1(✉)] and Jérôme Dupire[2]

[1] Department of Computer and Systems Science,
Stockholm University, Stockholm, Sweden
thomasw@dsv.su.se
[2] CNAM, Paris, France
jerome.dupire@cnam.fr

Abstract. While game accessibility is well researched, many game developers lack awareness of issues and solutions and there is no framework to support educators in teaching about game accessibility. This study is based on an international survey to accessibility researchers, as well as people in the game industry and related communities. The quantitative data shows the most weighted topics in a curriculum, and the qualitative data provides detailed quotes to explain how a curriculum framework could be designed. Results also show that there is a need to change attitudes to game accessibility, but also to focus on practice, basic concepts and needs of disabled in an introductory course, while an advanced course could focus more on theory and solutions which are harder to implement. Future research is to follow-up this study to further validate our conclusions.

Keywords: Games · Accessibility · Education · Framework · Awareness

1 Introduction

Game accessibility has been researched since the beginning of the game industry [1, 2] and there is a significant amount of publications, see e.g. [3]. During 2015 the Entertainment Software Industry (ESA) in the US, was allowed an extended waiver from the Communications and Video Accessibility Act (CVAA) [4]. The waiver excludes game software until January 2017, but requires game consoles and distribution platforms to be accessible. Thus, since 2015 game consoles now have accessibility options for the first time. However, there is still a lack of awareness of game accessibility among game developers [5, 6].

The problem is that while dedicated educators can create high-quality educational material for teaching about game accessibility, there is no framework explicating what knowledge is relevant for whom and in what order different topics should be introduced. It is not reasonable to expect all game educators to be experts in game accessibility (GA). Further, there are professional game developers who need to learn about GA without attending a school or have temporary employments [7] without access to workplace education. Also, updating the material for the rapidly evolving area of computer games requires collaboration to share work done by peers to be sustainable.

© Springer International Publishing Switzerland 2016
K. Miesenberger et al. (Eds.): ICCHP 2016, Part I, LNCS 9758, pp. 501–508, 2016.
DOI: 10.1007/978-3-319-41264-1_68

This in turn requires a structure for creating and sharing accessible Open Educational Resources (OERs) [8, 9].

The research questions are: How could a curriculum framework for game accessibility be designed? How could OERs for game accessibility be created and shared based on the framework? Answering these questions provides the prerequisites to support learning about game accessibility, and can be the basis for further discussions with e.g. IGDA Game Education SIG [10] Game Education and Game Accessibility special interest groups.

2 Method

A design science approach [11] was adapted for this study where requirements for a curriculum framework was defined based on literature and online resources [12, 13], evaluated with people in academia, industry, associations and others with interest in game accessibility. Data collection was done with a mix of open and closed questions in an international online survey. The survey questions were defined based upon topics found in research papers about game accessibility [3, 14] and a UNESCO toolkit [13]. The survey[1] was sent to more than one hundred researchers in game accessibility that published papers during 2011–2015 (to get current e-mail addresses), from several countries within EU, USA, as well as Brazil, Australia and Korea. Further, it was sent to an e-mail list of accessibility researchers, and to people in the game industry and various related communities. The closed questions about motivation were used to know more about e.g. the respondents' teaching experience and skills in game accessibility. The open question were analysed thematically and the closed questions were analysed with the median and the frequency of the responses.

3 Design of the Curriculum Framework

The curriculum framework for game accessibility is here defined as: A modular structure that support creating and sharing educational resources, as well as for teaching and learning about game accessibility. According to UNESCO [13] the following need to be considered for the curriculum: (1) Context: the audience is mainly game developers, attending a school or autodidacts; (2) Educational Policy: with the CVAA, game accessibility is no longer optional; (3) Broad Learning Objectives and Outcomes: high-level descriptions of knowledge and skills; (4) Structure of the Education System: with the broad context of school and autodidacts, the framework should be useful for all learners as far as possible; (5) Structure of the Curriculum content, learning areas and subjects: core, elective and optional subjects, as well as rationales for their inclusion and number of hours needed; (6) Standards of resources such as teacher qualifications and educational materials; (7) Teaching methodology i.e. approaches to implement the framework; and (8) Assessing student achievement related to learning

---

[1] The survey is still available online, for structure presentation purpose. See: https://goo.gl/1Dre1g.

goals. This paper focus on number (3) and (5) but also the educational material part of (6). Numbers (1), (2), (4) are given and (7), (8) can be followed up in a later study, when (3), (5), and (6) are set. The following sections reflect this selection.

3.1 Broad Learning Objectives and Outcomes

The main goal is awareness of game accessibility (GA) approaches, motivations, technical literacy, design methodology and communities. Related to UNESCO [13] the following are the overall objectives and outcomes to aim for: (1) Knowledge: what the main issues of GA are, as well as awareness of resources and current research; (2) Understanding: what the issues and resources mean, e.g. how guidelines must be used with care and understanding of the game and context; (3) Skills: be able to apply e.g. methods, code libraries, and tools to achieve GA; (4) Values: foster an understanding of why game accessibility is important for a sustainable industry beyond mere profit; (5) Attitudes: change attitudes and perception of this field among the community.

3.2 Structure of the Curriculum Content

According to UNESCO [13] the structure of curriculum content, learning areas and subjects should be described in the framework. There should also be a "brief description of each subject or learning area outlining the rationale for its inclusion in the curriculum and the contribution it makes to the achievement of the learning". Subject descriptions are beyond limitations in this paper but inclusion of subjects can be motivated based upon the survey results. An example curriculum can be designed based on p. 85 in [12] with learning outcomes defined as: (1) Introduced, (2) Transitional, (3) Emphasized. Potential learning outcomes are represented by the survey results in this paper.

3.3 Standards of Resources

To address Standards of resources [13] there is a need to explore: repositories for sharing; formats (editable, accessible); and also discuss how existing resources can be used and improved. Further, what skills and knowledge are needed, and for which learner profiles (designers, engineers, educators, and/or others)? Some knowledge may be common for all profiles and some may be specific. The educational material should be structured in a way that allows each individual to build his/her own course, according to his/her skills or context. Potential resources for educational material are e.g. accessible slides [15], research articles [14], statistics [3], simulations [16], games as tools for learning [17]; design methods [18–20]; and guidelines. To support Open Educational Resources [8] and giving contributors proper recognition and provide some control of how the work is used, the proposed license is Creative Commons Contribution (BY), No Commercial (NC), and Share Alike (SA).

4 Survey Results and Analysis

49 persons (mean age of 39 y.o.), mainly from Europe (36,17 %) and America (51,06 %), completed the survey over a 2 weeks period. A recurring opinion among respondents was the importance of framing the problem by explaining how game accessibility is important for all, including age related issues for "silver gamers" but also unskilled players. As the education is mainly for game developers (students and professionals), a focus of practice was mentioned be several respondents, but also "[p]ractice underpinned by principles and motivations". In other words, a first course should focus on practice, but this practice should be grounded in both theory and relevance for disabled.

Further, "to develop empathy for the people related to this problem" was expressed, where simulation of impairments can be useful: "The simulation and back-ground material about types of impairments need to be included upfront." The importance of developing empathy can be illustrated by a quote from another respondent who argued: "Game developers should not be restricted (in any way). disabled [sic!] people should rather learn to help themselves if they want to consume a specific game." This is exactly the type of attitude problem towards GA that has to change through education, especially as this respondent was a young academic, with no (self-reported) skills in game accessibility. The social model of disability is important, as one respondent said: "whether people are disabled when playing the game is entirely up to the designers and developers involved". In addition to simulation of impairments, "[s]tudents should also play the available accessible games".

A curriculum should be balanced between teaching needs of disabled gamers and how to address those needs. It is important to avoid misconceptions of complexity, as games can easily be more accessible by following basic game accessibility guidelines. These are often good design for all without "diluting to a lowest common denominator" as one respondent put it. However, another respondent noted that there are technology gaps for universally accessible mainstream games: "The technology may never exist to make every video game compliant in the same way accessibility on the Web." In any case, stressing how simple design decisions early on in the development process is still important: "to know how easy it can be to include more groups of players with simple design choices and some smart thinking". Yet another respondent noted that some game accessibility issues are complex and time consuming: "[Game developers] need to understand that many of those options are terribly time/tech intensive".

In addition to guidelines; design methods, basic concepts of impairments, disabilities and accessibility as well as hardware support were among the most important issues to address in a curriculum. Using good examples was one proposed approach: "Maybe show some examples of successful game accessibility modifications and how this impacts players with a disability". While bios and personas were rated as less important, one respondent explained his/her situation, which could be a good use case example: "I am handicapped myself, only able to play with one and a half hand (one hand is mostly paralyzed). So everything designed for controllers is inaccessible for me, as the usual two-stick-controller can't be used one handed or with not fully functional hands".

Pseudo code examples were preferred over language specific code libraries, except when solutions are readily available for implementation in a game engine: "It seems that articles containing code examples to support accessibility design methods would be more effective than creating libraries for specific languages". Related to how code solutions can lower the threshold for game developers, economic incentives were brought up: "As a developer, getting other developers to think about GA issues up-front is fundamental to getting features developed and time/resources allocated to working on this". Another respondent said: "It is also very important that there is incentive for them to make their games accessible through funding, knowledge about larger target audiences etc.". Similarly, a third person said: "key areas are being aware of what issues are, how common they are (are we missing out on a significant audience segment?) and legal requirements". Further, one respondent noted the need of funding research for game accessibility.

One respondent noted that the importance of various topics might vary with the type of class: "[I]s this a design class? If so, then design methods and understanding people will be the most important. If it's a development class, then software and hardware options may be more important. If it's more of a general theory class, then history, discussions of things like social/medical models of disability, or theories of games may be more important." In general though, history was not deemed very important for a basic introduction "but if a history of games class is available then perhaps a history of game accessibility would fit well with the material of that course". From a lifelong learning perspective, providing further resources is also important: "A single biographical example, 'further reading materials' on specific issues, legislation and so forth will hopefully inspire some of them to look into the matter more deeply".

These qualitative data were clearly confirmed by the analysis of the closed questions: design methods (95,74 %), guidelines (93,62 %) and the basic concepts of impairments (91,49 %) were the most weighted topics whereas history (14,89 %), bios (27,66 %) and persona (46,81 %) were the lowest ones. However, some slight but significant differences in these scores may appear when considering the profiles (academic, industrial, association, etc.) of the respondents, their declared GA skills or teaching habits. In order to design the curriculum framework, we can build upon these observations some hypothesis about the gaps that are to be filled for one group or another and, even, detect some misconceptions/misunderstandings inside a particular group.

5 Discussion

Twenty out of the twenty-seven academics in the survey do not teach GA at all or have done it just once[2]; seven teach it once a month. Possible reasons could be restrictions in time to design course material but also lack of integration in existing game education curricula. This may limit education about GA to an occasional lecture or assignment,

---

[2] On a semester time basis.

which is probably not enough to change attitudes such as the one quoted in the survey results. A curriculum framework is a first step in remedying this situation.

Based upon the survey and literature, a curriculum framework can be designed by dividing the empirical findings in the survey into two broad categories: (1) A basic level introduction should focus on practice with a balance between raising awareness of needs and framing problems versus methods to address those problems, especially what can be done with relatively little effort through software and hardware. Further, changing attitudes by gaining empathy of how it is to be disabled is important in a basic course, e.g. by using simulations and accessible games; (2) For more advanced level learners, content should focus more on current research, personas, law, statistics, and history but also go in depth with the technology gaps for universally accessible mainstream games. Further, implementation of more advanced and time consuming solutions should also be included, to enhance the game experience for all and reach even more gamers, e.g. through binaural audio and signing.

Depending on the type of class (design, engineering or theory) and if the education is basic or advanced the importance of topics may vary. In Table 1 a tentative curriculum framework is presented, which could be used as a model to discuss how to best implement a game accessibility curriculum in a specific context.

Table 1. Example curriculum with courses where learning outcomes are Not Applicable (N/A), (I)ntroductory, (T)ransitional, or (E)mphasized, and for what group (designers, engineers, all) and level (basic or advanced).

Learning outcomes	Basic level – for designers	Basic level – for engineers	Advanced level – for all
Understand basic concepts	E	E	N/A
Know the needs of disabled	E	E	N/A
Able to apply design methods	E	T	E
Awareness of the history	I	I	T
Know the scope of issues	I	I	E
Awareness of legislation	I	I	T
Awareness of funding	I	I	T
Experience of disabilities	I	I	T
Know-how of solutions	T	E	E

The different topics are marked as either: (1) Introduced: The outcome is not the focus of the course, but "course elements may provide either the knowledge, skills, or attitudes necessary for the ultimate achievement of the outcome" [12]; or (2) Transitional: More direct relationship between course and the outcome, i.e. "knowledge, skills, and/or attitudes (at least two of the three) required for the achievement of the outcome may be the focus of the course or course element, but the integration of all three is not" [12]; or (3) Emphasized: A direct relationship between the course and the outcome: "At least one element of the course focuses specifically on the complex integration of knowledge skills and attitudes necessary to perform the outcome" [12].

The most weighted topics (basic concepts and design methods) are here set as either Emphasized or Transitional for Designers and Engineers on the basic level. Designers have an emphasis on design methods, while engineers are more oriented toward implementing solutions in the game. Further, to know the needs of disabled was added with emphasis for both groups, which can be seen as an extension of under-standing the basic concepts. Also, both groups should gain empathy through experiencing the situation for disabled gamers, e.g. through simulation and playing accessible games. At the advanced level focus is more on theory but also on more advanced design methods and solutions.

6 Conclusions and Future Research

Our tentative conclusions are that the design of the curriculum framework should (1) Introduce GA by framing the problem, explaining user needs and stressing the change of attitudes; and (2) Teach how games can be designed to be more accessible. The need of a modular and flexible resource is obvious and efforts have to be done in that direction as well. Accessible OERs may be created and shared based upon a Creative Commons (BY, NC, SA) license. The next step is to get more feedback from disability organisations, as well as students who are aspiring game developers and collaboration with game industry efforts for game education. Further, graduation performance requirements aligned with what all game developers should know or be able to do after completing a course about game accessibility must be developed. We also aim to invite all respondents who provided their e-mail addresses in this survey to participate in our next study.

References

1. Hughes, K.: Adapting audio/video games for handicapped learners: Part 1. Teach. Except. Child. **14**(2), 80–83 (1981)
2. Burnham, V.: Supercade, 1st edn. The MIT Press, Cambridge (2001)
3. Yuan, B., Folmer, E., Harris, F.: Game accessibility: a survey. Univ. Access Inf. Soc. **10**, 81–100 (2011)
4. FCC: FCC Extends ACS Waiver for Video Game Software (n.d.). https://www.fcc.gov/document/fcc-extends-acs-waiver-video-game-software. Accessed 4 Jan 2016
5. Heron, M.: Inaccessible through oversight: the need for inclusive game design. Comput. Games J. **1**, 29–38 (2012)
6. Torrente, J., Serrano-Laguna, Á., Aguado, Á., Moreno-Ger, P., Fernández-Manjón, B.: Development of a game engine for accessible web-based games. In: Gloria, A. (ed.) GALA 2013. LNCS, vol. 8605, pp. 107–115. Springer, Heidelberg (2014)
7. Weststar, J.: Understanding video game developers as an occupational community. Inf. Commun. Soc. **18**, 1238–1252 (2015)
8. UNESCO: Open Educational Resources (n.d.). http://www.unesco.org/new/en/unesco/themes/icts/open-educational-resources/. Accessed 13 Jan 2016
9. Mavrou, K., Meletiou-Mavrotheris, M., Sallinen, M., Karke, A., Hoogerwerf, E.-J.: "ENTELIS" European Network for Technology Enhanced Learning in an Inclusive Society: State of the Art Report (n.d.)

10. IGDA Game Education SIG: IGDA Curriculum Framework: The Study of Games and Game Development (2008). http://c.ymcdn.com/sites/www.igda.org/resource/collection/0DBC 56DC-B7CB-4140-BF3A-22A9E92EC63A/igda_curriculum_framework_2008.pdf. Accessed 1 Dec 2015

11. Johannesson, P., Perjons, E.: An Introduction to Design Science. Springer, Switzerland (2014)

12. Maki, P.L.: Assessing for Learning: Buidling a Sustainable Commitment Across the Institution, 2nd edn. Stylus Publishing, Sterling City (2010)

13. UNESCO: Curriculum Design. Activity 1: The Structure of a Curriculum Framework. http://www.ibe.unesco.org/fileadmin/user_upload/COPs/Pages_documents/Resource_Packs/TTCD/sitemap/Module_3/Module_3_1_concept.html. Accessed 10 Jan 2016

14. Westin, T., Bierre, K., Gramenos, D., Hinn, M.: Advances in game accessibility from 2005 to 2010. In: Stephanidis, C. (ed.) Universal Access in HCI, Part II, HCII 2011. LNCS, vol. 6766, pp. 400–409. Springer, Heidelberg (2011)

15. W3C: W3C Presentation Guidelines. http://www.w3.org/WAI/training/accessible. Accessed 2 Sep 2015

16. Scott, M.J., Spyridonis, F., Ghinea, G.: Designing accessible games with the VERITAS framework: lessons learned from game designers. In: Antona, M., Stephanidis, C. (eds.) UAHCI 2015. LNCS, vol. 9177, pp. 547–554. Springer, Heidelberg (2015)

17. Grammenos, D.: Game over: learning by dying. In: Proceedings of SIGCHI Conference on Human Factors in Computing Systems, CHI 2008 (2008)

18. Grammenos, D., Savidis, A., Georgalis, Y., Stephanidis, C.: Access invaders: developing a universally accessible action game. In: Miesenberger, K., Klaus, J., Zagler, W.L., Karshmer, A.I. (eds.) ICCHP 2006. LNCS, vol. 4061, pp. 388–395. Springer, Heidelberg (2006)

19. Grammenos, D., Savidis, A., Stephanidis, C.: Unified design of universally accessible games. In: Stephanidis, C. (ed.) HCI 2007. LNCS, vol. 4556, pp. 607–616. Springer, Heidelberg (2007)

20. Grammenos, D., Savidis, A., Stephanidis, C.: Designing universally accessible games. Comput. Entertainment **7**, 1–29 (2009)

Identifying Existing, Accessible Touchscreen Games for People Living with Dementia

Phil Joddrell[1(✉)], Alexandra Hernandez[2], and Arlene J. Astell[1,2]

[1] The Centre for Assistive Technology and Connected Healthcare, ScHARR,
University of Sheffield, Sheffield, UK
{pmjoddrelll,a.astell}@sheffield.ac.uk
[2] Ontario Shores Centre for Mental Health Sciences, Toronto, Canada
hernandeza@ontarioshores.ca

Abstract. Devices featuring touchscreen interfaces are considered to be intuitive and there is growing evidence that people with dementia are able to use them. The challenge is in identifying suitable and accessible activities on these devices. This research is attempting to develop a shareable framework that can be used to identify available touchscreen apps suitable for people living with dementia. The framework is separated in to two stages: (1) app identification and (2) app testing. Five touchscreen gaming apps have been identified using the framework so far, four of which have been tested by people living with dementia. Following each applied use, the framework has been adapted in response to the observed outcomes. The applied use of the app selection framework to date indicates that it has the potential to be a reliable and valid method of identifying accessible apps for people living with dementia.

Keywords: Dementia · Apps · Touchscreen · Games · Framework

1 Introduction

A holistic approach to care can support people to live at home longer, as well as ensuring that the quality of life of people in receipt of care services are being maximised [1]. One area that was highlighted as a research priority in a survey of Alzheimer's Society members was in providing appropriate and stimulating recreational activities for people living with dementia [2]. Lack of activity, or boredom, is a problem reported for people with dementia both living at home and living in care services [3, 4]. Reducing boredom can contribute to the alleviation of signs of distressed behaviour which caregivers find difficult to deal with, therefore reducing the need for pharmacological interventions [5]. Activities that are engaging can increase positive emotions and decrease boredom [6]. Facilitating independent activity can be beneficial to avoid dependence on caregivers and to promote autonomy, and is possible at all stages of dementia progression, given the selection of appropriate activities [7].

Technology is increasingly being used in dementia care [8] and there are many examples of touchscreen devices being incorporated into these interventions [9–12]. It has been suggested that the touchscreen format is a more effective solution for providing assistive technology to people with dementia as it makes less demand of hand-eye

© Springer International Publishing Switzerland 2016
K. Miesenberger et al. (Eds.): ICCHP 2016, Part I, LNCS 9758, pp. 509–514, 2016.
DOI: 10.1007/978-3-319-41264-1_69

co-ordination when compared with a desktop computer using a mouse and cursor [13]. Many examples of technology application in this field have been in the form of 'assistive' devices [14], and often where the person with dementia is not the intended user [15]. Less attention has been paid to using technology to provide personal activity, which is surprising given technology's role in facilitating entertainment for other sectors of the population [16]. There are limited examples of studies that have investigated using touchscreens directly with people with dementia for leisure or entertainment purposes, either using original software [16, 17] or existing apps [6, 18]. The benefit to using existing apps or software is that there is wide availability from the outset and any potential risk of stigmatisation or exclusion through the design of population-specific technology is avoided.

An evaluation of existing touchscreen apps available in the Apple App Store was carried out with people living with dementia [19]. When offered a choice of ten different apps, a preference was indicated by the participants for activities that could be considered familiar. This notion was further explored in a recent study [20] where the choice element was removed and participants were asked to play either a familiar game or a novel game independently. Under these conditions, participants indicated an equally high level of enjoyment for both games, despite experiencing difficulties advancing through the familiar game. The conclusions drawn from this study were that people living with dementia are able to play touchscreen games independently, the selection of games does not necessarily need to rely solely on familiarity, and there is great potential in touchscreen gaming as an enjoyable activity.

The selection process for the two games in this study necessitated a systematic approach given the vast quantity of available apps for even the most specific game type. The purpose of the current paper is to describe this selection process and how it has evolved since its conception, with the overall aim of presenting a shareable framework that can be used to identify available touchscreen apps suitable for people living with dementia.

2   Framework

The selection process can be separated in to two stages; the first stage involves the identification of the *type* of app that is required (see Fig. 1); and the second stage involves the testing of an app or group of apps for suitability.

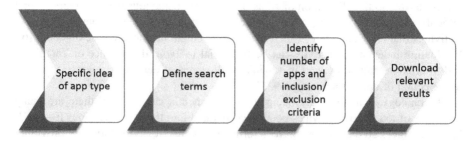

Fig. 1. Process for stage one of the app selection framework [21]

2.1   Stage One: Identification

The first stage requires a *specific* idea of the sought-after app, e.g. 'chess' or 'draughts' rather than 'board game'. The next step involves entering search terms into an app store, which will often be quite a straightforward task, as with the previous example where the search term could simply be 'chess'. Having entered the terms into the app store's search field, the next step is to decide how many apps are to be tested, or in other words, how thorough a search is necessary. For the aforementioned study, the authors decided that ten apps would be a reasonable and manageable figure, although this should be judged depending on the available resources and the volume of available apps. Before downloading, exclusion criteria may be required to ensure that the apps are relevant to the original brief. For example: whether to exclude apps above a certain level of cost; whether to exclude games with rule variations; or whether to exclude apps with superfluous design elements or themes. Identifying this information does not require each app to be downloaded, as it is possible to access titles, pictures, descriptions, reviews and costs all from within the app stores. The decision was made by the authors of the original study to use the rankings of the Apple App Store to inform the selection process, i.e. the top ten search results that met the criteria were downloaded. These rankings are defined by algorithms unique to each app store but commonly known as App Store Optimisation (ASO). For Apple, the primary factor is number of downloads, but there are also secondary factors such as keywords and visuals [22]. Therefore, by opting to download the top ten (or however many is required), an element of the selection process is deferred to the searched app store and its own ASO. This should be recognised as a potential bias but is an unavoidable consequence unless all of the search results are downloaded for testing (in excess of 500 results in the example of 'chess').

2.2   Stage Two: Testing

The second stage of the framework involves testing the app or apps that are under consideration against a set of review criteria (see Table 1 for an overview of stage 2). This stage can be utilised in isolation from the first stage, depending on the context. A situation that might require only the application of the framework's second stage would be if someone wanted to test a single app for suitability with people living with dementia, or if a developer wanted to test their own app for accessibility. The review criteria are currently presented across seven categories: interaction method; feedback; visual design; app features; customisation; obstacles; and age appropriateness. Each item within the categories has an ideal definition as to what constitutes an accessible app for people living with dementia based on an extensive literature review, the experience of one of the authors from designing touchscreen apps for people with dementia [23] and through the continued application of the framework.

The test process involves a thorough exploration of the app/s under consideration. Each app should be used for a sufficient length of time to ensure that all of the criteria can be confidently addressed before moving to the next app and repeating the process. After reviewing all of the apps under consideration, a decision can be made as to

Table 1. Overview of the review criteria featured in stage two of the app selection framework

Category	Description
Interaction method	How the app is primarily controlled, e.g. tap, drag-and-drop
Feedback	Responses the app provides to user interactions, e.g. animation, sound effects
Visual design	Aesthetics of the primary app screens, e.g. size of text and objects
App features	Presence of common features that improve accessibility for people living with dementia, e.g. inactivity prompts
Customisation	Extent to which the app can be personalised through the presence of customisation options, e.g. game speed, difficulty level
Obstacles	Presence or appearance of elements that could distract or obstruct the user's experience, e.g. adverts, social media links
Age appropriateness	Inclusion of design elements that could be considered patronising to an adult

whether any are suitable for use with people living with dementia and whether there is one app that can be highlighted as the most suitable for recommendation.

3   Application

The framework has so far been used to identify five gaming apps from fifty app tests using the criteria, four of which have been tested and received positively by people living with dementia in studies in the UK [20] and Canada. Across the two studies, sixty participants have tested one of the four identified apps (equally distributed across the cohort). The method utilised in these studies involves the use of video cameras to record the screens of the tablet device during gameplay, allowing for a greater depth of analysis of how participants interacted with the apps. The information learned from these analyses have contributed to the continued adaptation of the review criteria after each study. These adaptations have included the modification of existing items, addition of further categories (the customisation and age appropriateness categories were not in the original criteria) and the inclusion of a scoring system to rank the apps under review (available at [21]). In identifying the fifth app, four researchers applied the review criteria to the same twelve apps in isolation from one another and their scores were found to be highly reliable when tested for inter-rater reliability ($\alpha = .82$). This process is to be repeated multiple times in the future as more games are identified and as the criteria continues to be evolved.

4   Conclusions

Evidence collected to date indicates that the app selection framework has the potential to be a reliable and valid method of identifying apps that can be recommended for people living with dementia. Continued research will focus on the identification of more gaming apps with varied methods of user testing; an investigation of the usability of the framework by non-researchers (e.g. carers and clinicians); and the application of the framework to non-gaming apps.

References

1. Alzheimer's Society: Support. Stay. Save. Care and Support of People with Dementia in Their Own Homes. Alzheimer's Society (2011)
2. Alzheimer's Society: Challenges Facing Primary Carers of People with Dementia: Opportunities for Research (2012)
3. Harmer, B.J., Orrell, M.: What is meaningful activity for people with dementia living in care homes? A comparison of the views of older people with dementia, staff and family carers. Aging Ment. Health 12, 548–558 (2008)
4. Hellman, R.: Assistive technologies for coping at home and increased quality of life for persons with dementia. In: Cunningham, P., Cunningham, M. (eds.) eChallenges e-2014 Conference Proceedings, pp. 1–7. IIMC International Information Management Corporation (2014)
5. Department of Health: Prime Minister's Challenge on Dementia 2020, London (2015)
6. Leng, F.Y., Yeo, D., George, S., Barr, C.: Comparison of iPad applications with traditional activities using person-centred care approach: impact on well-being for persons with dementia. Dementia 13, 265–273 (2014)
7. NICE-SCIE: A NICE–SCIE guideline on supporting people with dementia and their carers in health and social care, London (2007)
8. Topo, P.: Technology studies to meet the needs of people with dementia and their caregivers: a literature review. J. Appl. Gerontol. 28, 5–37 (2009)
9. Armstrong, N., Nugent, C.D., Moore, G., Finlay, D.D.: Developing smartphone applications for people with Alzheimer's disease. In: Proceedings of the IEEE/EMBS Region 8 International Conference on Information Technology Applications in Biomedicine, ITAB, pp. 1–5. IEEE (2010)
10. Meiland, F.J.M., Bouman, A.I.E., Sävenstedt, S., Bentvelzen, S., Davies, R.J., Mulvenna, M.D., Nugent, C.D., Moelaert, F., Hettinga, M.E., Bengtsson, J.E., Dröes, R.-M.: Usability of a new electronic assistive device for community-dwelling persons with mild dementia. Aging Ment. Health 16, 584–591 (2012)
11. Zmily, A., Mowafi, Y., Mashal, E.: Study of the usability of spaced retrieval exercise using mobile devices for Alzheimer's disease rehabilitation. JMIR mHealth uHealth 2, e31 (2014)
12. González, L.C., Mashat, M.A., López, S.R.: Creating and updating models of activities for people with Alzheimer disease using JClic platform. In: Proceedings of the ICTs for Improving Patients Rehabilitation Research Techniques, pp. 356–361. IEEE (2013)
13. Wandke, H., Sengpiel, M., Sönksen, M.: Myths about older people's use of information and communication technology. Gerontology 58, 564–570 (2012)
14. Kerssens, C., Kumar, R., Adams, A.E., Knott, C.C., Matalenas, L., Sanford, J.A., Rogers, W.A.: Personalized technology to support older adults with and without cognitive impairment living at home. Am. J. Alzheimers Dis. Dement. 30, 85–97 (2015)
15. Smith, S.K., Mountain, G.A.: New forms of information and communication technology (ICT) and the potential to facilitate social and leisure activity for people living with dementia. Int. J. Comput. Healthc. 1, 332 (2012)

16. Astell, A.J., Alm, N., Dye, R., Gowans, G., Vaughan, P., Ellis, M.: Digital video games for older adults with cognitive impairment. In: Miesenberger, K., Fels, D., Archambault, D., Peñáz, P., Zagler, W. (eds.) Computers Helping People with Special Needs, pp. 264–271. Springer International Publishing, Cham (2014)

17. Riley, P., Alm, N., Newell, A.: An interactive tool to promote musical creativity in people with dementia. Comput. Human Behav. **25**, 599–608 (2009)

18. Lim, F.S., Wallace, T., Luszcz, M.A., Reynolds, K.J.: Usability of tablet computers by people with early-stage dementia. Gerontology **59**, 174–182 (2013)

19. Groenewoud, H., Schikhof, Y., Astell, A.J., Goumans, M., de Lange, J.: iPad happy games for people with dementia as pleasant and meaningful activity. In: Alzheimer's & Dementia, p. 181. Elsevier (2014)

20. Astell, A.J., Joddrell, P., Groenewoud, H., de Lange, J., Goumans, M., Cordia, A., Schikhof, Y.: Does familiarity affect the enjoyment of touchscreen games for people with dementia? Int. J. Med. Inform. **91**, e1–e8 (2016)

21. Joddrell, P.: AcTo Dementia. http://www.actodementia.com/guides/appselection

22. Neitz, R.: Extensive guide to App Store Optimization (ASO) in 2015. http://www.trademob.com/app-store-optimization-guide-apple/

23. Astell, A.J.: Developing computer games for people with dementia. Gerontechnology **9**, 189 (2010)

The Role of Small Robots in Designed Play Workshops in Centers of Adults with Cerebral Palsy

Isabel M. Gómez[(✉)], Rubén Rodríguez, Juan Jesús Otero,
Manuel Merino, Alberto J. Molina, and Rafael Cabrera

Department of Electronic Technology, Universidad de Sevilla, Seville, Spain
{igomez,almolina}@us.es,
hyrule2805@gmail.com, juanjesusotero@gmail.com,
{manmermon,rcabrera}@dte.us.es

Abstract. An experience that took place in ASPACE (Association of People with Cerebral Palsy in Seville) showed that the intervention with games based on tangible devices like small robots is a good alternative in the case of people with cerebral palsy (CP). The aim is to develop skills in three facets: cognitive, motor and social. From three to six sessions with seven subjects allowed obtaining information on the evolution of them and their involvement in the activity.

Keywords: Small robots · Cerebral palsy · Games therapy · Access to technology · Social skills improvement

1 The R&D or Application Idea

In this paper an event that took place in a center of adults with CP is described. In this center a game workshop made up one of several activities that they organized. The aim was studying new possibilities that can help to develop new skills in their users. In this workshop different alternatives for gaming are analyzed. The main idea is to study game accessibility for different user profiles and to familiarize them with technological solutions which can later be applied to communication, learning, etc. Videogames and little robots are used. The paper is focused on the robot alternative. Two options are tested. One of them is a ball robot called SPHERO manufactured by Orbortix [1]. The other one is homemade and is called CUBOT which consists of a vehicle manipulated by a cube. The origin of the name is a mixture of cube and robot.

2 The State of the Art in This Area

CP is a general term for a group of permanent, non-progressive movement disorders that cause physical disability in development, mainly in the areas of body movement. It is a central motor dysfunction affecting muscle tone, posture (and movement) resulting from a permanent, non-progressive defect or lesion of the immature brain but it might

© Springer International Publishing Switzerland 2016
K. Miesenberger et al. (Eds.): ICCHP 2016, Part I, LNCS 9758, pp. 515–522, 2016.
DOI: 10.1007/978-3-319-41264-1_70

also affect intellectual capabilities. This causes a lack of independence that diminishes self-esteem, entertainment opportunities and involvement in tasks. Since childhood, they get used to events happen without their participation and influence, the reason is that it is complicated they may have independent experiences. The access to technology improves the quality of life of people suffering from CP. It favors communication, integration and entertainment.

A European project which reveals two important aspects in the use of robots in game-based therapies for people with disabilities is described in [2]. The first is the lack of measurement scales for evaluating scenarios and game devices as well as its design. The second is the term Socially Assistive Robots, as intersection between Assistive Robots used in rehabilitation therapies and Social Interactive Robots, robots used like companion. Unlike in the case of Assistive Robotics, the social robots impact on quality of life is still unexplored due to the fact that social robots are still expensive and not largely widespread yet in educational or therapeutic settings; for these purposes, when developing new robot toys, a consistent framework should be anyway found and used.

In [3] the effects that the robot has on CP children s ability to participate in play were analyzed. The main types of play that can be observed in children younger than 8 years old are functional play and pretend play. Functional play is characterized by repetitive movements or actions that the child performs for the pleasure of exerting an impact on the toys (for example building a tower of blocks and then knocking them down). On the other hand, pretend play is make-believe play where children use toys in imaginative ways. The pretend level of play was not achieved with the robot, contradicting expectations.

In [4], a robotic arm system was used in the children s school. Children with disabilities will engage in play if the stimulus is adequate (i.e., the toy is interesting to the child) and the toy is physically accessible to them. Adapted robotic devices meet both of these criteria. Twelve children with severe physical disabilities, ranging in ages from 6 to 14, participated in this study. All of the children reacted positively to the robot. The robot generated tasks were more motivational for the children, and generated more interest and excitement than single switch tasks such as toys, appliances or computer-based activities.

In [5], the object of case study was to investigate the effect of a home-based robot intervention. The participant was a 4 year old girl using Lego Mindstorm robots. The results showed that playfulness increased a little more than in a play situation without robot.

In [6], SPHERO was proposed as the main device in the game. Several concepts arise in this paper. The first one emphasizes the idea of interactive technologies such as tools which have the ability to enhance the perception of individuals. Interaction can be done with physical objects. Those are tangible interfaces. The gameability concept is related to the quality of the user interaction with the game. A user centered approach is used. The disabled person takes an active part contributing to the adaptations of interfaces according to their needs.

In [7, 8] the goals are different because a robot therapy environment is used to perform physical rehabilitation.

As far as we could investigate, no studies were found based on using robots for therapies with CP adults. It is difficult too, the measure of the effect of interventions, there are not proper scales to do this. In this paper, our experience is described. An alternative based on low-cost robots to encourage and measure skills in this population. This is a preliminary study showing that the work on this line is promising and can be formalized and expanded in the future.

3   The Methodology Used

3.1   Participants

A group of seven users ranging from 24 to 43 (mean 33,8 ± 5,7) attending the day center of ASPACE took part in three to six sessions. In general these users have movement problems and very poor oral communication. Among them, there are varying social interactions and access to technology. The workshop s objective was to improve their shortcomings in these areas.

The sessions were led by an ASPACE therapist and a member of our team.

3.2   Materials

SPHERO and CUBOT are used.

SPHERO is a robotic ball with various internal motors to roll in any direction. It has lights and sounds too. There are several applications for mobile devices that allow one to control it. There are different kinds of games including augmented reality. Mobile devices communicate with SPHERO using Bluetooth (Fig. 1a).

Fig. 1. Left: SPHERO [1]. Right: CUBOT

CUBOT is a prototype we have built. It is formed by two devices, a little robot in the form of a motorized vehicle and a cube shaped control device. Controlling CUBOT is quite simple. Each face of the cube has a carved arrow on its surface that illustrates each action of the robot, turning the cube and therefore the face that is on the top. This changes the movement of the vehicle. Two Arduino Leonardo boards are in charge of controlling both devices. A three-axis accelerometer is installed in the cube to know its position. The LEDs provide lighting to each of the five arrows indications and the vehicle, different colors have been used, when cube and vehicle are connected the same colors appears in both, constituting a good feedback for the user. In addition, in the inside of the cube a little vibrator motor and a buzzer module are installed, these two components endow the cube with capacity to alert and inform the user of certain situations, for instance the proximity of an obstacle. The robot is based on a Rover 5 chassis by Dagu Electronics. On this chassis the Arduino Leonardo, a dual motor controller and an ultrasonic distance sensor were mounted. Cube and robot are connected using Bluetooth modules (Fig. 2).

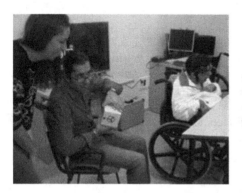

Fig. 2. Left: a user holds the cube in order to control the robot. Right: playing with SPHERO

3.3   Intervention

The planified Activities were different for CUBOT and SPHERO. The reason for this is due to the fact that the systems are controlled in different ways and not all the users are able to play with both.

CUBOT is controlled by turning the cube in five different positions. Motor skills can be improved in those cases where its use is possible (Fig. 2a). The subject is asked that turn the cube in several positions. Only spot tests could be performed with some users.

The activities with SPHERO were based on different circuits drawn on the floor that the robot had to follow. First the aim was that users were familiarized with the system and they had fun. Bottles were filled with sand to emphasize more the path to be followed in the circuit. The last goal was to pull the pins placed at the end of the circuit (Fig. 2b). In the following sessions a circuit with three items was used (Fig. 3). The users had to pass the items without crossing the lines of the circuit. If the lines were past, this was considered an error and counted then for the results. The time was also measured. Different sessions with this last circuit are done in order to notice the evolution in the skill to manipulate the robot.

SPHERO can be controlled through an application that was installed in a tablet or IPAD, so the access method was the touch screen or any other adaptation that can be used with the tablet. For instance one of the users controlled it with a licornio, but any other adaptation that allows simulating one touch in the screen would be possible.

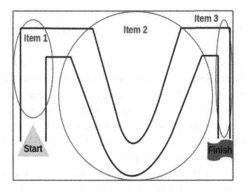

Fig. 3. SPHERO circuit

Additional goals to the main one, access to technology, can be obtained in this workshop:

- Motor skills. Controlling the robot by turning the cube in five different positions makes CUBOT an excellent tool to improve fine motor skills.
- Dissociation. In some cases CP people have problems in the perception of their environment. They should be able to increase their external attention focus (on the movements of the robot). In the case of CUBOT the robot lights up with the same color as the face of the cube when varying the action that is active, increasing the link between action and reaction between cube and robot.
- Coordination and orientation. Understanding and distinguishing concepts like left/right or forward/backward. Robots help to treat these orientation disorders while working with visual memory and the perception of spatial relationships.
- Temporal concepts. Working with robots, the educator can help to develop the temporal perception of the patient by marking certain guidelines in the control of the robot. He can ask the user to combine movements into a determined sequence, varying the time between actions or asking the user to do it at different speeds.
- Learning colors. In the case of CUBOT, the symbol in each face of the cube is light up with different colors, depending on the action that is being executed. SPHERO has different games related to colors

4   Results

The game workshop was well accepted in the center. The game using robots increase user enjoyment and motivation more than when they only engage video games. In general all participants showed a high interest to participate in games with CUBOT and SPHERO, but SPHERO was funnier for them.

Trials with CUBOT couldn t be formalized because in general people with CP have many difficulties in hand manipulation and only two of the users had enough skill to control CUBOT but with help. It can be observed, in any case, the high potential of CUBOT design for training the attention and orientation capabilities in the user. The original idea of doing control by turning the cube or the feedback that the user has due to the use of the same color in the cube and the vehicle to connect the different arrows symbols and the type of movement are very interesting and show great usefulness.

Tables 1 and 2 shows results in the sessions with SPHERO. In this case, at least three sessions could be realized with each user. Numbers of errors and time to complete the circuit were measured. Data show that the session 1 is clearly different from the rest. In general more time was required and more errors were committed in this session while in the rest of them the numbers are stabilized. User 6 accessed to the tablet with a licornio (Fig. 4), but this did not worsen the results. User 5 and 6 were in the group with great interest in took part in the activity, they did with too much errors, but the observation showed us that they acquired more control and security in the in subsequent replays, more sessions with them are needed in order to quantify their evolution.

Table 1. Numbers of errors for session with SPHERO

User	Session 1	Session 2	Session 3	Session 4	Session 5	Session 6
1	2	1	3	1	0	0
2	1	0	2	2	1	1
3	5	3	2			
4	5	2	3	1	3	1
5	Too many errors	Too much but less that in session 1	More security in the control and less errors			
6	2	2	1	0		
7	Need help but wants to do more sessions	Improve a little with help	Does it alone but with too much errors			

Table 2. Time for session with SPHERO

User	Session 1	Session 2	Session 3	Session 4	Session 5	Session 6
1	1 m 35 s	50 s	1 m 11 s	58 s	1 m 38 s	1 m
2	1 m 13 s	42 s	1 m 3 s	39 s	39 s	46 s
3	2 m 6 s	40 s	48 s			
4	1 m 12 s	50 s	38 s	1 m 11 s	55 s	44 s
5	1 m 30 s	52 s	52 s			
6	1 m 14 s	1 m 25 s	1 m 53 s	50 s		

Other aspects to be into account are the joy and willingness of users because they were accomplishing the proposed challenge. The feeling of being able to bowl without help was very fulfilling for them. They challenged each other and compare their results.

Fig. 4. An user control SPHERO with a licornio

5 Conclusion and Planned Activities

In the CP population, the use of small robots is a good option in activities using for develop skills related with technologies familiarization. Improvement in motor skill, coordination, temporal concepts is also reached. Games with family and friends enhance social relationships.

User acquire security and understand the control of this kind of robots in a short time, so they don t bored during the learning time and don t feel frustrated with the new technology. For people with CP, CUBOT has difficulties due to the needed control with the cube; an alternative can be adding another kinds of control it. An application for tablet expands the range of users. The use of color and vibration could be added to the application as reinforcement techniques in the same way as it is done with the cube.

More sessions must be developed in order to reach the initial objectives. On the other hand, therapist evaluation must be supported by objective scales that measure changes in users skills.

This kind of robots could be a good alternative for other kind of population; one clear case is the group with Autism Spectrum Disorder or ASD. These disorders have in common a significant alteration in three development areas: social-emotional skills, communication and interaction with people and restricted repertoire of interests and behaviors, usually accompanied by sensorimotor impairments. Working with a robot encouraged the patient to unfold with more simple rules than the reality ones; this reduces the confusion and the different sensory distractions of the real world that may be able to cause insecurity and anxiety. Exist several studies in this area of work between children with ASD and robots, most of them are centered in social-emotional skills [9, 10] and using high cost robots.

Acknowledgments. We would like to thank the staff at ASPACE Seville and Ruben Rodríguez who designed CUBOT.

References

1. SPHERO web page. http://www.sphero.com/
2. Besio, S., Caprino, F., Laudanna, E.: Profiling robot-mediated play for children with disabilities through ICF-CY: the example of the European project IROMEC. In: Miesenberger, K., Klaus, J., Zagler, W.L., Karshmer, A.I. (eds.) ICCHP 2008. LNCS, vol. 5105, pp. 545–552. Springer, Heidelberg (2008)
3. Adams, K., et al.: Using robots to access play at different developmental levels for children with severe disabilities: a pilot study. In: RESNA Conference (2015)
4. Cook, A.M., et al.: School-based use of a robotic arm system by children with disabilities. IEEE Trans. Neural Syst. Rehabil. Eng. 13(4), 452–460 (2005)
5. RiosRicon, A.M., et al.: Change in playfulness with a robotic intervention in al child with cerebral palsy. In: Assistive Technology: From Research to Practice: AAATE (2013)
6. Oliveira, E., Sousa, G., Magalhães, I., Tavares, T.: The use of multisensory user interfaces for games centered in people with cerebral palsy. In: Antona, M., Stephanidis, C. (eds.) UAHCI 2015. LNCS, vol. 9177, pp. 514–524. Springer, Heidelberg (2015)
7. Burdea, G.C., et al.: Robotics and gaming to improve ankle strength, motor control, and function in children with cerebral palsy–a case study series. IEEE Trans. Neural Syst. Rehabil. Eng. 21(2), 165–173 (2013)
8. Johnson, M.J., et al.: Design of a bilateral ADL task-oriented, robot therapy environment for children with cerebral palsy. In: The American Society of Biomecanic Conference (2013)
9. Begum, M., et al.: Measuring the efficacy of robots in autism therapy: how informative are standard HRI metrics? In: HRI 2015 (2015)
10. Costa, S., et al.: Using a humanoid robot to elicit body awareness and appropriate physical interaction in children with autism. Int. J. Soc. Robot. 7, 265–278 (2015)

How to Control a Mobile Game

A Comparison of Various Approaches for Visually Impaired People

Krzysztof Dobosz[✉] and Jakub Ptak

Institute of Informatics, Silesian University of Technology, Gliwice, Poland
krzysztof.dobosz@polsl.pl,
jakupta656@student.polsl.pl

Abstract. The aim of the study was the comparison of existing approaches of user interfaces for visually impaired people playing a mobile game. The mobile gamebook was taken into account as an example of the game. Seven different interfaces accessible for visually impaired people were studied analyzing the following aspects: interface reaction time, commands correctness, screen size influence, complexity of implementation, and number of available options. It was concluded, that perfectly accessible interface of a mobile game should consist of the lowest number of options as possible. When simple interfaces with limited number of options are designed, then swipes, multi-touch and sensors, due to the short reaction time and a high level of correctness of operations, are worth taking into account. The paper highlights, that the use of MVP design pattern allows developers to create mobile games with different methods of interaction, which can be changed in a runtime.

Keywords: Blind people · Visually impaired · Mobile games · Gamebook · Interaction

1 Background

Currently we can find many games in mobile application stores, like Google Play, App Store or Windows Phone Store. Some of them are simple text games, while others are graphically advanced 3D games. Also the number of mobile games adapted for blind people is still growing.

Support for mobile game developers starts on the level of operating systems. Leaders of mobile technologies, as Google and Apple, propose general solutions for visually impaired people, and they build them in their mobile operating systems [1]. They provide software developers with a rich set of guidelines. These guidelines also include rules for creating an interface for visually disabled people. Software developers taking them into account, proposed various ways to design the accessible user interfaces of mobile applications [2, 3].

However, there are no uniform solutions for control mobile applications, especially games. Additionally, blind users, because of the complexity of control, and the need to display detailed graphical information, cannot play all kinds of games. Therefore, the game accessibility was particularly defined [4].

© Springer International Publishing Switzerland 2016
K. Miesenberger et al. (Eds.): ICCHP 2016, Part I, LNCS 9758, pp. 523–529, 2016.
DOI: 10.1007/978-3-319-41264-1_71

Software developers should not throw the responsibility for the accessibility on the functionalities built-in mobile operating systems. They still have to experiment with the efficiency of different ways of interact, because mobile devices are increasingly powerful and built-in sensors more sensitive. The exploratory studies on non-visual mobile phone interfaces for games are provided for several years. Some of them are based on Semiotic Engineering principles [5], and emphasize communication through aural, tactile and gestural signs [6].

The aim of this study was the comparison of existing approaches of user interfaces for visually impaired people playing a mobile game. Although the problem of mobile applications design for visually impaired people is well known, this special kind of software is worth studying because of limited number of its options (functionalities).

The mobile gamebook [7, 8] was taken into account as an example of the game. The gamebook is any book that presents a world of fiction that allows the reader to participate in the story by making choices. The result of every choice is the selection of appropriate paragraph or page in the gamebook. Implementation of the gamebook in the form of mobile application is acceptable by visually impaired users because of game feedback. There is no need of graphical presentations, because the synthesized voice reading the content of paragraphs and descriptions of possible choices is enough to control the game state.

2   Research Software

The research software was a mobile gamebook for Android OS [9]. The existing game was rebuilt for conducted research needs. The expected solution needs to provide a fundamental set of gamebook functionalities and variety of user interfaces for them. The designed software architecture was adapted to these particular conditions. It is based on the Model-View-Presenter (MVP) design pattern (Fig. 1). Unlike the classical MVP approach, there is no need for a components layout defined by default in the XML file. The role of the view is taken over by the relevant objects activity [10], which being directly related to the user interface are able to capture the movement of a finger across the screen to read values from sensors and use other ways to interact with the device provided by the Android OS platform. This way, by creating multiple different views of activity objects we can obtain interchangeable interfaces. However, these interfaces require an additional object to the operation and use of the data from the model. Here, the presenter closely associated with the view, comes with the help. Based on events received view is called the specific functionality of the presenter, and the presenter in response manipulates a view to present the revised data. The functionality of the presenter is called using events received in the view. Then presenter manipulates the view to show the revised data in response.

Following user interfaces were implemented:

- Simple swipes – it uses touchscreen devices and it is based on the performance of gestures. It works by moving one finger across the screen in a particular direction. In addition, for the mobile gamebook, the interface has been enhanced with a double tap the screen.

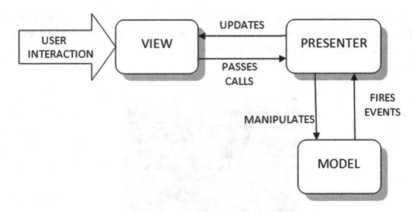

Fig. 1. MVP design pattern

- Multipoint swipes - it is an extension of previous interface. The user has the ability to execute a swipe with multiple fingers simultaneously. With this approach, the user can issue a command that will not only determine the direction of the gesture, but also carry information, how many indicators have been used.
- Multitouch - the user touches the screen with a certain number of fingers. Due to the requirements and usability, it is expected to make research an interface that supports up to five indicators at the same time,
- Braille keyboard – this virtual keyboard uses six screen subareas in a 2 × 3 pattern, related to the Braille dots. The user is able to control the application by entering the Braille code of appropriate letter representing proper option, i.e. "N" for the following part of paragraph: "...type N if you want to go to north..."
- Sensor - that uses the accelerometer sensor. It allows the user to specify the location of the device in three-dimensional space based on readings of the angular acceleration. This sensor is used to detect tilting the device in four directions: left, right, foreword, backward. In addition, for the gamebook functionality needs, it used the double-tap screen gesture.
- Speech recognition - it uses the speech recognition module provided by Google, namely the Voice Search application. The user communicates using commands. The interface includes limited number of commands. To save battery power and prevent unwanted diagnosis of speech, start of listening is after double-tap the screen.

These interfaces allow the user to control the application without the need of graphical presentation of content on the screen. The feedback uses a built-in speech synthesizer (Text-To-Speech) that reads the messages for the user. Mentioned interfaces were compared to the classical graphical interface running with the built-in screen reader (TalkBack) (Fig. 2). Its layout was composed of two parts: first presents the description of the paragraph in the high contrast mode, second one - includes screen buttons representing links to next paragraphs, and optionally a special one calling the dice roll. This interface was developed in the polish language version, because of polish spoken testers.

The independent part of the mobile application is used only for research purposes. Its functionality allows researchers to test each interface by verifying the correctness of commands and measuring the time of interface reaction.

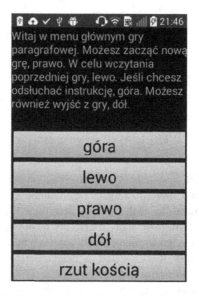

Fig. 2. Classic graphical interface of the gamebook

3 Procedure

Eleven visually impaired people aged 20–35 years, took part in this study. They had different levels of disability. All of them previously had used mobile devices with touchscreens. No one knew the Braille code. Separated set of test data was prepared for each interface. The test procedure involved drawing the task from the collection of test data. The overall time was not measured, because the structure of the sample gamebook allows to go from the start paragraph to the last one, using different paths. Then, the synthesizer read the command that should be done by the user adequately to the test interface. The procedure is repeated ten times for each interface.

The obtained results were analyzed taking into account the following aspects:

- Interface reaction time - the time between the end of voice command for the user and the recognition of the user's action.
- Commands correctness - the test result validation took one of the following values:
  - Correct - the command is recognized and matches the commands given by synthesizer,
  - Incorrect - the command is recognized, but it does not match the commands given by synthesizer,
  - Unrecognized - the command is not recognized by the test interface.

- Screen size influence – the study of interfaces used two devices (Pentagram Tab 8.5, LG L40) to test them in different configurations of hardware, but the most important were diagonals: 8 inches and 3.5 inches.

4   Results and Discussion

Obtained results are presented in the Table 1. Studies have shown that multi-gesture interfaces (multipoint swipes, Braille keyboard) are not effective for mobile game control.

Unfortunately, 33.81 % of Braille codes were unexpected values, similarly in the case of unrecognized values. During testing of this issue, it was noted that due to the split the screen into the constant six parts, the visually impaired user touches the screen quite often in areas other than intended. Introducing the Inpris Braille keyboard seems to be a good improvement of this kind of user interface.

Multipoint swipes interface also resulted in many unrecognized commands. Most of unrecognized gestures required the user to enter commands using four or five fingers, which often finished out of the screen. Such gesture was not properly completed and it was classified as incorrect.

Table 1. Comparison of command correctness and reaction times

Interface	User's commands [%]			Average reaction time [ms]
	Correct	Incorrect	Unrecognized	
Simple swipes	96,16	2,69	1,15	685
Multipoint swipes	57,46	34,81	7,73	978
Multitouch	98,64	1,36	0	554
Braille keyboard	27,62	33,81	38,57	2867
Sensor	97,37	2,63	0	504
Speech recognition	84,09	0	15,91	5589
Classical UI & TalkBack	98,32	1,68	0	3202

Users operated well with the other interfaces. The percentage of incorrectly entered commands is acceptable. Interfaces controlled by swipes, multi-touch and sensors resulted the shortest reaction time, while for the classical UI, a single time values were very divergent from about 500 ms to 12 s for operation. This discrepancy stems from the need to explore the screen and listen to the names of options to find the right button.

The slowest interface used speech recognition. It was about ten times slower than the fastest one. Such a poor result consists of listening initialization and need to communicate with the Google server for commands identification.

From the perspective of software developers and designers, there are also very important parameters of interfaces directly associated with their implementation:

- Complexity of implementation – it is estimated counting the logical (executable) lines of code (LLOC) of the source code [11]. In this measure, the result is independent of the formatting code that can be different for each developer. The measurements used the LocMetrics free software that explores lines of code written in C #, C++, Java and SQL.
- Number of available options – for the needs of the sample mobile gamebook, user interface has to use five control options. However, in many cases of gamebooks, the number of options in a paragraph is much higher. This number was verified for each interface. It can clearly show which of the interfaces can be used for projects requiring advanced, user interface.

The values in Table 2, indicate the number of lines responsible only for the user interaction. If we want to get the size of all lines of interface code, then we must con-sider the code that is responsible for the synthesis of speech: additional 88 LLOC.

Table 1. Comparison of command correctness and reaction times

Interface	User's commands [%]			Average reaction time [ms]
	Correct	Incorrect	Unrecognized	
Simple swipes	96,16	2,69	1,15	685
Multipoint swipes	57,46	34,81	7,73	978
Multitouch	98,64	1,36	0	554
Braille keyboard	27,62	33,81	38,57	2867
Sensor	97,37	2,63	0	504
Speech recognition	84,09	0	15,91	5589
Classical UI & TalkBack	98,32	1,68	0	3202

5 Conclusions

Analyzing obtained results, it can be concluded that the project objective is achieved. Perfectly accessible interface of a mobile game should consist of the lowest number of options as possible. When simple interfaces with limited number of options are designed, then swipes, multi-touch and sensors, due to the short reaction time and a high level of correctness of operations, are worth taking into account. However, if the reaction time is not so important, then a speech recognition interface and screen reader should be used.

If the designer needs an interface with bigger number of options, then speech recognition works very well because of theoretically unlimited number of available commands. The interface using multipoint gestures also allows the developer to design many options, but he should keep in mind that it works well only on tablet type devices, because of their larger touchscreens.

Unfortunately, the implementation of the Braille keyboard as a mobile game inter-face for the blind, completely failed. That prevents its use in a real mobile game for visually impaired people unknowing the Braille code.

Implementation of any of the tested methods of interaction does not require big effort of code written by the developer. The modular architecture of applications based on the model view-presenter design pattern allows developer to create mobile games with different ways of interaction, which can be changed in a runtime.

Acknowledgements. Publication financed by the Institute of Informatics at Silesian University of Technology, statutory research no. BK/263/Rau2/2015.

References

1. Adam, P.: iOS vs. Android Accessibility (2015). http://pauljadam.com/iosvsandroida11y/
2. Dobosz, K.: Designing mobile applications for visually impaired people. In: Visually Impaired: Assistive Technologies, Challenges and Coping Strategies, pp. 103–126 (2016)
3. Sierra, J., Togores, J.: Designing mobile apps for visually impaired and blind users. In: The Fifth International Conference on Advances in Computer-Human Interactions, pp. 47–52 (2012)
4. Archambault, D., Ossmann, R., Gaudy, T., Miesenberger, K.: Computer games and visually impaired people. Upgrade **8**(2), 43–53 (2007)
5. Souza, C.: The Semiotic Engineering of Human-Computer Interaction (Acting with Technology). MIT Press, Cambridge (2005)
6. Valente, L, Souza, C., Feijo, B.: An exploratory study on non-visual mobile phone interfaces for games. In: Proceedings of the VIII Brazilian Symposium on Human Factors in Computing Systems, pp. 31–39 (2008)
7. Demian's Gamebook Web Pages, Frequently Asked Questions (2015). http://www.gamebooks.org/show_faqs.php
8. Gamebook Adventures (2015). http://gamebookadventures.com/
9. Dobosz, K., Ptak, J., Wojaczek, M., Depta, T., Fiolka, T.: Mobile gamebook for visually impaired people. In: Miesenberger, K., Fels, D., Archambault, D., Peňáz, P., Zagler, W. (eds.) ICCHP 2014, Part I. LNCS, vol. 8547, pp. 309–312. Springer, Heidelberg (2014)
10. Potel, M.: MVP: model-view-presenter. The Taligent Programming Model for C++ and Java. Taligent, Inc. (1996)
11. LocMetrics, LocMetrics - C#, C++, Java, and SQL (2015). http://www.locmetrics.com/

Training Working Memory in Elderly People with a Computer-Based Tool

Sandra Rute-Pérez[1], Carlos Rodríguez-Domínguez[2],
María José Rodríguez-Fórtiz[2], María Visitación Hurtado-Torres[2(✉)],
and Alfonso Caracuel[1]

[1] CIMCYC, University of Granada, Granada, Spain
[2] ETSIIT, University of Granada, Granada, Spain
{mjfortiz,mhurtado}@ugr.es

Abstract. Working Memory (WM) is a fundamental system to allow the execution of many cognitive functions (learning, reasoning, reading, language comprehension, calculation, etc.) involved in daily activities. WM declines with aging but can be improved with training programs, including computer-based ones. This paper presents a free and open source web platform called VIR-TRAEL that consists of activities to train several cognitive skills, including WM. One of its activities, Objects Bag, is described as well as tests performed to show its effectiveness.

Keywords: Elderly people · Working memory · Computer-based cognitive training · Web platform

1 Introduction

Working memory (WM) is a multi-component system for short-term storage and manipulation of a given amount of information needed to successfully perform a wide range of complex cognitive tasks [1]. The WM model consists of four components: (1) the central executive for controlling the attentional process; (2) the phonological loop; (3) the visuospatial sketchpad for holding verbal and visual information; (4) and the episodic buffer for integrating information across space and time [1]. The WM is a fundamental system that allows the proper execution of many cognitive functions (learning, reasoning, reading, language comprehension, calculation, etc.) involved in daily activities [2]. Moreover, the WM is the component for updating and monitoring the executive function [3] and, consequently, it plays a central role in all goal-oriented behaviours.

However, WM declines in both normal [4] and pathological aging [5]. Although the exact causes of this decline are unknown, findings suggest impairments in the four components of the WM: deficit of efficiency [6] and speed of the central executive [7], and less capacity of the visuospatial sketchpad [8] and the phonological loop [7]. Therefore, to maximize the effectiveness of WM interventions, they should include activities aimed to improve its four components.

© Springer International Publishing Switzerland 2016
K. Miesenberger et al. (Eds.): ICCHP 2016, Part I, LNCS 9758, pp. 530–536, 2016.
DOI: 10.1007/978-3-319-41264-1_72

In this paper we present VIRTRAEL, a computer-based web tool that includes activities to train the WM. In particular, we will describe one of its key WM activities, namely Objects Bag, and the tests performed using it.

2 State of Art

Many computer-supported tools for training cognitive skills have been developed in the last few years. Cogmed (http://cogmed.com), Cognifit (http://cognifit.com), RehaCom (http://www.rehacom.co.uk) are the more frequently used computer-based WM training programs. Results with patients with acquired brain injury suggest that Cogmed can not only enhance WM but also cognition and psychological health [8]. However, the effectiveness of WM training is a controversial issue nowadays [9], especially when related to computer-supported training [10]. Melby-Lervag and Hulme [11] analysed the former three tools (and others) and suggest that none of those applications are supported by a detailed task analysis that might be expected to show improvements in the WM capacity. A large randomized controlled trial of this evidence in the elderly is being carried out, so data is currently unavailable [12].

In consequence, while there are some experiences with computer-supported trainings, their underlying theoretical models have not been proven to be suitable for improving WM.

In other work, Cameraio et al. [13] have analysed some training programs designed as serious games for stimulating mental abilities, and Rizo [14] has studied the advantages of virtual reality for the same objective. In both reviews, it can be observed that serious games and virtual reality may improve user involvement and experience during mental stimulation activities. Sík Lányi et al. [15] reviewed the usability and accessibility of 10 serious games that used virtual reality for improving cognitive skills that will help them in their working day. After their analysis they proposed design guidelines for serious games for use by people with intellectual and additional sensory impairments.

3 Method

The next subsection introduces VIRTRAEL as the underlying platform supporting the Objects Bag activity. Later, the Objects Bag activity itself is described, and the tests that were performed with it are summarized.

3.1 VIRTRAEL: A Web-Based Platform for Cognitive Stimulation in the Elderly

VIRTRAEL (formerly called PESCO [16]), http://virtrael.es, is an open source and free web platform developed at the University of Granada, Spain by a multidisciplinary group composed of psychologists, software engineers and doctors.

The platform integrates a computer-based cognitive training program and a set of supporting tools to allow communication between carers (therapists and informal carers) and users (older people), administration of their profiles and access privileges, planning of working sessions with activities for assessment and training, supervision, and evaluation of the users' performance.

VIRTRAEL provides 18 types of activities to evaluate and train the main cognitive skills: memory, attention, planning and reasoning. We have tested the concurrent validity of these activities and performed a previous pilot study to analyse the users' responses. Some of these activities include 3D virtual-reality environments [17].

Regarding its implementation, the platform is composed of integrated components, each of them related to different tools and functionality.

Standards technologies were used, because the key focus was on its portability, availability and extensibility, in order to allow anytime, anywhere use of the platform and easy integration of future enhancements. To achieve these goals, the contents of the activities are described using XML files. The code with the logic of the activities is written using JavaScript, and they are visualised using HTML and CSS (viewable in any web browser). A database is used to manage user profiles and to store measurements.

Usability and accessibility were other key points in the platform design. VIRTRAEL was developed taking into account several usability guides for elderly people and accessibility W3C recommendations [16], although the platform cannot be fully accessible because some activities require specific skills to be carried out using visual memory. Training Working Memory using the Objects Bag Activity.

This paper is focused on one of the activities of VIRTRAEL: Objects Bag. This activity was developed specifically to train WM. Its design, implementation and the measurements that the system takes to analyse user performance will be also described.

Objects Bag presents an avatar (a guide character) with a shopping bag while moving all around a city. Each time the avatar moves to a new place or shop depicted in a city map (Fig. 1), it can pick up or drop objects.

Fig. 1. A map with eight different places and instructions.

The quantities and specific objects to be picked up or dropped vary along the ride. Users are asked to pay attention and keep in their memory all operations performed by the avatar (Fig. 2).

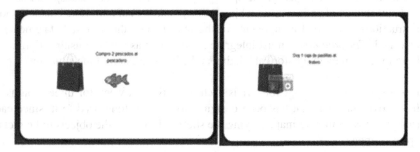

Fig. 2. Representation of how objects are introduced (left) into the bag or dropped (right).

To fully understand the task, written instructions are provided, and before starting the activity, a demonstration is done. Additionally, users must also practise through examples. Practices are repeated up to three times if their answers are incorrect. The activity begins when the user has performed the practice satisfactorily.

At the end, users are asked which items, and how many units of each one, are in the bag. The answer is provided through a selection panel (Fig. 3). The activity must be performed four times, varying the places and objects in each one.

Fig. 3. Final panel to choose the type and number of objects inside the bag.

Multiple characteristics make the Objects Bag activity suitable for improving WM:

- It is a complex *goal-oriented task* and therefore it requires the activation of all the four components of the WM. The *central executive* must allocate and control enough attention to input and manage the appropriate information. The *visuospatial sketch-pad* must hold and update visual objects. The *phonological loop* is activated by both instructions and verbal components of the objects, and the user self-statements or rehearsal. *Episodic buffer* must integrate every scene as a whole using information from long-term memory (for calculating and comprehension of the situation).

- It is a systematic training: four trials each time, twice a week for three months.
- It is a dynamic task that has been designed to avoid getting used to it, since each trial presents a different map, varying the shops, places and the objects to be picked up or dropped.
- In each trial the difficulty is graded, and it increases if more correct answers are provided.

VIRTRAEL performs several measurements while the users are performing this activity (and many others integrated into the overall platform), also allowing the therapists to supervise them. The measures that are taken are: time to read the instructions, total time to perform each trial, and the raw number of successes, failures and omissions (for each trial). To maintain and increase motivation for training, feedback is provided on the raw score achieved in each session. A visual feedback is also provided in the form of a bronze, silver or gold medal, depending on the performance level (Fig. 4). It is as a prize to the user.

Fig. 4. Feedback shown when the activity finishes. (English translation: "Congratulations. ¡It is not bad at all!. You have won a bronze medal. Let's continue training to get a silver or gold medal. You can repeat the activity by pushing the button).

To improve the applicability of the training to real environments, the Objects Bag activity presents an avatar resembling common activities that are done every day while shopping and walking around a city.

3.2   Tests

The effectiveness and usability of the Objects Bag was tested in a previous study with older people. Findings indicated that the experimental group of 36 users of VIRTRAEL showed a significant improvement in WM against a control group of 34 users who spent the same time doing recreational computer use [15]. Although this was not a randomized controlled trial, controls in the study design and specification of tasks and variables allow us to draw conclusions about the benefits of applying a scientific model to the training activities.

Some tests are currently being carried out again, since new activities have been added to the platform, including 3D activities and a recommendation system about nutrition. The usability of the activities has also been improved.

4   Conclusions and Planned Activities

Objects Bag is a specific activity and tool for computerized training of WM. It is integrated into VIRTRAEL, a free and open-source web platform. The activity has been designed following a theoretical evidence-based model of WM. It has demonstrated its usability for the elderly and its motivational qualities. Activities used in the Objects Bag tool are everyday activities, so future studies will determine whether the improvements made in WM are, in fact, transferred to real life, one of the main challenges of computer-based training.

Finally, the features of VIRTRAEL can provide a real social impact: it is a free and online tool that allows widespread use for training elderly people. Moreover, its use can be independent or supported by relatives or therapists, from homes, community classrooms, day centers, residences, etc. In fact, as its benefits are being demonstrated, some public institutions (such as the social services of municipalities of several villages and a regional consortium of business and local governments called Consorcio Fernando de los Rios) are interested in VIRTRAEL to train their elderly citizens. They are collaborating by providing resources and space for the tests.

The social and health impact of any action to minimize cognitive impairment would be enormous due to an aging population and the high rates of dementia. Objects Bag has also demonstrated the benefits of applying evidence-based models of neuroscience in tool design.

Acknowledgements. This project has been funded with support from the Regional Excellence Project TIC-6600, in Spain. We want to thank them and also the institutions that collaborate in the study, and the participating senior citizens.

References

1. Baddeley, A.: The episodic buffer: a new component of working memory? Trends Cogn. Sci. **4**, 417–423 (2000)
2. Jarrold, C., Towse, J.N.: Individual differences in working memory. Neuroscience **139**, 39–50 (2006)

3. Miyake, A., Friedman, N.P., Emerson, M.J., Witzki, A.H., Howerter, A., Wager, T.D.: The unity and diversity of executive functions and their contributions to complex "Frontal Lobe" tasks: a latent variable analysis. Cogn. Psychol. **41**, 49–100 (2000)

4. Cansino, S., Hernández-Ramos, E., Estrada-Manilla, C., Torres-Trejo, F., Martínez-Galindo, J.G., Ayala-Hernández, M., Gómez-Fernández, T., Osorio, D., Cedillo-Tinoco, M., Garcés-Flores, L., Beltrán-Palacios, K., García-Lázaro, H.G., García-Gutiérrez, F., Cadena-Arenas, Y., Fernández-Apan, L., Bärtschi, A., Rodríguez-Ortiz, M.D.: The decline of verbal and visuospatial working memory across the adult life span. Age **35**, 2283–2302 (2013)

5. Klekociuk, S.Z., Summers, M.J.: Lowered performance in working memory and attentional sub-processes are most prominent in multi-domain amnestic mild cognitive impairment subtypes. Psychogeriatrics **14**, 63–71 (2014)

6. Sebastian, M.V., Menor, J., Elosua, M.R.: Attentional dysfunction of the central executive in AD: evidence from dual task and perseveration errors. Cortex **42**, 1015–1020 (2006)

7. Titz, C.: Adult age differences in working memory: two complex memory span experiments. In: Handbook of Cognitive Aging: Causes, Processes and Effects, pp. 83–108 (2011)

8. Akerlund, E., Esbjornsson, E., Sunnenrhagen, K.S., Bjorkdahi, A.: Can computerized working memory training improve impaired working memory, cognition and psychological health? Brain Inj. **27**(13–14), 1649–1657 (2013)

9. Shipstead, Z., Redick, T.S., Engle, R.W.: Is working memory training effective? Psychol. Bull. **138**, 628–654 (2012)

10. Hulme, C., Melby-Lervåg, M.: Current evidence does not support the claims made for CogMed working memory training. J. Appl. Res. Mem. Cogn. **1**, 197–200 (2012)

11. Melby-Lervag, M., Hulme, C.: Is working memory training effective? Meta-Analytic Rev. Dev. Psychol. **49**(2), 270–291 (2013)

12. Flak, M.M., Hernes, S.S., Skranes, J., Løhaugen, G.C.C.: The memory aid study: protocol for a randomized controlled clinical trial evaluating the effect of computer-based working memory training in elderly patients with mild cognitive impairment (MCI). Trials **15**, 156 (2014)

13. Cameirao, M.S., Badia, S.B., Zimmerli, L., Oller, E.D., Verschure, P.F.M.J.: The rehabilitation gaming system: a review. Stud. Health Technol. Inform. **145**, 65–83 (2009)

14. Rizzo, K.: A swot analysis of the field of virtual reality rehabilitation and therapy. Presence: Teleoperators Virtual Environ. **14**(2), 119–146 (2005)

15. Sík Lányi, C., Brown, D.J., Standen, P., Lewis, J., Butkute, V.: Results of user interface evaluation of serious games for students with intellectual disability. Acta Polytech. Hung. **9**(1), 225–245 (2012)

16. Rute-Pérez, S., Santiago-Ramajo, S., Hurtado, M.V., Rodríguez-Fórtiz, M.J., Caracuel, A.: Challenges in software applications for the cognitive evaluation and stimulation of the elderly. J. NeuroEng. Rehabil. **11**(88), 1–10 (2014)

17. Rodríguez-Fórtiz, M.J., Rodríguez-Domínguez, C., Cano-Olivares, P., Revelles-Moreno, J. Rodríguez-Almendros, M.L., Hurtado-Torres, M.V., Rute-Pérez, S.: Serious games for the cognitive stimulation of Elderly People. In: SEGAH 2016, Orlando, Florida

Audible Mapper & ShadowRine: Development of Map Editor Using only Sound in Accessible Game for Blind Users, and Accessible Action RPG for Visually Impaired Gamers

Masaki Matsuo[1]([✉]), Takahiro Miura[2], Masatsugu Sakajiri[1], Junji Onishi[1], and Tsukasa Ono[1]

[1] Tsukuba University of Technology, 4-12-7 Kasuga, Tsukuba, Ibaraki 305-8521, Japan
mm122311@cc.k.tsukuba-tech.ac.jp,
{sakajiri,ohnishi,ono}@cs.k.tsukuba-tech.ac.jp
[2] Institute of Gerontology, The University of Tokyo, 7-3-1 Hongo, Bunkyo-ku, Tokyo 113-8656, Japan
miu@iog.u-tokyo.ac.jp

Abstract. Although many computer games have recently become diversified, plenty of effort and ingenuity is needed to produce games that persons with a total visual impairment can enjoy. Though some games for visually impaired persons have been developed, games that use only auditory information present challenges for sighted persons. Moreover, unfortunately, it is still difficult for visually impaired persons to play the same game with sighted persons and for sighted and visually impaired persons to share a common subject. To solve this problem, we developed a barrier-free game that both sighted and visually impaired persons can play using their dominant senses including visual, auditory and tactile senses. Moreover, we developed a map editor for a game developer with blindness and provided an integrated game development environment for them. In this paper, we describe the development and reflections of the barrier-free game and the map editor.

Keywords: Visually impaired persons · Inclusive game · 2D representation · Tactile map · Integrated game development environment for the blind

1 Introduction

Computer games have become so diverse that they have made their way into people's lives in the forms of arcade games (public business games), consumer games (home video games), PC games, etc. The latest forms of games have high pixel density and high-definition displays, which have increased the amount of

K. Miesenberger et al. (Eds.): ICCHP 2016, Part I, LNCS 9758, pp. 537–544, 2016.
DOI: 10.1007/978-3-319-41264-1_73

visual information that gamers receive. Therefore, visually impaired and fully blind people find it difficult to enjoy most of these games. People with normal vision can visually receive maps, texts, and other game information. However, for the visually impaired, the level of difficulty increases owing to their reliance on sound information to play the game. For the fully blind to play on their own, they need to associate the scenes and sound effects in the games and remember them. They also need to memorize everything from the menus and categories, and other orders of items, required to play the game. It takes extra effort on the part of visually impaired gamers to play regular games compared with people who have normal vision.

Recently, game development for the visually impaired has been making some progress. People with an interest in games that the visually impaired can play on their own or with assistance are posting and exchanging information on Audio-Games.net [1]. This website is a collection of information on games for the visually impaired. These games are called audio games, which the visually impaired can play using a screen reader. However, audio games are challenging for those with even normal vision to play, and these games offer more options to choose from. The issue is there are barely any games that the visually impaired and people with normal vision can play together.

With regard to game accessibility for the visually impaired, Yuan et al. reported on audio games and other types of games [2]. Game accessibility is a growing interest that can be reexamined by other researchers as well. Meisenberger et al. reported on the accessibility and interface requirements necessary for each type of disability [3]. Porter et al. interviewed game developers and game players with disabilities for a survey on game accessibility. The survey results shed a light on issues that occurred while playing games as well as game industry issues related to cost [4]. Zahand presented accessibility requirements for game developers from the standpoint of business values and game design [5].

The purpose of this research is to develop games that everyone can play, regardless of their visual acuity. We have developed an action RPG (role-playing game) that players with healthy vision, and those who are visually impaired, can play together. This may be the first game of its kind in the world. Many of the games classified as action RPGs require quick judgment based on screen information; hence, there is difficulty in playing the game without being able to view the information on screen. It is not easy for the visually impaired to develop such games on their own; producing and editing fields (topographic landscapes in games) would prove particularly challenging. Therefore, before we developed our game, we created a tool that allows the visually impaired to easily create fields on their own. In this journal we will describe a game map editor that enables the visually impaired to design games by listening to usable sounds. We will also explain the RPG games created by the map editor we developed, and introduce the user feedback and the evaluation overviews we received when we made the game public on the Internet.

2   Materials and Methods

2.1   Audible Mapper: A Map Creation Tool

Audible Mapper is a field creation tool with accessibility for the fully blind. We chose Hot Soup Processor (HSP) as a programming language to enable fully blind users to develop the game by using a screen reader [6]. The screen reader provides audio information on cursor locations, allowing the user to design 2D fields by typing on a keyboard. Figure 1 shows a fully blind user creating fields in our map editor. After surrounding the four sides of the map with walls Fig. 1(a), the user places more walls to build a map of his or her concept Fig. 1(b). Then the user can position objects such as treasure boxes Fig. 1(c).

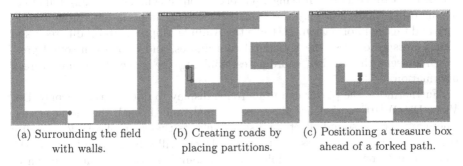

(a) Surrounding the field   (b) Creating roads by   (c) Positioning a treasure box
with walls.   placing partitions.   ahead of a forked path.

Fig. 1. An example of a map developed using our map editor. The red circle in the figure is the editor cursor. (Color figure online)

The details of this procedure are as follows: The editor allows the user to move the cursor using arrow keys on the keyboard, and to place tiles (for walls, waters, lava streams, etc.) and objects (treasure boxes, doors, etc.) by operating the number and letter keys. There is an option for the users to add different types of tiles and objects as needed. When moving the cursor, the user can also select the range and group the objects within the field to work on them all at once. To choose the range, the user must place the cursor on the corner of the area he or she wishes to select, and move the cursor while pressing the Shift key. A rectangular range will be selected when the user lets go of the Shift key. The objects within that range will be grouped and can be added and deleted all at once.

For the developer to know the cursor location at each point in time, the editor plays different sounds based on the cursor location. The horizontal direction of the cursor is expressed by asymmetry in the sound pressure; thus, the developer can find the lateral coordinate on the screen through sound image localization. Different sound pressures indicate the vertical direction of the cursor, allowing the developer to find the vertical coordinate on the screen. The developer can move the cursor over the map to get an entire picture of the screen with the sound effects. Regarding the changes in sound pressure when the cursor positions change, the lateral differences in the sound pressure are set at 2 dB and above [7,8] based on reports made by Hafter and Yost et al. The vertical differences are set at 1 db and above [9] based on reports made by Miller et al. The editor also generates sound effects for each of the tiles that the developer places.

2.2 ShadowRine: An Action RPG

This game is an action RPG game for those with regular vision as well as the visually impaired to play on their own. The game is played in the Windows operating system and is programmed to command DirectX for multimedia processing. HSP was used to develop both ShadowRine and the Audible Mapper.

Game players with normal vision can play ShadowRine just like a regular action RPG by visually following what occurs on screen. The visually impaired, on the other hand, can play the game by receiving information through auditory and tactile information. Just like the Audible Mapper, lateral differences in sound pressure express the horizontal coordinates, and changes in sound pressure represent the vertical coordinates, enabling the gamer to acquire screen information.

Furthermore, the player can use a touch display (a dot diagram display, Dot View, DV-2) [10] to visualize the screen in real time through the tactile senses. There are various sound effects and special effects that help players to visualize the screen. These effects assume that the players will rely on sound to play the game. The game uses lateral differences in sound pressure to show distances between objects such as enemies, items, and treasure boxes. ShadowRine also uses differences in sound pressure to show the vertical direction of objects. Screen readers can read out any text information from the game, which is compatible with major screen readers such as NVDA and SAPI as well as screen readers that automatically read clipboards. The dot display is used for tactile visualization. Among the visually presented screen information, accessible/nonaccessible spots in the field, and the positions of the player's character and enemies, are expressed by vertical movement of the pin in binarization. All of the information is in real time, allowing the players to visualize the field quickly and easily.

The basic operation of this game is to move the character (the player's assumed role) in both vertical and horizontal directions in the 2D field, similar to other conventional action RPG games. The field has accessible/nonaccessible spots and enemies that use various tactics to prevent the main character from progressing in the game. The player advances in the game by either avoiding or fighting enemies using weapons that he or she has gained. The game includes events and quizzes, which the player must clear to move the story along. It takes approximately 10 h to finish the entire game. Nonplayer characters are placed on the field, and they provide hints to help the player collect key items for a speed run. The game was designed for the players to sense all of these elements through the visual, auditory, or tactile senses. The game has three levels of difficulty for beginners and advanced gamers; there is a tutorial mode for the beginners.

3 Results and Discussion

3.1 Map Editor Experience Results

Figure 2 shows an example of a game map developed from the steps shown in Fig. 1. Figure 2(a) shows a map for the player to progress while relying on intuition (positions and routes are simple). Figure 2(b) shows a map for players to explore (positions and routes are difficult). Figure 2(c) shows a field for the players to strategize ways to collect treasure boxes. These maps are used in the game as parts of towns, dungeons, and fields where items are hidden.

Figure 2: (Left) Edits made in the field creation tool, and (right) results when applied to the game screen. (a) Towns in the game: Obtain information from the nonplayer character. (b) Dungeons in the game: Move forward by jumping over a valley. (c) Fields in the game: Swim in the waters to collect treasure boxes.

Audible Mapper allowed the fully blind to draw and design all the maps for the game quickly and efficiently. Until now, developers had to input the numbers directly onto the programming screen, and details for object placements proved difficult. Source code was also very complicated, and it took developers 20–30 min to create a single map. The Audible Mapper cut down the time from a few minutes to several tens of seconds, thus improving productivity.

An entirely blind developer used this mapper to create approximately 500 maps (24–32 squares) for the action RPG.

We also equipped the game with a field viewer based on this mapper to check the game screen. This feature allows gamers to play based only on auditory information. Visually impaired players with high gaming skills in various games are able to advance in the game by using this feature to receive map information on their current location.

To test the accessibility of this mapper for other visually impaired persons and those with normal vision, we conducted a simple survey targeting six people with weak vision, two entirely blind people, and one person with normal vision. We asked the participants to draw geometric shapes (squares, rectangles, and frames) based only on auditory information. We assessed their drawings based on three points: positioning, size, and corners of the walls. All participants were able to replicate the shapes correctly.

This result indicated a trend: the more the participants repeated the process, the less often they hit the wrong keys and the shorter the drawing time became. The participants answered a five-level questionnaire on visualization and accessibility by sound. The visualization of horizontal directions (lateral differences in sound pressure) averaged 4.14, and visualization of the vertical direction (changes in sound pressure) averaged 3.85. Those engaged in the field of music or those who had experience in playing audio games had an inclination to give higher evaluations. Accessibility averaged 4.43, and memorability averaged 4.57.

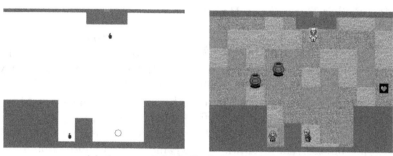

(a) A map of the hall of the novice in a town

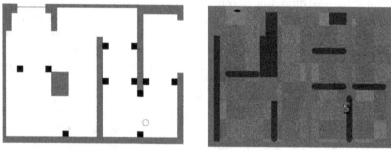

(b) A labyrinth with complex routes in a dangeon

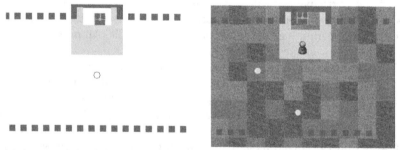

(c) A part of the field for getting used to "swimming" by aiming at a treasure

Fig. 2. Examples of maps created with the Audible Mapper (Left) and corresponding game maps (Right) (Color figure online)

3.2 Number of Game Downloads and Player Feedback

This game was released to the public for free via a website and other media on February 9, 2014. It has drawn attention as an action RPG for the visually impaired and has recorded 2,508 downloads.

An anonymous survey was conducted on the website beginning June 11, 2014, targeting users who have played the game. The investigation had two parts: a rating for the entertainment aspect of the game (selecting a from between 1–5) and free space to give feedback (good points and issues that needed improvement). Of 99 responders, 63 provided a rating of "5: Very Entertaining", and the overall rating averaged 4.6. The visually impaired expert game players ranked the game higher in general for its large field, long story, story variations, and speed-run modes with difficult dungeons and item-collection stages.

On the other hand, the visually impaired beginner game players commented that they became lost because the fields were too large, the system sounds were confusing, and jumping over the valley was too difficult. These issues were addressed by updating the field viewer, improving the tutorial mode, and adding sound effects when jumping over valleys. The survey was conducted in Japanese. However, 38 visually impaired users from outside Japan responded. (We tracked website access from areas outside Japan). They commented that they were looking forward to the launch of a new game, and made requests for English versions.

The information on our game was posted on AudioGames.net [10], and we discovered that English-speaking players with visual impairments were able to experience the game as well. User forums on the website documented experiences of visually impaired gamers and those with normal vision playing the game together.

4 Conclusion

We developed the Audible Mapper as a game development tool for the visually impaired developer to design games efficiently. Our mapper visualizes cursor positions on the screen using sounds, allowing the developer to draw maps by typing on a keyboard. An action RPG, ShadowRine, was successfully developed by combining sound visualization features and maps created on the mapper and tactile display. This game allows gamers with visual impairments and those with normal vision to play together. It was released online and is played by visually impaired gamers all over the world.

We plan to further our research in ways for the visually impaired and those with normal vision to game together. The Audible Mapper will also be improved so that even beginner visually impaired gamers can draw maps more efficiently. Detailed psychophysical experiments will be conducted to define the conditions required to draw by relying only on sounds. The Audible Mapper will be tested to determine its abilities in drawing existing topography or routes to a destination. We expect the Audible Mapper to become a tool for the visually impaired to draw maps and increase the types of information they can communicate.

544 M. Matsuo et al.

Acknowledgements. This work was partially supported by JSPS KAKENHI Grant Numbers 26285210, 15K04540, 15K01015.

References

1. AudioGames.net. http://www.audiogames.net/. Accessed 15 Jan 2016
2. Yuan, B., Folmer, E., Harris Jr., F.C.: Game accessibility: a survey. Univers. Access Inf. Soc. **10**, 81–100 (2011)
3. Miesenberger, K., Ossmann, R., Archambault, D., Searle, G., Holzinger, A.: More than just a game: accessibility in computer games. In: Holzinger, A. (ed.) USAB 2008. LNCS, vol. 5298, pp. 247–260. Springer, Heidelberg (2008)
4. Porter, J.R., Kientz, J.A.: An empirical study of issues, barriers to mainstream video game accessibility. In: Proceedings of the ACM ASSETS 2013, pp. 3:1–3:8 (2013)
5. Zahand, B.: Making Video Games Accessible: Business Justifications and Design Considerations. https://msdn.microsoft.com/en-us/library/windows/desktop/ee415219(v=vs.85).aspx. Accessed 15 Jan 2016
6. HSPTV!. http://hsp.tv/. Accessed 15 Jan 2016
7. Hafter, E.R., Dye, R.H., Nuetzel, J.M., Aronow, H.: Difference thresholds for interaural intensity. J. Acoust. Soc. Am. **61**, 829–834 (1977)
8. Yost, W.A., Dye, R.H.: Discrimination of interaural differences of level as a function of frequency. J. Acoust. Soc. Am. **83**, 1846–1851 (1988)
9. Miller, G.: Sensitivity to changes in the intensity of white noise and its relation to masking and loudness. J. Acoust. Soc. Am. **19**, 609–619 (1947)
10. Shadow Rine Full voice. http://audiogames.net/db.php?action=view&id=Shadow%20line%20Full%20voice. Accessed 15 Jan 2016

Memory Game and Special HCI Device in Stroke Therapy

Máté Godár, Veronika Szücs, and Cecilia Sik-Lanyi(✉)

University of Pannonia, Egyetem Street 10, Veszprem 8200, Hungary
godarmate@gmail.com, szucs@virt.uni-pannon.hu,
lanyi@almos.uni-pannon.hu

Abstract. The main goal of our project was to design and implement a serious-game application, which helps the older generation, stroke patients to complete the rehabilitation process or practise daily movements playfully. The patients, therapists, trainers, and family members can edit the levels in the game. The user can control the game via Microsoft Kinect sensor, which is one of the most popular HCI device.

Keywords: Serious game · Stroke rehabilitation

1 Introduction

1.1 The State of the Art in This Area

Virtual Reality (VR) based computer games have been recognized as a motivational tool in stroke rehabilitation in the last 20 years. The traditional exercises for practice movements are boring; moreover, the therapist's supervision is required. The VR based games are more and more popular, using different new input devices Microsoft Kinect sensor [1] or other hand free controllers. These devices are developed rapidly, the number of games for stroke rehabilitation in telemedicine systems are moderate.

2 The Methodology Used

Based on our earlier experiences in three years period StrokeBack Project [2, 4], it was concluded, that Hungarian Rehabilitation Centers have very similar need for serious games, as other European hospitals, or healthcare organisations. The target groups' needs were collected and identified in the previous project, these results were adapted to actual development. The application was developed in QT Integrated Development Environment, in C++ programming language. There was developed a Memory game, as a new application, there was developed a framework, which accomplish the control with a special HCI device, with Kinect sensor. There are three additional games, which are migrated onto the newly developed framework, and adapted the Kinect control ability to them. The complete application was tested by healthy users. The clinical tests started at the end of March 2016, at Budapest, at the Janos Hospital's Rehabilitation Center.

K. Miesenberger et al. (Eds.): ICCHP 2016, Part I, LNCS 9758, pp. 545–548, 2016.
DOI: 10.1007/978-3-319-41264-1_74

2.1   The R&D Work and Results

An easy to use Windows application was developed, with Microsoft Kinect control, and built into a flexible framework. On the application's start, the main menu appears, where the user can select the language for the game session first, than the kind of the game. These are shown on Fig. 1. At this moment four games are built in the framework: The Memory Game, The Gardener Game, The Pick And Save Game and The Fireworks Game. By pushing the Memory Game pictogram on the game selection screen, the game starts. On starting, the user have to choose a correct difficulty level, because the number of placed card pairs depends on difficulty. The game shows both of the cards about 5 s, than the cards are flipped.

During this time, the player can memorise the images on the cards, and when he/she plays, try to find pairs with similar pictures. The user can drag and flip the cards with using Microsoft Kinect sensor, of course. The correctly selected pairs are disappears from the desk.

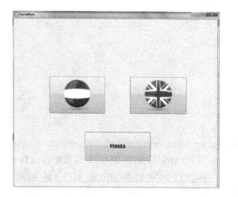 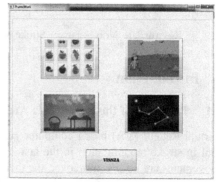

Fig. 1. The language menu (left) and the game select menu (right)

If the cards, which were chosen and flipped are different, then after 5 s these cards will flip back. The goal of the player is to find all possible pairs, and clear the screen from cards. When the user found all pairs, he/she gets the maximum points for the completed level.

After completing a level, he/she is able to choose from two further options: he/she can continue playing on the harder level, or he/she can step backward to the difficulty selector menu. The game rewards the user with points.

Control with Microsoft Kinect sensor - very good options for every players, who have any disabilities, which affects their arms, hands, fingers.

When Kinect control was implemented, the main goal was to create a very easy to use surface for the user. The selected middleware application was the FAAST. This is a very useful middleware application, and together with an installed OpenNI framework and NITE middleware the developer can immediately work with Kinect sensor from C++ code. The Fig. 2 shows the calibrating screen of the Kinect sensor with the help of OpenNi, NITE and FAAST middleware applications.

Fig. 2. The category selection (left) and Kinect calibration in the FAAST middleware (right)

Very important task was to implement a one hand control, via Kinect sensor. It has a great of importance, because stroke patients unfortunately are unable to equally use their arm.

There are a level editor for all of the games migrated to the framework. This is very important, because the therapists can personalize the games, and each patient, each player have a different skills with using games, every stroke patients have a different level of disability, and everyone need different complexity of the therapy.

2.2 The Scientific and Practical Impact or Contributions to the Field

The scientific and practical impact or contributions to the field are great of importance and multiple:

- To practise via gaming: more exciting, more incentive.
- To practise in smaller group or individually: less frustration
- More motivational rehabilitations, trainings mean: decrease the duration of rehabilitation.

3   Conclusion and Planned Activities

An easy to use application "Memory Game" and game framework were developed. The main importance of the game is the personality, gaming experience [3], use of modern HCI device (Kinect sensor). The users can play on step-by-step hardening levels. In this way this application is useful for any aging, useful for elderly people, for stroke patients. Only positive feedback was received during the tests. Despite the Kinect Sensor v1.0's inaccuracy the game is easy to use and easy to control, the playing with this game is very enjoyable. In the future we plan to perform more tests with stroke patients, and plan to implement other difficulty levels.

Acknowledgement. The paper and participation in the conference has been supported by "Stiftung Aktion Österreich- Ungarn", project number: 91öu6 (Conference participation AAA TE2015-ICCHP2016). The authors thank the support of colleagues of the Janos Hospital, Budapest and would like give special thanks to Ms. Ágnes Nyéki, and Mr. Tamás Dömök for their programming works.

References

1. https://news.microsoft.com/2010/06/13/kinect-for-xbox-360-is-official-name-of-microsofts-controller-free-game-device/
2. A StrokeBack Project. http://www.strokeback.eu/index.html
3. Sik Lanyi, C., Brown, D., Standen, P., Lewis, J., Butkute, V.: Results of user interface evaluation of serious games for students with intellectual disability. Acta Polytech. Hung. **9**(1), 225–245 (2012)
4. Sik Lanyi, C., Szucs, V.: Motivating rehabilitation through competitive gaming. In: Vogiatzaki, E., Krukowski, A. (eds.) Modern Stroke Rehabilitation Through e-Health-Based Entertainment, pp. 137–167. Springer International Publishing, Switzerland (2016). ISBN 978-3-319-21292-0

User Experience & Emotions for Accessibility

Introduction to the Special Thematic Session

Yehya Mohamad[(⊠)], Gaby Nordbrock, Henrike Gappa,
and Carlos Velasco

Fraunhofer Institute for Applied Information Technology (FIT),
Schloss Birlinghoven, 53757 Sankt Augustin, Germany
{yehya.mohamad, gaby.nordbrock, henrike.gappa,
carlos.velasco}@fit.fraunhofer.de

Abstract. This STS on user experience and emotions for accessibility is targeted towards the elaboration on the topics of user experience and affective computing approaches and their relation to accessibility of electronic content. Accessible design as crucial condition for disabled users to get access to electronic content, which is also beneficial for non-disabled users, e.g. because of adaptability of information presentation accessing web services via smartphones. Accessibility so far pays less attention to user experience or emotional aspects of interaction, though they are important factors for disabled persons in similar way as for non-disabled persons. Additional to accessibility, considering user experience and emotional aspects of user interfaces would help disabled users for example to easily and efficiently use information systems and overcome communication disorders. Concepts for support of emotional interaction can on the other side increase the usability of electronic services for disabled users.

Keywords: User experience · UX · Affective computing · Accessibility · Assistive technology · Sensors · GSR · Machine learning algorithm · Disabled person · Context · Emotion · Emotion management · User interface · e-Learning · Web-based

1 Introduction

Accessible design is a design process in which the needs of people with disabilities are specifically considered. Accessibility sometimes refers to the characteristic that products, services, and facilities can be independently used by people with a variety of disabilities[1].

Usable design considering user experience includes the practical, experiential, affective, meaningful and valuable aspects of human-computer interaction. Additionally, it includes a person's perceptions of system aspects such as ease of use, emotional aspects and efficiency. User experience may be considered subjective in nature to the

---

[1] http://www.washington.edu/doit/what-difference-between-accessible-usable-and-universal-design.

degree that it is about individual perception and thought with respect to the system. User experience is dynamic as it is constantly modified over time due to changing context of usage and changes to individual systems. Unfortunately, people with disabilities are not always included in user experience tests. Therefore, many products that perform well in user experience tests are not accessible to people with disabilities. Increasingly, accessible design considerations are being addressed by usability professionals. Usability shares some key goals with accessibility design. Designers in both disciplines seek to create product features that are easily discovered and operated by the user. Accessibility as indicated by W3C WCAG 2.0 is concerned with aspects of user interface that include[2]:

- Perceivable – Information and user interface components must be presentable to users in ways they can perceive. This means that users must be able to perceive the information being presented.
- Operable – User interface components and navigation must be operable. This means that users must be able to operate the interface.
- Understandable – Information and the operation of user interface must be understandable. This means that users must be able to understand the information as well as the operation of the user interface.
- Robust – Content must be robust enough that it can be interpreted reliably by a wide variety of user agents, including assistive technologies.

Usability is additionally concerned with aspects of the user experience that include:

- Learnability: Can users easily learn how to operate the product, and can they remember how to perform tasks when they return to the product the next time?
- Consistency: Are product features clearly and consistently labelled?
- Efficiency and effectiveness: Can users perform tasks with a minimal amount of effort and achieve their goals successfully?

There are different opinions about the relation between user experience and accessibility. E.g. should user experience and accessibility be the responsibility of the same team? When should designers think about the accessibility of a design? What types of disabilities may affect peoples' ability to use products. Another related dimension of user interfaces focuses on emotional aspects and cues. affective computing deals with this dimension and is not only about measuring someone's sensation; affective computing can be understood as the study concerning with the understanding, recognizing and expressing human emotions by designing computational systems that makes computers to be more adaptive and interact naturally with people [1, 2]. In addition to the work of accessibility experts, if:

- interface designers consider emotional aspects to help disabled persons to manage their emotions, and
- product designers apply user experience design principles, with a special focus on accessibility for people with disabilities, and

---

[2] https://www.w3.org/TR/UNDERSTANDING-WCAG20/intro.html#introduction-fourprincs-head.

- usability experts routinely include people with a variety of disabilities in usability tests,
- more products will become accessible to and usable by everyone.

2   Areas Covered by STS

The papers presented in this STS elaborate on questions including the following:

- How to conduct user studies with disabled persons in the context of wearables and affective computing?
- How to involve disabled user groups in the design of affective computing systems?
- How to design systems that allow for inclusion of disabled users in an agile human-centered product development practice?
- How to design and conduct complex usability studies involving disabled users?

In the following, an excerpt of the papers of this STS will be presented:

1. Kanako Takahashi et al. introduce a wearable ECG monitoring device designed for children with autism spectrum disorders (ASD). The results revealed that ECG measurement of three children with ASD were successfully performed during a therapeutic session. The device was applied easily by parents or therapists, and it was not necessary to explain ways of wearing the device. It can be said, that the device has a probability to estimate reliable HR and HRV during less motion therapeutictic activities.
2. Dimitris Spiliotopoulos et al. explore the use of speech enabled complex graphs that are designed to enable non-technical users to edit and appraise visually complex semantic structures. The authors report on the findings of how technically-savvy users and non-technical users experience the different modalities, make choices and identify each modality advantages and shortcomings as well as the ability of each user group to optimally exploit modality combination paths.
3. Yehya Mohamad et al. present a qualitative user study on elicitation and online detection of emotional states in users suffering from cerebral palsy (CP). The elicitation approach was based on the international affective digitized sound system (IADS-2) database. The body signal measurements were used to verify an online approach for the detection of emotional states. The results revealed high correlation between the findings in the study and the published standard IADS-2. These results have shown that the use of emotional sensitive systems for this user group is feasible and such a system will help them to manage their emotions and overcome communication obstacles.

3   Future Research Areas

The presented papers cover a wide area of topics in the focus of this STS.

There was until now little research on the cross roads between Accessibility, Usability, and Affective Computing. The relationship between accessibility and usability topics and probably to some extent the overlapping should be studied well and in more depth. Concerning affective computing, more work on tuning of the machine learning algorithms should be invested. Focusing future work on affective computing for disabled users on detection and relieve of stress rather than on detection of different emotional states and conducting more user studies with larger number of participants.

References

1. Calvo, R.A., D'Mello, S.: Affect detection: an interdisciplinary review of models, methods, and their applications. IEEE Trans. Affect. Comput. **1**(1), 18–37 (2010)
2. Picard, R.W.: Affective computing: challenges. Int. J. Hum.-Comput. Stud. **59**(1), 55–64 (2003)

A Smart Clothe for ECG Monitoring of Children with Autism Spectrum Disorders

Kanako Takahashi[1](✉), Soichiro Matsuda[2], and Kenji Suzuki[3]

[1] Department of Intelligent Interaction Technologies, University of Tsukuba,
1-1-1 Tennodai, Tsukuba 305-8573, Japan
kanako@ai.iit.tsukuba.ac.jp
[2] Faculty of Engineering, Information and Systems, University of Tsukuba,
1-1-1 Tennodai, Tsukuba 305-8573, Japan
matsuda@ai.iit.tsukuba.ac.jp
[3] Center for Cybernics Research, University of Tsukuba,
1-1-1 Tennodai, Tsukuba 305-8573, Japan
kenji@ieee.org

Abstract. We introduce a wearable electrocardiogram (ECG) monitoring device designed for children with autism spectrum disorders (ASD). The purpose of this study is to verify the quality of the ECG signals measured by the developed device during the therapeutic activity of children with ASD for the quantitative measurement of mental stress. The device is implemented in a clothe, and the ECG signals are captured at the wrists. ECG measurements of three children with ASD were successfully performed during therapy, and R-R intervals with a high reliability were obtained over 90 % of the duration of tasks that involve little movement.

Keywords: ECG monitoring · HR · HRV · Therapeutic environment · Children with autism spectrum disorders · Wearable devices

1 Introduction

Children with autism spectrum disorders (ASD) have difficulty expressing their feelings through actions during daily and therapeutic activities. Therefore, it is often difficult for parents and therapists to understand their feelings, and that may lead to problems such as panic or even therapy denial [1]. To resolve this problem, several studies have been recently conducted to examine the relationship between the behavior of people with ASD and their physiological state [2–5]. However, most such studies have been performed in limited or constrained environments, owing to the specifications of the measuring devices.

Cardiovascular-based indicators such as the heart rate (HR) and heart rate variability (HRV) can be used to estimate the inner state of a person. Researches have found that the HRV changes under acute psychological stress; therefore, the HRV has been used as an indicator of mental stress in several studies [4–8]. The HR and HRV can be acquired from both electrocardiogram (ECG) and

© Springer International Publishing Switzerland 2016
K. Miesenberger et al. (Eds.): ICCHP 2016, Part I, LNCS 9758, pp. 555–562, 2016.
DOI: 10.1007/978-3-319-41264-1_75

photoprethysmography (PPG). PPG measures the rate of blood flow, whereas ECG measures bioelectrical signals produced by heart activity. ECG is necessary for obtaining a reliable HRV [9,10].

We consider that the quantitative measurement of the mental stress during therapeutic activity helps therapists and parents understand the internal conditions of the child. Various systems are available for measuring ECG in the living environment. The Holter monitor is one of the most famous devices for obtaining ECG. Textile electrodes and capacitively coupled electrodes have also been proposed for obtaining ECG [8,11–14]. However, these systems are less suitable for measuring the ECG of children in the living environment because the usability of the device is not sufficient for children, parents, and therapists. Although the Holter monitor can measure ECG with a high accuracy, it requires parents or therapists to place wet-type electrodes on the chest of the child, and be careful about the condition of the device so that the electrodes are not removed. The textile electrodes are often embedded in the front of the garment and need a high pressure around the chest to ensure good contact with the skin. To achieve direct contact between the electrodes and the skin, parents or therapists must remove the clothe of the child, and then dress the child in a tight garment with the textile electrodes. This takes time, and the tight clothe increases the feeling of constraint for the child. We consider that smart textiles employed for children is still difficult. On the other hand, the accuracy of the measured ECG using capacitively coupled electrodes is unstable because the distance between the skin and electrode changes regularly during daily activities.

We have been developing a wearable ECG monitoring system for children [15] that can measure the ECG when the child wears regular clothe. Because we focus on the R-R interval from ECG regarding the mental stress, we adapted a bipolar lead from only three electrode at two different places on the body. The developed smart clothe has these electrodes on both wrist parts. We confirmed that an eight-years-old male child can use the device with minimal discomfort. Herein, we report the results of the ECG monitoring of children with ASD at therapeutic sessions using the developed wearable device.

2   System Overview

2.1   Signal Acquisition

Figures 1 and 2 show an overview of the developed system and the appearance of the device, respectively. The system consists of an electrode module, a signal amplifier, acceleration sensor module, and a monitoring part. The electrode module, the signal amplifier, and the acceleration sensor module are embedded in the clothe in order to increase the familiarity and enable use of the system in the living environment. The ECG signal is monitored in real time using a tablet-based wireless system.

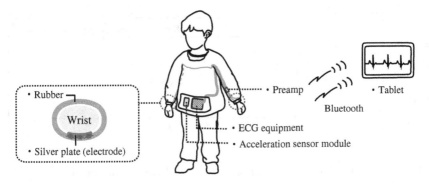

Fig. 1. System overview of the developed device. The ECG signals are measured at the wrist as the rubber presses the electrode to the skin. The ECG equipment amplifies the signal and transmits it to a monitor via a Bluetooth wireless connection.

Fig. 2. Appearance of the device.

Electrode Module. The electrode module is composed of pure silver plates and rubber elastics at the sleeves. Three electrodes (two main electrodes and one reference electrode) are used for measurement. The sizes of the main electrodes and reference electrode are 20 mm × 30 mm and 20 mm × 20 mm, respectively. The main electrodes are adhered to the palm side of each wrist. The reference electrode is adhered to the dorsal side of the left wrist. These positions are established naturally by wearing the device, as the electrodes are embedded in the garment. The length of the rubber elastics can be adjusted by using a hook-and-loop fastener to fit various outer perimeters of the wrist.

Signal Amplifier. ECG equipment was procured from Harada Electronic Industry Ltd. [16]. The signals are captured at a sampling frequency of 120 Hz after amplified by a factor of ∼800. Then, they are transmitted to the monitoring part via a Bluetooth wireless connection.

Acceleration Sensor Module. Three axes acceleration sensor module is installed in a pocket around the ECG equipment. The acceleration data is

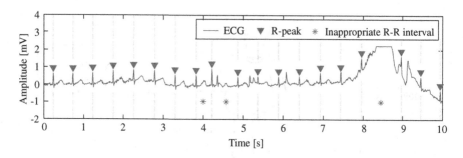

Fig. 3. Waveform of the application of the PT algorithm and range detector.

obtained at a sampling rate of 50 Hz and transmitted to the monitoring part via a Bluetooth connection.

Monitoring Part. The ECG data obtained by the receiver unit is processed to convert them into cardiac-potential values. Then, the ECG waveforms are displayed on the tablet or mobile device. Simultaneously, the ECG data and acceleration data are stored on a computer for offline data analysis.

2.2 R-R Interval Derivation

R-R intervals are needed to obtain the HR and HRV indices, which are related to the mental stress. The R-R intervals are the periods between adjacent R-peaks and can be calculated by detecting the R-peaks in the ECG waveforms.

We employed the Pan-Tompkins (PT) algorithm, which is one of the most common algorithm for detecting R-peaks [17]. This algorithm uses the slope, amplitude, and width information of the waveform. First, bandpass filtering is adapted to reduce various types of interference in the ECG signals. The next process is differentiation, followed by squaring to intensify the slope feature values and restrict the interference caused by T-waves. After the signal passes through a moving-window integrator, adaptive thresholds discriminate the locations of the R-peaks using feature values and several decision rules. To avoid deriving inappropriate R-R intervals due to misdetected R-peaks, we employed a range detector and we regard the interval from 450 ms to 850 ms as the acceptable range for R-R interval. Figure 3 shows a waveform of the application of the PT algorithm and range detector.

3   Experiments

The purposes of the experiments were to verify the acceptability of the developed device during therapeutic sessions and assess the degree of confidence in ECG signals during therapeutic tasks.

We recruited four male children with ASD and asked them to wear the developed device. This experiment was approved by institutional review board of Keio University, and was conducted after informed consent was obtained from the legally authorized representatives. Table 1 shows the chronological and development ages of the participants. The tasks were designed by the therapists to suit the ability of the participants. Table 2 presents types of tasks conducted during the sessions and a brief description of the behaviors exhibited in each task. An example of tasks for a participant throughout the therapeutic session is illustrated in Fig. 4. The duration of the entire session was ~60 min, and ECG were measured using the developed device. Additionally, the behaviors exhibited during the session were recorded by video cameras. We evaluated the quality of the ECG signals using the R-R intervals derived from the waveforms. First, the ECG data were divided into several datasets corresponding to the task durations. Then, the algorithm mentioned in the previous section was applied to each datasets. We used the datasets, which were longer than 2 s, to ensure the algorithm reliability. Furthermore, we calculated the measurement rate to assess the feasibility of the ECG monitoring during the therapeutic tasks. This rate is defined as the summation of durations where the R-R intervals were correctly

Table 1. Age of the participants.

Participant	Chronological age	Development age
A	5;5	1;10
B	4;7	2;0
C	5;8	4;0
D	3;8	Unknown

Table 2. Brief description of the tasks conducted during the therapeutic sessions.

Task	Activity
Exercise	Tossing rings toward a bar, holding the bar, or watching their play (ringtoss) from a sitting position
Motor imitation	Touching the head, shoulders, knees, eyes, ears, mouth and nose; raising the hand and clapping
Playing together	Passing a ball to the therapist; playing with toys on the floor
Manipulating	Assembling a toy
Card selection	Listening to the voice of the therapist, selecting a picture card that the therapist suggests from two or three cards, and passing the card to the therapist or touching the card
Reading	Watching the screen of a PC where words are displayed and reading out the words
Vocal imitation	Vocalization after watching the movement of the mouth of the therapist and listening to the sounds

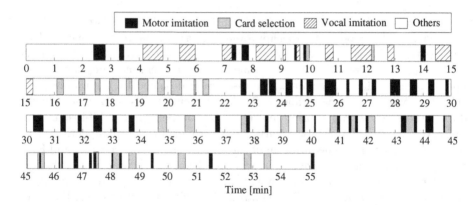

Fig. 4. An example of tasks for a participant throughout the therapeutic session.

obtained divided by the total duration of the task. After calculating the rate for each dataset, the average measurement rate was used as the index of quality of ECG during the task. On the other hand, we also calculated the activity volume to estimate the degree of movements during each task. The activity volume was considered as the average change of acceleration in all of three axes.

4   Results

Three of the four participants agreed to wear the developed device and wore it for the entire session (~60 min). The device was accepted easily by the parents and therapists, and it was not necessary to explain how to wear the device. Although one participant hesitated to use the device, we confirmed that children with ASD can use the developed device.

Table 3. Confident interval rate during therapeutic tasks.

Participant	Task	Total duration [s]	Measurement rate (SD) [%]	Activity volume (SD) [G]
A	Motor imitation	402	67.4 (±12.5)	0.40 (±0.13)
	Card selection	257	91.8 (±4.2)	0.18 (±0.02)
	Vocal imitation	360	83.7 (±7.8)	0.22 (±0.07)
B	Exercise	221	62.5 (±0)	1.44 (±0)
	Motor imitation	934	55.6 (±9.1)	0.84 (±0.25)
	Manipulating	420	69.9 (±0)	0.55 (±0)
	Reading	489	94.2 (±1.4)	0.48 (±0.02)
	Motor imitation	539	91.6 (±3.7)	0.34 (±0.08)
C	Playing	1196	67.9(±25.3)	0.54 (±0.03)
	Card selection	116	92.7(±4.0)	0.45 (±0.12)
	Reading	441	93.9(±4.8)	0.29 (±0.09)

Table 3 shows the results of the performance evaluation. Different measurement rate were seen in each task, and the card selection and reading task showed measurement rates of over 90 % in all the participants. The activity volume in each task is also shown in Table 3, and different activity volume were seen in each task.

5   Discussions and Conclusions

We introduced the results of applying a wearable ECG monitoring device to children with ASD. We confirmed that children with ASD can use the device during therapeutic sessions and that R-R intervals can be obtained during tasks that induce less motion. The measurement rate depended on the activity volume. The device is capable of obtaining ECG with high confidence when the activity volume is small. As shown in Table 2, the vocal imitation task involved only vocalization, and the body movements were far smaller compared with those with motion oriented tasks. These results suggest that reliable R-R intervals can be acquired during tasks that induce less motion, such as vocal imitation or reading. Therefore, we can say that the device have the potential to estimate reliable HR and HRV during less motion therapeutic activities.

In the experiment, three of the four participants accepted to wear the developed clothe. The reason that one participant did not agree to wear the device may have been associated with the degree to which the participant was accustomed to the therapy.

The potential applications of this device include mental state estimation. We plan to develop a system that can store the correct R-R intervals and automatically calculate the HR and HRV. We also plan to analyze the mental stress of children with ASD during therapeutic activities using the proposed device.

References

1. Scott, M.M., Chris, P.J.: Management of children with autism spectrom disorders. Am. Acad. Pediatr. **120**, 1162–1182 (2007)
2. Susannah, C., Katherine, M., Ann, M., David, H.: Psychophysiological responses to emotional stimuli in children and adolescents with autism and fragile X syndrome. J. Clin. Child Adolesc. Psychol. **44**, 250–263 (2015)
3. Rosalind, W.P.: Future affective technology for autism and emotion communication. Philos. Trans. R. Soc. B Biol. Sci. **364**, 3575–3584 (2009)
4. Elgiz, B., Emily, H., Damon, L., Amy, V.V.H., John, W.D., Stephen, W.P.: Emotion recognition in children with autism spectrum disorders: relations to eye gaze and autonomic state. J. Autism Dev. Disord. **40**, 358–370 (2010)
5. Chathuri, D., Judith, H.M., Shawn, E.C., David, Q.B., Takahashi, N.T., Gang, Y.: Atypical pupillary light reflex and heart rate variability in children with autism spectrum disorder. J. Autism Dev. Disord. **43**, 1910–1925 (2013)
6. Kim, H.K., Bang, W.S., Kim, R.S.: Emotion recognition system using short-term monitoring of physiological signals. Med. Biol. Eng. Comput. **42**, 419–427 (2004)

7. Kristina, S., Marc, T.P.A.: Measuring emotional arousal for online applications: evaluation of ultra-short term heart rate variability measures. In: Proceedings of the Affective Computing and Intelligent Interaction (ACII), pp. 2–5 (2013)
8. Mikko, P., Jarmo, V., Antti, V.: Night-time EKG and HRV monitoring with bed sheet integrated textile electrodes. IEEE Trans. Inf. Technol. Biomed. **16**, 935–942 (2012)
9. Schafer, A., Vagedes, J.: How accurate is pulse rate variability as an estimate of heart rate variability? A review on studies comparing photoplethysmographic technology with an electrocardiogram. Int. J. Cardiol. **166**, 15–29 (2013)
10. Guohua, L., Fang, Y.: Limitations of oximetry to measure heart rate variability measures. Cardiocasc. Eng. **9**, 119–125 (2009)
11. Pani, D., Dessi, A., Saenz-Cogollo, J.F., Barabino, G., Fraboni, B., Bonfiglio, A.: Fully textile, PEDOT: PSS based electrodes for wearable ECG monitoring systems. IEEE Trans. Biomed. Eng. **63**, 540–549 (2016)
12. Chae, Y.L., Kuk, J.J., Young, H.K.: A wearable healthcare system for cardiac signal monitoring using conductive textile electrodes. In: 35th Annual International Conference of the IEEE EMBS, pp. 7500–7503 (2013)
13. Kei, I., Yutaka, F., Gert, C., Akinori, U.: Noncontact sensing of electrocardiographic potential and body proximity by in-bed conductive fabrics. Comput. Cardiol. **40**, 523–526 (2013)
14. Ko, K.K., Yong, G.L., Jung, S.K., Kwang, S.P.: Capacitive-coupled ECG measurement and its applications for ubiquitous healthcare. In: International Conference on Convergence Information Technology, pp. 811–814 (2007)
15. Kanako, T., Kenji, S.: An ECG monitoring system through flexible clothes with elastic material. In: Proceedings of the 17th IEEE International Conference on E-Health Networking, Applications Services (Healthcom), pp. 300–305 (2015)
16. Harada Electronic Industry Ltd. http://www.h-e-i.co.jp/Products/h_r/ECG500.html
17. Jiapu, P., Willis, J.T.: A real-time QRS detection algorithm. IEEE Trans. Biomed. Eng. **32**, 230–236 (1985)

Study on Elicitation and Detection
of Emotional States with Disabled Users

Yehya Mohamad$^{(\boxtimes)}$, Gaby Nordbrock, Henrike Gappa,
and Carlos Velasco

Fraunhofer Institute for Applied Information Technology (FIT),
Schloss Birlinghoven, 53757 Sankt Augustin, Germany
{yehya.mohamad,gaby.nordbrock,henrike.gappa,
carlos.velasco}@fit.fraunhofer.de

Abstract. This paper presents the results of a qualitative study on elicitation and online detection of emotional states in users suffering from cerebral palsy (CP). Two questions stood in the focus of the study. Firstly, is an elicitation approach based on the international affective digitized sound system (IADS-2) database feasible for this user group? Secondly, is it possible to distinguish out of the measurements of the EDA sensor (Electro Dermal Activity) positive and negative emotional states? The results revealed high correlation between the findings in the study and the published IADS-2 standard [1]. These results has shown as well that it is possible to distinguish between positive and negative emotional states based on the measured EDA signals.

Keywords: Emotion · Cerebral palsy · Study · IADS · Sensor · EDA · Algorithm

1 Introduction

People with cerebral palsy (CP) who cannot control their movements and their facial expression are mostly unable to speak, so their means of communication are extremely limited. Electronic devices like pictogram based talkers supporting these users' interaction lack of possibilities to express the current emotional state like in nonverbal cues. Enabling them to do so would make it easy for them to express and manage their emotional states and make the communication with doctors and caregiver more efficient, which on the turn would improve outcome of therapies. There were many challenges accompanied with the involvement of this user group, one of them was the involuntary movements causing noise in the biofeedback signals measured out of EDA sensors. Another challenge was about the development of a methodology to test the correlation between the self-rating of the test participants (tps) and the IADS-2 database results. Furthermore, the measurement approach and the interpretation algorithms had to be defined and implemented.

The study was based on previous experience of the authors, who used Support Vector Machines (SVM) for the online detection of emotional states [2, 3].

For the purposes of this study, we have developed a framework for elicitation and measurement of CP users' body signals from the sensory inputs (EDA sensors) and

K. Miesenberger et al. (Eds.): ICCHP 2016, Part I, LNCS 9758, pp. 563–570, 2016.
DOI: 10.1007/978-3-319-41264-1_76

their interpretations. The emotion elicitation approach was based on one of the internationally known databases for the study of auditory affective processing: the International Affective Digitized Sounds (IADS) [1, 4]. For the assumptions in the current affective algorithms, we utilized findings in state of the art neuropsychological research, which revealed a differential processing of auditory stimuli, with pleasant (positive) and unpleasant (negative) valence, including a stronger activation by pleasant (e.g. laughing) relative to unpleasant (e.g. crying) sounds [6]. In self-report measures of emotion, unpleasant stimuli also tended to be assessed using more extreme scores for arousal than pleasant stimuli [5, 7]. Studies on auditory affective processing have also demonstrated sex differences in response to sounds [8, 9, 10]. Our model considers these findings by building models for every user, which comprise:

- The signal volume, which is given by its strength,
- Standard deviation of the signal.

Here we build the sum of both values and used it for the assertion, if the result is pleasant or unpleasant emotion. Providing an individual with online (real time) information about his or her own physiological state will help to increase the awareness about the own emotions of the user and therewith help to improve individual's emotional well-being. While there are meanwhile many commercially available tools that reflect body signals, especially on mobile devices, there is a lack of well-controlled validation studies.

2 Methodology

In order to evaluate the correlation between physiological signals of Electro Dermal Activity (EDA) of the tps and their self-ratings on how they felt while listening to different emotion-evocative sound stimuli. A test scenario was developed comprising a standardized test procedure as well as test materials like a questionnaire to gather personal data of the 15 tps, a scale for self-rating of emotions and a test protocol to note observations made during the tests by the test conductor. In order to get an overview of the arousal level of the test participants when listening to the sounds. The EDA-measurements were automatically recorded during the tests and stored in an XML file. A second XML file served for data collection of the test participants' self-ratings for each of the 24 sound stimuli.

2.1 Test Sample

The test sample for this user study was comprised of 15 tps, all of them suffering from CP with severe physical impairments. Most of them were categorized as level IV or V (most severe limitations) according to the 5-ary scale of the Motor Function Classification System (GMFCS), whereby 8 tps were classified as level IV, 6 tps as level V and 1 tp as level III. The test sample covered 6 female and 9 male tps, ranging from 23 to 60 years (mean age: 37.5), whereof 3 were between 50 and 60 years, 10 between 30 und 40 years and 3 under 30 years old.

2.2 Test Procedure

Due to possible fatigue of the CP tps and limited ability to concentrate, the test duration was limited to a maximum of 30 min. The average duration of each test session was 25 min. All tests followed a standard test procedure and were conducted by a psychologist and a physiotherapist. The psychologist knew the entire test participants (tp) personally, took over the communicational part with the tps including individual assistance in the rating procedure if necessary.

Fig. 1. Sensor placement at hand

A physiotherapist, familiar with people suffering from CP and experienced with the placement of the psychophysiological sensors from previous tests, fixed the sensors and operated the software for starting the audio play of sounds and storing the tp's ratings of their emotional states. At the beginning, the test conductor gave a short introduction about the main test goal, the duration of the test and the test procedure. The test participants were also informed about privacy issues, e.g. that the test data are processed anonymously. Then the EDA sensors were placed, mostly at the tp's left inactive hand. For 5 tps this was not possible due to high spastic, therefore the sensors were placed e.g. on one hand plus right or left forearm or on the left side of the body (see Fig. 1). After the sensors had been fitted, the measurement software was started and checked whether the sensors worked well, the first stimuli was used for checking purpose.

Fig. 2. 5-ary pleasant-unpleasant scale

With the sensor at place and working, the test procedure was explained in more detail, especially the meaning of the pleasant-unpleasant-rating scale with its 5 items (see Fig. 2) has been described. Furthermore, the test conductor pointed out that there would not be a right or wrong rating, but only the test participant's (tp) immediate personal experience with each sound was of interest, reflecting how he or she felt while hearing the sound. The first sound that was played, served as a test run to get the tps familiar with the specific test procedure of the audio play of the sounds and following rating. Shortly after the audio play ended, the tp was asked, which number on the rating scale is nearest to how she/he felt while listening to the sound. The tp's rating was entered and stored by the rating software. This procedure was repeated for all of the 24 test sounds. Some of the tps could verbally tell the chosen rating number or point to the associated item. In case, they were not able to do so the test conductor pointed to the items one after another from the right to the left and the tps affirmed their choices by e.g. the movement of his/her head, and/or a combinations of individual sounds, gestures or facial expressions. In rare cases, test conductor had to repeat the scanning of the rating scale, because the tp's rating could not be interpreted clearly. One tp (09) needed additional assistance due to problems with focalizing on the scale display and One tp (04) seamed not really to understand the meaning of the rating scale, so the test conductor had to scan through the items for several times repeating the meaning of the items. After all sounds had been rated the test conductor asked the test participant (tp) how easy it was to rate her/his emotional states and how exhausting it was for her/him to do the test. The test conductor ticked the scale item according to the tp's rating. After test session had finished, the test conductor completed the test protocol by observations made during the test.

2.3   Test Materials

The emotional self-rating was based on short emotion-evocative sound stimuli from the International Affective Digitized Sounds-2 (IADS-2) [2]. Due to time limitation 24 sounds were selected (each of 6 s). Thereof 8 sounds belonged to one of the 3 emotional categories: pleasant, unpleasant and neutral. The sequence of all 24 sounds has been created statistically (randomized) considering that 8 subsequences should always cover 1 sound from each of the 3 emotional categories. The same sequence of sound stimuli was presented to all tps. The test protocol contained instructions about the sequences within the test sessions (introduction, sensor placement, further explanation etc.) as well as how to explain the test goal and describe the items of the pleasant-unpleasant rating scale. The 5-ary pleasant-unpleasant scale (see Fig. 2) ranges from a smile to a frown and was presented in paper form. For data collection, a spreadsheet was used to gather personal data about the test participants (tps) as age, sex and type of CP and assistive technology used. The main utilities for data collection during each test sessions were two XML files gathering the recorded Electro Dermal Activity (EDA) measurements and the self-ratings of each test participant per sound in combination with the date, start- and finish times of each audio play of a sound over the whole session time. An additional protocol sheet in paper form was used in order to document the self-rating of the test participants (tp) on how easy or difficult the rating was for her/him and how exhausting it was to do the test. This was also rated on a 5-grade scale (from 'very easy' to 'very difficult' and from 'not exhausting' to 'very exhausting'). Additionally observations about behavior of the test participants or particular incidents or problems like higher motoric involvement, fatigue, or exhaustion either while listening to special sounds or while rating during the test session were also documented.

2.4   Technical Environment

The validation framework consists of hardware and software components. It utilizes EDA sensors, drivers and measurements software. The validation framework consists of a Java Application running in the background to make the required calculations and to manage the persistence of the results in an XML layer, where the results are stored in different XML files. This application captures the start and end time of every sound and the tp's rating. On the other side all raw signals and interpretations are as well captured in a different XML file. HTML5/Java Script/CSS3 for the user interface of the application presenting the sounds to the tp and allowing the tp to rate them individually.

3   Results

In this section, we present the results of the study based on the measurements as depicted in the previous sections. The results show that the pleasure self-reporting (valence) of the tps correlate very much with the results of users from the IADS-2 database, who do not suffer from CP. These findings confirm that the study methodology is working for users with CP and we can proceed to use the results to calculate affective states out of EDA sensors in order to find out if we can distinguish between positive and negative emotional states. The test results were categorized regarding the "Pleasure" (valence: pleasant, neutral or unpleasant) rating by the tps, when hearing a specific sound. High correlation was found in case of the measured arousal of tps compared to the arousal values collected in the IADS-2 database from none CP test participants. The correlation was less than the correlation of the "pleasure" parameter. The "pleasure" parameter is based on user rating in IADS-2 and study tps' rating, while the "arousal" parameter is based on user rating in IADS-2 and on real signal measurements in this study.

3.1   Pleasure Rating in Comparison to IADS-2 Database Rating

The most important test results regarding the emotional ratings showed that like in the IADS-2 tests the sound ratings for categories pleasant and unpleasant can clearly be distinguished (Table 1).

Table 1. Range of emotion rating of IADS-2 and this test

Sound category	Range of rating values (this study)	Range of rating values (IADS tests)
Pleasant	6.48–7.68	7.12–7.90
Neutral	4.08–6.84	4.33–5.26
Unpleasant	2.88–4.56	1.63–2.82

There is no overlap between the degree of pleasure for the pleasant sounds, ranging from 6.48 to 7.68 and the unpleasant ones, ranging from 2.88 to 4.56. According to the findings, the method applied for gathering emotional self-assessment can be considered as valid evaluation basis for people suffering from CP (see Fig. 2). The self-rating behavior of the test participants concerning their pleasure parameter when listening to the 24 sounds, showed a tendency to locate themselves via positive or negative ratings. Out of the 360 ratings 141 belonged to the category pleasant and 139 to unpleasant, whereas only 80 were of category neutral. The 8 sounds categorized as neutral in the IADS tests were rated rather positive or negative by the test participants (tps) within this study. This different rating behavior might be owed to the test situation. In contrast to the ratings within the IADS study, where the test participants (tps) did their ratings independently without support of another person. In this user study, the test conductor asked the tps how they felt about a sound after hearing it, which might have provoked the impression that they had to decide clearly whether they have a positive or negative emotion. In addition to these test conditions personal experiences and preferences might account for this outcome, e.g., some tps could not identify the (neutral) 'shovel' sound and therefore rated this sound rather negative or the sound 'rain' rated neutral in IADS was selected only 4 times as neutral, but 8 times as unpleasant and 3 times as pleasant.

Concerning the 16 sounds of the categories pleasant and unpleasant, where our investigations were focused on, the rating behavior matched the ones of the IADS tests, despite some minor differences. The rating values, reflecting the degree of pleasure the test participants felt when listening to the sounds, were a little lower for the pleasant sounds and on the whole higher (less negative) for the unpleasant sounds compared to the IADS ratings. The lowest rating of the sound "sports crowd" (6.48) seemed to be effected by individual attitudes. In accordance to the IADS results, the most negative rating applied to the unpleasant sound of a screaming woman with mean value of 2.88 (1.63 of IADS). As mentioned above, less negative rating values were determined for all unpleasant sounds, which might be caused by a general tendency of the tps to be more cautious about negative ratings. Furthermore, this tendency was increased by individual rating behavior due to personal attitudes, e.g., one tp rated some unpleasant sounds like car crash and fight as pleasant, because of his associations with action films, he likes very much.

3.2 Arousal Measurement in Relation to the Users' Self-ratings

In this perspective, we capture the tps' self-rating for each of the 24 sounds for all 15 users, which can have the values "pleasant (3)", "unpleasant (1)" or "neutral (2)". These average results for all 15 users are shown with a blue line in Fig. 3. During the self-rating, we have measured the arousal out of the EDA sensor's signal, and then we have mapped the resulting arousal value to a scale from 1–9 in accordance to IADS-2 scale. We display the resulting average arousal for all 15 users as a red line in Fig. 3. The results reveal high conformance between the self-rating and the measured arousal, which allow the assertion that it is possible to differentiate between positive and negative emotional states.

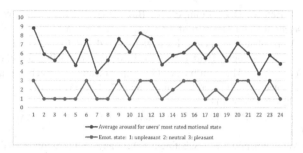

Fig. 3. Comparison of tps' ratings and the average of measured arousal (Color figure online)

4 Conclusions

Effective recognition of emotional states especially distinguishing between pleasant and unpleasant states plays an important role in general and for disabled persons in particular for users suffering from CP in order to compensate communication disorders, help them to achieve more autonomy, social inclusion and to support stress management. The processing of information captured from physio-psychological sensors like the EDA sensor provides an efficient way to detect users' emotional states. In this study, we aimed at the verification of our approach affective computing in supporting the interaction with users with CP. The investigated emotional features and developed algorithms including the data gathered in this part our work can be used as an input for the development of future adaptive HCI applications for disabled users especially CP users. There is more work to be done on the area of affective computing for disabled users:

- Further tuning of the algorithms
- Trying other Machine learning techniques (data mining algorithm methodologies) and combinations of them
- Combining the real time interpretation of data sources (sensors) e.g. EEG and EDA
- Focusing future work on affective computing for disabled user on detection and relieve of stress rather than on detection of different emotional states
- Conducting more user studies with larger number of participants.

Acknowledgements. The study was partially funded by the European Commission EC FP7-ICT; 2011-7-287774; ABC Augmented BNCI communication. The authors would like to acknowledge the support of the project partners AVAPACE and IBV, both from Valencia, Spain.

References

1. Bradley, M.M., Lang, P.J.: International affective digitized sounds (IADS): stimuli, instruction manual and affective ratings. The Center for Research in Psychophysiology, University of Florida, Gainesville, F.L. (1999)

2. Mohamad, Y., Hettich, D.T., Bolinger, E., Birbaumer, N., Rosenstiel, W., Bogdan, M., Matuz, T.: Detection and utilization of emotional state for disabled users. In: Miesenberger, K., Fels, D., Archambault, D., Peňáz, P., Zagler, W. (eds.) ICCHP 2014, Part I. LNCS, vol. 8547, pp. 248–255. Springer, Heidelberg (2014). doi:10.1007/978-3-319-08596-8_39

3. Mohamad, Y., Gappa, H., Nordbrock, G.: Experimental approach on affective aware systems for disabled users. Procedia Comput. Sci. **67**, 445–451 (2015). doi:10.1016/j.procs.2015.11.085. ISSN: 1877-0509

4. Bradley, M.M., Lang, P.J.: Affective reactions to acoustic stimuli. Psychophysiology **37**, 204–215 (2000)

5. Bradley, M.M., Codispoti, M., Sabatinelli, D., Lang, P.J.: Emotion and motivation I: defensive and appetitive reactions in picture processing. Emotion **1**, 276–298 (2001)

6. Sander, K., Scheich, H.: Auditory perception of laughing and crying activates human amygdala regardless of attentional state. Cogn. Brain. Res. **12**(2), 181–198 (2001)

7. Schirmer, A., Striano, T., Friederici, A.D.: Sex differences in the preattentive processing of vocal emotional expressions. NeuroReport **16**, 635–639 (2005)

8. Bradley, M.M., Codispoti, M., Sabatinelli, D., Lang, P.J.: Emotion and motivation II: sex differences in picture processing. Emotion **1**, 300–319 (2001)

9. Gohier, B., Senior, C., Brittain, P.J., Lounes, N., El-Hage, W., Law, V., Phillips, M.L., Surguladze, S.A.: Gender differences in the sensitivity to negative stimuli: cross-modal affective priming study. Eur. Psychiatry (2011). doi:10.1016/j.eurpsy.2011.06.007

10. Smith, N.K., Cacioppo, J.T., Larsen, J.T., Chartrand, T.L.: May i have your attention, please: electrocortical responses to positive and negative stimuli. Neuropsychologia **41**(2), 171–183 (2003)

Usability Evaluation of Accessible Complex Graphs

Dimitris Spiliotopoulos$^{(\boxtimes)}$, Despoina Antonakaki, Sotiris Ioannidis,
and Paraskevi Fragopoulou

Distributed Computing Systems, Institute of Computer Science,
Foundation for Research and Technology – Hellas, Heraklion, Greece
{dspiliot,despoina,sotiris,fragopou}@ics.forth.gr

Abstract. This work explores the use of speech enabled complex graphs that are designed to enable non-technical users to edit and appraise visually complex semantic structures. The standard usability evaluation that was performed previously employed young, computer-literate participants that were familiar with such concepts and tools. We report on the findings of how technically-savvy and technically challenged users experience the different modalities, make choices and identify each modality advantages and shortcomings as well as the ability of each user group to optimally exploit modality combination paths.

Keywords: Speech enabled graph · Usability · Accessibility · Non-technical users

1 Introduction

Visualization of data is used abundantly to convey complex semantic meaning [9] and facilitate data exploration [14]. As part of the latest data-driven visualization approaches, storytelling is also based on the visualization using descriptive complex design [11].

Auditory feedback was used successfully for the simple math graph [2] and more complex visual chart [3] accessibility for visually impaired users, as well as combination of haptic and auditory feedback [16]. Other approaches used natural language generation for fine tuned speech rendering of complex visual objects, such as graphs [4]. Evaluating such approaches constitutes a similarly challenging task, leading to works exploring ways to enable the user-driven design and usability evaluation of technologies for accessibility [1].

This work examines a domain of high societal impact that potentially affects all citizens of the democratic world. Policy modelling utilizes moderated crowdsourcing argumentation from social media that can enable policy makers and other users to visualize the citizen opinion. Policy models are represented and visualized as relational graphs, semantically linking policy components, entities and arguments with sentiment, the latter mined from social media [12]. Related works examined design considerations for creating effectively usable tools using social media data [5] and sentiment [8].

Dedicated e-participation and e-government tools designed for modelling policies present unique advantages to the policy makers [6, 10]. However, evaluations showed that severe weaknesses hinder the citizen adaptation, such as failure to understand the

K. Miesenberger et al. (Eds.): ICCHP 2016, Part I, LNCS 9758, pp. 571–574, 2016.
DOI: 10.1007/978-3-319-41264-1_77

visual structures [15]. Even policy makers find themselves not in possession of the required policy informatics-friendly competencies, skills, and attitudes to work on the policy formulation process [7]. It is, therefore, evident that, in order to include technologically marginalized citizens [17] to the new era of e-participation tools and processes, specific care should be made to facilitate the understanding of such visual representations.

2   Motivation and Experimentation

The main motivation for this work was to explore how accessibility practices may help towards using a complex interactive visual tool for policy design. A speech interface was developed as a result of the user driven design to enable improved navigation and editing of complex graphs (Fig. 1).

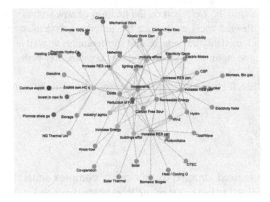

Fig. 1. A policy model

All interaction actions can be performed by either regular keyboard/mouse input or speech commands and automatic speech recognition [13]. The initial user evaluation by technically savvy users revealed that combined speech and normal (keyboard/mouse) interaction can help create and edit large complex graphs. However, it was also evident that less technology savvy users, mainly including older users, were not as successful at these tasks.

A follow up experiment was set up for exploring methods and practices to design inclusive interaction for non-tech-savvy users, essentially successfully enhancing their work output. Five participants that work in the field of policy modelling, hence familiar with the content, but do not traditionally use a computer (NTS group) and five policy formulation students that were not familiar with the interface, but considered themselves technically-savvy normal users (TSN group) were asked to explore the limits of their ability to follow the model complexity using any modality or combination they deemed optimal. The aim was to examine whether the choices of the two groups aligned and their feedback on the usability differentiated between them. Both groups were given ample time to familiarize with the interface, functionalities, the modalities and speech commands. The interaction of each participant were logged, including timestamps, providing interactional data for validation.

3 Results and Evaluation

The NTS group needed on average roughly twice the time to familiarize with the interface. The speech modality consistently took less time to familiarize with than the visual, the former averaging a 30 % longer than the TSN group, while the latter about 80 % longer on average. For simpler tasks (e.g. adding a new node) each user group opted for different modality as their main choice. Tasks considered as less complex were treated in a uniform manner, involving both modalities for optimal interaction. However, concrete differences were observed when the complexity of the graphs increased. The TSN group explored four times more possible combinations to achieve optimal results, mainly in understanding and keeping up with the graph semantic complexity (e.g. deciding where to link a new policy component).

The NTS group insisted on making themselves more involved with selected choices, identifying themselves as the factor that hindered their progress rather than the interface. Content creation was differentiated heavily between the two groups. The TSN participants followed a path of creating very descriptive, long texts that resulted in more cluttered graphs. The NTS group, with their expertise in paper and pen approach limited by the size of the paper itself, introduced abbreviation and provided feedback as to how that abbreviation should be part of the interface, essentially partially over-coming the visual modality disadvantage.

Acknowledgements. This work was supported by the FP7 Marie-Curie ITN iSocial funded by the EC under grant agreement No. 316808.

References

1. Bigham, J.P., Murray, K.: WebTrax: visualizing non-visual web interactions. In: Klaus, J., Zagler, W., Karshmer, A., Miesenberger, K. (eds.) ICCHP 2010, Part II. LNCS, vol. 6180, pp. 346–353. Springer, Heidelberg (2010)
2. Choi, S.H., Walker, B.N.: Digitizer auditory graph: making graphs accessible to the visually impaired. In: Proceedings from CHI 2010 Extended Abstracts on Human Factors in Computing Systems, pp. 3445–3450 (2010)
3. Elzer, S., Schwartz, E., Carberry, S., Chester, D., Demir, S., Wu, P.: Accessible bar charts for visually impaired users. In: Proceedings from Fourth Annual IASTED International Conference on Telehealth and Assistive Technologies, pp. 55–60 (2008)
4. Ferres, L., Lindgaard, G., Sumegi, L.: Evaluating a tool for improving accessibility to complex visual objects. In: Proceedings from 12th International ACM SIGACCESS Conference on Computers and Accessibility (2010)

5. Jung, H., Hong, S.R., Meas, P., Zachry, M.: Designing tools to support advanced users in new forms of social media interaction. In: Proceedings from 33rd Annual International Conference on the Design of Communication (2015)
6. Kamateri, E., Panopoulou, E., Tambouris, E., Tarabanis, K., Ojo, A., Lee, D., Price, D.: A comparative analysis of tools and technologies for policy making. In: Janssen, M., Wimmer, M.A., Deljoo, A. (eds.) Policy Practice and Digital Science, pp. 125–156. Springer, Switzerland (2015)
7. Koliba, C., Zia, A.: Educating public manager and policy analysts in the era of informatics. In: Janssen, M., Wimmer, M.A., Deljoo, A. (eds.) Policy Practice and Digital Science – Integrating Complex Systems, Social Simulation and Public Administration in Policy Research, pp. 15–34. Springer, Berlin (2015)
8. McGuire, M., Kampf, C.: Using social media sentiment analysis for interaction design choices: an exploratory framework. In: Proceedings from 33rd Annual International Conference on the Design of Communication (2015)
9. Olshannikova, E., Ometov, A., Koucheryavy, Y., Olsson, T.: Visualizing Big Data with augmented and virtual reality: challenges and research agenda. J. Big Data 2(1), 1–27 (2015)
10. Ruppert, T., Bernard, J., Kohlhammer, J.: Bridging knowledge gaps in policy analysis with information visualization. EGOV/ePart Ongoing Res. 221, 92–103 (2013)
11. Segel, E., Heer, J.: Narrative visualization: telling stories with data. IEEE Trans. Vis. Comput. Graph. 16(6), 1139–1148 (2010)
12. Spiliotopoulos, D., Dalianis, A., Koryzis, D.: Need driven prototype design for a policy modeling authoring interface. In: Marcus, A. (ed.) DUXU 2014, Part II. LNCS, vol. 8518, pp. 481–487. Springer, Heidelberg (2014)
13. Spiliotopoulos, D., Dalianis, A., Koryzis, D.: Speech enabled ontology graph navigation and editing. In: Antona, M., Stephanidis, C. (eds.) UAHCI 2015. LNCS, vol. 9176. Springer, Heidelberg (2015). doi:10.1007/978-3-319-20678-3_47
14. Stevens, J.-L.R., Rudiger, P., Bednar, J.A: HoloViews: building complex visualizations easily for reproducible science (2010)
15. Tambouris, E., Dalakiouridou, E., Panopoulou, E., Tarabanis, K.: Evaluation of an argument visualisation platform by experts and policy makers. In: Tambouris, E., Macintosh, A., de Bruijn, H. (eds.) ePart 2011. LNCS, vol. 6847, pp. 74–86. Springer, Heidelberg (2011)
16. Yu, W., Ramloll, R., Brewster, S.: Haptic graphs for blind computer users. In: Brewster, S., Murray-Smith, R. (eds.) Haptic HCI 2000. LNCS, vol. 2058, pp. 41–51. Springer, Heidelberg (2001)
17. Wöckl, B., Yildizoglu, U., Buber, I., Aparicio Diaz, B., Kruijff, E., Tscheligi, M.: Basic senior personas: a representative design tool covering the spectrum of European older adults. In: Proceedings from 14th International ACM SIGACCESS Conference on Computers and Accessibility, pp. 25–32. ACM, New York (2012)

Author Index

Printed in the United States
By Bookmasters